Equipment for Older or Disabled People and the Law

of related interest

Community Care Practice and the Law
Michael Mandelstam with Belinda Schwer
ISBN 1 85302 273 X

Disability and the Law
Jeremy Cooper and Stuart Vernon
ISBN 1 85302 318 3

Equipment for Older or Disabled People and the Law

Michael Mandelstam

Jessica Kingsley Publishers
London and Bristol, Pennsylvania

First published in the United Kingdom in 1997 by
Jessica Kingsley Publishers Ltd
116 Pentonville Road
London N1 9JB, England
and
1900 Frost Road, Suite 101
Bristol, PA 19007, U S A

Library of Congress Cataloging in Publication Data
A CIP catalogue record for this book is available from the Library of Congress

British Library Cataloguing in Publication Data
Mandelstam, Michael, 1956–
Equipment for older or disabled people and the law
1. Self-help devices for the disabled – Law and legislation
I. Title
362.4'028

ISBN 1-85302-352-3

Printed and Bound in Great Britain by
Athenaeum Press, Gateshead, Tyne and Wear

Contents

Acknowledgements

I would like to thank the many people who have made this book possible, whether by directly assisting with it – or by indirectly contributing through the advice they have given me in connection with other related pieces of work.

In particular, a number of civil servants in government departments – notably the Department of Health, Department of Environment and Department of Trade and Industry – have provided a truly public service. The Medical Devices Agency – especially Sue Wilkin and Tony Shipley (before his retirement) – has been most helpful.

Advice on specific aspects has been given by David Yelding (Research Institute for Consumer Affairs), Brid D'Ornellas (North & West Belfast HSS Trust), Ian Sherwood (British Surgical Trades Association), Judith Payling (Hampshire County Council), Beryl Steeden (College of Occupational Therapists), Lesley Bell (London Boroughs Occupational Therapy Managers' Group) – and many others. Thanks are due to the Disabled Living Centres Council – in the form of Tony Travis and Maggie Winchcombe – for generally encouraging me and kindly allowing me to draw (primarily for chapter 3) on material from *Going to Market?*, a report about the market for disability equipment which I completed for the Council early in 1996.

Because the book covers such a wide area of law, I have inevitably made use of several publications as pointers to the legal landscape. These include *Breach of Statutory Duty in Tort* (Stanton), *Consumer Law and Practice* (Lowe, Woodroffe), *Judicial Review Handbook* (Fordham), *Law of Contract* (Treitel), *Law of Torts* (Fleming), *Product Liability* (Stapleton), *Sale of Goods* (Adams,Atiyah), *Textbook on Torts* (Jones), *Winfield and Jolowicz on Tort* (Rogers).

I would like to thank my father for his comments and for assistance with the proofreading. Lastly, but certainly not least, Jessica Kingsley has been consistently a most supportive, encouraging and understanding publisher – along with her staff, Anna French, Charles Catton and Imogen Farrow.

Of course, all errors are my own, as are any opinions expressed – which do not, therefore, represent those of any employer for whom I have worked in the past or am currently working.

Disclaimer

Every effort has been made to ensure that the information contained in this book is correct, or at least represents a reasonable interpretation. However, not only is a book of this nature likely to contain errors, but the law is continually changing and is also – as the book reiterates many times – characterised by various uncertainties.

Furthermore, particular situations and disputes possess their own unique set of circumstances, and the reader should seek professional advice when attempting to solve particular problems, formulate legally sound policies etc. Thus, whilst the book aims to identify relevant legal considerations, it should not be seen as a simple recipe book for providing quick, definitive and blanket solutions.

The time of writing is generally April 1996, but – owing to legislative changes during 1996 on a number of fronts – it is, in key parts of the book, more recent. For example, included are the Housing Grants, Construction and Regeneration Act 1996, the Education Act 1996, the Community Care (Direct Payments) Act 1996 and the pivotal community care case, *R v Gloucestershire County Council, ex parte Barry* (Court of Appeal judgement).

Michael Mandelstam, November 1996

PART I

1. Introduction
2. Main themes of the book
3. Overview of provision of equipment in practice
4. Equipment and awareness of the law
5. When things go wrong
6. What statutory services and their staff can and can't do

CHAPTER 1

INTRODUCTION

COVERAGE

1. WHAT THE BOOK IS ABOUT

This book is about equipment (and home adaptations) which assist people with physical and sensory disabilities to overcome difficulties with everyday living. Put another way, it is about equipment to *make life easier.*[1] The book explains what equipment is available, how it is available, the legal basis for provision, and what can be done when things go wrong. For brevity, the term 'equipment' is sometimes used generally to include home adaptations.

The range of equipment covered in this book is very wide. It includes such common and well-known items as hearing aids, wheelchairs, walking sticks and electric toothbrushes – as well as less well-known equipment such as incontinence devices, page turners, electronic speech aids and environmental control systems for severely disabled people. Adaptations to people's homes, such as ramps, rails, through-floor lifts and structural extensions, though strictly not equipment, are also covered. These are but a few examples; Part 4 of the book begins to give an idea of the many products available.

Usefulness of equipment and adaptations

Equipment and adaptations are useful to many different types of people; for example, a wheelchair might assist a young person severely disabled with a high level spinal injury, a jar opener an elderly person with mild arthritis in the hands, large display computer software and hardware a child with a visual impairment, and a stairlift a person who is dying from a respiratory illness. Equipment and adaptations can enable people to manage and achieve the most basic functions and activities – such as sleep comfortably and safely, get out of bed, wash, hear, see, read, walk, talk, eat, drink and get out of the house. Perhaps the term *basic* should be underlined; the ability to manage such functions and activities is essential to people's independence and dignity. Wheelchairs and adapted cars enable people to get out to work and remain financially independent; and stairlifts and rails assist people to remain living in their own, rather than enter residential homes. The importance of such basic functions should perhaps be borne in mind when evaluating the practical consequences of the disorganised system of provision, rationing, and disputes – affecting people who are severely disabled, in substantial need, dying, or perhaps just wanting to be able to wash properly or get out to the shops. This is not about peripheral 'luxuries'.

The latest General Household Survey highlights the significant numbers of elderly people who are unable to perform a variety of ordinary actions and activities, such as bathing (8%), toenail cutting (31%), opening screw-top jars and bottles (10%), unaided shopping (16%), cleaning windows inside without help (20%), washing clothes by hand (7%), and household tasks requiring climbing (28%). These figures apply to people who are 65 years old or more; however, they rise significantly by age band. For example, although only 4% of people aged 65 to 69 require assistance with bathing, showering or washing, this figure rises to 14% for people aged 80 to 84 and to 21% for those of 85 years or more. And, whilst only 7% of those aged between 65 and 69 have problems getting out of the house and walking down the road, the figure rises to 37% for people aged 85 or over.[2] Equipment and adaptations are amongst the solutions which can assist people experiencing such difficulties.

System of provision: statutory and commercial

Disability equipment and home adaptations are provided through various public sector statutory services (the NHS, social services, housing, education and employment), the private sector and the voluntary sector. As a whole, the system is complex and confusing – as are some of its component parts, even if each is viewed in isolation. From the point of view of individual users of equipment, provision fits into two main systems of provision – the *commercial (market)* and the *statutory (welfare)* – but fares well in neither. The commercial market system entails *consumers* making contracts with sellers when they buy equipment. The statutory, welfare system is about providing equipment for *service users* on a non-contractual basis by statutory services – either free of charge or for a modest, statutory charge imposed or allowed by legislation. Provision of equipment by voluntary organisations sits somewhere in the gap between private and public sectors – variously providing equipment free of charge or selling it on a commercial basis.

Although statutory services provide large quantities of equipment and home adaptations, they have never possessed sufficient resources to meet all demands. On the other hand, the private sector retail market in disability equipment is not well-established. As a consequence, the voluntary sector steps in, where possible, to pick up the pieces. Add to this situation the fact that some people's physical needs are complex, that the use of equipment is anyway not determined solely by people's physical needs (eg psychological, environmental and social factors play a part), and that information and understanding of equipment and its provision is scarce – and the ingredients of a ragged system are in place.

Nevertheless, the dividing line between statutory and commercial provision is thinning. Not only does a 'mixed economy of care' mean that the public, private and voluntary sectors are working more closely together in delivering services, but also that people are being encouraged increasingly by cash-restricted statutory services to buy their own equipment. If they do so, they have stepped out of the welfare system into the marketplace. Furthermore, it is not just products labelled 'disability equipment' which people buy for themselves; a great many other products are sold as 'ordinary' equipment and are useful for people who have difficulties with certain everyday actions and activities. For instance, the following are advertised in newspapers or mail order catalogues without explicit mention of disability: large knobbed taps, easy-grip cutlery, car swivel seats, letter cages, grab rails for the bath, baths with hinged sides, long-handled gardening tools, large-button television remote controls – and so on. This means, too, that the gap narrows between special welfare provision for people's needs – and normal, everyday private purchase.

Thus, a review of the system of equipment provision requires a broad sweep – from the very specialist provision by statutory services of sophisticated environmental controls for severely disabled people at one extreme to the buying (by mail-order) of a letter cage to avoid the need to bend down at the other. The further consequence of the breadth of the system is that such a review has to take account of many different contexts and viewpoints. Any one context or view will not suffice, whether that of (a) the embattled voluntary organisation which produces disturbing reports about the dire needs of the people whom it assists, (b) government departments which tend to promulgate more optimistic views of the effects of their policies, (c) disabled people who claim that manufacturers over-price equipment, or (d) manufacturers who point to the inevitably high costs of production of equipment in a fragmented, specialist and 'difficult' market.

Equipment provision in a wider context

Of necessity, this book is not just about equipment provision closely defined. This is because equipment provision by statutory services is based on legislation and policy which governs the provision as a whole of welfare services such as community care, health, housing and education. Given that this system of welfare provision is so vast, some of its underlying principles can be helpfully explained by focusing on one particular aspect – such as equipment. For instance, s.2 of the Chronically Sick and Disabled Persons Act, which underpins equipment provision by social services departments, is also at the heart of community care legislation. Indeed, the Act, under which many other services can be provided as well, has been the main focus for legal challenge to the rationing of community care by local authorities.

Consequently, an understanding of equipment provision – whether by social services departments, the NHS or education authorities – necessarily brings with it an understanding of the legal principles governing an array of other services, from heart operations to orthopaedic surgery, toe-nail cutting to home help, and bathing services to speech therapy for children.

In the same vein, Part III of this book – which deals with areas of law such as negligence, contract, breach of statutory duty and judicial review – explains legal principles which apply to far more than disability equipment. For example, the duty of care owed by physiotherapists to patients (eg not to supply negligently crutches with worn tips) is conceptually and legally similar to the duty of a motorist to take care on the roads. And the contractual obligation of retailers to provide disability equipment of 'satisfactory quality' merely reflects the same general obligation which applies to the sale of all goods.

2. WHOM THE BOOK IS FOR AND WHOM IT IS ABOUT

The book has been written for:

- **people working in statutory services,** including practitioners, managers, purchasers and providers – in the NHS, social services, housing authorities, education authorities and schools and the Employment Service. Practitioners who need to know about equipment include occupational therapists, physiotherapists, speech and language therapists, hearing therapists, chiropodists, nurses (of various specialisms), medical doctors (of various specialisms), social workers, community care managers, environmental health officers, advisers on special educational needs, employment service officers and so on.
- **voluntary and advice-giving organisations:** for example, organisations for elderly people, for disabled people, or for people with particular medical conditions. Also information and advice centres such as Citizens' Advice Bureaux, community health councils, public libraries.
- **lawyers and other legal advisers**
- **users and potential users of equipment**
- **manufacturers and suppliers of equipment**

- **managers and staff of residential homes, nursing homes**
- **other private providers of health and social care**
- **university lecturers and students.**

The title of the book reflects the fact that older people form the biggest category of users of the equipment covered by this book – although many do not necessarily consider themselves to be disabled, and are not called so by many health and social care professionals. For example, in both social services departments and the NHS, a division between services for physically disabled adults (16–64 years old) and for elderly people is normally made.

Of course, this is not to suggest that all, or even most, older people need specialist equipment. As the latest General Household Survey, published by the Office of Population Censuses and Surveys, points out, many older people are fit and healthy.[3] For this reason – and also because assistive equipment can be quite 'ordinary' as well as specialised – the term 'disability equipment' is avoided in the title. Indeed, the line between 'ordinary' and 'disability' equipment is a fine one and continually shifting. For instance, electric tin openers, lever taps, remote control garage doors, or lightweight carpet sweepers are not thought of as disability equipment – but, a luxury for some, they might be essential to other people.

3. PURPOSE AND APPROACH OF THE BOOK

Length and detail of the book

It is difficult to know precisely how detailed to make the book. For readers who know little of the subject, a much shorter book, by way of an introductory text, might suffice. But the more knowledgeable reader already knows about the basic issues – and is looking for coverage of the more complicated problems.

Jargon is avoided as far as possible, whether that of therapists, social workers, managers, civil servants, or lawyers. Inevitably, some terms are used with which not all readers may be familiar – for example, 'criteria of eligibility' or even 'carers'. The dilemma between littering the text with abbreviations, and repeating the long names of Acts of Parliament and the names of organisations, has been resolved mainly in favour of the latter option – although, for example, the abbreviation CSDPA is used commonly for Chronically Sick and Disabled Persons Act. The problem of use of he/she in the text has been dealt with by using either one or the other in any particular sentence – usually 'he'. It should be noted, however, that most users of disability equipment are elderly and that women live longer than men; and also that members of some of the professions involved in equipment provision, such as occupational therapy and physiotherapy, are preponderantly female. The terms 'older people' and 'elderly people' are used interchangeably. The term 'disabled people' is used to refer to people who have a physical or sensory disability – although the difficulties in defining disability and disabled people are alluded to in Chapter 3.

Extensive references support the text and give the interested or specialist reader information in depth; the system of equipment provision spans many different interests and can only be understood with reference to diverse and elusive information sources. Rather than clutter the text excessively with legal case names, only those judged to be particularly relevant to the subject matter appear (in shortened form); otherwise full details are given in the numbered references to each chapter.

Selectivity

The book is necessarily selective – any one of the chapters could be expanded to form an entire book in itself. The selection has been based on various concerns expressed – either personally to the author or in print – by voluntary organisations, professionals, lawyers, suppliers, and users of equipment. Also, some names of organisations and equipment occur in the text; this is not an indication that these are in any way better than those which have not been mentioned.

Apart from selectivity within topics, other areas have been more or less excluded. These include the discretionary Social Fund (which is used to some extent to fund equipment for people's daily living needs), the Independent Living (1993) Fund, disability living allowance (including the mobility component), and the wider home renovation grant system. The law relating to fair trading is not covered – ie the Fair Trading Act 1973, Competition Act 1980, Resale Prices Act 1976, Restrictive Trade Practices Act 1976, and Articles 85 and 86 of the Treaty of Rome affecting the European Community. Also omitted are the Trades Description Act 1968, misleading price indications (s.20 of the Consumer Protection Act 1987), and references to particular sets of technical standards (whether solely British, or 'harmonised' European standards).

Application of the book in terms of the United Kingdom as a whole

Most of the content of the book applies broadly to the whole of the United Kingdom – but it has been written specifically with England in mind. For instance, separate welfare legislation and guidance governs the provision of equipment in Scotland and Northern Ireland – and even though most such legislation applying to England covers Wales as well, the Welsh Office issues its own guidance. In addition, health and social care in Northern Ireland is provided through unified health and social services boards (and trusts) – rather than through separate organisations as in the rest of the United Kingdom. In England and Wales, health authorities and NHS Trusts are responsible for health care, whilst social care is provided by social services departments; in Scotland, health boards (and NHS Trusts) and social work departments are responsible for health and social care respectively. The author is aware of the frustration which readers in Scotland and Northern Ireland sometimes experience when reading books such as this; the reason why the book does not deal with the whole of the United Kingdom in detail is simply a practical one – limitations of time and resources. Nevertheless it is hoped that the book will still be useful, since much of it is relevant to the whole of the United Kingdom – in principle, if not always to the letter.

Why write about disability equipment?

Equipment provision is complex. Of course, any subject looked at closely enough or from a particular angle can be made to appear impenetrable. However, the complexity affecting the provision of disability equipment can lead to difficulties and to things going wrong. The author's hope is that a thorough but clear explanation of the system will contribute to a better understanding and to improvements in provision.

Indeed, if the system of equipment provision worked smoothly and straightforwardly, the adage 'no news is good news' might apply – and there would be little need to write about it. But this is not the situation, and to a large extent the book has been written in response to longstanding practical problems. In addition, writing about legal issues anyway entails scrutiny of things going wrong.

Consequently, the book tends to examine uncertainties, ambiguities and shortcomings – ie the boundaries and breaking points of the system. This is not to deny the existence of good practice. As one writer on the provision of home adaptations put it, she could have very easily written a 'bad practice guide' – given both the level of complaints about adaptations which the Department of Environment receives and the disturbing reports of the local ombudsmen. Instead, heartened to find, amidst the gloom, so many examples of good practice, she wrote a report about 'finding ways to say yes' to people.[4] Indeed, it is surely good practice which will reduce the prevalence of mistakes, misunderstandings and disputes. Furthermore, some people receive not only innovative but also expensive services, such as community care packages provided by social services departments of £40,000 per year.[5]

Even so, there is sufficient evidence to suggest that the problems afflicting equipment provision are far from theoretical or minimal; a short review of the published evidence is to be found in Chapter 3.

Is there much money involved in equipment provision?

Money appears these days to be of paramount consideration. Government urges that judicious use be made of taxpayers' money and, for example, points out to local authorities that if they do not make reasonable charges for social services (including equipment), they will be placing an 'extra burden' on the local population.[6] Indeed, the law courts are prepared to hold that local authorities have strong 'fiduciary' duties (normally associated with e.g. duties of trustees to beneficiaries) to their local taxpayers. This happened in the 1983 case in which Bromley council successfully challenged the GLC's plans for public transport in London which had entailed additional rates payments.[7] The notion of a fiduciary duty owed by local authorities to ratepayers was traced back to a 1925 case, in which the House of Lords held that Poplar Council was paying its workers an excessively high wage (£4 a week), even though the legislation apparently allowed the Council to decide how much to pay.[8]

Examples of annual costs to the taxpayer of equipment and adaptations. From a financial point of view, does the provision of equipment and home adaptations by statutory services merit the concern of local and central government? Unless the tens of millions of pounds spent each year are to be passed over, the answer is in the affirmative. For instance, in 1993–1994, expenditure by social services departments in England on equipment and adaptations amounted to over £50 million, rising from about £37 million in 1991–2 and £39 million in 1992–3.[9] For major adaptations, housing authorities made payments for the year 1994–1995 of £89.2 million in mandatory, and £900,000 in discretionary, disabled facilities grants. In 1991–1992, the NHS issued over 170,000 wheelchairs at a cost of over £43 million.[10] Each year, the NHS is estimated to spend about £40 million on artificial limb services, £3 million on walking aids, £20 million on hearing aids, and £4 million on environmental control equipment.[11] In 1992, orthotic appliances, including surgical footwear, were reported to cost the NHS £70 million each year.[12] The cost of providing incontinence pads and appliances, through both NHS Trusts and prescription by general practitioners, was put at £68 million for the year 1989.[13]

Financial questions for central government, local government and the private sector about the provision of equipment and adaptations. There are at least two types of financial question which government, both local and central, might ask about the provision of equipment and adaptations through statutory services.

First, is too much money being spent, is effective use being made of public money, and what sort of outcomes are being achieved? Second, is too little money being spent on equipment, with the consequence that higher, overall costs are incurred by society in the longer term – and policies such as community care are hampered? For instance, if some people cannot obtain adaptations to their homes promptly, they may have to enter residential or nursing home care – at potentially great cost to the taxpayer. And, if a person does not receive assessment and advice about how to make her home environment safe, she might fall and require a costly stay in hospital. The stay becomes more costly still if there is subsequent delay in providing equipment and adaptations, and hospital beds consequently become 'blocked' because the person cannot be discharged.[14] Similarly, what sort of longer term costs (eg in terms of State benefits) are incurred by society when the Employment Service reports budgetary restrictions and a curbing of its Access to Work programme – including restrictions on the availability of equipment and adaptations to enable people to obtain or retain employment? And take, for instance, the trend in community care for authorities to target resources only on those with 'high priority' needs (risk to life and limb). Denied what is often only the small amount of advice or assistance needed, those at low risk soon move into a higher priority band of need and maybe into hospital or residential care – even though this could have been avoided. This issue concerns prevention rather than cure and is perhaps well illustrated by the children's rhyme: 'For want of a nail the shoe was lost...the kingdom was lost.'

On a different tack, does equipment for older and disabled people warrant the interest of manufacturers and retailers – whether they are selling to statutory services or direct to consumers? It would seem so. Surveys carried out by the Office of Population Censuses and Surveys in 1980s showed that well over four million people in Great Britain use one or more items of disability equipment.[15] It is estimated that several hundred thousand wheelchairs are in circulation at any one time – which, in principle, is a considerable sized market.[16] An additional factor is that older and disabled people require not just *specialist* equipment, but suitable, *ordinary* equipment. For example, some manufacturers and retailers have recognised such a need by producing milk cartons which are easy to open, television controls with large buttons, clothing for wheelchair users (which does not ruck up or have seams which cut into the user), shopping trolleys which provide support and a seat – and so on. Thus, the commercial potential for assistive, daily living equipment extends far beyond a narrow and specialist market to a much more general one. It also relates not just to the design, manufacture and potential availability – but also to how it is marketed for different, identified target groups. For instance, younger disabled people make up a very different market from older people whose bodies are undergoing various changes. Therefore, much might hinge on how and where equipment is advertised and sold, and what sort of image and lifestyle it conveys.

Apart from the obvious 'welfare' government departments (Health, Environment, Education and Employment) that might be asking these questions, the Department of Trade and Industry also has at least three possible areas of interest. First, it monitors accidents in the home and has produced guidance (in association with voluntary organisations) about home safety – which refers prominently to disability equipment. Second, it is the Department with responsibility for much consumer protection and product safety legislation. And third, it would presumably be keen to see United Kingdom companies exploiting a potentially large – but untapped – market for equipment.[17]

Why explain equipment provision in terms of law and practice?

As already stated, this book has been written for a range of different people, providers and users, professionals and non-professionals. Legislation and legal principles are emphasised, not to promote confrontation or the excessive 'legalisation' of society but to explain the basis for equipment provision. Indeed, the current system of provision is very much a legacy of statute, since equipment has largely been supplied via statutory services.

The book attempts to *bridge the gap between law and practice.* Thus, the legal reader gains an idea of what goes on in practice and, conversely, the reader who has a knowledge of practice can refer to the legal underpinning. The giving of *good* legal advice about obtaining equipment is near impossible, without appreciating the practical complexity and instability of the system of provision. Equally, people who are having difficulty in obtaining equipment from statutory services might sometimes need a knowledge of the law, if they are to be able to challenge the decisions of authorities effectively. And, the staff of authorities need a thorough awareness of the law if they are to balance, in legally sound fashion, people's needs with the limited resources available to meet those needs.

The book cannot hope to cover comprehensively every last aspect either of provision of equipment in practice, or of the legal issues. Amongst the reasons for this are that (a) local provision varies considerably, so that equipment provided in certain circumstances in one locality might not be in another, (b) both the meaning and practical application of legislation and legal principles covered by the book are not always straightforward, and (c) even if the law does seem clear, there is often an element of uncertainty as to how it might apply to the unique facts of any particular situation or dispute.

However, what the book does do is to provide a solid basis for assessing where those facts are likely to fit within the general legal, policy and practical framework of equipment provision – which does apply to all localities.

4. USING THE BOOK

How to use the book

The book is divided into four parts. For people unfamiliar with the subject, or at least parts of it, Chapters 1 to 6 provide an overview, and identify themes and principles. Each chapter generally begins with an introductory section, listing the main subjects covered and key points; most chapters also list a number of sample questions to illustrate common concerns. There are various ways to use the book, for example:

(i) The reader wants to find out how a particular type of equipment is provided. The item (eg wheelchairs) can be looked up via the A–Z list of equipment in Part IV of the book, to find out about types of chair, how provision works in practice, and which items statutory services might provide. The reader might then go to Part II of the book, to understand the legislation underpinning wheelchair provision by any one statutory service (eg the NHS, the Employment Service).

In relation to the safety of wheelchairs (and legal consequences), the reader will also be referred to Part I, Chapter 2 (where wheelchairs are used as an example to illustrate certain themes relating to safety and information about equipment). In addition, Chapter 5 contains an overview of various dispute procedures and legal remedies; whilst more detailed chapters in Part III deal with subjects such as common law negligence and product liability under the Consumer Protection Act 1987.

(ii) The reader wants an overview of the whole system of provision. In Part I, Chapter 3 looks at current provision; and Chapter 2 outlines various themes running through the practice, policy and law of equipment provision. From these two chapters, the reader is guided to various other parts of the book for greater detail.

(iii) The reader wants to understand how legislation and guidance affect staff in a particular statutory service. For instance, an occupational therapy manager might be concerned about whether her priority system is operating legally and according to principles of good administration. Chapter 6 (Part I) explains the effects of legislation and guidance in general, and what sort of duties they give rise to – as well as pointing the reader also to Chapter 17 in Part III, which explains how the courts intervene if authorities do not behave reasonably, legally and fairly. Chapter 7 (Part II) analyses legislation affecting provision of equipment by social services departments. In addition, Chapter 5 outlines the powers of the local ombudsman to investigate maladministration, whilst Chapter 7 summarises a number of ombudsman investigations into the policies, priorities and waiting lists operated by social services departments.

SUMMARY OF THE BOOK

PART I. Part I of the book provides an overview and discussion of the system of provision as a whole.

Chapter 2 (main themes). The main themes of the book are picked out, including, for example, the role of people's expectations in disputes, imprecision and uncertainties within legislation, unclear responsibilities for equipment, the tension between people's needs and the resources available to meet those needs, the 'empowerment' of users of services, and the difficulties of forming an objective view of how equipment provision is working in practice.

Chapter 3 (overview of system of provision). This chapter outlines the system of provision, pointing to what equipment can assist people, whom it can assist and how to get it.[18] It covers some of the factors which currently make the system confused and fragmented. These include the lack of a well-developed retail market, people's attitudes to using equipment, lack of information, and the dominant but sometimes disorganised activities of statutory services.

Chapter 4 (awareness of the law). Reasons are suggested why, increasingly, people need to know about the law.

For example, it appears that litigation, or the threat of it, is escalating as people's expectations become greater and lawyers step forward to inflate them further. And, when manufacturers and suppliers attempt to supply more equipment directly to consumers (and not just via statutory services), so the *law of contract* becomes more relevant to users of equipment – for example, in settling disputes about whether equipment is 'fit for its purpose', sufficiently durable or sold on unfair terms. Similarly, as statutory services are forced to adopt more sweeping rationing measures – affecting equipment and other services – so are they more likely to be challenged by means of *judicial review* in the law courts. In addition, various consumer safety legislation imposing criminal and sometimes civil liability is now in place. Stemming from European Community directives, this legislation applies both to products in general, and to 'medical devices' in particular; it affects not only manufacturers but also suppliers of equipment, including statutory services and voluntary organisations.

This chapter also considers the desirability of settling some types of dispute through informal negotiation, rather than through time-consuming, expensive and stressful litigation.

Chapter 5 (when things go wrong). This chapter sums up what people can do when things go wrong – whether they are purchasing equipment privately or obtaining it through statutory services. Possible courses of action are many, ranging from informal negotiation to formal legal action. Emphasising the general desirability of avoiding formal legal procedures where possible, the chapter summarises some of the advantages and disadvantages of the options available.

Chapter 6 (powers and duties). An explanation is given of how powers and duties expressed in legislation govern what statutory services their staff can and can't do. The legal status of Acts of Parliament, statutory instruments, guidance and charters is clarified. Also touched on is the legal relevance of statements made in Parliament, of standards and of clinical guidelines. As well as a general explanation of all of these, a number of ambivalent aspects, apt to create confusion and uncertainty, are highlighted.

PART II. Part II analyses the provision of equipment and home adaptations by a number of statutory services, and includes chapters devoted to the *NHS, social services, housing, education and employment.* Legislation, guidance and their practical consequences are covered, along with the setting of priorities, rationing, the attitude of the law courts, the use of complaints procedures, and the investigations of the ombudsmen. Separate chapters deal with residential homes, nursing homes and special provision for war pensioners.

Chapter 7 (social services). Considers how social services departments provide equipment within a complicated web of legislation, at the centre of which sits the Chronically Sick and Disabled Persons Act 1970. However, many other Acts of Parliament affect various aspects of provision, including community care assessments, the assessment of carers, children's legislation, charging for services, complaints procedures and (imminently) the making of direct financial payments to service users.

Chapter 8 (NHS). Looks at the broad and vague duties which govern the provision of NHS services, including various types of disability equipment. The flexibility of such duties is analysed and illustrated with reference to the types of rationing which health authorities adopt.

Chapter 9 (home adaptations). The various avenues for the provision of home adaptations are described, including housing authorities (via disabled facilities grants or minor works assistance), home improvement agencies and social services departments. The sometimes lengthy, badly organised and disruptive processes involved are pointed out, as well as the importance of adaptations in enabling people to remain in their own homes.

Chapter 10 (education). Summarises the provision of equipment for children and students with special educational needs, in primary, secondary, further and higher education. The making of statements of special educational needs is outlined, together with the implications of the distinction between 'educational' and 'non-educational' needs.

Chapter 11 (employment). Explains the Access to Work scheme operated by the Employment Service, under which both equipment and adaptations can be provided to enable people to gain or retain employment. Also looks ahead to the implementation of the Disability Discrimination Act 1995, and how it will affect the provision of equipment and adaptations in the workplace.

Chapter 12 (residential and nursing homes). Outlines the framework underpinning the provision of services and equipment for people living in residential and nursing homes. It explains how provision is governed by a hotchpotch of vague legislation, standards and contract terms.

Chapter 13 (war pensioners). Highlights briefly the special legislation and arrangements which allow war pensioners, and other related groups, special access to equipment in some circumstances.

PART III. In Part III various legal principles and actions are explained and illustrated by examples specifically relating to equipment provision by the public, private and voluntary sectors.

Chapter 14 (negligence). Sets out what is meant by a *duty of care, breach of the duty* (carelessness), and the *cause* of an accident and resulting harm. Well-established areas of negligence such as medical negligence and liability for defective products are contrasted with the uncertainty about the circumstances in which the courts will find social services departments and their staff negligent. The liability, both *vicarious* and *direct,* of employers for the acts of their employees and independent contractors is explained; this is particularly relevant as the mixed economy of care permeates welfare services and the delegation and contracting out of services proliferates. The rules affecting negligent advice, psychiatric injury, financial loss and damage to property are covered. Particular points which cause anxiety to professionals – such as the difference between carelessness and a simple mistake – are dealt with.

Chapter 15 (safe products, lifting and handling). Covers four main areas of legislation relating to consumer protection and health and safety – and variously affecting manufacturers and suppliers (including statutory services and voluntary organisations).

The *Consumer Protection Act 1987* (Part 1) imposes civil liability for defective products on manufacturers and suppliers (including statutory services and voluntary organisations); its meaning and practical consequences are considered. The *Medical Devices Regulations 1994* stipulate that medical devices placed on the market must conform to certain requirements of safety and performance and carry a CE Mark to indicate this conformity. Breach of the duties can lead to criminal, as well as to civil, liability. The uncertainties that still surround these Regulations are identified.

The *General Product Safety Regulations 1994* state that unsafe products must not be placed on the market. Lastly, the *Manual Handling of Loads Regulations 1992* impose duties on employers to eliminate or at least minimise the risk run by their staff when lifting people or inanimate loads. These Regulations are explained in the book, because of their implications for the use of equipment for lifting, handling and turning people.

Chapter 16 (contract). Outlines the law of contract, with specific reference to, for example, the quality of equipment (fitness for purpose, durability, freedom from minor defects), unfair agreements between consumer and seller, and why, legally, statutory services do not enter contracts when they loan equipment to individual service users.

Chapter 17 (judicial review). Illustrates how the law courts supervise the activities of statutory services and government departments by examining whether they have acted unreasonably, unfairly or illegally. Judicial review is the prime legal avenue for challenging the rationing decisions of statutory services. It has certain limitations, including the fact that the courts are concerned primarily not with what authorities do but that they do it in a proper manner. For example, whether authorities are denying equipment, home support services, hospital care or infertility treatment, the courts are concerned to establish only the lawfulness of such denial – not the practical impact on people's welfare.

This focus on what authorities are doing, rather than the individual rights and needs of service users, is reflected in the rule that damages are not normally available in connection with judicial review proceedings. Nevertheless, within these limits, judicial review can be an effective means of challenging and publicising the decisions of authorities; for example, most recently it has been used in the Court of Appeal to challenge the extent to which authorities can take account of resources when they assess people's needs for community care services (including equipment).

Chapter 18 (breach of statutory duty). Explains how breach of consumer protection (and health and safety at work) legislation can lead to criminal prosecution and sometimes to civil liability as well. However, the existence of civil liability is very much dependent on the context – and it is reasonably well-established in the field of health and safety at work. However, the courts are most reluctant to find authorities liable for breach of duties imposed on, for example, the NHS, social services departments or education authorities.

PART IV. The final Part of the book consists of a full A–Z list of *equipment types* to give the reader an idea of the range of products available. Details are given of which statutory services are likely to provide particular products. Where appropriate, the function of the equipment is explained, together with summaries of the practical aspects of how it is provided.

Notes

1 See e.g. Research Institute for Consumer Affairs (1995). *Equipment for an easier life: a guide to products and where to get them.* London: RICA.

2 Office of Population Censuses and Surveys (1996). *Living in Britain: results from the 1994 General Household Survey.* London: HMSO, chapter 6.

3 *Ibid.*

4 Heywood, F. (1994). *Adaptations: finding ways to say yes.* Bristol: University of Bristol, School of Advanced Urban Studies, p.v.

5 Social Services Inspectorate (Booth, L.; Strettle, T.; Paul, D.) (1995). *Inspection of community services for physically disabled people in the London Borough of Wandsworth, 28 June – 12 July 1995.* London: Department of Health, p.22.

6 LAC(94)1. Department of Health. *I. Charges for residential accommodation: CRAG amendment No 2. II. Charges for non-residential adult services under section 17 of the Health and Social Services and Social Security Adjudications Act 1983.* London: DH, para 18.

7 *Bromley London Borough Council v Greater London Council* [1983] 1 AC 768 (HL).

8 *Roberts v Hopwood* [1925] AC 579 (HL).

9 *Hansard,* House of Commons, Written Answers, 14 June 1995, cols 563–564.

10 Royal College of Physicians of London (1995). *The provision of wheelchairs and seating: guidance for purchasers and providers.* London: RCP, p.5.

11 Based on figures kindly provided by the NHS Supplies Authority.

12 Bowker, P.; Rocca, L.; Arnell, P.; Powell, E. (1992). *A study of the organisation of the orthotic services in England and Wales: report to the Department of Health.* Salford: Salford Health Authority Physiotherapy Service; University of Salford, Department of Orthopaedic Mechanics; North Western Orthotic Unit, p.95.

13 Sanderson, J. (1991). *An agenda for action on continence services.* London: Department of Health, pp.5–6.

14 Hodges, C. (1996). Plugging the gaps to unblock beds: waiting for OT services or equipment often delays hospital discharge. *Therapy Weekly:* 28 March 1996, p.6.

15 Martin, J.; White, A.; Meltzer, H. (1989). (Office of Population Censuses and Surveys). *Disabled adults: services, transport and employment. OPCS Surveys of disability in Great Britain: report 4.* London: HMSO.

16 Pointed out by Sir John Harvey Jones on the Channel 4 programme, *People first: we have the technology* (by Circle Productions, September 2nd 1995).

17 Royal Society for the Prevention of Accidents; Care & Repair; Department of Trade and Industry; Department of Health (1992). *Keep safe: ideas for older people and those with disabilities.* Birmingham: ROSPA.

18 A threefold division used by the European Commission project, Handynet, to develop its database of Community-wide product types, suppliers and legislative framework.

CHAPTER 2

MAIN THEMES OF THE BOOK

COVERAGE

1. Expectations about equipment
   - Expectations: unreasonable behaviour: examples
   - Expectations: poor communication and information-giving: examples
   - Expectations: muddled organisational arrangements: examples
   - Raising false expectations in public
   - Inevitable clash of expectations.
2. Information, instructions and safe equipment
   - Instructions, warnings, labelling, information
   - Examples: wheelchairs and walking aids.
3. Imprecise legislation and uncertainty about the law
   - Why is some legislation imprecise?
   - Does precise legislation make things easier
   - Uncertainty about the law
   - Guidance or legislation?
4. Tension between people's needs and resources
   - Can people's need for equipment be defined by money?
   - Independent assessments of people's needs
   - Inequitable provision.
5. Grey areas of provision: who provides what equipment?
   - Geographical boundaries between services.
6. Equipment provision: a statutory or commercial system?
   - Problems affecting both statutory and commercial provision of equipment
   - Bridging the divide between statutory and commercial provision
   - Collision of public, private and voluntary sectors in providing equipment.
7. Empowerment of service users and legal rights
   - Effect of complaints
   - What legal rights do people and organisations have.
8. Information: finding out what is happening in 'reality'.

Key points

The following themes run through the book.

Expectations about equipment. Disputes, whether between service users and statutory services, or between consumers and private companies, sometimes arise because of the disappointed expectations of at least one of the parties. This might be because of deliberately unreasonable behaviour by one party, organisational muddles, poor communication and information-giving, the raising of false expectations – or genuinely insoluble problems leading to an unavoidable clash of expectations. Some legislation even defines the safety and quality of equipment ultimately in terms of people's expectations – eg the Consumer Protection Act 1987 (Part 1 concerned with liability for defective products) and the Sale of Goods Act 1979 (concerned with the satisfactory quality of equipment).

Information, instructions and safe equipment. The safe and effective use of equipment can depend on the provision of adequate information, instructions and warnings. These can be decisive as to whether legal liability is established under, eg, the law of negligence, the law of contract, the Consumer Protection Act 1987, the General Product Safety Regulations, or the Medical Devices Regulations.

Wheelchairs illustrate well a number of aspects of equipment provision relevant to this book including expectations, safety, information, quality and the potential for dispute.

Imprecise legislation and uncertainty about the law. A range of legislation is covered in this book, relating to the provision of welfare services, consumer protection, and health and safety at work. Some of the Acts of Parliament and Regulations covered have the appearance of being very much more precise than others, and although even the more detailed and unambiguous legislation does not provide all the answers as to 'what the law is', the less precise legislation provides even fewer.

Tension between people's needs and resources. The tension between people's needs and the resources available to meet them is sometimes plain. It affects how statutory services deliver and ration services – and raises the sensitive issue of how far the professional and clinical judgements of staff are influenced by a knowledge of what resources are available.

The tension between protecting individual consumers and wider economic issues also informs, eg, the way in which the Consumer Protection Act 1987 provides a defence for manufacturers of defective products. The defence reflects public policy considerations about the degree of risk to consumers that is acceptable in society – when new products are researched, developed and placed on the market.

Grey areas of provision: who provides what? A confluence of vague legislation, a shortage of resources, and the sometimes complex needs of disabled and elderly people leads to grey and sometimes murky areas of provision. Authorities attempt to divide up responsibilities for equipment and other services. This is often a difficult task, whether the rationale adopted for such a division is one relating to the purpose, r the type, of equipment. It becomes even more difficult when authorities are short money and are tempted to 'pass the buck' to other authorities, to voluntary ations or simply into thin air. When this happens, both gaps and overlaps in can occur.

At best, uncertain responsibilities can allow for flexible provision; at worst, they lead to a denial of responsibilities, confusion amongst both service users and professionals, and delayed provision – or even non-provision – of equipment. The resulting local variations can lead to glaring inequities, when provision is determined by postcode rather than need, and by chance rather than rational policy.

Equipment provision: a statutory or commercial system? Equipment is provided through the *statutory* (or *welfare*) system run by statutory services, and the *commercial (market)* system involving the private sale of equipment to consumers. One system, the latter, is based on the law of contract, the other not – but both display shortcomings in relation to equipment provision for individuals. However, to some extent, a *mixed economy of care*, the culture of *purchasers and providers*, and the viewing of users of statutory services as 'customers' or even 'consumers' – means that the barriers between the public, private and voluntary sectors are being lowered.

Empowerment of service users and legal rights. A fundamental tension exists between the plentiful rhetoric about the empowerment of service users, and the hard decisions that statutory services have to make about the level of provision in their area. Despite a welter of activity aimed at giving people (or making them aware of) entitlements in the form of complaints procedures, charters, consultation exercises, and provision of information about services – welfare legislation confers on people few, if any, legally enforceable rights to services. It is not always realised that even the right to life-saving medical treatment or equipment does not exist. This is underlined by the difficulty facing service users when they attempt to challenge rationing decisions in the courts. Thus, complaints procedures and charters are in some respects ultimately toothless, since they cannot resolve the basic tension between resources and people's needs – even if they are capable of providing relatively simple and effective solutions to some other types of dispute. This suggests an inherent contradiction in providing avenues of redress which cannot, in their very nature, deal with root causes.

Difficulty in finding out what is happening 'in reality'. There are two main reasons why it seems increasingly difficult to summarise the system of equipment provision and related services. First, there is a tension between the different views and objectives of different sectors – central government, local government, voluntary organisations, equipment users, equipment manufacturers and suppliers, and lawyers. Second, the system of equipment provision, like many other welfare services, is increasingly fragmented as purchasers, providers – and associated good and bad practices – proliferate.

1. EXPECTATIONS ABOUT EQUIPMENT

Many disputes between service users and statutory services, and between consumers and private companies, seem to arise because of misplaced or confused expectations. Expectations might not be fulfilled when one party behaves unreasonably, when a breakdown in communication or information-giving occurs, organisational arrangements are confused, public expectations are falsely raised – or when transactions are so riddled with tensions that a clash of expectations between the two people is inevitable, even though neither is behaving unreasonably or thoughtlessly.

In considering the role of expectations, it should be noted that far from being defined in absolute, objective terms, products which are legally unsafe under the Consumer Protection Act 1987 (Part 1) are defined ultimately in terms of people's expectations. Similarly, under the Sale of Goods Act 1979, products of unsatisfactory quality (and therefore giving rising to breach of contract) are defined as what reasonable people would 'regard as satisfactory'. Possibly surprising, this emphasises that 'legal' faults in equipment relate to more than an objective set of physical properties.

Expectations: unreasonable behaviour: examples

If people buy stairlifts which don't work – and retailers or manufacturers then place obstacles in the way of prompt replacement or refund – they are quite rightly disappointed. Conversely, sellers might reasonably be upset if people buy electric wheelchairs which are clearly sold for indoor use only, use them out of doors, have an accident on uneven ground and complain.

Expectations: poor communication: examples

If people are promised explicitly that within a month they will be assessed for a shower by an occupational therapist, they might well begin to be upset six months later when they have heard nothing. The misplaced expectation might arise not because of the wait itself but because of inaccurate, or lack of, information. If waiting times were long, then a thoughtless promise should not have been given in the first place. If the waiting times escalated after the promise was given, then people should have been informed. Indeed, the local ombudsman has sometimes found maladministration not because people have had to wait, but because they were not told what was happening.

Misunderstanding can easily arise. For instance, a family asks a social worker whether the grandparent living at home can have a wheelchair. The social worker says 'probably' without really thinking, and explains that a community physiotherapist will have to carry out an assessment. The family understands this as a 'yes' and that the purpose of the assessment is simply to identify the right type of wheelchair. The physiotherapist carries out the assessment and refuses to prescribe a wheelchair because she judges that the grandparent does not meet the criteria of eligibility. Perhaps the house is unsuitable for wheelchair use; he might derive only minimum benefit from it; or he might even do much better without a wheelchair and regain limited walking ability. The family, feeling that it has been misled, complains.

If an NHS wheelchair service publicises its criteria of eligibility, but applies them inconsistently, and changes them informally from month to month and from case to case – depending on the money available – service users will not know what to expect. The criteria of eligibility of local authorities are sometimes expressed in such a way as to confuse everybody – users, carers, voluntary organisations and staff alike. For example, priority bands might be defined in unhelpful terms such as: '"Limited independence – one major difficulty may exist or twenty per cent less severe difficulties"'.[1]

Expectations: muddled organisational arrangements: examples

When terminally ill people are confronted with dense bureaucracy in local authorities – eg, being assessed by three different sections of a social services department in the space of a month, and still failing to obtain necessary and timely assistance such as an essential telephone – then complaints (albeit posthumous, on the deceased's behalf) might well be made to the local ombudsman.[2] The position is similar if disabled people have to wait four years before being assessed by social services departments.

An example taken from a recently published investigation by the local ombudsman for Wales illustrates how expectations can sink in a sea of disorganised practice. The investigation is notable because, apart from the misplaced expectations of the applicant, it illustrates a number of aspects of provision which can go wrong. These include the social services department's failure to provide a professional assessment, probable breach of the statutory duty of assessment (by losing control of the assessment to another agency), attempts at saving money (employing an occupational therapist assistant unsupported by an occupational therapist, and not using NHS therapists because they were too expensive), the division of responsibilities between authorities, the difference between powers and duties (eg here, mandatory or discretionary grants) – and so on[3]:

> Following treatment for cancer, a woman living alone had difficulties in managing at home. Supported by Macmillan nurses to some extent, she needed more help and wished to have an additional room in which a carer could stay overnight. The social services department purportedly assessed her and made a recommendation to the district council that such an adaptation/extension was necessary and appropriate, and so qualified for a disabled facilities grant. The district council refused to provide one, explaining that the proposed adaptation did not come under the mandatory category of grant, but only under the discretionary; and the council had a policy of not awarding discretionary grants.
>
> Relying on Circular guidance from the Department of Health and Department of Environment – which stated that in such circumstances (ie rejection by the district council of a social services recommendation) the social services department had a continuing duty to meet the person's needs – the woman asked the social services department for help. In the course of refusing, the department disowned its previous recommendation to the district council. It transpired that, at the relevant time, the occupational therapy assistant involved had no substantial support or supervision from a qualified occupational therapist; and the possibility of using NHS therapists had been rejected on grounds of cost. As a consequence, and unknown at the time to the director of social services, the original assessment had

been delegated to another organisation altogether (a home improvement agency) – and the recommendation, made without the use of qualified staff (eg therapists), had been forwarded as its own and without question by the social services department to the district council.

During this process, and whilst other work was being carried out on her house (by means of a renovation grant from the district council), the roof was removed. Realising that for an extra £5500 the extra room she needed could be added in the attic there and then, the applicant borrowed the money, expecting that since social services had recommended the room, she would (one way or another) eventually receive the grant money for it. Of course, she never did.

The ombudsman found that at no time had the disabled facilities grant been promised – and so he would not immediately recommend reimbursement of the £5500. However, he did recommend that the social services department assess whether the adaptation was required under the CSDPA 1970 – and, if so, to reimburse her the full cost. He pointed out that social services had throughout failed to assess the woman's needs properly. He asked the county council to pay her £500 anyway.

Some investigations of the health service ombudsman into hospital discharges expose a catalogue of false expectations and poor communication on all sides. For instance, a medical consultant might assume or expect that the social services department will have services and equipment in place when a person goes home from hospital – even though he has not confirmed this with them. The family of the patient being discharged of course assumes that the doctor knows what he is doing. However, the social services department is unaware of the speed of events. The consequence is premature and disorganised discharge from hospital.[4] Indeed, one study of negligence cases involving orthopaedic surgeons found that 'communication failure' was the most common contributory cause, including simple misunderstandings, poor use of English and a failure to write things down.[5]

When consumers buy equipment, false expectations can be fostered by lack of information. The company which does not mention, either orally or in writing, its hefty, additional delivery and installation charge for equipment can scarcely be surprised when the consumer complains. Of course, were this a deliberate policy of concealment, it would amount to unreasonable (see above), rather than merely inadvertent, behaviour.

Raising false expectations in public

More generally, people are sometimes confused about what to expect from statutory services. They might hear from politicians that community care is a great success and that the NHS is more efficient than ever before; but this leaves them ill-prepared for seeing their elderly parents spending nights on trolleys in hospital corridors or their children denied suitable wheelchairs. Indeed, government departments might highlight examples of good practice, whilst ignoring the bad – rather than seek out and present a balanced picture.[6]

Sometimes the meaning of statements made in Parliament is not necessarily clear to those MPs or to some readers of Hansard (the record of Parliamentary proceedings) who are not well-informed about the relevant legal backdrop. For instance, in response to questions about NHS rationing, an elliptical reply is sometimes given to the effect that everybody has access to the NHS on the basis of clinical need. This might suggest that the clinical needs of everybody will be met. In fact, this is neither the legal position nor the situation in practice; sometimes people who have a clinical need are denied services and equipment, if there is a local shortage of resources and other people are deemed to be in *greater clinical need.* The courts have upheld this interpretation of the NHS Act 1977 by health authorities. However, although the original reply is quite correct, its implications are not obvious to the uninitiated.

To take a similar, specific example. In response to questions (addressed to the Secretaries of State for Health and for Wales respectively) about government policy on the provision of incontinence pads, an identical answer was given within the space of a few days in the House of Commons. This was that health authorities and NHS Trusts were 'under a general obligation to provide these services where the need exists and in the light of their resources and priorities'.[7] Correct as far as it goes, such an answer is brief, is more about the legal situation than policy, and does not spell out the practical significance of 'general obligation' and 'resources and priorities' – ie that health authorities have considerable scope to ration pads and therefore precisely not to meet people's needs.

Another example occurred when the government was asked to comment on a survey showing that nearly 50% of health authorities were rationing incontinence supplies. Rejecting use of the word 'rationing', it instead answered rather euphemistically that it accepted that GPs and incontinence advisers 'have to assess the individual's needs'. And, asked about the availability of pads to people in residential homes, the government replied that 'pads are available free through the district nursing service' and that residents of such homes should be treated in exactly the same way as people living in their own homes.[8] Again, the answer is quite correct from the legal and practical points of view. But, again, for the unwary, it did not make clear that even people living in their own homes can be denied pads in the light of resources and priorities – and that equal treatment can lead to non-provision as well as provision. Plainer speaking was left to a Welsh Office spokesman who was reported to say simply that health authorities had no statutory duty to supply incontinence aids. This comment was made when, responding to Welsh Office guidance about equal provision for people in their own homes or in residential homes, a health authority had threatened to withdraw provision of pads altogether, because of the costs of such equal treatment.[9]

The criticism one might be tempted to make of these Parliamentary exchanges does not necessarily focus on the fact that people are being denied services and equipment (that is a separate issue) – but that franker exchanges do not take place. Perhaps, it might be argued, Opposition parties are not interested in honest debate and would only attempt to exploit (for party political advantage) more open statements made by government. Whatever the explanation, it is arguable that it is disabled people and older people who are the losers. Sometimes, in debate, notably in the House of Lords, blunter views do emerge which introduce social realities. For example, the rationing of pads might appear to a health authority or NHS Trust to be a justifiable efficiency-saving measure; but from the point of view of those in need, it can be 'downright stupid and cruel'.[10] Indeed it might be pointed out that[11]:

> 'The general public who are healthy and well have no idea that at such a basic level people who are incontinent are having many problems. They are having to buy pads or have them rationed or cut off. The mother of a spastic daughter who cannot speak and is doubly incontinent, living in a Cheshire Home, was told that she would have to pay for her daughter's incontinence pads as the Cheshire Home has nursing home status. The mother has to choose between supplying her daughter with pads or giving her a holiday. She cannot afford to do both. Other people have been told that they cannot have the pads which are the most suitable for them. If this goes on there will be an increase in pressure sores and all sorts of problems costing the health service millions of pounds. In addition to this, there are difficulties for carers who may find dealing with other people's urine and faeces none too pleasant. If people do not have adequate pads, life will become unbearable.'

Inevitable clash of expectations

Some situations by their very nature tend to preclude a coincidence of expectations of two people; yet neither might be to 'blame', in terms either of deliberately unreasonable, or of merely thoughtless, behaviour. For example, a lack of resources might force health authorities or NHS Trusts suddenly to withdraw the provision of incontinence pads, to restrict the provision of wheelchairs or to limit home help services. Housing authorities have found themselves denied adequate money from central government in order to meet the demand for renovation and disabled facilities grants – which they have a legal duty to provide. So, no matter how carefully and conscientiously they might have planned, authorities might be left with little choice but to adopt one form of rationing or another. Some service users, even if provided with information about what is happening, will none the less be distressed since, inevitably their expectations will have been dashed and their needs left unmet. And, urged by government to produce ever more publicity about services and about standards of service, authorities might stimulate increased demand for equipment which they cannot afford to meet.

Similarly, the private sale and purchase of some disability equipment can raise awkward questions about the expectations of both sellers and buyers. For instance, if people buy an electric wheelchair or scooter, there is far more to be considered than whether they buy the right size and can operate it in the showroom. Is there somewhere to store it at home, can they get it in and out of their house, are they (or is somebody else) capable of maintaining it safely, are they aware of, and can they afford, the maintenance costs? Have they got the motivation and opportunity to use it? What happens if the wheelchair breaks down or the batteries run down when it is in use, leaving a person stranded, unable to get home and not knowing what to do? That person is far more vulnerable than the average motorist whose car breaks down; indeed, such experiences might be distressing to the point that the person never uses the wheelchair again.[12]

How many of these issues should salesmen bring to the attention of buyers? And what if salesmen can see that the person's condition is such that within six or nine months, the scooter will no longer be of use? Should they point this out? Sometimes users or their families complain, but who is to 'blame'? Salesmen are there to sell products and to provide advice about them; they are not rehabilitation therapists whose job it is to assess people's disabilities. At least some of these problems do not appear capable of easy solution, and are anyway not confined to sellers and consumers; for instance, in the 1970s the Parliamentary ombudsman found himself embroiled[13]:

> 'Having been loaned an electrically-propelled three-wheeled vehicle by the DHSS, a woman gave it up shortly afterwards, claiming (on medical grounds) that she was unable to use it. In the meantime she had paid £88 to the local social services department towards the cost of facilities to park the vehicle and to recharge the batteries. She tried to have this sum reimbursed by the DHSS on the grounds that it should never have prescribed the vehicle in the first place – in which case she would not have paid the money to social services. On the facts of the particular case, she failed.'

2. INFORMATION, INSTRUCTIONS AND SAFE EQUIPMENT

When people buy equipment, the Sale of Goods Act 1979 states that it must be of satisfactory quality which, in turn, is defined as what reasonable people would regard as satisfactory (see Chapter 16). Similarly, defective products under the Consumer Protection Act 1987 (Part 1) are defined ultimately in terms of people's expectations (see Chapter 15). This is a little surprising, since it seems obvious that an exploding toaster is unsatisfactory or unsafe. However, the defective toaster clearly fits the expectation test – ie nobody expects it to do this – and there are other examples which more obviously justify an appeal to expectations.

Nevertheless, not all legislation defines unsafe or unsatisfactory products in such terms. For example, the two Acts mentioned in the paragraph immediately above impose civil liability. Other legislation, imposing criminal liability, does not use the language of expectation but refers instead to the risks posed by products – eg, the General Product Safety Regulations 1994, the Medical

Devices Regulations 1994, and the Health and Safety at Work Act 1974 (s.3) (see Chapter 15 for all of these).

In any event, whether considering people's expectations about equipment or the more objective notion of risk, it seems clear that information, instructions, warnings, and labelling are axiomatic to the safe use of equipment. If a shower seat is provided with instructions that clearly state a particular weight capacity, then the product is not defective either in terms of that physical property or the expectations of purchasers. If such instructions are missing, then arguably it might be defective under both tests; and this sort of factor might be decisive as to people's liability in negligence, in contract, under the Consumer Protection Act 1987, under General Product Safety Regulations 1994 – and so on.

Instructions, warnings, labelling, information

Because of a general lack of knowledge about equipment (see p.70) and disabled people's special physical and sensory needs – safety, performance and quality demand in practice the special attention of manufacturers, retailers and statutory services. For example, instruction booklets provided with cars do not generally tell able-bodied people how to get in and out. But should wheelchair booklets contain instructions about how to get in and out of chairs, since wheelchair transfers can be difficult, lead to accidents and cause physical injury? In any event, the following suggests poor practice;

> An elderly woman (with a balance disorder and sensory/tactile impairment in her hands) goes to a well-known, large and reputable equipment supplier to buy a walker (a four-wheeled walking frame) complete with brake-handles, a seat and a basket. Served by an assistant who candidly admits she does not know how the product works, the woman comes away – having spent over £200 – with no instruction booklet whatsoever. Only weeks later does a physiotherapist acquaintance explain to her how to 'lock' the brakes – *for safety*, when she is resting on the seat.

A research report into aids and equipment for elderly people commissioned by the Department of Trade and Industry and published in 1992, concluded that most of the disability equipment it had assessed was safe. True, some items fell a 'little short of the mark' – such as a knife with an unstable cutting action, a step stool which tilted during foreseeable types of use, a wheeled gardening tool with a sharp axle and ill-fitting seat, and anti-slip tape which failed to perform in the manner advertised. However, while the report found few products inherently unsafe, it noted that many more were supplied with inadequate instructions. Most of the instructions that were supplied related to assembly only; aspects such as safe use, cleaning and maintenance of the equipment were inadequately dealt with.[14]

Of course, in principle, the safe use of equipment should not always have to be grounded in instructions or information at all – a point illustrated recently by the Research Institute for Consumer Affairs[15]:

> When the brakes of a wheeled walking frame broke because of how they had been used, it was arguable that the manufacturer should have stated clearly in the brochure how to operate the brakes. According to therapists, it was foreseeable that users of such frames would grip the brakes hard and often – precisely the type of usage that caused the failure this instance. In addition, the frame had broken because the handles had been extended by the user too far; but the manufacturer could likewise have made clear how the handles were to be adjusted. However, an alternative solution to providing fuller instructions might simply have lain in better design; the brake cables could have been thicker and the frame manufactured so as to prevent over-extension of the handles.

Extra instructions would then not have been necessary. In any event, no amount of instruction will help in some circumstances – eg, if many elderly purchasers of a gardening or kitchen gadget (designed for people with poor dexterity) have difficulty handling the fiddly screws provided for assembly.[16]

Examples: wheelchairs and walking aids

Wheelchairs illustrate well the issues surrounding the safe and effective use of equipment and the importance of information and instructions.

It is thought that, overall, 20,000 accidents involving wheelchairs occur each year.[17] However, this figure is based on the home and leisure accident surveillance statistics (HASS and LASS) published annually by the Department of Trade and Industry; and these contain no information about causes.[18] Thus, some of the accidents might be unrelated to the characteristics of the wheelchair; for instance, road accidents involving wheelchairs might be no more avoidable than any other accident involving cars, bicycles or pedestrians – they are simply an inevitable concomitant of mobility.[19] Furthermore, as pointed out generally elsewhere in this book, people's needs for, and use of, equipment is determined to greater or lesser extent by the surrounding environment. So it is with wheelchair accidents; some involve unguarded staircases, kitchen work-surfaces (eg spilling boiling water), uneven surfaces, high kerbs – and so on.[20]

Nevertheless, there is evidence that at least some of these accidents could be avoided; arguably, basic instructions about how to use equipment properly are essential. For example, information about safe transfer in and out of wheelchairs could help prevent accidents – and even death.[21] Similarly, instructions about how to operate the wheelchair on different surfaces might play a similar preventative role.[22] It might be important to underline the usefulness of wheelchair lap straps; and training in the use of wheelchairs generally might be required for both users and carers.[23] Of course, the giving of warnings, instructions and training are no guarantee that people will use equipment properly; and, eg, the staff of statutory services (with legal liability in mind) might be well-advised to obtain written confirmation from users, or at least keep a clear record, that such information has been given.[24] In practice, a lack of resources can mean that NHS Trusts have to compromise and provide face-to-face instruction only for users with more severe or complicated disabilities or with highly specialist chairs.[25]

Training and instructions are not necessarily designed to remove all risk, since (i) this is not possible, and (ii) people must be allowed to decide to take risks. For example, some physiotherapists teach children to propel themselves up and down steps and stairs in their wheelchairs.[26] If taught properly this is safe for children – just like riding a bicycle – but there is always the chance of an accident, as there is for everybody in all walks of life.

It is difficult to stipulate how detailed to make instructions and warnings if legal liability is to be avoided – given, eg, the varying characteristics and abilities of different wheelchair users – and the differences in the wheelchairs themselves. The level and specificity of instruction could also reasonably vary, depending on whether it stems from the commercial retailer or the specialist NHS therapist. Clearly, the retailer's responsibility for identifying every last implication of the consumer's medical condition or disability is less than that of a therapist for her patient. Certainly, from a legal point of view, it is bad practice if NHS patients are loaned wheelchairs without receiving instructions, even though the local NHS procedures themselves stipulate that they should be provided. They might contain, eg, information about maintenance, pumping and tyre pressures – and at the same time state the user's obligations to look after and to clean the chair – and to report any problems.[27]

There are even further complications for therapists. If most cushions 'bottom out' fairly regularly with heavy use[28], and put users at risk of pressure sores, whose responsibility is it to ensure that cushions are replaced – the user or the professional? The answer is probably both. The British Society for Rehabilitation Medicine states that managers 'of NHS Special Seating Services need to recognise that they are responsible for ensuring that there are frequent inspections to maintain the seating system in safe and good working order'.[29] But, equally, it should be made clear to users that they need to be alert to problems. However, maintenance arrangements will differ; powered wheelchairs might require annual maintenance checks, non-powered chairs triennial checks, and some chairs (eg standard attendant propelled models with puncture-proof tyres) might require even less.[30]

Poorly maintained wheelchairs

Sometimes, problems with equipment are less obviously connected to instructions and information; for instance, the 'inadequate, poorly maintained and incomplete' wheelchairs in hospitals'.

Indeed, the potential problems with wheelchairs – both in hospital and at home – are legion, relate to safety, performance and satisfactory quality and quite rightly create concern that wheelchairs can become 'chariots of fear'.[31] For example, upholstery wears and tears, seats sag, people develop pressure sores, inappropriate cushions make people hot and clammy, poor suspension can cause considerable discomfort, inadequately inflated tyres might occasion erratic steering or brake failure, brakes can work loose and need constant adjustment, and brake handles are sometimes too stiff or awkwardly positioned. Foam coverings on armrests might be inadequate, become worn and expose sharp edges; missing or defective footplates leave feet unprotected. Heel straps might not work or make Achilles tendons sore; and, if they are worn away, exposed upright footrest spikes inflict lacerations and penetrating foot injuries.[32]

Wheelchair users can suffer harm, not just from ill-maintained wheelchairs, but also from poor prescription by professionals or inappropriate purchase. For example, badly fitting wheelchairs and special seating can result in poor respiratory function, pressure sores, muscle fatigue, depression, discomfort and pain, progressive deformity (especially in children), loss of function due to poor upper limb control and hand-eye coordination.[33]

However, even in relation to this catalogue of wheelchair ills, instruction and information remain relevant to increasing the awareness of both the staff of statutory services and individual users.[34]

Safety: walking aids

The provision of walking aids by statutory services requires alertness to safety aspects. For example, crutches might exhibit broken, ill-fitting or loose joints, cracks or distortions. After long use, some crutches, both metal and wooden, snap. Wing nuts can work loose and become worn, and the spring-loaded buttons on metal crutches need to be checked to ensure they are in working order. Rubber tips (often referred to as ferrules) frequently become worn and put people at risk on slippery or wet surfaces – though it should be explained to users that they should check ferrules regularly and request replacements as necessary. Thus, the safe provision of crutches involves not just the condition of the hardware but also instruction in use and maintenance.[35]

Walking frames can develop similar problems including bending, deformation, fracture, protruding screws (which can damage people or furniture as well as weaken the frame), handgrips which are cracked, split, loose or too hard (and thus cause ulnar nerve palsies), worn ferrules. One reason why frames can become weakened is that when people fall whilst using their frame, they might all on the frame and thus weaken it.[36]

Incorrect use of walking aids is common, as are walking sticks of the wrong height; and even NHS patients issued with walking frames might not receive instructions. People's mental ability also affects effective and safe use of walking aids.[37]

3. IMPRECISE LEGISLATION AND UNCERTAINTY ABOUT THE LAW

Legislation determines what people and organisations can and can't do. For example, it places duties on social services departments to arrange for the provision of equipment, a duty on the Secretary of State for Health to provide a comprehensive health service, a duty on manufacturers not to place unsafe products on the market – and on employers to try to ensure that staff do not risk injury through lifting people.

It would seem to follow that the more detailed and precise legislation is, the better is everybody informed about what they can and can't do – and what they are entitled to and what not. The consequence ought to be a reduction in dispute and litigation, since legal advice would be clearer and more certain – and people generally wish to avoid disputes that are doomed to failure. Accordingly, it would seem to follow also that legislation would always be precise and detailed; however, this is by no means always the case.

For example, some welfare legislation is endemically imprecise. This might be by omission; the NHS Act 1977 does not mention specific services or equipment, referring only to services at very general levels, such as medical, nursing, after-care, illness prevention, and so on. Alternatively or additionally, imprecision could be by way of vaguely expressed duties. For instance, the duty to provide medical and nursing services, anyway non-specific, is further clouded by the qualification that they need only be provided so far as 'necessary to meet all reasonable requirements'. And, by way of good measure, community care was introduced with exceptional brevity by the NHS and Community Care Act 1990, leaving many central processes – such as assessment of people's needs – legally undefined.

Nevertheless, not all welfare legislation is so minimalist. In contrast to community care legislation, the Education Act 1996 (following its predecessor, the Education Act 1993) does put in place a detailed, statutory scheme of assessment for children with special educational needs (see Chapter 11). And, the Chronically Sick and Disabled Persons Act 1970, though leaving 'need' undefined, does list specific welfare services that authorities should consider providing (see Chapter 7). Outside of the welfare field, a range of legislation deals in detail with matters relevant to equipment, including the sale and supply of goods, product safety and unfair terms in consumer contracts – whilst the common law of negligence boasts a wealth of concepts and axioms.

Two obvious questions arise. The first is about *why* some legislation is imprecise. The second is concerned with whether precise legislation – intended to clarify the law – does actually make life simpler and, eg, avoid the need for people to take disputes to court.

Why is some legislation imprecise?

There are several reasons why legislation is drafted imprecisely. First, there is sometimes a balance to be achieved between flexibility and inflexibility. For instance, if the NHS Act 1977 listed every service and type of equipment that could be provided, the Act would have to be changed every month, as new products or new treatments became available. In other words, an impossibly detailed Act would be self-defeating. Such legislation would impose a strait-jacket on authorities – not only impeding innovation, but also giving retrograde authorities an excuse not to step outside the 'exhaustive' statutory detail contained in the legislation. This sort of argument might explain why s.2 of the Chronically Sick and Disabled Persons Act 1970, though mentioning specific services, defines neither 'need' nor the circumstances in which it is legally 'necessary' for authorities to meet that need (see p.158).

The wording of legislation cannot foresee every particular circumstance in life that is likely to arise. For instance, in order to equip the law courts to deal with a great variety of circumstance, legislation dealing with unfair contract terms leaves much to what the judges consider 'reasonable' (albeit with a statutory list of suggestions about what unfairness might look like). Similarly, the Consumer Protection Act 1987 (Part 1) vaguely consigns the safety of products to the expectations of consumers – whatever they might be. The Medical Devices Regulations allow potential offenders a defence that they employed 'due diligence'. And employers only have to ensure that staff do not risk injury by lifting people and loads, so far as is 'reasonably practicable'.

There are also less impressive reasons why legislation is sometimes vague. The government of the day might recognise the complexity or sensitivity of the area of life with which the legislation is dealing – and so simply 'duck' the issues. Alternatively, draftsmen might simply make mistakes or express themselves unclearly.

Does precise legislation make things easier?

In some respects, clear legislation obviously helps to convey an understanding of what the law is. For instance, the Unfair Contract Terms Act 1977 explicitly states that contracts cannot exclude liability for personal injury or death caused by negligence. The Sale of Goods Act 1979, too, puts in place a solid statutory framework, governing contracts for the sale and supply of goods. And, even welfare legislation such as the Chronically Sick and Disabled Persons Act 1970 places an absolute duty on authorities to make arrangements for the provision of equipment – once they have accepted that there is a need which it is necessary for them to meet.

However, in other respects, precise legislation does not put an end to complexity and dispute. For example, the Education Act 1996 imposes detailed duties concerning the assessment of children's special educational needs – right down to the form such assessments should take, and the distinction between a child's *educational* and *non-educational* needs at school. Yet, still uncertainties arise – eg, about whether the need for speech therapy, or a through-floor lift, should be classified as educational or non-educational. It is almost as though for every answer given by legislation, another question is posed. Indeed, the fact that the Education Act 1996 is so detailed seems almost to have stimulated rather than averted, legal dispute. Such has been the stream of judicial review cases in the last decade, that a Special Educational Needs Tribunal now diverts complaints and challenges away from the law courts (see p.274).

Even when legislation does establish apparently clear and detailed rules, uncertainties seem inevitably to lie in wait one step beyond. For instance, the Sale of Goods Act 1979 states that goods should be of satisfactory quality. But what makes goods of satisfactory quality? Apart from referring to people's expectations, the Act lists a number of aspects including fitness for purpose, freedom from minor defects and durability. But what does durability mean – eg, in relation to a wheelchair or walking frame used by all sorts of people in different circumstances and in diverse ways? Here, the Act does not provide the answer.

Indeed, over-precision might be positively counter-productive. For instance, the Sale of Goods Act 1979 has been described as delightful to read and of apparently 'limpid clarity', but deceptively so because[38]:

> 'the draftsman has been so concise as to render an apparently self-evident proposition quite ambiguous… The excessive use of definitions is one of the curses of modern legislation and more often than not seems only to obscure than to illumine the meaning. Fortunately, the legislature is sometimes prepared to recognise that certain words are wholly undefinable. Thus the word 'possession' appears in innumerable statutes, but Parliament has wisely chosen not to attempt a definition.'

It should also be noted that some areas of law are still scarcely governed by legislation – eg, the law of negligence is still rooted in the common law.

Uncertainty about the law

The effect of imprecise legislation is that people do not know what the law is. In the welfare field in particular, such legislation allows much to be decided by individual authorities in the light of their local policies, priorities and resources. For example, without any change in legislation, the NHS has been increasingly rationing services and equipment, whilst social services departments are imposing more charges on service users.

Such flexibility, as already mentioned above, can be both good and bad for authorities and service users. Authorities might relish the freedom, but at the same time lament the lack of direction given them by central government. Likewise, service users might praise those authorities which exercise their powers to provide high quality services – but be powerless to challenge the same authorities when policies change and provision is reined back. Furthermore, when authorities render their responsibilities obscure by hiding behind vague legislation, service users – unable to ascertain exactly who should be providing what equipment either in principle or practice – might become thoroughly bewildered.

If legislation is unclear, then until particular questions and disputes reach the law courts, uncertainties persist. For instance, the approach that the courts would take to the definition of a 'medical device' (in the Medical Devices Regulations 1994) is currently unknown; and for some 25 years, people could only speculate about how the courts would interpret the duties of social services departments to provide equipment under s.2 of the Chronically Sick and Disabled Persons Act 1970.

Even when the courts do actively intervene, it is clear that the law is not a fixed entity, but is constantly moving and changing. Judges disagree with one another, adapt the law on a case-by-case basis and sometimes overrule previous decisions. A recent House of Lords (*X v Bedfordshire CC*) case about the negligence of local authorities and their staff in relation to children illustrates well the difficulties the judges experience when trying to understand the rights of individuals in the context of welfare services.[39] And, in the NHS context, judicial disagreement was illustrated when the Court of Appeal overruled the High Court (*R v Cambridge HA, ex parte B*) – on the very same day the latter had ruled that a health authority should re-think its decision not to provide lifesaving treatment for a child with leukaemia.[40]

When dealing with the common law, such as the law of negligence, judges actively and continually 'make law' as they add to, and modify, the body of rules that has been established in the law courts over the centuries. When analysing legislation, they interpret, and sometimes re-interpret the meaning (and sometimes underlying purpose) of legislative words, phrases and clauses.

Guidance or legislation?

In order to fill out the framework that legislation puts in place, government issues substantial quantities of guidance. Guidance plays a particularly important role within the welfare state, encouraging authorities to act in particular ways and to change policies as circumstances, finances and people's needs change. Similarly, a series of guidance notes and bulletins has been issued by the Medical Devices Agency about the Medical Devices Regulations 1994, which cover the safety and performance of a wide range of medical devices. Such guidance explaining legislation usually contains the proviso that it does not represent, but merely interprets, the law. Even so, judges sometimes disagree amongst themselves when attempting to establish the weight and precise legal status of guidance. For example, during a recent Court of Appeal case about s.2 of the Chronically Sick and Disabled Persons Act 1970 and community care generally (*R v Gloucestershire CC, ex parte Barry*), the legal effect of, eg, community care policy guidance, community care practice guidance, a Social Services Inspectorate letter and an old DHSS Circular issued in 1970, was discussed.[41]

One advantage of relying on guidance, rather than legislation, is that it facilitates the administration of welfare or regulatory systems. A disadvantage in some circumstances is that guidance, unlike legislation, is not placed before Parliament. If the balance between guidance and its governing legislation tips too far toward the former, fears grow that government has too free a hand.

Whether passing detailed or vague legislation, government finds itself confronted by a tension. It talks of deregulation and minimal interference by the State and a reduction in legislation.[42] However, regulatory directives of the European Community have continued to pass into United Kingdom law apace, whilst, generally, society at large is becoming increasingly 'legalised' as the amount of legislation passed by Parliament proliferates steadily.[43] Yet, equally, without detailed legislation, government instead feels obliged to issue large quantities of guidance.

4. TENSION BETWEEN PEOPLE'S NEEDS AND RESOURCES

Very apparent throughout the book is the tension between people's needs and the resources available to meet them.

Conflicts emerge at all levels when people's needs plainly outstrip the resources available to statutory services – particularly since major national surveys have shown that people with disabilities tend to be poorer on average than the rest of the population. Less likely to have sufficient money to purchase privately the equipment and home adaptations they need, many disabled people remain dependent on statutory services or assistance from voluntary organisations.

Statutory services are constantly striving to meet people's needs with limited resources. In the past, much rationing of equipment and services has proceeded silently, although now it is increasingly publicised and sometimes challenged in the law courts. For example, a child in Cambridge is denied possibly life-saving treatment for leukaemia[44], people's home help services are removed or reduced in Gloucestershire[45], and in Lancashire the social services department refuses to support an elderly lady in her own home – insisting instead that she must go into a nursing home because it is cheaper.[46] Difficult local decisions have to be made by individual professionals, managers, social services committees.

The law affecting defective products is also framed by considerations of resources and needs. For instance, the courts have traditionally been hesitant in finding negligence when products have been badly designed – because of complicated questions of public policy about the risks that society should be exposed to when new products are developed. Legislation dealing with product safety has to protect consumers without placing excessively onerous burdens on business. Thus, under the General Product Safety Regulations 1994, products are defined as unsafe if their use involves more than the minimum risk considered acceptable and consistent with a high level of protection of health and safety. The words, *minimum risk*, *considered acceptable* and *high*, indicate quite reasonably that the elimination of all risk in all circumstances is simply not feasible.

Can people's need for equipment be defined by money?

The law courts and the ombudsmen generally accept that, one way or another, authorities can take account of resources when deciding what people really 'need' and what services will be provided.

From one point of view, this is difficult to understand. It is one thing to say that a person has a need which cannot be afforded; but it is quite another to state that a person does not have a particular need, because there is not enough money. Yet both the NHS and local authorities are coming close to embracing this latter type of approach – and the courts appear to be more or less going along with it. Thus (*R v Cambridge HA ex parte B*), when a High Court judge told a health authority not to 'toll the bell of tight resources', after it had refused to treat a seriously ill child, the Court of Appeal swiftly overturned the judge's decision.[47] And in a 1995 High Court case (*R v Gloucestershire CC, ex parte Mahfood*) about the withdrawal of home help services under s.2 of the CSDPA, the judge concluded that local authorities could take account of resources when assessing people's needs.[48] Nevertheless, the approach of the courts has not been all one way. The *Mahfood* case went to the Court of Appeal and was overturned in June 1996 (see below).

The argument on behalf of service users is as follows. It is accepted that local authority judgements are likely to vary (since professional judgements by their very nature differ) – and so will never be objective in the sense that there is always one 'right answer'. Thus, the courts have held that two assessments – even by the same person – of the same child's special educational needs might result in different conclusions (see p.438). Similarly, the ombudsman investigated the following case:

> Three different assessments by the social services department had been made – resulting in recommendations of a vertical lift, a straight stairlift and finally a curved stairlift (the last of which a woman, with multiple sclerosis, actually wanted). The authority explained this by saying that all the decisions were professionally and technically correct and ultimately had been based on individual judgement. The essential element in the last assessment was that the user's personal feelings and circumstances were given greater weight. The ombudsman recognised possible shortcomings in the original recommendation of the vertical lift (because of the obvious disruptive effect it would have had). However, (since he is not empowered to question professional judgements) he would not criticise this as maladministration, even though subsequent assessments resulted in different conclusions; this was because the original decision 'followed a proper assessment and was not inherently perverse or arbitrary'.[49]

In any event, the argument runs, assessments should not be influenced by resources. The counter-argument is that the assessment of people's needs cannot but be influenced by resources – and that this is envisaged as a matter of course in Acts of Parliament, whether or not they state this explicitly.

Taking a resource-driven approach raises important questions about whether people's health and social care needs should be measured in terms of money. In issue is not only people's well-being, but also the integrity of professionals, who can very easily introduce affordability into their assessments of people's needs. Yet there is a clear incentive for them to do just this; less fuss is likely to result if they state that a person is not in need – rather than that she is in need, but that there is no money to do anything about it. All this is in sharp contrast to a recent decision in the courts about the treatment of sewage demanded by a European Community directive. In a dispute about how the limits to an estuary should be measured, the High Court ruled that in any event, cost – which the government had taken account of, because sewage treatment in *estuary waters* is more expensive than in *coastal waters* – could not be relevant to deciding a feature of physical geography.[50] The courts have *not* generally been prepared to take such a direct approach to people's medical or social needs – eg, by reminding authorities that resources cannot sensibly determine whether somebody really needs an electric wheelchair or needs a stairlift. However, in June 1996 (*R v Gloucestershire CC, ex parte Barry*), the Court of Appeal did take such an approach when reaching a decision which, intuitively at least, appeals to common sense. One of the judges stated simply that, under s.2 of the Chronically Sick and Disabled Persons Act 1970, the defining of people's needs in terms of money would lead to a logical absurdity: if there was no money, nobody could, by definition, be in need. However, the decision was not unanimous (another of the three judges dissented), and it remains to be seen whether the decision will survive an appeal to the House of Lords.[51]

Independent assessments of people's needs

One view is that people's needs should be assessed independently, so that authorities (eg social services or education) would not then be able to influence the outcome of assessments with an eye to available resources. However, embraced on any large scale this would merely exacerbate the mismatch between the needs and expectations of people, and the resources available to meet them. From the point of view of authorities, this would be a recipe for chaos, since they would be able to exercise even less control over their budgets than they do currently. Glaringly, community care guidance mirrors this tension by advocating strongly that assessments be, if not independent, at least 'needs-led', and be conducted irrespective of available services. Yet, at the same time, it warns authorities to beware of recording needs they cannot afford to meet.

From time to time, the question of whether local authority staff can conduct assessments fairly – because they are aware of the limited resources available – actually comes before the courts (see p.441). Independent assessment is an issue which the local ombudsman also sometimes grapples with:

> In one case, following a tortuous succession of disagreement and misunderstanding about adaptations for a severely disabled young man – between a district council (housing authority), county council (social services department) and the family – the ombudsman recommended that the county council should agree to fund an independent assessment, which both councils would then consider.[52] In another investigation, the ombudsman did not uphold a complaint that the clerk to an education authority's appeals panel could not be sufficiently independent, since he was an employee of the authority.[53]

In a third case, the ombudsman found that, without the report from an independent educational psychologist – paid for by the mother of a child with special educational needs – the child's needs would not have been fully identified by the authority. He recommended that the authority pay compensation towards the expense incurred for the report.[54] And, a woman with back problems, who was applying for adaptations to assist with food preparation and bathing, did not receive support for the application from the NHS hospital where she had been having treatment. Instead, she went privately to an orthopaedic consultant who wrote a letter to the social services department, stating that her condition did merit the adaptations. Although nothing apparently came of this letter, the NHS hospital changed its opinion some months later and eventually the application proceeded.[55]

From these ombudsman investigations, it can be seen that whatever the legal position, independent assessments are in practice being resorted to. They might be referred to when people take their complaints against social services departments to the final, Review Panel stage; eg, a disabled living centre (see p.82) or an independent occupational therapist might assess how safely and effectively a person with multiple sclerosis can use a stairlift – after she has been denied it in line with the local authority's policy. In similar vein, in one investigation the ombudsman called in the College of Occupational Therapists to assess the professional soundness of an authority's decision to class as low priority the needs of a child with special seating needs.[56]

Inequitable provision

Differing local policies and priorities, affecting how people's needs are identified and how they are met, leads to inequitable provision – varying not only between geographical areas, but also within the same areas from year to year, and sometimes from month to month. For example, reporting on community care in March 1996, the Audit Commission confirmed the continuing and significant differences between authorities in terms of the proportion of people they assess, the criteria of eligibility they apply, the services they provide and the charges they make for them.[57]

5. GREY AREAS OF PROVISION: WHO PROVIDES WHAT EQUIPMENT?

One consequence of imprecise legislation, is a blurring of responsibilities between authorities in the welfare field. Provision of equipment, notoriously, falls time and again into the resulting grey areas. In addition, problems are exacerbated by the admitted difficulties in defining who disabled people are and what type of needs they have, and in distinguishing 'disability equipment' from 'ordinary equipment' (see p.64).

For both authorities and service users, the existence of grey areas could, in principle, be either advantageous or disadvantageous. It allows authorities to escape excessively onerous demands and instead to pass the responsibility to somebody else. However, the drawback for any one authority is that whilst it can pass the buck, it might also receive it. For service users, this blurring of responsibilities could, in principle, allow for flexible provision of equipment and services; if one avenue is not open, another might be. For instance, in one case investigated by the local ombudsman, a disabled woman applied unsuccessfully to a local authority *environmental health department* for a *renovation grant.* She was advised instead to apply for a *disabled facilities grant* (which required initial assessment by the *social services department*). However, whilst waiting for the assessment, she obtained the adaptations through the assistance from the *Social Fund* (administered by the Department of Social Security).[58] But, equally, if authorities deny responsibility and pass the buck – the buck might never stop, as it moves from authority to authority, from authority to voluntary organisation and finally, perhaps, into thin air.

Authorities divide up responsibilities in terms primarily of the *purpose* for which equipment is required (eg to meet a health or social care need) and secondarily by the *type* of equipment (eg incontinence equipment as health care equipment and therefore NHS responsibility). However, attempts at hard and fast division of responsibilities for equipment between services is likely to fail for at least three reasons. First, people's needs can be complex and changing – and do not fit neatly into statutory pigeon-holes. Second, attempts are made to construct logical divisions on the back of legislation too imprecise to support them. Third, even if such divisions could work in practice in spite of their flimsy foundation, authorities – faced with budgetary pressures – sometimes exploit the uncertainties for their own ends and unravel attempts to create workable arrangements. Further explanation and examples are given in Chapter 3 (see pp.73–80).

Geographical boundaries between statutory services

Different statutory services do not necessarily have co-terminous boundaries. For example, a London borough's boundaries might – or might not – follow the boundaries of a health authority. And, a county council covering a large geographical area might embrace a considerable number of health authorities and NHS Trusts. Fragmentation in the health service has spread with the advent of NHS Trusts, potentially hindering the achievement of practical cooperation and agreed policies with other statutory services, such as social services departments. Although health authorities (some of which have merged) remain the purchasers of health care – and thus arguably the focus of NHS cooperation with other services – the extent to which they become involved with the details of equipment policy and practice is by no means clear. For instance, a health authority might purchase a wheelchair service from an NHS Trust, but it is the Trust which might make detailed rationing decisions – and decide, eg, how far it can afford to provide wheelchairs for children at school. Such decisions affect children with special educational needs – a field itself subject to fragmentation as budgetary and management responsibilities have leant towards schools and away from education authorities.

Further complexity exists. Metropolitan local authorities and a number of new (from April 1996) 'unitary authorities' combine functions – ie the same authority has both a social services, education and housing department. But, elsewhere county councils have responsibility for social services and education, whilst smaller district councils have carried out the housing function. Thus, a large county council might have to reach a number of separate and differing agreements with district councils within its area. Joint guidance from the Department of Health and the Department of Environment has stressed the 'fundamental importance' of cooperation – pointing in 1992 to the example of Hampshire County Council which had agreed county-wide 'overall principles' for home adaptations with the 13 district councils within its boundary.[59]

6. EQUIPMENT PROVISION: A STATUTORY OR COMMERCIAL SYSTEM?

Equipment is provided through the public, private and voluntary sectors. Statutory services have dominated provision of disability equipment to individuals; in the past, the private sector sold mainly to statutory services, rather than to individual users of equipment. The voluntary sector has attempted to fill the gaps between public and private sector provision.

This state of affairs means that equipment has been rooted in a statutory (welfare) system of provision. From a legal point of view, equipment is being provided to individuals on a non-contractual basis, either free of charge or for modest charges stipulated or permitted by legislation. Any contracts which exist are made between manufacturers (or suppliers) of equipment and statutory services. The consequences of this system are that since people are in receipt of public, statutory services, they do not have private, contractual rights enforceable through law courts – whether in respect of any 'right' to provision or of the quality of equipment.

In contrast to the statutory system is the commercial (free market) system of provision. Based on contractual transactions in the 'marketplace', this entails individuals striking bargains and entering legal agreements. In the context of this book, the commercial system operates when consumers buy equipment from retailers and manufacturers.

The Welfare State is seen by some to create a culture of dependency and to deny the notion of individuals as free agents, bargaining their way through life, and taking responsibilities for their own actions. If this emerged as a 'right-wing' view during the 1980s, it now attracts a number of unexpected allies. For instance, some disability organisations support this view – critical as they are of health and social care professionals who, they believe, have 'medicalised' disability, expanded their own 'empires', and attempted to make disabled people more, rather than less, dependent.[60]

Problems affecting both statutory and commercial provision of equipment

Both welfare and model markets face a number of problems. In practice, statutory services do not have the resources to meet everybody's needs for equipment; in addition, they have often struggled to identify the limits of their responsibilities. It has also been suggested that – because it is the staff of authorities who ultimately make decisions about what should be provided – equipment ends up not being used, when it does not correspond with what disabled people have requested. Nevertheless, this view should be contrasted with the findings of the General Household Survey that mobility equipment was used most when prescribed by professionals, rather than obtained by users themselves or their relatives.[61]

At the same time, a flourishing retail market in disability equipment does not exist at present. There are a number of reasons for this, including the previous dominance of the marketplace by statutory services, consequent lack of marketing strategies aimed at individuals, a dearth of knowledge and information about equipment on the part of public and professionals, stigma associated with the use of equipment, and the affordability of equipment in relation to older people's and disabled people's resources.

Bridging the divide between statutory and commercial provision

The gap between statutory and commercial provision is being bridged by the mixed economy of care. This development is summarised in the next section. However, in addition, there are three other points of note.

First, some legal principles span both types of provision. For example, under the law of negligence, individuals have the right to sue for compensation if they have suffered harm because of somebody else's carelessness. Although this right is a *private law* right, it is available not only against private bodies but also, at least in some circumstances, public sector bodies as well. Thus, although a user of equipment has no private law contractual rights against statutory services, he or she can sue (eg an NHS Trust) in negligence.

Second, there is no shortage of legislation designed to protect consumers in the marketplace; eg, the Sale of Goods Act 1979 (eg quality of goods), the Consumer Protection Act 1987, the Unfair Terms in Consumer Contracts Regulations 1994, and the General Product Safety Regulations 1994. It is unclear whether such legislation should be seen as belonging to the welfare type, protecting consumers – or simply as a mechanism for safeguarding the free market by ensuring that a 'level playing field' exists on which consumers can bargain freely. This ambiguity is reflected by European Community directives affecting products; they have a direct bearing on consumer safety but their 'preambles' emphasise that the overall purpose is to break down trade barriers between Member States. Nevertheless, it has been suggested that the significance of legislation affording consumer protection is that there are now *two laws of contract* – one governing purely commercial, the other consumer, agreements.[62]

Third, it could be argued that remedying the lack of information – a problem affecting both the users and providers of statutory services, as well as private consumers – would likewise not be an extension of the Welfare State, but a pre-condition for the working of the market. Whether this information is provided by the private, public or voluntary sectors, it would enable people to enter private, contractual transactions well-informed and in a reasonably strong bargaining position; as a result, competition would be stimulated.[63]

The existence of consumer safeguards and information is particularly important in the disability equipment field for a number of reasons. Few people are familiar with disability equipment in any detail, and so less likely to make the informed choices they would expect to be able to make when they buy most other types of everyday product. In addition, when people are ill, anxious about their changing or changed physical abilities, and threatened by loss of their physical independence, they might be particularly vulnerable and 'snatch' at potential (and expensive) solutions without the relevant information. Mistakes can be expensive and demoralising. And, a proportion of older people who buy equipment might have some slight mental impairment short of legal incapacity (eg those suffering from the early stages of dementia, or language impairment following a stroke) that could affect their ability to make informed choices – or to digest the small print of contracts of sale.

Collision of public, private and voluntary sectors in providing equipment

The contract culture and mixed economy of care that now permeates the provision of welfare services means that voluntary organisations and private companies are involved increasingly in the delivery of statutory services. The following examples illustrate the sometimes innovative, but sometimes uncomfortable, results which occur when public and independent sectors collide.

Accountability and liability of statutory services

The proliferation of purchasers, providers, independent contractors, sub-contractors etc raises questions about accountability. For instance, is it for health authorities as purchasers to lay down detailed policy and set criteria of eligibility for wheelchair provision – or can they leave it up to the providers, the NHS Trusts to do this? If they choose the latter course, is it not a matter of the tail wagging the dog – and how might a judicial review court react, when it finds an absence of health authority policy? After all, it is to the health authority that the Secretary of State delegates his or her powers.

When the discharge of a patient from hospital goes wrong, blame might be shifted from health authority to hospital NHS Trust to community NHS Trust and back again.[64] And, who is liable if a private company, under contract to an NHS Trust, negligently supplies to a person's home a defective and dangerous walking frame which causes an accident – the company, the NHS Trust, or the health authority (see Chapter 14)?

From service user to private consumer

There are a number of ways in which users of statutory services are moving, actually or superficially, towards becoming 'customers' or 'consumers'.

For example, it appears that some authorities are increasingly suggesting that people buy some types of equipment for themselves. When this happens, a person ceases to be a service user dealing with statutory services, but becomes a consumer dealing with the private sector – or perhaps a supplicant dealing with a voluntary organisation.

Under various provisions of NHS legislation, health authorities can make payments to other independent and public sector bodies who are providing services. The making of these payments, and the way in which they can or can't be used, is convoluted.[65] It is possible that in some circumstances, these other bodies can make charges for services which, if provided by the NHS, would be free. For example, a voluntary organisation might loan wheelchairs for a hire charge or provide toe-nail cutting services in return for a small charge. The legality of such charges is likely to depend on the type of payment made by the NHS to the independent organisation and on how the agreement is expressed.

Central government has been keen to promote the idea of a pseudo-contractual relationship between service user and statutory services.[66] This can have beneficial effects, insofar as users contribute to their own assessments and can make complaints about poor services. Furthermore, forthcoming schemes will involve equipment users actually becoming consumers, albeit state-aided: these are direct payments by social services departments to service users, and voucher provision to NHS wheelchair users (see p.178 and p.519). And the Motability scheme – through which people use a weekly State benefit (the mobility component of the disability living allowance) to pay for cars (sometimes adapted) – already functions along the same lines (see p.478). In addition, some social services departments allow people to select their own small items of equipment – eg, simple kitchen aids.

However, in other ways, the contractual, 'customer approach' to the provision of statutory services seems dubious both in theory and in practice. The notion of contract entails two parties, of equal bargaining strength, concluding an agreement of their own free will. But when people go to statutory services, they usually have no choice – they have to use their local social services department and cannot go to the neighbouring one. Second, people often go to statutory services not from choice – but precisely because they have run out of choices. Third, the provision is generally not enforceable by service users, and certainly not in contract; neither legislation, nor charters, nor local policy documents give service users contractual rights. In addition, people are not always competent consumers. For example, it has been reported that some people prefer general medical practices or schools which have slick, comfortable, expensively furnished waiting areas – irrespective of the quality of medical services or education provided.[67] In the field of disability equipment, there is certainly a danger that if people have inadequate information and advice about equipment, they will choose inappropriately, or even be deterred from choosing anything at all.

Contracting out services: purchasing, providing and statutory duties

Social services departments are beginning to contract out their disability equipment services to independent organisations in the private or voluntary sector. Much of this contracting out concerns 'operational' activities such as delivery, maintenance, collection and recycling. Substantial efficiency gains and better services are reported where such contracting out has taken place. Similarly, a number of occupational therapists who used to work in statutory services are now operating independently and contracting with local authorities. It is reported even that some independent organisations, private and voluntary, are undertaking assessment. This can result in more efficient assessment practices – such as the clearing of long waiting times.

However, a legal complication has to be guarded against. For example, community care assessment is a statutory function imposed explicitly by legislation – and it is *authorities* which have ultimately to be satisfied that people are in need. Depending on the particular arrangements of contracting out, and the way they are expressed, authorities run a possible risk of delegating such decision-making illegally (see p.140).

In addition, these agreements to contract out equipment services have raised some disquiet, amongst both smaller companies and the voluntary sector, about fair trading matters. The concern has surrounded the potential for abuse by large companies which operate as both manufacturer and supplier – and so have every incentive, when delivering equipment on behalf of statutory services, to supply their own products rather than those of their rivals. This could be to the detriment of those rivals, as well as to service users who might not receive the most appropriate item. The answer would seem to lie in stringent contracts and efficient monitoring, to ensure that such concern remains ill-founded.

An irony of the contract culture, which has so virulently infected statutory services, is that legislation states that NHS purchasers and providers (ie health authorities and NHS Trusts) do not actually make proper contracts when they enter into agreements with one another.[68] And whilst local contracting and purchasing can result in better specified, targeted and publicised local services, it can also lead to discontinuous provision and the fragmentation of expertise, as has occurred to some extent in, eg, the case of the NHS wheelchair service (see p.516).

Finally, in the area of residential care, independent homes and local authorities find themselves confronted by a potpourri of overlapping provisions and obligations. For example, the provision of facilities and equipment in homes is governed by the requirements imposed by legislation, by guidance and standards laid down by local authorities (in their capacity as registration authorities), and by contractual terms agreed with local authorities (in their capacity as purchasers of care). All three sets of provisions – the legislation, the registration standards and the contractual terms – differ to some extent and might be inconsistent. From the point of view of independent home owners, insult is added to this injurious state of affairs, by their belief that local authorities inspect their own homes more leniently than they inspect independent homes.

7. EMPOWERMENT OF SERVICE USERS AND LEGAL RIGHTS

A constant theme pursued by central government is the importance of enabling service users to participate and to complain. For instance, community care guidance emphasises that service users should participate fully in assessments. And the Education Act 1996 puts into place a statutory assessment scheme overflowing with opportunities for parents to question and to appeal against the decisions of education authorities. Social services departments are obliged to operate complaints procedures, the whole of the NHS complaints system is being reformed and the country is awash with both national and local charters.

Nevertheless, amidst this flurry of activity, there are significant tensions. Decisions about people's entitlements generally remain for authorities to take: community care guidance spells out the message that, in the event of conflict between authority and user, it is the authority that makes the final decision. Indeed, to suggest, as the guidance does, that conflicts sometimes occur is something of an understatement. It also fails to discuss properly the invidious position that social care practitioners find themselves in, caught in the 'crossfire' between the needs of service users and the financial constraints imposed upon them. Practitioners might find themselves blamed by service users for decisions which are quite beyond their control. Thus, Gloucestershire County Council became entangled in a High Court judicial review with the voluntary organisation, RADAR – even though the authority's director of social services felt that he and RADAR were really on the same side.[69] Or, as the chairman of the social services committee of the authority put it, 'we are caught between a rock and a hard place. We have to provide the best service we can with the money we have got'.[70]

Effect of complaints

Rhetoric about the empowerment of users requires qualification. On the one hand, charters and complaints procedures do offer users of services a means of cheap, quick redress. Their ostensible purpose is to achieve informal settlements of disputes and to ensure that people are not treated poorly by statutory services. Indeed, there is every reason to suppose that the published investigations of the health service ombudsman represent only the tip of a great deal of poor treatment and services received by NHS patients. However, at least the ombudsman publicly exposes a sample of these and recommends remedies for some individual patients and relatives. On the other hand, charters, complaints procedures and even the recommendations of the ombudsman do not offer legally enforceable remedies.

One of the consequences of encouraging authorities to set standards and people then to complain about them, is to raise expectations. They might well need raising – some people's expectations err towards the modest or even non-existent. For example, different generations of people who are deaf and blind might have very different ideas about what statutory services can, or should, provide. An older generation might have been hidden away by parents or relatives and so led very narrow, unstimulating lives. Younger people, better educated and aware of more opportunity, might expect very much more.[71]

Nevertheless, at another extreme, if a culture of complaint takes *excessive* hold, then complaining and confrontation can become a habit. Inflated expectations can lead to vexatious, frivolous and unreasonable complaints, made by those people who are not in the most need. In addition, complaints procedures often require a substantial commitment of resources[72] – at the expense of direct provision of services. Indeed, the government itself has recognised that empowerment of service users should not be all one-way. If public authorities have responsibilities towards citizens, then so too should citizens have responsibilities to behave reasonably towards those authorities.[73] For instance, general practitioners should not be called out for trivia in the middle of the night.

Some complainants gain deserved apologies, services or compensation. However, complaints procedures are to some extent flawed even in their own terms. First, their purpose is not only to give individuals redress, but also to enable authorities to identify and eradicate recurrent problems – and so improve services. But, if authorities are being forced, through lack of resources from central government, to cut back services – and 50% of complaints are precisely about the effects of the harsh policies that ensue – the existence of complaints procedures to deal with such issues is something of a red herring.[74] It is a bit like allowing people to attempt to go up on a down-escalator; some forthright individuals might benefit by complaining successfully, and policies which are inadequate for reasons unrelated to resources might subsequently change for the benefit of all. But, where resources are in issue, it is difficult to see how complaints procedures can provide an overall solution for service users in general.

Second, encouragement of the resolution of the majority of complaints against statutory services informally and internally is an attractive approach – but suffers from the flaw that such procedures need to be, and need to be seen to be, impartial. The fear is that, too often, they are likely to favour the authority rather than the complainant. The same problem affects how trade associations are viewed, rightly or wrongly, when they offer to conciliate between their members and consumers. Third, some confrontation is likely to spill over towards more independent avenues of redress, such as the local ombudsman or the law courts. Ironically therefore, informal dispute resolution procedures, designed to prevent such escalation, might precipitate litigation in some circumstances.

What legal rights and obligations do people and organisations have?

Generally speaking, people have little absolute right to equipment provided by statutory services – provision is for authorities and their staff to decide on. This situation is probably little appreciated. Consequently, the word 'right' is often used rather loosely in a non-legal sense. For example, the Patient's Charter refers to rights – but these are not rights enforceable in a court of law by individuals. And, perhaps falling into a similar trap, recent Department of Health advice to the staff of residential care homes refers to the 'right' of residents to receive chiropody services from the NHS or to buy them privately. Yet, as a matter of law, there is no enforceable 'right' to receive chiropody from the NHS – and it means little to talk of a resident's right to buy something with his or her own (scarce) money.[75] And, an Age Concern report, about the long waiting lists which affect the provision of equipment and adaptations by social services departments, concludes that older people are being denied their legal rights to basic equipment.[76] Perhaps this could have been put slightly differently; it is surely that people are being denied the equipment because it is unclear exactly what legal rights, if any, they actually have. Indeed, it is this very issue, centred around the provision of services and equipment under s.2 of the CSDPA 1970, which is being fought out in the law courts at the present time (see p.160).

The law courts are not well equipped to deal with claims about the provision of discretionary welfare services. The legislation underlying these services is essentially 'collectivist', passed for the good of society in general, not of particular individuals.[77] So, rather than recognise and enforce private law rights of individual people and award financial compensation, the courts tend to use judicial review – eg, to hear challenges to the rationing decisions of authorities. The primary purpose of the courts in judicial review is not to enforce the rights of the individual but to ensure that public bodies are not abusing their powers – and are acting reasonably, legally and fairly. Put simply, the courts are not so much concerned that authorities deny equipment to service users, as that they should do so in a proper and fair manner.

In contrast to a lack of 'rights' in relation to the provision of welfare services, individuals do enjoy private law rights in other fields of law. If people's 'neighbours' are negligent and cause injury, people have the right to compensation in the law courts. If people buy defective equipment, they have a right to compensation in contract; and if the product causes damage or injury, they can bring a case for compensation under the Consumer Protection Act 1987. The courts sometimes become ensnared in arguments about whether such private law rights can be enforced against statutory services. For instance, negligence is well-established in the NHS context, if it concerns the common law duty of care that healthcare staff owe towards their patients. But if it concerns *policy* matters, such as the suffering caused by the withdrawal of incontinence pads, the courts will generally not find liability in negligence. Judicial review is more appropriate in relation to policy matters, and even then the courts will intervene only very reluctantly.

It is perhaps the lack of legally enforceable rights enjoyed by the users of statutory services that makes it imperative that other effective means of redress are available. In a wider sense, however, it seems clear that the collective rights given to the population to benefit from, eg, the NHS, can only be enforced by the will and policies of both central and local government. Such rights would seem to lie in the field of politics, not law, although lawyers and academics might urge that the courts play a more active role[78] – perhaps as the High Court did in the case (*R v Cambridge HA, ex parte B*) involving a child with leukaemia (though it was overruled immediately by the Court of Appeal).[79] However, were the courts to become more involved in such matters, they would be offering only a panacea and not a cure – and more public money would be diverted toward lawyers instead of patient care. Indeed, some of the provisions of welfare legislation such as the NHS Act 1977 represent, perhaps, little more than policy statements, rather than tangible legal obligations and rights. If so, they are unlikely to be maintained or rescued in any substantial sense by judicial activity.

8. INFORMATION: FINDING OUT WHAT IS HAPPENING 'IN REALITY'

A large body of guidance from central government affects statutory services; local authorities and the NHS are urged to produce ever more publicity; whilst, from all quarters, a seemingly endless stream of ever-glossier reports and studies on aspects of provision continues to pour forth. Thus, information seems to be more important than ever – and the following are a few examples of information issues relevant to the system of equipment provision.

It is becoming increasingly difficult to summarise how the system of equipment provision works in practice. Long since fragmented – one of the reasons for the introduction of the Chronically Sick and Disabled Persons Act 1970 was the uneven provision of equipment and other services by local authorities[80] – the system of provision is now even more so. This is partly because of the development of an increasingly complex system of purchasers, providers and a mixed economy of care (see p.42). It is also partly due to the relinquishing, by central government, of direct responsibility for administering the provision of equipment such as wheelchairs, artificial limbs and environmental control systems. For instance, the practices of local wheelchair services are likely to diverge increasingly, reflecting local circumstances, policies, priorities and resources. Where once criteria of eligibility were imposed by central government and thus of national application, this no longer happens. Consequently, it becomes very much more difficult, if not impossible, to provide a summary of a 'national' wheelchair service.[81]

Other evidence of the difficulty in obtaining information came in Parliament in May 1995. Asked to list statutes, statutory instruments, circulars, advice notes and departmental letters affecting 'care in the community' – together with details such as title, date, summary, availability to the public, cost etc – the government's answer was curt and in the negative; 'this information could be provided only at disproportionate cost'.[82] This response is suggestive both of the complexity of the mass of legislation and guidance, and of the difficulty of maintaining an informed overview; and if central government cannot do so, it is scarcely surprising if statutory services and other organisations also fail to.

Expectations and views about the provision of welfare services seem to be increasingly disparate, depending on who is expressing them. For example, reports from the Department of Health tend to concentrate on the 'success' of community care policies. Perhaps this is justified from a financial, management, and organisational point of view; in this sense, there probably have been significant achievements. But, ask a local or a national voluntary organisation, and a very different picture sometimes emerges. Long waiting lists, people being excluded altogether from services, confusion, people sent home prematurely from hospital, people worried about losing their houses to pay for care, increased and unreasonable charges for home help services – and so on. It is hard not to conclude that, in some respects, a polarisation of opinion has taken place – despite recent government guidance about the need for 'partnership' between all involved in community care.[83]

Similarly hard to reconcile are views that reflect widely differing perspectives on the disability equipment industry. One argument maintains that manufacturers deliberately keep the market small, overpricing equipment and exploiting disabled people. The counter view is that the market is a difficult one to expand, that it consists of many small markets rather than one large one, that small production runs are costly, and that research and sales overheads are high (see p.72).

Finally, much importance is placed on the availability of information – almost, it seems, in the belief that by publicising problems, they will disappear. For example, both social services departments and health authorities are urged to publicise the criteria of eligibility that they use to regulate people's access to services. Such publicity can clearly assist people to understand what services are available and in what circumstances – but is by no means a magic wand which guarantees the 'success' of an authority's policy. For example, the effectiveness of criteria of eligibility depends on how carefully they have been drawn up, how clearly they are expressed, whether they are actually adhered to – and what their consequences are in practice. Thus, taking the last of these considerations, criteria which have been carefully developed, well-publicised and are consistently followed, might nevertheless still cause dispute and upset if they have the effect of denying people the levels of service and equipment that they require. In which case, the criteria, and the policy they represent, might be a notable administrative achievement, but a failure in terms of effective welfare provision.

Notes

1 Quoted in: Social Services Inspectorate (Horne, D.; Walker, M.) (1995). *Inspection of community services for physically disabled people in Cornwall.* Bristol: Department of Health, p.22.
2 Commission for Local Administration in England (94/C/0399). *Report on investigation into a complaint against Salford City Council.* York: CLAE, 1996, p.12.
3 Commission for Local Administration in Wales (95/0227). *Report by the local government ombudsman on an investigation into a complaint against Dyfed County Council.* Cardiff: CLAW, 1996.
4 Health Service Commissioner (W.113/84–85). *Failures in care and communication.* 2nd report 1984–1985. HC 418. London: HMSO, 1985.
5 Woodyard, J. (1990). Orthopaedic negligence: the tip of the iceberg? *British Journal of Hospital Medicine:* September 1990; 44, pp.163–166.
6 Wintour, P. (1994). Civil servant seeks cheery care stories. *Guardian:* 14 April 1994, p.8.
7 *Hansard,* House of Commons, Written Answers, 17 January 1996, col 595, Mr Bowis. And: *Hansard,* House of Commons, Written Answers, 22 January 1996, col 98, Mr Bowis.
8 *Hansard,* House of Commons, Oral Answers, 22 March 1996, cols 121–122, Mr Bowis.
9 McPherson, D. (1993). Inco supplies threaten to dry up in Gwynedd. *Care Weekly:* 5 August 1993, p.4.
10 Baroness Masham quoted in: Holden, G. (1990). What is the bottom line? *Disability Now:* March 1990, p.9.
11 *Hansard,* House of Lords, 3 April 1990, col 1342, Baroness Masham.
12 Campbell, F., Ross, F. (1990). Dealing with wheels: factors to consider when patients need a wheelchair. *Community Outlook:* October 1990, pp.23–26.
13 Parliamentary Commissioner Administration (C.867/V). *Actions in connection with the loan of an electrically propelled three-wheeler.* London: HMSO, 1976.
14 ICE Ergonomics (1992). *An ergonomics investigation into aids and equipment for elderly people.* London: Department of Trade and Industry, pp.33–35.
15 RICA (1996). Consumer clinic: is this walking frame defective? *Disability Now:* March 1996, p.12.
16 See eg discussion about ease of assembly of equipment: ICE Ergonomics (1992). *An ergonomics investigation into aids and equipment for elderly people: carried out on behalf of the Consumer Safety Unit, Department of Trade and Industry.* London: Department of Trade and Industry, p.34.
17 Dudley, N.J.; Cotter, D.H.G.; Mulley, G.P. (1992). *Clinical Rehabilitation* 1992; 6, pp.189–194.
18 The latest set of statistics includes figures for a wide range of consumer products, including wheelchairs, walking frames, artificial limbs etc: Consumer Safety Unit (1995). *Home accident surveillance system: report on 1993 accident data and safety research.* London: Department of Trade and Industry.
19 Chariots of fear: wheelchair-related accidents. *The Lancet:* 21 November 1992; 340, pp. 1263.
20 See eg: Dudley, N.J.; Cotter, D.H.G.; Mulley, G.P. (1992). *Clinical Rehabilitation* 1992; 6, pp.189–194.
21 Jill Calder, C.; Lee Kirby, R. (1990). Fatal wheelchair-related accidents in the United States. *American Journal of Physical Medicine and Rehabilitation:* August 1990; 69(4), pp.184–190.
22 Eg Gray, B.; Hsu, J.D.; Furumasu, J. (1992). Fractures caused by falling from a wheelchair in patients with neuromuscular disease. *Developmental Medicine and Child Neurology:* 1992; 34, pp.589–592.
23 Dudley, N.J. (1993). Wheelchair safety. (Letter). *The Lancet:* 23 January 1993; 341, p.246.
24 Brennan, M.T.; Thomson, A.R. (1990). Product liability and the medical profession. *Journal of the Royal Society of Medicine:* December 1990; 83, pp.807–808.
25 Smith, S.; Goddard, T. (1994). *Wheel power? Case studies from users and providers of the NHS wheelchair services.* London: Spastics Society, p.17.

26 Friend, B. (1986). Mastering the 'wheelie' opens up the road to freedom. *Therapy Weekly:* 21 August 1986; 13(8), p.4.
27 Aldersea, P. (1996). *National prosthetic and wheelchair services report 1993–1996.* London: College of Occupational Therapists, Part 2, p.31.
28 Campbell, F.; Ross, F. (1990). Dealing with wheels: factors to consider when patients need a wheelchair. *Community Outlook:* October 1990, pp.23–26.
29 British Society for Rehabilitation Medicine (1995). *Seating needs for complex disabilities: a working party report of the British Society of Rehabilitation Medicine.* London: BSRM, p.48.
30 Aldersea, P. (1996). *National prosthetic and wheelchair services report 1993–1996.* London: College of Occupational Therapists, Part 2, pp.15, 29–31.
31 Chariots of fear: wheelchair-related accidents. *Lancet:* 21 November 1992; 340; 1263.
32 Drawn from: Mulley, G.P. (1989). Standards of wheelchairs: awful can only get better. *British Medical Journal:* 6 May 1989; 298, pp.1198–1199.
33 See eg: Campbell, F.; Ross, F. (1990). Dealing with wheels: factors to consider when patients need a wheelchair. *Community Outlook:* October 1990, pp.23–26. Also: Royal College of Physicians (1995). *The provision of wheelchairs and special seating: guidance for purchasers and providers: report of a working group of the Royal College of Physicians.* London: RCP, p.9.
34 See eg: Sadler, C. (1989). Wheelchair comfort. *Community Outlook:* November 1989, pp.4–8.
35 Potter, B.; Angus Wallace, W. (1990). Crutches. *Physiotherapy:* 3 November 1990, pp.1037–1039.
36 Mulley, G. (1990). Walking frames. *British Medical Journal:* 7 April 1990; 300, pp.925–927.
37 Simpson, C.; Pirrie, L. (1991). *Physiotherapy:* March 1991; 77(3), pp.231–234.
38 Goode, R. (1995). *Commercial law.* Harmondsworth: Penguin, pp.23, 198.
39 *X (minors) v Bedfordshire County Council* [1995] 3 All ER 355 (HL).
40 *R v Cambridge Health Authority, ex parte B* [1995] 1 FLR 1055 (QBD and CA).
41 *R v Gloucestershire County Council, ex parte Barry; R v Lancashire County Council, ex parte Gilpin and RADAR* (1996) (CA) (7–10 May 1996, CO/95/1779, CO/95/1134, transcript).
42 See eg: *Deregulation and Contracting Out Act 1994.*
43 See eg: Galanter, M. (1992). Law abounding: legalisation around the North Atlantic. *Modern Law Review:* January 1992; 55(1), pp.1–24.
44 *R v Cambridge Health Authority, ex parte B* [1995] 1 FLR 1055 (QBD and CA).
45 *R v Gloucestershire County Council, ex parte Mahfood and Others, R v Islington London Borough Council, ex parte McMillan* (1996) 160 LGRevR 321 (QBD).
46 *R v Lancashire County Council, ex parte Ingham and Whalley* (1995) (QBD) (5 July 1995, CO/774/95, CO/108/95, transcript).
47 R *v Cambridge District Health Authority, ex parte B* [1995] 1 FLR 1055 (QBD & CA).
48 *R v Gloucestershire County Council, ex parte Mahfood and Others, R v Islington London Borough Council, ex parte McMillan* (1996) 160 LGRevR 321 (QBD).
49 Commissioner for Local Administration in England (94/C/1563). *Report on an investigation into complaint against Sheffield City Council.* York: CLAE, 1996, pp.10–12.
50 *R v Secretary of State for the Environment, ex parte Kingston upon Hull City Council* (1996) (QBD), *Times,* 31 January 1996.
51 *R v Gloucestershire County Council, ex parte Barry; R v Lancashire County Council, ex parte Gilpin and RADAR* (1996) (CA) (7–10 May 1996, CO/95/1779, CO/95/1134, transcript).
52 Commission for Local Administration in England (93/B/3111 & 94/B/3146) *Report on investigation against South Bedfordshire District Council and Bedfordshire Council.* Coventry: CLAE, 1996, pp.27–28.
53 Commission for Local Administration in England (93/B/3567). *Report on investigation into a complaint against Cambridgeshire County Council.* Coventry: CLAE, 1995, p.22.
54 Commission for Local Administration in England (94/C/2021). *Report on investigation into a complaint against Cumbria City Council.* York: CLAE, 1995, pp.16–19.
55 Commission for Local Administration in England (94/C/2750). *Report on investigation into a complaint against Liverpool City Council.* York: CLAE, 1996.
56 Commission for Local Administration in England (93/C/3660). *Report on investigation into a complaint against Rochdale Metropolitan Borough Council.* York: CLAE, 1995, pp.8–9.

57 Audit Commission (1996). *Balancing the care equation: progress with community care.* London: Audit Commission, p.33.

58 Commission for Local Administration in England (94/A/2369). *Report on investigation into a complaint against the London Borough of Islington.* London: CLAE, 1995, pp.5–6.

59 DoE 10/92; LAC(92)12. Department of Environment; Department of Health. *Housing and community care.* London: HMSO, p.8.

60 Oliver, M. (1990). *Politics of disablement.* London: Macmillan, pp.49–54.

61 Foster, K.; Jackson, B.; Thomas, M.; Hunter, P.; Bennett, N. (Office of Population Censuses and Surveys) (1995). *1993 General Household Survey.* London: HMSO, p.83.

62 Brownsword, R. The philosophy of welfarism and its emergence in the modern English law of contract. In: Brownsword, R.; Howells, G.; Wilhelmsson, T. (eds) (1994). *Welfarism in contract law.* Aldershot: Dartmouth Publishing Company.

63 Collins, H. Disclosure of information and welfarism. In: Brownsword, R.; Howells, G.; Wilhelmsson, T. (eds.) (1994). *Welfarism in contract law.* Aldershot: Dartmouth Publishing Company.

64 *Hansard,* House of Commons Debates, Health Service Commissioners Bill, 25 January 1996, col 540, Mr David Hinchcliffe.

65 For a summary of the position, see: NHS Executive (1995). *Arrangements between health authorities and NHS Trusts and private and voluntary sector organisations for the provision of community care services.* London: Department of Health.

66 See eg discussion in: Plant, R. (1992). Citizenship, rights and welfare. In: Coote, A. (ed) (1992). *The welfare of citizens: developing new social rights.* London: Institute of Public Policy Research; River Oram Press.

67 Discussed in: *Analysis* presented by Andrew Dilnot of the Institute for Fiscal Studies: broadcast on Radio 4 on Thursday 9th November 1995.

68 *NHS and Community Care Act 1990,* s.4.

69 Valios, N. (1995). Gloucestershire in the dock again. *Community Care:* 19–25 October 1995, p.1.

70 Judges force rethink. *Disability Now:* February 1996, p.7

71 Social Services Inspectorate (1989). *Sign posts: leading to better services for deaf–blind people.* London: Department of Health, pp20–21.

72 Simons, K. (1995). *I'm not complaining but... complaints procedures in social services departments.* York: Joseph Rowntree Foundation; Community Care, p.26.

73 Hencke, D. (1995). Keep up to the mark, Major tells 'irresponsible' citizens. *Guardian:* 5 December 1995.

74 Simons, K. (1995). *I'm not complaining but... complaints procedures in social services departments.* York: Joseph Rowntree Foundation, Community Care, pp.88–89.

75 Social Services Inspectorate (1995). *Responding to residents: messages for staff from inspections of local authority residential care homes for older people.* London: Department of Health, p.12.

76 See: Salvage, A. (1996). *Stuck on the waiting list: older people and equipment for independent living.* London: Age Concern England, p.42.

77 See eg Atiyah, P.S. (1995). *Law and modern society.* 2nd edition. Oxford: Oxford University Press, p.128.

78 See eg: Parkin, A. (1996). Allocating health care resource in an imperfect world. *Modern Law Review:* November 1995; 58(6), pp.867–878.

79 *R v Cambridge Health Authority, ex parte B* [1995] 1 FLR 1055 (QBD and CA).

80 *Hansard,* House of Commons Debates, 5th December 1969, col 1856, Alfred Morris.

81 See eg: Swaffield, L. (1996). Wheelchair services: last look for first step forward? *Therapy Weekly:* 4 April 1996. Referring to the major report: Aldersea, P. (1996). *Report of the National Prosthetic and Wheelchair Services Project.* London: College of Occupational Therapists.

82 *Hansard,* House of Commons, Written Answers, 4 May 1995, col 275, Mr Bowis.

83 Department of Health (1995). *Building partnerships for success: community care development programmes.* London: DH.

CHAPTER 3

OVERVIEW OF PROVISION OF EQUIPMENT IN PRACTICE

COVERAGE

1. Importance of disability equipment in society
   - Equipment is not always the solution.
2. Range of disability equipment
   - Types of equipment
   - Whom equipment can assist.
3. Definition of disability equipment
   - What to call equipment collectively
   - Different methods of defining equipment
   - Disability equipment or ordinary equipment?
4. How and by whom is equipment provided?
   - Problems in the system of provision
   - Provision of equipment by statutory services
   - Provision of equipment by manufacturers and suppliers
   - Provision of equipment by voluntary organisations
   - Equipment activities of disabled living centres and other specialist centres.

Key points

This chapter provides an overview of how the system of equipment provision works in practice and how it is characterised by a kaleidoscope of diverse and sometimes ill-defined products, views, motives, and concepts.

The potential importance of equipment to society is explained and how people can be assisted to manage everyday functions and activities. Some of the difficulties affecting provision are indicated, including problems of defining both disability equipment and the people who use it. These difficulties of definition affect, for example, statutory services when they attempt to divide up responsibility for provision, Customs and Excise officers when they attempt to apply VAT legislation – and the marketing strategies of the private sector when it determines what equipment to sell, to whom, and in what image.

Identified also are various factors which contribute to an under-developed consumer/retail market in equipment and to the lack of accessible information about what is available. Finally, the role of the public, private and voluntary sectors is outlined.

Questions people ask

- What is disability equipment?
- With what sort of functions and activities can disability equipment assist people?
- What is the difference between 'disability' equipment and 'ordinary' equipment?
- Why is disability equipment not more conspicuous in the High Street?
- Why is the division of responsibilities between statutory services for equipment such a problem in practice?
- Why has most disability equipment been provided in the past through statutory services?
- What types of equipment can be zero-rated for VAT purposes?

1. IMPORTANCE OF DISABILITY EQUIPMENT IN SOCIETY

Equipment helps us all to do things all the time; the car gets us to work, remote controls operate the television and the lift takes us to the twentieth floor of an office block. We cannot get away from equipment; indeed, it is often maintained that one of the defining features of the human race is that it uses tools.[1] As Professor Heinz Wolff of Brunel University has long argued, disability equipment products are no more than 'tools for daily living'.

The availability and use of equipment for people who are having particular difficulties with everyday activities is important for society – from the point of view both of individuals and of government policy and public expenditure. For example, an electronic speech and writing aid can enable an individual child to communicate and participate at school – and so go on to gain qualifications and earn a living. An outdoor, electric wheelchair might allow a young person to get out of the house, to work, earn a salary and not claim means-tested state benefits. A long-handled shoe horn and appropriate shoes can enable an elderly person with swollen feet to walk to her lunch club. This might assist her to maintain muscle strength and so be at less risk of falling and fracturing her hip. It could also mean that she maintains social activity, thereby keeping her spirits up and depression at bay. An effective hearing aid might reduce the risk of an elderly person in a hospital being dismissed as 'vague' or 'going senile' and being hindered from recovery and appropriate discharge home.

Equipment and adaptations have received some attention from central government in relation to its Health of the Nation strategy. They were specifically mentioned in the Health of the Nation Green Paper[2] as a cause for concern – but they did not survive to become a key area in the ensuing 1992 White Paper. However, one of these key areas is accidents; and underlined is both the high incidence of elderly people falling in their own homes and the preventative role of the NHS, social services, housing and environmental health departments.[3] At least part of this prevention surely includes the provision of, and/or advice about, equipment and adaptations.

Much of the equipment covered by this book can be classed unproblematically as 'daily living' equipment in a broad sense – whether it is required (according to statutory services) for health, social, educational or employment needs. However, as a consequence of shorter hospital stays and community care policies, the NHS is loaning increasing quantities of 'medical' equipment to people at home. For example, parents of 'technologically dependent babies' use nasal or gastric feeding tubes, suction equipment, nebulisers, ventilators feeding pumps, catheters at home.[4] 'High-tech' packages of care, some including drugs and equipment, are provided increasingly for people with cystic fibrosis, HIV/AIDS or cancer – or for people receiving renal dialysis, specialist feeding, anti-coagulant treatment.[5] Such a trend is in effect conveying such equipment, once the province of hospitals, into people's daily lives at home.

Equipment is not always the solution

Of course equipment is not always the sole answer to people's needs and might not be the answer at all. For example, the management of diabetes can involve using equipment such as syringes, needles and blood count monitors – but crucially it involves also education and support from NHS diabetes advisers and teams. And residents of nursing homes are sometimes inappropriately catheterised, because this is an 'easier' way of dealing with incontinence than assisting people to re-establish bladder control.

A shortage of adequately trained staff on a hospital ward can mean that people become dependent totally on wheelchairs or walking frames instead of being encouraged and assisted to regain mobility, independent of equipment. Yet, sometimes the situation is exactly the opposite. Use of a good quality wheelchair can be the most suitable solution, physically and psychologically, for a disabled person.[6]

People might not want to use equipment, even if it would appear to offer a solution. This might be because of pride or because of a reluctance to introduce into the home environment hardware which will have a physically or psychologically disruptive effect. Sometimes there is a middle way; an elderly person with a disorder of balance might refuse to use a walking frame to go out, but be quite happy to push a shopping trolley which acts as a walking support. Alternatively, confidence is at stake. For instance, a notable Social Services Inspectorate report on community care suggested that people's decisions about whether to stay at home or go into residential care were influenced more by fear and anxiety than physical frailty.[7]

Sometimes, it is the removal or rearrangement of existing equipment that might be required in order to make a home environment safer – for instance, the removal of slippery rugs and mats or the rearrangement of dangerously projecting furniture.

And, a final example (perhaps atypical) illustrates some of the complications, including the different viewpoints of professional and user, the difficulty of establishing what a person's 'needs' are, the division of responsibilities between statutory services, the degree to which statutory services should attempt physical or psychological rehabilitation rather than just handing out equipment – and so on:

> A woman has an accident, injures her back, and is forced to give up work. Three years later she is involved in a car accident and sustains head and leg injuries. For three days in hospital, her slightly confused answers and behaviour are attributed to the anaesthetic. She is discharged with a pair of crutches. She is visited by a community physiotherapist, but despite advice and assistance, she will not, or cannot, use the crutches – and thus prevents the fracture from mending and risks permanent disability.
>
> The physiotherapist suspects that her inability to use the crutches is for perceptual, rather than physical, reasons. Indeed, there is no reason, she believes, why the woman will not be able to walk normally again. However, the woman refuses even to consider seeing a doctor. Instead she wants a lightweight wheelchair from the NHS and to be rehoused in property more suitable for her apparent disability. Not only is the physiotherapist aware that the NHS wheelchair service might refuse to provide such a chair, but also that it is not even clear which wheelchair service or housing authority the woman should approach. This is because she has a home in one area, but has been living for nearly a year in another area with a friend – and dispute could well arise about which authorities are responsible for meeting her needs.

It can be seen that the provision of equipment may be very far from being a simple equation of matching people's physical needs to the right hardware.

2. RANGE OF DISABILITY EQUIPMENT

The book covers a very wide range of equipment, in terms of product types, the functions it can assist with, and the groups of people who can benefit from it.

Types of equipment

Disability equipment includes, for example, artificial limbs, diabetes equipment, easy-grip cutlery, electric toothbrushes, electronic speech aids, footwear, hearing aids, incontinence equipment, magnifiers, oxygen equipment, page turners, stoma care equipment, walking aids, wheelchairs. These are but examples from a long list – unknown to many people, including both professionals and members of the public – which is expanded in Part IV of this book.

Whom equipment can assist

Equipment is useful to people in many different situations and for diverse reasons. Young or old, severely or mildly disabled, it might assist people in their own homes, sheltered housing, residential homes, nursing homes or hospitals, schools or colleges, or at work.

Equipment can assist older people with mild arthritis or younger people with a progressive condition such as multiple sclerosis, motor neurone disease or HIV/AIDS. Handrails around the home can help a person who is a bit 'shaky' because of muscle-wasting. More dramatically, environmental control systems can enable people with a spinal injury to control their environment – even though they are paralysed below the neck and have head, mouth or even eyebrow movement only.

The examples of relevant medical conditions are numerous and, for the purpose of this book, not worth listing. The reason for this is that even two people with exactly the 'same', diagnosed, condition can have very different needs for equipment or adaptations. Much depends on what the individual person wants, on his or her environment and on carers. For instance, of two people, both with severe arthritis, one might need a wheelchair, the other not – because the first person would rather walk painfully than use the equipment. Even if both of them did decide to use wheelchairs, only one might need widened doorways or ramps, because the other might live in a house already having suitable doorways and easy access. And, lastly, only the first person might need or want jar openers, electric tin openers, or a personal alarm – because the second might have a carer (eg a spouse) who does everything in the kitchen and watches over the person's safety. Some carers are dismissive of equipment because they regard it as intrusive or a slight on their caring abilities.

Equipment in terms of everyday actions and activities

For the purposes of this book, it is more useful to analyse people's needs for equipment in terms of everyday function than medical condition. The following is a list of some of the everyday actions and activities with which equipment can assist. It will be noted that these are applicable to everybody and not just to people who are sometimes stigmatised as 'the disabled' or 'the old' – as though they were a race apart:

1. **Body functions:**
    - **breathing:** eg oxygen concentrators, oxygen cylinders, nebulisers, ventilators;
    - **sleeping:** eg special cushions, pressure relief mattresses, bed rails;
    - **hearing:** eg personal hearing aids, flashing doorbells;
    - **speaking:** eg electronic speech aids, communication boards and charts, eye transfer frames;
    - **seeing:** eg low vision aids, magnifiers;
    - **managing incontinence:** eg accessible lavatories, pads, bedding, catheters, enuresis alarms;
    - **managing a stoma:** stoma care equipment;
    - **controlling blood sugar levels:** diabetes equipment;

- **supporting or immobilising parts of the body:** orthotic appliances including braces, calipers, orthopaedic footwear, surgical collars, trusses.

2. **Actions:**

- **sitting up in bed:** eg backrests, adjustable beds, overbed tables;
- **getting in and out of bed:** eg hoists, high beds;
- **getting down the stairs:** stairlifts, vertical lifts, downstairs extensions avoiding need to use the stairs;
- **getting about the house:** eg handrails, low/no doorway thresholds, wide doorways, non-slip rugs, walking aids, wheelchairs, riser chairs).

3. **Activities:**

- **washing:** eg walk-in baths, wheelchair-accessible washbasins, electric toothbrushes, toothpaste tube holders, long-handled brushes;
- **going to the lavatory:** eg floor- and wall-fixed rails, raised toilet seats, automatic 'washing'/bidet lavatories, commodes;
- **preparing food in the kitchen:** eg accessible stoves, low work surfaces, cooker guards, jar openers, electric tin openers;
- **eating and drinking:** eg special cutlery, crockery, non-slip mats;
- **doing general household tasks:** eg high level sockets, plugs with handles, helping hands/reaching sticks;
- **getting out and about:** eg ramps up to the front door, outdoor electric wheelchairs and scooters, adapted cars, artificial limbs;
- **working:** eg standup wheelchairs (eg to work at a drawing board), large display computers (for people with low vision), stairlifts;
- **reading:** eg talking books, page turners, braille equipment and documents;
- **writing:** eg writing frames and guides, weighted cuffs, computers with easy-control switches;
- **safety:** eg bodyworn alarms which automatically dial an emergency number when triggered.

3. DEFINITION OF DISABILITY EQUIPMENT

Defining the equipment covered by this book is difficult. Detailed definition aside, it is not even clear what collective name to give to the diverse products. In addition, the question runs into wider fields of debate about how to define disability and how to view the place of disabled people in society. For example, is the inability of some people – to open milk cartons or get into a cinema in a wheelchair – due to their individual disabilities or to the wider failings of society in not ensuring the existence of suitable cartons or cinemas? Is it an individual or an environmental problem?

What to call equipment collectively

A number of different terms or phrases are currently used to refer to equipment. These include:

- aids and adaptations
- aids to daily living
- assistive devices
- daily living equipment
- disability equipment
- equipment for an easier life
- equipment for independence
- medical devices
- technical aids
- tools for daily living.

The problem facing manufacturers, suppliers, voluntary organisations and statutory services is to choose a name which conveys the most meaning to the most people. This is not necessarily easy. For example, many older people who find it difficult to walk up the stairs do not think of themselves as disabled; nor, doubtless, do the millions of people who wear spectacles or contact lenses. In similar vein, the advertisements that appear in Sunday newspapers for stairlifts, thus making it easier to get in and out, do not mention the terms 'disability' or 'disabled'. Whether the sellers believe that the terms are stigmatising or simply meaningless to many people, the concept of disability is clearly no part of the marketing strategy.

Different methods of defining equipment

Defining equipment is a problem. As already explained, there are many types of equipment and many different groups of people whom it can assist.

Assisting disabled people with difficulties?

It is unsatisfactory to define disability equipment as *equipment which assists people with difficulties in everyday activities.* This is because such a definition applies to us all when we use a car or a train to travel 50 miles in a day – because we are physically incapable of walking that distance, either at all or in what is nowadays considered a reasonable length of time.

If one maintains that disability equipment is *equipment which disabled people use,* then the question arises immediately as to who, exactly, disabled people are (see below). And, even if disabled people could be exactly identified (which they can't), which of the equipment that they use merits the label 'disability equipment'? For example, a wheelchair user might be using a wheelchair, a teacup and a low-level kitchen work surface. The wheelchair is an item of disability equipment, the teacup not – but what about the low-level kitchen work surface?

Definition by statutory purpose

For administrative and legal reasons, statutory services tend to define equipment and adaptations by *primary purpose*, namely, whether it is for health care, social care, housing, education or employment. At a secondary level, they also divide up their responsibilities by *type of equipment.* Some of the conceptual and practical difficulties affecting these definitions and divisions are explained later in this chapter.

Individual or social and environmental need for equipment?

There are two very different ways of viewing disability and the need for equipment.

On the one hand, disability is viewed exclusively as an *individual* problem. For instance, there is something 'wrong' with the person who cannot get up a steep flight of stairs in time to get to the lavatory – and who consequently appears to be incontinent. And people in wheelchairs or with difficulties in walking, who cannot get into buildings because there are no ramps, suddenly become 'the disabled'.

On the other hand, disability can be viewed *socially and environmentally.* Thus, the lack of a downstairs lavatory is the real problem, not the incontinence, which would 'evaporate' if the person could get to the lavatory in time. In fact, a recent booklet on health and well-being for older people demonstrates this environmental approach. Produced by the Department of Health, it talks about making the home safe, rather than overcoming individual disabilities. Thus, it warns against floor hazards such as electric wires, magazines and slippery mats, as well as recommending the use of items such as non-slip bath mats, grab rails and one-handed trays.[8] The recently passed Disability Discrimination Act 1995 takes exactly the approach that there is something wrong with the environment and with society. For example, it attempts to improve disabled people's access to employment, goods and services, and education.[9]

Community care policies often do not take account of general social and environmental, as well as individual, problems. For example, problems of inaccessible transport, buildings, houses and leisure facilities can cause as many difficulties as the medical conditions and functional disabilities of individual people.[10] And, some years ago, an investigation by the Parliamentary ombudsman demonstrated the tension between taking a medical and an environmental approach[11]:

> A man who had suffered a stroke made a good recovery and his employers offered to re-employ him; however, even using public transport, he would have to walk over four miles a day to and from work – a distance he felt he could not manage. He applied to the DHSS for a three-wheeled invalid vehicle, but was rejected because, tested out of context at the DHSS centre, his walking ability was judged by the medical officer to be too good – even though it was accepted that he might not be able to walk to work, especially in bad weather.

The justification for this approach was that (1) the DHSS had to adhere to strictly defined criteria in order to keep within the available resources, and (2) the availability of adequate public transport was not a relevant factor for the purpose of the medical assessment. The ombudsman sympathised with the complainant but did not challenge the decision of the DHSS.

Sometimes at least, the solution to people's needs might reflect a general, social issue. A social services department might, instead of providing assistants to do people's shopping, encourage or even pay local shops to make home deliveries. This reflects a wider problem; for example a recent report by Mintel notes that if local shops generally are to survive the onslaught of supermarkets, they have to offer value-added services – such as home deliveries to anybody who wants them.[12] Even so, solutions are seldom straightforward; when local authorities save money on home helps by persuading elderly people to use mail order shopping schemes, the social isolation of those people might increase as a result.[13]

Shopmobility schemes, which hire out electric wheelchairs and scooters to people in shopping centres, meet the needs of the local population *generally*, rather than the needs of particular, identified individual people. A recent study of these schemes by the Automobile Association has shown that they not only assist people who use the vehicles, but also bring economic benefit to their host towns and cities; the spending power of people who use the schemes is considerable.[14]

Impairment, disability and handicap

Attempts to define disability often refer to the threefold distinction to be found in the classification of the World Health Organisation: impairment, disability and handicap.[15]

Broadly, these categories are respectively about (1) loss or abnormality in psychological, physiological structure or function (eg loss of use of legs), (2) the resulting restriction on 'normal' activities (inability to walk), and (3) resulting social disadvantage (inability to apply for a job in a building with no wheelchair access). It has been argued that equipment has contributed much to the medical diagnosis and treatment of impairment; is contributing increasingly to the overcoming of disability; but, alone, cannot overcome handicap because of the wider social questions involved.[16]

Medical models of disability. Even therapists and rehabilitation doctors, ostensibly those most involved with trying to assist disabled people, sometimes stand accused of using the *individual-problem* and *medical model* approach to disability in order to further their own professional interests. This, it is claimed, can make disabled people more, rather than less, dependent. Some people have protested strongly about what they view as the paternalistic, prescriptive and empire-building approach of some professionals.[17] They believe that disability should not be confused with medical need. This is logical. If a person in a wheelchair gets appendicitis, she becomes a patient – but not because of the wheelchair. Similarly, if the operation is unpleasant, leads to complications and she suffers depression, this is because of the operation – again, not because of the wheelchair.

From the medical point of view, whilst it is vital for professionals to take into account people's perceptions of their own disabilities – only to do so could invite a move 'from medicine to quackery'[18], since all notion of objectivity starts to disappear. It has also been pointed out that advocating a social model to the exclusion of medical considerations can go too far, resulting in conceptual muddles rather than models, and working against disabled people by denigrating the prevention and cure of particular medical conditions.[19]

However, these considerations by no means invalidate the view that disabled people should have control (to the extent anybody does) over their own lives. Many of their needs are not medical at all but concern simple, everyday living – about which they themselves are best placed to make decisions. In any case, at its most positive, the debate is not about excluding professionals, but about re-defining their role, so that they provide advice, services and equipment in a less patronising and prescriptive manner.[20] The Community Care Direct Payments Act 1996, debated in Parliament in early 1996, reflects this approach. When in force, it will enable certain groups of people to receive payments from social services departments, so that they can buy their own services and equipment.

OPCS surveys of disability: equipment. The medical model of disability was not adopted by the Office of Population, Censuses and Surveys (OPCS) when it carried out major disability surveys in the 1980s. Instead, people were asked for their view of whether they had difficulties with everyday acts and activities, such as reaching and stretching, eating, drinking, locomotion and so on.

Although this still constituted the individual rather than the environmental approach (see above), it did not attempt to measure disability in terms of diagnosed medical condition. However, as a result, the waters were muddied as far as equipment was concerned. For example, some people who were using heart pacemakers, spectacles or hearing aids replied in the negative when asked if they had difficulties in walking, seeing or hearing. This was because, using these products, they were not experiencing difficulties in everyday living (precisely because the equipment was effective), and so did not show up in the survey as disabled.[21]

Asking the right questions about people's situations. Professor Mike Oliver has illustrated the difference between asking questions which portray problems as belonging to individuals – and those that point to problems in society at large. For instance, the OPCS asked people what it was about themselves that made it difficult for them to hold, grip or turn things. Instead, it could have asked about the design defects in jars, bottles and tins that made them difficult to hold, grip or turn.[22] This alternative view of disability has commercial, as well as theoretical or ideological, value. For example, the Institute of Grocery Distribution has not only commissioned research into the openabilty of items such as cartons and cans, but also stimulated practical changes to products on the shelves of shops. The Institute noted the 'dramatic' changes occurring in the demography of the population, the increase in the number of people over 65 years old – and that many 'packs are notoriously difficult to open by all ages never mind elderly and arthritic people'.[23]

Disability: financial or physical disadvantage?

A major aspect of disability is money. The OPCS surveys showed a significant link between disability and economic disadvantage; many disabled people are poor. Two outstanding reasons for this are that (1) disabled people have less chance of earning money, or as much money, as the rest of the population, and (2) that disability can increase everyday living costs which State-provided benefits might not compensate for.[24] Disabled people undoubtedly incur extra daily living costs because of their disability – including the capital costs of buying equipment. Not all of this might be 'disability equipment' – for instance, a microwave oven might be needed, because the person cannot manage the cooker.[25] A 1994 survey of people, 16 to 64 years old and with very 'severe and appreciable' disabilities, found that the average cost of equipment and home adaptations to disabled people and their families was £5,700 and to statutory services was £4,400.[26] And a survey by the Joseph Rowntree Foundation found numerous extra costs incurred by parents with disabled children, including laundry, clothing, heating, bedding, medical supplies, furniture replacement – and special equipment and home adaptations.[27]

In one sense, people with the money to pay for all the equipment, adaptations and care they need cease to be 'disabled'. Indeed, it has been argued that disability is in fact a political, administrative and financial – rather than a clinical or medical – category.[28] As one study of disabled people found: 'those in work, irrespective of disability, were able to buy more and promote their independence'.[29] In addition, the link between ill-health generally and low income continues to be of wider concern – but is beyond the scope of this book.[30]

Disability equipment or ordinary equipment?

Obviously, not all the products required by a disabled person are disability equipment items. What becomes clear is that, owing to their fluidity, the terms 'disability' and 'disability equipment' defy straightforward definition. Consequently, unsatisfactory consequences follow when legislation, or at least those who execute and enforce it, attempt to impose hard and fast rules. VAT legislation is a case in point as is the operation of the Social Fund.

The status and context of some equipment is neither stable nor, from a logical point of view, predictable. Spectacles are not generally regarded as disability equipment, though logically they should be, since they are clearly designed to assist people with visual problems. And it is possible that if baths with hinged sides and stairlifts continue to be widely advertised in the national press, they will cease eventually to be regarded as disability equipment (as they have perhaps been in the past). Everyday magazines and newspapers, and not specialist disability publications, will become the established and natural home of advertisements for such equipment. For instance, *Which?* magazine recently carried a feature on how to 'adapt your home', highlighting various products such as ramps, stairlifts, lever taps, extra bannister rails, pull-out ironing boards – and so on.[31] Once equipment becomes available on the general market, it comes within the public gaze and begins to lose any stigma it might otherwise have – at least in the eyes of some people. Thus, the line between relatively unknown 'disability' equipment, and 'ordinary' equipment is thin and changes over time.[32]

Furthermore, some equipment is *coincidentally* useful to disabled people. A television remote control unit is a lazy convenience for one person, but for another person, chair-bound, it is essential for managing a disability. Along the same lines, a recent publication by the Research Institute for Consumer Affairs investigated the dimensions of 'ordinary' cars in order to provide information for people with special needs for easy access.[33] In other words, rather than looking at disability equipment, the publication looks at the aspects of ordinary equipment that are relevant to disability. Similarly, when another recent issue of *Which?* evaluated microwave ovens, it took account of how conveniently the appliances could be used by elderly people and other people with poor eyesight or dexterity problems.[34] In the same vein, a broadsheet newspaper might carry a feature page on disability which includes advertisements not only for stairlifts but also for mail order famous brand perfumes – on the basis that disabled people might have difficulty getting out to the shops but need perfume as much as anybody else.[35]

Children under five years old: mobility component of disability living allowance. The distinction between ordinary and specialist equipment is utilised to determine eligibility for the mobility component of disability living allowance, a State benefit.

The legislation in question governs cash payments to disabled people who can benefit from 'facilities for enhanced locomotion' – perhaps for an adapted car or electric wheelchair. However, the payments are not available for children who are under five years old – on the basis that *all* children under that age require mobility equipment (eg pushchairs or prams). Thus, at the age of four a pushchair is ordinary equipment, but it is disability equipment at the age of five.[36] This distinction is not necessarily convincing. There is clear evidence that disabled children under five years old incur extra costs directly related to a lack of mobility, including additional transport, telephone, clothing, footwear, heating and laundry.[37]

Social services departments: not providing ordinary equipment? Some social services departments state that certain products, such as non-slip bath mats, bath seats and reaching sticks, constitutes ordinary everyday equipment which everybody needs. Therefore, the argument goes, the authority, after assessing people's needs for such equipment, is under no obligation to provide it. For example, under s.2 of the Chronically Sick and Disabled Persons Act 1970, the authority can probably argue that though a person needs the equipment, it is not 'necessary' for it to make provision (see p.163). This would be argued on the basis that such equipment is 'ordinary' and so can be bought easily and cheaply at a pharmacy.

Similarly, social services departments might operate a policy to the effect that safety items such as car seats, fireguards and stair gates will only be provided for children who need them beyond the 'normal age'.[38]

VAT legislation: designed for disability or designed solely for disability? The law concerning VAT illustrates well the considerable difficulty in establishing whether some equipment is 'disability equipment' and whether it is eligible for VAT zero-rating.

For example, in relation to equipment generally, VAT legislation makes the distinction between equipment *designed* for disabled people (as well as other people) and equipment *designed solely* – ie for disabled people only. Only the latter is capable of attracting zero-rating, if it is sold to an individual disabled person who signs the appropriate form confirming his disability. This would seem to be a clear distinction, but in practice it is not. Continual confusion and uncertainty arises about exactly what equipment qualifies for zero-rating. (In contrast to VAT legislation, the Medical Devices Regulations 1994 (see p.371) state that medical devices are those that are *intended* by manufacturers to be used for disability – but not *intended solely* for that purpose.[39] This would appear to invite even more uncertainty).

The requirement, that equipment be designed solely for disabled people, could exclude equipment which is designed for disability – but is intended to be used by other 'non-disabled' people as well. For instance, overbed tables might come into this category, as the VAT Tribunal explained[40]:

> 'We are of opinion, however, that the particular value of the table to the chronically disabled is by no means sufficient to enable us to infer that the table was solely designed for them, and an inspection of the tables...confirms our view. We asked ourselves: does the appearance and method of operation of this table suggest to us, using the words with their ordinary and natural meaning, that it was designed "solely for use" by a chronically disabled person? We can only say that the table struck as eminently practicable and convenient for all sorts of hospital patients and was not designed with a particular class in mind.'

TENS machines, for pain relief, have been given zero-rating status – but only after the manufacturer had argued that, although they were used in practice for acute as well as chronic pain, they had been originally designed solely for those with chronic pain.[41] And ordinary hearing aids which compensate for mild hearing loss do not qualify for zero-rating – but more powerful hearing aids, such as powerful pocket amplifiers, might do.[42]

The requirement that equipment be designed solely for disabled people does not apply to all equipment however. For example, in the case of some equipment (obviously designed for disability) such as adjustable beds, chair lifts, stair lifts, hoists and lifters, the legislation states only that they should be designed – not designed solely – for use by invalids. And for commodes, special bidet lavatories, and 'frames or other devices for sitting over or rising from a sanitary appliance', even the 'invalid' specification is omitted.

Motor vehicles qualify if they have been designed or adapted to carry a disabled person in a wheelchair or stretcher and not more than five other people. Also qualifying for zero-rating are clothing, footwear, wigs, wheelchairs – and equipment such as oxygen concentrators, ventilators, and renal dialysis units. Emergency alarm systems designed to be capable of operation by disabled people and linking either to a control centre or to friends/relatives qualify. Zero-rating applies to home adaptations needed by a disabled person, such as ramps, widened doorways and passages – and extended/adapted bathrooms, washrooms or lavatories.[43]

In practice, local VAT officers or the VAT Tribunal are likely to take into account the original design and patent of a product, how it is advertised and the context in which it is sold. For example, an electric riser chair, advertised in a disability magazine, is more likely to qualify for VAT zero-rating than if it is sold as a luxury item in an ordinary furniture shop. This could discourage manufacturers and retailers from developing a broader retail market, which, in turn, would reduce the stigma of disability equipment and give many more older people access to it. Similarly, in the case about overbed tables, the VAT tribunal, when rejecting the claim that the tables were designed as accessories to the special King's Fund hospital bed – and therefore eligible for zero-rating – consulted the manufacturer's catalogue. It found safety rails, lifting poles, transfusion poles and swivel buffer units listed as accessories – but not overbed tables.[44] Much depends on the local VAT officers. The interpretation of one local office will not necessarily accord with that of another – and even the same office might reassess, and change, its view.

Recently, confusion arose about VAT charged on an off-road wheelchair and on computer equipment provided for visually impaired people. Even the government found itself having to backtrack, one day stating in the House of Lords that the wheelchair did attract VAT, a few days later admitting that it did not – having apparently become muddled about whether it was a motor vehicle or a wheelchair and applied the wrong rules.[45] However, in the case of the computer equipment, more complicated issues surfaced. For instance, basic computer hardware (personal computer and printer) might be sold with a speech synthesizer and special software. It could then be uncertain whether the whole system can be zero-rated, or only those elements of it that are designed solely for disabled people. The answer might even depend on whether people bought different components of the system at different times, rather than at the same time – or hinge on the proportion or percentage of the total system that is comprised of specialist components.[46]

Just as Parliament becomes confused, so too might the consumer faced with a specialist mail order catalogue. For instance, a longhandled dustpan and brush is deemed eligible – but a lightweight, longhandled mop not. A 'contour general purpose turner' (eg for taps) is eligible, but not a foldaway key turner. And an electric plug with a built-in handle does qualify for VAT, whereas a detachable moulded 'plug-pull' for electric plugs does not.[47]

Social Fund. Similar problems sometimes affect the Social Fund (operated by the Department of Social Security), through which people suffering financial hardship can sometimes obtain loans or grants for clothing, household appliances or, sometimes, special equipment including disability equipment. For example, community care grants (and budgeting loans) cannot be given for any medical, surgical, optical, aural or dental items. This is on the basis that the NHS could provide them. Nor can community care grants be given for expenses which a local authority has a duty to meet.[48]

Local Social Fund officers have the power to provide assistance with a range of everyday equipment which people need – from cookers to washing machines and from wheelchairs to incontinence pads. Nevertheless, such assistance should, according to the legislation, only be provided on the assumption that such items are not available through other statutory services. Inevitably, this has led to difficulties. For example, in one case which went to judicial review (*R v Social Fund Inspector, ex parte Connick*), a woman had been denied incontinence pads on the grounds that they were needed for a medical problem, and that they were medical, and therefore excluded, items. The judge found that the officer had applied the wrong test and gave two examples to illustrate this; just because a handkerchief is needed for a runny nose or a bowl for a bout of vomiting, neither item thereby becomes 'medical'.[49] Furthermore, a previous decision by a Social Security Commissioner had similarly pointed out that cotton sheets or duvets would not be excluded items simply because they were required in connection with a medical condition.[50]

A Social Fund advice note, issued subsequent to the judicial review case, stated that a twofold test should be applied. First, if the item is 'an item of ordinary, everyday use', then it is not medical and therefore not excluded – for instance, cotton sheets, non-allergic bedding/curtains, built-up shoes and beds with adaptations. Second, if it is not an everyday item, then the question should be asked whether it could 'be reasonably regarded as dedicated to the cure, alleviation, treatment, diagnosis or prevention of a medical condition'? If so, then it is an excluded, medical item and not within the power of a Social Fund Officer to provide assistance with.[51]

An advice note on wheelchairs was also issued. It concluded that wheelchairs cannot be regarded as items of ordinary, everyday use – although 'Buggy Majors' (for children up the age of 10) could perhaps be. However, generally speaking, neither can wheelchairs be regarded as diagnosing, alleviating, treating or curing a medical condition. Thus, the note concluded, wheelchairs are not automatically excluded on the grounds that they are medical items, but may be if they can be provided elsewhere – for example, through the NHS or through the Motability scheme.[52] In any event, assistance with electric wheelchairs (which can cost over £2000) is sometimes available in practice through the Social Fund.[53]

4. HOW AND BY WHOM IS EQUIPMENT PROVIDED?

The system of disability equipment provision is undoubtedly confused. The bulk of provision has been dominated by statutory services, in particular social services departments and the NHS. A consequence, or at least a correlative, of this situation, is that a flourishing retail market in disability equipment has failed to develop. In turn, this has meant that competition in the private sector has not been stimulated by consumer pressures, the population at large has remained ill-informed about equipment, the market has remained small – and prices are perceived to have remained high.

Filling the many gaps between the public and private sectors, are voluntary organisations, both local and national, which give advice, financial assistance or loan equipment themselves. Finally, a number of specialist centres or organisations of expertise merit separate mention. These include disabled living centres, communication aids centres, educational technology centres, specialist rehabilitation units in the NHS, and special residential schools for severely disabled children.

Problems in the system of provision

The overall system of equipment provision is flawed in a number of obvious respects, as is demonstrated by the propositions listed below.

As a recent report put it, the three main planks of provision are vitiated by practical problems. *Begging* from voluntary bodies involves the drawbacks of charity (eg people's reluctance to approach a charity), *buying* requires that people have money and information (which many people do not have) and that a conspicuous market exists (it does not). Finally, *borrowing* from statutory services is subject to the resources – and sometimes to the whim – of the lender.[54]

(i) **There appears to be a widespread need for assistive equipment.** Surveys by the Office of Population, Censuses and Surveys (OPCS) in the 1980s showed that there are over 6 million disabled people in Great

Britain, of whom over 4 million use special items of equipment for assistance with everyday activities.[55]

The population is ageing, and as it does so and people's bodies change (eg people become less dextrous, less able to get in and out of the bath or to get up and down the stairs), the potential need for assistive equipment grows.

(ii) **People are poorly informed about equipment.** The lack of a well-established retail market means that, in general, people have difficulties finding out about equipment. One reason is that information about equipment has, in the past, been aimed by manufacturers and suppliers mainly at professionals in statutory services – rather than direct at individual consumers.

Disabled living centres (see p.82) provide a focus of expertise where people can try out equipment, compare different products and receive impartial advice. However, there are only about 40 of these centres in the United Kingdom. They remain little known not only to much of the general public but also to many social care and health care professionals. A further hindrance is that a significant proportion of people who could benefit from equipment is physically or psychologically housebound – and so does not get to see those products that are available in the High Street.

As a result, disabled people, older people and their friends and relatives know little about the availability and usefulness of equipment.[56] Even if people know that equipment exists, they might have little idea of where to find it, or at least specialist information and advice about it.[57] Thus, many are not in a position to buy equipment – even if they could afford to do so. In addition, this lack of information might even make it more difficult for people to contribute fully to assessments by statutory services and to the planning of appropriate solutions – because they are so unfamiliar with the equipment options available.

(iii) **Some people cannot afford to buy equipment.** Many people who need equipment might be unable to afford to buy it. The OPCS surveys found that disabled people were likely to have lower incomes than the rest of the population, principally because of the extra costs of disability and because disabled people have fewer opportunities to earn money. Whilst some people can afford to buy an electric scooter for £3,000, others, without any savings at all, and relying on state benefits, will find even £12.99 for a reaching stick prohibitive.[58]

(iv) **Disability equipment has a poor design and image.** Poor design of products is another factor hindering the development of a retail market in equipment. Supplied through statutory services and institutions, some disability equipment has tended to be *engineered* rather than *designed.* Displayed in a shop-window, it has said loud and clear to people, 'you are a cripple'.[59] As already mentioned, many catalogues have, in the past, been aimed at professionals working in hospitals – not at individual consumers seeking equipment for their personal use and ownership. It is one thing for professionals to provide equipment for other people, but quite another for people to buy their own products for use in their own homes. Thus, whilst many disability equipment products have, in the past, been functional and safe, they have not always been easy to use or aesthetically pleasing.

There are now at least some signs of change. For example, crutches and wheelchairs are available in a range of colours; and specially designed ranges of wheelchair clothing include trousers with flattened seams which do not cut into people's legs, and jackets without too much material which bunches up.[60] The Centre for Applied Gerontology at the University of Birmingham applies the *Owlmark* to equipment which is particularly suitable for use by older people.[61] When evaluating domestic appliances, *Which*? magazine sometimes considers the convenience or ease with which products can be used by older or disabled people. And the Research Institute for Consumer Affairs (RICA), which is linked to the Consumers' Association, evaluates equipment for disabled people and older people – and publishes results in its own publications.

(v) **People are reluctant to use equipment.** People might be reluctant to use equipment for a number of reasons, even when they do find out about it. It might be unattractive, or, as an unknown quantity, people might be afraid of it or even hostile. They might not want to clutter up their home environment with, for instance, hoists, rails and wheelchairs.

As people get older, they might find it difficult to admit that they are becoming less able and to accept the changes happening to their bodies. Carers might almost become 'jealous' of equipment because it seems to be a slur on their caring abilities. The vagaries of domestic relationships sometimes interfere; for example, a man might resent the intrusion of equipment provided for his wife to such an extent that he deliberately prevents her using the multi-adjustable (single) hospital bed on loan from the NHS – and removes the raised lavatory seat that has been provided for her. However, once overcome through advice and information, people's general reluctance to use equipment might subside.[62]

(vi) **Statutory services are unable to meet all needs for equipment.** Statutory services such as social services departments and the NHS are unable to meet everybody's equipment needs. For example, the NHS in England and Wales routinely rations incontinence pads, nebulisers, communication aids and specialist wheelchairs.

Social services departments have for many years operated long waiting lists, and people who are deemed to be low priority have had to wait months or even years for assessments. Many departments are now tightening their criteria of eligibility for assessment, services and equipment, whilst some have, in any case, more or less ceased to provide certain types of equipment such as special cutlery and simple bath aids.

Yet, the advent of community care will in principle mean an increased demand for equipment and adaptations, to enable people to remain in their own homes. Accordingly, the increasingly restrictive criteria of eligibility would appear to fly in the face of the needs of many vulnerable people. Nevertheless, because, generally speaking, people have no absolute legal rights to equipment – provision will continue to be subject to local resources, priorities and rationing. This means that what people get, and sometimes whether they get anything at all, can depend on where they live – since one social services department can be more generous than another.

(vii) **There is no well-established retail market.** The lack of a flourishing retail market in disability equipment means that people find out about equipment with difficulty. Even when they do find out about it, there is often a lack of information through which products can be evaluated and compared. This might cause competition to be restricted and prices to remain high.

There are conflicts of opinion as to why a flourishing market has not developed. Some argue that the market is not large, cohesive and waiting to be exploited – but is instead made up of a number of small markets, of different product types for different, small groups of people. Production runs are of limited size, thus precluding low unit costs. Prices are therefore justified given the research, production, marketing and sales costs associated with disability equipment. Sales visits to people's homes can involve considerable time being spent on assessing whether the equipment will be suitable for the person's disability and home circumstances. People's lack of information and awareness about equipment is also an obvious hindrance; as is some people's resistance, out of pride, to using equipment. All these are obstacles in the way of profitable exploitation of the equipment market.

Others retort vehemently that manufacturers and suppliers deliberately exploit disabled people by maintaining a small, 'niche' market of over-priced goods which are invested with a false mystique. Statutory services are also blamed – for having stifled initiative, development and competition amongst manufacturers and retailers.

Whatever the truth of these conflicting views, some manufacturers and suppliers clearly do believe that there is a large market and are trying to expand it in a variety of ways (see below).

(viii) **Voluntary organisations try to fill the gaps in the system.** Voluntary organisations fill important gaps between the public and private sectors. There is some concern that these gaps are widening as statutory services struggle to cope with the demands being made on them. However, *over-reliance* on charity is not a desirable option from the point of view of an efficient system of provision. Some people, out of pride, will simply not approach a charity for assistance, even if it is their own children, rather than themselves, who are in need. In any case, even when approached, a voluntary organisation can only give assistance if it has the resources to do so; and increasing demands will strain those resources.

Provision of equipment by statutory services

As explained above, statutory services divide up their responsibilities according to the primary purpose for which equipment is needed. These divisions of responsibility are to some extent artificial and, in any case, less than robust. Indeed, the existence of grey areas has long been recognised – along with the hope that authorities will come to sensible local arrangements, so that service users do not suffer from delay in provision or even non-provision. The general position is as follows:

- **NHS:** health-related including medical, nursing, therapy and chiropody equipment
- **social services departments:** daily living equipment and home adaptations
- **housing and environmental health departments:** home adaptations
- **education authorities and schools:** equipment and adaptations for special educational needs
- **employment service:** equipment and workplace adaptations for work-related needs.

More specifically, for example, community care practice guidance identifies incontinence laundry, disability equipment, washing/dressing, bathing, lifting/transferring, rehabilitation with mobility as equipment and services which could fall either to the NHS or to social services departments.[63]

It was pointed out in Chapter 2 that the division of responsibilities between services is of limited practical effectiveness for a number of reasons – the legislation is vague, people's needs are complex and do not easily fit into statutory pigeon-holes, and authorities with little money sometimes exploit the uncertainties in order to evade potential responsibility for equipment (see p.40).

Artificial divisions of responsibility?

In principle, the *NHS* provides equipment for people's needs, so far as they are met by the provision of medical, nursing and after-care services – and by services for the prevention of illness or the care for people who are ill. *Social services departments* meet people's social care needs and, specifically in relation to equipment, their needs for facilities for greater safety, comfort or convenience. Housing authorities have powers and duties to assist people in a number of different ways with home adaptations. *Education authorities* and schools provide equipment for children's special educational needs, whilst the *Employment Service* (through Placement, Assessment and Counselling Teams known as PACTS) can provide equipment and adaptations for people's needs at work.

From the administrative and legal point of view, this division of responsibilities appears to be necessary, logical and undemanding. However, in practice, there are significant complications. From the point of view of service users, equipment is for getting on with daily life, whichever statutory service provides it. Consequently, the sometimes fine division between what is supposed to be health care and social care equipment is likely to leave users bewildered – especially when provision is delayed or even obstructed altogether as a result. Such problems can be exacerbated when limited resources force authorities to adhere to rigid demarcation lines – thus 'passing the buck' to other authorities, or perhaps away from statutory services altogether and towards the voluntary sector.

Avoidance of duplication of equipment provision. The effects of vague legislation become more pronounced when the meaning of one imprecise Act of Parliament rests on a reference to another similarly imprecise Act.

Thus, some legislation is drafted with the intention that duplication of provision should be avoided; so what can or must be provided under one statutory provision is not also provided under another. For example, the Secretary of State is empowered to provide, for war pensioners, equipment or services which cannot be provided under other legislation. Similarly, the provision of medical items is excluded by the Social Fund (not dealt with in this book) on the grounds that they can be provided under the NHS. And, under s.29 of the National Assistance Act 1948 (and therefore, presumably s.2 of the CSDPA 1970), social services departments cannot provide any 'services required to be provided under the National Health Service Act 1977'. The problem which emerges very clearly is that when legislation (eg the NHS Act 1977) is vague, it becomes impossible to tell exactly what can or cannot be provided under it.

The question facing, for example, the Secretary of State (in relation to war pensioners) or Social Fund Officers, might be whether eg powered nebulisers can be provided under the NHS Act 1977. It can be asked in four different ways. First, can the NHS provide them in principle (ie is it legally empowered to)? Second, does it, nationally, provide them in practice? Third, does the applicant's local NHS Trust provide them generally? And finally, will that particular NHS Trust provide one to this particular applicant? Certainly, from the point of view of restricting provision, the Secretary of State or the Social Fund officers could ask themselves the first question and hide behind a fog of uncertainty. Yet, from the point of view of the applicant, the last question is most favourable; ie, whatever the position in principle, will the NHS Trust provide him with a nebuliser in practice? If not, the Secretary of State or the Social Fund will assist. Yet, adoption of this last option invites abuse, in so far as it tempts the NHS to refer people to these other avenues as often as possible.

In one judicial review case, a Social Fund inspector had refused to assist with incontinence pads, on the grounds that they were medical items which the local NHS could supply. One of the issues discussed in the case was whether the pads were items which the health authority would provide. The authority had indeed stated that it supplied pads in principle – but it transpired that the particular applicant did not qualify for provision in practice, because she did not meet the eligibility criteria of terminal illness or regular, double incontinence. The case was decided against the Social Fund inspector. On this point, in this case, the judge therefore favoured the asking of the fourth type of question referred to above – ie the one most favourable to the applicant.[64]

As for social services departments and the NHS, the acknowledged overlap in provision of disability equipment items, makes it difficult to see how the 'anti-duplication' clause can be applied very easily. One solution would be to argue that, by definition, provision by social services amounts to social care, by the NHS to health care – and that, therefore, social services departments simply *cannot*, legally or logically, duplicate NHS provision. This might sound like casuistry, but without it, it is difficult to see how, for example, a social services department and NHS Trust could both be providing walking aids locally – and legally.

Examples of grey areas of equipment provision. Buck-passing or migration of responsibilities is facilitated by imprecise and vague legislation, and by acknowledged *grey* areas which exist between the NHS and social services departments in particular – but also between all the statutory services providing equipment.

For example, bathing services, traditionally provided by NHS district nurses, are now provided increasingly by social services departments. When this happens, the bathing in effect becomes a *social care* rather than *health care* service, and is given by personal care assistants rather than district nurses. Significantly, because the bathing is then provided under different legislation, financial charges can be made by social services departments – whereas the NHS does not have this power.[65] The highly porous divide between services is illustrated by the person who receives visits from both NHS district nurses and social services home care staff. On one occasion, the latter places the person on a commode, but cannot not return for five hours. As a result, the person develops a pressure sore, which, in turn, means that the district nurses have to visit more frequently to give wound care and to help the person get on and off the commode.[66]

There are many examples involving equipment which illustrate grey and confused areas of responsibility. One survey identified in particular beds, mobility equipment, children's equipment and communication equipment as falling into these grey areas.[67] Two bed-raising blocks (to tilt a bed for bodily fluid drainage) might be an NHS responsibility; but four blocks (to raise the height of the bed for easier transfer to and from bed) come under social services. A person might even receive two wheelchairs – one from the NHS and one from the social services department.[68] Wheelchairs for children are provided by the NHS or sometimes by education authorities or schools. Hoists can be provided by the NHS or social services departments; and stairlifts by social services or housing departments. Equipment might be provided by some social services departments for people who cannot get in and out of the bath easily – but other departments might only treat bathing needs as a high priority if people have specific medical needs (eg they suffer from a skin condition requiring daily immersion). Conversely, many social services departments will not provide footstools and legstools if they are required for medical reasons – but might do if they are needed for non-medical reasons.

The NHS might accept responsibility for providing some of the equipment a person needs on leaving hospital – but only up to six months after discharge. Thereafter, continuing needs (eg for a commode, a hoist, bathing aids) would be referred to the social services department.[69] Arguments can break out about which service is going to pay for what. For example, dispute – or perhaps simply indecision – about a £400 standing frame for an adult wheelchair user might circulate between NHS community physiotherapists, a social services department occupational therapy manager and the manager of a joint equipment store. The frame is needed so that he can stand up for periods in the day (eg to assist bowel movement, use muscles, and relieve the pressure of constant sitting); the indecision over whether it is a 'health' or 'social care' need, and thus who will pay, persists because of the cost. Thus, sometimes people are unable to obtain equipment through statutory services, either at all or within a reasonable time, and have to request assistance from voluntary organisations or pay for it themselves if they can afford to. The way in which responsibilities are divided varies from place to place and from time to time, depending on local needs, resources and priorities.

One survey, conducted in 1990, indicated a host of variable practices. It found that only some social services departments visited to assess people for chemical commodes; of those that did provide these items, some supplied the fluid, others did not; and of those that did, some charged for it. Some departments supplied special beds and mattresses regularly, others did not. Some were prepared to issue replacement bath mats, but others had discontinued the practice. In some areas, social services departments provided all commodes, in others the NHS did, in still others social services supplied them in certain circumstances – for example, for night-time use. High seat chairs might be provided regularly when an existing chair in the home could not be adapted, be provided following an assessment by a hospital occupational therapist, not be provided at all, or be provided only in exceptional circumstances. The survey also asked, appropriately, whether authorities had policies on 'grey area equipment'; predictably some did and others didn't.[70]

Nor are children exempt from some of these problems, especially since children's physical and mental development can mean that equipment has to be replaced far more often than for adults – with correspondingly greater expense. For instance, posture/support equipment such as lying boards, wedges and standing frames might be classed as social care equipment to be provided by social services – or as health care equipment to be provided by the NHS. And disputes about whether a child needs a wheelchair in the playground for primarily health or educational reasons, are about who is going to pay – the

NHS, the education authority or neither. Indeed, government guidance, on the development of local authority plans for children's services in general, acknowledges the persistent criticism made about the lack of coordination in services for disabled children and their families.[71] A 1996 report on the wheelchair service expressed its particular concern that the needs of children and students were not being met, because authorities were arguing about who should provide wheelchairs. This adversely affects, for example, the various skills (physical, social and psychological), self confidence, and independence of children and young people.[72]

Joint working between authorities. Overlapping and grey areas of responsibility do not necessarily mean poor services. In theory, they could enable statutory services to respond flexibly and to the advantage of service users. For many years joint working between authorities has been encouraged in policy documents and stipulated in various legislation.[73] One recent manifestation of this is known as the *joint commissioning* of services by statutory authorities; and for many years some authorities have been running joint equipment stores to which both NHS and social services practitioners have access. However, even Department of Health guidance on joint commissioning emphasises the financial and legal difficulties of pooling budgets.[74]

Community care guidance emphasises the importance of joint working and cooperation, but there are obvious weaknesses.[75] Although housing and health services are clearly vital to any notion of people remaining in their own homes, neither are defined as community care services. Therefore, such crucial services continue to be provided by authorities other than social services departments (housing departments and the NHS), empowered under different legislation and holding different aims and objectives. In addition, although community care legislation imposes a duty on social services departments to invite, when appropriate, the NHS and housing department to assist in the assessment of people – neither of these two statutory services has a duty to accept the invitation.[76]

The nebulous effect of this type of legislation and guidance has been confirmed by the law courts. The House of Lords (*R v Northavon DC, ex parte Smith*) has stated that it is not for the courts to enforce cooperation between authorities, even if the duty of cooperation, albeit a qualified one, is stated in legislation as in s.27 of the Children Act 1989.[77] This states that other authorities such as housing, health, education must comply with requests for help by the social services department 'if it is compatible with their own statutory or other duties and obligations and does not unduly prejudice the discharge of any of their own functions'.

Similarly, the duty of health authorities to assist education authorities in respect of the special educational needs of children is subject to whether the health authorities consider it reasonable to assist given their available resources.[78] How much more nebulous is community care legislation which does not even specify two-way cooperation. It merely states that social services departments have a duty, when appropriate, to invite housing authorities and the NHS to assist in community care assessments. However, the invitees have no duty, not even one qualified by available resources, to respond.[79] Nevertheless, although the courts might feel unable to step in, the local ombudsmen sometimes do intervene; for example, when authorities, or even different departments within the same authority[80], fail to communicate with each properly.

Local joint equipment stores, shared by the NHS Trust, social services department and sometimes education authority, have long been viewed as one way of improving the system of equipment provision. Depending on the arrangements operated by any one particular store, the bureaucratic barriers between statutory services are broken down to greater or lesser extent. Nevertheless, a joint store is not a guaranteed solution, since each statutory service still has to contribute annually to the budget, and disputes can still easily occur.

Indeed, ever tighter budgets and 'efficiency drives' are leading to apparently greater levels of rationing of services. In order to justify such rationing and defend it against legal challenge, authorities are likely to formulate policies which exploit the grey areas to their own financial advantage.

History of equipment provision

A stream of reports over the last 25 years has consistently pointed to the shortcomings in the provision of equipment and home adaptations. Some have looked at provision generally, others at particular aspects. Those reports that deal with particular types of equipment – such as wheelchairs – are referred to in Part IV of this book, under the relevant heading in the A–Z list.

It should be emphasised that good practice is sometimes to be found reported – for example, some social services departments have reduced the length of their waiting lists, and there are innovative and effective schemes in some localities for carrying out minor home adaptations. However, overall, the findings of the reports mentioned below do paint a gloomy picture; indeed a good practice document on equipment provision, published by the Department of Health in 1992, admitted that it had been 'very difficult to find a good all-round service'.[81]

In 1968, the British Medical Association found glaring defects in the system generally, caused by a fragmented system of provision which hindered communication between professionals and patients and meant that few people were aware of what was available.[82] Twenty years later, a King's Fund report on services for physically disabled people found that the supply of equipment was the 'single most confused area of service provision for disabled people'.[83] The Audit Commission noted in 1992 that, for many people, the provision of equipment and home adaptations represented 'a frustrating clash between the immediacy of need and bureaucracy at its worst'.[84] Most recently, in March 1996, an Age Concern England report summarised the plight of some older people who, if they are not at immediate physical risk, are obliged to wait for months or even years for assessment by social services departments.[85] A RADAR report, issued in October 1994, highlighted how many people are failing to obtain the services, including equipment and adaptations, that they need under s.2 of the CSDPA.[86] In 1995, SCOPE noted that the effects of deficiencies in the provision of equipment by statutory services are exacerbated by the high cost of equipment purchased privately.[87] A detailed study, published in 1992, analysed equipment provision in one health authority from the perspective of district nurses; it drew the overwhelming conclusion that the system of provision was confusing and inefficient, as well as frustrating, patchy, inequitable, unresponsive to need, and under-funded.[88]

The national picture that emerges from these reports is reflected at more local level as well. Age Concern London, having investigated home support services for older people in 1995 in London, found inconsistent and complex policies, procedures and practice in relation to the provision of equipment and adaptations.[89] And a 1995 report produced by Sesame, a voluntary organisation in Kent, found that 85% of parents of disabled children experienced problems in obtaining equipment such as wheelchairs, walking frames, incontinence aids, footwear – at all, in time, or of the appropriate type.[90] And, children, as well as adults might suffer from poorly organised provision. Reporting nationally n 1994 on services for children in need, the Audit Commission stated that the problems included:[91]

> 'over-bureaucratic approaches, confusion over who could order what equipment, arguments over the source of funding, repeated assessments by different agencies, lack of flexibility in meeting needs, long delays – sometimes so long that the child outgrew the size of the item ordered – and no way for parents or children to know whether, or when, they might receive their equipment.'

It should be emphasised that it is not just service users who become confused about provision of equipment by statutory services; a number of the above-mentioned above reports point out that many professionals do not know how the system works and so are unable to provide service users with either equipment itself or accurate information about how to get it. To take a specific example:[92]

> A recent House of Commons Select Committee report carries an example of a man who was admitted to hospital and immediately recognised by nurses to be at risk of pressure sores. They believed that special pressure relief equipment was not available; in fact senior staff later stated that it could have been obtained. When the patient was subsequently transferred to another hospital and assessed, the second hospital recorded that he was at extremely high risk in relation to pressure sores on the 'Waterlow' scale. The Committee noted that this 'confusion on the availability of such important equipment is a most serious failing and in this instance meant that the patient remained in unnecessary discomfort, his condition worsening'.

Provision of equipment by manufactures and suppliers

It has already been noted that a strong retail market in disability equipment does not at present exist; some of the possible reasons for this have also been given. Nevertheless, the OPCS disability surveys found over four million users of disability equipment. Given an ageing population, the market for such equipment 'should', in principle, be expanding. And certainly some manufacturers and suppliers, fully convinced that a large market does exist, are attempting to enlarge and develop it.

Summarised under the eight headings immediately following are the main ways in which individual consumers can purchase equipment.[93]

(i) **Pharmacies.** Some pharmacies display more or less equipment on the premises; many more carry mail order catalogues through which people can order equipment.

(ii) **Specialist shops.** A number of specialist disability equipment shops exist. Some sell only small items for use around the house, such as reaching sticks, jar openers and tap turners. But most sell, in addition, larger items, particularly electric wheelchairs and scooters, and electric riser and recliner chairs. One reason for this is that the profit margin on, and turnover of, the smaller, cheaper items is generally too low to be commercially viable.

(iii) **Superstores.** A company called Keep Able has pioneered the concept of disability equipment superstores. Situated in large warehouse premises, Keep Able offers a wide range of equipment, the space to try it out and expert advice. The advent of these stores (there are two at present) has been widely welcomed.

(iv) **Ordinary shops.** Some equipment, useful for older people and disabled people, can be found in ordinary shops. For example, easy-grip cutlery can be bought in chain stores such as Sainsbury's or Boots. And bathroom grab rails, special gardening equipment and plugs with handles can be bought in DIY stores such as B&Q.

(v) **Specialist mail order catalogues.** A number of specialist mail order catalogues are now being aimed increasingly at consumers, rather than just at statutory services. Their design and image is being improved to convey the idea that the products are consumer goods rather than medical appliances. For example, a recent catalogue launched by Coopers Healthcare and Boots includes good quality general information about how equipment is relevant to people's everyday living, as well as photographs illustrating people, both younger and older, using products.[94] And, for example, a company called Rolli-Moden has produced a glossy, attractive fashion catalogue of clothing for wheelchair users.

(vi) **Generalist mail order catalogues.** Some of the mail order catalogues (eg Innovations) that arrive regularly in the weekend newspapers feature a number of items of equipment useful for older or disabled people. These might be described in the catalogues as being just *easy to use* (eg television remote controls with big buttons), or more explicitly as useful for older people (eg talking clocks or letter cages to minimise bending down) – though still without necessarily mentioning age or disability prominently or at all.

(vii) **National newspapers.** Certain types of equipment are currently advertised regularly in mainstream newspapers, often in weekend supplements, but sometimes on main pages during the week. Typically, electric scooters, stairlifts and special baths appear widely.

(viii) **Specialist newspapers for disabled people and older people.** These typically carry many advertisements for equipment.

Provision of equipment by voluntary organisations. It is difficult to measure how much equipment – or advice and information about it – voluntary organisations provide, directly or and indirectly. Nevertheless, the diversity of activity, and probably the scale, is substantial.

At both national and local level, some organisations are heavily involved in equipment provision. An obvious example is the British Red Cross. It has over 900 branches (each one an independent charity), some larger, some smaller, but all loaning equipment, generally for people's short-term needs. Items loaned include wheelchairs, walking aids, commodes, bath seats and urinals. In 1993, over 224,000 items of equipment were loaned.[95] Some specialist organisations (eg the Motor Neurone Disease Association) have a national scheme which supplements equipment provided by statutory services – providing, for example, electric riser and recliner chairs and 'lite-writers'.

Many other voluntary bodies sometimes loan equipment or offer financial assistance. A glance at the Directory of Social Change's annual guide to grants for individuals in need, begins to give an idea of the broad scope of assistance available.[96] Voluntary organisations, just like statutory services, tend to operate criteria of eligibility in order to ensure that their assistance is targeted most effectively. For example, the Joseph Rowntree Foundation's Family Fund is prepared to help families with washing machines, required because of their children's disabilities – but not with incontinence supplies or nappies (deemed by the Fund to be the responsibility of the NHS).[97] In addition, some organisations are wary of excessive publicity because of the demand for assistance that might be generated but could not be met.

Organisations, such as Age Concern England, Arthritis Care and the Disabled Living Centres Council have collaborated with disability equipment suppliers, such as Homecraft Supplies and Keep Able, to produce mail order catalogues of daily living equipment. Other voluntary organisations sell equipment themselves; for example, the Royal National Institute for the Blind sells a wide range of products.

Filling the gaps between the public and private sectors

Voluntary organisations fill the gap between what people receive from statutory services and what they buy privately. This role is suggested by a number of studies or surveys of people with motor neurone disease[98], multiple sclerosis[99], terminal cancer[100] or with equipment needs generally.[101] They found that people with several items of equipment obtained them variously through social services departments or the NHS, private purchase and assistance from voluntary organisations. Nevertheless, of some concern at present is that, as statutory services increasingly ration and restrict provision, extra demands fall on the voluntary sector. For example, the Red Cross has recently announced that, such has been the increased pressure to loan wheelchairs for short-term periods, it is planning to 'charge' the NHS (eg obtain some financial assistance for running local, short-term loan schemes). The increase in demand is attributed to the increase in day surgery and shorter hospital stays.[102]

In addition, equipment might feature prominently amongst the enquiries that voluntary organisations receive. For instance, a 1992 survey found equipment featured in 43% of enquiries received by the Greater London Association of Disabled People and the British Council of Organisations of Disabled People.[103]

Voluntary organisations and contractual work for statutory services

Sometimes, voluntary organisations undertake formal contractual work for statutory services. For example, the British Red Cross in Leicestershire has for many years run a joint equipment store on behalf of the local NHS and social services department. Some social services departments are now contracting with independent disabled living centres to carry out *fast-track* assessments of people who need items of bathing equipment. And for many years voluntary organisations have acted as agents for local authorities in providing specialist services for people with sensory impairments.

The advantage of the prevailing 'contract culture' for voluntary organisations is increased opportunity for much needed income. The danger is that they will begin to lose independence of approach and activity as more restrictive contracts replace the grant payments which tended to leave them greater liberty.[104]

Equipment activities of disabled living centres and other specialist centres

A number of specialist centres exists, variously assessing for, adapting, making and selling equipment. The following does not constitute an exhaustive list but is merely by way of example.

Disabled Living Centres

There are about 40 disabled living centres (DLCs) throughout the United Kingdom. Some are part of NHS Trusts or of social services departments, whilst others are independent voluntary organisations. Open to both members of the public and professionals, they display and demonstrate a wide range of equipment, from special cutlery to electric wheelchairs and hoists. Expert staff are able to give impartial advice about equipment, face-to-face, by telephone and by letter. Some DLCs sell limited ranges of equipment, and some are in the process of making increasingly formal contracts with social services departments.

These centres enable people to compare like-products in terms of function, quality and price. In the absence of a flourishing retail market and of accessible information about equipment, the potential role of DLCs can scarcely be overestimated. However, they remain relatively few, and many people, both the general public and professionals, remain unaware of them.[105] The centres are represented at a national level by the Disabled Living Centres Council.[106]

Communication aids centres, educational technology centres and other specialist centres

A number of communication aids centres (CACs), based usually in hospitals and staffed by speech and language therapists, display, demonstrate and give advice about speech and writing equipment for people with communication difficulties. Sometimes CACs can loan equipment for trial periods (see p.480). In addition, educational technology centres (eg the ACE centres in Oxford and Oldham) assess children and young people who have communication difficulties for the use of speech and writing aids.

Various other organisations and centres offer expertise in equipment matters. These include specialist NHS rehabilitation centres and spinal injury units, as well as those hospitals or centres that continue to offer long-term stays for some severely disabled people. Some NHS Trust hospitals have rehabilitation or bio-engineering departments, whose staff are able to make and adapt equipment for people's individual needs – for example, seating, postural, communication and mobility.

In addition, an organisation of Rehabilitation Engineering Movement Advisory Panels, known as REMAP, designs and constructs customised, one-off items of equipment for disabled people, whose needs cannot be met by other available products. The organisation consists of a network of about 100 panels, each consisting of some 20 volunteers. Some of these, such as therapists, doctors and social workers, *identify* needs and problems; others, professional engineers and craftsmen, *solve* the problems. Equipment is made or adapted free of charge for individual disabled people.[107]

Toy libraries

Throughout the United Kingdom toy and leisure libraries loan, free or for a small charge, toys or equipment to disabled children. The libraries are run in a variety of ways – by parents, voluntary organisations, libraries, social services departments, NHS Trusts and education authorities. The range of equipment can include jigsaws, books and cassettes, dolls – and toys with, for example, the following functions: developmental, construction, sit and ride, musical/sound, pull-along, soft and electronic.[108]

Notes

1 See eg: Diamond, J. (1991). *The rise and fall of the third chimpanzee.* London: Vintage, p.328.
2 Department of Health (1991). *The health of the nation: a consultative document for health in England.* London: HMSO, p.97.
3 Secretary of State for Health (1992). *The health of the nation: a strategy for health in England.* London: HMSO, pp.108, 118.
4 Beresford, B. (1995). *Expert opinions: a national survey of parents caring for a severely disabled child.* York: Joseph Rowntree Foundation; Community Care, pp.10–11.
5 EL(95)5. NHS Executive. *Purchasing high-tech health care for patients at home.* Leeds: Department of Health, 1995.
6 Stachura, K. (1994). Professional dilemmas facing physiotherapists. *Physiotherapy:* June 1994; 80(6), pp.357–360. Refers to points made in Oliver, M. (1992). *Power and ideology in the rehabilitation enterprise: the social construction of walking.* (Paper at COHERE conference, Glasgow in 1992).
7 Social Services Inspectorate (1994). *The F Factor: why some older people choose residential care.* London: Department of Health.
8 Department of Health (1995). *Health and well-being: a guide for older people.* London: DH, pp.49–50.
9 See eg Department of Social Security (1995). *A brief guide to the Disability Discrimination Act 1995.* London: DSS. See for more detail: Gooding, C. (1996). *Blackstone's guide to the Disability Discrimination Act 1995.* London: Blackstone Press.
10 See eg. Ellis, K. (1993). *Squaring the circle: user and carer participation in needs assessment.* York: Joseph Rowntree Foundation, p.41. Also: Arnold, P.; Bochel, H.; Brodhurst, S.; Page, D. (1993). *Community care: the housing dimension.* York: Joseph Rowntree Foundation, p.12.
11 Parliamentary Commissioner for Administration (C.283/V). *Refusal to provide a three-wheeled vehicle.* 3rd report for session 1975–76. HC 259. London: HMSO, 1976.
12 Reported by: Nuttall, N.; Hornsby, M. (1995). High streets doomed, report claims. *The Times:* 1st November 1995.
13 Mail-order shopping row. *Disability Now:* March 1996, p.3.
14 Automobile Association (1995). *Shopmobility: good for people and towns.* Basingstoke: AA.
15 World Health Organisation (1980). *International classification of impairments, disabilities and handicaps: a manual of classification relating to the consequences of disease.* Geneva: WHO.
16 Cornes, P. (1991). Impairment, disability, handicap and new technology. In: Oliver, M. (ed) (1993). *Social work: disabled people and disabling environments.* London: Jessica Kingsley.
17 See eg. Oliver, M. (1990). *Politics of disablement.* London: Macmillan, pp.49–54. Abberley, P. (1995). Disabling ideology in health and welfare – the case for occupational therapy. *Disability and Society:* 1995; (10)2, pp.221–232.
18 Haggard, M. (1993). *Research in the development of effective services for hearing-impaired people.* London: Nuffield Provincial Hospitals Trust, p.17.
19 Low, C. (1996). Disability models or muddles. *Therapy Weekly:* February 1996; 22(29), p.7
20 See eg: French, S. (1994). Attitudes of health professionals towards disabled people: a discussion and review of the literature. *Physiotherapy:* October 1994; 80(10), pp.687–693. Campbell, J. (1996). Their own agenda. *Therapy Weekly:* 22 February 1996, p.4.
21 Martin, J.; Meltzer, H.; Elliot, D. (1988). *Office of Population Censuses and Surveys. Prevalence of disability among adults. OPCS surveys of disability in Great Britain: report 1.* London: HMSO, pp.8–10.
22 Oliver, M. (1990). *Politics of disablement.* London: Macmillan, pp.7–8.
23 Moore, E.J. (1995). *Grocery packaging openability: an open or shut case?* Watford: Institute of Grocery Distribution, p.77.
24 Martin, J.; White, A. (1988). (Office of Population Censuses and Surveys). *Financial circumstances of disabled adults living in private households.* OPCS surveys of disability in Great Britain: report 2. London: HMSO, p.xviii.
25 Thompson, P. (1990). *Short changed by disability.* London: Disablement Income Group, pp.27–28.
26 Hull, R.; Prouse, P.; Sherratt, C.; Brennan, P.; Townsend, J.; Frank, A. (1994). Capital costs of supporting young disabled people at home. *Health Trends:* 1994; 26(3), pp.80–85.
27 Beresford, B. (1995). *Expert opinions: a national survey of parents caring for a severely disabled child.* York: Joseph Rowntree Foundation; Community Care, p.16.

28 Stone, D.A. (1985). *The disabled state.* London: Macmillan, p.27.

29 Hull, R.; Prouse, P.; Sherratt, C.; Brennan, P.; Townsend, J.; Frank, A. (1994). Capital costs of supporting young disabled people at home. *Health Trends:* 1994; 26(3), pp.80–85.

30 See eg: Townsend, P.; Davidson, N., Whitehead, M. (1992). *Inequalities in health: the Black Report and the Health Divide.* London: Penguin (the seminal Black Report originally published in 1980); and a more recent summary: British Medical Association, Board of Science and Education (1995). *Inequalities in health.* London: BMA.

31 Research Institute for Consumer Affairs (1996). Adapt your home. *Which?:* May 1996, pp.18–22.

32 See eg research conducted for the Department of Trade and Industry: Jane Oldfield Associates (1991). *Home and leisure accident research: physical disability and consumer safety.* London: DTI, p.36.

33 Research Institute for Consumer Affairs (1995). *Ability car guide.* London: RICA.

34 See eg: Convenience cooking: microwave ovens. *Which?:* December 1995, pp.12–15.

35 Kirby, H. (1995). Dressed for a smooth ride. Disabled Living. *The Times:* 1 May 1995, p.21.

36 For the rules governing the mobility component of the Disability Living Allowance, see: *Social Security Contributions and Benefits Act 1992*, s.73.

37 Howard, M. (1994). *Too young to count: the extra mobility-related costs of disabled children under five.* London: Disability Alliance.

38 Eg London Boroughs Occupational Therapy Managers Group (1992). *Occupational therapists' criteria for the loan of equipment to people with disabilities.* London: LBOTMG, p.27.

39 SI 1994/3017. *Medical Devices Regulations 1994*, r.2.

40 *Princess Louise Scottish Hospital v C&E Comps* [1983] VAT Tribunal Reports 19

41 See note in: *Physiotherapy*: March 1994; 80(3), p.188.

42 As in the case of the Royal National Institute for Deaf People's pocket amplifier, the 'Crystal', which Customs and Excise eventually agreed should be zero-rated in early 1996. And see: HM Customs & Excise (1994). *VAT reliefs for people with disabilities: 1 August 1994. VAT Notice 701/7/94.* London: HM C & E. This notes that training aids for deaf children and specialised aids for people with severe hearing impairment may qualify for zero-rating.

43 Value Added Tax Act 1994, Schedule 8, Group 12. And see also: HM Customs & Excise (1994). *VAT reliefs for people with disabilities: 1 August 1994.* VAT Notice 701/7/94. London: HM C & E.

44 Princess Louise Scottish Hospital v C&E Comps [1983] VAT Tribunal Reports 191 (see Note above).

45 *Hansard,* House of Lords, 24 January 1996, Vehicles for the disabled: VAT rating, cols 1030–1033. *Hansard,* House of Lords, 15 February 1996, Vehicles for the disabled: VAT rating, col 720.

46 This type of issue arose in 1995/1996 over computers and printers supplied to disabled people by Dolphin Systems (of Worcester).

47 *Chester-care* catalogue (Homecraft Supplies).

48 These rules are contained in the Social Fund Directions, to which Social Fund officers work. For a summary and details, see: McKenny, J.; Simmons, D.; Tait, G.; (with Emma Knight). *National welfare benefits handbook. 25th edition.* London: Child Poverty Action Group, p.372.

49 *R v Social Fund Inspector, ex parte Connick* [1994] COD 75.

50 Social Security Commissioner decision CSB/1360/1986.

51 Independent Review Service for the Social Fund (1993). *Advice note number 7: Direction 12(j): 'a medical, surgical, optical, aural or dental item or service'.* Birmingham: IRS.

52 Independent Review Service for the Social Fund (1994). *Advice note number 13: wheelchairs: Directions 12(j), 23(b).* Birmingham: IRS.

53 Independent Review Service for the Social Fund (1995). *Social Fund Commissioner's Report 1994/95.* London: HMSO, pp.73–77 (detailed example of a decision involving provision of a kerb-climbing electric wheelchair.

54 Mandelstam, M. (1996). *Going to market? Products and equipment for older people and disabled people: an overview of current provision.* London: Disabled Living Centres Council.

55 Martin, J.; Meltzer, H.; Elliot, D. (1988). *Office of Population Censuses and Surveys. Prevalence of disability among adults. OPCS surveys of disability in Great Britain: report 1.* London: HMSO, pp.8–10.

56 See generally: Research Institute for Consumer Affairs: a) (1984). *Aids for people with disabilities: a review of information services.* London: RICA, – and b) (1994). *Equipment for an easier life: a guide to products and where to get them.* London: RICA. Also: Wade, G. (1995). *Pilot study of*

patient views of equipment provision. Hull: Royal Hull Hospitals. And: Coopers & Lybrand (1988). *Information needs of disabled people, their carers and service providers.* London: DHSS.

57 Winchcombe, M. (1995). *Equipment for easier living survey.* Winchester: Hampshire County Council Social Services Department, pp.9–10. Research Institute for Consumer Affairs (1995). *Equipment for an easier life: RICA booklet evaluation in Hampshire.* London: RICA, p.9.

58 See eg: Titley, J. (1995). *Just about coping: Age Concern's spending diary survey of older people.* London: ACE, p.6: most respondents of the survey would have spent an extra £10 (which they did not have) on food, clothing, heating and other bills.

59 Hogan, P. Building bridges: designing for elderly people. *Access By Design:* 67, pp.14–16.

60 Kirby, H. (1995). Dressed for a smooth ride. *The Times:* 1st May 1995.

61 Nayak, U.S.L. (1995). *Elders-led design.* (reprinted from *Ergonomics in Design,* January 1995, pp.8–13.

62 Research Institute for Consumer Affairs (1995). *Equipment for an easier life: RICA booklet evaluation in Hampshire.* London: RICA, p.8.

63 Social Services Inspectorate; Social Work Services Group (1991). *Care management and assessment: managers' guide.* London: HMSO, p.86. Based on: National Association of Health Authorities and Trusts (1990). *Care in the community: definitions of health and social care: developing an approach: a West Midlands study.* Birmingham: NAHAT.

64 *R v Social Fund Inspector, ex parte Connick* [1994] COD 75 (QBD).

65 On the problems which such grey areas pose community nurses, see: Northway, R. (1996). The health and social care divide: bridging the gap. *Nursing Standard:* 14 February 1996; 10(21), pp.43–47.

66 Elliott, M. (1995). Care management in the community: a case study. *Nursing Times:* 29 November 1995; 91(48), pp.34–35.

67 Eg London Boroughs Occupational Therapy Managers Group (1992). *Occupational therapists' criteria for the loan of equipment to people with disabilities.* London: LBOTMG, Appendix 1, p.12.

68 Social Services Inspectorate (Cope, C.; Watson, A.; Tweedale, L.) (1996). *Inspection of community services for physically disabled people in Wirral: 9–20 October 1995.* Manchester: Department of Health, pp.28, 39.

69 Eg: Social Services Inspectorate (Booth, L.; Strettle, T.; Paul, D.). *Inspection of community services for physically disabled people in the London Borough of Wandsworth, 28 June – 12 July 1995.* London: Department of Health, p.32.

70 Eg London Boroughs Occupational Therapy Managers Group (1992). *Occupational therapists' criteria for the loan of equipment to people with disabilities.* London: LBOTMG, Appendix 1, pp.5–9.

71 Department of Health; Department for Education and Employment (1996). *Children's services planning: guidance.* London: DH, DfEE, p.4.

72 Aldersea, P. (1996). *National prosthetic and wheelchair services report 1993–1996.* London: College of Occupational Therapists, Part 2, pp.10–13.

73 *NHS Act 1977,* s.22: cooperation between the NHS and social services – and joint consultative committees.

74 Department of Health (1995). *An introduction to joint commissioning.* London: DH, p.7.

75 Social Services Inspectorate, Department of Health; Social Work Services Group, Scottish Office (1991). *Care management assessment: managers' guide.* London: HMSO, p.21: the first priority: to establish community care assessment arrangements 'in negotiation with other care providers'.

76 *NHS and Community Care Act 1990,* s.47.

77 *R v Northavon District Council, ex parte Smith* [1994] 3 All ER 313 (HL).

78 *Education Act 1996,* s.322.

79 *NHS and Community Care Act 1990,* s.47.

80 Commission for Local Administration in England (92/C/3162). *Report on investigation into a complaint against Lancashire County Council.* York: CLAE, 1995, p.14: apparent failure of education department to inform social services department about a child's residential/educational needs.

81 Department of Health (1992). *Equipped for independence?* London: DH, p.1.

82 British Medical Association (1968). *Aids for the disabled.* London: BMA, pp.8, 35.

83 Beardshaw, V. (1988). *Last on the list: community services for people with physical disabilities.* London: King's Fund Institute, p.27.

84 Audit Commission (1992). *Homeward bound: a new course for community health.* London: HMSO, p.18

85 Age Concern England (1996). *Stuck on the waiting list: older people and equipment for independent living.* London: ACE.
86 Keep, J.; Clarkson, J. (1994). *Disabled people have rights: final report on a two year project funded by the Nuffield Provincial Hospitals Trust.* London: RADAR.
87 Lamb, B.; Layzell, S. (1995). *Disabled in Britain: counting on community care.* London: SCOPE, p.50.
88 Ross, F.; Campbell, F. (1991). *If it wasn't for this wheelchair, I might as well be dead: a study of equipment and aids for daily living in the community.* London: St George's Hospital Medical School, p.85.
89 Age Concern London (1995). *Home comforts: home support for disabled older people.* London: Age Concern London.
90 Parkes, L. (1995). Out of sight, out of mind: an audit for the future. *Sesame,* pp.21–24.
91 Audit Commission (1994). *Seen but not heard: co-ordinating community child health and social services for children in need: detailed evidence and guidelines for managers and practitioners.* London: HMSO, p.28.
92 Select Committee on the Parliamentary Commissioner for Administration (1996). *Report of the Health Service Ombudsman for 1994–95. Third report. HC 39.* London: HMSO, p.xi.
93 For a range of examples of how equipment is marketed, see: Mandelstam, M. (1996). *Going to market? Products and equipment for older people and disabled people: an overview of current provision.* London: Disabled Living Centres Council.
94 Hodges, C. (1995) ...and living aids to boot. *Therapy Weekly:* October 12 1995; 22(15), p.6.
95 Information kindly supplied by Mary Coleman of the British Red Cross.
96 Casson, D.; Brown, P. (1994). *A guide to grants for individuals in need. 1994/1995 edition.* London: Directory of Social Change.
97 Joseph Rowntree Foundation (1995). *The Family Fund.* York: Joseph Rowntree Foundation (leaflet).
98 Harper, J. (1989). Aids to daily living: help for the enduring. *Therapy Weekly:* 17 August 1989, pp.7–9.
99 Southampton MS Survey Research Team (1989). *Multiple sclerosis in the Southampton District.* Southampton: University of Southampton, Rehabilitation Unit and Department of Sociology and Social Policy, pp.124–5.
100 Marie Curie Memorial Foundation (1989). *Study of the Marie Curie Community Nursing Service.* London: MCMF, pp.144–155.
101 Martin, J.; White, A.; Meltzer, H. (1989). (Office of Population, Censuses and Surveys). *Disabled adults: services, transport and employment. OPCS surveys of disability in Great Britain: report 4.* London: HMSO, pp.46–59.
102 Voucher scheme due for powered wheelchairs. *Therapy Weekly:* 22 February 1996; 22(32), p.1.
103 Disabled Living Foundation (1993). *Disability equipment information project: draft report.* London: DLF, pp.40–41.
104 For a summary of some of these issues, see eg National Council for Voluntary Organisations; Association of Directors of Social Services (1995). *Community care and voluntary organisations: joint policy statement.* London: NCVO, ADSS, pp.5–6. Also: Cervi, B. (1994). Contracts and campaigning. *Community Care* (Inside): 25–31 August 1994.
105 For a picture of what Disabled Living Centres do, where they are, what they are, what they look like etc, see: Parnell, R.; Lupton, C. (1994). *Equipped for change: a study of Disabled Living Centres & the social care market.* London: Disabled Living Centres Council. Also: Parnell, R. (1993). *Equipped for life: a national survey of Disabled Living Centres and their services.* London: Disabled Living Centres Council.
106 For a summary of the Council's present aims and activities, see: Swaffield, L. (1996). Aids to daily living: the 37 steps. *Therapy Weekly:* B, pp.6–7.
107 See Stirling, R. (1995). *REMAP Yearbook 1995.* Sevenoaks, REMAP G
108 Head, J.; Barton, P. (National Toy Libraries Association) (1987). *Toy libraries in the community: the report of a survey of community toy libraries.* London: Eltan.

CHAPTER 4

EQUIPMENT AND AWARENESS OF THE LAW

COVERAGE

1. Why law is increasingly intrusive
    - Litigation and a culture of blame
    - European directives on the safety of equipment
    - Judicial review of statutory services providing equipment
    - Expectations of service users and consumers
    - The role of lawyers.
2. Disputes about equipment and the law
    - Avoiding the law courts
    - Litigation and the interests of society
    - Common sense and informal resolution of differences
    - Going to court
    - Knowing what the law is.

Key points

This chapter suggests that staff of statutory services, manufacturers and retailers, and voluntary organisations increasingly require a knowledge of law – in relation to, for example, the law of negligence, product safety and consumer protection, and judicial review. It also emphasises the desirability, where possible and appropriate, of avoiding resort to the law and of settling disputes by means of common sense and negotiation – ie of achieving non-legal rather than legal solutions. Of course the law courts do sometimes represent the appropriate solution if people are to gain compensation or access to services, or if important points of law need to be tested.

Questions people ask

- Are people more likely to sue nowadays, and is there more legislation to be aware of?
- Should somebody always be to blame for an accident?

- Can a knowledge of the law assist the prevention, or the informal resolution, of disputes?
- What disadvantages are there to litigation?

1. WHY LAW IS INCREASINGLY INTRUSIVE

In practice, law threatens to intrude increasingly on the field of disability equipment. For example, negligence litigation – or at least the threat of it – seems to be growing in society generally. It is thought that, whereas 20 years ago people would generally accept mistakes in medical treatment as an inevitable risk, now they sue.[1]

In addition, a range of consumer protection legislation affecting products is now in place, including the Consumer Protection Act 1987, General Product Safety Regulations 1994, Medical Devices Regulations 1994, Unfair Terms in Consumer Contracts Regulations 1994, Unfair Contract Terms Act 1977 and the Sale of Goods Act 1979. Thus, depending on the circumstances, manufacturers, retailers, statutory services or voluntary organisations which supply equipment run the risk of falling foul of any – or even all – of these legal provisions. Similarly, as statutory services increasingly ration services and equipment, their decisions are exposed to increased challenges and sometimes to judicial review in the law courts.

One silver lining to increased regulation and legislation is that, in a culture of blame and litigation, a certain amount of immunity is being conveyed. For instance, if manufacturers ensure that their products conform to the requirements of safety and performance stipulated by European Union directives, then they know that they are relatively safe from litigation. Or, for example, occupational therapists in social departments, concerned about negligence, product liability, rationing and maladministration – might implement thorough procedures to minimise the risk of legal challenge.

Thus, health and social care professionals might ask service users to sign a form indicating that proper instruction in the use equipment has been given. Records of equipment might be kept for at least 11 years, so that, asked to identify the original manufacturer of a defective product, statutory services can do so and avoid liability under the Consumer Protection Act. The head technician of a social services department might ensure that his staff work to detailed instructions about the type of fixing required for handrails and grabrails if they are to be installed safely in people's homes. In addition, managers might try to ensure that people who 'shout loudest' or most persuasively do not jump the waiting list – and thereby put the authority at risk of findings of maladministration by the ombudsman.

Given the variety of law that, for example, statutory services and their staff can fall foul of, the obvious advice to give professionals is they should simply be 'careful'. However, this is by no means always straightforward, particularly in the field of equipment and adaptations. For instance, as a matter of good practice, occupational therapists might ensure that when they recommend particular items, they should conform to relevant British or European technical standards – for instance, ramps, stairlifts or showers. But, in addition, therapists have to take account of the physical and cognitive ability of particular users, as well as the effect of any alterations to equipment necessitated by a person's disability. For example, even if British Standards are adhered to with respect to, for instance, baths, showers, and thermostatic mixing valves – these items will not be necessarily be safe for a particular disabled person – especially if an unusual alteration has had to be made. Therapists have to consider the risk of scalding from shower mixer units, and the safety of ramps not only for the user but also for carers and members of the public who might use them. Thus, adherence (when possible) to a technical standard might only represent a minimum standard of care that needs to be taken[2] – in fact, more careful, additional assessment and specification might be required in some circumstances.

Furthermore, in order to avoid findings of maladministration by the ombudsman, and even adverse judicial review by the law courts, local authorities and their staff can find themselves embedded in a set of contradictions. Reacting to individual people in considerable need, it is only too easy to apply criteria of eligibility and priority inconsistently, especially since such criteria cannot take account of all situations. And, whilst policies should be consistently applied, they should not be applied absolutely rigidly since, unable to cater for exceptions, they run the risk of 'fettering the discretion' of an authority and adverse judicial review in the law courts. In addition, therapists might find themselves caught between respecting the choice of a service user who is opposed to the use of a hoist in the home – and the health and safety interests of his carers and local authority staff who are put at risk from continuing to lift him manually. This is not to mention the Manual Handling of Loads Regulations 1992, imposing obligations on employers to minimise the lifting of loads undertaken by their staff.

Litigation and a culture of blame

Negligence litigation is apparently increasing generally in society, spreading possibly from the United States and importing a culture of blame and the belief that every adverse event 'ought' to be somebody's fault. Taken to excess, such an attitude is of course unhealthy – it generally ignores the fact that life is not a cast iron certainty for any of us. For example, it should be obvious to people who wander to the end of the Cobb at Lyme Regis that they might slip on algae which are visible, and that it is not appropriate to sue the local council – however, it needed the Court of Appeal to point this out to the 'victim'.[3] And an extreme example is reported to have occurred in the United States, when police staged a bogus accident between a bus and a car. Between the time of the accident and the arrival of an ambulance, a number of bystanders had boarded the bus, hoping to claim compensation for having been involved in the accident. Instead they were arrested.[4] And, in this country, parents might plan to a sue theatre company because their children have been frightened by a production of Peter Pan.[5]

It has been suggested that 'one of the biggest factors in the growth of litigation against professionals, particularly in the NHS, has been an undermining of public trust in the professions which is partly a product of a general reticence to own up to making mistakes, both individually and collectively'.[6] Whatever the reasons for increasing litigation, fear of it is rife. The Department of Health has recently created a new 'insurance' scheme for NHS Trusts (see p.320), and, as a whole, the NHS is awash with documents about *risk-management*, focusing on how to avoid negligence litigation. For example, in the years 1990–1991 and 1991–1992, the value of claims settled by the NHS amounted to about £53 million and £51 million respectively.[7] For 1994, the cost to the NHS is thought to have been about £125 million, rising to £150 million in 1995. The escalation is such that, even from within the legal profession, calls have come for a reform to the system to make it more just and economic. For instance, there might be a case for hospital mediation schemes to deal with smaller claims when explanations and apologies, rather than money, are often people's prime aim.[8] And, in the field of council housing, some authorities spend up to 10% – and even 25% – of their housing repair budgets on litigation brought by tenants in connection with a failure to carry out the repairs.[9]

There is no shortage of home and leisure accidents, as the Department of Trade and Industry's annual statistics demonstrate. Disability equipment, including wheelchairs and walking aids, features along with many other everyday items which are involved in these accidents. However, the statistics do not reveal the causes of accidents, only the products involved; it might be that few are avoidable in the reasonable sense of the word, and still fewer caused by products inherently unsafe.[10] Nevertheless, there is clearly a possibility that if a culture of blame spreads *excessively*, then an incident which is one day unavoidable, becomes avoidable the next, and, on the third day, one caused by negligence.

Litigation and the interests of society

It might not appear to be in society's interest that the fate of elderly women, wishing to remain in their own homes, should be decided (months after they have died) in the High Court and then Court of Appeal through the logic chopping of barristers (*R v Lancashire CC, ex parte Ingham*)[11] – even if the proceedings are fair, thorough, and detailed. It is not clear that such cases further the cause of people's welfare in general and in the long term – since not only are the issues connected closely to policy, but there are seldom any villains of the piece. Social services departments or health authorities, often 'in the dock', usually sympathise with the plight of their users of services – but suffer from a shortage of resources which forces them to make unpleasant decisions. Furthermore, as was pointed out by Lord Justice Hirst during the recent community care case in the Court of Appeal (*R v Gloucestershire CC, ex parte Barry*), about services provided under s.2 of the CSDPA 1970 – even if the service users won the case, the victory could prove to be illusory if it led to local authorities acting more defensively and cautiously.[12]

Nevertheless, the bringing of such cases – with assistance from organisations such as the Royal Association for Disability and Rehabilitation or the Public Law Project – is socially useful. Vulnerable individual people are assisted, and 'test' cases can affect many thousands of other people, and so are of general public interest. Indeed, the proliferation of community care court cases was predicted from the moment the relevant legislation came into force. It was almost as though, faced with insoluble contradictions and highly sensitive issues, central government had to some extent abdicated responsibility deliberately (rather than inadvertently) and was leaving the difficult decisions to the law courts. Whether this is the best way of introducing major new policies is a debatable matter.

Away from rationing decisions, the desire always to find someone to blame and to sue is a disturbing trend. Overworked healthcare professionals live in fear that any mistake – made, for example, in a hospital casualty department besieged by 322 patients in one day – might result in harm to the patient and in possible legal action.[13] Though understandable in terms of the harm individual people have suffered, it is difficult to see how it is in society's wider interests that NHS patients should sue hospitals, on the basis of mistakes made by dedicated, but overwhelmed, nurses. So too, could the value be doubted of making it easier to sue social services staff for mistakes or omissions they make in assessment – if it means placing additional pressure on staff such as the four community care assessors handling up to forty hospital discharge referrals in two days.[14] Although anxiety can result in greater care being taken by professionals, it can also lead to defensive practices which are not necessarily in the best interests of service users. Furthermore, it is by no means certain that litigation, or even the threat of it, is the optimum means of improving professional practices – or whether it even does so at all.

The courts recognise the difficult issues. In one case, the mother of a premature baby sued a health authority when the baby became blind shortly after birth, allegedly because of the negligent administration of excess oxygen. One of the judges stated that:[15]

> Before addressing these questions, we must face up to a problem which must oppress many of those who have to deal with cases of this kind... Here we have a medical unit which would never have existed but for the energy and public spirit of Dr. _______. If the unit had not been there, the plaintiff would probably have died. The doctors and nurses worked all kinds of hours to look after the baby. They safely brought it through the perilous shoals of its early life. For all that we know, they far surpassed on numerous occasions the standard of reasonable care. Yet it is said that for one lapse they (and not just their employers) are found to

> have committed a breach of duty. Nobody could criticise the mother for doing her best to secure her son's financial future. But has not the law taken a wrong turning if an action of this kind is to succeed?

Yet the court did go on to find negligence – only for the House of Lords to overturn the decision on the grounds that it could not be proved that it was the oxygen which had caused the blindness.

In any case, the system of tort, allowing people to sue for negligence and win compensation, is recognised to be inefficient and inequitable.[16] For example, it is reported that claims against the NHS have trebled in the last five years, that most are settled for less than £10,000 but only after an often long and expensive legal process, that most claims are legally aided, and that the majority (60% to 75%) are clearly without merit and get nowhere near the courts (yet it is estimated that in 1994 about 12,000 such claims cost the taxpayer over £21 million).[17] And, an increase in litigation merely serves to make the overall system of provision even less efficient – with large sums of money being spent on the legal process. Surely, the money could be spent more equitably than in what is now an extravagant lottery? If you have an accident and can find somebody to blame, you might win substantial compensation, possibly from a public service such as the NHS. If, however God or chance is to blame, you will not get a penny. Either way, it seems that lawyers stand to gain.

When 2000 firms of solicitors assembled 17,000 people to bring a group action in relation to Valium and Ativan, most of the cases failed – yet £35 million in legal aid was paid to lawyers and medical experts.[18] Indeed, when unsuccessful attempts were made to maintain this action against the prescribers (health authorities and general practitioners), as well as the producers of the drugs, the Court of Appeal stated that the 'National Health Service has better things to spend its money on than lawyers' fees…'.[19] And, even for those who do find someone to blame and who win their cases, the levels of damages awarded might be subject to chance, rather than to a clear idea of what personal injuries should be worth.[20] It has been suggested that personal first-party personal injury insurance schemes, much like property insurance, might provide a more equitable system of compensation.

European Community directives on the safety of equipment

Despite government intentions to promote deregulation for industry and business, new legislation – based on European Community Directives – is increasingly affecting manufacturers, suppliers, statutory services and voluntary organisations. For instance, under the banner either of consumer protection or of health and safety at work, legislation introduced in the 1990s applies to medical devices, general product safety and the manual handling of loads (see Chapter 15). Organisations failing to comply with this legislation run the risk of criminal, as well as the possibility of civil, liability. At the same time, compliance (eg with the Medical Devices Regulations 1994) entails administrative costs – which, whilst not onerous for larger organisations with sophisticated quality control systems already in place, might be prohibitive for the smaller firm.

Judicial review of statutory services providing equipment

Judicial review allows the law courts to supervise public bodies, including the statutory services covered in this book, by ensuring that they act reasonably, legally and fairly (see Chapter 17). In the context of this book, it is arguable that increased judicial review of statutory services is an inevitable consequence, not necessarily of intrusive judges, ferreting lawyers and querulous service users – but of significant changes occurring within statutory services.

The general duty, laid down in the NHS Act 1977, to provide a comprehensive health service could almost be viewed more in the way of a general policy statement, than a legal provision giving rights to people. It is the means by which postwar governments, bound by a common consensus, could deliver a national health service – the effectiveness of which will depend not on the law courts but on the commitment of the government of the day. It is difficult not to agree with the approach taken in 1980 by Lord Denning in the Court of Appeal, that the NHS could not be expected to deliver every last piece of high technology and state-of-the-art treatment. And, it was not generally for the law courts to intervene, since the making of NHS priorities was a matter of policy and politics.[21] Similarly, in a case (*Wyatt v Hillingdon LBC*) involving provision of services by a social services department under s.2 of Chronically Sick and Disabled Persons Act 1970, the Court of Appeal stated that it was not for the courts to interfere with the provision of comforts for the sick and disabled.[22]

However, increasingly, far more than expensive technology is denied to people. Rationing can affect the most basic services to vulnerable, and sometimes to dying, people. As a consequence, government and statutory services sometimes take refuge behind the legislation. When this happens, judicial review can be used to examine important points of law and principle affecting basic aspects of the daily life of not just one person, but many; for example, the case (*R v Gloucestershire CC, ex parte Mahfood*) brought by several residents of Gloucestershire against the County Council's decision to withdraw or reduce home support services, had consequences for up to 1500 people.[23]

Furthermore, whilst it could be argued that such matters are for policymakers and politicians rather than the law courts, it does seem that resort to law is sometimes precipitated as much by government and local authorities as service users and their lawyers. For example, some answers given in the House of Commons bear all the marks of having been legally prescribed, sometimes down to the last syllable (which is not to be deviated from).[24] And, rather than expand on policy (which after all is what really determines NHS provision) in Parliament, refuge might be taken by government ministers behind the vague language of statute. Perhaps not surprisingly, other lawyers, acting on behalf of service users, might pick up the gauntlet and attempt to mount legal challenges. Similarly, it is arguably an invitation to do legal battle, if central government issues guidance openly inviting social services departments to circumvent statutory duties under s.2 of the CSDPA 1970 by means of wordplay.[25]

Expectations of service users and consumers

Although many avenues of redress open to service users and consumers fall short of the law courts, nevertheless, an increase in people's expectations can lead to more confrontation generally – some of which, in turn, can lead to litigation.

Organisations such as the Consumers' Association, the National Consumer Council and Citizens' Advice Bureaux encourage people to be aware of, and enforce, their rights. Similarly, charters for public services set down standards of service which people should be entitled to; and emphasis is placed on the effective use of complaints procedures within those services. Up to a point this is a good thing. For example, individual consumers are at a potentially great disadvantage in relation to statutory services and large companies; hence, for example, the protection afforded consumers by various provisions contained in legislation such as the Sale of Goods Act 1979, and the Unfair Terms in Contracts Regulations 1994.

Charters promote, in principle at least, good practice in statutory services. Community care guidance encourages the participation of service users both in the general planning of services, as well as in individual assessments of people's needs for services. Complaints procedures in social services departments are designed to enable service users to challenge what they perceive to be unfair decisions. This sort of redress is important, given the disparity in bargaining power between, say, a vulnerable, elderly man with communication problems – and the managers who are making priorities, allocating resources, and rationing people's services and quality of life.

Expectations and their part in disputes, complaints procedures and consumers have already been discussed in Chapter 2 – both generally and in relation to disability equipment, a field of activity which throws up its own particular problems.

The role of lawyers

Lawyers are becoming more active in their efforts to identify people who can be persuaded to sue for compensation.[26] For example, 'ambulance-chasing' might involve advertising in hospital accident and emergency departments. Law firms might place advertisements on the London Underground and in local newspapers[27]; whilst marketing firms compile and sell to solicitors lists of 'victims' who – with suitable encouragement – might be prepared to sue.[28] Some solicitors are reported to be using the Internet to alert people to the legal implications of harm they might have suffered – for example, in respect of faulty products or poor professional services.[29]

The role of solicitors is delicately balanced. On the one hand, some can be seen as self-seekers who feed off the fears and concerns of victims. Others, for example those who take on 'group' actions in respect of faulty products, might see themselves as assisting powerless victims to take on big business and thus provide a fundamental freedom essential in a complex democracy.[30] Nevertheless, the issue is not totally clearcut; for example, in relation to a group action against the manufacturers and prescribers of benzodiazepine, it has been pointed out that there were[31]:

> 'nearly 5,000 actions, many of them of doubtful merits and viability, and others with very small claims, brought with the assistance of legal aid – and most could not otherwise have been contemplated – requiring the defendant companies and prescribers to incur expenditure on irrecoverable costs of many millions... Win or lose, whether or not causation could be proved or the limitation period relied on, the defendants were quite literally at the mercy of the plaintiffs. Even so, with all the financial mayhem caused by their litigation, the plaintiffs were highly unlikely to collect a penny piece between them, come what may.' [Because, even if they won, they would have to repay the costs incurred by the Legal Aid Board on their behalf.]

Whilst the Law Society insists on holding a line between informing people of their rights and encouraging excessive litigation, it is not clear where that line is.[32] Lawyers might admit that encouraging people to sue local authorities is probably not the most desirable solution to a social problem, but maintain that it is better than nothing.[33] In addition, a recent change in the law now allows solicitors to offer 'no win, no fee' arrangements in actions for personal injury (excluding, at present, medical negligence). In one way, such an arrangement encourages the attitude, 'you might as well sue, there is nothing to lose'. A more positive way of viewing the new arrangements is that they will allow people to sue who have a good case, but who previously could not have afforded to do so. In addition, they might offset to some extent the increasing restrictions placed on eligibility for legal aid.

2. DISPUTES ABOUT EQUIPMENT AND THE LAW

Many decisions, occurrences and transactions are underpinned potentially, one way or another, by the law – whether by legislation or by a common law principle, such as negligence. In other words, if lawyers look into something, they will be able to analyse it legally. Indeed, on one view, law 'is everywhere: all actions, all relationships, even many facts and events which appear to be purely physical phenomena, can be (and sometimes must be) described in legal terms and slotted into legal classifications'.[34]

But just because law is widely applicable, it is not necessarily always to the fore. Indeed, it is quite possible and perhaps often desirable to go through daily life unaware of the hidden legal implications and consequences of some of our actions. Nevertheless, when disputes arise, or threaten to arise, for one in ten, one in a hundred or one in a thousand people, a knowledge of the law is sometimes essential for the parties involved – not only so that the disputes can be solved easily, but so that sometimes they can be avoided in the first place.

When shops replace faulty goods, they are doing so out of good business practice, not necessarily because the law forces them to do so. Similarly, when social services departments assess people, they often might not explicitly record under what legislation the assessment has taken place – for instance, s.47 of the NHS and Community Care Act 1990, s.4 of the Disabled Persons (Services, Consultation and Representation) Act 1968, or s.45 of the Health Services and Public Health Act 1968. However, whilst it might not matter most of the time if a social services department cannot demonstrate what legislation it has acted under – it might do if the law courts become involved. For instance, during the hearing of a recent Court of Appeal case about community care services (*R v Gloucestershire CC, ex parte Barry*), it became clear that one of the county councils involved could not show under what Act it had assessed an elderly woman; one of the judges pointed out in passing that, because of this, a court could technically (the point was not actually being decided in this case) find that the council had acted beyond its powers – in that it had been spending public money without a statutory basis for doing so.[35]

Differences and disputes arise every day between consumers and companies and between service users and statutory services. Sometimes a dispute can be viewed in black and white. Unreasonable consumers might mistreat their wheelchairs, but expect their money back nine months after purchase; while the unreasonable seller of a surgical belt might omit to mention, at the time of the sale, that there is a substantial and additional charge for fitting it. Sometimes service users demand the impossible of community therapists, thereby denying other people in greater need the services of those staff. And there are thoughtless health authorities and NHS Trusts who threaten to withdraw, at a stroke, the supply of incontinence pads – without reassessing people individually to see what their needs really are.

However, other situations are less straightforward and arise through genuine misunderstanding, with no 'fault' attaching to either party. Ultimately, some conflicts might be unavoidable. Of necessity, authorities do ration wheelchairs, speech therapy, home help services or home adaptations. Accidents involving defective products do occur, even if manufacturers have been careful – as do arguments about whether an expensive electric wheelchair was appropriate for the complex needs of the buyer when he bought it. Indeed, the law courts sometimes recognise, in negligence cases, that what they are doing is not apportioning moral blame, but deciding how the costs of accidents should be borne in society – by unlucky victims, unlucky defendants, insurance companies, hospitals etc. On some occasions, they might explicitly state that they are imposing liability on the party better able to bear the loss. For instance, a surveyor will normally be insured for negligence, and so can better bear the loss of his negligent survey – than can the housebuyers who relied on it.[36]

Avoiding the law courts

On a practical level, becoming embroiled in legal disputes carries with it a cost in terms of money, time and stress. Even if people win their legal actions, they might still have to pay costs which can reduce, or even wipe out, the compensation they have won. It is true that the small claims procedure of the County Court, legal aid, and the recently introduced 'no win, no fee' arrangements are designed to assist some people to pursue remedies through the courts. Not least, for example, people are far more likely to complain to the Office of Fair Trading, than to use the small claims procedure in the County Court.[37]

If it is desirable in many situations to avoid resort to the law, lawyers and the law courts, then why include these aspects in this book? By way of answer, it might be useful to make a threefold distinction. First, disputes can often be solved or even avoided without reference to the law at all. Second, a knowledge of the law might sometimes help resolve or avoid disputes, even though lawyers are not resorted to. In both these cases, disputes might be handled through the complaints or conciliation procedures of trade associations, the complaints procedures of social services departments, assistance from community health councils or advisory centres, or the intervention of an MP or councillor etc. And, well-informed about the law, large organisations might adopt safe and thorough procedures to reduce the risk of litigation.

Either way, whether or not 'the law' is referred to, neither lawyers nor the law courts need enter the picture (though advice organisations might do). For example, conciliation or arbitration might tend to apply a broad measure of 'fairness' rather than detailed legal rules. Indeed, the Lord Chancellor's Department makes just this sort of point in a recent booklet encouraging people to resolve disputes out of court.[38] And, as the National Consumer Council acknowledges, from the 'point of view of the consumer there is a balancing act between making existing court procedures more accessible and recognising that for many people the court is not the most appropriate forum for them to resolve their disputes'.[39]

Third, a knowledge of the law is of course utilised once lawyers, and possibly the law courts, become involved.

Common sense and informal resolution of differences

Disputes do not have to be analysed in legal terms and in some circumstances it is preferable for people to resolve their differences informally by using common sense. After all, it should be sufficient to demonstrate that a person who has just had her incontinence pads withdrawn, or who cannot afford to pay for home help, is in real 'need'. Such matters are surely meant (at least in a welfare state) to concern ultimately benevolence, humanity and care – not money and legal terminology. Similarly, if a retailer has imposed completely unreasonable hidden costs in a transaction, it should be enough to point this out, if not to the retailer, then to the relevant trade association. Such a situation should ideally be capable of solution on the basis of an informal application of fairness, rather than resorting to the law of contract.

The changing or replacing of goods is a specific instance of common sense, in the guise of good business practice, conscience and plain dealing between individuals. For example, the daughter of an elderly woman who has just died might approach the supplier of an electric scooter bought by her mother six months ago but barely used. The mother was perfectly sure that she wanted the scooter and was encouraged by her husband at the time. The scooter had beneficial psychological effects in terms of the independence it potentially offered, even if, as things turned out, it was actually little used. If the daughter makes a friendly and frank approach, the supplier might do something to help – for example, take the scooter back and refund half the money, or suggest secondhand dealers. On the other hand, if the daughter behaves aggressively – claiming that the salesman should never have sold the scooter in the first place and that the full cost should be refunded – the supplier might well react negatively. Certainly, in some circumstances, there might be a difference between advising a consumer about his or her 'legal rights', and suggesting the best and most practical solution to the dispute.

Another example concerns the consultant who is about to discharge an elderly couple (one has had a heart attack, the other a stroke) prematurely from hospital, but changes his mind when relatives make a strong case and he begins to see the couple as human beings with aspirations, rather than faceless patients. The relatives explain that the couple are both 'tough' and independent, and that it is premature to consign them to a residential or nursing home without giving them the chance to benefit first from rehabilitation and return to their own home. Along these lines, the health service ombudsman has observed that it is 'of value for the nurse or doctor to remember that what is routine for them is unique both for the patient and the patient's family'. Indeed, he suggests that complaints should be dealt with by NHS staff 'rationally and honestly' rather than defensively – ie in a common sense fashion.[40]

Prompt and thoughtful action by an organisation can help avoid confrontation and actually be the best solution for all concerned. For example, an occupational therapist in a social services department might instruct her staff to respond immediately to any reports of accidents in people's homes involving equipment or adaptations the department has provided. Thus, when a man rings up, irate because his disabled mother has fallen and been injured when using a stairlift, a therapist visits immediately, spends some hours with the man and his mother and talks through events. Initial threats of possible litigation subside as it becomes clear that what has happened was a genuine accident due neither to a want of instruction about how to use the lift nor to inappropriate prescription – it was 'just one of those things'.

Knowing what the law is

In some circumstances a knowledge of the law is valuable for all sides, even though litigation might still remain a last resort.

Knowledge of the law is quite distinct from litigation. An MP, councillor or community health council chairman who intervenes is perfectly capable of pointing out that an NHS Trust is breaking the law if it is charging families for surgical footwear. At little cost, a solicitor can write a letter to an authority or to a retailer, setting out the legal position and demonstrating the undesirability of litigation. Similarly, in the face of unclear legislation, local authorities need to have a good knowledge of the law if they are to anticipate and avoid legal actions being brought against them. (Nevertheless, if legislation is particularly vague or uncertain, a knowledge of it may provide neither authorities nor service users with adequate information about the strength of their respective legal positions.)

It might be tempting to maintain that judicial review (see Chapter 17) need not concern local authority staff – except for the fact that legal challenges about the rationing decisions of authorities are made precisely by way of such review. And, since rationing is increasing all the time, so awareness of judicial review becomes all the more important. In the same vein, the distinctions, overlaps and inconsistencies between areas of law such as negligence, contract, breach of statutory duty and the Consumer Protection Act 1987 could be written off as legal curiosities. But, in an increasingly litigious society, everybody – whether manufacturers, suppliers, statutory services, claimants seeking damages – can become ensnared. This is not to mention the introduction into English law, through the influx of European Union directives, of additional legal obligations – bringing in their wake legal, financial and administrative implications for manufacturers, suppliers and employers.

Going to court

There sometimes appear to be good reasons for going, or at least threatening to go, to court. If a person has been so severely injured as to need substantial amounts of money in the future for the costs of care, equipment and lost earnings – going to court might be the only way to ensure that these costs are met. For example, in the case of a car accident, an insurance company might deny that its client was liable – or a hospital might deny liability for an operation which has gone badly wrong.

Following a car accident and a broken neck, a young woman might need a phrenic nerve stimulator to enable her to breathe, personal care costing £170,000 per year, and a range of other daily living equipment. Even an award of £3.4 million, carefully managed, could be exhausted if she lives a long time.[41] A man might suffer severe burns which prevent him pursuing his career as a guitarist – thus denying him both income and personal fulfilment.[42] And there would seem to be every moral justification for suing a large tyre manufacturer which conceals the existence of a faulty type of tyre from the Department of Transport – even though the fault caused 300 incidents, including at least one fatal accident.[43] As the Welfare State appears increasingly unable to cope with the demands made upon it, so people who decide not to sue in negligence might in the future have less chance of assistance in coping with disabilities following from an accident.

Even so, this type of 'full compensation' is only available when other people are proved to be at fault and when they (or their insurance companies) are able to pay. But there are many people who are born, or become severely disabled, without such fault. This suggests that such a system of compensation is something of a lottery.

People also go to court for reasons other than damages. For example, if an authority, desperately trying to balance its budget, starts arbitrarily to withdraw services from vulnerable people, then a judicial review case might be effective. Even if it is difficult for service users to win against authorities when welfare and rationing are involved, such cases do sometimes raise public awareness about what is happening to the more vulnerable members of society. For example, a 1995 case involving the denial of treatment to a 10-year old child with leukaemia reached the Court of Appeal, attracted much publicity, and has generated a continuing debate – not only about the case itself, but even the way in which it has been reported and discussed in the Press.[44]

Nevertheless, most disputes fail to reach the law courts, even once lawyers have become involved. They are settled one way or another beforehand; indeed, as pre-trial procedures – such as gathering evidence, commissioning expert reports, interviewing witnesses, exchanging documents – progress, costs begin to mount and the incentive for both parties to settle increases in proportion.

Notes

1 Laurance, J. (1995). Litigious patients 'are threatening NHS medical care'. *The Times:* 10 April 1995.

2 London Boroughs Occupational Therapy Managers Group (1988). *Occupational therapists' criteria for the provision of home adaptations in the homes of people with disabilities.* London: LBOTMG (section 1: Access).

3 *Staples v West Dorset District Council* (1995) (CA), *The Times:* 28 April 1995.

4 Appleyard, B. (1995). We take up reckless pursuits, but want the real world to insulate us against all possible risks. *Independent:* 26 July 1995.

5 Parents sue theatre over Peter Pan 'nightmare'. *The Times:* 4 March 1996.

6 Jones, M. (1995). (Editorial). *Professional Negligence:* 1995; 11(3), p.77.

7 Fenn, P.; Hermans, D.; Dingwall, R. (1994). Estimating the costs of compensating victims of medical negligence. *British Medical Journal:* 6 August 1994; 309, pp.389–391.

8 Gibb, F. (1996). Accidents do happen. *The Times:* 6 February 1996.

9 (News item). 'Don't blame us' say solicitors. *Solicitors Journal:* 15 March 1996; 140(10), p.244.

10 ICE Ergonomics (1992). *An ergonomics investigation into aids and equipment for elderly people: carried out on behalf of the Consumer Safety Unit, Department of Trade and Industry.* London: Department of Trade and Industry, p.35. Concluded that although some equipment fell a little short of the safety mark, the majority was reasonably safe.

11 *R v Lancashire County Council, ex parte Ingham and Whalley* (1995) (QBD) (5 July 1995, CO/774/95, CO/108/95, transcript).

12 *R v Gloucestershire County Council, ex parte Barry; R v Lancashire County Council, ex parte Gilpin and RADAR* (1996) (CA) (7–10 May 1996, CO/95/1779, CO/95/1134): from the author's own notes of the case.

13 Eg account of pressurised staff: Pilkington, E. (1996). Health service faces lethal cocktail of problems, BMA chairman warns: 'It's quite frightening, so much is happening, you are terrified you will miss something crucial'. *Guardian:* 12 January 1996.

14 Social Services Inspectorate (Booth, L.; Moore, L.; Hunter, I.). *Inspection of home care services: London Borough of Hammersmith and Fulham, 5–19 October 1995.* London: Department of Health, p.26

15 *Wilsher v Essex Area Health Authority* [1986] 3 All ER 801 (CA) (at 810).

16 See generally: Cane, P. (1993). *Atiyah's accidents, compensation and the law.* 5th edition. London: Butterworths.

17 Harris, J. (1996). Peace deals: the bill to the NHS for medical negligence damages is escalating, as a battle develops on all fronts to reduce the number of claims. *Health Service Journal:* 16 May 1996, (Medical Negligence insert, pp.1–2).

18 Toynbee, P. (1996). Legal leeches are bleeding the NHS: the rise in medical negligence cases is bad news for just about everyone except opportunistic lawyers. *Independent:* 28 February 1996.

19 *AB and Others v John Wyeth and Brother Ltd and Another* [1994] 5 Med LR 149 (CA).

20 Hilborne, N.; Ames, J. (1996). City lawyer slates damages 'lottery'. *Law Society Gazette:* 13 March 1996, p.3.

21 *R v Secretary of State for Social Services, ex parte Hincks and Others* (1980) 1 BMLR 93 (CA).

22 *Wyatt v Hillingdon London Borough Council* (1978) 76 LGR 727 (CA).

23 *R v Gloucestershire County Council, ex parte Mahfood and Others, R v Islington London Borough Council, ex parte McMillan* (1996) 160 LGRevR 321 (QBD). And also: *R v Gloucestershire County Council, ex parte Royal Association for Disability and Rehabilitation* (1995) (QBD) (21st December 1995, CO/2764/95, transcript).

24 Consider, for example, the identical answers given to separate questions asked (on different days) of the Secretary of State for Health in England, and the Secretary of State for Wales about incontinence pads: *Hansard,* House of Commons, Written Answers, 17 January 1996, col 595, Mr Bowis. And: *Hansard,* House of Commons, Written Answers, 22 January 1996, col 98, Mr Bowis.

25 CI(92)34. Social Services Inspectorate. *Implementing caring for people: assessment.* London: Department of Health, 1992, paras 13, 24.

26 Generally on advertising: Samples, C. (1996). Adding value: most lawyers use advertising to promote their practices. *Law Society Gazette:* 6 March 1996; 93(9), p.22.

27 The front page of local newspapers may carry four separate advertisements from different firms – headed, for example, 'personal injury', 'accident compensation' or 'have you been injured'. *Camden New Journal:* 28 March 1996 (719), p.1.

28 Gibb, F. (1995). Lawyers snap up lists of accident victims. *The Times:* 30 November 1995.

29 Internet helps firms seek out business. *Law Society Gazette:* 7 February 1996, p.16.

30 Day, M. (1995). Public service or ambulance chasing? *The Times:* 14 February 1995.

31 Puxon, M. (1994). Commenting on: *AB and Others v John Wyeth and Brother Ltd and Another* [1994] 5 Med LR 149 (CA) (pp.154–155).

32 Ford, R.; Wilkinson, P. (1995). Law chiefs question plan to help victims sue over accidents. *The Times:* 11 August 1995.

33 (News item). 'Don't blame us' say solicitors. *Solicitors Journal:* 15 March 1996; 140(10), p.244.

34 Atiyah, P.S. (1995). *Law and modern society.* 2nd edition. Oxford: Oxford University Press, p.80.

35 *R v Gloucestershire County Council, ex parte Barry; R v Lancashire County Council, ex parte Gilpin and RADAR* (1996) (CA) (7–10 May 1996, CO/95/1779, CO/95/1134): from the author's own notes of the case.

36 *Smith v Eric S Bush* [1989] 2 WLR 790 (HL): in which case surveyors, reporting to a building society, were held nevertheless to have a duty of care (in negligence) to the prospective mortgagors (ie house-buyers) who relied on the negligent report.

37 Lowe, R.; Woodroffe, G. (1995). *Consumer law and practice.* 4th edition. London: Sweet & Maxwell, p.211.
38 Lord Chancellor's Department (1995). *Resolving disputes without going to court.* London: LCD, p.11.
39 National Consumer Council (1993). *Settling consumer disputes.* London: NCC, p.40.
40 Reid, W. (1996). Righting wrongs: the value of complaints for NHS users and providers. *Nursing Standard:* 6 March 1996; 10(24), p.19.
41 Ballantyne, A. (1995). 'I just hope that Christopher Reeve is as lucky as me'. *Times:* 20 June 1995.
42 Conn, D. (1996). Legal insult added to personal injury. *Independent:* 6 February 1996.
43 Victor, P. (1996). Dunlop in 'faulty tyres cover-up'. *Independent:* 5 March 1996.
44 Entwistle, V.; Watt, I.; Bradbury, R.; Pehl, L. (1996). Media coverage of the Child B case. *British Medical Journal:* 22 June 1996; 312 (7046), pp.1587–1591.

CHAPTER 5

WHEN THINGS GO WRONG

COVERAGE

1. What to do when things go wrong
   - What do people want when they complain?
   - Choosing a procedure when thing go wrong
   - Categorising avenues of complaint and redress
   - Are procedures of redress only for the benefit of individuals?
2. Settling things without using, or threatening to use, the law courts
   - Avoidance or informal resolution of disputes
   - Charters, complaints procedures and monitoring officers
   - Conciliation, mediation and arbitration
   - Ombudsmen.
3. Using, or threatening to use, the law courts
   - Diverse legal rules and procedures
   - Uncertainties of legal principles and procedures
   - How the law courts make rules and reach decisions.
4. Obtaining information from statutory services about equipment provision
   - Obtaining general information
   - Obtaining personal information.

Key points

A number of avenues can be used by people to complain, seek redress and sometimes claim damages if things go wrong. Some of these avenues tend toward the informal or at least the 'non-legal' in the sense that they do not involve the law courts. Others involve, or at least threaten to involve, the law more formally. Overall, there is sometimes a bewildering array of options. Therefore, people need to be aware of the rules governing the use of these different options, what the likelihood of success is – and, if they are successful, what sort of satisfaction, redress or compensation is available.

This chapter explains the use of both non-legal avenues of complaint, such as the ombudsmen, complaints procedures and charters covered in Part II of this book – as well as the formal legal procedures that apply if people pursue legal actions using the principles and concepts described in Part III. Further detail can be found in those

Parts of the book; this chapter provides the reader with an overview. In addition, users of statutory services might require access to both general or personal information when challenging decisions; the last part of this chapter outlines how such information can be obtained.

Questions people ask

- When should people take legal action instead of using less formal alternatives such as the complaints procedure or the ombudsman?
- Is it worth knowing about the law even if only to threaten or to bargain, rather than actually go to court?
- How relevant is the law at all to what actually goes on in practice?
- Is the law clear, and how can one assess the chances of winning the case?
- When people invoke the law, why do they do so? Is it worth the expense, time and stress?
- If you wish to go to law, how do you know which 'bit' of the law is relevant? For example, should an action be brought in negligence, consumer protection, contract or judicial review?

1. WHAT TO DO WHEN THINGS GO WRONG

People need to decide what sort of redress they want, followed by the procedure most likely to provide that redress. This might not be straightforward; depending on circumstances, some avenues are simply unusable, others are usable but do not offer the desired remedy (eg financial compensation), and others still might entail both excessive stress and uncertainty about the outcome.

What do people want when they complain?

People do not always use the most appropriate avenue of redress. For example, there is evidence that at least some people are driven to seek damages for negligence against the NHS, not because they want money, but because they have failed to obtain explanations and apologies at an earlier, informal stage. Given the amount of time and money now expended on clinical negligence cases, there is every incentive for NHS Trusts to settle disputes away from lawyers and the law courts. For patients, too, the incentive might be great, since medical negligence actions remain difficult to win (see p.331).

People's motives for pursuing legal actions can be many and varied. Apart from financial compensation, they might want apologies, explanations, revenge, knowledge that similar incidents will not occur in the future, publicity – and so on. As one editorial in the Lancet put it, the motives of NHS patients might stem from *altruism, naked truth or recompense.*[1] Assuming that they have not received serious injury for which they will sue anyway (eg for loss of earnings and future care), a full explanation might 'defuse the anger, upset and resentment'.[2] Professional staff should not straight away admit that they have been negligent since that issue can only be decided properly by a professional body, a court of law, an inquiry etc.[3] However, they can say candidly and sympathetically that they are sorry about what has happened, without thereby imputing the blame to themselves.[4] Indeed, an admission that a mistake has been made is not necessarily to concede negligence.

If simple and effective types of redress are not easily available at the outset of a complaint, people might end up going to court. For instance, if authorities operate complaints procedures defensively, complainants might be unable to obtain the information and explanation they want and so feel impelled to commence a legal action. Ironically, the authority might have withheld the information precisely because of its fear that the information was sought for the purpose of, or would provoke, litigation.[5]

Choosing a procedure when things go wrong

Sometimes people are clear about what sort of redress they want and which procedure to use.

For instance, the members of a family might be distressed about how their grandmother was treated in hospital, following a minor heart attack. Denied a bath and hairwash for six weeks because of staff indifference, allowed unnecessarily to remain incontinent of faeces on account of drugs she was given, and given no exercise or rehabilitation, she might become despondent, depressed and suffer further deterioration in her health. The final straw might come when the family is told on the telephone that she has been discharged home – in fact, it is later 'discovered' that she is still on the ward, but not before the family has suffered considerable anxiety. In this case, the family might be willing to receive a genuine apology and an undertaking to improve practices. The hospital complaints procedure ought to suffice if not at the informal, then at the formal, stage. If the procedure failed, it would be open to the family to make a complaint to the health service ombudsman.

If, through somebody else's negligence, a young woman suffers a high level spinal injury in a car accident which leaves her severely disabled and reliant on high levels of personal support and expensive equipment for the rest of her life, she will probably need to seek a high level of financial compensation. Tangible and sometimes large amounts of financial damages can be obtained. In the case of people who are badly injured, this can be essential; they might require expensive equipment such as wheelchairs, pressure relief beds or environmental control systems, costing in total many thousands of pounds. If the insurance company does not concede liability, then they might have to go to court.

However, choosing the right procedure is sometimes not so easy. For example, if a man is denied acute hospital care and dies as a consequence, his family might have a choice of using the NHS complaints procedure, taking legal action for negligence, or seeking judicial review. Yet none of the three choices might be quite right. First, hospital complaints procedures are not designed to pay out large sums in compensation – yet the family might need precisely to claim financial damages because it has been deprived of its main income. Second, a negligence action could be attempted, but it might well fail because (1) the case might be about a hospital 'closing its doors' to a patient, rather than careless treatment (see p.322) – and (2) the shortage of beds might relate to matters of policy and resources – with which the courts are reluctant to interfere. Finally, judicial review might succeed if it could be shown that the shortage of beds was caused by the unreasonable, unfair or illegal decision or action of the hospital. However, this would be difficult to prove, and in any case damages are not available in judicial review proceedings.

Weighing up which procedure to use

When choosing a particular procedure, people need to be aware of the practicalities, both advantageous and disadvantageous.

For instance, pursuing a legal action for negligence can take years, and be expensive and stressful. At the end of it all, the person might lose the case and have to pay not only the costs of his own lawyer but also those of the other side. A person who is legally aided is generally insulated from paying costs if the case is lost; however, if the case is won, he or she will have to repay costs to the Legal Aid Board out of the damages obtained. Even under the new 'no win, no fee' arrangements, a person who loses the case still has to pay the other side's costs – although these could be covered by insurance companies, on payment of a premium by the person who is suing. It is often difficult to predict what the courts are going to decide in any particular case.

More optimistically, the other side might settle the dispute quickly and favourably without the case ever getting to court. And the small claims procedure used in the courts, for claims of up to £3000 (but only up to £1000 in personal injury cases), is intended to be easy to use and ideal for seeking small amounts of compensation for defective goods.

Other procedures also need to be carefully considered before they are used. For instance, complaints procedures of social services departments offer, in principle, a speedy, informal and effective method of receiving apologies, overturning unfavourable decisions and obtaining services. However, principle is not always reflected in practice. The same might also go for the complaints procedures of trade associations (see below).

There are other, easily overlooked factors. For instance, vulnerable patients in hospital might be reluctant to complain, in case they are victimised as a result; they might also wish to avoid causing trouble for staff whom they like or sympathise with.[6] Indeed, people who are knowledgeable about their entitlements might be characterised by social services staff as 'demanding', 'grabbing' or 'fussy'.[7]

Categorising avenues of complaint and redress

Disputes can be conducted through a number of avenues, ranging from informal negotiation to the law courts. Although different 'remedies' involve clear differences of procedure, there are also significant overlaps.

For example, the distinction between formal and informal complaints is vague. Formal complaints procedures themselves have 'informal' stages – and statutory services struggle to identify, classify and deal with informal complaints. There are even uncertainties about the difference between 'complaints', 'comments', 'criticisms', 'feedback' – and so on. And a dispute taken to solicitors might be resolved by a quick, informal settlement before the action has even begun – even though formal, legal action was clearly in prospect.

Principles and concepts are sometimes common to more than procedure. For example, the judicial review courts investigate unreasonableness, illegality and unfairness; the local ombudsman sometimes employs these concepts when investigating maladministration. Both the law courts in applying judicial review, and the ombudsman, generally question the procedures that authorities have followed – not the merits of the actual decisions and the welfare needs of the individual concerned, nor the effects of policies, priorities and rationing (so long as these have been legally and properly implemented).

Similarly, social services department review panels (which sit at the third and final stage of the complaints procedure) sometimes take a similar approach. Indeed, ensuring that decisions have been taken according to procedure, at the expense of considering whether 'justice' has been done to the complainant, is sometimes referred to as 'ombudsman-proof' decision-making.[8]

There are other areas of overlap between procedures. For instance, the ombudsmen are generally not supposed to undertake investigations in circumstances where the complainant could take more formal legal action. But they regularly exercise their power to waive this condition, when they feel that it is not reasonable to expect people to do this. Thus, cases that could in principle have been heard in the law courts as judicial review or even negligence actions, might instead be investigated by the ombudsman. In any event, pursuing one course does not necessarily preclude another. For instance, if people are dissatisfied with the outcome of conciliation offered by trade associations, they can still go to the county court. But on the other hand, if people go to independent arbitration, then only in very limited circumstances can they resort to a court if they are still not satisfied.

Are procedures of redress only for the benefit of individuals?

Most complaints revolve around individual people. For example, making a complaint to a social services department or a trade association is very much about the individual person seeking redress – as is suing a manufacturer for negligence.

However, some avenues of redress revolve ultimately less around the individual complainant, and rather more around the activity of the person or organisation being complained of. For example, although individuals might indirectly benefit from a judicial review decision by the law courts, the judges are *primarily* concerned with ensuring that the authority is acting properly –

rather than with the welfare of the individual. When people complained (*R v Gloucestershire CC, ex parte Mahfood*) that their home help, provided under s.2 of the CSDPA 1970 had been removed, the courts were concerned with *the way* in which, *not the fact* that, this had been done.[9] This function of judicial review – ie the supervision of the way in which public bodies behave – is reflected in the fact that damages are not available in judicial review cases. In contrast, whilst the local ombudsmen also investigate *how* authorities have made decisions, rather *what* they have decided, they do recommend explicitly individual solutions and sometimes compensation.

A criminal prosecution for breach of safety regulations can result primarily in a fine or imprisonment – compensation for the victim is a secondary consideration, although it is sometimes obtained. Similarly, a person can make a complaint to a professional body, for instance, the General Medical Council. However, the purpose of any disciplinary action taken by the Council is to censure or punish the offending doctor – not to provide compensation to the victim of bad practice.

Another form of regulation, even further removed from individual complaints, concerns the inspection and registration of services. For instance, inspectorates at both national and local level inspect social services provided by local authorities, including residential care, day services, home support services, and occupational therapy services for equipment and adaptations. Inspections can obviously benefit residents if they expose problems and deficiencies and catalyse change; but their primary purpose is not to compensate individuals for any harm, loss or discomfort suffered.

Can groups of people take action?

Legal actions are usually individual affairs, although sometimes a number of cases might be heard together; for instance, challenges (*R v Gloucestershire CC, ex parte Mahfood*) to the withdrawal of home help services under s.2 of the CSDPA 1970 were brought in the High Court by several elderly people and heard together. The decision in the case affected hundreds of other people who were in the same position in Gloucestershire.[10] Furthermore, by the time the case reached the Court of Appeal (*R v Gloucestershire CC, ex parte Barry*), it was obviously seen by the courts (as well as service users and their advisers) to be a matter of principle and public interest affecting other people in the future – since, of the two individuals whose cases were heard, one was now dead and the other had since had his services restored by the county council.[11] Nevertheless, the Court of Appeal was prepared to hear the cases over three days. The local ombudsman sometimes investigates a number of cases together – for example, if a number of people complain at the same time about how an authority has introduced charges for social services.[12]

A development new to English law is the pursuing of group or multi-party actions, in which litigation is conducted by a steering committee on behalf of a number of plaintiffs. Such actions are particularly relevant in cases involving products, prescription drugs, or disasters.[13] There are other ways in which a decision affecting one person, will in fact affect many others. If one resident successfully protests about the closure of a residential home, then other residents stand to gain.

Points of principle and public interest

Sometimes a voluntary organisation might be allowed to bring a case on behalf of a particular person or persons with a view to gaining a *declaration* (see p.449) – ie a statement of the law affecting many other people as well. For example, in 1995 the Royal Association for Disability and Rehabilitation gained a declaration against Gloucestershire County Council, to the effect that it was unlawful for the council to have withdrawn services from people before it had reassessed their needs according to revised criteria of eligibility for services.[14] And, in 1996, it joined the daughter of the original applicant (who had died in the interim) to take a judicial review case (about the provision of home support services) to the Court of Appeal (*R v Lancashire CC, ex parte Gilpin and RADAR*), following an adverse decision in the High Court.[15] An independent advice centre might make a posthumous complaint to the local ombudsman on behalf, for example, of a man with AIDS to whom the local authority had denied 'appropriate and essential services and facilities' (including a telephone).[16] Thus, when people have died, but their cases are pursued in judicial review or through the ombudsman, points of principle and public interest affecting many people might be at issue.

More generally, the ombudsmen not only award compensation to the individuals concerned, but also sometimes recommend improvements to policies and procedures – which, if implemented, are clearly of benefit to many other people, as well as the original complainant.

2. SETTLING THINGS WITHOUT USING, OR THREATENING TO USE, THE LAW COURTS

Avoidance or informal resolution of disputes

A potential dispute can sometimes be avoided altogether. For example, the person who buys a pickup stick which does not work properly will normally take or send it back to the shop to get a replacement, repair, credit note or money back. The shop is not under a general legal obligation to settle in this way (though it might be bound by particular contract terms), but will normally do so as a matter of good business practice. Likewise, a phone call and discussion about a proposed reduction in the number of incontinence pads supplied weekly by the local, community NHS Trust could result in an acceptable agreement being reached. The desirability of settling things informally is stressed in Chapter 4.

Local representatives, such as councillors, MPs, community health councils or voluntary bodies can sometimes intervene effectively. For example, councillors might act when they realise that the strict criteria of eligibility for equipment provision, that they themselves approved in Social Services Committee earlier in the year, are affecting people in their own ward adversely. Apart from stimulating the benevolent side of councillors and MPs, hardship amongst constituents is not a votewinner.

Some years ago, when concern arose about the provision of powered nebulisers by the NHS, local community health councils protested to their local health authorities – and the national body representing these councils wrote to the Secretary of State for Health.[17] Following this episode, involving heated exchanges in Parliament, guidance was issued by the Department of Health and the Welsh Office to clarify the legal position. And, in the last two years, the Royal Association for Disability and Rehabilitation has been in contact with a number of social services departments on behalf of individual people denied community care services.

Charters, complaints procedures, monitoring officers

Charters might be of some assistance in obtaining the provision of statutory services or apologies. In principle, they offer an informal and speedy solution to disputes. In practice, they might be vitiated by their apparent lack of legal enforceability and their selective and limited scope (see p.145).

The complaints procedures of particular statutory services are explained in other chapters. At best, in response to a wide range of complaints, they can offer speedy and effective remedies which do not involve complicated questions of law, lawyers or expense. People might obtain the services previously denied them – or at least apologies. Complaints procedures are not generally designed to pay financial compensation as a matter of course, but occasionally it is offered.[18] At worst, procedures are poorly organised, take too long and are applied narrowly. Defensive reactions can easily characterise the reactions of staff, even though apologies and explanation might be all that is required to defuse the situation.[19]

In addition – and it is difficult to see how authorities could manage it otherwise – most complaints procedures inevitably provide only limited, if any, opportunity to challenge the priorities and policies underlying rationing decisions.[20] The inevitable suspicion lurks that because complaints procedures are operated from within the very body (ie the social services department) being complained of, they will not be sufficiently independent.[21] Doubts about the impartiality of the 'inhouse' complaints or appeal procedures of local authorities surface from time to time in the investigations of the local ombudsmen and in the law courts (see p.441). Judges sometimes insist that complaints procedures should be used instead of judicial review in the law courts. This makes it even more important that complaints procedures should be effective.

Codes of practice of trade associations might stipulate that complaints procedures be well-publicised – and complaints be treated seriously and promptly, and be resolved, if necessary, with assistance from local authority trading standards officers, consumer advice centres or Citizens' Advice Bureaux. In the field of disability equipment, there are several codes of practice produced by sections of the BSTA (British Surgical Trades Association). These include the Rehabilitation Products Section, the British Association of Wheelchair Distributors, and the Mobility Vehicles Section. The procedures of trade associations can work well, although, again, there might be misgiving about whether the trade association will deal evenhandedly between its member company and a consumer. Nevertheless, it is not necessarily in the interests of the association to over-protect erring members – since its reputation, together with that of other members, stands to suffer.

Local authority monitoring officers have a duty to report whether the proposals, decisions or omissions of local authorities either breach – or are likely to breach – legislation or a code of practice. They also have a duty to report on actual or possible maladministration or injustice perpetrated by the authority.[22] In some circumstances, monitoring officers might be a useful avenue of approach when attempting to persuade an authority to re-think a policy or particular decision.

Conciliation, mediation and arbitration

Alternative dispute resolution generally

Because of the costs, time and stress of going to court various forms of *alternative dispute resolution* exist. There is much in their favour. A useful summary of available procedures, and their advantages and disadvantages, is contained in a booklet published recently by the Lord Chancellor's Department called *Resolving disputes without going to court.*[23] Legal complexity might be avoided in alternative dispute resolution, in favour of a more general concept of fairness. Whilst speedy and practical remedies might be facilitated, concern exists just outcomes might be hindered in some circumstances.

Conciliation and mediation

The principles involved in conciliation and mediation are similar. A neutral third party assists the parties in dispute to reach agreement but, ultimately, those in dispute have to agree to the solution – the third party cannot impose it (in contrast to arbitration).

The codes of practice of trade associations might offer a conciliation service, whereby the association steps in to resolve a complaint which has not been settled between its member and a consumer. Conciliation is provided free and does not affect a person's rights to resort to other means of redress, including the law courts. The Chartered Institute of Arbitrators offers a Consumer Dispute Resolution Scheme which includes a conciliation process.[24]

Because of disquiet about the increasingly costly litigation engulfing the NHS, mediation and arbitration have been proposed as alternatives for solving even medical negligence disputes.[25] So far, such proposals have not been widely adopted – although mediation is being pioneered in some NHS Trusts.[26] It has been suggested that because the causes of some medical conditions can be many, and often remain unknown in individual cases, alternative dispute resolution will prove no more effective than the law courts.[27] However, this view misses the point that more open, less confrontational methods of resolution will precisely help people to understand both the complications of the case and the point of view of the other party.[28]

Arbitration

There are two main types of arbitration. One is the County Court small claims procedure. The other operates outside of the courts. Arbitration generally is governed by the Arbitration Acts 1950 to 1979 (although new legislation is imminent) and by the Consumer Arbitration Agreements Act 1988. Basically, this last Act states that the code of practice of a trade association cannot force a consumer to go to arbitration.

Arbitration outside the courts: trade association schemes. Arbitration is a more formal process that might be offered either as part of individual consumer contracts or as part of a code of practice of a trade association. Arbitrators are often appointed through the Chartered Institute of Arbitrators. They will consider only written evidence and will give reasons for their decisions. Their decisions are final and legally binding. Arbitrators have 'the widest discretion permitted by law to resolve the dispute in a just, speedy, economical and final manner in accordance with natural justice'.[29]

The advantages of arbitration are that it offers (in principle at least) quick and informal redress at low cost, it is private, and the binding decision reached can be enforced if necessary through a county court. The disadvantage is that a dissatisfied party cannot challenge the decision subsequently by going to court, except to appeal on grounds of procedure or a mistake of law – for example, if the arbitrator has shown bias.[30] Evidence suggests that many people are unaware of the arbitration schemes of trade associations, with the consequence that they are little used.[31]

County court small claims procedure. Civil legal actions involving claims of not more than £3,000 are automatically referred for arbitration by a district judge as part of the county court small claims procedure. This rule applies neither to actions for personal injury if the sum being claimed is over £1000, nor to other cases which are complex in terms of fact or law.[32]

The small claims procedure is designed to give people quick and easy access to the courts, avoiding expense and cumbersome legal procedure. Legal aid is generally not available, but legal representation is not prohibited. This can result in an imbalance between legally represented companies and unrepresented consumers.[33] The £3000 limit for automatic referral has been effective from January 1996; the previous figure was £1000. Some concern exists that more serious cases (in terms of value) will now be dealt with by arbitration and further tip the balance against poor, individual consumers.[34]

There is evidence that, in the past at least, consumers have been ill-informed about the small claims procedure.[35] It is used more commonly as a debt collection procedure by businesses against consumers, than by consumers against companies.[36] Facilities for disabled people are patchy; for example, 27% of courts have no level or ramped access, 54% are without accessible toilet facilities, whilst very few courts provide facilities for people with visual or hearing impairments. Although the majority of people who use the small claims courts are satisfied with how their cases are handled in court, problems arise afterwards. For example, 36% of successful plaintiffs fail to recover the money they are entitled to, whilst over 46% find themselves in the position of having to enforce their judgements – frequently unsuccessfully.[37]

Ombudsmen

There are a number of ombudsmen including, for example, the banking, insurance and legal. However, this book concentrates mainly on the decisions of the local government, health service and Parliamentary ombudsmen.

The ombudsmen are generally limited to investigating maladministration – that is the procedures followed by public bodies, rather than the substance of their policies or the professional judgements of their staff, such as doctors, nurses and social workers. In this they resemble the judicial review courts, who look at *how* authorities make decisions, but not *what* they decide. Furthermore, the ombudsmen cannot directly challenge policies, priorities and the allocation of resources. However, the Parliamentary ombudsman has pointed out in his latest annual report that further reductions in the number of civil servants will lead inevitably to increased maladministration and to more complaints.[38] Therefore, the ombudsman will not challenge those cuts and the underlying policy explicitly, but will be doing so implicitly by making more adverse findings of maladminstration against public bodies.

The ombudsmen are not hemmed in by formal legal procedure, nor are they are bound by the formal system of precedent (ie following previous decisions: see p.123) to which the courts adhere. The ombudsmen strive to reach consistent and fair decisions, taking account of the detailed circumstances of each case. This means that if there has been delay in service provision (eg in providing home adaptations or in producing statements of children's special educational needs), what can be predicted is not the outcome but only that the ombudsman will have applied fairness to the dispute. Thus, before finding maladministration, the ombudsmen will look at the reasons for the delay; and, even if there has been maladministration, they will also consider, before recommending compensation, whether or not complainants have suffered injustice.

In addition to maladministration, the health service ombudsman can investigate also failure in a service and failure to deliver a service which there is a duty to provide. The local ombudsmen, though without this additional remit, are not wholly disadvantaged, since they sometimes state that failure to carry out a duty amounts to maladministration in any case. Legislation passed during 1996 has extended significantly the health service ombudsman's powers by allowing him to investigate clinical, as well as administrative, decisions. Nevertheless, even without these additional powers, the health service ombudsman has sometimes been able to investigate what appear to be professional judgements – when the foundation of those judgements is administratively flawed (eg the 'clinical' decision has been taken on the basis of obviously inadequate information).

The great advantage of using the ombudsmen is that they are independent, generally make thorough investigations and are not afraid to rule against authorities. Indeed, in the context of this book, they have made many relevant investigations into, the provision of equipment, adaptations, continuing NHS care, discharge from hospital, and communication between authorities/staff and service users. Unlike the judicial review courts, the local ombudsmen regularly award financial compensation, the health service ombudsman sometimes. The ombudsmen are not meant to take up cases which people could otherwise pursue in the law courts – but they have a discretion to waive this restriction in particular cases. Sometimes, if there are several aspects to a single complaint, some might be dealt with in a court case, others in an investigation of the ombudsman.[39]

Possible disadvantages to using the ombudsmen are that, in principle at least, public bodies are not obliged to follow their recommendations (eg for financial compensation). In any case, the complaints procedures of authorities are meant to be used first, before ombudsmen are resorted to.

The function of the health service ombudsman is explained further elsewhere (see p.219); that of the local ombudsman immediately below.

Local ombudsman

A number of decisions of the local ombudsmen are referred to in this book, particularly in Chapters 7 and 9, since they have carried out many investigations into the provision of home adaptations and daily living equipment. They have also investigated numerous disputes concerning the assessment and meeting of children's special educational needs (see Chapter 11).

Local ombudsmen investigate maladministration and the injustice caused. There are several, men and women, covering broad tracts of the country. They are not meant to take on cases which could be dealt with by a court of law, a tribunal or a government minister – but frequently waive this requirement. For instance, the ombudsmen would not normally expect people to instigate judicial review proceedings. Normally, they cannot investigate more than 12 months after the occurrence of the incident complained of. The ombudsmen can recommend financial compensation or any other lawful remedy, but only if injustice was caused.

The injustice for which compensation is recommended might be obvious (eg award for repairs which the complainants had to pay for themselves, failing the renovation grant they should have received), or perhaps slightly less so (eg the equivalent cost of speech therapy sessions a child with special educational needs should have received but did not). Less tangible still, but equally capable of meriting compensation is the stress, anxiety and uncertainty suffered, for example, by parents as a result of the maladministration of an education authority towards their child – even if the latter did not itself actually suffer injustice. Local authorities are specifically empowered to pay compensation recommended by the ombudsman but are not obliged to. If authorities do not accept the ombudsman's recommendations, even after a second report, they can be forced to publish the report in a local newspaper.

In principle, the investigation of maladministration brings with it certain limitations. Like the judicial review courts, ombudsmen are investigating not what authorities are doing, so much as how they are doing it. Thus, the ombudsmen are sometimes prepared to accept that authorities have no choice but to operate long waiting lists. But they will, for example, find fault with authorities that have no proper policy about waiting times or operate such a policy unfairly. For similar reasons, the ombudsmen will not, in principle at least, question the professional judgements of staff. Despite these limitations the ombudsmen carry out flexible investigations, and are quite prepared to rule against authorities on a variety of grounds.

Legislation does not define maladministration. The law courts have pointed out that maladministration is not necessarily unlawful, and that lawful maladministration is not for the courts, but for the ombudsman, to deal with.[40] However, the converse does not hold; the ombudsman is quite prepared to find maladministration if the law has been broken (eg when a housing authority exceeds the statutory timescale for dealing with applications for renovation grants). In addition, it has been suggested that the ombudsmen apply notions of fairness and natural justice in their investigations.[41] In the absence of a statutory definition of maladministration, the office of the local ombudsman has published 42 axioms of good administration.[42] The following is a selection (in paraphrase):

> Authorities and their staff should be aware of the law. Criteria of eligibility should be clear, relevant and applied consistently but allow for exceptions. Policies and rules should be communicated to service users and misleading statements avoided. Codes of practice and government Circulars should be taken account of and followed unless there are good reasons for not doing so. Decisions must be made on the basis of all relevant, but excluding irrelevant, factors. Reasons for adverse decisions should be given. Delegation of functions should be legal and appropriate. Adequate records should be maintained. Disputes should be solved informally if possible, but otherwise more formally and impartially.

Overall, only 3% to 4% of disputes coming to the attention of the local ombudsmen result in formal investigations. And, of these formal investigations, only about 3% result in findings of maladministration; although the 16% that are settled before investigations are completed would, taken to their conclusion, probably result in findings of maladministration.[43]

3. USING, OR THREATENING TO USE, THE LAW COURTS

This book covers the following areas of law: negligence, contract, breach of statutory duty and judicial review. It also deals with specific consumer protection and safety legislation relevant to equipment – including product liability, general product safety, medical devices, and the manual handling of loads. The details of these legal principles and legislation are explained and discussed in Part III of the book, whilst the general advantages and disadvantages of using lawyers and the law courts have been dealt with in Chapter 4.

Each of these areas of law is itself complicated and subject to limitations, uncertainties and change – and so is sometimes difficult to understand. And, if just one specific Act of Parliament is difficult to grasp, how much more difficult is it to give a unified picture or overview of a number of different areas of law. Nevertheless, an overview can be helpful. The following headings therefore represent a few of the considerations that need commonly to be borne in mind by those using the law.

Diverse legal rules and procedures

Different areas of law reflect not only different principles and concepts, but also contain unexpectedly divergent and detailed rules. The following are a few examples:

(i) **Bringing legal actions in time.** Time limitations vary; there are different periods of time, from the date of the relevant event (eg an accident or decision made by a public body), within which a legal action must be started. Thus, a legal action involving personal injury must be brought within three years, involving property damage within six years – and a judicial review action within six months. However, some time limits can be waived.

(ii) **Availability of financial compensation.** Compensation might generally be available in one area of law (eg negligence) but not in another (eg judicial review); and some types more readily obtainable in one area than another. For instance, pure financial loss (eg money wasted on a defective product, but with no personal injury or property damage caused) is generally not obtainable in negligence, but is standard in an action for breach of contract.

(iii) **Permission to bring a legal action.** Bringing a judicial review case requires preliminary 'permission' – whereas bringing a private action for breach of statutory duty, for breach of contract or negligence does not.

(iv) **Using more than one legal principle.** Sometimes a legal action can be brought under more than one legal head, for instance, negligence and breach of statutory duty, or negligence and contract. This can be an advantage – if the action fails on one principle, it might succeed on another.

If a person has bought a defective wheelchair which has caused an accident, personal injury and damage to property (eg clothing), she could try to sue the retailer in contract – and the manufacturer (with whom she does not have a contract) under the Consumer Protection Act 1987 or in negligence or both. Not only could she sue both at the same time, but if one of them has disappeared, or is not financially worth suing, then she can still sue the other. However, she cannot of course gain 'double-recovery' (ie the full amount of damages twice over).

Indeed, a person might have 'concurrent' liability in both contract and tort (of which negligence is a part); and there might be distinct advantages in using one rather than the other. For instance, if a person is suing for financial loss only (eg when he loses money, having relied on poor, professional advice), then the obvious legal action is breach of contract (if there was one). On the other hand, it might sometimes be easier to prove that the harm resulting from, for example, negligent advice or treatment (eg from a private physiotherapist) was foreseeable in negligence, than to prove it in contract (depending, though, on the wording and circumstances of the contract). And, the Court of Appeal recently affirmed that in relation to a single transaction, a professional's *duty of care* in negligence might be greater than his contractual duty to exercise *reasonable care and skill.* This was in a case brought against a firm of solicitors and an estate agent in connection with a £5.8 million property transaction.[44]

Uncertainties of legal principles and procedures

Within each area of law are uncertainties which make the outcome of cases difficult to predict. This is because the legal principles and procedures are not static. Case by case, the courts develop the law, giving meanings and then revised meanings to words, and introducing explicitly or implicitly public policy considerations. The following are a few examples.

Challenging the decisions of public bodies: judicial review

Judicial review (see Chapter 17) has been a rapidly expanding area of law in the last fifteen years or so – meaning that the law courts are still busily exploring and trying to define its limits. Put another way, they have been considering how far they can or should challenge and overrule the decisions (eg about equipment provision) of public bodies. The meaning and application of concepts changes over time and with context.

Providing equipment carelessly: negligence

The law of negligence (see Chapter 14), too, continually changes. Judges formulate what they think they mean by a 'duty of care' – only to modify or even reject the formulation at a later date.

For instance, by the early 1980s, it was feared by some that the law of negligence was developing too rapidly and becoming over-extended. Stemming from a case in the 1930s involving ginger beer and a decomposed snail (*Donoghue v Stevenson*)[45], negligence was now lapping at everybody's door – whether the Home Office for failing to control Borstal boys[46] – or local authorities for the financial loss caused to home owners by their negligent inspection of house foundations.[47] There was a danger that the law of negligence would increasingly be used to recover compensation for financial loss (not just personal injury or damage to property). This was tantamount to legal heresy, since recovery for financial loss traditionally lies in the law of contract.[48]

In response, the House of Lords tried to halt such uncontrolled development by stating in 1990 that the law, if it was to advance, should do so incrementally and cautiously. Furthermore, it overruled one of its own decisions and stated that local authorities should not, after all, be liable for financial loss caused by negligent inspection of house foundations.[49] Nevertheless, since that apparent brake on development, the perception more recently is that the law of negligence is probably expanding again.[50]

In any case, one of the areas in which the ambit of negligence remains unclear is that of local authorities. Whilst they are found negligent for broken paving stones or leaving mud on the road – the courts experience difficulty in deciding, for example, in what sets of circumstances liability should be imposed on social services departments and their staff (see p.308).

Predicting what the courts will decide in different contexts and different circumstances

To some extent, each legal principle operates both contextually and non-contextually. For instance, fairness is one of the principal concepts of judicial review. One aspect of fairness is that reasons should be given for decisions. However, the courts rule that, in order to act fairly, public bodies need to give reasons for their decisions in some contexts only; in others they need not.

Under the law of negligence, we owe a duty to our 'neighbours' to be careful. This duty of care is normally traced back to the *Donoghue v Stevenson* case. The case was important because it established that the manufacturer of a product owes a duty of care to a consumer, even though neither come into contact with each other. Following this case, the duty to be careful to one's neighbours has become the mainstay of the law of negligence and is now applied in many different types of situation (see p.306).

The tension between 'universal' (non-contextual) and 'local' (contextual) concepts can make it both easier and more difficult to predict judicial decisions. For instance, in one case about home renovation grants, it was uncertain whether the court would extend the necessity to give reasons to this particular context: it did not.[51] In contrast, the duty of care owed by medical doctors to patients is well entrenched and taken for granted. Whereas in cases involving social workers, the duty of care would have to be argued, because to date, social workers have been largely immune in negligence actions (see p.308). However, in those situations when a duty of care is taken for granted, the outcome of the case does not automatically follow. For instance, typically a court might find that although the doctor breached his duty of care, this breach was not the cause of the accident (see p.331).

Practical uncertainties: judges and judicial reasoning

One view of how the law courts work is that there is a fixed and certain canon of law, against which judges measure, logically, the facts and circumstances of each individual case. This suggests that objective, 'scientific' legal decisions are made by judges who function as expert interpreters of fixed statute law (legislation) and common law (the body of rules and principles law developed by the judges themselves).

This view of how the law works is probably a socially useful one. It encourages a belief in the objectivity and impartiality of the judges – and thus respect and deference to the very legal system itself. It also implies a considerable degree of certainty and inevitability in the outcome of legal cases: a sufficient knowledge of the law ought to enable accurate prediction.

However, this view of the law only represents part of the picture; there are a number of respects in which legal decision-making is more complicated, arbitrary and unpredictable.

Judicial reasoning: facts, law and conclusion – or facts, conclusion and law? One view of how judges make decisions is that they (i) look at the facts of a case, (ii) consider the law, (iii) apply the law to the facts and (iv) then reach a conclusion. However, this view – implying that there is always a 'right' answer which judges will alight on if they use the correct analytical formula – has been dismissed as a 'fairy tale' by at least one eminent judge.[52] Instead, another suggestion is that sometimes judges look at the facts of the case, decide what a just outcome should be, and only then formally identify and interpret the law to fit the desired outcome. This is a form of arguing 'backwards' by making the law fit into the facts rather than the facts into the law.[53]

Inevitability of legal decisions? The idea, given a certain set of facts, that legal decisions are inevitable (or 'repeatable' in the scientific sense of experimental method) scarcely stands up. First, no two cases are alike and each is defined by unique events, circumstances and individual characters. As Lord Denning put it in one case about disputed care orders for children: 'This case is of legal significance, but more of human interest. I will start with the human side: because that always has its bearing on the legal side'.[54]

Second, even if two cases are very alike, there is plenty of room for different judges to take different views of very similar circumstances. Third, the doctrine of precedent (described below) means that decisions can be overturned in some cases. For instance, the High Court might decide a case, the Court of Appeal come to the opposite conclusion, only for the House of Lords to restore the original High Court decision. This process is currently affecting Gloucestershire County Council in a case directly relevant to this book – concerning, as it does s.2 of the Chronically Sick and Disabled Persons Act 1970. The High Court ruled that the council could take account of resources when assessing people's needs[55]; the Court of Appeal (in a 2:1 split decision) ruled that it could not; and the case is now likely to go to appeal in the House of Lords.[56] More haphazardly, successful appeals and overturning of decisions might depend, not on the justice of the case but on whether a person is motivated or can afford to appeal in the first place.

Even in the House of Lords, the highest UK law courts, the five judges can radically – if politely – disagree with one another. The lack of inevitability of decisions was perhaps demonstrated in the *Donoghue v Stevenson* case, already referred to above. The decision was a 3:2 majority in favour of finding a duty of care owed by the manufacturer of the offending ginger beer bottle; but one of the dissenting judges suggested dryly that though such a duty and its consequences might have been found amongst the laws of ancient Babylon, it had no place in English law.[57]

If judges in the same court disagree, the case is decided on a majority, rather than a unanimous, verdict; and, sometimes, the dissenting views of the losing minority in such cases can turn out to be of longer term significance than those of the majority. They are sometimes 'resurrected' and form the basis for development of the law in a later case. This happened in a case establishing the principle that professionals can be liable in negligence for the financial loss they cause other people through careless advice or careless statements. The actual case was lost by the plaintiff; but the principle was established for the future.[58]

Variations between different judges and lawyers. Much might depend on individual judges and lawyers. Judges are, after all, human beings and not computers; so they inevitably have differing approaches and sympathies. For instance, it has been suggested that the outcome of some cases in contract law reflect the various leanings of judges towards consumer-welfarism, market-individualism, formalism (sticking to the rule book, come what may) or realism (moulding the rules to ensure reasonable results).[59]

Decisions in some cases might depend on such conceptual leanings and thus on which judge happens to be conducting a case on any particular day. For example, in a 1995 case about health authority rationing (*R v Cambridge HA, ex parte B*), the High Court judge's allusion to a right to life (in connection with the European Convention on Human Rights) was one which probably few other judges would have made.[60] And, over a long period, Lord Denning became known as the defender of the 'little man' against powerful institutions, for instance, in cases about farmers and banks.[61] Even so, this approach did not necessarily spill over into cases concerning statutory services, where he bowed to the inevitable constraints of welfare legislation – whether in connection with homeless people[62] or substantial delay in providing NHS orthopaedic treatment.[63]

Apart from the judges, the lawyers who are involved in the case might affect the outcome in various ways. These could include the uneven expertise of opposing barristers, poor presentation of the argument on the day, an omission to take a particular line of reasoning (which, therefore, the judges do not consider when reaching their decision), a barrister who has mostly failed to master her brief, a barrister's misreading of a judge's sense of humour – and so on. Such factors are a reminder about the 'human' elements of a court case – no matter how important the issues.

Outcome of cases influenced by considerations of public policy. A further difficulty in predicting how the courts are going to react is that they sometimes import considerations of public policy. Although they are not always explicit about it, they might look to the wider effects of possible decisions, before deciding the actual outcome of a particular case. Sometimes the courts state quite candidly that it is all a question of policy. Recently, for instance, when denying a soldier's claim that he had been injured through the negligence of a gun commander in the Gulf War, the court said, when dismissing the claim[64]:

> 'How wide the sphere of the duty of care in negligence is to be laid depends ultimately on the court's assessment of the demands of society for protection from the carelessness of others.'

So, for example, one reason for not finding social services departments negligent – or for forcing health authorities to provide detailed reasons for their decisions – is that it would not be in society's interest. The money and time of authorities is better spent providing services than fighting what might become a flood of litigation (*X v Bedfordshire CC*).[65]

The contrast between an approach based on policy and one based on a 'direct chain of reasoning' was highlighted by the Court of Appeal itself in a medical negligence case:[66]

> Unsure about how to apply the test of whether alleged negligence had actually caused harm to a baby, the court felt it should follow a previous House of Lords case involving the National Coal Board, dermatitis caused by dust and a failure to provide showers.[67] This case had been decided against the Board, because although the effect of the failure to provide showers could not be precisely measured in terms of causing the dermatitis, the absence of showers clearly made a 'material contribution'. Further, as a matter of policy, it was the employer rather than the employee who should suffer from such a difficulty in producing evidence about causation. In the later case, the Court of Appeal had to decide whether it, too, could take such a policy-based approach, rather than a painstaking evidential one about causation. It decided on the former (policy) course, only to be overturned by the House of Lords at a later date.

How the law courts make rules and reach decisions

As already explained, the outcome of court cases is beset by a number of uncertainties – conceptual and practical. However, even when cases have been decided, it is not necessarily easy to state exactly 'what the law is' – or at least to explain what you mean when you state 'this is what the law now is'. In spite of a system of precedent, by which lower courts are meant to follow the decisions of higher courts, the state of the law can remain doubtful. For example, judges sometimes circumvent precedent by *distinguishing* cases, and decisions can be *overruled* by higher courts. Not least, some legal questions never get to the law courts at all and so remain subject to speculation.

The system of precedent and consistency of judgements

The law courts operate through a system of *precedent*; this means basically that if a decision is made in a higher court, then lower courts must follow that decision in similar cases. Higher courts might find themselves *persuaded* to follow lower courts, but are not bound to. The hierarchy of courts for civil (as opposed to criminal cases) cases is County Court, High Court, Court of Appeal and House of Lords. There are various rules that determine the court a case must be started in.

County Court cases are not reported and do not bind any other court; the county court is generally used in simpler cases and where large sums of damages are not being claimed.

The High Court hears more complex cases (eg medical negligence or judicial review) and those that involve larger sums of money. It is not bound to follow itself (ie other High Court decisions are persuasive but not binding) but must follow the Court of Appeal. The decisions of the Court of Appeal bind the courts below it; it is usually, though not always, bound by its own decisions – but, in any case, must follow the House of Lords. House of Lords decisions bind all the courts beneath it; but since 1966, the House of Lords may overrule itself – although this happens rarely.

For example, in May 1996, two cases involving community care and the CSDPA 1970 – and thus relevant to equipment provision – were heard together in the Court of Appeal. This followed High Court decisions which were, on the whole, unfavourable to service users.[68] The judgement of the Court of Appeal is likely to be significant, since it will set a precedent which can only be overruled by the House of Lords.

No two cases are the same – 'distinguishing' cases

No two cases are exactly the same; even if there are striking similarities, it is open to a judge to point to certain details making the case different from one previously decided. Consequently, even if a similar, previous case has been decided by a higher court, the judge in a lower court could try to reach a different decision – by finding a way around the precedent and thus 'distinguishing' the present case.

For example, the judge might need to decide whether the principles, laid down previously, about the negligence of local authority social workers – should apply as well to local authority occupational therapists. Certainly, therapists are professionals working for the same type of authority under the same type of legislation; but, equally, they could be regarded as having quite different functions (compare a therapist recommending the installation of grab rails with a social worker dealing with child abuse). With this in mind, the lower court might be able to choose whether or not to 'follow' the principle established in the previous case.

The system of precedent is therefore an aid to predictability but not an exact indicator.

Getting to court

The establishing of precedent depends of course on cases getting to court in the first place. Many cases never get that far, falling by the wayside for a number of different reasons.

Both users and providers of equipment might baulk at the cost of the action – the users giving up the action, or the providers settling out of court, if this seems the cheapest option. Another reason for statutory services to settle out of courts is to avoid the risk of an unfavourable precedent being established. This could lead to an increase of obligations to many other service users, not just to the person or persons bringing the particular case – and could prove very much more costly than simply settling the present case without an admission of liability.

An example of such a pattern of settlement seems to have occurred in relation to s.2 of the CSDPA 1970. For many years, legal advice from the Department of Health and elsewhere was that once need was identified, the local authority was under a strict duty to see that the need was met. Though this advice was persuasive to many local authorities – and pointed the way to out-of-court settlements – it was not 'the law', because it had never been fully tested in the law courts. This finally happened in 1995 (*R v Gloucestershire CC, ex parte Mahfood*), when the legal advice was actually borne out, though only up to a certain point.[69]

Influence of Europe on the law of the United Kingdom

An added 'wild card' to the doctrine of precedent described immediately above concerns Europe; namely the legislation of the *European Community* (EC) and the *European Convention on Human Rights* (ECHR).

Although the House of Lords is the highest court in the United Kingdom, it has now been accepted that, where it applies, European Community law is supreme. This means that the House of Lords has to follow rulings by the European Court of Justice, the court of the European Community. The system of European Community law, and how it relates to UK law, cannot be explained in any detail here; however, it is particularly relevant to this book in respect of, for example, the Consumer Protection Act 1987 and Regulations covering medical devices, general product safety, unfair contract terms, and the manual handling of loads (see Chapter 15). The important point to bear in mind is that not only does this legislation impose duties on manufacturers, suppliers, statutory services, employers etc – but that the original European Community directives, on which the UK legislation is based, do so as well. For example, it is possible that if a case were brought under the Consumer Protection Act 1987, a UK court might find that the Act did not correctly reflect the original Directive. In such circumstances, the court might 'reinterpret' or stretch the meaning of the Act – or even refer the matter to the European Court of Justice.

The situations in which European law applies to the United Kingdom are primarily economic – for example, product performance and safety, employment rights, fishing rights – since the European Community has hitherto been an economic union, devoted to breaking down trade barriers. However, European law can arise in unexpected guises. For example, as emphasised throughout this book, statutory services normally have discretion to decide what level of provision to make. Nevertheless, the English High Court (*R v Chief Constable of Sussex, ex parte International Trader's Ferry*) recently held that a decision to restrict the policing of animal rights protests was a breach of European law. Livestock exports were at stake, and a failure to allow them to proceed breached article 34 of the Treaty of Rome (which prohibits quantitative restrictions on exports). The court explained that authorities could not successfully argue a defence of public policy (under article 36) because civil disturbances could not afford such a defence, so long as the resources were available to deal with them at a cost which was not disproportionate.[70]

The European Convention on Human Rights and Fundamental Freedoms (the ECHR) – quite distinct from European Community legislation – is basically a list of human rights. The UK is a signatory to the convention, but it is neither a part of, nor can it overrule, United Kingdom law. However, if there is some unclarity in UK law, then judges will try to decide a case in line with the Convention. If it cannot be so interpreted – or if the UK law in question is clear and is inconsistent with the Convention – then the UK law prevails. The ECHR has relatively little application to the subject matter of this book, although it can arise on occasion. For instance, it arose in relation to whether a health authority is infringing a child's 'right to life' (under article 1 of the ECHR) when it refuses to provide lifesaving treatment because of lack of resources (*R v Cambridge, ex parte B*). The judge in the High Court, whilst acknowledging that the Convention could not be used as a 'statutory text' in a United Kingdom court of law, nevertheless suggested it could be used as 'persuasive legal authority'. He referred to it in a ruling which was favourable to the patient – only to be overruled firmly and immediately by the Court of Appeal.[71]

4. OBTAINING INFORMATION FROM STATUTORY SERVICES ABOUT EQUIPMENT PROVISION

In order to obtain services or challenge decisions, people need information – personal, general or sometimes both. For instance, if a person is aggrieved that he or she has been denied a kerb-climbing wheelchair, it is important to have access to general information, such as the policy and criteria of eligibility of the local NHS wheelchair service. It might also be necessary for the person to see his or her own personal record, with details of the results of the assessment for the wheelchair. Putting the two types of information together, it might become clear that the staff who carried out the assessment did not apply the criteria properly. In this case, a complaint might succeed.

Obtaining general information

In practice, in order to find out what services and equipment are available under what conditions, people need information from statutory services. This could come in many forms, such as leaflets, posters, items on the radio, charters and community care plans.

For information to be effective, account needs to be taken of people with sensory impairments or with limited understanding of English. It needs to be made accessible to the extent that people who require it are likely to be able to obtain it. In addition, information needs to be comprehensible and informative – but, if cluttered with the jargon of professionals, it is unlikely to be.[72] If it is too vague, it will not be informative and either put people off or raise false expectations. If it is too detailed, then it might equally be impenetrable and incomprehensible – as well as hindering authorities from acting flexibly. Indeed, authorities have, in the past, sometimes been reluctant to publish their detailed criteria of eligibility determining who can get what services or equipment. This avoids the adverse publicity excited by stringent criteria, but it also allows authorities to apply criteria flexibly in the light of people's individual needs and the resources available. However, increasing pressure from central government (in the form of law and policy) on authorities to produce more publicity and information, makes this sort of strategy less viable.

Information provision by social services departments

As far as legislation goes, social services departments have a range of specific duties to publish community care plans, to produce publicity about complaints procedures – and to provide information duties to both the public generally and individual service users about equipment (and other) services under s.2 of the CSDPA 1970 (see p.166).

People have a statutory right of access to most local authority social services committee meetings and to associated documents – dealing with, for example, policies about equipment provision.[73] However, documents made available should not contain certain types of information – for instance, information about individuals who are receiving services or financial assistance.[74]

Openness in the NHS

Service users might require additional types of normally unpublished information – or simply the information authorities were meant to (but have failed to) publish anyway. For instance, a patient might wish to challenge the rationing decisions of health authorities or NHS Trusts. Under the *Code of practice on openness in the NHS*, authorities and NHS Trusts must publish, or otherwise make available, information on a range of topics including available services, changes to policies and services, and responsibilities for the management and provision of services. In addition, NHS Trusts and authorities can be asked for other information, which they should normally send within 20 days. Charges can be made for supplying information in response to such requests.

Although the code of practice does not have the force of law, the Department of Health clearly expects authorities and NHS Trusts to comply with it. It states that if people are dissatisfied about a refusal to provide information, delay in doing so, or any charges imposed for it, then they can complain to the person responsible for the operation of the code. If they remain dissatisfied, they should complain to the chief executive of the particular NHS Trust or authority. Beyond that, it would be open to them to take complaints to the health service ombudsman.[75]

Special education: information about policies

School governing bodies are obliged to publish various information relating to their policy on special educational needs and its implementation. Included within a wide range of matters to be covered are 'facilities for pupils with special educational needs at the school including facilities which increase or assist access to the school by pupils who are disabled'.[76] Education authorities also have a duty to publish general information about their special education policies and arrangements.[77]

When various amendments to education legislation made by the Disability Discrimination Act 1995 come into force (probably during 1996), education authorities and further education colleges (both in respect of further education), and higher education institutions (in respect of higher education) will be obliged to publish 'disability statements' containing information about the facilities they provide for disabled people.[78]

Open government: central government information

Alternatively, information might be sought from central government. In principle, this should be easier to obtain than in the past, in the light of the *Code of practice on access to government information*, published in 1994 by the Cabinet Office under the banner of the Citizen's Charter. It should be said that some government departments, parts of government departments, and individual civil servants have always been more helpful than others, when asked to provide information. It seems that this variation in approach is being continued, even under the new code, since departments are making contrasting financial charges under the code – ranging from the generous to the prohibitive.[79]

Obtaining personal information

Social services: personal records

Under the Data Protection Act 1984, people have the right of access to information held about them in computer form, subject to certain safeguards; access can be refused if serious harm would come either to the applicant or to anybody else as a result of disclosure.

In addition, under the Access to Personal Files (Social Services) Regulations 1989 people can get to see information still held manually. They have to apply in writing, pay a small fee and provide adequate information about their identity, so that the information can be found. If other people are referred to in the information, their consent has to be obtained before the information is made available to the applicant. As in the case of the Data Protection Act, there are restrictions; for example, the information can be withheld if it is likely that serious physical or mental harm to the applicant or anybody else would result from its disclosure.[80]

Although personal information about other service users (eg for purposes of comparison and establishing whether a policy has been applied consistently) is not obtainable by individuals, the local ombudsman (for example) sometimes looks at how other service users have been treated in order to judge whether a particular complainant has been unfairly dealt with.

Personal health records

Various legislation affects people's rights to see information about themselves, including their medical records. This includes the Data Protection Act 1984 and the Access to Health Records Act 1990. Generally speaking, NHS patients have no absolute right of access to personal information; access is subject to certain limitations.

In summary; first, access can be denied under legislation if disclosure would result in serious harm either to the patient or somebody else. Second, it can be denied under legislation because of the date, or the form in which, the record was made. For example, if the record was made before 1st November 1991 and was in hard copy, rather than in electronic form, then neither the Access to Health Records Act 1990 nor the Data Protection Act 1984 applies. In such a case, there is no statutory right of access at all. Third, where the common law applies (as in the situation just outlined), a right of access does exist, but again a qualified one; it is subject to what a court considers to be the 'best interests' of the patient.[81]

Sometimes, in order to demonstrate fault on the part of healthcare practitioners and managers, access to other people's records can be very useful. Equally, this is very difficult to achieve, given the proper concern to preserve confidentiality. Nevertheless, in one case the judge directed that the notes of other patients could be referred to, albeit with code names. This was to ascertain whether the delay in treating a particular patient was justified because of the urgency of other cases in the ward at the time.[82]

Special education: personal records

Parents of children have a right of access to relevant reports and their child's school record. Young people over the age of 16 years have the same right in respect of relevant reports and their own record.[83] However, access to statements of special educational needs requires the parents' consent (except in certain circumstances prescribed in regulations).[84]

An authority's failure, for example, to keep adequate records of the process of the assessment of a child's special educational needs might be deemed maladministration by the ombudsman – even if the explanation given by an educational psychologist is that copious notes would not be helpful when sensitive and confidential information was at issue, and would lead to a defensive approach.[85]

Notes

1 Suing the doctor: altruism, maked truth, or recompense? (Editorial). *Lancet:* 25th June 1994; 343, pp.1582–1583.

2 Ritchie, J.; Davies, S. (1995). Professional negligence: a duty of candid disclosure: doctors should explain in full when care has gone wrong. *British Medical Journal:* 8th April 1995; 310. pp.888–889.

3 Davies, R.H. (1995). Professional negligence: negligence cannot be decided by offending doctor. (Letter). *British Medical Journal:* 24th June 1995; 310, p.1671.

4 Tingle, J.H. (1994). Adopting strategies to reduce healthcare litigation and complaints. *British Journal of Theatre Nursing:* 7th October 1994; 4(7), pp.17–18.

5 Harpwood, V. (1994). Medical negligence claims and NHS complaints. *Professional Negligence:* 1994; 10(3), pp.74–81.

6 Simons, K. (1995). *I'm not complaining but...: complaints procedures in social services departments.* York: Joseph Rowntree Foundation; Community Care, p.35.

7 Ellis, K. (1993). *Squaring the circle: user and carer participation in needs assessment.* York: Joseph Rowntree Foundation, p.22.

8 Simons, K. (1995). *I'm not complaining but...: complaints procedures in social services departments. York: Joseph Rowntree Foundation; Community Care, p.12.*

9 *R v Gloucestershire County Council, ex parte Mahfood and Others, R v Islington London Borough Council, ex parte McMillan* (1996) 160 LGRevr 321 (QBD)

10 *R v Gloucestershire County Council, ex parte Mahfood and Others, R v Islington London Borough Council, ex parte McMillan* (1996) 160 LGRevR 321 (QBD). The case was brought by three other people against Gloucestershire County Council and one other person against the London Borough of Islington.

11 *R v Gloucestershire County Council, ex parte Barry; R v Lancashire County Council, ex parte Gilpin and RADAR* (1996) (CA) (7–10 May 1996, CO/95/1779, CO/95/1134).

12 Commission for Local Administration in England (90/A/2675, 2075, 1702, 1273, 1228, 1172). *Report on investigation into complaint against Essex County Council.* London: CLAE, 1991.

13 See eg: Day, M.; Balen, P.; McCool, G. (1995). *Multi-party actions: a practitioner's guide to pursuing group claims.* London: Legal Action Group.

14 *R v Gloucestershire County Council, ex parte RADAR,* 21 December 1995 (QBD) (transcript).

15 *R v Gloucestershire County Council, ex parte Barry; R v Lancashire County Council, ex parte Gilpin and RADAR* (1996) (CA) (7–10 May 1996, CO/95/1779, CO/95/1134).

16 Commission for Local Administration in England (94/C/0399). *Report on investigation into a complaint against Salford City Council.* York: CLAE, 1996.
17 Letter sent by the Association of Community Health Councils for England and Wales, dated 15th January 1992.
18 Harpwood, V. (1994). Medical negligence claims and NHS complaints. *Professional Negligence:* 1994; 10(3), pp.74–81. Also: Simons, K. (1995). *I'm not complaining but...complaints procedures in social services departments.* York: Joseph Rowntree Foundation; Community Care, p.59.
19 Reid, W. (1996). Righting wrongs: the value of complaints for NHS users and providers. *Nursing Standard:* 6 March 1996; 10(24), p.19.
20 Simons, K. (1995). *I'm not complaining but...: complaints procedures in social services departments.* York: Joseph Rowntree Foundation; Community Care, pp.88–89.
21 Simons, K. (1995). *I'm not complaining but...: complaints procedures in social services departments. York: Joseph Rowntree Foundation; Community Care, pp.50–51.*
22 Local Government and Housing Act 1989, s.5.
23 Lord Chancellor's Department (1995). *Resolving disputes without going to court.* London: LCD.
24 Chartered Institute of Arbitrators (1995). *The Consumer Dispute Resolution Scheme.* London: CIA (folder containing rules, guidance notes and a suggested clause for inclusion in consumer contracts).
25 See eg Morgan, R. (1994). Medical negligence disputes: alternatives to litigation. *British Journal of Obstetrics and Gynaecology:* March 1994; 101, pp.185–187.
26 Dyer, C. (1995). Right place to say you're wrong. *The Guardian:* 7 November 1995.
27 Palmer, R.N. (1994). Legal action and medical negligence. (Letter). *Lancet:* 19th February 1994; 343, p.484.
28 Barton, A. (1994). Legal action and medical negligence. (Letter). *Lancet:* 12th March 1994; 343, p.674.
29 Chartered Institute of Arbitrators (1995). *The rules of the Consumer Dispute Resolution Scheme.* London: CIA, pp.3–4.2
30 Eg *Turner v Stevenage Borough Council* (1995) (Chancery Division), Times: 7 December 1995: concerning the asking of an interim payment by the arbitrator in a dispute between the council and a tenant of a lockup garage.
31 National Consumer Council (1993). *Settling consumer disputes.* London: NCC, p.7.
32 SI 1981/1687. *County Court Rules 1981,* Order 19, r.3(2).
33 Eg National Consumer Council (1994). *Handling small claims in county courts: response to the National Audit Office.* London: NCC, p.2.
34 Smerin, J. (1996). Small claims. *Law Society Gazette:* 10 January 1996; 93(1), p.14.
35 National Consumer Council (1987). *Small claims in the County Court in England and Wales: response to the Lord Chancellor's Department.* London: NCC.
36 See eg summary in: White, R.C. (1991). *The administration of justice.* 2nd edition. Oxford: Blackwell, p.176.
37 National Audit Office (1996). *Handling small claims in the County Courts.* London: HMSO.
38 Parliamentary Commissioner for Administration (1996). *Annual report for 1995: fourth report, session 1995–96.* London: HMSO, p.2.
39 See eg: *R v Local Commissioner for Administration for the North and East Area of England, ex parte Bradford Metropolitan City Council* [1979] 1 QB 287 (QB): a dispute about children in care, in which two out of four complaints by the mother were to be dealt with by the ombudsman, and the other two by the courts.
40 *R v Inland Revenue Commissioners, ex parte National Federation of Self-Employed Builders and Small Businesses* [1982] AC 617 (HL).
41 Williams, T.; Goriely, T. (1994). Big idea – any effect: the Charter complaints system as an alternative to statutory rights. *New Law Journal:* 1994; 144(6661), pp.1164–1165.
42 Commission for Local Administration in England (1993). *Good administrative practice.* London: CLAE.
43 Thomas, P. (1994). The maladministration business: what the Local Government Ombudsman can and cannot do. *Solicitors' Journal:* 1994; 138(7), 178–179.
44 *Holt and another v Payne Skillington (A Firm) and Another* (1995) (CA), Times: 22 December 1995.
45 *M'Alister (or Donoghue) (Pauper) v Stevenson* [1932] AC 562.

46 *Home Office v Dorset Yacht Co* [1970] AC 1004 (HL).
47 *Anns v Merton London Borough Council* [1978] AC 728 (HL).
48 *Junior Books Ltd v Veitchi* [1093] 1 AC 520 (HL): the plaintiffs sued a subcontractor (with whom they had no contract) for the financial loss incurred by a negligently installed floor.
49 See eg *Murphy v Brentwood District Council* [1990] 2 All ER 908 (HL): inadequate inspection by local authority of foundations of house.
50 Eg: Greenfield, S.; Osborn, G. (1995). A new dawn for negligence? *Professional Negligence:* 1995; 11(2), pp.53–58.
51 *R v Bristol City Council, ex parte Karelene Bailey and Dennis Bailey* (1995) 159 LGRR 221 (QBD).
52 Lord Reid, see: Lee, S. (1988). *Judging judges.* London: Faber and Faber, p.3.
53 Lee, S. (1988). *Judging judges.* London: Faber and Faber, pp.40–45.
54 *R v Local Commissioner for Administration for the North and East Area of England, ex parte Bradford Metropolitan City Council* [1979] 1 QB 287.
55 *R v Gloucestershire County Council, ex parte Mahfood and Others, R v Islington London Borough Council, ex parte McMillan* (1996) 160 LGRevR 321 (QBD).
56 *R v Gloucestershire County Council, ex parte Barry; R v Lancashire County Council, ex parte Gilpin and RADAR* (1996) (CA) (7–10 May 1996, CO/95/1779, CO/95/1134).
57 *M'Alister (or Donoghue) (Pauper) v Stevenson* [1932] AC 562 (Lord Buckmaster).
58 *Hedley Byrne & Co Ltd v Heller & Partners Ltd* [1964] AC 465: involving reliance by one company on a careless statement made by a bank about the financial health of another company.
59 Adams, J.; Brownsword, R. (1987). *Understanding contract law.* London: Fontana, p.55.
60 *R v Cambridge Health Authority, ex parte B* [1995] 1 FLR 1055 (QBD and CA).
61 *Lloyds Bank v Bundy* [1975] QB 326 (CA): an elderly farmer had acted as guarantor for bank loans to his son which were not repaid: the court held that since both father and son used the same bank, there had been a conflict of interest and the bank should have insisted that the father take independent advice before agreeing the guarantee.
62 *Southwark London Borough Council v Williams* [1971] Ch 734 (CA): involving homelessness, squatters, empty council housing, s.21 of the National Assistance Act 1948 (duty to provide residential accommodation).
63 *R v Secretary of State for Social Services, West Midlands Regional Health Authority and Birmingham Area Health Authority, ex parte Hincks* (1980) 1 BMLR 93 (CA).
64 *Mulcahy v Ministry of Defence* (1996) 146 NLJLR 334 (CA): Neill, LJ quoting from Lord Pearce in Hedley Byrne & Co Ltd v Heller & Partners [1963] 2 All ER 575.
65 *X (Minors) v Bedfordshire County Council* [1995] 3 All ER 353 (HL) (at 381).
66 *Wilsher v Essex Area Health Authority* [1986] 3 All ER 801 (at 829).
67 *McGhee v National Coal Board* [1972] 3 All ER 1008 (HL).
68 *R v Gloucestershire County Council, ex parte Barry, R v Lancashire County Council, ex parte Gilpin and RADAR* (7–10 May 1996, CO/95/1779, CO/95/1134).
69 *R v Gloucestershire County Council, ex parte Mahfood and Others, R v Islington London Borough Council, ex parte McMillan* (1996) 160 LGRevR 321 (QBD).
70 *R v Chief Constable of Sussex, ex parte International Trader's Ferry Ltd* (1995), *Independent:* 28 July 1995 (QBD).
71 *R v Cambridge Health Authority, ex parte B* [1995] 1 FLR 1055 (QBD and CA).
72 SSI (1991). Social Services Inspectorate. *Getting the message across: a guide to developing and communicating policies, principles and procedures on assessment.* London: HMSO.
73 Rights of access are under the *Local Government Act 1972*, ss.100A-K and the Public Bodies (Admissions to Meetings) Act 1960.
74 *Local Government (Access to Information) Act 1985; Local Government Act 1972,* Schedule 12A, Part 1.
75 NHS Executive (1995). *Code of practice on openness in the NHS.* Leeds: Department of Health.
76 See Education Act 1996, s.317(5)–(6) (the last subsection added by the *Disability Discrimination Act 1995* and due to come into force mid-1996). Also: SI 1994/1048. *Education (Special Educational Needs) (Information) Regulations 1994.*
77 SI 1994/1421. *Education (School Information) (England) Regulations 1994,* Schedule 1.

78 See amendments made by s.30 of the *Disability Discrimination Act 1995*, affecting ss.5, 8, 62 of the Further and Higher Education Act 1992, and s.15 of the Education Act 1996.

79 Dynes, M. (1994). £100 a photocopy is price of public's 'right to know'. *Times:* 9 November 1994. And see: Cabinet Office (1995). *Open government: code of practice on access to government information.* London: Cabinet Office, Appendix 4.

80 SI 1989/206. *Access to Personal Files (Social Services) Regulations 1989.*

81 *R v Mid Glamorgan Family Health Services Authority & Another, ex parte Martin* [1995] 1 WLR 110 (CA). For a discussion of the shortcomings of this test in terms of 'medical paternalism' and excessive control over personal health information, see: Feenan, D. (1996). Common law access to medical records. *Modern Law Review:* January 1996; 59(1), pp.101–110.

82 Dimond, B. (1995). *Legal aspects of nursing.* 2nd edition. Hemel Hempstead: Prentice Hall, pp.54–55. Referring to: *Deacon v McVicar and Another* (QBD) (7 January 1984, unreported).

83 Under the *Data Protection Act 1984* and the *Education Reform Act 1988.*

84 SI 1994/1047. *Education (Special Educational Needs) Regulations 1994,* r.19.

85 Commission for Local Administration in England (93/B/3567). *Report on investigation into a complaint against Cambridgeshire County Council.* Coventry: CLAE, 1995, pp.4, 18–19.

CHAPTER 6

WHAT STATUTORY SERVICES AND THEIR STAFF CAN AND CAN'T DO

COVERAGE

1. Hierarchy of documentary sources of law and policy
2. Duties and powers: what authorities and their staff can and can't do
   - Acting reasonably, fairly, legally and according to administrative good practice
   - Different types and strengths of duty
   - Statutory instruments, directions and approvals.
3. Guidance, codes of practice, charters etc
   - Guidance
   - Charters
   - Statements made in Parliament
   - Standards and clinical guidelines: some legal implications
   - Locally produced guidance and guidance produced by national bodies.

Key points

This chapter outlines how legislation and guidance determine what authorities and their staff can and can't do. Policy-makers, managers and practitioners all need to be aware of what their obligations are. On one level, this is important when decisions about rationing are taken at planning and policy level; on another, when assessment decisions are taken about individual people. From the point of view of service users who wish to challenge the behaviour of authorities, such an awareness is equally necessary.

The distinction, and the sometimes fine line, between general, 'target' duties and the stronger duties towards individual people is explained – as is the difference between duties and powers. In addition to legislation, guidance is prevalent, particularly in the field of statutory services, but its legal effect is sometimes uncertain. The legal implications of charters, statements made in Parliament, standards and clinical guidelines are also covered.

Questions people ask

- What do the words in legislation really mean; for example, what is the difference between something which an authority *shall* provide and something it *may* provide?
- Is an authority under a stronger obligation if it must provide services for *any person*, rather than for the *local population* in general? What implications do such distinctions in wording have for social care and health care practitioners in their day-today activities – and for users of services?
- How important is it to look as well at guidance from central government? Are there different types of guidance?
- What entitlements do charters give people?
- How important is it when politicians speak in Parliament – can what they say be cited as evidence about what a piece of legislation really means? For example, if social services departments are manipulating and changing what they mean by 'need', can they be challenged by citing what Alf Morris, the author of the Chronically Sick and Disabled Persons Act 1970, said when the Bill was debated in Parliament in 1969 and 1970?

1. HIERARCHY OF DOCUMENTARY SOURCES OF LAW AND POLICY

In principle, a 'pecking order' applies to documentary sources of the law and policy relating to statutory services:

(i) Legislation and law reports. At the top are *Acts of Parliament, statutory instruments* (often referred to as *regulations*), *directions* and *approvals.* These all have the force of law and give authorities various duties and powers (see below).

Law reports, too, are a primary source of law and are to be found in various series of published law reports. The decisions contained in them set precedents and thus form a body of legal rules (see p.123). For example, it is an Act of Parliament (s.2 of the Chronically Sick and Disabled Persons Act 1970) which imposes the duty on local authorities to provide equipment in certain circumstances; but it is a 1995 High Court case (*R v Gloucester CC, ex parte Mahfood*) which confirmed the nature of the duty – ie that it is an absolute (ie a strong) one. This case was reported quite promptly in the Times newspaper, and then more fully some 9 months later in the Administrative Law Review Reports.[1] Thus, for example, managers and policymakers in social services departments need to know about both the Act and the case if they are to understand the implications for themselves, their staff and service users.

Alternatively, the law reports might have to be looked to wholly for some areas of law; for example, the law of negligence is rooted in the common law and thus to be found set out (albeit in scattered form) in the law reports, not in legislation. For instance, if the CSDPA 1970 is the rock on which equipment provision is based, so a law report published in 1932 (*Donoghue v Stevenson*: about a snail in a bottle of ginger beer) underpins negligence actions by consumers against manufacturers, as well as the law of negligence more generally.[2]

European Community law is very influential and ultimately overrules any conflicting UK legislation; its particular relevance to this book is explained in Chapter 15.

(ii) Guidance etc. Occupying the middle order, are the *codes of practice*, *guidance* and *charters* of various types issued by central government. The legal force of guidance can vary, depending not only on its type – but also on how judges choose to interpret its force. However, conceptually, guidance is quite distinct from legislation; it merely states, with greater or lesser strength of language, how authorities should exercise the duties and powers which have, however, already been imposed by legislation. The 'bottom line' is that, although the courts will consider the effect of government guidance carefully, they have the power to state that it is inconsistent with the legislation and to disregard it. Whereas they cannot 'strike down' Acts of Parliament in this way.

(iii) Standards, clinical guidelines. Lower down the order are standards and clinical guidelines produced nationally (whether or not by central government). Not in themselves law they too, like guidance, sometimes have legal implications. For instance, they might generally be useful evidence, in a court of law, of acceptable practice. And, for example, the conformity of products to 'harmonised' European technical standards, can carry with it a legally sanctioned presumption that certain legislation (relating to product safety and performance) is being complied with (see p.363).

In addition to guidance produced by central government, local statutory services also produce a profusion of local guidance. This category of document is of little legal significance – except for the fact that both the judicial review courts and the ombudsmen often scrutinise it as evidence of whether authorities are behaving reasonably, fairly, legally, or according to good administrative practice.

(iv) Statements made in Parliament and ombudsman decisions. Finally, but not necessarily least, because they are something of a 'wild card', come particular statements made in Parliament which, in some circumstances, the courts may refer to in order to clarify the meaning of legislation. Obviously, if so deployed, such statements take on considerable legal significance.

Another odd category is the reports of the ombudsmen. They do not have the legal significance of law reports and so neither set precedents, nor constitute a body of legal rules. Indeed, the recommendations of ombudsmen (eg the health service or local ombudsmen) are not even legally binding upon individual authorities. Nevertheless, occasionally ombudsman reports do have a much wider and more effective impact; for instance, in the much-publicised 'Leeds' report published in 1994, the health service ombudsman found that the denial of continuing NHS care to a severely disabled man amounted to a failure in service.[3] This finding led to the Department of Health issuing firm guidance to restrain health authorities from discarding too many of their responsibilities; though whether the government's anxiety was focused on the potential legal implications of what health authorities were doing, or simply on the bad publicity (and the electoral consequences) – is not totally clear.

In practice, it will be seen from the various examples below that the application of this pecking order is not necessarily straightforward. For example, legislation, at the top of the pile, is sometimes so sparse or vague that much of what happens in practice is determined by guidance – which sometimes gains an elevated status in disputes.

2. DUTIES AND POWERS: WHAT AUTHORITIES AND THEIR STAFF CAN AND CAN'T DO

Generally speaking, the decisions and actions of statutory services are framed either by *duties* or *powers*. Duties state what authorities must do; *powers*, what they can do if they want, but don't have to.

Duties and powers are created by legislation in the form of Acts of Parliament. If neither the duty nor the power to do a particular thing is contained in legislation, then authorities act illegally if they proceed to do it, because they are acting outside their duties and powers. Duties are often expressed in legislation by use of the word *shall*; and powers by the word *may*.

For example, social services departments have a *duty* under s.47 of the NHS and Community Care Act 1990 to assess any person who appears to be in need of community care services. They also have a duty to make arrangements for the provision of equipment under s.2 of the CSDPA 1970, if they feel it is *necessary* in order to meet a disabled person's needs. In contrast, they have the power, but no duty, under s.45 of the Health Service and Public Health Act 1968 to promote the welfare of elderly people. This could include equipment provision.

And, under s.1 of the NHS Act 1977, health authorities and NHS Trusts *cannot* make charges for equipment, unless specified elsewhere in legislation. Consequently, they can charge for elastic hosiery and wigs, since these are specified in separate regulations. But they have no power to charge NHS patients for walking aids or orthopaedic footwear; when they do so, they are acting outside their powers (ultra vires) and thus illegally (see p.213).

Acting reasonably, fairly, legally and according to administrative good practice

Apart from acting in accordance with the duties and powers contained in Acts of Parliament, public bodies also have to act reasonably, fairly and legally. If they do not, they can be judicially reviewed by the courts (see p.424). These principles are not stated in legislation, but belong to the body of administrative law applied by the courts to ensure that public bodies follow certain rules and do not abuse their powers.[4] The principles of judicial review are to be found scattered within the published law reports of legal cases; such published cases represent a primary source of law and so are akin to legislation in status.

In addition, authorities need to act according to the principles of good administration if they are to escape adverse findings by ombudsmen. In practice terms, the *local ombudsman* investigates complaints against social services departments, housing departments and education authorities; the *health service ombudsman* complaints against the NHS; and the *Parliamentary ombudsman* complaints against the Employment Service and other government departments (eg against the Secretary of State for Health or for Education – for taking too long to deal with an appeal or a complaint). The health service ombudsman's remit is formally wider than that of the other ombudsmen and extends beyond maladministration (see p.219). The investigations of the ombudsmen are published – and the office of the local ombudsman (the Commission for Local Administration in England) has published a booklet setting out axioms of good administration.

Thus, although this chapter explains that statutory services generally enjoy considerable freedom when formulating and applying policies, careless authorities are quite capable of running foul of both the judiciary and the ombudsmen.

Different types and strengths of duty

The operation of powers and duties might appear to be straightforward – but is not for a number of reasons.

Strong and weak duties

Duties are of different types and of varying strengths.

For example, equipment, together with many other NHS services, is provided under sections 1 and 3 of the NHS Act 1977 (see Chapter 8). These sections contain duties expressed in general terms. Individual people are not mentioned – ie the legislation does not state that those services must be provided for each and every person who needs them. Such duties are perceived to be of the general, weaker type, because they are difficult to pin down and enforce in relation to any one particular person. Sometimes they are referred to as 'target' duties and perceived to be so weak, as to amount to little more than powers in respect of any one particular service. For example, though the Act imposes a general duty to provide nursing services, it is up to the authority to decide whether, as part of those nursing services, it will provide incontinence pads to people in residential homes. It may do, but is not obliged to. Thus, in one case concerning the Education Act 1944 and a similarly broad duty to provide sufficient schools, the judge stated that failure to make the prescribed provision in a particular situation does not, in itself, amount to a breach of duty.[5]

By contrast, both s.47 of the NHSCCA 1990 concerning community care assessment and s.2 of the CSDPA 1970 relating to equipment provision contain duties relating to *any person* – that is, each individual and not just the population at large. This second type of duty is perceived to be stronger and, in principle at least, easier to enforce through the law courts.

Thus, the duty under s.2 of the CSDPA has been characterised explicitly by the courts as 'absolute' (*R v Gloucestershire CC, ex parte Mahfood*).[6] but the duty under s.3 of the NHS Act 1977 as precisely not (*R v Secretary of State and Others, ex parte Hincks*).[7]

Qualified duties

Duties are sometimes qualified and 'weakened' by surrounding wording.

For example, the duty under s.2 of the CSDPA to provide equipment and other services is in fact expressed as follows. The duty operates only if the authority is *satisfied* that it is *necessary* to *make arrangements* to provide *facilities* for a person's greater safety, *comfort* or *convenience*. All the italicised terms are for authorities to interpret or define in their local policies, priorities and criteria of eligibility. They are not defined by central government either in legislation or guidance.

Thus, given identical circumstances, one authority might decide that a person is in need, another that he is not. Or, both might agree that he is in need, but the first authority state that it is *necessary* for it to meet the need, the second that it is not necessary. And, an authority might or might not decide that special cutlery or bathmats fall within the *facilities* it will provide.

In addition to liberal and flexible interpretation of words in legislation, the law courts sometimes even add their own extra words to give authorities greater leeway in which to carry out their duties. For example, in one case (*R v Secretary of State for Social Services and Others, ex parte Hincks*), the Court of Appeal decided that the duty of the NHS to provide health services should be read as if it was qualified by the words 'within the resources available' – even though there is no trace of those words in the relevant part of the NHS Act 1977.[8]

The courts do sometimes impose limits on the discretion of authorities to act as they please under vague legislation. For instance, they might disagree with an authority's expression of *satisfaction*, if it is clear that the authority lacked adequate grounds on which to make a decision. For instance, in 1976 (*Secretary of State for Education and Science v Tameside MBC*), the House of Lords ruled that a Labour Secretary of State for Education had insufficient grounds to be 'satisfied' that a local education authority had behaved unreasonably when it decided to alter plans concerning comprehensive schools.[9] And, in a community care case under s.2 of the CSDPA (*R v Gloucestershire CC, ex parte Mahfood*), the judge suggested that an authority could scarcely claim to be satisfied that a person did not need services, if he was at severe physical risk.[10] Likewise, some limits might be placed on the expression, 'where it appears'. On this basis, it is just possible that the courts might state that an assessment must be given to a person who actually was obviously in need – whether or not the authority had conceded the appearance of need, which is the statutory condition for assessment.[11]

The line between duties and powers

If the courts did not place some limits on the discretion of authorities, then the line between *individual duties* and *general duties*, and between general duties and powers would break down. If authorities were allowed total freedom to decide whom to provide services for, then there would presumably be no point in legislation imposing one type of duty or power rather than another. This point was made during the hearing of a recent Court of Appeal case (*R v Gloucestershire CC, ex parte Barry*) about the obligations of local authorities under s.2 of the CSDPA 1970. The danger was that if the courts allowed authorities to take resources into account when assessing people's needs, the strong s.2 duty intended to give individual disabled people 'rights' would collapse – leaving it scarcely to be distinguished from the more general duties and powers governing other community care services.[12]

Nevertheless, the line between powers and duties can be thin. As already explained above, the general duty of the NHS to provide comprehensive services is so vague, that, in respect of any one service, it is often regarded as no more than a power. Similarly, the thin line was illustrated by the debate over the Community Care (Direct Payments) Bill. One clause stated that 'an authority may, if the person consents, pay to him...'. This is a power. A proposed amendment stated that an 'authority shall not unreasonably refuse a disabled person access to direct payments...'. This is a duty, albeit one still qualified by the condition that it be reasonable to perform it.[13] The purpose of such an amendment is, therefore, not to create an absolute duty, but merely to place some limits on the wide discretion otherwise given to authorities.

Occasionally, however, the courts might hold that a power amounts to a duty. In one case, the Minister of Agriculture refused to refer a complaint about the Milk Marketing Board to a committee of investigation. He was not under a duty to refer all complaints, but merely had the power to do so under the Agricultural Marketing Act 1958. But the House of Lords held that not to refer this sort of complaint would be frustrating the very purpose of the Act.[14]

Courts wary of intervening in the case of vague and qualified duties

Although the courts will intervene sometimes (see immediately above) when welfare legislation is vague, they will generally be wary of doing so. For example, in the context of child care, they have highlighted the imprecision and generality of certain terms in legislation (see p.462). Indeed, a duty might be so imprecise that a court will not rule against a local authority because it is too difficult to say under what circumstances the duty could ever be breached. And even if the courts sometimes find that a clear duty does exist and has apparently been breached, they still might not award a substantial remedy such as damages. Instead, they might aver that Parliament, when framing the legislation, did not intend that individuals could pursue authorities through the courts and gain compensation for breach of duty (see p.463).

However, other welfare legislation allows the courts to identify more easily whether an authority has breached its duty. For instance, the duty to make arrangements for provision of equipment under s.2 of the CSDPA – once the authority has accepted that such provision is necessary – is an 'absolute' duty. Even if this duty is breached as it was recently (*R v Gloucestershire, ex parte Mahfood*)[15], the courts are likely to censure authorities in judicial review proceedings – rather than award damages to individuals in private law cases brought in negligence or for breach of duty (see Chapters 17,14,18 respectively). This merely emphasises the collectivist nature of welfare legislation; even when it imposes the stronger type of duty towards individual people, enforceable (private law) individual rights are generally not created.

Authorities must not follow policies too rigidly

Inevitably, authorities make policies to guide their decisions when they are exercising their powers and duties. Indeed, without policies to guide staff, authorities would be in danger of presiding over inconsistent and arbitrary practices. For instance, a social services department can make a policy about the circumstances when it will provide stairlifts under the duty imposed by s.2 of the CSDPA 1970. Similarly, a housing authority can have a policy that it will not provide home repair assistance (HRA) to people who need minor adaptations to their homes; under the Housing Grants, Construction and Regeneration Act 1996, it has a power, but not a duty to provide HRA.

However, in both these types of example, authorities must not be too rigid in their approach; they must always leave room to consider the exceptional case justifying a departure from their policies. If authorities do not retain such flexibility, they might undergo judicial review by the courts and be found at fault for *fettering their discretion* (see p.446).

Who is empowered to carry out duties or exercise powers?

If legislation places duties and powers on authorities, then those authorities – and nobody else – are obliged to exercise them. However, sometimes the relevant legislation allows delegation. For example, the Secretary of State delegates his duty to provide health services to health authorities; and the Local Government Act 1972 allows local authorities to delegate functions to officers and committees. In addition, for example, the National Assistance Act 1948 (s.30) allows authorities, when making arrangement to provide services, to employ as its agents independent organisations. The latter might be contracted to provide the delivery, maintenance, recall and recycling of equipment.

However, authorities have to be careful. For instance, a local authority might be empowered to delegate assessment of people's need for equipment to its employed officers (eg occupational therapists), but there is no power to delegate the whole assessment process (including the final decision about needs and services) to independent organisations.[16] The latter could contribute toward the assessment, by offering advice and opinion, but could not legally take the final decision – which must remain for the authority to take. The authority 'should genuinely keep the decision in its own hands'.[17] If challenged, it might need to be able to demonstrate that one of its own officers takes the final decision in every case. On the same theme, the local ombudsman has pointed out that legislation places the duty to identify and assess children with special educational needs 'squarely on the shoulders' of local education authorities. Thus, whilst authorities can delegate aspects of these tasks to, for example, teachers, they retain the overall duty and accountability.[18]

In the present culture of increased contracting with voluntary organisations, commercial companies and independent occupational therapists, it is not always clear whether the mark is being overstepped. The courts themselves disagree sometimes. For example, two recent High Court decisions conflicted on the issue of whether the investigation by a housing authority of people's homelessness could be delegated to housing associations – to the extent that the authority ceased to play a dominant role in the investigation. The first case suggested it could not, the second that it could, so long as the ultimate decision remained for the authority. Indeed, in the second, the judge pointed out that it could be to the applicant's advantage if the housing association (rather than the local authority) conducts the interview/assessment, since the 'decision-maker (the local housing authority) can be detached from the fact-gathering process, thereby removing any suggestion of bias'. However, he also adverted to another consequence of such delegation – namely, that housing associations, unlike housing authorities, are not directly susceptible to judicial review.[19]

In contrast to these two cases, in which the precise extent of the delegation was perhaps not entirely apparent, a recent investigation by the local ombudsman describes blatantly bad practice. A social services department had delegated an assessment for a home adaptation to a local, independent, home improvement agency. The assessment was carried out by non-professional staff, was nevertheless accepted without question by the social services department, and forwarded as a recommendation for the adaptation to the local district council. At a later date, the director of social services disowned the assessment, questioned its competence and admitted that he had not even known that assessments were being delegated to the agency.[20]

Reassessments and reviews of people's needs for equipment

One question emerging from community care cases involving s.2 of the CSDPA 1970 is how to analyse legally the reassessment or review of people by local authorities (as advocated by community care guidance) – and any subsequent increase, reduction or removal of services or equipment, whether precipitated by a change in the person's own needs, or in the resources the authority has available.

The answer seems to be a) that if an authority has a duty (under s.47 of the NHS and Community Care Act 1990) to assess people who appear to be in need of services, then once it is providing services, the authority knows that the recipients are people in need – and that their needs are likely to change.

Aware of this, it should therefore reassess their needs regularly; this sort of argument could be used by service users, unable to obtain review and reassessment. It has also been suggested that s.12 of the Interpretation Act 1978 is relevant; it states that duties or powers imposed by legislation can be performed from time to time as the occasion requires. An authority might cite this Act to justify a reassessment – even if a service user was not so keen, since the purpose might be to reduce or withdraw services.

In fact, were an authority not to reassess people and to go on supplying services or equipment to people for whom they were not necessary – then it might be acting outside its powers; for example, provision under s.2 of the CSDPA is only sanctioned by the presence of need and the necessity for an authority to meet it.

Statutory instruments, directions and approvals

Considerable uncertainty about the duties and powers of authorities can arise because of documents other than Acts of Parliament (known as primary legislation).

Statutory instruments, also known as regulations are secondary legislation. Directions and approvals too have the force of law. All are issued by central government under the express authority of primary legislation. Directions lay down duties, and approvals powers. For example, under the NHS Act 1977, regulations introduce the annual increases in charges for wigs, abdominal and spinal supports, surgical brassieres and Drug Tariff appliances. And, under s.45 of the Health Service and Public Health Act 1968, approvals give local authorities the power to provide equipment for old people.

3. GUIDANCE, CODES OF PRACTICE, CHARTERS ETC

Beyond Acts of Parliament, statutory instruments, Directions and Approvals, lies the hazy territory of *guidance, guidelines, codes of practice, Circulars, Letters, charters* issued by central government – all of which explain, interpret and amplify duties and powers already laid down in legislation.

But even this apparently clear division between legislation, directions and approvals on the one hand, and guidance on the other is not as clear as it might be. For instance, in 1995 the High Court resolved a dispute about whether certain statements made in the 'Red Book', issued by the Department of Health and dealing with general practitioner finances, amounted to directions or guidance. One of the reasons for the uncertainty was that the statements were not explicitly labelled as directions – but the court nevertheless found that they were *in fact* directions and therefore mandatory. The decisive factor was that the language used was 'clear' and at times 'peremptory' and so had the ring of directions. However, the judge did make the point that the Secretary of State could have saved a lot of time and money if she had followed the normal practice of calling a direction by its proper name – a direction.[21]

Guidance

The world of statutory services brims with guidance, some of it issued decades ago but still current. Apart from the practical problem of keeping abreast with what has been issued and which of it remains current, there are sometimes additional legal difficulties. Essentially, though not possessing the force of law, some guidance is of a stronger variety. Authorities can fall foul of the law courts and the ombudsmen if they fail to follow it – or at least fail to take it into account sufficiently when, making decisions.

Guidance of different strengths

Guidance falls into various categories. For example, some is issued explicitly under a particular section of an Act of Parliament and, in principle, this is stronger than guidance not so issued. Thus, community care policy guidance, referring to the importance of disability equipment and adaptations, is made explicitly under s.7 of the Local Authority Social Services Act (LASSA) 1970.[22] This Act states that authorities have a duty to 'act under' any guidance issued under it. To confuse matters even more, it is not always clear whether or not guidance has been issued explicitly under this Act or not. The Department of Health view is that guidance is only made under that section if it states that it is.[23]

There is some debate about what 'act under' really means; at one extreme, does it mean obey to the letter or, at another, does it mean 'have regard to generally'? Disputes can arise about whether guidance is issued under the statutory authority of an Act of Parliament and about its legal effect. This happened when Mrs. Gillick protested about the giving of contraceptive advice by general practitioners to people under the age of sixteen years without parental consent – the five judges in the House of Lords could not reach a unanimous decision about the legal effect of the guidance issued by the Department of Health and Social Security.[24]

Nevertheless, in one community care case (*R v North Yorkshire CC, ex parte Hargreaves*) about the provision of respite care, the judge stated that a breach of statutory policy guidance meant that the authority had acted unlawfully.[25] This seemed to elevate the guidance to the status of legislation – which it clearly is not. In any event, the community care policy guidance is stronger than the practice guidance; the former is what authorities 'need' or are 'expected' to do, the latter is to 'help authorities decide' how to do it.[26] And, in another case (*R v Islington LBC, ex parte Rixon*) about the provision of educational and recreational facilities under s.2 of the Chronically Sick and Disabled Persons Act 1970, the judge held that authorities were not free, having considered community care *policy guidance*, simply to reject it. They had normally to follow it, could deviate to some extent if there were good reasons which were part of an identifiable decision-making process – but could not take a substantially different course. Likewise, he stated that even the community care *practice guidance* (which did not have the status of the policy guidance) authorities had to have regard to – for example, when implementing care plans.[27]

Such guidance, whether policy or practice, is to be contrasted with a mildly worded *Health Notice* issued by the DHSS in 1988, inviting health authorities to 'consider' providing district incontinence services and equipment.[28] The shortcomings of such weak guidance have been pointed out in Parliament by concerned members of the House of Lords.[29]

Uncertainty of effect of guidance

'The law' is determined by legislation and by the decisions of the law courts. Thus, whilst guidance can usefully suggest or interpret, it cannot state authoritatively what the law is.

For instance, a DHSS Circular in 1970 took the view about the provision of equipment and services under s.2 of the CSDPA, that criteria of need were to be determined in the light of resources.[30] In effect, this was saying that authorities could decide about people's needs, with at least some reference to how much money the authority had, or chose to make, available. However, that was only the government's view of an Act which in fact had been introduced by a private member, Alf Morris MP, who, when piloting his bill through Parliament, had made no such provisos.

It took many years for that view to be tested properly in the law courts. As it has transpired, the view was more or less confirmed in the 1995 case (*R v Gloucestershire CC, ex parte Mahfood*) involving the withdrawal of home help services because of lack of money.[31] Nevertheless, until that case was heard, nobody was really sure what the legal position was, even though the Circular had been relied on by authorities for 25 years. And even this 1995 judicial decision in the High Court was appealed against. In any event, the potential fragility of central government's interpretation of legislation was illustrated in 1995 by the House of Lords (*R v Wandsworth LBC, ex parte Beckwith*). The Department of Health had stated in a Circular that social services departments had a duty to provide directly at least some residential care for all adult groups. The court stated that this interpretation of part of the National Assistance Act 1948 was entitled to respect – but was, quite simply, 'wrong'.[32] And, faced with a plethora of community care guidance of various provenance and status, the High Court (*R v Gloucestershire CC, ex parte RADAR*) has politely pointed out that some of it is difficult to follow, unclear and even misleading.[33] More recently, the Court of Appeal (*R v Gloucestershire CC, ex parte Barry*) paid considerable attention to community care guidance, when examining s.2 of the CSDPA 1970 in particular. One of the judges pointed out that it was unsurprising that amidst all the policy guidance, Circulars and guides, both sides in the dispute found passages to support their arguments.[34]

Ombudsmen sometimes support adverse findings against authorities by referring to the failure of authorities to follow relevant guidance. For example, in one case about discharging a person from hospital, the health service ombudsman insisted that the health authority should have followed Circular guidance and provided written information about who was going to pay for private nursing home fees.[35]

Given the broad sweep and generality of the NHS Act 1977, the specific guidance on hospital discharge seemed to assume an added importance in this investigation – as the only useful pointer to what should have been happening.

Identifying guidance and whether it is current or obsolete

In the absence of reliable and accessible listings by government, everybody – authorities, voluntary organisations, lawyers – is sometimes in doubt about what guidance has been issued, which is current and which obsolete.

For example, it appears that, in the past, Circular guidance has sometimes been cancelled unintentionally. Despite the 'default' cancellation date placed on the Circular, the policy had been, in fact, intended to continue. For example, a letter issued by the Department of Health on community care assessments (for all services including equipment) was issued in December 1992, cancelled in March 1994, but the gist of the guidance within it was almost certainly not meant to be cancelled or doubted so swiftly.[36]

Even cancelled guidance can continue to be of some use legally as evidence of government policy; and, in any case, the message it contained might remain valid. For example, a 1991 Circular about charging for equipment by the NHS has now been cancelled, but its interpretation of the NHS Act 1977 remains a useful reminder to NHS Trusts not to make illegal charges.[37]

Charters

Under the banner of the Citizen's Charter, which emphasises the importance of complaints and redress procedures, charters have proliferated.[38] In the context of this book, these include the national NHS Patient's Charter, and the framework laid down by the Department of Health for local community care charters.

National charters refer to standards and rights, breach of which can justify a complaint; for example, dissatisfied patients are encouraged to write to the chief executive of the relevant NHS Trust if a charter provision has been broken. If patients are still dissatisfied, the NHS Executive can bring pressure to bear on local NHS Trusts – and patients can refer the matter to the health service ombudsman.

However, charters – even national ones – do not confer legal rights on users of services. The legal status of charters is uncertain and it has been suggested that, merely aspirational, they are of no legal effect but could be viewed as some form of customer guarantee.[39] In principle, central government might have the choice of developing charters which reflect primarily (i) market forces, (ii) the interests of suppliers of services, (iii) the interests of suppliers and consumers balanced, or (iv) a welfare model in which standards are imposed on suppliers irrespective of cost. It is contended that the charters in this country, under the general banner of the Citizen's Charter, reflect model (ii), and so do not necessarily reflect the concerns of users of services.[40]

To sum up. On the one hand, the charters offer a simple, direct and cheap route to obtaining apologies, redress and services from the NHS. On the other hand, if this route of complaint fails, patients still have to use other routes to sort out complaints, such as the ombudsman or ultimately the law courts. In this latter respect, charters can be viewed as nebulous, and yet one more obstacle to obtaining proper, legal redress.[41] Nevertheless, breach of a charter might indicate maladministration to the ombudsman or even serve as evidence in a judicial review case before the law courts.

Statements made in Parliament

Traditionally and officially, the law courts cannot refer to what has been said in Parliament (and reported in Hansard) when interpreting legislation. To a large extent this remains true but, whereas until recently there were likely to be very few exceptions[42], now there are likely to be more. This is because the rule has been relaxed; if the meaning of particular clauses in legislation is unclear, then statements made by ministers or other promoters of a Parliamentary Bill can be referred to in court – so long as such statements are themselves clear.[43] And, if European Union legislation is relevant (as it might be when the UK legislation under scrutiny is implementing a European directive), the courts might be prepared to allow even broader reference to Hansard – so that the overall purpose of the UK legislation, not just its meaning, can be clarified.[44]

For example, it could well be argued that community care legislation is ambiguous or obscure in some places; if a court were to accept this, then reference to what was said by the Secretary of State for Health and other ministers might be permissible in court. Similarly, if a dispute were to arise about the meaning of the duty to provide equipment under s.2 of the CSDPA, then reference might be allowed to what Alf Morris MP, the promoter of the original Bill, said at the time – for example, that the purpose of the legislation was to give rights to disabled people, and to ensure both good practice and equitable provision of local authority services.

The recent relaxation of the rule is a helpful concession in attempting to ascertain what Parliament intended when an Act was passed. For example, in the recent Court of Appeal of case (*R v Gloucestershire CC, ex parte Barry*) about community care and s.2 of the CSDPA 1970, the judges alluded to what Parliament 'must have intended' – though Hansard was not, in the event, resorted to.[45]

Standards and clinical guidelines: some legal implications

Standards and clinical guidelines – even if produced nationally by central government or other professional bodies – do not have the force of law but might have legal consequences.

In the context of a number of European directives relating to the technical performance and safety of products, 'harmonised' European standards are significant because compliance with the standard carries with it the presumption that the broad 'essential requirements' (which do have legal force) are also being complied with (see p.363).

In the context of statutory services, standards have proliferated in the face of the increased attention being paid to quality and cost. They are used to evaluate, modify, improve and sometimes formally inspect services. For instance, the Social Services Inspectorate (SSI), which inspects local authority services including both residential and non-residential services, takes a standard-based approach to inspection. It employs sets of standards, backed up by criteria and evidence-to-be-looked-for. The reports of SSI findings are written explicitly against these standards. And recently, the government issued a booklet designed to assist the NHS in improving clinical effectiveness by utilising research information – ie to encourage 'evidence-based' medicine.[46] The College of Occupational Therapists (COT) publishes a number of detailed documents setting standards of practice. Areas of work covered include referral to OTs, home visiting with hospital patients, services for people with physical disabilities, therapeutic services in people's own homes and so on.[47]

Nevertheless, the legal implications of standards are sometimes uncertain. First, those based closely on legislation need to be distinguished from those that merely represent good practice advocated by professionals.[48] For instance, a standard about assessment for equipment by social services departments might state that the need for telephone and radio must be considered. Such a standard or criterion would be reflecting what s.2 of the CSDPA states explicitly. But another standard, advocating that the potential for use of infra-red control technology around the house should also always be considered, would not be based on the express wording of legislation. This is because, whilst radio and telephone are mentioned in the CSDPA, infra red environmental controls are not – at most they are implied by the words *adaptations or facilities* (for safety, comfort or convenience).

Sometimes a mismatch occurs between the impossibly high standards set centrally by a professional body – and the reality of everyday practice. Lack of resources and local under-staffing can force practitioners to act in a fashion inconsistent both with standards and with what they have been taught when qualifying as, for example, nurses or therapists.

There is some concern that the existence of standards could work against practitioners when complaints and legal actions are brought against them – ie that they might be hoist by their own petard of stated good practice. Standards are not directly enforceable by users of services, since they have no legal force. Nevertheless, a departure from the standards could be used as evidence of carelessness and therefore of negligence.[49] For the same reason, there is a danger that clinical guidelines (eg for occupational therapists) could encourage defensive treatment. Even when they are not needed or are inappropriate, they might still be used because they are seen to represent essential good practice.[50] Indeed, if standards are set too high and are publicised, they might generate unrealistic expectations amongst service users – who then make more, and sometimes unreasonable, complaints.[51] Indeed, to take a cynical view, a hospital might be far better off legally with a set of standards at the foot of its beds on the general theme of the 'patient comes first' and 'dignity' – rather than with specific statements displayed in elderly care wards about patients' rights to have so many baths a week, or so much rehabilitation (where it is appropriate) from therapists.

Locally produced guidance and guidance produced by national bodies

In addition to guidance produced by central government, statutory services also produce their own local guidance. This has no formal legal effect; often, it is based on central guidance, which itself is only expanding upon and interpreting legislation. However, local guidance might be an indication to judicial review courts of whether an authority is exercising its duties powers reasonably, fairly and legally. It might also furnish the ombudsmen with evidence of whether authorities are acting according to the axioms of good administration.

Sometimes guidance is produced by professional bodies. This, too, has no legal effect but again might be useful evidence of accepted practice. For example, in the early 1970s, the Association of County Councils and the Association of Metropolitan Authorities produced Circular guidance on the provision of telephones under s.2 of the Chronically Sick and Disabled Persons Act 1970.[52]

Notes

1 *R v Gloucestershire County Council, ex parte Mahfood and Others, R v Islington London Borough Council, ex parte McMillan* (1996) 160 LGRevR 321 (QBD).

2 *M'Alister (or Donoghue) (Pauper) v Stevenson* [1932] AC 562.

3 Health Service Commissioner (E.62/93–94). *Failure to provide long term NHS care for a brain damaged patient. 2nd report 1993–1994.* London: HMSO.

4 See full discussion in: Craig, P.R. (1994). *Administrative law.* 3rd edition. London: Sweet & Maxwell, chapter 1.

5 *R v ILEA, ex parte Ali* (1990) 2 Admin LR 822: referred to in a community care case: *R v Islington LBC, ex parte Rixon* (QBD), *The Times:* 17 April 1996.

6 *R v Gloucestershire County Council, ex parte Mahfood and Others, R v Islington London Borough Council, ex parte McMillan* (1996) 160 LGRevR 321 (QBD).

7 *R v Secretary of State for Social Services, West Midlands Regional Health Authority and Birmingham Area Health Authority, ex parte Hincks* (1980) 1 BMLR 93 (CA).

8 *R v Secretary of State for Social Services, West Midlands Regional Health Authority and Birmingham Area Health Authority, ex parte Hincks* (1980) 1 BMLR 93 (CA).

9 *Secretary of State for Education and Science v Tameside MBC* [1977] AC 1014 (HL).

10 *R v Gloucestershire County Council, ex parte Mahfood and Others, R v Islington London Borough Council, ex parte McMillan* (1996) 160 LGRevR 321 (QBD).

11 *R v Secretary of State for Health, ex parte United States Tobacco International* [1992] 1 QB 353: where a duty to consult with people who appeared to be substantially affected was in fact

tantamount to a duty to consult with anybody who actually was substantially affected. This example used in: Fordham, M. (1994). *Judicial review handbook*. Chichester, Wiley, p.247.

12 *R v Gloucestershire County Council, ex parte Barry; R v Lancashire County Council, ex parte Gilpin and RADAR* (1996) (CA) (7–10 May 1996, CO/95/1779, CO/95/1134): from the author's own notes of the case.

13 *Hansard,* House of Lords, 15 January 1996, Community Care (Direct Payments) Bill, cols 391–394.

14 *Padfield v Minister of Agriculture, Fisheries and Food* [1968] AC 997 (HL).

15 *R v Gloucestershire County Council, ex parte Mahfood and Others, R v Islington London Borough Council, ex parte McMillan* (1996) 160 LGRevR 321 (QBD).

16 *Local Government Act 1972,* s.101.

17 Wade, H.W.R.; Forsyth, C.F. (1994). *Administrative law.* 7th edition. Oxford: Oxford University Press, p.351 (and see pp.347–351).

18 Commission for Local Administration in England (94/B/0524). *Report on investigation into a complaint against Leicestershire County Council.* Coventry: CLAE, 1994, p.9.

19 First case: *R v West Dorset District Council, ex parte Gerrard* (1995) 27 HLR 150 (QBD). The second, later case, is: *R v Hertsmere Borough Council, ex parte Woolgar* (1996) 160 LGRevR 261 (QBD).

20 Commission for Local Administration in Wales (95/0227). *Report by the local government ombudsman on an investigation into a complaint against Dyfed County Council.* Cardiff: CLAW, 1996.

21 *R v Secretary of State for Health, ex parte Manchester Local Committee and others* (1995) (28 March 1995, transcript, CO/189/94).

22 Department of Health (1990). *Community care in the next decade and beyond: policy guidance.* London: HMSO. Issued with joint Circular, making clear that the guidance was issued under LASSA 1970, s.7: EL(90)5, LAC(90)12. Department of Health. *Community care: policy guidance.* London: DH, 1990.

23 The point was raised in the Court of Appeal: *R v Gloucestershire County Council, ex parte Barry; R v Lancashire County Council, ex parte Gilpin and RADAR* (heard 7–10 May 1996).

24 *Gillick v West Norfolk Area Health Authority* [1986] 1 AC 112 (HL).

25 *R v North Yorkshire County Council, ex parte Hargreaves* (1994) 26 BMLR 121 (QBD).

26 Department of Health (1990). *Community care in the next decade and beyond: policy guidance.* London: HMSO, p.3. See also: Social Services Inspectorate, Department of Health; Social Work Services Group, Scottish Office (1991). *Care management and assessment: practitioners's guide.* London: HMSO, p.5.

27 *R v Islington Borough Council, ex parte Rixon* (1996) (QBD), The Times: 17 April 1996.

28 HN(88)26; HN(FP)(88)25; LASSL(88)8. *Health service development: the development of services for people with physical or sensory disabilities.* London: DH, Annex A, xx.

29 See the comments of Baroness Masham, Baroness Seear and Baroness Blatch (opposing them) in: *Hansard,* House of Lords, NHS and Community Care Bill debate, 7 June 1990, cols. 1588–1596.

30 DHSS (12/70), DES 13/70, MHLG 65/70, ROADS 20/70. Department of Health and Social Security; Department of Education and Science; Ministry of Housing and Local Government; Ministry of Transport. *The Chronically Sick and Disabled Persons Act 1970.* London: DHSS, para 7.

31 *R v Gloucestershire County Council, ex parte Mahfood and Others, R v Islington London Borough Council, ex parte McMillan* (1996) 160 LGRevR 321 (QBD).

32 *R v Wandsworth London Borough Council, ex parte Beckwith* [1996] 1 FCR 504 (HL).

33 *R v Gloucestershire County Council, ex parte Royal Association for Disability and Rehabilitation* (1995) (QBD) (21st December 1995, CO/2764/95, transcript).

34 *R v Gloucestershire County Council, ex parte Barry; R v Lancashire County Council, ex parte Gilpin and RADAR* (1996) (CA) (7–10 May 1996, CO/95/1779, CO/95/1134, transcript).

35 HSC (E.62/93–94). Health Service Commissioner. *Failure to provide long term NHS care for a brain damaged patient.* 2nd report 1993–1994. HC 197. London: HMSO, 1994.

36 CI(92)34. Social Services Inspectorate. *Implementing caring for people: assessment.* London: Department of Health.

37 Eg EL(92)20. NHS Management Executive. *Provision of equipment by the NHS.* London: Department of Health.

38 *The Citizen's Charter: raising the standard.* London: HMSO, pp.42–43.

39 Barron, A.; Scott, C. (1992). Citizen's Charter Programme. *Modern Law Review:* 1992; 55(4), pp.526–546.

40 Rawlings, P. (1994). Consumerism and the Citizen's Charter. *Consumer Law Journal:* 1994, pp.3–8.

41 Williams, T.; Goriely, T. (1994). Big idea – any effect: the Charter complaints system as an alternative to statutory rights. *New Law Journal:* 1994; 144(6661), pp.1164–1165.

42 Such as the case of *Pickstone v Freemans PLC* [1989] AC 66, where, with help from Hansard, the House of Lords interpreted amendments made by 1983 Regulations to the Equal Pay Act 1970.

43 *Pepper (Inspector of Taxes) v Hart* [1993] AC 593 (HL).

44 *Three Rivers District Council and Others v Bank of England (No 2)* (1995) (QBD), *Independent:* 22 December 1995.

45 *R v Gloucestershire County Council, ex parte Barry; R v Lancashire County Council, ex parte Gilpin and RADAR* (1996) (CA) (7–10 May 1996, CO/95/1779, CO/95/1134, transcript).

46 NHS Executive (1996). *Promoting clinical effectiveness: a framework for action in and through the NHS.* Leeds: Department of Health.

47 From: the publications list of the College of Occupational Therapists, 1995.

48 A comparable question arose over the status of Department of Health guidance about children. Confusion arose over the deregistration of a childminder for smacking a child. It was held by magistrates that a local authority had applied government guidance too strictly in a particular case. The High Court found in favour of the decision of the magistrates. See eg: Status of guidance should be clarified. *ADSS News:* April 1994, p.4.

49 Dimond, B. (1994). Standard setting and litigation. *British Journal of Nursing:* 1994; 3(5), pp.235–238.

50 Austin, C.; Herbert, S.I. (1995). Clinical guidelines: should we be worried? *British Journal of Occupational Therapy:* November 1995; 58(11), pp.481–484.

51 Tingle, J. (1994). Legal implications of standard setting in nursing. *British Journal of Nursing:* 1992; 1(14), pp.728–731.

52 Association of County Councils; Association of Metropolitan Authorities (1971). *Chronically Sick and Disabled Persons Act 1970: provision of telephones as amended by ACC/AMA letter 20/4/72.* London: ACC; AMA.

PART II

7. Provision of equipment by social services departments
8. Provision of equipment by the NHS
9. Provision of equipment in residential and nursing homes
10. Provision of home adaptations by housing authorities and social services departments
11. Provision of equipment for pupils and students with special educational needs
12. Provision of equipment and adaptations for work
13. War pensioners: provision of equipment and adaptations

CHAPTER 7

PROVISION OF EQUIPMENT BY SOCIAL SERVICES DEPARTMENTS

COVERAGE

1. Type of equipment and practitioners involved
2. Mosaic of legislation governing equipment provision
   - Overview of the legislation
   - (i) Provision of equipment and adaptations: Chronically Sick and Disabled Persons Act 1970, s.2
   - (ii) Provision of information about equipment: CSDPA 1970, s.1
   - (iii) Welfare services for disabled people: National Assistance Act 1948, s.29
   - (iv) Request for assessment: Disabled Persons (Services, Consultation and Representation) Act 1986
   - (v) Provision of equipment and adaptations for older people: Health Service and Public Health Act 1968
   - (vi) Provision of laundry equipment: NHS Act 1977
   - (vii) Community care assessment: NHS and Community Care Act 1990, s.47
   - (viii) Safeguarding and promotion of the welfare of children in need: Children Act 1989
   - (ix) Assessment of carers: Carers (Recognition and Services) Act 1995
   - (x) Provision of adequate staff: Local Authority Social Services Act 1970, s.6
   - (xi) Charges for equipment: Health and Social Services and Social Security Adjudication Act 1983, s.17
   - (xii) Direct payments for equipment and services
3. Complaints
   - Complaints procedures of social services departments
   - Default powers of the Secretary of State
   - Community care charters
   - Local ombudsman.

4. Operation of priorities, criteria of eligibility and waiting times for equipment
   - Waiting lists and priorities
   - Innovative solutions?

Key points

This chapter focuses in particular on s.2 of the Chronically Sick and Disabled Person Act (CSDPA) 1970, which is the main statutory channel for equipment provision by the social services departments of local authorities. In summary, s.2 provides that if authorities believe that it is necessary for them to meet a person's needs, then they have a duty to make arrangements to provide equipment and various other services. The detailed implications of this duty – including its strengths and weaknesses for both authorities and service users – are spelt out, especially in the light of recent community care cases which have reached the law courts.

However, the CSDPA itself sits enmeshed in a complicated web of other welfare legislation underpinning, for example, welfare services in general, children's services, services for older people, laundry facilities, community care assessments, requests for assessments, charges for equipment, direct payments to service users and complaints procedures. On top of all this sits a range of Department of Health guidance, whilst authorities themselves produce local community care charters, setting out local standards of service (and equipment) provision.

In order to carry out their statutory duties within the resources available, social services departments adopt various policies, priorities, criteria of eligibility and systems of waiting lists. Nevertheless, local authorities are faced with an ageing population, people's increasing needs and expectations, and a shifting of responsibilities – in line with community care policies – from the NHS to social services departments. Yet they have limited budgets. In addition, local authorities have long pleaded another excuse for deficiencies in provision equipment; namely, the shortage of occupational therapists – professionals employed by social services departments to ensure that equipment and adaptations are provided expertly, appropriately and safely.

Consequently, authorities adopt various policies and strategies to manage the inevitable conflict between needs and resources. For example, they might decide to cease providing items of equipment costing less than £15.00 (on grounds that people can afford to buy it), high seat chairs (because they are expensive) or bathing equipment (deemed to be low priority, desirable but not essential). Furthermore, authorities have long operated priority systems involving long waiting times for assessment, particularly for those people whose needs are deemed to be of a low priority. Such policies and procedures are not always implemented legally and according to the principles of good administration. When they are not, then authorities run the risk of judicial review by the law courts and findings of maladministration by the local ombudsman. This risk is not theoretical. A number of community care cases have reached the High Court (and even the Court of Appeal and the House of Lords) in the last three years or so. Though not dealing with equipment in particular, some have concerned s.2 of the CSDPA which governs equipment provision, as well as various other services; they are therefore highly relevant to this book. As well, the local ombudsmen have, over many years, conducted numerous investigations into the operation by social services departments of waiting lists and priority systems applied to equipment and home adaptations.

Even so, if authorities proceed with a knowledge of the relevant legislation and of good administrative practice, they are likely to be able to make priorities and ration services more or less at will, with little danger of significant interference from either the courts or the ombudsmen.

Questions people ask

- What can a person do if she is forced to wait two years for an assessment?
- What if an authority provides a stairlift but then decides, a year later, to take it away again, even though the physical needs of the user of the lift have not changed? In effect, is it permissible for authorities to reassess people according to new, stricter criteria, in order to remove or reduce services?
- Can social services departments make charges for equipment?
- Can authorities decide to stop supplying altogether certain types of equipment such as bath mats or special cutlery?
- Can authorities safely, in the legal sense, say that they will never provide a person with an electric wheelchair?
- What is the legal position if two people with similar needs and in similar circumstances are assessed differently, so that one receives services and the other does not? And does it make a difference if they are residents of the same authority or of different authorities?
- What is the legal position when authorities contract out equipment services, including assessment, to independent organisations?
- If authorities are charging people for equipment, what can people be asked to pay?
- What if occupational therapists allow people on assessment waiting lists to 'jump the queue', either out of kindheartedness, or simply as a way of dealing with a 'vexatious' person who is 'shouting loudly' and thereby wasting everybody's time?

1. TYPE OF EQUIPMENT AND PRACTITIONERS INVOLVED

The range of equipment typically provided by social services departments is extensive and includes, for example, items for: the *toilet* (eg raised lavatory seats), *bath* (eg bath boards, bath lifts), *bed* (eg. overbed tables), *sitting* (eg highback chairs, riser chairs), *dressing* (eg stocking aids, longhandled shoehorns), *eating and drinking* (eg. special cutlery, plate guards), *cooking* (eg safety pans), *washing* (eg tap turners, longhandled brushes, toothpaste squeezers), *general household* (eg helping hands, cleaning and laundry equipment), *reading* (eg magnifiers, page turners) – and so on. Part IV of this book gives many more examples. It should also be borne in mind that, legally, authorities are empowered in some circumstances to provide many other products, including those thought of as 'ordinary' rather than 'disability' equipment (eg microwave ovens, letter cages, television remote controls). On the whole, such 'ordinary' equipment is unlikely to be provided in practice – although, for example, high seat chairs and occasionally washing machines (eg out of a special budget for people with HIV/AIDS) are sometimes available.

Children's daily living equipment which might be provided by social services departments includes, for instance, special beds and cots, special seating systems and chairs, posture equipment (eg boards, wedges and frames for lying, standing and kneeling), toilet equipment (eg musical potties), special car seats and harnesses, eating and drinking equipment, communication aids, toys for play/development and so on.

Equipment is provided through a range of social services staff including occupational therapists (identified by a variety of titles) and their assistants, occasionally physiotherapists, rehabilitation officers for blind and partially-sighted people, specialist social workers for deaf people, and social workers generally. For disabled children, services and equipment are often provided through multi-disciplinary teams known by a variety of names including child assessment centres, child development teams and special needs teams. How these teams are organised and operate is likely to vary from place to place. Members are likely to include, for example, social workers, therapists, nurses, doctors such as paediatricians.

2. THE MOSAIC OF LEGISLATION

The legislative basis for provision of equipment is without doubt complicated, spanning over 45 years and entailing at least nine Acts of Parliament. In addition, there is an abundance of guidance of various types and status, focusing especially, for example, on the Children Act 1989 and the NHS and Community Care Act 1990.

The main focus for equipment provision is s.2 of the Chronically Sick and Disabled Persons Act 1970, although this is now densely hedged round by various other legislation. Consequently the legal framework for provision of equipment by social services departments is at best complicated and at worst confused – since it is not always clear how some of these Acts relate to others. In particular, it should be noted that although the CSDPA does retain a considerable degree of importance because of the strong duties it imposes on authorities, it sits now firmly within the wider community care system of assessment and care management introduced by the NHS and Community Care Act 1990.

Overview of the legislation

The following is a brief summary of the relevant legislation that underpins the provision of equipment and adaptations by social services departments:

(i) **Provision of equipment and adaptations: Chronically Sick and Disabled Persons Act 1970, s.2.** Section 2 of the Chronically Sick and Disabled Persons Act (CSDPA) 1970 imposes the most explicit duty to provide equipment and adaptations for both children and adults. The duty is a strong one towards individual people; if an authority is satisfied that it is necessary for it to meet a person's needs, then it has a duty to make arrangements for provision.

(ii) **Provision of information about equipment.** Under s.1 of the CSDPA, local authorities have a duty to publish information, and inform individual service users, about services and equipment.

(iii) **Welfare services for disabled people.** The CSDPA (s.2) is itself an extension of more general welfare duties and powers towards disabled people, stemming from s.29 of the National Assistance Act 1948 (this applies, however, only to adults). The s.29 duties are general ones owed by authorities to the local population, not towards individual people.

(iv) **Request for assessment.** The Disabled Persons (Services, Consultation and Representation) Act 1986 applies both to children and to adults. It strengthens the CSDPA by placing duties on authorities to assess disabled people for services available under s.2 of the CSDPA, if requested by those disabled people or by their carers. The duty is a strong owed towards individual people. Under the 1986 Act, authorities must also have regard to the needs of carers.

(v) **Provision of equipment and adaptations for older people: Health Service and Public Health Act 1968.** Under the Health Service and Public Health Act 1968 (s.45), authorities have the power, but not the duty, to provide equipment and adaptations for 'old people'.

(vi) **Provision of laundry equipment: NHS Act 1977.** Under s.21 and Schedule 8 of the NHS Act 1977, social services departments have a power to provide laundry facilities (eg washing machines) to households for which it is providing, or could provide, home help services.

(vii) **Community care assessment: NHS and Community Care Act 1990, s.47.** The NHS and Community Care Act 1990, s.47, the hub of community care, places a strong duty on authorities to assess individuals who appear to be in need and to decide if they need services or equipment. It applies only to adults. This section, too, strengthens the CSDPA by removing the need for people receiving a community care assessment, to request an assessment under s.4 of the 1986 Act (see above). However, this section fails to clarify the exact relationship between an assessment under the CSDPA 1970 and a community care assessment.

(viii) **Safeguarding and promotion of the welfare of children in need: Children Act 1989.** In parallel with community care legislation, s.17 of the Children Act 1989 places a general duty on authorities to safeguard and promote the welfare of children in need. It also states that authorities may make an assessment under s.2 of the CSDPA 1970 at the same time as they make an assessment under the Children Act 1989.

(ix) **Assessment of carers: Carers (Recognition and Services) Act 1995.** The Carers (Recognition and Services) Act 1995 places a strong duty (ie towards individual people) on authorities, when they assess adults or children under community care or child care legislation. If requested, the authority must assess the needs of carers, including children or young people who are caring for somebody – and then take this assessment into account when deciding what services are needed by the person being cared for.

(x) **Provision of adequate staff: Local Authority Social Services Act 1970, s.6).** The Local Authority Social Services Act 1970 (s.6) places a duty on authorities to provide adequate staff for social services functions.

(xi) **Charging for equipment and services: Health and Social Services and Social Security Adjudications Act 1983, s.17.** The Health and Social Services and Social Security Adjudications Act 1983 (s.17) gives authorities the power to make charges for certain non-residential services (including equipment) – as does s.29 of the Children Act 1989. (The duty to make charges for arranging the provision of residential or nursing home accommodation lies in s.26 of the National Assistance Act 1948).

(xii) **Direct payments for equipment and services.** Lastly, the Community Care (Direct Payments) Act, when in force, will enable social services departments to make direct cash payments to certain groups of people.

(i) Provision of equipment: Chronically Sick and Disabled Persons Act 1970

Section 2 of the Chronically Sick and Disabled Persons Act 1970 (CSDPA) imposes a strong duty on local authorities to make arrangements for the provision of *home adaptations* and *additional facilities* for the *greater safety, comfort and convenience* of individual adults and children. The duty arises when an authority:

> 'is satisfied in the case of any person to whom that section [s.29 of the National Assistance Act 1948] applies who is ordinarily resident in their area that it is necessary in order to meet the needs of that person for that authority to make arrangements for all or any of the following matters, namely...the provision for that person in arranging for the carrying out of any works of adaptation in his home or the provision of any additional facilities designed to secure his greater safety, comfort or convenience.' (square brackets added)

Additional duties are also imposed for the provision, in particular, of television, telephone and wireless. Other services too are listed (including holidays, meals and practical assistance in the home) but are not covered by this book.

Obligations of social services departments under s.2 of the CSDPA: conflict between duty and resources

The CSDPA, introduced as a private member's Bill in Parliament and thus 'uninvited' by government, continues to be unwelcome in some respects to both central government and local authorities.[1] At the heart of community care legislation, it is 'dangerous' because its strong legal force threatens to limit the wide discretion of authorities to determine when to provide services and equipment.

Authorities fear that, once they have decided that it is necessary for them to make arrangements to meet a person's needs, they then have an absolute duty to make those arrangements. Therefore, if authorities assess too many people in relation to available resources, they could be in the position of having to provide services and equipment for which they do not have the money. Plainly, this situation creates potential conflict.

For 25 years, government guidance appeared to accept the existence of this absolute duty.[2] However, the law courts had never directly verified that such an absolute duty would exist even in the face of a lack of resources.[3] Finally, in 1995 a case concerning home help provision under s.2 of the CSDPA, was heard in the High Court (*R v Gloucestershire CC, ex parte Mahfood*). The outcome both confirmed and qualified the duty. It was confirmed in the sense that once the need for services or equipment has been assessed, an authority cannot simply take them away because it does not have enough money. But what the court gave with one hand, it took away with the other. It ruled that the absolute duty can be circumvented simply by reassessing people's needs, according to new, stricter criteria – reflecting how much money the authority has available. Following reassessment, the authority could decide that it was not, after all, necessary to make any arrangements to meet a person's needs.[4] However, in June 1996 (*R v Gloucestershire CC, ex parte Barry*), the Court of Appeal ruled that authorities could not take resources into account when assessing or reassessing people[5]; the case is now likely to be appealed to the House of Lords.

A further refinement to the arguments used to alter or reduce services occurred when an authority claimed that it could no longer afford to provide home support services for an elderly lady (*R v Lancashire CC, ex parte Ingham*). Instead, she would have to enter a nursing home. Part of the authority's argument seemed to be that it had never been under an absolute duty to provide the home support services, since strictly speaking they were not absolutely 'necessary'. Therefore, the authority was quite at liberty to alter its provision (ie to nursing home care), so long as that provision did not fall below the level of what really was 'necessary' to meet the person's needs.[6]

The outcome of the Gloucester case at the High Court stage, basically unfavourable to service users, might not have been what the author of the CSDPA, Alfred Morris, originally had in mind[7]; the Court of Appeal decision is probably more in line with his intentions. Nevertheless, even the High Court decision did not make life easy for the 'victorious' authority, Gloucestershire County Council. The council was faced with the expense of reassessing hundreds of people, and was even taken to court for failing to reinstate people's services prior to that reassessment (*R v Gloucestershire CC, ex parte RADAR*).[8] It was subsequently threatened with still further judicial review – for failing to restore a person's home cleaning services following the reassessment, on the grounds that the reassessment had taken account of costs only.[9]

Gloucestershire case: the High Court. The position the High Court (*R v Gloucestershire CC, ex parte Mahfood*) took was that although resources could be taken account of in an assessment (or reassessment) under s.2 of the CSDPA

1970, they were only one of several factors which need to be considered in each individual person's case. Therefore, a decision based on resources alone was susceptible to challenge; and the court, whilst accepting that resources are relevant, even to 'needs-led assessment', did not give authorities a free hand to deny people services solely on grounds of money. It suggested also that, beyond a certain point, it would be unreasonable for authorities to deny assistance to people who are at serious physical risk. (The ombudsman, too, has found maladministration when an authority denied the request for a telephone to a dying man who had AIDS on the grounds simply that the budget was exhausted).[10] What the court appeared not to accept is that the assessment of people's needs should be entirely free of resource considerations (see generally Chapter 2).[11] The judge's summing up of all this was as follows (square brackets added):

> **[taking account of resources, but meeting needs of people at severe risk]** 'that a local authority is right to take account of resources both when assessing needs and when deciding whether it is necessary to make arrangements to meet those needs. I should stress, however, that there will, in my judgement, be situations where a reasonable authority could only conclude that some arrangements were necessary to meet the needs of a particular disabled person and in which it could not reasonably conclude that a lack of resources provided an answer. Certain persons would be at severe physical risk if they were unable to have some practical assistance in their homes. In those situations, I cannot conceive that an authority would be held to have acted reasonably if it used shortage of resources as a reason for not being satisfied that some arrangement should be made to meet those person's needs.'
>
> **[balancing exercise between need and resources]** 'On any view s.2(1) is needs-led by reference to the particular needs of a particular disabled person. A balancing exercise must be carried out assessing the particular needs of that person in the context of the needs of the others and the resources available, but if no reasonable authority could conclude other than that some practical help was necessary, that would have to be its decision.'
>
> **[absolute duty once the authority has accepted the necessity of meeting a person's needs, irrespective of resources]** 'Furthermore, once they have decided that it is necessary to make the arrangements, they are under an absolute duty to make them. It is a duty owed to a specific individual and not a target duty. No term is to be implied that the local authority is obliged to comply with the duty only if it has the revenue to do so. In fact, once under that duty, resources do not come into it'.
>
> **[reassessment must take account of all relevant factors not just resources]** 'It would certainly have been open to the Gloucestershire county council to reassess the individual applicants as individuals, judging their current needs and taking into account all relevant factors including the resources now available and the competing needs of other disabled persons. What they were not entitled to do, but what in my judgement they in fact did, was not to reassess at all but simply

cut the services they were providing, because their resources in turn had been cut. This amounted to treating the cut in resources as the sole factor to be taken into account, and that was, in my judgement, unlawful'.

Gloucestershire case: the Court of Appeal. In June 1996 (*R v Gloucestershire CC, ex parte Barry*), the Court of Appeal overturned the High Court (*R v Gloucestershire CC, ex parte Mahfood*) – and ruled (in a 2:1 split decision) that authorities could not take account of resources when assessing (or reassessing) the needs of disabled people under s.2 of the CSDPA 1970. In summary, the two majority judges could not see how people's needs can sensibly be assessed in the light of a third party's resources. Indeed, one referred to the Shorter Oxford English Dictionary for the meaning of 'need', and alluded to the logical absurdity of taking resources into account – if an authority had no resources, then, by definition, no disabled person could have any needs.[12] The approach of the majority is intuitively attractive; even the High Court recognised its forcefulness, when rejecting it. However, the dissenting judge in the Court of Appeal supported the High Court's view that resources must inevitably be able to be taken into account; and this is a more 'realistic', if unattractive, view. Thus, whether the Court of Appeal's decision will survive an appeal to the House of Lords must be open to some doubt.[13]

Other aspects of the duty to provide equipment and services under s.2 of the CSDPA 1970

When attempting to deal with the conflict between needs and resources, there are a number of aspects to s.2 of the CSDPA which sometimes, but not always, enable authorities to alleviate the duty imposed on them. These are summarised immediately below:

The CSDPA duty applies only to people who are ordinary residents of the area. The duty under s.2 of the CSDPA applies only to people who are ordinarily resident within the area of an authority. Thus, authorities sometimes deny that a duty exists on the basis that people are not ordinary residents. Although Department of Health guidance about ordinary residence has stipulated the use of dispute procedures by local authorities, the definition of ordinary residence is legally a matter for the courts to settle (see p.436).[14]

The CSDPA duty applies only to people who qualify under the National Assistance Act 1948. The duty applies only to people eligible for assistance under s.29 of the 1948 Act: ie substantially and permanently 'handicapped' people and people who are blind, deaf or dumb. Therefore, there is no duty to provide equipment under the CSDPA for anybody else. However, authorities need to be wary about adopting stringent policies excluding people from assessment and services, since Department of Health guidance urges a generous, rather than a parsimonious, definition of disability (see p.168).

The local authority must be satisfied that it is necessary for it to make arrangements to meet people's needs. An authority must be satisfied that it is necessary to make arrangements for the provision of people's needs. This obligation, by no means straightforward, allows authorities perhaps more leeway than is commonly recognised.

Satisfaction. The term 'satisfied' is crucial in the legislation. It is the term that describes the making of the final decision by an authority about whether to arrange provision of equipment. Authorities have a wide and subjective discretion to decide whether they are satisfied that people need equipment. Once an authority has expressed itself to be satisfied, it comes under a strong duty to make arrangements to meet people's needs – although even this duty can be ameliorated or removed if the authority reassesses and downgrades these needs. It is for authorities, not service users or anybody else, to be satisfied.

The term 'satisfied' is generally treated by the courts as a subjective one. This means that, on the whole, it is for individual authorities to decide whether they are satisfied about need, not for the law courts to impose objective rules or conditions about when authorities should be satisfied.[15] However, this might not be the whole picture; as explained above, a court might rule that it was unreasonable not to recognise the needs of a person who would be put at severe physical risk, were he to be denied practical assistance in the home.[16]

It is important to note that it is for authorities to be satisfied, not service users or even independent advisers. The legislation clearly states this. If, instead, it read something like, 'if a person is in need, then an authority must provide', then it could be argued that need could be determined as much by service users as by authorities – or at least by independent professionals, experts, advisers or even the courts (see ??). However, as the legislation stands, it is for authorities to be satisfied. Thus, community care guidance issued by the Department of Health explains that, though it is good practice for service users to participate fully in assessments, it is for authorities to make final decisions about people's needs.[17]

In 1986, the High Court made it quite plain in a case about services provided under s.2 of the CSDPA, where decision-making power lay (*R v DHSS, ex parte Bruce*). The judge stated that an authority's decision could not be challenged successfully unless it had made a decision about a person's needs which was irrational, to the extent that no other local authority could have made the decision.[18] This state of affairs would appear to give authorities unbridled power to do much as they please.

Need. The concept of need is not objective, and the notion that need is a highly elastic commodity has been reinforced in Parliament by government ministers of different persuasions, from Barbara Castle in 1975 ('of course ¿need" is an imprecise concept')[19] to Margaret Thatcher in 1985 ('it is for the local authority to assess need and to determine how it should best be met').[20] More recently, advice issued by the Social Services Inspectorate in 1992 suggested that authorities could avoid legal problems by distinguishing between people's needs and preferences. The former would trigger a duty under the CSDPA, but the latter would not.[21] There are in fact two levels at which authorities deal with the concept of need.

The first is at the planning and policy level, when an authority formulates the criteria of eligibility people have to meet in order to qualify for services. It is to this level which the Court of Appeal's recent judgement in the Gloucestershire case (see above) is particularly relevant. For instance, 1970 DHSS guidance on s.2 of the CSDPA had emphasised that criteria of need were to be determined in the light of resources.[22] The Court of Appeal commented that such guidance was of limited use in determining what the Act really means – since it was merely government guidance interpreting an Act resulting from a private member's (not a government) Bill.[23]

The second is at the level of individual assessment, when an authority decides whether a particular person meets those criteria. At this second level, the concept of need can be a difficult and variable one, since, even in a world of unlimited resources, there is plenty of scope for differences of professional opinion. Indeed, more complications and possible solutions exist in the social than the medical context, because of a broader range of unpredictable factors.

Authorities would thus seem to have wide discretion to vary their interpretation of need; they could try to define it, for example, in terms of criteria of eligibility which few people could meet in practice. Few services would then be provided.[24]

Is it necessary for the authority to make arrangements? The duty under s.2 of the CSDPA only arises if an authority is satisfied that it is necessary for it to make arrangements for provision. These words provide authorities with an escape route. For instance, an authority might assess that a person needs a stairlift. But if the person's daughter, who is financially well-off, voluntarily offers to buy it herself, then it is clearly not necessary for the authority to provide the lift. Similarly, having assessed that a severely disabled person with arthritis needs an electric riser/recliner chair, an authority might seek financial assistance from local voluntary organisations. Only if it failed in this attempt might the authority then accept that it was now 'necessary' for it to make the arrangements itself – and provide the chair.[25] And, when investigating a case about home support services, the ombudsman accepted that, although a 35-year old who was severely physically disabled 'needed' 24-hour home care, the authority simply did not have the resources to provide this directly. Instead, it provided some of the services, whilst applying to the Independent Living Fund (ILF) for extra finance. (Although the application eventually succeeded, the ombudsman found maladministration because the authority, before making it, had failed to ensure that the man was receiving a particular benefit, on which ILF support depended. This caused delay).[26]

In assessing whether the arrangements – whether or not made by the authority – are adequate the courts might react more or less generously to service users. For example, in one controversial homelessness case (*R v Hillingdon LBC, ex parte Pulhofer*), the House of Lords emphasised that, when considering the term 'accommodation' (which housing authorities had a duty to secure the provision of) in the relevant homelessness legislation, authorities should not preface the term with words such as 'reasonable' or 'appropriate'. This meant that an authority would be discharging its legal duty even if it made available accommodation unfit for human habitation.[27]

However, there are circumstances in which the duty to make arrangements – after assessment of the necessity of meeting a person's needs – might 'hang around the neck' of an authority. For instance, joint guidance (from the Department of Health and Department of Environment) states that a social services department might assess the need for home adaptations and refer a person to the housing department for a disabled facilities grant. However, if the housing department for some reason does not or cannot assist, then the duty to meet the need 'returns' to social services.[28] More broadly, it is arguable that if a need for any equipment at all is assessed, but not met elsewhere (for whatever reason), then the local authority's duty to make arrangements remains. In such circumstances, direct provision might be the only remaining solution.

Such a sweeping and continuing duty might give authorities pause for thought. For example, in the past local authorities have sometimes assessed that people need outdoor, electric wheelchairs. Few authorities provide these and so would normally give advice about them, refer people to the NHS, or perhaps assist people to obtain alternative funding. However, if all this were to fail then it could be argued that the authority might itself be obliged to provide the wheelchair in some circumstances. Indeed, the local ombudsman has suggested that authorities cannot just dismiss their responsibilities for such items[29]; in practice, social services departments do sometimes still loan manual wheelchairs[30]; and, it is thought that in the 1970s particularly, a number of authorities did directly assist people to obtain electric wheelchairs.

Thus, this duty is sweeping not only because it continues and returns to the authority in some circumstances, but also because the range of equipment implied by facilities for greater safety, comfort or convenience (see below) is immense.

Facilities and adaptations for greater safety, comfort or convenience

The word 'equipment' is not mentioned in s.2 of the CSDPA. Instead authorities have a duty to make arrangements for the provision of assistance with home adaptations, and for the provision of 'facilities' for people's 'greater safety, comfort or convenience'. The last three terms, taken at face value, can clearly cover a huge range of equipment, including flashing alarm systems or handrails for safety, special chairs, beds, wheelchairs, raised cooking surfaces, stairlifts and downstairs lavatories. The unusual might also be covered – for example, a padded box/playpen for a 12-year-old girl with severe epilepsy to prevent her banging her head at home (as a temporary measure in advance of providing £6000 for the parents to pad the walls of one room in the house).[31]

Duty in relation not only to safety but also to comfort and convenience? The duty under section 2 covers all three terms, *safety, comfort* and *convenience.* This could mean that authorities which only ever assess and make arrangements for people's safety are in breach of their duty. For example, some authorities state explicitly, or at least imply, that people's needs for leisure equipment (eg for the garden) or even some bath equipment is such a low priority that those people are unlikely ever to be assessed – or will have to wait a very long time. This is tantamount to declaring that an authority is not going to carry out its duty to assess disabled people in apparent need (under, for example, s.4 of the Disabled Persons (Services, Consultation and Representation) Act 1986). Yet the legislation does not list safety, comfort or convenience in an order of priorities – and the local ombudsman has noted that the duty to assess people is no less in non-urgent than in urgent cases. Indeed, he referred not only to the potential danger, but also to the 'extreme discomfort' and the 'inconvenient' accommodation, in which a disabled woman had to live – whilst waiting four years and eight months for the simple aids that eventually made such a difference to her life.[32]

In a similar vein, the High Court decided a case against an authority in relation to holidays provided under s.2 of the CSDPA (*R v Ealing LBC, ex parte Leaman*). The authority had stated that, because of lack of resources, it would consider giving assistance only with its own, but not with privately organised holidays. This was clearly not consistent with the wording of the Act which refers to both types of holiday; as the judge put it, the authority was wrong.[33]

A further point for authorities to note is that s.2 of the CSDPA says nothing about providing specialist equipment – eg equipment designed solely for disabled people. This means that authorities which do not provide some types of equipment – on the basis that it is *ordinary* equipment (eg a bath mat) which everybody uses – are probably using a legally irrelevant consideration to justify non-provision. It is true that other reasons could be sought to justify this approach. For example, the authority might decide that it is not necessary to provide a non-slip bath mat, because the person could buy it cheaply at a nearby pharmacy or by mail order. But the fact that the bath mat is ordinary, cannot by itself justify non-provision. On the same basis, some authorities might only consider providing a high seat chair for a person who already has some sort of easy chair (albeit an unsuitable one) – since they (understandably) do not wish to take on the 'ordinary' job of furnishing people's houses.[34] If the person could not obtain the chair elsewhere (eg private purchase or assistance from a voluntary organisation) – and assuming she 'needed' it according to the authority's criteria – then it is not clear that this sort of explanation for non-provision is legally defensible.

The word 'greater' should also be noted. This comparative word suggests that even if a person is, for example, already safe or comfortable to some to extent – a request could be made for further safety or comfort.

Thus, the broad and unspecified range of equipment which could be covered by s.2 of the CSDPA adds to the onerousness of the duty and to the imperative that authorities place limits on what they will provide.

Provision of telephone, television and radio

Apart from arrangements for the provision of facilities and adaptations generally (see immediately above), s.2 of the CSDPA also imposes a similar duty in relation to specific items of equipment, namely, telephone, television and radio. An authority has a duty to make arrangements for the provision of, or for assistance to help the person to obtain, any of these items – if the authority is satisfied that it is necessary in order to meet the person's needs. The implications of terms such as 'make arrangements' have already been discussed above.

In 1971, the Association of County Councils (ACC) and Association of Metropolitan Authorities (AMA) issued a joint Circular (note: not a government Circular: see p.148) which offered guidance on the provision of telephones. In summary[35]:

> People would qualify if, in the view of an authority, they lived alone, or were frequently alone – or lived with a person who was unable, or could not be relied on, to deal with an emergency or maintain necessary outside contacts. In *addition* to this, the person either (a) would have a need to get in touch with a doctor, other health worker or helper and would be in danger or at risk without a telephone; or (b) be unable to leave the dwelling in normal weather without assistance or have seriously restricted mobility – and need a telephone to avoid isolation. Also, there should be no friend or neighbours willing and able to help.

Central government guidance for England seems never to have been issued in respect of any of these items – telephone, television or radio. However, guidance on telephones was issued in Scotland and Northern Ireland and contained similar criteria to the AMA/ACC guidance.[36] And, in Northern Ireland, the DHSS gave guidance on the provision of televisions by health and social services boards (HSSBs): the person had to be housebound and living alone, or confined to a room which meant that television was needed in that particular room. As well as providing the sets, the licence fees of eligible applicants could be paid.[37] The Northern Ireland DHSS also issued guidance stating that HSSBs should provide batteries free of charge for people who had radio sets provided by the British Wireless Fund for the Blind.[38]

(ii) Provision of information about equipment: CSDPA 1970, s.1.

Under s.1 of the CSDPA, local authorities have a twofold duty.

First, they must ensure that information is published about welfare services provided under the umbrella of s.29 of the National Assistance Act 1948 (see below). The duty is very much a general one, and probably difficult to enforce except in extreme circumstances. For instance, the information has to be published from 'time to time', in a manner which authorities 'consider appropriate' and is to be 'general' information. This leaves a very great deal to authorities to decide about when, how and what they publish.

Second, authorities have a much more specific duty to each individual user of services. An authority must inform him or her about any other services – whether or not they are services the authority provides – which the authority believes he or she needs. This might include information about, for example, NHS physiotherapy, a voluntary organisation's wheelchair loan scheme, an advice service on disability benefits – and so on. There are at least two explicit limitations to the extent of the authority's duty; the first hinges on the authority's 'opinion' of whether the information is needed. The second affects information about services not provided by the authority and limits the obligation to information, the 'particulars' of which the authority has in its possession.

Except in a case of blatant non-performance of such duties, the publishing of information is a difficult activity for the courts to interfere with. Information provision is such an open-ended activity, and what is sufficient for one person, might be quite inadequate for another. For instance, one education case concerned the duty of a local authority to publish 'particulars' including school admissions arrangements and admissions policy. It was alleged that the published booklet failed to give sufficient information about 'traditional catchment areas' and that therefore parents might make 'hopeless' choices without knowing that they were doing so. The booklet did refer to 'catchment' areas but did not specify which they were. The judge summed up as follows[39]:

> 'The statutory requirement is to publish information about the policy... That does not require that every nut and bolt of what is to be done has to be spelt out in the information to be provided... It seems to me that the policy was quite adequately set out in the booklet when one adds to it the information which the booklet said was available at various places. It was open to the applicant to ask questions about the admissions and catchment areas... It does not seem to me that the applicant was underinformed or in any way misled.'

The ombudsman has investigated a case in relation to s.1 of the CSDPA, when the giving of inaccurate advice to a partially-sighted woman meant that she lost financial State benefits. One point of view put forward by the authority was that though it had a duty to direct people to relevant information sources, this did not extend to the provision of direct advice on welfare rights. Nevertheless, the ombudsman found that advice had been given, it was inaccurate, and therefore amounted to maladministration.[40]

(iii) Welfare services for disabled people: National Assistance Act 1948, s.29

The National Assistance Act 1948 (s.29) gives authorities a variety of general powers and duties to make arrangements for promoting people's welfare. It applies to people who are over 18 years of age who are blind, deaf or dumb, have a mental disorder, or are 'substantially and permanently handicapped by illness, injury or congenital deformity or such other disability as may be prescribed'.

Section 2 of the CSDPA only applies at all if the authority has *functions* under s.29 of the 1948 Act. Therefore, a person who does not qualify for services under the latter cannot benefit from provision of equipment under the CSDPA.

Directions and approvals made under s.29 specify what authorities respectively have a duty to provide, and what they have a power to provide if they wish.[41] These include a general duty towards ordinary residents – and power towards other people – to provide a social work service and other advice and support. It is probable that equipment could be provided under this duty and power without reference to the CSDPA – although the explicit provisions and stronger duty under the CSDPA remain the obvious focus.

Inclusive or exclusive definition of disabilities?

Guidance issued by the Department of Health states that authorities should adopt a broadly inclusive, rather than narrowly exclusive, definition of substantial handicap.[42] During the passing of the NHS and Community Care Bill through Parliament, the government stated that community care assessment is intended to be open to a wide range of people according to need, rather than to those with a prescribed range of medical, or other, conditions.[43]

Authorities might emphasise 'substantial and permanent' disability, when trying to target their services and to limit the number of people they are required to help. For instance, they might state that it is for the NHS to provide for people whose needs are likely to last less than six months. On this basis, a social services department might refuse to provide daily living equipment for a person discharged from hospital who is recovering from a fractured femur.[44]

However, sometimes the local ombudsman intervenes when authorities have tried to justify long waiting times and priorities by reference to substantial handicap. They might argue that they have to set priorities, so as to ensure that they are at least meeting their duties towards people with severe disability. However, this stance raises at least two questions. First, it is certain that some people with appreciable, albeit not immediately life-threatening, disability can end up waiting for a long time. Second, the local ombudsman has pointed out that, in any case, it is sometimes difficult for authorities to identify the extent of a person's disability and needs *before* an assessment has taken place (see below). This could lead to a finding of maladministration on the basis that the authority was using an inadequate method to evaluate priority.[45] In fact, if those people with lower priority needs are considered not to be substantially and permanently handicapped (under s.29 of the 1948 Act), then the authority should not be considering making provision for them under s.2 of the CSDPA 1970 – since if it did so, it would be exceeding its powers under the legislation (see p.433). (In some circumstances, an authority might instead claim that those people whose needs are in fact very low priority are not substantially and permanently handicapped at all – but that provision is contemplated under s.45 of the Health Service and Public Health Act 1968 (see below), which imposes a mere power to assist older people in similar ways to the 1970 Act).

Authorities have a duty under s.29 to maintain registers of people to whom the section relates.[46] The usefulness and effectiveness of registers has long been in doubt and at most it is thought that they have functioned as planning, rather than identification, tools.[47] People's eligibility for services is not supposed to be governed by whether or not they are actually registered.[48] However, registration is necessary for visually impaired people to qualify for certain State benefits; and it might, for example, give people on council waiting lists priority.

(iv) Request for assessment: Disabled Persons (Services, Consultation, Representation) Act 1986

Section 4 of the DP(SCR)A 1986 places a duty on authorities to assess a person's needs for services under s.2. of the CSDPA 1970, if requested to so by the person or a carer. This strengthens s.2 of the CSDPA by removing a loophole – namely that authorities might attempt to evade their s.2 duties by failing to assess people at all. Clearly, if authorities did not assess people, then they would never know if people were in need. In fact, it is arguable, on principles of public law[49], that the loophole did not in fact exist; the government, too, denied its existence. Nevertheless, the passing of the Act put the matter beyond doubt.[50]

The NHS and Community Care Act 1990 (s.47) makes even this request for assessment unnecessary in some circumstances. If an authority is assessing, under the 1990 Act, a person who appears to be disabled, then the authority has an automatic duty to assess people also under the 1986 Act for CSDPA services. It also has a duty to inform the person that this is what is happening.

Department of Health practice guidance has somewhat confused matters by stating that people who are disabled (according to s.29 of the National Assistance Act 1948) should be offered a 'comprehensive assessment' under s.4 of the 1986 Act, irrespective of the level of the need presented.[51] The muddle seems to be twofold. First, although the guidance states that such comprehensive assessments are legally prescribed, a High Court judge (in *R v Gloucestershire CC, ex parte RADAR*) has commented that he could find no support in the legislation for this statement.[52] Second, the same guidance states elsewhere that most people who require community care are likely to be disabled[53]; whilst other guidance states that comprehensive assessments should be kept to a minimum.[54] This smacks of inconsistency. Whatever was intended, the local ombudsman has expressed the implications – for example, finding maladministration when an authority failed to conduct a 'full assessment' of a disabled man who had been referred to a domiciliary support service.[55]

The local ombudsman sometimes finds that authorities are failing in their duties to assess people. For example:[56]

> A woman had applied to the social services department for assistance in storing her electric wheelchair (on which she was highly dependent) to protect it from the weather and vandals. The authority's criteria were in the form of an exhaustive list, and stated that assistance could only be provided for people with a life-threatening condition, a rapidly deteriorating physical condition, or for those who could not otherwise leave hospital or residential care.
>
> Having received the woman's request for assessment, the council replied by letter that since she did not appear to meet the criteria, she would not receive a visit. This was nothing if not final – but, when asked by the ombudsman to explain this, the authority attempted to put a different gloss on it, stating that 'each case is considered on its own merits and even if not meeting the criteria could still be deemed high priority'. Unimpressed by this explanation, the ombudsman concluded that the authority was not meeting its statutory duty either to assess the woman when requested (under s.4 of the Disabled Persons (Services, Consultation and Representation) Act 1986) – or to consider providing assistance with facilities for greater safety, comfort or convenience under s.2 of the CSDPA 1970.

Under s.8 of the 1986 Act, when assessing the needs of a disabled person for welfare services, an authority also has a duty to 'have regard' to whether a carer can continue to give substantial amounts of care on a regular basis. This duty does not apply if the authority is already assessing a carer under the Carers (Recognition and Services) Act 1995 (see below). The Act seems to apply only to people already providing care; and a duty to have regard to somebody's needs imports neither the duty to assess people nor to provide for their needs.

(v) Provision of equipment and services for older people: Health Service and Public Health Act 1968

Approvals made under the Health Service and Public Health Act 1968 (s.45) give authorities, in relation to 'old people', the power, but not the duty to:

> 'provide practical assistance in the home, including assistance in the carrying out of works of adaptation or the provision of any additional facilities designed to secure greater safety, comfort or convenience.'

These words were repeated two years later in s.2 of the CSDPA 1970. It might therefore seem odd that this power under the 1968 Act has been allowed to remain in force. However, there are some circumstances in which it might be relevant. First, some older people might not qualify for provision under the CSDPA because they do not come within the definition of substantial handicap included in s.29 of the National Assistance Act 1948. Second, if an authority's power to make charges for equipment under s.2 CSDPA 1970 were to be challenged successfully (unlikely but possible, see p.177) – then, if the person in question were elderly, the authority could make the charge under the 1968 Act – under which the power to charge is quite explicit (see below). Third, if an authority chose to make provision under this Act, it would face far fewer legal obstacles when reducing or withdrawing provision of equipment services, than it would under the CSDPA 1970.

(vi) Provision of laundry equipment: NHS Act 1977

Under the NHS Act 1977, local authorities have the power (but not the duty) to provide laundry facilities for households either receiving, or eligible for, home help services provided by the authority.[57] This is a general duty owed to the local population and not to individual people.'Laundry facilities' could include equipment; so this legislation gives authorities the explicit power to provide people with, for example, washing machines or tumble driers.

(vii) Community care assessment: NHS and Community Care Act 1990, s.47

Section 47 of the NHS and Community Care Act 1990 is at the centre of community care. It places an explicit duty on social services departments to assess people who appear to be in need of community care services; and then to decide whether to provide any of those services to meet the identified needs:[58]

> 'where it appears to a local authority that any person for whom they may provide or arrange for the provision of community care services may be in need of any such services, the authority...shall carry out an assessment of his needs for those services; and...having regard to the results of that assessment, shall then decide whether his needs call for the provision by them of any such services.'

As already explained immediately above, the Act also places a separate duty on authorities if, during a general community care assessment, the person being assessed appears to be disabled. In that situation, the authority also has to assess the person for services, including equipment, under s.2 of the CSDPA:[59]

> 'If at any time during the assessment of the needs of any person under subsection (1)(a) above it appears to a local authority that he is a disabled person, the authority- (a) shall proceed to make such a decision as to the services he requires as mentioned in section 4 of the Disabled Persons (Services, Consultation and Representation) Act 1986 without his requesting them to do so under that section; and (b) shall inform him that they will be doing so and of his rights under that Act.'

Although the CSDPA remains a sharp focus for equipment provision, the 1990 Act has had far-reaching effects on the activities of social services departments – and to some extent assessment under the 1986 and 1970 Acts seem to have become subsumed under general community care procedures. A number of themes run through the community care guidance issued by the Department of Health. These include joint working between authorities, planning and assessment of the needs of the local population, publication of community care plans, making of priorities, determining different levels of assessment, imposing criteria of eligibility, user empowerment and participation in planning and assessment, complaints – and so on.[60] All of these apply to community care in general, but equally to equipment provision in particular. This book cannot deal with these themes in depth; this section concentrates on *assessment.*

Community care services

It is important to bear in mind that the 1990 Act does not itself create 'community care services'. Instead, they are defined with reference to legislation existing previously:

- National Assistance Act 1948 (ss. 21 and 29: residential and nursing home care, and welfare services)
- Health Service and Public Health Act 1968 (s.45: services for older people, including equipment)
- NHS Act 1977 (s.21 and Schedule 8: laundry and home help facilities)
- Mental Health Act 1983, s.117.

The CSDPA 1970 is not defined explicitly as a community care service. The question therefore arises as to whether, in law, provision of equipment under s.2 of the CSDPA is a community care service or not. The answer seem to be that it is a community care service if it is an integral part of s.29 of the National Assistance Act; otherwise it is not. By accident or design, the NHS and Community Care Act appears to have left the question unhelpfully open. Some years ago (*Wyatt v Hillingdon LBC*), the Court of Appeal appeared to treat s.2 of the CSDPA as governed wholly by s.29 of the 1948 Act.[61] However, a recent High Court decision apparently casts some further doubt on the relationship between the two Acts[62]; and a comment made by the Court of Appeal in 1996 also suggests that s.2 of the 1970 Act is not to be regarded as part of the community care regime.[63]

In practice, government guidance and advice assumes consistently that provision of equipment under s.2 of the CSDPA 1970 is community care provision.[64] The practice of local authorities seems to assume the same, since assessment and provision of equipment takes place within the community care framework. In fact, there has hitherto been little evidence that authorities make a distinction between assessment under the 1990 Act and under the 1970 Act – even though, by law, authorities are meant to inform people that they are being assessed under s.4 of the Disabled Persons (Services, Consultation and Representation) Act 1986 for s.2 (of the 1970 Act) services.[65] Whatever the correct position, the question is not pointless. If services and equipment provided under s.2 of the CSDPA are not, in law, community care services, then there is no power to make charges for those services and equipment (see below).

In any event, long before the advent of mainstream community care legislation, authorities had in fact been applying priorities and criteria of eligibility to assessment for, and provision of, equipment and adaptations.[66] Evidence of this is provided by the large number of investigations made over the years by the local ombudsman into the priorities, criteria of eligibility and waiting times. To some extent, this state of affairs foreshadowed and rehearsed the more organised and formal rationing of community care now occurring.

Community care assessments

The NHS and Community Care Act 1990 puts in place an assessment regime with remarkable brevity. The detail is left to policy guidance and practice guidance issued by the Department of Health.[67]

The legislation itself states that authorities must assess any individual person who appears to be in need of community care services. Having carried out the assessment of those needs, they must then decide whether the needs call for the provision of services. Social services departments also have a duty to request the local NHS or housing authority to assist in the assessment. The fact that neither has a duty to accept the invitation significantly weakens the community care legal framework and fails to reflect the importance attached by policy guidance to cooperation between different types of authority.[68]

A detailed analysis of community care guidance is not appropriate here – although is available elsewhere.[69] Nevertheless, there are a few particular points to note. First, community care *policy guidance* states that the preferred aim of community care is to provide support, including disability equipment and adaptations, for people in their own homes.[70] Second, the *practice guidance* lays great weight on what amounts to a potentially daunting series of hurdles for people to jump before being entitled to services. For example, by using priorities, levels of assessment and criteria of eligibility, authorities are asked to control who will be assessed, how quickly they will be assessed, what sort of assessment they will get, whether they will qualify for services – and, if they do qualify, which services will be provided, at what level and how promptly.

Third, community care policy guidance emphasises that assessment should be 'needs-led'; ie that people's needs should be assessed separately from considerations about service provision.[71] This is to try to ensure that people receive services that reflect their assessed needs, rather than have the assessment of their needs determined by what type of services happen to be available locally. Praiseworthy in principle, the 'needs-led' approach has proved very much more difficult to put into practice for a number of reasons. One obvious one is that authorities have limited resources, and are fearful that if they acknowledge people's needs, they will incur legal obligations, notwithstanding the lack of money. Thus, in practice, whatever people's needs, authorities tend, for example, to set a weekly limit on the costs of providing home care services.[72] Alternatively, authorities might simply raise the threshold of eligibility from time to time, enabling the reduction, withdrawal – or withholding in the first place – of equipment and services.

(viii) Safeguarding and promotion of the welfare of children in need: Children Act 1989

Various provisions of the Children Act 1989 have a bearing on equipment provision for disabled children.

First, s.17 states that authorities have a general duty to 'safeguard and promote the welfare of children within their area who are in need...by providing a range and level of services appropriate to those children's needs'. This duty is a general one towards children in need amongst the local population. It can be contrasted with the stronger duties towards *individuals* contained in some other welfare legislation, such as s.2 of the CSDPA and s.47 of the NHSCCA 1990 covering equipment provision (amongst other services) and community care assessments respectively.

Second, although community care services do not generally apply to children, s.2 of the CSDPA does.[73] The Children Act 1989 states that when assessing children in need, authorities can at the same time make an assessment under the CSDPA 1970.[74] Thus, authorities have potential duties towards individual children to meet their needs for equipment and adaptations.

Third, under the Children Act 1989, authorities have a duty to 'minimise the effect on disabled children within their area of their disabilities' and to 'give such children the opportunity to lead lives which are as normal as possible'.[75] And if a local authority is providing accommodation for a disabled child (eg by placing the child with a family, a relative or in an institutional home) then it has a duty to ensure (so far as 'reasonably practicable') that the accommodation is suitable for the individual child's particular needs.[76] Both of these duties, the one general, the other towards individual children, can quite clearly have implications in respect of equipment and adaptations.

Finally, authorities also have general duties concerning the identification of local needs, the keeping of registers, and the publication of information about their own and other services (eg those of voluntary and other statutory bodies).[77] These duties run parallel with those that authorities have in respect of adults under the CSDPA 1970 and the National Assistance Act 1948 (see above).

(ix) Assessment of carers: Carers (Recognition and Services) Act 1995

The Carers (Recognition and Services) Act 1995 places a duty on authorities, when assessing an adult person's needs for community care services, to assess (if requested) also the ability of a carer to provide or continue to provide a 'substantial amount of care on a regular basis'. Having done so, the authority must then take into account the assessment of the carer when deciding whether the other person's needs warrant the provision of services. This duty appears to apply both to carers who have already been caring and those who are about to start. There is no definition of substantial and reasonable care; thus, as Department of Health policy guidance makes clear, not all carers will qualify for an assessment, – and it is for authorities to supply their own definitions.[78]

There is no subsequent duty to provide services directly for carers – but merely to take into account the carer when deciding what services or equipment the person being cared for should receive. However, if it appears to local authorities that carers have community care needs of their own, then the carers themselves should also receive community care assessments.[79]

The same duty applies when an authority is assessing a child under either Part 3 of the Children Act 1989 or s.2 of the CSDPA 1970. The 1995 Act applies to young carers (ie children) as well as adults. Any young carers who are themselves deemed to be 'children in need' under the Children Act 1989, might qualify in their own right for services under that Act.[80]

The Act came into force on the 1st April 1996 and is clearly relevant to equipment. For instance, provision of a stairlift and other lifting equipment (such as a hoist) can remove the daily risk of injury to family members who carry a person up and down the stairs every day, and get him in and out of bed. Thus the local ombudsman has investigated the plight of family where a man with motor neurone disease had to be carried up and down the stairs by his 15-year-old son, 76-year-old mother or 11-year-old daughters.[81] Like so much of the legislation, policy and practice described in this book, the Act might have resulted from various motives. For example, it has the potential not only to alleviate the plight of many carers – but also to save public money being spent (eg on residential care), since it has been suggested that the value of informal care to the economy is about £34 billion a year.[82]

(x) Provision of adequate staff: Local Authority Social Services Act 1970, s. 6

Under s.6 of the Local Authority Social Services Act (LASSA) 1970, local authorities have a duty to ensure that directors of social services departments have adequate staff to assist them in their functions. Challenging an authority's performance of such a general duty is difficult, precisely because of the vagueness and the 'imperfect obligation' created. However, if sufficient and relevant evidence is obtained, it might be possible to argue a case – for example if Social Services Committee minutes show continual but unsuccessful requests for adequate staffing levels.[83]

One of the enduring excuses pleaded by social services departments for the long waiting lists that exist for assessment for equipment and adaptations, is the shortage of qualified staff (ie occupational therapists). Sometimes referring to s.6 of LASSA, and sometimes not, the local ombudsman will not necessarily accept this excuse. For instance, he found maladministration specifically in relation to this duty – when waiting times for equipment and adaptations had long been reported to, known by, but not tackled by the social services committee of a local authority. An excerpt from the report gives the background which justified his finding that the particular complaints he was investigating:[84]

'reflect a wider failure in the delivery of the occupational therapy service in the Borough. It is apparent that delays in assessments were widespread – there is evidence of long delays being suffered by many applicants and of large backlogs of applicants awaiting assessment in all categories. As long ago as 1987 the then manager of occupational therapy was aware that even when fully staffed the service could not cope with all new or outstanding referrals, and these problems were reported to the [Social Services] Committee in January 1988 when the new posts of Occupational Therapy Assistants were created. But after the introduction of Project '90 the situation was not properly monitored, and inadequate records of numbers awaiting assessment and of waiting times were kept. It seems that decentralisation of the service and a reduction in the number of staff available for occupational therapy work led to increased backlogs, and it was not until the service was re-centralised in February 1992 that the problem began to be properly monitored, investigated and dealt with. The above failures amount to maladministration.'

(xi) Charges for equipment: Health and Social Services and Social Security Adjudication Act 1983, s.17

This Act, abbreviated to the HASSASSA 1983, gives authorities the power to make charges for services provided under specified, social services legislation.[85] This is

- s.29 of the National Assistance Act 1948: welfare services for disabled people;
- s.45 of the Health Service and Public Health Act 1968: welfare services for older people;
- s.21 and Schedule 8 of the NHS Act 1977: home help and laundry facilities.

What are the practical consequences for users of equipment? Authorities might in principle provide, and charge for, equipment under the National Assistance Act; and, similarly, under the Health Service and Public Health Act. Laundry facilities under s.21 of the NHS Act 1977 could also include equipment (eg a washing machine). Charging policies vary considerably between authorities, and are sometimes portrayed not only as a means to recoup costs, but also as a rationing tool – since people might cease to request a service or equipment, or even not request them in the first place. Furthermore, even if people do find the money, it might be at the cost of forgoing other basic household items – and cause them considerable anxiety about how they will pay perhaps higher charges in the future as their needs become greater.[86]

The Department of Health has encouraged authorities to make charges for their services, although a government White Paper stated that advice, assessment, social work support and occupational therapy cannot be charged for.[87] This position has been reiterated by other advice from the Social Services Inspectorate.[88] Sometimes the encouragement has even been in the form of veiled threats relating to the obligations of authorities to local taxpayers.[89] In response to this and to increasingly strained budgets, many authorities are introducing both new and higher charges for various services. A number of studies have reported these changes but have paid little attention to equipment

– probably because charging for it has not been widespread. Nevertheless, some authorities do charge – in the form of one-off payments or hire charges, that might or might not depend on means-testing. Sometimes the arrangement is more complex. For instance, an item of equipment might be loaned free but the user asked to pay a maintenance or service charge – for example, for maintenance of a stairlift, the weekly emptying of a chemical toilet, the fluid for a chemical commode, or an annual charge of £58 for maintenance of a special bath.[90]

There might be practical difficulties; for instance, the cost of administering a charging system can sometimes outweigh the financial benefits. An alternative is simply to suggest that people buy the equipment themselves – whether small items such as bath mats from a pharmacy, or larger, more expensive, items such as a high-seat chair.

The legislation gives authorities the power to enforce the payment of charges by taking an action for civil debt.[91] However, non-payment of charges does not appear to give authorities the power to stop provision, simply because a person is not paying.

Can authorities charge users for equipment under s.2 of the CSDPA?

Some uncertainty exists about whether authorities can make charges under section 2 of the CSDPA. The HASSASSA 1983 gives authorities explicit power to make charges under s.29 of the National Assistance Act 1948 but fails to mention the CSDPA. Consequently, if section 2 of the CSDPA is viewed as an extension and 'as part' of the 1948 Act, then charges can be made. This view is expressed by government advice.[92] However, if it is not an integral part of the 1948 Act, then there is no power to make charges (see below); this alternative view has been aired by some lawyers, but has not been tested explicitly in the courts.

Distinction between income generation and covering costs

In any event, when charges are made, they can only be made to the extent that the authority is satisfied that it is reasonably practicable for the person to pay them.[93] For those people who can afford to pay, Social Services Inspectorate advice suggests that a reasonable charge is one that takes account of the full cost of providing a service. This should include capital, managerial and other overheads directly related to provision – but not costs connected to purchasing nor to operating a system of charges.[94] However, there is a distinction between recovering the costs of a service and raising money (eg by local taxation) or generating income. Local government legislation empowering authorities to raise money[95] does not apply to charges made under the HASSASSA 1983 and authorities therefore need to distinguish between covering costs and raising money.

Charges under the Children Act 1989

Local authorities also have the power to make charges for services provided for children in need under sections 17 and 18 of the Children Act 1989 – other than for advice, guidance or counselling. The charge may be such as they consider reasonable. Charges may not be made of a person in receipt of certain benefits. The parents are charged if a child is under 16, and the child if he or she is over 16 year of age; and charges can be recovered as a civil debt.[96]

(xii) Direct payments for equipment and services.

The Community Care (Direct Payments) Act 1996 will (when in force in 1997) enable social services departments to make direct cash payments so people can buy their own services and equipment.

Debated issues have included whether authorities will be *obliged* to make such payments if requested (they will not), which groups of people will benefit (only adults between the age of 16 and 64 years, with physical, sensory or learning disabilities – or with some types of mental or other illness), whether payments will cover the full costs of employing carers (eg national insurance, statutory sick pay), whether payment can be made to close relatives as carers (they will not be), whether maintenance costs of equipment will be covered, how often payments can be made to replace worn equipment – and so on.[97]

The Secretary of State will have the power to make regulations in order to implement the detail of the basic scheme imposed by the Act.

3. COMPLAINTS

Complaints procedures of social services departments

Under s.7 of the LASSA 1970, and associated regulations and directions made under it, authorities have a duty to establish and operate complaints procedures in relation to their social services functions for adults.[98] The complaints procedure must be coordinated by a named officer and include *informal*, *formal* and *review* stages. Time limits are prescribed, and written responses and notifications of decisions are obligatory at various stages of the procedure. At the review stage, the panel must contain an independent person.

In relation to children's services, s.26 of the Children Act 1989 places a duty on authorities to set up complaints procedures. Complainants can include children, parents, people with parental responsibility and anybody else the authority thinks has sufficient interest.[99] Children's complaints procedures are described by Department of Health guidance as 'broadly compatible' with adult procedures – thus allowing common administrative structures for both.[100] One significant difference between adult and children's procedures is that in the case of the latter, an independent person must be involved from the start.[101] Sometimes it is uncertain which procedure is the most appropriate to use – and, for example, the ombudsman might find maladministration if an authority has no policy to guide staff on this.[102]

Complaints in practice

The complaints procedure is likely to be seen by the courts as the first and preferable means of solving complaints – and they might be unwilling, for example, to carry out judicial review of authorities if complaints procedures exist – or at least have not been used first.

In the main, it might be advantageous for people to use complaints procedures, since this will normally be easier than going through the courts. However, complaints procedures need to be of good quality if people are to be encouraged to rely on them. The solutions on offer too, might determine whether people's complaints can be resolved satisfactorily; for example, in many cases, people might simply want explanation, apology or rectification of the fault. Complaints procedures should normally be able to offer these solutions. But if people want and need financial compensation, then the procedures might be inadequate, since Department of Health guidance states that such compensation will not generally be the objective.[103]

In terms of practice, there is evidence that formal complaints by adults are not always resolved within the statutory timescales (normally 28 days, otherwise three months maximum).[104] Failure to adhere to such timescales might result in findings of maladministration by the local ombudsman.[105] In addition, there is no statutory timescale stipulated for informal complaints, and so considerable delay is possible even before the formal stage is reached. Considerable confusion about how to categorise and record informal complaints is reported.[106] One way around this problem would be for complainants to omit the informal stage altogether – a possibility envisaged by policy guidance in special cases.[107]

Some disquiet and uncertainty surrounds the scope of the investigations of review panels at the final stage of the complaints procedure – and the effect of recommendations they make to local authorities.[108] First, it is unclear whether review panels can question only the procedures local authorities have followed in reaching their decision – or whether they can question the overall merits of decisions as well by considering again all aspects of the case from scratch.[109] On this question, a report by the Social Services Inspectorate suggests that the implications of Department of Health guidance are that the role of panels should be broader, rather than narrower.[110] Second, it is unclear to what extent authorities must follow the recommendations of review panels. One court case suggested that authorities should basically follow them (*R v Avon CC, ex parte M*)[111], another that there was no such rule (*R v North Yorkshire CC, ex parte Hargreaves*).[112] However, in a third case in early 1996, the judge stated that although an authority's failure to comply with the recommendations was not itself unlawful, the greater the departure, the greater the need for cogent, articulated reasons to be given for non-compliance (*R v Islington LBC, ex parte Rixon*).[113] And, the local ombudsman, investigating the loss of State benefits incurred by a partially-sighted woman following inaccurate advice from a local authority, criticised the adequacy of a review panel's recommendations. He recommended additional compensation of £4,220 (reflecting the value of the lost benefits), as opposed to the £750 suggested by the review panel.[114]

Sometimes staff might be insufficiently trained or impartial in their approach to complaints[115] – and it is only the final (review panel) stage of social services complaints procedures for adults which requires the participation of an independent person. And even the involvement of an independent person might not be decisive; for example, they might disagree with the final decision of the Panel – but not be able to overturn the decision.[116]

Default powers of the Secretary of State

In addition to the complaints procedure, s.7D of the LASSA also provides for *default powers* which can, if necessary, be enforced by a court of law. The Secretary of State can make an order declaring that an authority has not complied with its duty. The order can also contain directions to ensure that the duty is complied with. However, the Secretary of State can only exercise these default powers if a local authority has failed to do its duty 'without reasonable excuse'. If necessary, the Secretary of State can enforce such an order by a court order.

In practice, although the Department of Health sometimes informally investigates complaints with a view to applying the default powers, they have apparently never been formally used – either under s.7 of the LASSA 1970, or in their former guise under s.36 of the National Assistance Act 1948. Similar default powers are given, in s.84 of the Children Act 1989, to the Secretary of State in relation to children's services.

The non-use of these default powers has, on occasion, been challenged, albeit unsuccessfully – for example, through the High Court and through the Parliamentary ombudsman. In the first instance, a case (*R v DHSS, ex parte Bruce*) was brought in the law courts against the Department of Health and Social Security for failing to use its powers against an authority that had not assessed a person's need for assistance with a holiday under s.2 of the CSDPA.[117] In the second, a complaint was made to the Parliamentary ombudsman when the DHSS responded particularly slowly in deciding whether to employ its default powers – in relation to an authority which had withdrawn assistance for holidays, again under s.2 of the CSDPA. Although he found slowness and elements of maladministration, the ombudsman found no absolute failure to act. In the event, the DHSS was not forced to decide whether to take action, because the authority restored the assistance.[118]

Community care charters

Apart from the statutory complaints procedure explained above, social services departments will, from April 1996, be operating local community care charters. The role of charters has already been discussed in relation to the NHS (see p.145), but unlike the Patient's Charter, community care charters will not be national and so will set diverse standards. A framework document produced by the Department of Health asks that charters should contain specific standards to be 'as tightly defined as possible'.[119]

The framework document specifically mentions equipment and adaptations and suggests that standards should be set so as to apply to the time between completion of assessment and delivery – and to reliability, repair and replacement. There should also be 'specific standards' applying to the assessment process from first referral to first response, from that response to the beginning of the assessment and from there to completion of the assessment.[120]

One problem facing authorities is to find a way a middle way between filling their charters with excessive detail and filling them with vague statements. In the first case, they risk inflexibility and will be inviting complaints when people point out that the reality does not correspond with the theoretical detail. Equally, vague statements will mean little to service users and might also result in actual, or at least apparent, arbitrary and inequitable provision of services.[121] One partial solution suggested by the Department of Health is to couch standards in terms of 'normal performance' – for example, 90% of letters to be answered within 10 working days. It is also suggested that some standards, especially those relating to the provision of specific services, should be 'selective'.[122]

The Department of Health's framework document states what should happen if things go wrong: they should be put right, full explanations and apologies be given and lessons learnt. In addition, people's rights to make representations and complaints to the social services department and to the ombudsmen should be explained. Nevertheless, the language of the framework document is, inevitably, cautious. It states repeatedly that people should be 'entitled to expect' certain standards of service. This seems to suggest that entitlement is to the expectation only – not to actual services themselves.

Local ombudsman

The local ombudsmen have investigated many cases of alleged maladministration in relation to equipment and home adaptations. A number of examples are given throughout this chapter, whilst the powers and remit of the local ombudsmen are summarised in Chapter 5.

4. OPERATION OF PRIORITIES, CRITERIA OF ELIGIBILITY AND WAITING TIMES FOR EQUIPMENT

A practical method of easing the duty imposed by s.2 the CSDPA is for authorities to operate priorities, criteria of eligibility and waiting lists. Community care practice guidance has emphasised the importance of such devices in the context of community care in general.[123] In fact, Circular guidance issued in 1970 about the CSDPA advised authorities to determine eligibility criteria (ie who qualifies for services) in the light of resources[124]; and for many years before the implementation of the NHS and Community Care Act 1990, authorities regulated access to equipment and adaptations by such means. Thus, the balancing of needs against resources is nothing new.

Although the law courts have in the past rarely ventured into this area (but this pattern is now altering with the advent of community care), the local ombudsmen have done so many times. Their investigations are instructive and illustrate well the practical difficulties facing both local authorities and the people who need equipment.

Waiting lists and priorities

For many years, problems have afflicted assessment and provision of equipment and adaptations under s.2 of the CSDPA. The most common of these has probably been the excessive delay in assessing people – waiting times have been measured not only in months but in years.[125] Plainly expressed, waiting times can span one day, 730 days – or be 'infinite'.[126] Detrimental consequences can follow, not only for individual people who are in need, but arguably also for statutory services. If people's needs for equipment and adaptations are not met reasonably promptly because they are deemed to be of low priority, then people's ability to cope is reduced. The subsequent costs to statutory services, in terms of high levels of home support services, hospital stays or residential care might be far greater than the cost of timely intervention.[127]

Nevertheless, as emphasised in Chapter 1, good practice can be found as well as bad. For instance, a particular local authority might deal with 99% of referrals for equipment or adaptations in six weeks, have an average waiting time per person of 1.2 weeks and a target time (mostly achieved) for the delivery of equipment of two weeks from the date of order.[128] And, even though there might be long waiting times for the supply of equipment such as stairlifts or electric riser chairs, even after assessment (someone might have to die before one becomes free) – overall, delivery times might look respectable. For example, the Audit Commission's latest performance indicators show that about 80% of small items of equipment is provided within three weeks of being ordered.[129]

The local ombudsmen, who have investigated many cases of delay, generally accept that priorities have to be made. However, they will find maladministration if, for example, priorities and eligibility criteria have been applied unfairly, if they have not been publicised properly, or if people have been inadequately informed about what is happening to their applications. Nor will the ombudsmen necessarily accept the excuse, often pleaded, that the authority is short of occupational therapists. The following summaries are a few examples of ombudsman investigations.

A woman who lived with her mentally and physically handicapped daughter approached the local authority for assistance with home adaptations in December 1991. The mother could not carry her daughter up the stairs – and the daughter's condition was deteriorating. In July 1992 she was visited, a ramp was ordered and she was advised to apply for a disabled facilities grant – which she did in September 1992. The ombudsman accepted that a subsequent wait of 14 months for the assessment for the grant was reasonable, since the authority had applied its 'category 3' criteria properly. However, maladministration did occur, because the authority regarded the date of her request for help from September 1992 instead of the earlier date of December 1991; this caused extra delay.[130]

Nevertheless, it is clear that long waiting times alone will not necessarily constitute maladministration – though the language of the ombudsmen often makes it clear that they are weighing up each case carefully. When faced with an authority's contention that the duty to provide assistance under s.2 of the CSDPA 1970 is an obligation which does not have to be carried out immediately – and that 'some delay is acceptable' – the ombudsman noted that 'whether or not any particular delay is so excessive as to constitute maladministration will depend on the facts of the individual case'.[131] Thus, in a case when the ombudsman looked at the authority's waiting list more widely, he found no maladministration. He took account of how the authority had attempted 'positively and creatively' to circumvent the national shortage of occupational therapists and the recruitment freeze – whilst reducing a waiting list, standing at 1500 in 1988, to 849 in 1992. He concluded in measured language:[132]

> 'I have given very careful consideration to this question of whether, in all the circumstances, this delay amounts to maladministration. I conclude that, given the particular resource and staffing difficulties faced by the Council, this delay is not so unreasonable as to amount to maladministration in this case.'

But, in another case, the ombudsman found it totally unacceptable that a woman should have waited for three years for an assessment – even though her needs had been categorised as low priority. She had arthritis, asthma and sciatica which made it difficult to use the bath; following a fall and hip fracture, she could no longer use it at all. Looking more generally at the authority's approach to the problem of disability assessments and waiting lists, the ombudsman found that, though long aware of the problems, the authority had done little to solve them. He had no hesitation in finding maladministration.[133] And, when a woman waited 56 months for an assessment – and, more generally, the authority had even gone so far as to close its non-urgent waiting list – the ombudsman found maladministration for 'serious failures'. He noted that the closing of the list meant that the authority might have been failing to carry out its duties – since any disabled person was entitled to request and receive an assessment (see p.169). The woman's problems had arisen following a spinal injury and were clearly not trivial:[134]

> 'As a result she experiences considerable pain when standing, sitting and walking, and has to spend most of her time lying in a horizontal position. She has been registered with the Council as a 'physically handicapped' person since January 1989. She has found it particularly difficult to use the WC independently, to take baths without assistance and to put on socks and shoes. She has been unable to

stand and wash dishes at the kitchen sink because it is positioned at an inconvenient height. She has been unable to open security locks on the doors and windows to the flat to provide a means of escape in case of fire. When she is at home alone the locks are left unbolted so that she can escape quickly in case of fire.'

Priorities and professional judgement

Priorities and eligibility criteria for equipment and adaptations will normally be drawn up and applied on the basis of the knowledge and experience of occupational therapists. For example, the guidelines on equipment provision, drawn up by the London Borough Occupational Therapy Managers Group (and probably made use of in a significant number of authorities), are the result of considerable professional expertise.[135]

Therefore, in one sense, the application of detailed priorities and criteria amounts to the deployment of professional judgement – an aspect of local authority decision-making which the local ombudsmen are not empowered to challenge. Nevertheless, sometimes they come close. In one case, the mother of a profoundly mentally and physically disabled boy had asked for a reassessment of his needs; he had outgrown the toilet and seating equipment provided previously. Provision of a toilet aid took eight months and of new seating thirteen months. The authority explained that a shortage of occupational therapists in general, and of paediatric therapists in particular, was at the root of the delay – and necessitated the priority system that had been applied. The ombudsman took the unusual step of obtaining an opinion from the College of Occupational Therapists, which expressed its alarm that the child's needs had been categorised as a low priority. He went on to conclude that the authority's system of priorities was 'over-simple', and failed to provide simple solutions in complex cases (ie to 'tide people over' until a full assessment), and to recognise urgent cases other than 'emergencies'.[136]

The ombudsman sometimes questions professional judgements in an indirect way if it is clear that they have not been made on the basis of relevant information. For instance, he found maladministration when an authority placed a man (who had suffered several strokes) in a low priority category – having paid more attention to an incomplete occupational therapy assessment and a visit made by an officer who was neither professionally nor medically qualified, than to a medical certificate from the man's general practitioner.[137]

Adopting and administering policies fairly

The ombudsman will accept that authorities can have policies on equipment, so long as they are not so rigid as to amount to a blanket policy or a 'fettering' of the authority's discretion (see p.446). Thus, applying a policy which makes the presumption that people with multiple sclerosis will not be provided with stairlifts does not amount to maladministration – if, although the lift was initially refused, the applicant was told how to appeal. She had made the point that, whereas the authority regarded multiple sclerosis as the 'falling down disease', symptoms can be very different from individual to individual and that her own prognosis was uncertain. In the event, she obtained the stairlift and used it successfully.[138] Similarly, when an authority began to ration its home help services, its policy was to reduce or remove cleaning and laundry, rather than shopping (deemed more essential), help. However, the particular complainant – a diabetic, an amputee and suffering from double incontinence – considered that he was exceptionally vulnerable to infection, and so placed great store on cleanliness and hygiene. The ombudsman, uncovering no evidence that the authority had considered his medical needs, found maladministration; he also criticised the fact that the policy of priority had not been expressly presented to members of the social services committee.[139] Equally, however, authorities should apply their policies and priorities equitably and consistently. Thus, in one case the ombudsman could well understand the complainant's anger that had she lived a few hundred yards away, so as to fall within the area of another team (within the same borough), she might have waited only five months instead of four years and eight months.[140]

In another investigation, the ombudsman made a finding of maladministration because although the complainant's needs had been correctly categorised according to the authority's policy, five other people (in a sample of 45) had been incorrectly given priority ahead of the complainant – even though the occupational therapists had, on the face of it, 'good' reasons for doing this. For instance, incorrect priority might have been given to one person because of the OTs' 'soft-hearted' response to a comment on the application form, which referred to 'living on borrowed time'. In another, it was given out of fear that the escalating epileptic fits reported by the woman would make her more vulnerable. And, in a third, two sisters might have been given priority because they lived together, both had needs and one had made previous requests. The fact that the ombudsman found maladministration shows what an onerous task confronts occupational therapists. In this case their 'fault' appeared to arise from the sympathy they showed to individual people in need, and their failure to act as inflexible administrators. This is emphasised also by noting the condition of the people who were wrongly given priority – and who would otherwise have been due to wait 15 months. For example, one of the sisters had Crohn's Disease, arthritis, trouble with her back and knees and was unable to bathe. The other sister reported osteo-arthritis in the spine, hips and knees, had been unable to bathe for several years, and only had a strip wash if helped to wash her back. And the person living on borrowed time reported asthma, emphysema, osteo-arthritis – and difficulty in breathing, and managing steps or stairs.[141]

Indeed, not only will the ombudsman acknowledge the importance of priority systems, but also criticise their absence – since without them, authorities will be unable to ensure that those in most need receive assistance more quickly. Thus, failure to respond promptly to budgetary shortfalls by applying priorities resulted in delay in providing a stairlift – during which time, the disabled woman (with chronic asthma, bronchitis, emphysema and severe arthritis in the hands and spine) fell down the stairs and was admitted to hospital. The ombudsman found maladministration not only on account of the delay, but also because the family had not been informed adequately about was happening.[142] And, it is not enough that an authority has a bare waiting list system – the ombudsman has found maladministration when insufficient information was gathered at an early stage, preventing the authority from identifying the urgency with which it should intervene. This happened in the case of a woman who had suffered several strokes, used a wheelchair frequently and could not use a bath at all, and who, after two years, had still not been assessed.[143]

Staff shortages

Sometimes the ombudsman will accept staff shortages as an excuse for delay in assessment. For instance, when a woman with arthritis and a lump on her spine (causing pain and limiting her mobility) applied for a renovation grant, a period of some 10 months elapsed from her first approach to final approval of the grant (a disabled facilities grant, as it turned out). Given the difficulty the authority was experiencing in recruiting and deploying occupational therapists, the ombudsman accepted that it had to make judgements and priorities on the basis of the need. Thus, the time taken was not unreasonable and there was no maladministration.[144] And if an authority has clearly made considerable efforts – by, for example, offering recruitment and retention packages, seconding an NHS therapist, setting up an assessment clinic, and appointing both temporary and permanent staff – the ombudsman might not find maladministration.[145] In another case, an elderly woman, confined to a wheelchair, waited seven months for assessment; the ombudsman stated that this was unacceptable, pointing out that if 'such expertise is not available councils need to find an alternative way of meeting their statutory responsibilities'. Subsequently, the council did increase its staffing levels by means of temporary and part-time contracts.[146] However, any alternatives must be appropriate; for example, the ombudsman will not condone social services departments that allow assessments for adaptations to be undertaken by unqualified staff of independent agencies – a situation arising because at the relevant time the occupational therapy assistant of the authority was not supported or advised by any occupational therapists and because the authority had rejecting using NHS therapists as too expensive an option.[147]

Although the ombudsman mostly investigates delay in assessment, sometimes the delay in provision of equipment or adaptations follows the assessment. For instance, the ombudsman has found maladministration when a ramp was provided 16 months after its provision was agreed, and the authority could give no reasons for the delay. As a result, the applicant, a wheelchair user, was denied safe and convenient access to his property.[148]

Innovative solutions?

Some authorities attempt to improve provision by reorganising service structures, introducing fast-track assessment and sometimes self-assessment procedures.[149] This last might involve people assessing themselves and selecting their own equipment from the local authority store. Legal concerns (eg about negligence litigation) are assuaged by limiting the type of equipment available in this way to products with minimal safety implications – for example, reaching sticks rather than bath boards. Where service users literally visit a 'drop-in' centre and walk out carrying small items of equipment – without having been formally assessed – it is arguable that, strictly speaking, legislation is not being adhered to. This is because, as already explained, under the legislation it is for authorities to decide what individual people need – not for those people themselves (see p.46). However, since self-assessment seems to be a common-sense arrangement, few people are likely to challenge it. Nevertheless, objections could conceivably be raised by service users if they felt that the procedure was being used to deflect, rather than to meet, their needs. It is also possible that a disgruntled local taxpayer might argue that resources were being used unlawfully.

Alternatively, following assessment, people are sometimes advised to buy their own equipment. Authorities might find this option attractive, although practice apparently varies. Some authorities ask people to buy smaller items of equipment, others might ask them to buy the larger, more expensive items as well. Up to 75% of the equipment loaned by local authorities might consist of small, cheaper items. This means that some people at least can afford them. On the other hand, if such small items only represent 25% of the total of the authority's expenditure on equipment, then the scope for savings, on small items alone, is obviously limited.[150] Having made an assessment, authorities might not make an outright refusal to provide equipment – for example, a stairlift – but point out that a long waiting list exists, and that the person might like to consider buying it instead. Alternatively, some people, dismayed at the length of local waiting lists, might pay for their own equipment and adaptations anyway – sometimes hoping (usually in vain) that the authority will reimburse them.[151]

Some authorities, in order to improve efficiency and effectiveness, contract out their whole equipment services to private companies. Typically, the contractor takes on delivery, maintenance, collection and recycling. These can be classed as *operational* activities. There has been some controversy about such contracts, in relation to the law of fair trading (ie where the contracted supplier is also a manufacturer and thus tempted to favour its own products).[152] The assessment process itself is sometimes contracted out also, either to private companies or to independent occupational therapists. For example, the latter might be brought in to reduce, within an 18-month period, a waiting list of five years to one.[153] Authorities need to be sure to retain the ultimate decision-making responsibility about people's needs – since assessment and the decision about what services people need are explicit statutory functions imposed on authorities by s.2 of the CSDPA 1970, s.4 of the Disabled Persons (SCR) Act 1986, and s.47 of the NHS and Community Care Act 1990.

Notes

1 For a summary of its history, successes and failures, see: Darnborough, A.; Kinrade, D. (1995). *Be it enacted...25 years of the Chronically Sick and Disabled Persons Act 1970.* London: Royal Association for Disability and Rehabilitation.

2 See the view put forward in the joint Circular: DHSS 12/70; DES 13/70; MHLG 65/70; ROADS 20/70. Department of Health and Social Security; Department of Education and Science; Ministry of Housing and Local Government; Ministry of Transport. *The Chronically Sick and Disabled Persons Act 1970.* London: DHSS, DES, MHLG, MoT, 1970, para 7. The view that a binding duty arises under s.2 of the CSDPA was reiterated forcibly in: CI(92)34. Social Services Inspectorate. *Implementing caring for people: assessment.* London: Department of Health, 1992 (now formally cancelled).

3 See eg Schwehr, B. (1995). The legal relevance of resources – or a lack of resources – in community care. *Journal of Social Welfare and Family Law:* 1995; 17(2), pp.179–198.

4 *R v Gloucestershire County Council, ex parte Mahfood and Others, R v Islington London Borough Council, ex parte McMillan* (1996) 160 LGRevR 321 (QBD).

5 *R v Gloucestershire County Council, ex parte Barry; R v Lancashire County Council, ex parte Gilpin and RADAR* (1996) (CA) (7–10 May 1996, CO/95/1779, CO/95/1134, transcript).

6 *R v Lancashire County Council, ex parte Ingham and Whalley* (1995) (QBD) (5 July 1995, CO/774/95, CO/108/95, transcript).

7 Alf Morris (1995: letter). Home care denied to the disabled. *The Times:* 24 October 1995.

8 *R v Gloucestershire County Council, ex parte Royal Association for Disability and Rehabilitation* (1995) (QBD) (21st December 1995, CO/2764/95, transcript).

9 Judicial review follows refusal. *Community Care:* 1–7 February 1996; 1104, p.1.

10 Commission for Local Administration in England (94/C/0399). *Report on investigation into a complaint against Salford City Council.* York: CLAE, 1996.

11 *R v Gloucestershire County Council, ex parte Mahfood and Others, R v Islington London Borough Council, ex parte McMillan* (1996) 160 LGRevR 321 (QBD).

12 *R v Gloucestershire County Council, ex parte Barry; R v Lancashire County Council, ex parte Gilpin and RADAR* (1996) (CA) (7–10 May 1996, CO/95/1779, CO/95/1134, transcript).

13 *R v Gloucestershire County Council, ex parte Barry; R v Lancashire County Council, ex parte Gilpin and RADAR* (1996) (CA) (7–10 May 1996, CO/95/1779, CO/95/1134, transcript).

14 LAC(93)7. Department of Health. *Ordinary residence.* London: DH.

15 See eg the comments of Sir Thomas Bingham MR and Peter Gibson LJ about the subjectivity of terms such as 'satisfied', 'appears', 'general duty', 'reasonable steps' etc in *M (a minor) v Newham London Borough Council, X and others (minors) v Bedfordshire County Council* [1994] 4 All ER 602 (CA).

16 *R v Gloucestershire County Council, ex parte Mahfood and Others, R v Islington London Borough Council, ex parte McMillan* (1996) 160 LGRevR 321 (QBD).

17 Social Services Inspectorate, Department of Health; Social Work Services Group, Scottish Office (1991). *Care management and assessment: practitioners' guide.* London: HMSO, p.53.

18 *R v Department of Health and Social Security and Others, ex parte Bruce* (1986) (QBD), The Times, 8 February 1986 (and see LEXIS, 5 February 1986).

19 *Hansard,* House of Commons, Oral Answers, 5th August 1975, cols 219–220, Barbara Castle.

20 *Hansard,* House of Commons, Written Answers, 31 January 1985, col 294, Prime Minister.

21 CI(92)34. Social Services Inspectorate. *Implementing caring for people: assessment.* London: Department of Health, 1992, para 24 (now formally cancelled).

22 DHSS 12/70; DES 13/70; MHLG 65/70; ROADS 20/70. Department of Health and Social Security; Department of Education and Science; Ministry of Housing and Local Government;

Ministry of Transport. *The Chronically Sick and Disabled Persons Act 1970.* London: DHSS, DES, MHLG, MoT, 1970, para 7.

23 *R v Gloucestershire County Council, ex parte Barry; R v Lancashire County Council, ex parte Gilpin and RADAR* (1996) (CA) (7–10 May 1996, CO/95/1779, CO/95/1134, transcript).

24 One option envisaged by the Audit Commission in relation to community care generally: *Taking care: progress with care in the community.* London: Audit Commission, 1993, p.5.

25 Salvage, A. (1996). *Stuck on the waiting list: older people and equipment for independent living.* London: Age Concern England, pp.14–15.

26 Commission for Local Administration in England (94/C/1027). *Report on investigation into a complaint against the Humberside County Council.* York: CLAE, 1995, pp.10–11.

27 *R v Hillingdon London Borough Council, ex parte Pulhofer* [1986] 1 AC 484 (HL).

28 DoE 10/90; LAC(90)7. Department of Environment. *House adaptations for people with disabilities.* London: DoE, 1990, paras 15–16.

29 Commission for Local Administration in England (91/C/0565 & 92/C/1400). *Report on investigation into a complaint against North Yorkshire County Council & Harrogate Borough Council.* York: CLAE, 1993.

30 Eg Social Services Inspectorate (Cope, C.; Watson, A.) (1996). *Inspection of community services for physically disabled people in Wirral.* London: Department of Health, p.28.

31 (News item). Leicestershire defends its decision on padded 'coffin'. *Local Government Chronicle:* 23 February 1996, p.6.

32 Commission for Local Administration in England (91/A/0482). *Report on investigation against the London Borough of Hackney.* London: CLAE, 1993.

33 *R v London Borough of Ealing, ex parte Leaman* (1984) (QBD), The Times, 10 February 1984 (and see LEXIS, 6 February 1984)

34 See eg: London Borough Occupational Therapy Managers' Group (1992). *Occupational therapists' criteria for the loan of equipment to people with disabilities.* London: LBOTMG, p.22.

35 Association of County Councils; Association of Metropolitan Authorities (1971). *Chronically Sick and Disabled Persons Act 1970: provision of telephones as amended by ACC/AMA letter 20/4/72.* London: ACC; AMA.

36 SW7/1972. Social Work Services Group. *Telephones for severely disabled persons living alone.* Edinburgh: Social Work Services Group, 1972. And: HSS(OS5A)5/78. Department of Health and Social Services. *Telephones for the handicapped and elderly.* Belfast: DHSS, 1978.

37 HSS(PH)5/79. Department of Health and Social Services. *Help with television.* Belfast: DHSS.

38 HSS(OS5A)4/76. Department of Health and Social Services. Belfast: DHSS.

39 *R v Bradford Metropolitan Borough Council, ex parte Sikander Ali* [1994] ELR 299 (QBD).

40 Commission for Local Administration in England (93/A/3738). *Report on investigation into a complaint against East Sussex County Council.* London: CLAE, 1995, pp.12–15.

41 *Secretary of State's Directions and Approvals under section 29(1) of the National Assistance Act 1948* (attached to LAC(93)10).

42 LAC(93)10. Department of Health. *Approvals and directions for arrangements from 1 April 1993 made under schedule 8 to the National Health Service Act 1977 and sections 21 and 29 of the National Assistance Act 1948.* London: DH, Appendix 4. This appendix updates, with little change, previous Circular guidance.

43 *Hansard,* House of Lords, 10 May 1990, cols 1590–1591, Baroness Hooper.

44 Salvage, A. (1996). *Stuck on the waiting list: older people and equipment for independent living.* London: Age Concern England, p.32.

45 Commission for Local Administration (92/C/0670). *Report on investigation into a complaint against Bolton Metropolitan Borough Council.* York: CLAE, p.7.

46 LAC(93)10. Department of Health. *Approvals and directions for arrangements from 1 April 1993 made under schedule 8 to the National Health Service Act 1977 and sections 21 and 29 of the National Assistance Act 1948.* London: DH, Appendix 2.

47 Toplis, E.; Gould, B. (1981). *A charter for the disabled.* Oxford, Blackwell, p.100.

48 LAC(93)10. Department of Health. *Approvals and directions for arrangements from 1 April 1993 made under schedule 8 to the National Health Service Act 1977 and sections 21 and 29 of the National Assistance Act 1948.* London: DH, Appendix 4.

49 Eg not to have assessed people would have frustrated the purpose of the Act – which was to decide whether people needed services and, if so, to provide them: see generally: Fordham, M. (1994). *Judicial review handbook.* Chichester: Wiley, pp.240–246, 309.

50 See explanation in: LAC(87)6. Department of Health and Social Security. *Disabled Persons (Services, Consultation and Representation) Act 1986: implementation of sections 4, 8(1), 9 & 10.* London: DHSS, 1987, para 3.

51 Social Services Inspectorate, Department of Health; Social Work Services Group, Scottish Office (1991). *Care management and assessment: practitioners' guide.* London: HMSO, p.43.

52 *R v Gloucestershire County Council, ex parte Royal Association for Disability and Rehabilitation* (1995) (QBD) (21st December 1995, CO/2764/95, transcript).

53 Social Services Inspectorate, Department of Health; Social Work Services Group, Scottish Office (1991). *Care management and assessment: practitioners' guide.* London: HMSO, p.44.

54 CI(92)34. Social Services Inspectorate. *Implementing caring for people: assessment.* London: Department of Health, 1992, para 9 (now formally cancelled).

55 Commission for Local Administration in England (93/A/4250). *Report on investigation into a complaint against Westminster City Council.* London: CLAE, 1996, p.17.

56 Commission for Local Administration in England (93/C/1609). *Report on investigation into a complaint against Sheffield City Council.* York: CLAE, 1995, p.8.

57 *NHS Act 1977,* s.21, Schedule 8.

58 *NHS and Community Care Act 1990,* s.47(1).

59 *NHS and Community Care Act 1990,* s.47(2).

60 Social Services Inspectorate, Department of Health; Social Work Services Group, Scottish Office (1991):

Care management and assessment: practitioners' guide. London: HMSO.

Care management and assessment: managers' guide. London: HMSO.

61 *Wyatt v Hillingdon London Borough Council* (1978) 76 LGR 727 (CA): where it was held that the 1948 Act governed complaints and appeal procedures in relation to s.2 of the CSDPA.

62 *R v Gloucestershire County Council, ex parte Mahfood and Others, R v Islington London Borough Council, ex parte McMillan* (1995) (QBD), Times Law Reports, 21 June 1995 (see transcript for this point, which relates to the implications of subsection 29(6) in relation to home help provided under the NHS Act 1977, schedule 8 and the under the CSDPA).

63 *R v Gloucestershire County Council, ex parte Barry; R v Lancashire County Council, ex parte Gilpin and RADAR* (1996) (CA) (7–10 May 1996, CO/95/1779, CO/95/1134, transcript).

64 See detailed analysis in: Mandelstam, M. (1995). *Community care practice and the law.* London: Jessica Kingsley, pp.189–192.

65 *NHS and Community Care Act 1990,* s.47.

66 See eg appendices 2 and 3 of the following book, detailing examples of priorities and criteria obtained in 1988/1989 (but numbers of which had been applied already for some years): Mandelstam, M. (1990). *How to get equipment for disability.* 1st edition. London: Jessica Kingsley, pp.397–424.

67 Social Services Inspectorate, Department of Health; Social Work Services Group, Scottish Office (1991):

Care management and assessment: practitioners' guide. London: HMSO.

Care management and assessment: managers' guide. London: HMSO.

68 See eg: Department of Health (1990). *Community care in the next decade and beyond: policy guidance.* HMSO, London, paras 2.3, 3.32.

69 For a detailed breakdown of community care law, policy and practice, see: Mandelstam, M. (1995). *Community care practice and the law.* London: Jessica Kingsley.

70 Department of Health (1990). *Community care in the next decade and beyond: policy guidance.* London: DH, p.27.

71 Department of Health (1990). *Community care in the next decade and beyond: policy guidance.* London: DH, para 3.15.

72 Eg: Social Services Inspectorate (Horne, D.; Walker, M.) (1995). I*nspection of services for physically disabled people in Cornwall, July 1995.* Bristol: Department of Health, p.25.

73 See: *CSDPA 1970,* s.28A.

74 *Children Act 1989,* schedule 2, part 1, para 3.

75 *Children Act 1989*, schedule 2, part 1, para 6)

76 *Children Act 1989*, s.23(8)

77 *Children Act 1989*, schedule 2, part 1, para 1.

78 Department of Health (1996). *Carers (Recognition and Services) Act 1995: policy guidance.* London: Department of Health, para 11.

79 Department of Health (1996). *Carers (Recognition and Services) Act 1995: policy guidance.* London: Department of Health, para 17.

80 Department of Health (1996). *Carers (Recognition and Services) Act 1995: policy guidance.* London: Department of Health, para 13.

81 Commission for Local Administration (88/A/303). *Complaint against the London Borough of Newham.* London: CLAE, 1988, para 21.

82 Arksey, H. (1996). Missed target. *Community Care:* 28 March – 3 April 1996, pp.24–25.

83 Clements, L. (1992). Duties of social services departments. *Legal Action Journal:* January 1994, p.21.

84 Commission for Local Administration (92/A/4108). *Report on investigation against the London Borough of Redbridge.* London: CLAE, pp.2, 17.

85 *Health and Social Services and Social Security Adjudication Act 1983*, s.17.

86 Chetwynd, M.; Ritchie, J. (in collaboration with: Reith, L., Howard, M.) (1996). *The cost of care: the impact of charging policy on the lives of disabled people.* York: Joseph Rowntree Foundation, p.85.

87 Secretaries of State (1989). Secretary of State for Health; Secretary of State for Social Security; Secretary of State for Wales; Secretary of State for Scotland. *Caring for people: community care in the next decade and beyond.* London: HMSO, p.29.

88 Social Services Inspectorate (1994). *Advice note for use by Social Services Inspectorate: discretionary charges for adult social services (section 17 of Health and Social Services and Social Security Adjudications Act 1983).* London: Department of Health, p.2.

89 LAC(94)1. Department of Health. *I. Charges for residential accommodation: CRAG amendment No 2. II. Charges for non-residential adult services under section 17 of the Health and Social Services and Social Security Adjudications Act 1983.* London: DH, para 18.

90 Commission for Local Administration (93/C/2475). *Report on investigation against Leeds City Council.* York: CLAE, 1995, p.8.

91 *Health and Social Services and Social Security Adjudication Act 1983*, s.17.

92 Social Services Inspectorate (1994). *Advice note for use by Social Services Inspectorate: discretionary charges for adult social services (section 17 of Health and Social Services and Social Security Adjudications Act 1983).* London: Department of Health, p.1.

93 *Health and Social Services and Social Security Adjudication Act 1983*, s.17.

94 Social Services Inspectorate (1994). *Advice note for use by Social Services Inspectorate: discretionary charges for adult social services (section 17 of Health and Social Services and Social Security Adjudications Act 1983).* London: Department of Health, p.3.

95 See eg: *Local Government Act 1972*, s.111.

96 *Children Act 1989*, s.29.

97 See eg: Kestenbaum, A. (1996). I*ndependent living: a review.* York: Joseph Rowntree Foundation, pp.20–23.

98 LASSA 1970, s.7 gives the Secretary of State the power to make regulations requiring authorities to establish complaints procedures. Regulations, SI 1990/2244, state that authorities must do so. The real detail, however, is given in the *Complaints Procedures Directions 1990* which are made under s.7B of LASSA 1970 – which states that authorities must comply with Directions. The Directions are contained in the policy guidance, *Community care in the next decade and beyond.* London: HMSO, 1990.

99 *Children Act 1989*, s.26(3).

100 Department of Health (1991). *Children Act 1989 guidance and regulations: volume 3: family placements.* London: HMSO, p.108.

101 SI 1991/894. *Representations Procedure (Children) Regulations 1991.* London: HMSO, r.5.

102 Commission for Local Administration in England (93/C/2893). *Report on investigation into a complaint against Manchester City Council.* York: CLAE, 1995.

103 Social Services Inspectorate, Department of Health (1991). *The right to complain: practice guidance on complaints procedures in social services departments.* London: HMSO, p.14.

104 Eg Social Services Inspectorate (1993):

Progress on the right to complain: monitoring social services complaints procedures. London: DH, p.30.

Inspection of complaints procedures in local authority social services departments. London: DH, pp.36–37.

105 Commission for Local Administration (92/A/3725). *Report on investigation against the London Borough of Haringey.* London: CLAE, 1993.

106 Social Services Inspectorate (1996). *SSI inspection of complaints procedures in local authority social services departments: third overview report: January 1996.* London: Department of Health, pp.26–29.

107 Department of Health (1990). *Community care in the next decade and beyond: policy guidance.* London: DH, p.68.

108 See eg Parsloe, P. (1994). Balancing user choice and resource constraints: the role of review panels in social services departments. *Policy and Politics:* 1994; 22(2), pp.113–118.

109 Dean, H. (1995). Social care provision: problems of redress. *Legal Action:* December 1995, p.8.

110 Eg Social Services Inspectorate (1993). *Inspection of complaints procedures in local authority social services departments.* London: DH, p.29.

111 *R v Avon County Council, ex parte M* [1994] 2 FCR 259 (QBD): a dispute about the choice of residential care for a person with learning disabilities.

112 *R v North Yorkshire County Council, ex parte Hargreaves* (1994) 26 BMLR 121 (QBD).

113 *R v Islington Borough Council, ex parte Rixon* (QBD), The Times, 17 April 1996.

114 Commission for Local Administration in England (93/A/3738). *Report on investigation into a complaint against East Sussex County Council.* London: CLAE, 1995, pp.14–15.

115 Eg: Commissioner for Local Administration (92/A/3725). *Report on investigation against the London Borough of Haringey.* London: CLAE, 1993.

116 Simons, K. (1995). *I'm not complaining but...: complaints procedures in social services departments.* York: Joseph Rowntree Foundation; Community Care, p.44.

117 *R v Department of Health and Social Security and Others, ex parte Bruce* (1986) (QBD), Times 5 February 1995.

118 Parliamentary Commissioner for Administration (C.799/81). Assistance under Chronically Sick and Disabled Persons Act 1970. In: *Selected cases 1982 – volume 3.* Fifth report – session 1981–82. London: HMSO.

119 Department of Health (1994). *A framework for local community care charters in England.* London: DH, p.9.

120 Department of Health (1994). *A framework for local community care charters in England.* London: DH, pp.14, 17.

121 See eg discussion about criteria of eligibility in general: Audit Commission (1993). *Taking care: progress with care in the community.* London: Audit Commission, p.4.

122 Department of Health (1994). *A framework for local community care charters in England.* London: DH, p.30.

123 Social Services Inspectorate, Department of Health; Social Work Services Group, Scottish Office (1991):

Care management and assessment: practitioners' guide. London: HMSO.

Care management and assessment: managers' guide. London: HMSO.

124 DHSS 12/70; DES 13/70; MHLG 65/70; ROADS 20/70. Department of Health and Social Security; Department of Education and Science; Ministry of Housing and Local Government; Ministry of Transport. *The Chronically Sick and Disabled Persons Act 1970.* London: DHSS, DES, MHLG, MoT, 1970, para 7.

125 See eg Social Services Inspectorate (1993). *Occupational therapy: the community contribution: report on local authority occupational therapy services.* London: Department of Health, p.11.

126 Stalker, K.; Jones, C.; Ritchie, P. (1995). *Occupational therapy: changing roles in community care: a report to the Social Work Services Inspectorate for Scotland.* Edinburgh: Scottish Office Home and Health Department, p.19.

127 Salvage, A. (1996). *Stuck on the waiting list: older people and equipment for independent living.* London: Age Concern England, pp.16–19.

128 Social Services Inspectorate (Booth, L.; Strettle, T.; Paul, D.) (1995). *Inspection of community services for physically disabled people in the London Borough of Wandsworth, 28 June – 12 July 1995.* London: Department of Health, p.9.

129 See: Audit Commission (1996). *Local authority performance indicators: volume 1, education, social services, libraries and expenditure.* London: HMSO, pp.24, 30.

130 Commission for Local Administration in England (93/A/2536). *Report on investigation into a complaint against London Borough of Waltham Forest.* London: CLAE, 1994, pp.13–15.

131 Commission for Local Administration in England (90/C/2203). *Discontinuation report on investigation into a complaint against Wakefield Metropolitan District Council.* York: CLAE, 1992, p.2.

132 Commission for Local Administration in England (92/A/1693). *Report on investigation into a complaint against London Borough of Lewisham.* London: CLAE, 1993, pp.24–25.

133 Commission for Local Administration (92/A/4108). *Report on investigation against the London Borough of Redbridge.* London: CLAE, pp.12, 16–17.

134 Commission for Local Administration in England (91/A/0482). *Report on investigation against the London Borough of Hackney.* London: CLAE, 1993.

135 See eg: London Borough Occupational Therapy Managers' Group (1992). *Occupational therapists' criteria for the loan of equipment to people with disabilities.* London: LBOTMG.

136 Commission for Local Administration in England (93/C/3660). *Report on investigation into a complaint against Rochdale Metropolitan Borough Council.* York: CLAE, 1995, pp.8–9.

137 Commission for Local Administration in England (91/B/0254 and 91/B/0380). *Report on investigation into a complaint against Leicester City Council and Leicestershire County Council.* Coventry: CLAE, 1992, p.18.

138 Commission for Local Administration in England (94/C/1563). *Report on investigation into a complaint against Sheffield City Council.* York: CLAE, 1996, p.12.

139 Commission for Local Administration in England (93/A/4250). *Report on investigation into a complaint against Westminster City Council.* London: CLAE, 1996, pp.17–18.

140 Commission for Local Administration in England (91/A/0482). *Report on investigation against the London Borough of Hackney.* London: CLAE, 1993, p.20.

141 Commission for Local Administration in England (92/A/1693). *Report on investigation into a complaint against London Borough of Lewisham.* London: CLAE, 1993, pp.17–24.

142 Commission for Local Administration in England (93/B/4453). *Report on investigation into a complaint against Wolverhampton Metropolitan Borough Council.* Coventry: CLAE, 1995.

143 Commission for Local Administration in England (91/C/1852). *Report on investigation into a complaint against Wirral Metropolitan Borough Council.* York: CLAE, 1993.

144 Commission for Local Administration in England (94/A/2369). *Report on investigation into a complaint against the London Borough of Islington.* London: CLAE, 1995.

145 Commission for Local Administration in England (92/A/1693). *Report on investigation into a complaint against London Borough of Lewisham.* London: CLAE, 1993, p.24.

146 Commission for Local Administration in England (94/C/0964 & 94/C/0965). *Report on investigation against Middlesbrough Borough Council and Cleveland County Council.* York: CLAE, 1996, p.10.

147 Commission for Local Administration in Wales (95/0227). *Report by the local government ombudsman on an investigation into a complaint against Dyfed County Council.* Cardiff: CLAW, 1996.

148 Commission for Local Administration in England (93/B/3956). *Report on investigation into a complaint against Sandwell Metropolitan Borough Council.* Coventry: CLAE, 1995, pp.9, 19.

149 See eg: Social Services Inspectorate (1994). *Quality occupational therapy services: report of the SSI seminars, February/March 1994.* London: Department of Health, pp.5, 11–12.

150 Figures cited in: Social Services Inspectorate (Shipley, C; Raw, D) (1991). *Managing aids to daily living services.* Bristol: Department of Health, p.4: a survey of equipment provision in South West England.

151 Salvage, A. (1996). *Stuck on the waiting list: older people and equipment for independent living.* London: Age Concern England, p.18.

152 See eg Robinson, K. (1995). Contractual controversy. *Hospital Equipment Supplies:* September 1995, p.13; Travis, A. (1995). Tender mercies. *DLCC News*; Spring 1995, pp.14–15.

153 Mapp, S. (1996). Two's company. *Therapy Weekly:* 25 January 1996.

CHAPTER 8

PROVISION OF EQUIPMENT BY THE NHS

COVERAGE

1. Type of equipment provided by the NHS, and practitioners involved
2. A comprehensive health service
   - Comprehensive provision of NHS services and equipment?
   - Duty to provide medical, nursing, care and after-care services
   - Relationship between professional judgements and resources
   - Discharge from hospital and equipment provision
   - Restricting or withdrawing provision
   - Methods of rationing NHS services and equipment.
3. Provision of equipment by general practitioners
   - Drug Tariff equipment
   - Referral and advice-giving by general practitioners in relation to equipment
   - Offering consultations to patients who are 75 years old or over
   - Home care equipment: provision by fundholding general practitioners.
4. Charges for NHS equipment
   - Failing to provide equipment at all
   - Selling of equipment by NHS occupational therapy departments
   - Shops on NHS premises.
5. NHS complaints
   - New complaints procedure (from April 1996)
   - Patient's Charter
   - Health service ombudsman
   - Default powers of the Secretary of State
   - Complaints to professional bodies.

Key points

The NHS provides significant quantities of disability equipment each year, spending tens of millions of pounds on wheelchairs, artificial limbs, walking aids, incontinence equipment, home nursing equipment, orthotic appliances and footwear, environmental control systems, hearing aids, communication/speech aids – and so on. Nevertheless, services as a whole for physically disabled and older people – including the provision of equipment – often do not command a high priority within the NHS. For example, over the last decade specific criticism has been levelled at the provision of each of these types of equipment; the substance of this criticism is given in Part IV of this book under the relevant headings.

This chapter analyses how the NHS Act 1977 imposes vague duties and gives health authorities wide discretion to decide local policies, priorities and rationing. The potential conflict between objective professional judgements and judgements influenced by the availability of resources is highlighted. The role of general practitioners in equipment provision is outlined, including the powers of fundholding GPs to provide an extended range of home care equipment for their patients. NHS charges for equipment are analysed along with the confusion which seems to arise quite regularly about them. Both the 'old' and 'new' (operative from April 1996) procedures for NHS complaints are set out, as is the function of the health service ombudsman and the role of the Patient's Charter. The remit of professional disciplinary bodies is briefly dealt with.

Conflict between people's needs and resources. More generally, the functioning of the NHS is coming under greater scrutiny; in particular, the rationing of services and equipment has become an increasingly public debate. Difficult decisions are affecting NHS managers, practitioners and patients alike. Sometimes the debate finds its way to the law courts and into Parliament – but more often into the newspapers and on to television. This chapter tries to explain the basic conflict between the duty of the Secretary of State and health authorities to provide a comprehensive health service – and the seemingly inevitable limits on the resources available. Both the legal approach to, and the practical consequences of, that tension are explained.

The evidence would suggest that, in the *normal* – if not the *legal* – sense of the word, comprehensive services are simply not being provided. For example, the supply of incontinence pads is sometimes withdrawn or restricted to people in residential homes or even their own homes, people are asked to buy their own nebulisers, parents cannot obtain suitable wheelchairs for their children, bathing aids are no longer provided because they are deemed to be for social rather than health needs – and so on. Outside of the equipment field, the absence of comprehensive services are only too evident, from older people refused physiotherapy, children in school denied adequate speech therapy – and patients left on trolleys in hospital corridors, or even turned away from hospitals because of a shortage of beds.

The conflict between people's needs and limited resources is normally – but not always – resolved in favour of central government, health authorities and NHS Trusts. This is because legislation is so vague that individuals have very few, if any, enforceable legal rights to services. Specific services or equipment are not mentioned; and, at root, the Secretary of State's duty to provide medical and nursing services (including equipment) generally extends only so far as 'reasonable requirements' demand. Similarly, he has a duty to provide facilities for the prevention of illness, for the care of people who are ill, and for the after-care of people who have been ill – only so far as he considers that they are 'appropriate'. It is hard not to conclude that provision of equipment by the NHS rests not on the bedrock of people's clinical needs, but on the shifting sands of resources. When conflicts between people's needs for services and limited resources reach the law courts, they are resolved in favour of the latter. The health service ombudsman, too, has usually – but not always – upheld the powers of the NHS to make rationing decisions. This state of affairs suggests that the provision of a 'comprehensive' national health service is not amenable to judicial enforcement in any substantial sense. Instead, the way in which the relevant sections of the NHS Act 1977 are applied in practice, depends on the will of incumbent governments.

Questions people ask

- When can health authorities and NHS Trusts ration incontinence pads?
- Can authorities loan nebulisers to people for three months, then take them back and tell people that they will they have to buy their own?
- Is it legal when authorities decide that people over 65 years of age cannot have physiotherapy treatment and the equipment which goes with it?
- Can an NHS wheelchair service refuse to provide a wheelchair for a person who has less than six months to live, on the grounds that his need is not 'permanent'?
- What about the person, with four weeks to live, who following an in-depth assessment from various professionals, is told that he can go home – only to find that all the hospital's special beds are already on loan, and his family will have to buy or hire one privately?
- Can NHS Trusts legally make charges for orthopaedic footwear?

1. TYPE OF EQUIPMENT PROVIDED BY THE NHS, AND PRACTITIONERS INVOLVED

The NHS provides many different types of equipment, including artificial limbs, wheelchairs, walking aids, incontinence pads, stoma care equipment, hearing aids, surgical shoes, respiratory equipment and pressure relief beds.

Equipment is provided by a range of NHS staff who work either in hospitals or in the community health services. These include occupational therapists, physiotherapists, speech and language therapists, chiropodists, orthotists, specialist nurses and medical consultants. General practitioners (GPs), pharmacists, dentists, ophthalmologists and opticians also prescribe or supply equipment as part of 'general medical services'.

2. A COMPREHENSIVE HEALTH SERVICE

Most NHS equipment is provided under the broad language of the NHS Act 1977 which refers to the provision of a *comprehensive* health service and of *medical, nursing* services – and services for the prevention of illness, care of people who are ill, and after-care for those who have been ill. Thus, most types of equipment, as well as specific services (eg occupational therapy) are not mentioned.

There are, however, some specific references. The provision of electric wheelchairs appears to be governed explicitly by s.5 of that Act which confers a power (though not a duty) to provide invalid carriages.[1] Ironically, despite this specific reference, most NHS wheelchair services have only provided indoor –

and not outdoor – user-controlled electric wheelchairs. The situation is now poised to change, following an announcement by the Department of Health in early 1996. Interestingly, change will come about not through legislation but simply through a change of policy by central government expressed in guidance.[2] This illustrates a point made elsewhere (see p.35) that once a legislative framework is in place, much of the detailed policy and practice is controlled by government without recourse to the Parliamentary process.

Also specifically mentioned in legislation is equipment which can be charged for, including wigs, surgical brassieres and spinal supports – whilst equipment itemised in the Drug Tariff (a list made under regulations), prescribed by general practitioners for their patients and also by hospital doctors for hospital outpatients, also attracts prescription charges.

Overall, it is clear that health authorities have great discretion to do more or less what they want – so long as they act legally, fairly and reasonably and so avoid judicial review by the courts (see Chapter 17). They can make local priorities, allocate resources accordingly and so ration services. Although the legislation does refer to duties, they are so general and vague that – in respect of providing any particular equipment to an individual patient – it is arguable that they have the effect only of powers (see p.136), which are much weaker than duties. This means that the authority can, but does not have to, provide equipment for any individual. Put simply, people do not have a legal right to health care.[3]

Comprehensive provision of NHS services and equipment?

Most equipment provision is governed by sections 1 and 3 of the NHS Act 1977. The first of these sections places a duty on the Secretary of State (and, by delegation, on health authorities[4]):

> 'to continue the promotion in England and Wales of a comprehensive health service designed to secure improvement...in the physical and mental health of the people of those countries, and...in the prevention, diagnosis and treatment of illness, and for that purpose to provide or secure effective provision of services in accordance with this Act.'

This duty embraces all and nothing. It gives the Secretary of State the ability to provide all manner of health services; yet, equally, the term comprehensive cannot be given a tangible meaning. For instance, asked in Parliament for a list of services provided by the NHS, the government could only reply that the NHS provides a 'comprehensive' range of services.[5] Also, the duty is towards people in general and not towards each individual person; this makes the duty even more difficult to enforce (see p.137).

Comprehensiveness and total exclusion of NHS services

It is sometimes suggested that total exclusion of a particular service might offend against the notion of comprehensiveness.[6] For example, could an authority decide that it would not provide nebulisers or wheelchairs at all? The answer seems unclear; in one case the Court of Appeal expressly stated that one could not pinpoint one hospital or one area and point to a shortcoming, because the Secretary of State had to consider the country as a whole.[7] This sort of reasoning suggests that even total removal of specific services will not breach the general duty to provide comprehensive services. Of course, if *all* medical or all nursing services were removed in a particular area, then the courts could more easily intervene, since they are referred to explicitly in the legislation. In a case to some degree comparable (*R v Hertfordshire CC ex parte Three Rivers DC*), a dispute had arisen between a county council and a district council over public transport services, including services for elderly and disabled people. The county council had a duty to secure what it considered to be 'appropriate' public transport services; the court suggested that whilst the council could legally make various cuts to its services, its decision might have been flawed 'if it were demonstrated that a community within the district had been left without any public passenger service at all.'[8]

Nevertheless, possibly with a view to avoiding this sort of question, for example, a Department of Health report about plastic surgery states that 'no procedure should be totally excluded' when priorities are made.[9] When health authorities have been explicit about rationing, they are unlikely to exclude provision of a service totally – except perhaps when they argue that the service is elective, cosmetic and nothing to do with health at all, or at least of doubtful effectiveness.[10] Nevertheless, there might always be good clinical reasons for providing most services at least in some individual cases.[11] An additional legal reason for not operating such blanket exclusions is that authorities might offend against the legal principle of *fettering discretion* and so risk judicial review by the law courts (see p.446).

Thus, what total exclusion of a service really means is by no means straightforward. A health authority might not formally purchase a particular service but maintain that, in exceptional circumstances, it would ensure that it was available. This might be via 'extra-contractual' referral. The authority could then argue that it was not excluding a service *totally*.

Identifying comprehensiveness: levels of services and provision

A second difficulty about the notion of comprehensiveness concerns identification of what a service really is and at what level in the NHS one finds it.

Services can be identified at a high level. For example, if they are identified as *community nursing* or *therapy*, then only complete removal of all community nurses and all therapists would amount to total non-provision, and trigger doubts about whether a comprehensive service was being maintained. Absence of mere aspects of these services would not amount to total exclusion of whole services. On this argument, refusal of the community nursing service to provide bathing equipment, as a matter of policy, would amount only to exclusion of an aspect; and similarly, if the therapy directorate refused to provide hearing therapy or communication aids.

But if services are identified at a lower level, then the picture changes, theoretically at least. If bathing equipment, hearing therapy or communication aids were to be regarded as services in their own right – then their removal might constitute total exclusion of services. Indeed, from whose point of view is total exclusion of service to be regarded – from that of patients or of health authorities? For example, a health authority might decide, on the basis of local priorities and resources, to restrict the provision of incontinence pads to people in their own homes – and cease to provide them for people in residential homes. From the point of view of those in residential care, there is no service at all. But, from the standpoint of the authority, there is no total exclusion since people in their own homes are continuing to receive the pads.

There appears to be no clear answer to these questions.

Duty to provide medical, nursing care, and after-care services

Section 3 of the NHS Act 1977 is more detailed than section 1 (see above). However, it is still, from the standpoint of particular services or types of equipment, vague. The duty is placed on the Secretary of State (though delegated to health authorities) to:

> 'provide throughout England and Wales, to such extent as he considers necessary to meet all reasonable requirements...medical, dental, nursing and ambulance services...such facilities for the prevention of illness, the care of persons suffering from illness and the after-care of persons who have suffered from illness as he considers are appropriate as part of the health service.'

Terms such as 'considers', 'appropriate' and 'reasonable requirements' give both the Secretary of State and health authorities enormous discretion to decide what services to provide. The detailed content of 'medical', 'nursing', 'care' and 'after-care' services is unspecified. And, even terms such as 'prevention' and 'illness' are capable of diverse interpretation.

For example, one health authority might consider that in order to meet all reasonable requirements, it should provide electronic speech aids for children to use in school. Another health authority might decide the opposite and leave it up to the education authority or the children's parents to provide the equipment.

As already observed, a health authority would be acting unlawfully if it failed to provide any medical, nursing or after-care services at all. However, the section does not specify *which* medical and nursing services should be provided. For example, it does not state that every health authority must provide, or purchase the services of, consultants in rehabilitation medicine or of specialist stoma care nurses. Similarly, this section of the NHS Act 1977 says nothing about equipment. For example, no hint is given about whether consultants should prescribe communication aids as part of medical services. And it does not hint at whether the community nursing services must provide incontinence pads for people in residential or nursing homes as part of nursing services.

Nevertheless, the health service ombudsman has entered where the law courts have feared to tread. He has attempted to grapple with the vagueness of s.3 and, in one notable case (*Leeds*), ruled against an authority which had a policy not to provide long-term care for patients with neurological conditions. He investigated the failure, as a matter of policy, to provide continuing NHS care for a severely disabled patient. Referring at the beginning of the report to the duty to provide after-care services, the ombudsman went on to find a failure in service and that this failure was unreasonable. The person was doubly incontinent, could not eat or drink unassisted, could not communicate, and had a kidney tumour, cataracts in both eyes and occasional epileptic fits.[12]

NHS guidance about equipment

As explained in the first chapter of this book, there is, in addition to legislation, a mass of guidance issued by the Department of Health issued to fill out the statutory framework. This guidance includes Circulars and Letters – most notably, health service guidelines (HSG) and executive letters (EL) – although there are a number of other series as well.

Some of this guidance relates explicitly to equipment: for example, Circulars on incontinence pads, NHS charges for equipment, or orthotics contracts. Other guidance is relevant to equipment implicitly, for example, a Circular about chiropody services. Most of this guidance is dealt with under the relevant headings in Part IV of this book.

Relationship between professional judgements and resources

Of concern to both practitioners and patients alike is the effect of restricted resources on professional and clinical judgements. Clearly there is a difference between saying that a patient is in need, but that there are no resources to meet the need – and denying that there is a need in the first place. The former approach would appear to be the greater preserver of professional integrity but is also likely to produce more upset and bad publicity than the latter. It is not certain how the NHS is handling needs for equipment which cannot be met; is the need for a specialist wheelchair being denied or are staff and managers honestly admitting that there is no money? It might even be doubted whether, in practice, the two approaches can be disentangled at all. More generally, this raises the question, discussed in Chapter 2, of just how tangible or useful the concept of 'need' really is when it is employed in relation to provision by statutory services.

Lack of resources and clinical need

As already explained in Chapter 2, some statements made in Parliament, designed to reassure questioners about people's access to a national health service, are sometimes less than informative. Typically, they tend to claim that people's access to NHS treatment and services is governed by judgements about their clinical need.[13]

In one sense, such statements are literally true; if two people need NHS services urgently and the one in greater need receives services ahead of the other, then a 'clinical' decision has indeed been made. In another sense, the statements mean little, since they are phrased so as to remain true not only when people gain access to services, but also when services are being denied to people. This is because a judgement about a person's 'clinical need justifying NHS treatment' is made relative to other people's needs at the time and to available resources. So, if some people's clinical needs are *greater* than other people's, the latter might go without services. Of course, if a patient denied services dies or otherwise suffers as a result, it is little consolation for him or his family to know that the denial was made on the basis of clinical need. Politicians seem loath to admit that access to NHS services is governed so inexorably by resources. Yet, the level of clinical need triggering service provision is highly flexible and unpredictable; depending on demand for services and competing priorities, it can vary from day to day and from week to week in the same hospital. Statements made by the NHS Executive, in answer to astute enquiries by the health service ombudsman about the availability of NHS continuing care, confirm this picture that not every patient who is in need will necessarily receive NHS services.[14]

Because of the flexible nature of clinical need, the notion of equitable provision of NHS services and equipment evaporates; and the boundary between clinical and financial decision-making appears precarious. Behind the respectable cloak of clinical judgements, priorities are made, rationing organised and people denied services. It is difficult to accept the language of those politicians who attempt to imply that it is clinical decision-making which leaves people on trolleys in corridors all night. Nevertheless, sometimes discussion of resources cannot be kept out of Parliamentary debate fact, as happened when the failure to provide intensive care beds was highlighted.[15]

In addition, the government's political drive to reduce hospital waiting times according to crude, undiscriminating time limits can distort clinical judgement. One consultant pointed out that the:[16]

> 'major incentive for surgery appears to be a management decision...to remove all those who have been waiting more than one year for their operation regardless of [clinical] priority.'

Indeed, it has been pointed out that the distinction between clinical judgement and the allocation of resources broke down in the Court of Appeal case in 1995 – about Cambridge health authority's refusal to treat a child with leukaemia.[17] On the one hand, the authority had told the child's parents that the decision was made not on financial grounds but in the best interests of the child. However, subsequently, the authority told the court that the decision was based on the allocation of resources, the Secretary of State referred at the time to a 'medical judgement on funding', the High Court told the authority that it must do more than 'toll the bell of tight resources', and the Court of Appeal referred to the greatest good of the greatest number in the face of limited budgets.[18] This all suggested that the issue was about resources. Therefore, if a child dying of leukaemia cannot insist on treatment, what chance of success do parents have when they try to insist on a more suitable wheelchair for their severely disabled child?

Judicial interference with professional judgements and the allocation of resources. The law courts are normally reluctant to interfere with the clinical decisions of health professionals.[19] More generally, they hesitate similarly to become involved with the allocation of resources and rationing by authorities. Thus, the wide discretion of the NHS to make difficult decisions has been upheld in a number of circumstances, including waiting times for people in need of orthopaedic treatment (*R v Secretary of State and Others, ex parte Hincks*)[20], postponement of operations for babies with heart conditions (*R v Birmingham HA, ex parte Walker and R v Birmingham HA, ex parte Collier*)[21], lifesaving treatment for a child with leukaemia (*R v Cambridge HA, ex parte B*)[22] and infertility treatment (*R v Sheffield HA, ex parte Seale*).[23]

The judges might rely on the existing, vague wording of the NHS Act 1977. They might even read extra words into the legislation to give authorities yet more room for manoeuvre. For instance, in the *Hincks* case in the Court of Appeal, Lord Denning (though notable in other contexts for siding with the 'little man'[24]), recited s.3 of the NHS Act 1977 but added the following italicised words of his own: 'to meet all reasonable requirements *such as can be provided within the resources available*'.

This made it quite clear that authorities could argue lack of resources even in the face of a clinical need for treatment. And, in the *Cambridge* case, the Court of Appeal did not insist that the authority produce evidence of how it had allocated its scarce resources – on the grounds that even this degree of accountability would place a counter-productive burden on the authority. Both the *Hincks* and *Cambridge* cases were judicial review cases brought to show that authorities had acted unreasonably, unfairly or illegally (see p.426). Not only their outcome, but also the judgements handed down, indicate the reluctance of the courts to intervene.

Clinical judgement or maladministration: the ombudsman. The health service ombudsman has usually (but see the *Leeds* case above) upheld the wide discretion of health authorities to allocate resources and make priorities – even though his remit does allow him to investigate a failure in a service, or failure to provide a service which there was a duty to provide. However, if the delay or non-provision of services or equipment is due to maladministration, then he will make findings against health authorities and NHS Trusts. Hitherto, the ombudsman has been unable to investigate purely clinical judgements – however, this situation has changed with effect from 1st April 1996 (see p.219).

The following represent a selection of investigations, mostly involving equipment; some are investigations of the Parliamentary ombudsman, reflecting the fact that certain equipment, such as wheelchairs, limbs and invalid vehicles, used to be administered centrally by the Department of Health:

(i) **Ombudsman investigations into delay.** In one case, the ombudsman found that an 18-month wait for a hearing aid was due to inadequate resources – but that the allocation of resources was for the authority to manage. Because there was no maladministration, he could not make a finding against the authority.[25] In an earlier case, he accepted the Welsh Office's explanation that the careful allocation of resources justified non-provision by the NHS of a commercial hearing aid and of batteries for it.[26]

Delay in provision caused by simple inefficiency, rather than a lack of resources, might however attract adverse findings by the ombudsman. And, if the provision of a special wheelchair is delayed by six months, the patient dies without ever receiving it, and the NHS wheelchair service is notified of his death and cancels the order – the ombudsman will take a dim view of the actions of the wheelchair service when it subsequently sends letters to the man's widow, asking whether her husband is benefiting from the wheelchair.[27]

When investigating the provision of special boots, the ombudsman did not find maladministration because the delay of several months was owing mainly to factors beyond the control of the health board – such as the time taken by the manufacturer to make the boots.[28] Likewise, difficulties and delay in the provision of a suitable artificial limb will not amount to maladministration – if the confusion and misunderstanding that occurred was due in large part to the complex needs of the disabled person.[29] Similarly, the long wait for each of the three artificial limbs made for another complainant over a period of seven years did not amount to maladministration. This was because although the artificial limb and appliance centre (ALAC) and limb fitting centre (LFC) had not always followed correct procedures, most of the delay was caused by the medical condition of the person, industrial action at the contractor's (ie the maker of the limbs) factory and the complainant's own inability to keep appointments.[30]

In cases involving various causes of delay, the ombudsman weighs up carefully whether to 'blame' statutory services. For instance, when a woman with severe rheumatoid arthritis had to wait over two years for a suitably modified invalid car, the delay was caused in part by the privately contracted manufacturers and repairers involved, over whom the DHSS had little control. Nevertheless, the ombudsman still criticised the DHSS for delay in processing the order, sending the wrong order, prolonging excessively the consultations about the required type of steering wheel and seat belt, and generally acting with a lack of urgency.[31] And, a delay of nine months in the provision of surgical shoes did amount to maladministration. Although the main cause of the delay was a mistake by the shoe fitter (employed by a private company) over whom the ombudsman had no jurisdiction, the hospital staff also contributed – they had run short of casts, and the progress of the order had not been checked and monitored.[32]

(ii) **Administrative defects in clinical judgements?** Time and again, the ombudsman has explained that his legal remit has prevented him from questioning the allocation of resources by authorities made on the basis of clinical judgement, unless maladministration has occurred. (Though, as mentioned above, his powers have been recently extended to cover clinical aspects of decision-making). For these reasons, he has not interfered when women over ninety or children under three years old are allegedly receiving inadequate community nursing services[33] or speech and language therapy respectively.[34] And, if the absence of an operating theatre at an orthopaedic hospital and a shortage of anaesthetists results in long waiting times and the making of difficult decisions about people's clinical priority, the ombudsman will not make adverse findings.[35]

However, even without the legal power to question clinical judgements, the ombudsman is sometimes able to undermine them. For example, if a patient is discharged from hospital on the basis of obviously faulty or missing information, then 'relevant factors' have not been taken into account. The 'clinical' judgement is, consequently, administratively flawed.[36] The ombudsman has quite rightly recognised that a clinical veneer should not obscure the administrative faults which occur when hospitals attempt to clear beds in over-hasty fashion – with an eye on resources, rather than the individual patient.

Sometimes the decision is obviously not clinical. For example, in one case the ombudsman found that it was unreasonable not to loan crutches to a person leaving hospital. This finding was made on the basis that the decision to withhold the crutches had been made, not by a doctor on clinical grounds – but by a technician who had been worried about stock levels. The ombudsman stated that the crutches should have been withheld only for a medical, and not for an administrative, reason.[37]

Nevertheless, in other cases, the ombudsman has been unable to question judgements about people's needs. One investigation involving the prescription of contact lenses illustrated how the concept of 'need' can fluctuate; and that, whatever the need, money might be the decisive factor. In the course of various delays and referrals, a person was assessed by one hospital eye service as needing contact lenses, but by a second as not needing them. Finally, it became irrelevant whether he really 'needed' them or not, because he was denied them in any case by a third hospital – which, as a matter of policy, had decided not to provide any ophthalmic services obtainable elsewhere. The ombudsman explained that he could not investigate differing levels of services between hospitals; nor could he question the clinical, as opposed to the administrative, decisions that had been made. And he could not, in the absence of evidence of maladministration, question the third hospital's policy, since it was based on a formal review of services. However, although he did not uphold the complaint that the health authority (in relation to the third hospital) had failed to provide a service which it should have provided – he did find that inadequate explanation had been given to the patient.[38]

Discharge from hospital and equipment provision

When people leave hospital and require equipment or home adaptations, information, or adequate consultation, then cooperation with other services and voluntary bodies – and timely, well-organised discharge arrangements – are often essential. The health service ombudsman has investigated many times the arrangements, or lack of them, made when people are discharged from hospital. This is not surprising, given the longstanding problems afflicting hospital discharge practices.[39] Indeed, advice from the Department of Health and professional organisations elsewhere refers to the need for timely and appropriate provision of equipment and adaptations when people leave hospital.[40]

For example, in the Friday afternoon rush to discharge people, a patient might be sent home with a part missing from feeding apparatus, with the consequence that the district nurse cannot feed him.[41] The health service ombudsman might fault a consultant who, having assured the husband of a woman with Huntingdon's Chorea that she would receive equipment and home adaptations, then failed to find out from the social services department and local voluntary bodies whether they could in fact provide these.[42] Similarly, hospital staff failed a patient administratively, because, although they knew that she would require substantial support from social services at home, they failed to ensure that they were discharging her into an environment where that support would be available.[43]

When a woman complained that she could not manage to bathe her husband twice a day when he was discharged from hospital, the ombudsman could not directly attack the doctor's clinical decision to discharge him. Instead, he ascertained that the decision had been affected by a lapse in communication between staff; this meant that inadequate consideration had been given to the consequences of the discharge and the home circumstances. In addition, there was little evidence of adherence to Circular guidance about discharge and no system of recording discharge arrangements on patient records. This was maladministration.[44]

On another occasion, a 68-year-old woman was discharged home needing, as the complainant maintained, oxygen equipment, a commode and a raised toilet seat. The ombudsman criticised the discharge decision on the basis of 'insufficient thought'. Although he could not question the clinical decision about the oxygen equipment, he found that the need for a commode had been assessed over a week before the discharge, and before the woman's condition had deteriorated even further. The arrangements for the commode and the toilet seat should therefore have been made prior to discharge in any event.[45]

Restricting or withdrawing provision

The import of the above paragraphs is that health authorities can often do much as they please. However, this freedom is qualified to the extent that they should make decisions reasonably, fairly and legally and so preclude adverse judicial review by the law courts (see p.426). Similarly, they need to avoid maladministration, failure in service or failure to provide a service at all (which they have a duty to provide) – if they are to escape the reach of the health service ombudsman.

These qualifications need to be borne in mind by health authorities and NHS Trusts not only when people are first assessed and provided with equipment or other services – but also when an authority or NHS Trust wishes to reduce or withdraw provision. Thus, the Department of Health itself sometimes passes down cautionary advice. For example, guidance has warned against too sudden a withdrawal of incontinence supplies from people.[46] Such a warning was given probably for legal as well as benevolent reasons.

First, health authorities should probably 'play it safe' by reassessing individual patients before withdrawing a service – so that they cannot be accused of operating a 'blanket policy' and therefore *fettering their discretion* (see Chapter 17 on judicial review). This is because, in principle at least, they must retain the ability to take account of individual, perhaps exceptional, needs.[47] Second, reassessment gives patients notice that their service might be reduced or withdrawn – thus satisfying perhaps patients' *legitimate expectation* (another judicial review concept) about what services they will receive. Third, reassessment followed by withdrawal or reduction of service might make it quite clear that an authority has not breached its common law duty of care (ie the decision was in accord with proper procedure and good professional practice) – and so reduce the risk of a negligence action (see p.315), if the patient suffers harm after the withdrawal or reduction.

Methods of rationing NHS services and equipment

Both the legislation and decisions of the courts, analysed above, give authorities a wide discretion to set priorities and ration services; and in practice this is what happens. Health authorities have always rationed services and equipment to some extent. Rationing is not new although it is now receiving increased publicity in the face of escalating expectations, needs and technology.

For instance, in the case of equipment, rationing is commonplace, including the failure (in the past at least) of most health authorities to provide people with user-controlled electric wheelchairs for outdoor use, the reduction and sometimes withdrawal of the provision of incontinence pads, the inability of the NHS sometimes to fund communication aids, the longstanding limiting of NHS chiropody services and equipment to priority groups of people, or restrictions on the loan of nebulisers (thus forcing of people to buy, or otherwise obtain, their own). Some years ago, the health service ombudsman even investigated – and did not censure – a health authority's decision to base the provision of chiropody services on means-testing.[48]

Since the term rationing is an emotive one, government sometimes prefers to use terms such as *priority-setting* or *resource allocation.* Resource limitations lead to restrictions on services, although somewhere there is a distinction to be made between the inevitability of at least some rationing – and the rationing brought on by excessive underfunding.[49] Rationing might involve adjusting levels of services, some up, some down. Alternatively it might require the withdrawal of services altogether – or at least from some groups of people.[50] Rationing devices include, for example[51]:

- *deterrence* (eg operation of eligibility criteria, 'weeding out' referrals or otherwise controlling access to services through screening/receptionist procedures)
- *deflection* (eg passing the buck' to other agencies, statutory or voluntary, by quibbling over the definitions of people's needs and the type of agency which is therefore responsible for meeting those needs)
- *dilution* (eg reduction in the standards and levels of provision of particular services)
- *delay* (eg operation of waiting lists).

Explicit or implicit rationing?

Much of the rationing in the NHS has, up to now at least, not been explicit. However, health authorities do sometimes openly ration elective treatment such as cosmetic surgery (eg for tattoos, varicose veins, adult bat ears) and infertility treatment. Such public admissions or declarations of rationing are usually followed by unfavourable publicity.

It has been pointed out that rationing is achieved as much by *non-decisions* as by *decisions,* simply by perpetuating existing levels of provision.[52] Although there might be no overt admission that this is happening, it appears that such silent rationing has afflicted NHS provision of equipment for disabled or elderly people (see p.78). This is despite the fact that these people have for decades been amongst the groups labelled priority by government.[53] Sometimes the silence is broken when stories of age-related rationing come to light whether it be related to incontinence pads, nebulisers, cancer, renal failure or breast screening. With them come the protests that, in any case, such rationing policies are based on mistaken beliefs – for example, about the level of successful clinical outcomes for older people.[54]

Alternatively, although an authority might state what its priorities are, they might turn out to be merely 'aspirational'. That is, they represent general intentions only and are not backed up with specific funding. So, for example, services for elderly people might be 'high on the shopping list' of health authority priorities but in reality receive little money.[55]

Even when priorities are publicised and specifically funded by an authority, the information imparted to the onlooker is limited. A statement of priorities does not explain which other services, not mentioned, will consequently be neglected and to what extent. Even the statement that over the next two years a health authority will spend so many million pounds on community services discloses limited information. True, it might show that the authority is spending a quarter the amount of money on community services it is spending on acute services – and twice that being spent on children's services. But such broad statements are not necessarily predictive of the levels of specific services nor sudden threats of withdrawal of, for example, incontinence pads from hundreds of people, whether it be in Scarborough[56] or Leicestershire.[57]

Levels of rationing

Rationing policy can be identified at, for example, four levels: *government, health authority, service,* and finally *individual practitioner* level.[58]

For example, central government might suggest that authorities develop services for disabled people; and a health authority then states which particular disability services it will develop. The managers of each of those particular services then set out their own detailed criteria and policies. Lastly, individual practitioners decide which of their patients qualify for service provision, perhaps with an eye on the budget or on their own workloads.

The government White Paper, *Health of the Nation,*[59] identified 'key areas' including heart disease, stroke, cancer, and accidents. Towards the end of the paper, brief mention is made of how these are relevant to elderly people and to people with physical and sensory disabilities. But how these aspirations at government level finally manifest themselves at practitioner and patient level are difficult to pinpoint. Yet it is at this fourth, *individual level* that the meaning of rationing becomes clear, when, for example, terminally ill people are refused wheelchairs or special beds which would enable them to go home,[60] or older people are denied services because of their age.[61]

Answers to the rationing question?

Answers are not easy. For example, explicit rationing might not be the solution and instead create as many difficulties as implicit measures.[62] It has been pointed out that informal clinical rationing by doctors avoids political controversy[63] and also might obscure the difficult ethical issues raised.[64] If the decisions to be made involve almost impossible value judgements and 'tragic choices', then allowing access to health care to resemble a lottery might be superficially justified.[65] Another suggestion has been that it is desirable to 'muddle through elegantly'.[66] In line with one of the themes identified in Chapter 2 – 'user empowerment' – the public is sometimes consulted about what form local rationing should take. However, this is no straightforward exercise; apart from the difficulty in obtaining a substantial and representative response, the public might express morally debatable preferences which would result in inequitable services.[67]

The term equity is sometimes mentioned in connection with the NHS. But is it equity of *equal health*; *equal access* to health services; or *equality of actual use* of the NHS? In similar vein, the concept of need as a basis for priorities and rationing is also fraught with difficulty. For example, should government and authorities equate *need* with the size of a health problem; ie the larger the problem, the greater the resources to be allocated? Or should need be measured by taking account of people's capacity to benefit from services, in a practical, attainable sense?[68]

Certainly, services for elderly or disabled people, including equipment provision, would seem not to conform with the House of Commons Health Committee's principle of equity. This refers to all patients having 'high quality health care according to their assessed need' without age, sex, ethnicity, occupation, social class or geography affecting service availability or speed of delivery'.[69]

Furthermore, many people's idea of equity includes the assumption of consistency of service from place to place. The Secretary of State for Health's argument that rationing should be local and based on clinical priorities[70] sounds rational but is likely to produce visible inequalities. It is surely inequitable that a person might obtain an NHS electronic communication aid in one locality but not in another. It is of limited use to explain to somebody denied assistance because he is, as it were, living in the wrong place, that (despite appearances) such denial is really equitable, because it is in line with local priorities.

3. PROVISION OF EQUIPMENT BY GENERAL PRACTITIONERS

The role of general practitioners (GPs) in equipment provision can be explained fourfold.

First, GPs prescribe equipment listed in the Drug Tariff. Second, they are the focus or trigger (ie through referral) for equipment provision by other professionals such as district nurses, therapists and chiropodists. Third, GPs have duties to give patients advice about local authority services and, more specifically, have a duty to offer annual consultations and home visits to patients who are 75 years of age or over. Fourth, the role of GP fundholders in equipment provision has potentially increased from April 1996 when they were given powers to purchase an extended range of equipment on behalf of their patients.

The services provided by general practitioners are known as *general medical services*. Each general practitioner works under *terms of service* laid down in regulations and constituting a contract between practitioner and the local health authority.[71]

Drug Tariff equipment

GPs have the power to prescribe a range of drugs and appliances listed in a book known as the Drug Tariff and published monthly by Her Majesty's Stationery Office.[72] The appliances include, for instance, incontinence devices (but not pads, except in Scotland), elastic hosiery, stoma care appliances, oxygen cylinders, oxygen concentrators and diabetes equipment.

Prescriptions are normally dispensed by pharmacists who have a duty to make necessary arrangements for the measuring and fitting of appliances.[73] Some general practitioners dispense prescriptions as well – for example, in rural areas where there are no pharmacists. In addition, centres known as dispensing appliance centres (DACs) offer specialist supply and fitting services for NHS-prescribed equipment such as incontinence and stoma care devices.[74]

Pilot schemes have allowed some nurses in certain areas to prescribe certain appliances.[75] They are listed in a separate part of the Drug Tariff and in the *Nurse Prescribers' Formulary* – and include elastic hosiery, urinary catheters and appliances, stoma care products, and diabetes equipment.

Prescription by general practitioner or by hospital consultant?

Disputes sometimes arise between hospitals and GPs about who should issue regular prescriptions for appliances or drugs for patients who are under the care of both hospital and GP. In the past, limited budgets have sometimes tempted hospitals inappropriately to transfer prescribing responsibility to GPs. With the advent of indicative prescribing amounts for GPs, the potential for dispute has increased, since the incentive to shift responsibility for prescription – and thus financial responsibility – now works in both directions.

Guidance issued by the Department of Health states that GPs should have the confidence to prescribe items, and that they should not find themselves in the position of having to prescribe for conditions with which they are not familiar. Hospital consultants have full responsibility for inpatients and outpatients, and when patients are discharged, the hospital pharmacy should have prescribed drugs and dressings for at least seven days. When the condition of patients is stable, a shared care arrangement between consultant and GP might be possible. The guidance notes that consultants should retain responsibility if items are only available through hospitals or if there are supply problems.[76]

Referral and advice-giving by general practitioners in relation to equipment

General practitioners might employ, work with, or frequently refer patients to, other professionals such as NHS district nurses, therapists and chiropodists – all of whom provide equipment.

When fundholding GPs purchase NHS or private services, or non-fundholders refer patients to other NHS services, they are in effect sometimes purchasing, or referring people for, equipment as well. For example, a fundholder might buy the services of a private physiotherapist to treat an office worker's stiff neck and provide her with a cushion – or of an NHS physiotherapy service to provide treatment, including the provision of walking aids. Any such equipment, which is not listed on the Drug Tariff or otherwise specified, must be provided free of charge if provided as part of NHS treatment.[77]

GPs have a specific contractual duty, under their terms of service, to give advice, 'as appropriate, to enable patients to avail themselves of services provided by a local social services authority'.[78] Since social services departments are major providers of equipment, this duty is clearly pertinent to equipment provision.

Offering consultations to patients who are 75 years old or over

GPs have a duty to offer annual consultations and home visits to patients aged 75 or over, and are obliged to consider a number of matters affecting the health of these patients (examples, not from the legislation, of equipment are added in brackets) including[79]:

- *sensory functions* (eg hearing aids, low vision aids, environmental layout and colour contrasts)
- *mobility* (eg wheelchairs, walking frames, home adaptations)
- *physical condition* including continence (eg incontinence appliances)
- *social environment* (eg a whole range of equipment).

Equipment is an important part of such consultations and assessments, since a significant number of people is likely already to be using, or to have a need for, it. For example, one study of GP patients of 75 years or over found that walking sticks were being used by 30% of people, bath aids by 29%, stair rails by 28%, high chairs by 22%, front door rails by 15% and toilet aids by 14%.[80]

Home care equipment: provision by fundholding general practitioners

From April 1996, GP fundholders may purchase on behalf of their patients an extended range of equipment, which has been added to the list of goods and services fundholders are empowered to provide. The three main categories listed are orthotic equipment, orthopaedic footwear and, thirdly, therapy and home care equipment. This last category includes breast prostheses, cervical collars, communication equipment, continence equipment, hoists, nebulisers, special beds and mattresses, suction equipment, syringe drivers and walking aids. The list is almost certainly not meant to be exhaustive, although it is delimited by a number of definite exclusions: hearing aids, prostheses (except breast prostheses), wheelchairs, environmental control equipment, and any equipment costing more than £6000. Wigs, fabric supports and elastic hosiery (for all of which there are NHS prescription charges) are also excluded.[81]

How GPs will exercise these new purchasing powers is not yet known. For example, they might run their own equipment services directly, or contract out assessment and provision to other statutory services, voluntary organisations or private companies. The guidance as a whole points to the already existing avenues of provision – for example, social services departments – but does little to advise GPs on how to make sense of the profusion of different providers of equipment.[82] Thus, the new powers given to fundholders introduce the potential both for increasing the coordination of equipment provision (eg because, overall, people see their GP more than any other health or social care professional) – but also for even more complexity and fragmentation than already exists. One particular concern is that general practitioners' knowledge about disability and disability equipment is variable and often poor.[83]

4. CHARGES FOR NHS EQUIPMENT

Legislation states quite clearly that, unless otherwise specified, charges cannot be made for NHS services and equipment.[84]

Specified appliances are listed in the Drug Tariff, prescribed by general practitioners and dispensed by pharmacists or dispensing appliance centres. They are also prescribed by hospital doctors. The standard prescription charge for each Drug Tariff item is, from April 1996, £5.50. In addition, statutory charges apply to the prescription of wigs (£46, £120 or £175 depending on composition), spinal supports (£28.30) and surgical brassieres (£19.25) for hospital outpatients (GPs cannot prescribe these).[85] Various exemptions apply to prescription charges depending on factors such as people's medical condition, financial status and age. The exemptions are for:[86]

- people in receipt of income support, family credit, disability working allowance or members of a family of someone who does receive these[87]
- people in receipt of low income
- people under 16 years old, or under 19 and in full-time education
- people of pensionable age (60 years old)[88]
- women who have given birth within the last 12 months
- war pensioners (and related groups) if the prescription is needed for the 'accepted disablement'
- people with the following medical conditions
    - permanent fistula (including caecostomy, colostomy, laryngostomy, ileostomy which require continuous use of surgical dressing or appliance)
    - forms of hydro-adrenalism (including Addison's disease) for which substitution therapy is essential
    - diabetes insipidus and other forms of hypo-pituitarism
    - diabetes mellitus (except if treatment is by diet alone)
    - hypoparathyroidism
    - myasthenia gravis
    - myxoedema
    - continuing physical disability which confines people to their homes (unless helped by somebody else to get out)
    - epilepsy requiring continuous anti-convulsive therapy.

In addition, no charges can be made for equipment supplied to NHS inpatients.[89] But, if an inpatient is assessed for a specified appliance, but it is only supplied and fitted when he has left hospital, then he will be an outpatient for the purposes of paying the prescription charge.

A partial reduction of charges is possible on the basis of low income for wigs, spinal supports and surgical brassieres – but not for Drug Tariff items.[90]

The NHS may make charges for repairing or replacing equipment, whether or not it originally attracted a charge, if this is necessitated by the 'act or omission' of the person.[91] The exercise of this power has sometimes attracted controversy, for example, in relation to the repair and replacement of expensive hearing aids used by children. In addition, hospitals can, in some circumstances, charge insurance companies for the cost of treatment for in-patients and out-patients following road traffic accidents. They can also charge an emergency treatment fee from the users of motor vehicles for immediate treatment or examination.[92]

However, no other equipment supplied by the NHS to NHS patients – such as walking frames, speech aids, hearing aids and incontinence pads – can be charged for. This would appear to be a straightforward legal and practical state of affairs, but in fact it is not. For example, it appears that some staff and managers in health authorities and NHS Trusts remain unaware of the law; and, from time to time, the Department of Health and Welsh Office issue guidance as a reminder.[93] There is an informed view that an undercurrent of illegal charging has existed in the NHS for many years. Sometimes it does surface in the Press[94], the investigations of the health service ombudsman[95], Parliament[96] or community health councils[97] – concerning, for example, illegal charges for children's orthopaedic footwear or nebulisers. And, in one VAT Tribunal case in 1974, it was never made clear how a woman – who, it was agreed, was receiving NHS treatment – came to pay £9.66 plus £0.96 to the company which made and fitted the belt, instead of the normal NHS prescription payable to the hospital.[98]

Because of the difficulties of ensuring the return of equipment, some hospitals charge deposits. For instance, this encourages people to return crutches which they have left hospital with (hospitals can lose hundreds of pairs of crutches annually)[99], or to return transit wheelchairs to hospital entrances when they have finished their visit (coin-in-the-slot is one method of).[100] On the assumption that such deposits do not amount to a 'charge', such schemes would not breach s.1 of the NHS Act 1977.

Failing to provide equipment at all

The question of charging is sometimes clouded by the little-appreciated irony that though the NHS cannot charge for most equipment, it does have the discretion simply not to provide it at all.

For example, some years ago considerable political heat was generated in the House of Commons about alleged charging for powered nebulisers by the NHS. If those hospitals concerned had been directly charging people, then they would indeed have been breaking the law. However, if they had instead been telling people to go away and buy their own, then they would have been within the law. Though the latter was legal in principle, nevertheless, such a blanket policy of withdrawing services runs the risk of adverse of judicial review (see p.446).

Occasionally, disputes about these matters reach the health service ombudsman, whose investigations illustrate how easily misunderstanding occurs. For example[101]:

> A woman suffering from sclerosis of the first and third vertebrae, had been receiving treatment from physiotherapists at a military hospital. The woman and her husband decided that the transcutaneous nerve stimulator (TENS) machine was so effective that her life would be much improved if she could use it at home. They bought a machine at a cost of £108 and claimed reimbursement from the health authority. The woman claimed that she had been advised by the sergeant physiotherapist to buy her own machine; and indeed the latter had supplied the address of a manufacturer, whilst the lieutenant physiotherapist had signed a certificate, recording his full agreement that the woman obtain the machine. On the other hand, the physiotherapists denied putting any pressure on the woman to make the purchase; and all were agreed that no promise of reimbursement had been made.
>
> A further confusing factor was that, whilst the physiotherapists stated that there was no possibility of their loaning TENS machines beyond one month (on a semi-permanent basis), the health authority stated that a longer loan might in fact have been possible; but, in any event, the woman had not been informed of this. The ombudsman found that the health authority had not acted maladministratively in refusing to reimburse the cost of the machine – but that it was most unfortunate that the woman and her husband had not been informed of the possibility of a loan. The eventual outcome was a happy one; the health authority agreed to buy the machine from the woman and her husband – and then loan it back to them.

One trend, reported to be widespread, has seen NHS district nurses provide fewer bathing services, whilst personal care assistants employed by social services departments have been taking on more. Where this occurs, the result is that the bathing can be charged for, since it is no longer being provided by the NHS. Similar concern has arisen over the powers health authorities have to make payments to organisations in the independent sector and to other authorities.[102] Depending on the precise arrangements, it is thought that services which would have been provided free of charge by the NHS – if provided at all – might be routinely charged for by the organisation receiving the payments. For instance, a voluntary organisation might receive NHS money to employ chiropodists to visit elderly people 'on behalf' of the NHS – but go on to make charges, which the NHS could not have made, had it been providing the service directly.

Selling of equipment by NHS occupational therapy departments

For many years, occupational therapy departments have sold small items of daily living equipment, often on the basis that they are for people's social care, rather than their medical or health care needs. The reason is that although people might eventually receive the item from a social services department, time and effort is saved if they can get the equipment straight away at the hospital. This selling of daily living equipment has taken place generally on a not-for-profit basis.

However, a few years ago, the Department of Health advised the College of Occupational Therapists that such selling is probably illegal and that it would instead be preferable for therapists to refer people to a hospital shop run by a voluntary organisation. This would then mean that NHS staff would not directly be receiving cash.[103] The advice caused some disquiet amongst occupational therapists, because of how well-established the practice had become and because of the adverse effects its cessation would have on patients.[104]

The uncertainty of the legal position is suggested by an investigation a few years ago by the health service ombudsman. A hospital occupational therapy department had charged a small sum for a pickup stick. The ombudsman noted that the statutory responsibility for provision of such equipment had lain with social services. But, because of imminent delay, the patient didn't want to wait. The ombudsman concluded that the charge for the stick was justified.[105]

The position is further complicated, because NHS Trusts can operate *income generation* schemes, so long as certain conditions are met. In particular, the schemes must not interfere with provision of NHS services.[106] Charges should also be commercially realistic, since the schemes are intended genuinely to generate income and to be run on business principles. Thus, if the equipment is defined as meeting social care needs, rather than NHS health care needs, then the selling of it is clearly not interfering with NHS provision. And the business condition would be met if schemes generate income. Therefore, and somewhat ironically, the selling of equipment by NHS occupational therapists is more likely to be legal if it generates a profit than if it is run on a not-for-profit basis.

There is a precedent for arguing that daily living equipment can be sold as part of income generation, so long as it clearly does not meet a health need which the NHS would normally deal with. Guidance from the Department of Health about income generation suggests that, for example, although free hospital transport should be available to patients with medical needs, those whose need for transport is primarily social (eg because of lack of access to public transport) could be charged for transport (eg a hospital car service).[107]

Shops on NHS premises

Sometimes shops are to be found in hospitals selling hearing aids or footwear. At best, such arrangements increase choice and are probably to be welcomed; but, at worst, the scope for abuse is considerable, since people could be at risk of being 'persuaded' – or subtly forced – to buy their equipment privately, rather than obtain it free of charge through the NHS. For example, the range of NHS special footwear available in a particular hospital might become increasingly restricted, whilst people might at the same time be informally advised that they would be much better off buying from the shop. Their needs might even be reassessed and reclassified as social rather than clinical – or as clinical, but so low a priority that they do not qualify for provision.[108]

The National Committee for Professionals in Audiology has produced guidelines on the private dispensing of hearing aids in association with the NHS. The guidelines state that, for example, financial benefit must not go directly to staff (who might be working in both an NHS and private capacity), but only to the hospital, authority or unit. No pressure of any kind must be put on patients to buy privately. If patients are being guided toward a particular private supplier, they should also be informed of other private suppliers. Advertising of private hearing aids within the hospital should be balanced and not excessive or misleading – and a 30-day money-back guarantee is to be encouraged.[109]

Department of Health draft guidance, too, emphasises that patients should be given the opportunity to see NHS aids first and be put under no pressure to buy privately.[110]

5. NHS COMPLAINTS

NHS complaints procedures have recently been overhauled and simplified – the new procedures have been effective from April 1996. However, for the sake of completeness, both the old and the new systems are summarised below.

NHS complaints procedures have been characterised as fragmented, confusing and complicated. Past problems have included unhelpful procedural differences relating to clinical and non-clinical complaints, limits on the jurisdiction of the health service ombudsman (see below), lack of information about procedures, and delays in handling complaints and appeals.[111] Also it seems that in the past some health authorities have not operated efficient and open complaints procedures. For example, rather than promote a complaint, a health authority might instead terminate the investigation if negligence is uncovered – despite DHSS guidance to the contrary.[112] Indeed, guidance about the new complaints system warns against hostile and defensive reactions, pointing out that an open and sympathetic approach is more likely to avert, than to stimulate, litigation.[113] However, the guidance also states that if a complainant 'explicitly indicates an intention to take legal action' then the complaints procedure should be discontinued. This reflects too a Court of Appeal ruling that it is not unreasonable for an authority to abort the procedure when faced with legal proceedings.[114]

One view is that good communication between NHS staff and patients, with less emphasis on 'fault' and an adversarial stance, might result in fewer complaints.[115] Complainants might feel 'compelled' to take legal action as a last resort, simply because they cannot obtain satisfactory responses and acknowledgement of their grievances through ordinary complaints procedures. Certainly, there is every incentive for patients not to take legal action since negligence is difficult to prove, litigation can take a long time, the stress might be considerable and the action be a financial gamble for the complainant.[116] In summary the old system operated as follows:

(i) **Old system: main hospital complaints procedure.** Hospital complaints which were not about clinical matters were investigated by the hospital complaints officer. Health authorities had to appoint designated complaints officers to receive formal complaints and to ensure that they are acted upon – and also assist with informal complaints. Arrangements had to be in place to enable staff to try to resolve complaints informally and otherwise to advise complainants how to make formal complaints. Formal complaints had to be in writing and made within three months of the incident complained of, although this time limit could be waived. Responses to formal complaints were to be prompt. Authorities had to ensure that complaints procedures are properly publicised.[117]

(ii) **Old system: clinical complaints procedure.** The clinical complaints procedure could involve up to three stages if necessary. At the first stage, the consultant involved responded to an oral or written complaint. At the second, the complainant could refer the matter to health authority staff (eg the director of public health). At the third stage an independent professional review would be set up. The review would involve investigation by two consultants working in the same specialism as the consultant against whom the complaint had been made. The review procedure was not intended to be used if legal action is likely.[118]

(iii) **Old system: complaints against general practitioners.** The Family Health Services Authority complaints procedure was for complaints against practitioners providing *general medical services* in the community: general practitioners, dentists, opticians and pharmacists. It consisted of an informal procedure, sometimes involving lay conciliation, in less serious matters. However, a formal procedure was invoked if there was an allegation that the practitioner had broken his or her terms of service.[119]

New complaints procedure (from April 1996)

In the light of the criticism of NHS complaints procedures, encapsulated finally in the Wilson report, *Being Heard*[120], a new, unified NHS complaints procedure is being implemented.

The new procedure is effective from April 1996 by means of Directions made under the NHS Act 1977 and the Hospital Complaints Procedure Act 1985. Amendments have also been made to NHS Regulations affecting *family health services* provided by general practitioners, dentists, ophthalmologists and pharmacists. In addition, the powers of the health service ombudsman have been extended through an Act of Parliament.

In summary, the new procedure is as follows.[121] It covers complaints against NHS Trusts, health authorities and family health services practitioners. Essentially, informal local resolution should be attempted, before the setting up of an *independent review panel.* If both procedures fail to resolve a dispute, resort can be had to the health service ombudsman, who will be able to investigate clinical, as well as administrative complaints (see below). The following paragraphs are based on a summary of the substantial guidance on implementation issued by the Department of Health in March 1996 – which in turn paraphrases, and expands upon, the various directions and regulations.[122] In outline the new system is as follows:

(i) **Establishing complaints procedures.** NHS Trusts and health authorities must establish a written complaints procedure; family health service practitioners will also be obliged to operate procedures approved by the health authority.

Complaints procedures must be publicised. NHS Trusts and health authorities must have a designated complaints manager who is not an employee to act as convener for independent reviews (see below). Complainants can include current or former patients or their representatives. Complaints must be made within 6 months of the relevant incident, although this limit can be waived in some circumstances. If negligence is probably at issue, the complaints procedure should not be abandoned unless expressly requested by the complainant.

(ii) **Local resolution of complaints.** NHS Trusts and health authorities must have a clear local resolution (ie informal) procedure – as must family health services practitioners in their practice-based complaints procedures. Attempts should be made to complete full investigation and resolution of complaints within 20 days in the case of NHS Trusts and health authorities, and 10 days in the case of family health services practitioners.

(iii) **Independent review panels.** Complainants, if dissatisfied with the local resolution process, can request the setting up of an independent review panel. The convener must decide whether to set up such a panel on the basis of a signed statement by the complainant. If the convener decides not to set up the panel, the complainant can ask the convener to reconsider – or instead refer the complaint to the health service ombudsman.

Independent review panels must consist of three members, including a lay chairman, a convener or alternative, and a purchaser (eg a health authority non-executive or GP fundholder) in the case of NHS Trusts, or independent person in the case of health authorities. If the complaint is about clinical matters, two independent clinical assessors will advise the panel. The panel must be given access to relevant records, including clinical ones. The complainant can be accompanied by another person but not by somebody legally qualified acting in a legal capacity. The panel has no executive authority over any actions by the NHS Trust, health authority or family health services practitioner. The panel's final report must be sent to various people including the complainant.

Dissatisfied complainants can approach the health service ombudsman. Time limits to be achieved by panels, from notice of setting up of the panel to final letter on action to be taken on the panels's findings, are six months for NHS Trusts and health authorities, and three months for family health services complaints.

Patient's Charter

The function of charters has already been outlined in Chapter 6. The Patient's Charter is of national application although it is reflected also in local charters, which could, for instance, set standards above – but presumably not below – those set out in the national document.

The Patient's Charter refers to various rights, guarantees, standards, targets, performance levels, and expectations.[123] Nevertheless, the 'rights' are not straightforward legal rights, because they cannot be enforced directly in a court of law. Instead, if people wish to complain under the Charter, they should write to the chief executive or general manager (rather than the complaints officer) of the hospital.[124] If complainants remain dissatisfied they can ask the health service ombudsman to investigate.[125] In addition, the NHS Executive (part of the Department of Health) might exert informal pressure on NHS Trusts.

Health service ombudsman

The health service ombudsman is legally empowered to investigate (i) *failure in service,* (ii) *failure to provide a service* which there is a duty to provide, and (iii) *maladministration* which has allegedly caused *injustice* or *hardship.*[126]

The booklet issued to the public by the ombudsman's office gives examples of maladministration: avoidable delay, failure to follow proper procedures, rudeness or discourtesy, not explaining decisions, and failure to deal with complaints fully and promptly.[127] However, because the ombudsman's remit covers not only maladministration but also provision and failure of services, he can investigate the standards and delivery of patient care as well.[128] In the past, the ombudsman has been unable, legally, to question the clinical judgements of NHS staff about the diagnosis, treatment and care of patients. However, this situation has changed with effect from April 1996.[129] One obvious reason for this change is that the ombudsman has sometimes been hampered in investigating complaints containing both administrative and clinical aspects – since he could investigate only the former, even when the two aspects could not sensibly be disentangled. In addition, the ombudsman can investigate complaints about the provision of information concerning how the NHS operates locally (eg policy on wheelchair provision); for example, refusal to provide information, a delay of over four weeks in obtaining the information, or financial charges made.[130]

In principle, the health service ombudsman wields broader powers than the local ombudsman – since failure within a service, or failure to provide a service, would appear to provide a better opportunity to challenge rationing decisions than that afforded the local ombudsman by the general maladministration ground alone. In fact, in the absence of maladministration, the ombudsman has not often ruled against authorities for rationing services – although has done so in a few notable cases, including the 'Leeds' case involving the denial of nursing care to a severely disabled person (see p.200).

Formal limits to the powers of the health service ombudsman

The ombudsman cannot investigate a case if there is an alternative means of remedy or redress (eg a negligence action), unless he is satisfied that it would not be reasonable to expect the complainant to pursue this other remedy. For instance, if a person was injured by a defective wheelchair, he or she might have a strong legal case under the Consumer Protection Act 1987 or in negligence. But, the ombudsman might accept that, on financial or other personal grounds, the person cannot, for various reasons, reasonably be expected to pursue the matter through the law courts.

Hitherto, the ombudsman has been unable to investigate complaints about GPs, dentists and pharmacists (unless they work in a hospital), though he has been able to investigate the handling by FHSAs of complaints against those practitioners. This has changed from April 1996.[131]

The ombudsman will not normally accept a complaint about something which happened over a year before, but may do if he thinks that it would be reasonable. A complaint must be made in writing to the ombudsman, and have first been made to the relevant NHS body which must have had a 'reasonable opportunity' to investigate the complaint first. Under the new NHS complaints procedure, it is expected that the ombudsman would only exceptionally take up complaints which had not first passed through the procedure. However, the most common complaint investigated by the ombudsman is precisely the handling of complaints by the NHS.[132] (It has been suggested that because, under the new NHS complaints procedures, the convener (see above) will be a member of the health authority or NHS Trust, the decision about whether to proceed to a review panel is not an independent one. This might lead to dissatisfied complainants and an excessive number of referrals to the ombudsman).[133]

Generally, the ombudsman's investigations are perceived to be thorough but are sometimes criticised as lengthy – for example, an average of 45 weeks in 1992–1993.[134]

Penalties and remedies

Legislation does not enable the ombudsman to impose binding, formal penalties on health authorities and NHS Trusts. However, in practice, he makes recommendations about how the injustice or hardship suffered by a patient should be remedied. This might be by means of an apology and an undertaking to review and change certain policies – or might even be financial compensation (eg for nursing home fees unjustly incurred following an authority's refusal to provide NHS care).[135]

Default powers of the Secretary of State

The Secretary of State has the power to declare an authority to be in default, if it has not carried out its functions in accordance with the NHS Act 1977.[136] It seems that no default order has ever been issued.

Complaints to professional bodies

In addition to NHS complaints avenues, it is possible for patients to complain to professional bodies such as the General Medical Council, the United Kingdom Central Council (UKCC) for Nursing, Midwifery and Health Visiting and various other bodies representing, for example, physiotherapists, occupational therapists and chiropodists.

These bodies investigate professional misconduct. Disciplinary action may include the cautioning, suspension or even the striking off of practitioners from the relevant professional register. Consequently, the primary aim of the hearings of these professional bodies is not to compensate complainants but to enforce standards of professional practice.

The explanatory booklet produced by one of these bodies, the UKCC, gives examples of misconduct which can lead to nurses, midwives and health visitors being struck off:

- falsification of, or failure to keep, essential records
- failure to protect the interests of patients
- reckless and 'wilfully unskilful' practice
- 'abuse' of patients by improper withholding, or excessive giving, of drugs which have been prescribed – or the giving of drugs which have not been prescribed.

However, as in the case of formal legal actions, there are defences to liability which invoke *reasonableness* or similar notions. For example, it is not misconduct if the practitioner failed 'to achieve the impossible in the particular circumstances'; or if she had exercised 'careful and conscientious' judgement 'reasonable in the circumstances and at the time the decision was taken'. Furthermore, even if misconduct is established, the practitioner might not be struck off if, for instance, he had committed an 'error' rather than a 'culpable act'.[137] In 1994, the General Medical Council dealt with 84 doctors charged with serious professional misconduct. Twenty seven were struck off, and all but 10 were found guilty of some offence.[138]

The decisions of such professional bodies can be contested in the courts; for example, at the end of 1995 the Privy Council held that the General Medical Council had been entitled to find that seriously negligent treatment could amount to serious professional misconduct – for which the doctor in question had been struck off.[139]

The purpose of the Medical (Professional Performance) Act 1995, not yet in force, is to enable the medical profession to regulate itself, by giving the General Medical Council powers to act against doctors who have worked to a 'seriously deficient standard of professional performance'.[140] How the concept of serious deficiency will be applied is as yet unclear.[141]

Notes

1 'Invalid carriage' is further defined in Schedule 2 of the *NHS Act 1977* as being 'a mechanically propelled vehicle specially designed and constructed (and not merely adapted) for the use of a person suffering some physical defect or disability and used solely by such a person'. This definition would presumably exclude the provision of essentially non-powered wheelchairs with an add-on power pack – a practice adopted by some NHS wheelchair services.

2 HSG(96)34. *Department of Health. Powered indoor/outdoor wheelchairs for severely disabled people.* London: DH.

3 Brazier, M. (1992). *Medicine, patients and the law.* 2nd edition. London: 1992, p.23.

4 SI 1996/708. *National Health Service (Functions of Health Authorities and Administration Arrangements) Regulations 1996.*

5 *Hansard,* House of Commons, Written Answers, 28 November 1995, col 613, Mr Sackville in reply to Ms Harman.

6 Dimond, B. (1994). How far can you go? [Boundaries of NHS responsibilities to pay for long-term care]. *Health Service Journal:* 14th April 1994, pp.24–25.

7 *R v Secretary of State for Social Services, West Midlands Regional Health Authority and Birmingham Area Health Authority, ex parte Hincks* (1980) 1 BMLR 93 (CA).

8 *R v Hertfordshire County Council, ex parte Three Rivers District Council* (1993) 157 LGR 526 (QBD).

9 *Report of the project team: plastic and reconstructive surgery,* para 6: sent out with EL(93)58. *Plastic surgery – issues for purchasers and providers.* NHS Management Executive, Department of Health, 1993.

10 Timmins, N. (1995). Operations halted as rationing row erupts. *Independent,* 27 August 1995.

11 Health Committee (1995). HC 134–i. *Priority setting in the NHS: purchasing.* Volume 1. London: HMSO, p.xxxiv.

12 Health Service Commissioner (E.62/93–94). *Failure to provide long term NHS care for a brain damaged patient.* 2nd report 1993–1994. London: HMSO.

13 Eg: *Hansard,* House of Commons, Written Answers, 24 November 1995, col 456, Mr. Hague: 'Decisions on the appropriateness of a particular treatment are a matter for clinical judgement'.

14 Quoted in: Health Service Commissioner (W.194/89–90). *Inability to provide NHS care for man in need of a hospital bed.* In: 2nd report 1990–1991. HC 482. London: HMSO, 1991.

15 *Hansard,* House of Commons Debates, Health Provision (Bradford), 24 January 1996, cols 325–332.

16 Quoted in: *Hansard,* House of Commons Debates, National Health Service, 20 January 1994, col.1083, Mr Davis.

17 *R v Cambridge Health Authority, ex parte B* [1995] 1 FLR 1055 (QBD and CA).

18 Price, D. (1996). Lessons for health care rationing from the case of child B. *British Medical Journal:* 20 January 1996; 312, pp.167–169.

19 See eg: *Re J (a minor) (wardship: medical treatment)* [1992] 4 All ER 614 (CA): in which Lord Donaldson said that he could not envisage the circumstances in which it would be right to require a doctor to treat a patient contrary to the doctor's professional judgement and duty to the patient.

20 *R v Secretary of State for Social Services, West Midlands Regional Health Authority and Birmingham Area Health Authority, ex parte Hincks* (1980) 1 BMLR 93 (CA).

21 *R v Central Birmingham Health Authority, ex parte Collier* (1988), Times 6 January 1988 (Lexis 6 January 1988) (CA). *R v Central Birmingham Health Authority, ex parte Walker* (1987) 3 BMLR 32 (QBD and CA).

22 *R v Cambridge Health Authority, ex parte B* [1995] 1 FLR 1055 (QBD and CA).

23 R *v Sheffield Health Authority, ex parte Seale* (1994) 25 BMLR 1 (QBD).

24 *Lloyds Bank v Bundy* [1975] QB 326 (CA): in which Lord Denning supported an elderly farmer against the bank which was trying to take possession of his farm, following an ill-advised guarantee and charge which the farmer executed in relation to the farm.

25 Health Service Commissioner (W.371/83–84). *Delay in providing hearing aid.* 4th report 1983–1984. HC 476. London: HMSO, 1984.

26 Parliamentary Commissioner for Administration (5/915/78). *Failure to provide a suitable hearing aid. 4th report for session 1978–79. HC 302.* London: HMSO, 1979.

27 Parliamentary Commissioner for Administration (C.794/K). *Provision of a wheelchair. 5th report for session 1976–77. HC 528.* London: HMSO, 1977.

28 Health Service Commissioner (SW.47/83–84, SW.54/83–84). *Hospital care and arrangements made for weekend at home for elderly patient.* HC 33. 1st report for 1984/85 London: HMSO, 1984.

29 Parliamentary Commissioner for Administration (15/313/77). *Difficulties over an artificial limb. 3rd report for session 1977–78.* London: HMSO, 1978.

30 Parliamentary Commissioner for Administration (C309/87). *Failure to respond properly to requirements for an artificial leg.* 5th report for session 1987–88. HC 430. London: HMSO, 1988.

31 Parliamentary Commissioner for Administration (C98/77). *Supply of a modified invalid car.* 1st report for session 1977–78. HC 126. London: HMSO, 1978.

32 Health Service Commissioner (W341/77–78). *Delay in supply of surgical shoes.* 1st report for session 1979–80. HC 302. London: HMSO, 1979.

33 Health Service Commissioner (SW.28/84–85). *Care of an elderly patient.* 1st report 1985–1986. HC 27. London: HMSO, 1985.

34 Health Service Commissioner (W.783/85–86). *Failure in speech therapy service.* 3rd report 1987–1988. HC 232. London: HMSO, 1988.

35 Health Service Commissioner (W.224/78–79). *Waiting time for orthopaedic treatment.* 1st report 1978–1979. London: HMSO, 1979.

36 Health Service Commissioner (W.286/86–87). *Discharge arrangements made for domiciliary care.* In: 4th Report 1987–1988. HC 511. London: HMSO, 1988.

37 Health Service Commissioner (WW.3/79–80). *Refusal to provide crutches.* 1st report 1981–1982. HC 9. London: HMSO, 1981.

38 Health Service Commissioner (W.707/85–86). *Provision by hospital eye service (HES) of contact lenses.* 3rd report 1987–1988. HC 232. London: HMSO, 1988.

39 Marks, L. (1994). *Seamless care or patchwork quilt: discharging patients from acute hospital care.* Research Report 17. London: King's Fund Institute.

40 Eg Department of Health (1994). *Hospital discharge workbook: a manual on hospital discharge practice.* London: DH. See also: British Geriatrics Society; Association of Directors of Social Services; Royal College of Nursing (1995). *The discharge of elderly persons from hospital for community care: a joint policy statement.*

41 *Hansard,* House of Commons, 11 February 1996, National Health Service Staff, col 814, Ms Harriet Harman.

42 Health Service Commissioner (W.40/84–85). *Proposals to discharge younger chronic sick patient.* 2nd report 1984–1985. HC 418. London: HMSO, 1985.

43 Health Service Commissioner (W.420/83–84). *Discharge arrangements for an elderly, immobile patient.* London: HMSO, 1984.

44 Health Service Commissioner (SW.82/86–87). *Unsatisfactory discharge arrangements.* 4th report 1987–1988. HC 511. London: HMSO, 1988.

45 Health Service Commissioner (W.24/84–85 and W.56/84–85). *Failure in care and communication about discharged patient.* 2nd report 1984–1985. HC 418. London: HMSO, 1985.

46 EL(91)28. *Continence services and the supply of incontinence aids.* NHS Management Executive, Department of Health, 1991.

47 Elliston, S.; Britton, A. (1994). Is infertility an illness? *New Law Journal:* 11 November 1995; 144(6671), pp.1552–3. The authors discuss the denial of treatment for infertility on the basis of age.

48 Health Service Commissioner (W.68/77–78). *Use of 'means test' by NHS.* 2nd report 1977–1978. HC 343. London: HMSO, 1978.

49 Smith, R. (ed) (1993). *Rationing in action.* London: British Medical Association, p.ix.

50 Harris, T. (1993). Consulting the public. In: Smith, R. (ed) (1993). *Rationing in action.* London: British Medical Association, p.161.

51 Hunter, D.J. (1993). *Rationing dilemmas in health care.* Birmingham: National Association of Health Authorities and Trusts, p.11.

52 Klein, R.; Redmayne, S. (1992). *Patterns of priorities: a study of the purchasing and rationing policies of health authorities.* Birmingham: National Association of Health Authorities and Trusts, p.21.

53 Hunter, D.J. (1993). *Rationing dilemmas in health care.* Birmingham: National Association of Health Authorities and Trusts, p.9.

54 Royal College of Physicians (1994). *Ensuring equity and quality of care for elderly people: the interface between geriatric medicine and general (internal) medicine.* London: RCP. Grimley Evans, J. (1993). This patient or that patient? In: Smith, R. (ed) (1993). *Rationing in action.* London: British Medical Association.

55 Klein, R.; Redmayne, S. (1992). *Patterns of priorities: a study of the purchasing and rationing policies of health authorities.* Birmingham: National Association of Health Authorities and Trusts, pp.15, 17.

56 *Hansard.* House of Commons Debates: National Health Service, 21 October 1991, col 676, Mr. Robin Cook.

57 Eg *Hansard:* Written Answers, 20th December 1990, cols.347–348, Mr. Dorrell replying to Mr Janner: concerning the proposed withdrawal of incontinence pads from 400–500 residents of residential care homes in Leicestershire.

58 See eg: Hunter, D.J. (1993). *Rationing dilemmas in health care.* Birmingham: National Association of Health Authorities and Trusts, p.9.

59 Secretary of State for Health (1992). Cm 1986. *Health of the nation: a strategy for health in England.* London: HMSO, pp.116–123.

60 *Personal communication:* Senior NHS therapist, 1995.

61 Eg *Hansard:* Oral Answers, 14th April 1994, col 415, The Prime Minister replying to Mrs. Beckett: concerning a BBC radio 'Today' report; *Hansard:* Written Answers, 19th April 1994, col 474, Dr. Mawhinney replying to Mr. David Young: 'It is the duty of all health authorities to ensure that people of all ages have access to acute care, and that specialist care is available to those who suffer with chronic conditions due to the aging process'. This statement unhelpfully ignores authorities' wide powers to deny services to individuals on the basis of priorities and resource allocation.

62 Hunter, D.J. (1993). *Rationing dilemmas in health care.* Birmingham: National Association of Health Authorities and Trusts, p.12.

63 Hunter, D.J. (1993). *Rationing dilemmas in health care.* Birmingham: National Association of Health Authorities and Trusts, p.10.

64 Smith, R. (1993). *Rationing: the search for sunlight.* In: Smith, R. (ed) (1993). Rationing in action. London: British Medical Association.

65 See eg: Calabresi, G.; Bobbit, P. (1978). *Tragic choices: the conflicts society confronts in the allocation of tragically scarce resources.* New York: W.W. Norton.

66 Hunter, D.J. (1995). Rationing: the case for 'muddling through elegantly'. *British Medical Journal:* 1995; 311, p.811.

67 See eg: Bowling, A. (1996). Health care rationing: the public's debate. *British Medical Journal:* 16 March 1996; 312, pp.670–674.

68 Mooney, G.; Gerard, K.; Donaldson, C.; Farrar, S. (1992). *Priority setting in purchasing: some practical guidelines.* Birmingham: National Association of Health Authorities and Trusts, pp.9–12.

69 House of Commons Health Committee (1995). *Priority setting in the NHS: purchasing.* Vol 1. London: HMSO, p.lvii.

70 Bottomley, V. (1993). Priority setting in the NHS. In: Smith, R. (ed) (1993). *Rationing in action.* London: British Medical Association, p.27.

71 SI 1992/635. *National Health Service (General Medical Services) Regulations 1992.* (As amended).

72 The power to publish the Drug Tariff stems from the following regulations: SI 1992/662. *National Health Service (General Pharmaceutical Services) Regulations 1992*, r.18.

73 SI 1992/662. *National Health Service (General Pharmaceutical Services) Regulations 1992,* schedule 2, para 5.

74 For a thorough analysis of the market for appliances and the role of dispensing appliance contractors and pharmacy contractors, see: Touche Ross (1994). *Department of Health reimbursement and remuneration of appliances report.* London: Touche Ross. (For the Department of Health).

75 Nurse prescription is governed by the *Medicinal Products: Prescription by Nurses etc Act 1992.*

76 EL(91)127. NHS Executive. *Responsibility for prescribing between hospitals and GPs.* London: Department of Health, 1991.

77 *NHS Act 1977*, s.1.

78 SI 1992/635. *National Health Service (General Medical Services) Regulations 1992*, Schedule 2, para 12.

79 SI 1992/635. *National Health Service (General Medical Services) Regulations 1992,* Schedule 2, para 16.

80 Iliffe, S.; Haines, A.; Gallivan, S.; Booroff, A.; Goldenberg, E.; Morgan, P. (1991). Assessment of elderly people in general practice 2: functional abilities and medical problems. *British Journal of General Practice:* January 1991, pp.13–15.

81 HSG(95)19. NHS Executive. *GP fundholding: list of goods and services.* Leeds: Department of Health, pp.9, 15. This list of good and services is made under s.15(7)(b) of the *NHS and Community Care Act* 1990 and r.20 of SI 1993/567, *NHS (Fundholding Practices) Regulations* 1993.

82 See advice in: HSG (95)64. NHS Executive. *GP fundholding: inclusion of community specialist nursing and other services in standard and community fundholding from 1 April 1996.* Leeds: Department of Health.

83 Eg McMullan, J.J. (1988). General practitioners and disability. *Journal of the Royal College of General Practitioners;* April 1988, pp.191–192. Phillips, A. (1996). General practitioners' knowledge and use of a disabled living centre. *British Journal of Occupational Therapy:* February 1996; 59(2), pp.79–83.

84 *NHS Act 1977*, s.1.

85 SI 1989/419. *NHS (Charges for Drugs and Appliances) Regulations 1989* r.3 (as amended).

86 SI 1989/419. *NHS (Charges for Drugs and Appliances) Regulations 1989* r.6 (as amended).

87 SI 1989/419 cross-refers here to: SI 1988/551. *National Health Service (Travelling Expenses and Remission of Charges Regulations 1988* (as amended).

88 In October 1995, the government lowered the age limit for men from 65 to 60 following a ruling by the European Court of Justice that the unequal age limits between men and women were discriminatory and contravened EC Directive 79/7/EEC. See: HSG(95)52. NHS Executive. *Change to prescription charge exemption arrangements.* London: Department of Health.

89 *NHS Act 1977*, schedule 12, para 1.

90 SI 1988/551. *National Health Service (Travelling Expenses and Remission of Charges Regulations 1988* (as amended).

91 *NHS Act 1977*, s.82. And: SI 1974/284. *NHS (Charges for Appliances) Regulations 1974*, r.6.

92 See: HSG(95)24. NHS Executive. *Road Traffic Charges.* London: Department of Health, 1995.These charges can be made under the *Road Traffic Act* 1988, ss.157–159. The amount of the charges is controlled by: SI 1995/889. *Road Traffic Accidents (Payments for Treatment) Order 1995.*

93 See eg EL(91)129. NHS Executive. *Charging NHS patients.* London: Department of Health, 1991. Also: EL(92)20. NHS Executive. *Provision of equipment by the NHS.* London: Department of Health, 1992. From the Welsh Office, see: FHSL(W)115/91. *Charging NHS patients.* Cardiff: Welsh Office, 1991. Also: FHSL(W)21/92. *The provision of powered nebulisers under the National Health Service.* Cardiff: Welsh Office, 1992.

94 Patients charged illegally. *Therapy Weekly* 1992; 18(34), p.1.

95 Health Service Commissioner (1992) (W.226/91–92). *Refusal to provide orthoses to a child free of charge.* 1st report 1992–1993. HC 32. London: HMSO.

96 *Hansard.* House of Commons Debates: National Health Service, 21 October 1991, col 662, Mr. William Waldegrave, Secretary of State for Health, and Mr. Rhodri Morgan.

97 Eg letter (15 January 1992) from the Association of Community Health Councils to Virginia Bottomley, Secretary of State for Health about nebulisers.

98 *Mary Payton v The Commissioners* (1974) 1 VATTR 140.

99 Potter, B.; Angus Wallace, W. (1990). Crutches. *Physiotherapy:* 3 November 1990; 301, pp.1037–1039.

100 Jones, J. (1996). Hospital levy on wheelchairs. *Observer,* 18 February 1996.

101 Health Service Commissioner (W.263/83–84). *Reimbursement of cost of privately purchased medical equipment.* 1st report for 1984/85. HC 33. London: HMSO, 1984.

102 For a summary of the complicated situation, see: HSG(95)45. NHS Executive. *Arrangements between health authorities and NHS Trusts and private and voluntary sector organisations for the provision of community care services.* London: DH.

103 Letter dated 9th June 1992: *Provision of equipment by the NHS: EL(92)20.*

104 Eg Regional Occupational Therapy Advisory Group North West Thames (1992). *Statement on EL(92)20.*

105 Health Service Commissioner (W.340/80–81). *Care and treatment provided for a paralysed patient at home. 2nd report 1981–1982. HC 372.* London: HMSO, 1982.

106 *Health and Medicines Act 1988,* s.7(8).

107 Department of Health (1989). *Income generation: a guide to local initiative.* London: DH, para 45.

108 Tomkin, Z. (1991). Footing the bill: the orthopaedic department at Guy's Hospital is trying to cut costs by offering patients stock shoes where possible, or inviting them to go private. *Therapy Weekly:* 1991; 18(9), p.4.

109 Rendell, R. (1994). *Ethical guidelines for commercial dispensing of hearing aids in association with the NHS.* National Committee for Professionals in Audiology.

110 See draft guidance: Department of Health (1995). *Hearing aid services provided by audiology departments.* London: DH.

111 National Consumer Council (1993). *Consumer concerns 1993: a consumer view of health services: the report of a MORI survey.* London: NCC, pp.29–37. Also: Consumers' Association (1993). *NHS complaints procedures: the way forward.* London: CA. Also: Association of Community Health Councils for England and Wales (1993). *NHS complaints procedures: a submission to the Complaints Review Committee.* London: ACHCEW.

112 Consumers' Association (1993). *NHS complaints procedures: the way forward.* London: CA, pp.17–18.

113 NHS Executive (1996). *Complaints: listening...acting...improving: guidance on implementation of the NHS complaints procedure.* London: Department of Health, p.16.

114 *R v Canterbury & Thanet District Health Authority, ex parte F and W* [1994] Med LR 132 (CA).

115 Consumers' Association (1993). *NHS complaints procedures: the way forward: policy report.* London: Consumers' Association, p.14.

116 Association of Community Health Councils for England and Wales (1993). *NHS complaints procedures: a submission to the Complaints Review Committee.* London: ACHCEW, p.35.

117 The hospital complaints procedure has operated under the *Hospital Complaints Procedure Act 1985,* Directions made under s.17 of the NHS Act 1977 (carried in HC(88)37) and guidance contained in: HC(88)37. Department of Health and Social Security. *Hospital Complaints Procedure Act 1985.* London: DHSS.

118 Department of Health and Social Security. HC(81)5. *Health service complaints procedure.* London: DHSS, 1981.

119 FHSA complaints procedures stem from Regulations made under the NHS Act 1977: SI 1992/664. *National Health Service (Service Committees and Tribunal) Regulations.*

120 Wilson, A. (Chairman) (1994). *Being heard: the report of a review committee on NHS complaints procedures.* London: Department of Health.

121 The following is summarised from: NHS Executive (1995). *Interim guidance on implementation of the NHS complaints procedure.* London: Department of Health.

122 NHS Executive (1996). *Complaints: listening...acting...improving: guidance on implementation of the NHS complaints procedure.* London: Department of Health. (An outline of the legislative framework of the new complaints system is given on p.3).

123 Department of Health (1995). *The patient's charter & you.* London: DH. And see: HSG(92)36. NHS Management Executive. *Patient's Charter: monitoring and publishing information on performance.* London: Department of Health, 1992.
124 Department of Health (1995). *The patient's charter & you.* London: DH.
125 As he did in Scotland in relation to waiting times and information given to a patient about them: Health Service Commissioner (SW.81/92–93). *Rights under the Patient's Charter. 1st report 1993–1994. HC 30.* London: HMSO, 1993.
126 For the ombudsman's powers, see: *Health Service Commissioners Act 1993.*
127 Health Service Ombudsman for England (1996). *Do you have a complaint about the service you have received from the NHS? How the health service ombudsman can help you.* London.
128 Health Service Commissioner (1993). *Annual report for 1993–94.* London: HMSO, p.2.
129 *Health Service Commissioner's (Amendment) Act 1996:* amending the *Health Service Commissioner's Act 1993.*
130 Health Service Ombudsman for England (1996). *Do you have a complaint about the service you have received from the NHS? How the health service ombudsman can help you.* London.
131 *Health Service Commissioner's (Amendment) Act 1996:* amending the *Health Service Commissioner's Act 1993.*
132 NHS Executive (1995). *Interim guidance on implementation of the NHS complaints procedure.* London: Department of Health, p.33.
133 Harris, T.; Simanowitz, A. (1996). Concern for NHS complaints system. (Letter). *The Times:* 3 April 1996.
134 House of Commons Select Committee on the Parliamentary Commissioner for Administration (1993). *The powers, work and jurisdiction of the ombudsman.* First report, volume 1. London: HMSO, paras 12–13.
135 Eg Health Service Commissioner (E.264/94–95). *Discharge to private nursing home. In: Report of the Health Service Commissioner: selected investigations completed April to September 1995.* 1st report for session 1995–1996. HC 11. London: HMSO, 1995.
136 *NHS Act 1977,* s.85.
137 United Kingdom Central Council for Nursing, Midwifery and Health Visiting (1993). *Complaints about professional conduct.* London: UKCC, pp.8–11.
138 Howard, G. (1996). The medical 'courts' that can try a doctor's crimes. *The Times:* 16 January 1996.
139 *McCandless v General Medical Council* (1995) (PC), *The Times:* 12 December 1995.
140 Summarised: Barton, A. (1995). Powers for GMC against incompetent doctors. *Lancet:* 18 November 1995; 346, p.1355.
141 Marquand, P. (1996). Protecting patients. *Solicitors Journal:* 8 March 1996; 140(9), pp.222–223.

CHAPTER 9

PROVISION OF EQUIPMENT IN RESIDENTIAL AND NURSING HOMES

COVERAGE

1. Equipment provision in residential homes
    - Duty of independent residential homes to provide equipment and adaptations
    - Specification of equipment in contracts for residential care
    - Duty of social services departments to provide equipment for the individual needs of residents
    - NHS provision of equipment for people in residential homes
    - Prescription of equipment by general practitioners.
2. Equipment provision in private nursing homes
    - Duty of nursing homes to provide equipment and adaptations
    - Specification of equipment in contracts for nursing home care
    - NHS provision of equipment for people in nursing homes
    - Prescription of equipment by general practitioners
    - Practical consequences of confused responsibilities.

Key points

The provision of equipment for people in residential homes and nursing homes is an ill-defined area of provision. There are various reasons for this.

First, there are several categories of residents in homes. Some residents might be paying wholly for themselves, but many will be paid for either wholly or partly by the Department of Social Security, the social services department or an NHS Trust. A resident's category can affect, in principle, how equipment is provided. Second, the services provided for residents are based on, and influenced by diverse legislation. Third, many residents – even those paying for themselves – do not have detailed, formal contracts with the homes providing their care. As a result, neither they nor their relatives, are easily able to enforce the provision of particular services or equipment. Fourth, the regulation of residential and nursing homes (and of the availability of equipment and adaptations within them) is achieved by (i) vague *legislation* (which anyway does not apply to homes run directly by local authorities), (ii) the variable *standards* imposed on homes by local authorities and health authorities (in their registering capacity), and (iii) the variable *contract terms* imposed by the same local authorities when they purchase care from the homes.[1] Even, taking one aspect of this regulation – standards, for example – their composition is likely to vary from authority to authority, and their enforcement may also vary from inspector to inspector within the same authority.[2]

The practical consequence of this situation is that, when problems arise, it can be difficult to identify who should be providing what equipment. The boundaries between provision by the home itself, the NHS, social services department or residents (and their relatives) are indistinct. This lack of clarity, reflected in law and practice, is not for want of helpful and detailed guidance; for example, a number of useful good practice documents have been produced by the Social Services Inspectorate, the National Association of Health Authorities and Trusts and the Centre for Policy on Ageing.

Questions people ask

- Who will provide and pay for incontinence pads in residential homes and nursing homes?
- How detailed are the contracts local authorities draw up with homes – and do they specify who should be providing particular nursing services, therapy services and equipment?
- Do social services departments provide daily living equipment needed by individual residents?
- Will NHS physiotherapists visit nursing home residents and loan them, for example, special walking frames?

1. EQUIPMENT PROVISION IN RESIDENTIAL HOMES

Provision of equipment in residential homes is subject to legislation that governs:

- the duties of home owners (excluding local authorities) to provide certain services and facilities
- the duties of social services departments to provide residential care either directly or by purchasing it from the independent sector
- the duties of social services departments to provide equipment for residents' individual requirements
- the duties of health authorities to provide health services to the population at large; and
- the provision of general practitioner services.

Duty of independent residential homes to provide equipment and adaptations

Regulations made under the Registered Homes Act 1984 contain a list of services and facilities to be provided by private homes 'having regard to the size of the home and the number, age, sex and condition of residents'. The list includes specific reference to the[3]:

- making of adaptations and providing facilities necessary for physically disabled people
- employment of suitably qualified and competent staff adequate for the well-being of residents
- reasonable accommodation and space
- adequate and suitable furniture, bedding, curtains, screens and related equipment
- adequate washing facilities and lavatories
- adequate light, heating and ventilation
- sufficient and suitable kitchen and eating equipment
- access to public telephone and ability and arrangements to allow residents to communicate with others privately whether by post or telephone.

Equipment and adaptations covered by the Regulations form part of the services provided by a residential home. In practice, the existence of suitable facilities, in terms of disability equipment and adaptations, is likely to vary. Wheelchair ramps might be commonplace, but the availability of other equipment less so.[4]

The Regulations are vague in so far as specific disability equipment is not mentioned – and the duty to provide those items which are listed is qualified by words such as 'appropriate' and 'adequate'. The wide discretion conferred on homes could easily be criticised, since vagueness makes enforcement problematic. However, it might be equally unreasonable to stipulate (not only in legislation, but also in standards), for example, how many bath hoists a home should have. This is because the number of hoists reasonably required varies, depending not only on the number and medical condition of residents, but also on the physical features of the home and the types and ages of the staff.[5]

Standards and good practice guidance

Various guidance sets out good practice for the provision of services and equipment in residential homes. *Home life* was published by the Centre for Policy on Ageing in 1984.[6] This code of practice received government approval in 1986 Circular guidance[7] and was referred to in the main community care policy guidance issued in 1990.[8] It refers not only to the need for a range of equipment and adaptations – but also to their proper fitting, repair, the support of residents in using them, and staff training. It has recently been published in a revised form under the title, *A better home life.* Home owners are, however, likely to wish to avoid prescriptive contracts or standards – as reaction to a draft of the revision suggested. Adverse comments surfaced in the House of Commons about the recommended use of chemical toilets rather than commodes, low window sills – and to the disapproval expressed of residents being treated as objects of charity (eg through activities involving carol singing or harvest festival goods).[9]

In 1989, the Social Services Inspectorate (SSI) published *Homes are for living in*, a model of good practice to be used for evaluation of the quality of life in residential homes. It contains a number of references to equipment and adaptations under various headings such as premises, privacy, dignity and independence.[10] More recently, the Inspectorate's inspections of residential homes are carried out according to a set of explicit standards and criteria. For example, inspectors check how well the environment allows people to use walking frames or wheelchairs, as well as for the presence of adequate handrails, special baths or alarms.[11] Most recently, a comprehensive guide to health care in residential homes published by Age Concern England has been endorsed by a Chief Inspector letter from SSI. It contains references to equipment and adaptations throughout.[12]

Registration and inspection of residential homes

Local authorities are responsible for registering and inspecting independent residential homes; whilst those homes run by authorities themselves are inspected by the Social Services Inspectorate of the Department of Health.

Authorities may refuse to register, or may de-register, independent homes which provide inadequate premises and equipment. Appeals can be made to Registered Homes Tribunals which sometimes consider, amongst many other aspects of homes, equipment and premises. Registration and inspection is not primarily a means by which individual residents can seek redress – although, clearly, residents stand to benefit. Further sanctions exist, because it is a criminal offence to breach the Regulations specifying the services and facilities that must be provided.[13] Before prosecution, local authorities have the power to issue notices ordering a home to comply within a certain time limit.[14]

Registered Homes Tribunals sometimes consider the adequacy of equipment and adaptations when hearing appeals in disputes between local authorities and home owners. They have found, for example, whilst it is understandable that staff should encourage residents to use lavatories, it is not acceptable that commodes should be inappropriately denied to residents. Similarly, even though staff might believe that a particular resident is better off without her walking frame, they should not discourage its use excessively. And, although, residents sometimes use call-bells or buzzers inappropriately (eg for attention-seeking), it is poor practice for the home to place them out of reach of residents.[15] Shortcomings might include excessively small bathrooms without grab handles on baths or walls, or the difficulty residents with walking frames or wheelchairs had in using the lavatories and closing the doors.[16] And, the absence of a lift might contribute to the 'restricted and depressing life' of residents.[17]

Specification of equipment in contracts for residential care

Considerable uncertainty sometimes surrounds what equipment and other services people are entitled to in residential and nursing homes. Typically, for instance, it might be unclear who is going to provide and pay for incontinence pads. The reasons for the uncertainty are several and relate in part to the absence or vagueness of contracts.

If residents are supported financially by a social services department, then it is the latter and not the resident who has the contract with the home; therefore, the resident cannot enforce the contract directly, because he or she is not a party to it. Furthermore, the contract might simply not specify in detail who should be providing what.[18]

Alternatively, if a resident is making his or her own arrangements, there might still be no detailed contract. Given the amount of money involved (several hundred pounds a week), it seems remarkable that formal, detailed contracts between home and resident are reported to have been the exception rather than the rule.[19] This general lack of adequate contracts is not for want of eminent recommendation – for example, by *Home Life: a code of practice for residential care* (1984)[20] which was endorsed by the DHSS and by the influential Wagner report on residential care.[21]

For the sake of clarity and enforcement, clear agreements, with detailed terms and conditions, would be desirable for all concerned. Even where the local authority enters into a block contract with a home for a specific number of beds, it might be preferable to create a contractual relationship also between home and resident, thereby aiding enforcement and clarity.[22] The Continuing Care Conference has published a framework contract for use in residential and nursing homes.[23] Contracts might go some way to rectifying the mismatch between the facilities residents want – such as locks on their doors or physiotherapy – and what they actually get. Otherwise, hopes, expectations and reality might not coincide.[24]

Duties of social services departments to arrange for residential accommodation: content of contracts and equipment

Under community care legislation, local authorities have duties to provide residential accommodation.[25] They can provide it directly or by arrangement with providers from the independent sector. It is open to authorities to specify contractual terms relating to the provision of equipment by independent residential homes. The High Court has confirmed that such terms can be stricter than the requirements imposed by legislation governing what homes must provide (see above section).[26] Confusion can also arise, since the local authority acts both as registration authority and as the placer of contracts – yet the conditions (including specification of required equipment) of registration and of the contract might differ.

Duty of social services departments to provide equipment for the individual needs of residents

As explained above, contracts made by local authorities with independent residential homes might in practice refer specifically to equipment. However, in addition, the duty social services departments have under s.2 of the CSDPA to provide equipment applies, in principle, as much to people living in residential homes as to people remaining in their own homes.[27] Circular guidance issued by the Department of Health in 1986 explained that, whilst homes might provide equipment for general use, residents might have additional, individual needs for equipment which could be met separately by local authorities.[28] In principle, the duty would apply irrespective of how residents are funded, and whether they are in independent or local authority residential homes.

However, in practice, social services departments might tend, as a matter of policy, to regard the needs of people in residential care as a lower priority than those in their own homes. Perhaps reflecting this state of affairs, an SSI report in 1988 found that only 63% of social services departments provided 'personal aids', 70% 'special equipment' and 50% 'personal special clothing' for residents.[29]

The access of residents to equipment might not depend simply on resources or their wishes. For instance, in one local authority residential home, the bedroom set aside for respite care did not have a television because of a policy of promoting contact between the occupant and the other residents of the home.[30]

NHS provision of equipment for people in residential homes

Health authorities have duties towards the general population to provide medical, nursing and after-care services (see p.199). These duties apply as much to people in residential accommodation as to people in their own homes.

Guidance from the Department of Health confirmed this interpretation of the law by stating that the NHS continues to have responsibility for providing a range of community health services. These include district nursing, specialist nursing services (eg advice about incontinence), nursing equipment, physiotherapy, chiropody, and speech and language therapy.[31] In practice, however, because people in residential homes are in a formal care setting and are not living alone, their needs are often regarded as lower priority than those of people still living in their own homes.[32] Therefore, as with NHS services in general, provision of equipment for residents is governed by local policies, priorities and rationing and varies from area to area and from home to home.

Some health authorities adopt policies not to provide certain services or equipment to people in private residential care. This is despite the fact that, if such policies are rigid and do not allow for exceptions, authorities might run the risk of judicial review in the law courts on the grounds that they are *fettering their discretion* (see p.446). For example, a report published by the Social Services Inspectorate in 1988 examined the extent to which its 1977 *Memorandum of guidance* (see above) had been followed in residential homes run by local authorities. The answer was that it had been – but patchily. More particularly, 69% of health authorities provided 'personal aids', 24% 'special equipment' and 17% 'personal special clothing' for residents.[33]

More recent reports by SSI on residential care suggest continuing uncertainty. Good practices are found – but so are poor. For example, the provision of therapy services by health authorities might be limited, absent or charged extra to residents.[34] Chiropody services might be subject to long waiting times or withdrawn altogether, leaving residents to purchase services privately. Assistance from occupational therapists in assessing equipment for daily living might be 'very good' – but elsewhere, it could be limited. And physiotherapy services might be generally unavailable.[35]

Prescription of equipment by general practitioners

Home owners have a duty to make adequate arrangements for residents to see their GPs and dentists.[36] Thus, in principle residents retain access to NHS equipment prescribable by GPs – the range of which has been considerably extended for fundholding GPs from April 1996. In addition, GPs can refer their patients on to hospital consultants and sometimes directly to other NHS practitioners, such as therapists and chiropodists, who supply equipment.

2. EQUIPMENT PROVISION IN PRIVATE NURSING HOMES

Provision of equipment in private nursing homes is governed by legislation covering:

- the duty of home owners to provide certain services and facilities
- the duty of social services departments to purchase nursing home care for people who need it
- the general duties of health authorities to provide health services to the population at large
- the provision of general practitioner services.

Duty of nursing homes to provide equipment and adaptations

Regulations made under the Registered Homes Act 1984 contain a list of services and facilities which must be provided by homes 'having regard to the size of the home and the number, age, sex and condition of the patients'. The list includes specific reference to[37]:

- 'adequate medical, surgical and nursing equipment'
- 'adequate professional, technical, ancillary and other staff'
- 'adequate accommodation' for each patient
- adequate furniture, bedding, curtains, screens, floor covering
- adequate wash basins and baths
- adequate light, heating and ventilation
- adequate food, kitchen and eating equipment
- provision of public telephones.

Any equipment covered by these regulations should be provided as part of the services provided by a nursing home and included within the fees paid to it – whomever those fees are paid by.

Registration and inspection of nursing homes

Health authorities are responsible for registering and inspecting nursing homes. They may refuse to register, or de-register, homes which provide inadequate premises and equipment. Appeals can be made to Registered Homes Tribunals which sometimes consider, amongst many other aspects of homes, equipment and premises. Registration and inspection is not primarily a means by which individual residents can seek redress – although, clearly, residents stand to benefit.

It is a criminal offence for homes to breach the Regulations in respect of the services and facilities which must be provided by homes.[38] However, before prosecution, health authorities have the power to issue notices ordering a home to comply within a certain time limit.[39]

Registered Homes Tribunals sometimes consider the adequacy of equipment and adaptations when hearing appeals in disputes between health authorities and home owners. For example, the absence of a lift, which means that top-floor residents were isolated, might be unacceptable.[40] On the other hand, a narrow staircase and a stairlift which did not travel quite to the top of the stairs was not deemed to be a problem, so long as the residents on the second floor of the home were ambulant – and had no trouble negotiating the staircase.[41] Tribunals might consider the capacity of particular rooms to accommodate hoists[42] – especially in view of the Manual Handling of Loads Regulations 1992.

Specification of equipment in contracts for nursing home care

The corresponding section above, dealing with residential homes, is generally applicable to nursing homes.

NHS provision of equipment for people in nursing homes

The nature of the provision by health authorities and NHS Trusts for people in private nursing homes, depends on whether they are NHS patients or not. However, there has for many years been uncertainty about precisely what services and equipment any one NHS authority or Trust will be prepared to provide. Both the theory and the practice is outlined below.

Provision of equipment for NHS patients

Health authorities and NHS Trusts sometimes pay for private nursing home beds directly when, for various reasons, they are unable or do not wish to treat or care for NHS inpatients on NHS premises. Guidance from the Department of Health has emphasised that, in such circumstances, patients should receive exactly the same services as they would have received had they remained on NHS premises. There should be no disparity in services and patients should not be persuaded to pay for other services they do not need.[43] For instance, as NHS inpatients, people cannot be charged for any equipment provided.[44]

NHS equipment provision for other nursing home residents

Health authorities have the power to provide services and equipment for residents of nursing homes, even if they are not being financed directly by the NHS. Nowhere does the NHS Act 1977 seems to outlaw such provision, although, traditionally, some health authorities have been reluctant to make it. Thus, authorities are as free to provide equipment for nursing home residents as for the rest of the population. Department of Health guidance has tried to explain. However, not only is the guidance far from resolute, but it does not, in any case, apply to all categories of resident.

The guidance (*HSG(92)50*) states that basic nursing and incontinence provision should be made and paid for by nursing homes and not by the NHS. The NHS should be responsible for provision of specialist nursing advice, for example, about incontinence or stoma care – but only so far as resources and priorities allow. The NHS can provide chiropody as well as therapy services, including physiotherapy, occupational therapy, and speech and language therapy. Again, however, such provision is to be subject to resources and priorities.[45] Subsequent guidance (*HSG(95)8*) issued about NHS responsibilities for the continuing care of people states that specialist medical or nursing equipment – not available through prescription and normally only available through hospitals – may be provided by the NHS. The one example given of such a specialist item is 'specialist feeding equipment'.[46] However, when still later guidance (EL(96)8) claims that NHS responsibilities are clear, a note of caution must be sounded – since there is no consensus about the definition and practical application of the term 'specialist equipment'.[47] Of course, local health authorities, NHS Trusts and social services departments can 'fill out' the Department of Health guidance by agreeing in detail what equipment they will and won't provide or pay for in nursing homes – for instance, deciding who is responsible for electrically operated, pressure relief mattresses.[48] Nevertheless, how well such agreements work depends on their initial quality, how they are administered in practice, the commitment of all parties (including nursing homes) – and, of course, whether people's needs are met. For instance, it would be possible to reach an amicable and workable agreement in managerial, administrative and financial terms which, however, leave a certain number of people's needs unmet.

The guidance, however, applies only to people placed in nursing homes by social services departments. It does not apply to people paying for themselves or with the preserved right to financial support from the Department of Social Security.[49] Indeed, earlier guidance still, issued during the 1970s and referred to from time to time in the House of Commons, had stated that therapy services were, in general, not to be provided by the NHS.[50]

Prescription of equipment by general practitioners

Home owners have a duty to make adequate arrangements for residents to see their GPs and dentists.[51] Thus, in principle, residents retain access to NHS appliances prescribable by GPs – the range of which has been considerably extended for fundholding GPs from April 1996.

In addition, GPs can refer their patients to hospital consultants and sometimes directly to other NHS practitioners such as therapists and chiropodists who supply equipment.

Practical consequences of confused responsibilities

In practice, variations and uncertainty result from the overlapping and confused responsibilities for the provision of equipment and services in nursing homes. It might not be clear whether the equipment will be provided by (i) the home itself as part of the fees, (ii) the home (but charged extra to residents), (iii) the NHS free of charge, (iv) residents and their relatives at their own expense.

The reasons for the uncertainties are not difficult to find. The legislation is vague; for example, the Regulations (see above) fail not only to clarify whether 'professional staff' or 'other staff' means therapists and chiropodists – but also what is meant by nursing equipment. By way of assistance, the National Association of Health Authorities and Trusts supplies a *Handbook on the registration and inspection of nursing homes.*[52] This book, with its supplement[53], covers a wide range of provision in nursing homes, including the provision of equipment, appliances and adaptations. Nevertheless, DHSS Circular guidance, which recommends the handbook, emphasises that it amounts to advice only and is therefore not legally binding.[54]

If the detailed responsibilities of nursing homes are unclear, so too are those of the NHS. As already indicated, the relevant guidance from the Department of Health gives with one hand but takes away with the other. The NHS is responsible for providing specialist nursing advice, therapy and chiropody services for residents – but the extent of such services 'is a matter for health authorities' judgement taking account of the resources available and competing priorities'.[55]

Different NHS policies for different categories of resident?

The latest Department of Health guidance applies only to people placed and funded in nursing homes (since April 1993) by social services departments in nursing homes under community care legislation. However, there are other categories of nursing home resident. For example, residents might be paying for themselves privately, be funded by the Department of Social Security (if they went into the home before April 1993), or be contractually placed in the home by the NHS (eg when there is no hospital bed available, but NHS inpatient care is still required). This means that a health authority's policy of provision to nursing homes might differ, depending on the category of resident. Therefore, residents of the same home might have access to different services because of how they are funded.

The practical upshot of such distinctions could be that a visiting NHS therapist or nurse might be able to treat one resident but not another in the same home – even if the second resident was in greater clinical need.

Health authorities face other problems in determining policies which are both sensitive to individual needs and legally and administratively sound. For example, the condition and needs of different residents in nursing homes can vary greatly. If so, a blanket policy not to provide therapy services to nursing home residents or to treat them all as low priority could scarcely be justified.[56]

If applied rigidly, without taking account of exceptional cases and individual circumstances, such a policy could fall foul of the legal principle of 'fettering discretion' (see p.446) and be judicially reviewed by the courts.

Examples of varied NHS provision. One Age Concern study of chiropody services in private nursing homes in London found the NHS providing for all, some or no residents, depending on the home.[57] It is likely to be a matter of chance whether residents receive NHS physiotherapy or occupational therapy services[58]; even the Secretary of State for Health admitted in 1989 that provision of NHS services in nursing homes was variable.[59] For instance, a survey of homes in Lincolnshire found that physiotherapy and occupational therapy were available in 70% of homes and that residents paid extra for such therapy in 20%.[60] Not only residents, but also home owners might be confused about entitlements to statutory services.[61]

Contracts placed by local authorities with nursing homes (or residential homes) are likely to vary; for example, some stipulate that incontinence pads are covered by the fees; others might not.[62] The position might become unclear if a nursing home does provide incontinence pads – but only certain types. If residents have special needs – for example, for more expensive pads with extra absorption capacity – they might have to pay extra. Or, general occupational therapy or physiotherapy classes might be provided free by the home; but if residents need individual treatment – including equipment – then they or their relatives might have to pay for it themselves. Sometimes homes state that they provide 'occupational therapy' – although, in fact, the 'therapy' is provided by nursing staff and not qualified therapists.[63]

Notes

1 Day, P.; Klein, R.; Redmayne, S. (1996). *Why regulate? Regulating residential care for elderly people.* Bristol: Policy Press.

2 See eg: Day, P.; Klein, R.; Redmayne, S. (1996). *Why regulate? Regulating residential care for elderly people.* Bristol: Policy Press, p.15. Also: George, M. (1996). Conflicting interests: independent care providers say local authorities should be stripped of their joint role of purchasing and inspecting care homes. *Community Care:* 28 March – 3 April 1996, pp.28–29.

3 SI 1984/1345. *Residential Homes Care Regulations 1984,* r.10.

4 Social Services Inspectorate (1995). *Responding to residents: a report of inspections of local authority residential care homes for older people.* London: DH, p.51.

5 Day, P.; Klein, R.; Redmayne, S. (1996). *Why regulate? Regulating residential care for elderly people.* Bristol: Policy Press, p.22.

6 Centre for Policy on Ageing (1984). *Home life: a code of practice for residential care. A report of a working party sponsored by the Department of Health and Social Security and convened by the Centre for Policy on Ageing under the chairmanship of Kina, Lady Avebury.* London: CPA.

7 LAC(86)6. Department of Health and Social Security (1986). *Registration of residential homes.* London: DHSS.

8 Department of Health (1990). *Community care in the next decade and beyond: policy guidance.* London: DH, p.52.

9 *Hansard,* House of Commons Debates, Rest Homes, 24 January 1996, cols 317–324.

10 Social Services Inspectorate (1989). *Homes are for living in: a model for evaluating quality of care provided, and quality of life experienced, in residential care homes for elderly people.* London: HMSO.
11 See eg Social Services Inspectorate (1994). (Ormiston, H.; Sarkar, R.; Stafford, C.). I*nspection of residential care for older people: Cheshire Social Services Department, September 1994.* Manchester: Department of Health, pp.54–57.
12 Roberts, A. (1995). *Health care in residential homes.* London: Age Concern England.
13 *Registered Homes Act 1984,* s.49.
14 SI 1984/1345. *Residential Homes Care Regulations 1984,* r.20.
15 Department of Health. *Decisions of Registered Homes Tribunals 261–270,* decision 268.
16 Department of Health. *Decisions of Registered Homes Tribunals 1–62,* decision 36.
17 Department of Health. *Decisions of Registered Homes Tribunals 1–62,* decision 46.
18 Social Services Inspectorate (1993). *Achieving the change in SSI Central Region: fifth report on the implementation of caring for people. Regional summaries, September 1993.* London: Department of Health, p.13.
19 Age Concern England. *Vulnerable elderly people and community care: decision making and mental incapacity.* Briefings series. London: ACE, p.6.
20 Centre for Policy on Aging (1984). *Home Life: a code of practice for residential care.* London: CPA, p.18.
21 Wagner, G. (1988). *Residential care: a positive choice.* London: HMSO, p.116.
22 See eg Ashton, G. (1995). Elderly people and residential care (2). *Solicitors Journal:* 13 October 1995, pp. 1010–1012.
23 Continuing Care Conference (1995). *Framework contract between residential care provider and resident.* London: CCC.
24 See eg: Counsel and Care (1992). *From home to a home: a study of older people's hopes, expectations and experiences of residential care.* London: Counsel and Care, pp.13–19.
25 National Assistance Act 1948, s.21. And Directions: LAC(93)10. Department of Health. *Approvals and Directions for arrangements from 1 April 1993 made under Schedule 8 to the National Health Service Act 1977 and sections 21 and 29 of the National Assistance Act 1948.* London: DH.
26 *R v Newcastle-upon-Tyne Council, ex parte Dixon* (1994) 158 LGRevR 441 (QBD).
27 Ie under s.2 of the *Chronically Sick and Disabled Persons Act 1970,* and s.45 of the *Health Service and Public Health Act 1968.*
28 LAC(86)6. Department of Health and Social Security (1986). *Registration of residential homes.* London: DHSS.
29 Social Services Inspectorate (1988). *Health in homes: a review of arrangements for health care in local authority homes for elderly people.* London: Department of Health, p.112.
30 Social Services Inspectorate (Brown, D.; Fraser, J.; Macrowan, R.; Thompson, R.) (1995). *Inspection of services for older people with dementia in the community: Northumberland, September 1995.* Gateshead: Department of Health, p.17.
31 HSG(92)50. NHS Executive. *Local authority contracts for residential and nursing home care: NHS related aspects.* NHS Management Executive, Department of Health, 1992.
32 See eg evidence which emerged in a health service ombudsman investigation: Health Service Commissioner (W.360/77–78). *Failure to provide a community nursing service. 1st report 1979–1980.* London: HMSO, 1979.
33 Social Services Inspectorate (1988). *Health in homes: a review of arrangements for health care in local authority homes for elderly people.* London: Department of Health, p.112.
34 Social Services Inspectorate (1993). *Achieving the change in SSI Central Region: fifth report on the implementation of caring for people. Regional summaries, September 1993.* London: Department of Health, p.13.
35 Social Services Inspectorate (1995). *Responding to residents: a report of inspections of local authority residential care homes for older people.* London: DH, pp.45–46.
36 SI 1984/1578. *Nursing Homes and Mental Nursing Homes Regulations 1984.* London: HMSO, 1984, r.12.
37 SI 1984/1578. *Nursing Home and Mental Nursing Homes Regulations 1984,* r.12.
38 Registered Homes Act 1984, s.49.
39 SI 1984/1578. *Nursing Homes and Mental Nursing Homes Regulations 1984,* r.15.
40 Decision 29. Department of Health. *Decisions of Registered Homes Tribunals 1–62.*

41 *Department of Health. Decisions of Registered Homes Tribunals 1–62.* Decision 27.

42 Department of Health. *Decisions of Registered Homes Tribunals 271–280.* Decision 271.

43 HC(81)1. Department of Health and Social Security. *Contractual arrangements with independent hospitals and nursing homes and other forms of co-operation between the NHS and the independent medical sector.* London: DHSS, Annex.

44 *NHS Act 1977,* schedule 12, para 1.

45 HSG(92)50. NHS Executive. *Local authority contracts for residential and nursing home care: NHS related aspects.* NHS Management Executive, Department of Health, 1992.

46 HSG(95)8; LAC(95)5. Department of Health. *NHS responsibilities for meeting continuing health care needs.* London: DH, 1995, annex A, para G.

47 EL(96)8; CI(96)5. Department of Health. *NHS responsibilities for meeting continuing health care needs: current progress and future priorities.* London: DH, 1996, section C, para 16.

48 Clode, D. (1996). A tight ship. *Community Care:* 21–27 March 1996, pp.18–19.

49 HSG(92)50. *Local authority contracts for residential and nursing home care: NHS related aspects.* NHS Management Executive, Department of Health, 1992.

50 Circulars: HRC(74)16. *Statutory provisions: charges under section 2(2) of the National Health Service Reorganisation Act 1973. DHSS, 1974;* HC(78)16. *NHS chiropody services.* DHSS, 1978. And see eg: *Hansard,* House of Commons, Written Answers, 22 May 1992, col 301, Mr Yeo.

51 SI 1984/1578. *Nursing Homes and Mental Nursing Homes Regulations 1984.* London: HMSO, 1984, r.12.

52 *Registration and inspection of nursing homes: a handbook for health authorities.* Birmingham: NAHA, 1985.

53 *Registration and inspection of nursing homes: a handbook for health authorities: 1988 supplement.* Birmingham: NAHA.

54 HC(84)21. *Registration and inspection of private nursing homes and mental nursing homes (including private hospitals).* DHSS, 1984.

55 HSG(92)50. *Local authority contracts for residential and nursing home care: NHS related aspects.* NHS Management Executive, Department of Health, 1992, Annex, para 10.

56 See eg. Royal College of Nursing (1992). *A scandal waiting to happen? Elderly people an and nursing care in residential and nursing homes.* London: RCN; Todd, J. (1990). Also: Office of Population Censuses and Surveys, Social Survey Division. *Care in private homes: a qualitative study carried out by Social Survey Division of OPCS on behalf of the Department of Social Security.* London: HMSO, pp.7–13. And: Darton, R., Wright, K. (1990). The characteristics of non-statutory residential and nursing homes. In: Parry, R(1990). *Privatisation: research highlights in social work 18.* London: Jessica Kingsley, pp.66–67.

57 Collyer, M.; Hanson-Kahn, C. (1989). *Feet first: a reappraisal of footcare services in London.* London: Age Concern Greater London.

58 Chartered Society of Physiotherapy (1992). *Survey of physiotherapy services to older people resident in private nursing homes.* London: CSP; Bond, J. *et al.* (1989). *Evaluation of continuing-care accommodation for elderly people: volume 4: the 1984 and 1987 surveys of continuing-care institutions in six health authorities.* Newcastle: University of Newcastle upon Tyne, School of Health Care Sciences, Health Care Research Unit, pp.53–54.

59 *Hansard.* House of Commons Debates, July 12th 1989, col.980, Kenneth Clarke.

60 North Lincolnshire Community Health Council (1991). *Nursing homes in North Lincolnshire: survey.* Lincoln: North Lincs CHC.

61 Challis, L.; Bartlett, H. (1987). *Old and ill: private nursing homes for elderly people.* London: Age Concern England, p.58.

62 Social Services Inspectorate (1993). *Achieving the change in SSI Central Region: fifth report on the implementation of caring for people. Regional summaries, September 1993.* London: Department of Health, p.13.

63 Challis, L.; Bartlett, H. (1987). *Old and ill: private nursing homes for elderly people.* London: Age Concern England, p.59.

CHAPTER 10

PROVISION OF HOME ADAPTATIONS BY HOUSING AUTHORITIES AND SOCIAL SERVICES DEPARTMENTS

COVERAGE

1. Types of adaptation and practitioners involved
2. Different avenues for the provision of home adaptations
   - Home adaptations and community care
   - Powers of housing authorities to adapt their own stock
   - Disabled facilities grants
   - Minor works assistance (Home repair assistance)
   - Home improvement agencies
   - Provision of home adaptations by social services departments
   - Provision of home adaptations by housing associations.
3. Maintenance of adaptations
4. Complaints

Key points

This chapter outlines the various avenues people can pursue in order to modify their homes. These include the powers and duties of local housing authorities to adapt their own stock, award disabled facilities grants, provide home repair assistance – as well as the duty social services departments have to provide adaptations. The importance of suitable housing for people to live in should not be underestimated; though home adaptations are not (in the main) defined legally as part of community care services, it is difficult to see how they can, in practice, form anything other than a central plank of community care.

That said, the present system of provision of home adaptations is complex and confusing – for a number of reasons. First, housing authorities have a number of different duties and powers, by means of which they can provide, or assist disabled people with, home adaptations. Second, the line between major adaptations, minor adaptations and equipment is sometimes far from clear. Nevertheless, where this line is drawn can determine whether the item will be provided as equipment or a minor adaptation by the social services department – or as a major adaptation by the housing (or environmental health) department. Despite a tradition of good cooperation between these different departments, confusion can arise. A further twist is that, if housing authorities do not assist with adaptations, then social services departments sometimes fund even major adaptations as well.

Third, the practical arrangements for major adaptations can be complex, time-consuming and highly disruptive. Often, initial assessments are carried out by social services departments – but there are sometimes long waiting times involved. Means-tests conducted by housing authorities entail calculations about how much grant a person qualifies for, if any, and form another administrative hurdle. The arrangements for adaptations can involve several departments either within a single local authority or spread over more than one (eg depending on whether it is a metropolitan or county council: see p.40). Occupational therapists, environmental health officers, technical officers, architects, surveyors, builders and sub-contractors might all be involved. Major adaptations can take months or years to complete; investigating many such delays, the local ombudsman sometimes finds maladministration.

On a more positive note, despite the many problems that do arise, there are many examples of good practice to be found and ways of 'saying yes' to people.[1] As community care guidance policy guidance states, home adaptations are an important part of assisting people to remain in their own homes and maintain a good quality of life. Some of this good practice is achieved by home improvement agencies (HIAs) which coordinate and facilitate the process of adaptations, and particularly minor ones, for older people.

N.B. Housing Grants, Construction and Regeneration Act 1996

This chapter should be read bearing in mind that relevant parts of this Act will come into force at the end of 1996, superseding provisions of the Local Government and Housing Act 1989.

Minor works assistance is abolished and replaced by *home repair assistance.* Broadly, the new scheme extends eligibility for assistance – in grant payment or materials – with repairs, improvements or adaptations to a dwelling (including a mobile home or house boat). Applicants must be at least 18 years old and be owner-occupiers, tenants (but not council tenants) or have a right of occupation. The dwelling must be the sole or main residence of the applicant or of the elderly, infirm or disabled person being cared for. Another condition of eligibility – receipt of State benefits – is also relaxed in the case of elderly, disabled or infirm people. The amount of assistance available for an applicant is £2000 in any one year and £4000 within a three year period.

The *disabled facilities grant* (DFG) system remains much the same, although mandatory *renovations grants* are abolished. However, there are some changes. The criteria for mandatory DFGs have been modified; they now refer to safety, as well as placing greater emphasis on access to a bath or shower. Regulations will allow discretionary DFG to be added to mandatory DFG where the cost of the mandatory work exceeds the mandatory grant limit – this was not possible previously. Furthermore, reasons will have to be given by housing authorities when they refuse applications for grants; this will in effect override a High Court ruling that reasons need not be given (see p.433). Another change is that although authorities will still have to notify applicants of approval or refusal of applications within six months, they will also be empowered, following approval, to delay the payment of mandatory disabled facilities grants for up to 12 months from the date of application. The Act also broadens the definition of disability, making it wider than the one social services departments work to under the National Assistance Act 1948 (see p.168).

It should be emphasised that his chapter has been written without the benefit of new guidance on home repair assistance and DFGs, due to be published at the end of 1996.

Questions people ask

- What is the difference between a major adaptation and a minor adaptation and between an adaptation and equipment?
- If a housing department refuses to assist with an adaptation, does the social services department have a duty to help?
- Why do home adaptations sometimes take so long?
- How many ways are there of funding a home adaptation?
- Is there a legal timescale within which housing authorities must process applications for disabled facilities grant – and what if they do not keep to it?
- What are home improvement agencies and how can they help?

1. TYPES OF ADAPTATION AND PRACTITIONERS INVOLVED

Home adaptations include handrails, extensions, conversions, low kitchen surfaces, through-floor lifts, ramps, widened doorways, raised electric sockets – and so on. Many examples are given in the A–Z list of equipment and adaptations in Part IV of this book. Not all adaptations need be major in scale, and even the minor variety might be effective. For example, a light fitting in the porch adds to safety, convenience and value; and reachable window catches, central heating/radiator controls and switches can all make life much easier for everybody.[2]

Successful home adaptations, both major and minor, can make a great difference to people's lives, enabling them to do what many people take for granted – take a bath or shower, get to the lavatory, prepare food in the kitchen or get in and out of the front door. They can enable people to return from hospital to a suitable environment – and so avoid readmission, or entry to a residential or nursing home.[3]

Nevertheless, a major adaptation to a home can be a complex process, the successful outcome of which is by no means guaranteed. Even if it is ultimately successful, misunderstandings, irritations, delays and shortcomings can be expected along the way. The adaptation might never be completed if clients die or their relationships break up before completion. People's disabling condition might change unpredictably, or the original plans might not have taken account of predictable future needs.[4] Alternatively, plans might simply have been badly drawn up resulting in, for example, rails and wash basins installed at the wrong height, or an unusable bath plumbed in.

A range of personnel might be involved, including for example, occupational therapists, social workers, housing officers, environmental health officers, technical officers, architects, surveyors, builders, sub-contractors, home improvement agencies.

2. DIFFERENT AVENUES FOR THE PROVISION OF HOME ADAPTATIONS

Local authorities – ie housing departments or environmental health departments – are responsible for assisting people with adaptations to their homes. There are a number of channels for such assistance, including disabled facilities grants (DFGs), home repair assistance and the powers of authorities to adapt their own stock. Social services departments have legal responsibilities too. They assess people for adaptations, provide minor adaptations, refer people to housing authorities – and sometimes, more unusually, assist with major adaptations as well.

Housing associations also carry out adaptations to their property using their own funding arrangements – although disabled facilities grants can also be applied for by housing association tenants.

Home adaptations and community care

Home adaptations, for the most part, do not come under community care services as defined by the NHS and Community Care Act 1990. (Arguably, adaptations provided by social services departments are part of community care – assuming it is accepted that services provided under s.2 of the CSDPA are community care services: see p.172). It is surprising that a policy, the explicit and preferred aim of which is to enable people to remain in their own homes through provision of adaptations (and other services)[5], should omit to place them legally at its centre.

The 1990 Act does, however, place a duty on social services departments if they think that people have housing needs, to 'invite' housing authorities to participate in community care assessments.[6] However, the Act places no duties on housing authorities to respond to that invitation, to carry out an assessment, or ultimately to provide adaptations. Although it might be good practice for housing authorities to respond, there would appear to be little legal pressure on them to do so.

Government guidance does recognise the major role of housing in community care and in enabling people to live independently in their own homes.[7] Nevertheless, commentators have pointed out that housing has merited too low a priority in community care legislation, policy, planning and implementation.[8] One consequence of this, as observed by a Department of Health consultation paper, is that a person's need for community care does not, as a matter of course, entitle a person to suitable housing.[9]

Powers of housing authorities to adapt their own stock

Under the Housing Act 1985 housing authorities have powers to 'alter, enlarge, repair or improve' their housing stock; and to 'fit, furnish and supply a house' with 'all requisite furniture, fittings and conveniences'.[10]

Therefore, although council house tenants can apply for disabled facilities grants (see below), local authorities do have the power to carry out adaptations without operating a formal grant scheme at all. Thus, there is nothing, for example, to stop an authority providing ramped access, or handrails, for its dwellings as part of these general functions towards its own stock. For council tenants, there are distinct advantages if housing authorities use their housing revenue or capital programme finance to fund adaptations. The process costs the tenants nothing and might be quicker, but practices vary to a considerable extent.[11]

However, even if authorities do offer such adaptations, and in a manner generally favourable to tenants, the latter should still be given the choice of deciding whether to apply for a disabled facilities grant instead – since it is their statutory right.[12] This means that authorities need to publicise and explain both schemes (ie their own, and the DFG) evenhandedly; failure to do so is maladministration in the eyes of the local ombudsman.[13] Indeed, there does seem to be sporadic confusion about the ability of council tenants to obtain disabled facilities grants. In another ombudsman investigation, a tenant who had just moved into a new property, applied to have the bath replaced with a shower and asked for ramps and handrails. He was 77 years old, had artificial hips and knees, acute arthritis, specially built up shoes – and had moved to be near family and to avoid admission to residential care. The council refused to provide these as part of its duties to adapt its own stock – and also failed to inform him about disabled facilities grants. This was maladministration.[14]

When adapting their own stock, housing authorities are likely to adopt different approaches. For instance, major adaptations (funded from capital accounts) might only be considered if no other suitable council housing is available – whereas minor adaptations (funded from housing revenue accounts) might be more easily obtained. However, the financial dividing line between adaptations classed as major and those as minor, might be set as low as £300 in one authority, but up to £1000 in another. Some housing authorities impose means-tests when considering applications for minor adaptations – and others do not. The means-tests might themselves differ – and anyway contrast with the policy of social services departments in the same authorities not to impose means-tests when approving minor adaptations in private property.[15]

Disabled facilities grants

Legislation, regulations and guidance specify in considerable detail how *disabled facilities grants* (DFGs) should work; only the main points can be dealt with here.

Local authorities assist with adaptations through DFGs, which are a part of the wider renovation grant system. Owner occupiers, council tenants, private tenants and housing association tenants can apply.[16] Private tenants might require the permission of their landlords, and sometimes the agreement of other tenants. Both these requirements can cause problems. For example, other tenants might object to a ramp running along a wall on the grounds that the wheelchair user, or other users of the ramp, will be able to overlook their bedrooms.

This chapter does not deal with the wider system of renovation grants, of which disabled facilities grants are a part. Generally speaking, if a dwelling is unfit, according to a statutory definition, a mandatory renovation grant has been available; otherwise discretionary grants are available for other repairs and improvements. The Housing, Construction and Regeneration Act 1996 changes this system by removing mandatory grants. However, some people, who apply for renovation grants and are refused, might still qualify for a disabled facilities grant on other grounds.

Changes to disabled facilities grants

The Housing Grants, Construction and Regeneration Act 1996 introduces changes to the system of disabled facilities grants. One of these is that authorities will be able to defer payment of grants for up to 12 months. In response, Age Concern England has pointed out that most elderly people who need adaptations for access to the bath or lavatory need them immediately – few are able to wait.[17] Nevertheless, it is clear that in practice many authorities have been unable to comply even with the current six-month statutory time limit for dealing with applications (see below). Other changes have been outlined above.

Duty to approve grant applications

The duty placed by the Housing Grants, Construction and Regeneration Act 1996 on authorities to approve applications for DFGs is a strong one. First, the duty is expressed to be towards an individual 'applicant', rather than the population in general (see p.137). Second, the legislation lays down certain statutory assessment procedures and criteria. The latter relate to any one of more of following purposes:[18]

- 'facilitating access by the disabled occupant to and from the dwelling or building in which the dwelling or, as the case may be, flat, is situated
- making the dwelling or building safe for the disabled occupant and other persons residing with him
- facilitating access by the disabled occupant to a room used as the principal family room
- facilitating access by the disabled occupant to, or providing for the disabled occupant, a room used or usable for sleeping
- facilitating access by the disabled occupant to, or providing for the disabled occupant, a room in which there is a lavatory, or facilitating the use by the disabled occupant of such a facility

- facilitating access by the disabled occupant to, or providing for the disabled occupant, a room in which there is a bath or a shower (or both), or facilitating the use of the disabled occupant of such a facility
- facilitating access by the disabled occupant to, or providing for the disabled occupant, a room in which there is a washhand basin, or facilitating the use of the disabled occupant of such a facility
- facilitating the preparation and cooking of food by the disabled occupant
- improving any heating system in the dwelling to meet the needs of the disabled occupant or, if there is no existing heating system in the dwelling or any such system is unsuitable for use by the disabled occupant, providing a heating system suitable to meet his needs
- facilitating the use by the disabled occupant of a source of power, light or heat by altering the position of one or more means of access to or control of that source or by providing additional means of control; and
- facilitating access and movement by the disabled occupant around the dwelling in order to enable him to care for a person who is normally resident in the dwelling and is in need of such care'.

Most of the statutory criteria concern access to the accommodation in its present state; however, those that refer to the provision of facilities do allow in principle for the extension of a property – for example, a bathroom or bedroom (but not, for example, since it is not listed, a living room extension). If an authority is *satisfied* that any of these criteria are met, then subject to certain other conditions (see below), the application must be approved; the authority has a duty to do so.[19]

If applications are made for facilities such as a play area for a disabled child or a sterile room for peritoneal dialysis – which do not meet the statutory criteria for a mandatory disabled facilities grant – a discretionary, rather than mandatory, grant might have to be applied for.[20] Similarly, authorities might deem as discretionary the provision of extra living space for a carer to stay, because it would benefit somebody other than the disabled person – and would therefore not be 'necessary' and 'appropriate' under the legislation. Investigating such a decision, the ombudsman gave no definitive answer as to whether this was a correct interpretation of the law – but did not find the approach 'obviously flawed'.[21]

Discretionary grants are defined in legislation as those which do not meet the criteria for mandatory grants, but which are for the purpose of making the dwelling 'suitable for the accommodation, welfare or employment' of the disabled person.[22] Authorities are not obliged to award discretionary grants in any particular case, and can have a general policy of not awarding them; however, such a policy must be sufficiently flexible to allow awards in exceptional circumstances. Authorities which fail to incorporate such flexibility in their policies, will be vulnerable to adverse judicial review in so far as they have 'fettered their discretion' (see p.446).

If disputes were to get to court, the wording of the Act might be examined in detail in order to decide whether, for example, a proposed adaptation fell into the mandatory or discretionary category. For example, in one case (*R v Bristol CC, ex parte Naqvi*), a person had applied for a mandatory renovation grant to convert a property, consisting of a flat and a shop, into a house. The housing authority concluded that the application did not qualify for a mandatory grant because it was not for the improvement or repair of an existing dwelling (ie which would retain its identity after the works) – but was a work of conversion which entailed provision of an entirely new dwelling. Therefore, it could attract only a discretionary grant. The court found that the authority was entitled to reach this conclusion.[23]

Other conditions about which the authority must be satisfied

Even if the statutory criteria (see above) are met, the legislation states that the housing authority has to be satisfied that the proposed adaptation is '*necessary and appropriate*' for the applicant's needs. It must also be satisfied that it is '*reasonable and practicable*' to carry out the adaptation in the light of the age and condition of the building.[24]

For instance, it might be necessary and appropriate to provide a ramp or platform lift to enable a person to go in and out of a house; but if the steps up to it are very steep and narrow, neither solution might be reasonable and practicable from a technical point of view.[25] In addition, legislation has prevented an authority approving a grant application, if the house will remain unfit for human habitation even after the proposed adaptation has been carried out. This is reported to cause some people, especially elderly people, to withdraw applications, because, for example, they wish to avoid the disruptive effect of remedial work.[26] The Housing Grants, Construction and Regeneration Act 1996 relaxes this requirement that the property be fit on completion of DFG works, by giving authorities the discretion to waive the rule.[27]

As to whether the adaptation is necessary and appropriate, the housing authority is under a duty to consult the social services department of a separate local authority. In practice, this usually means that a social services occupational therapist (OT) will carry out an assessment and make a recommendation. However, it need not be a social services OT; given the shortage of OTs, long waiting lists and findings of maladministration by the local ombudsmen, some social services departments make use of independent OTs, NHS OTs, OT assistants, senior social workers or Care and Repair agencies.[28]

Previous guidance from the Department of Health and the Department of Environment (to be replaced at the end of 1996) suggests that social services departments should approach assessment flexibly, without imposing strict boundaries on what work is acceptable. However, authorities should make the distinction between what is *desirable* and what is actually *needed*. Thus, a person might request a downstairs lavatory, but the authority decide that a stairlift is more appropriate. The guidance also states that the impact on family and carers should be assessed, as should the future, foreseeable needs of the disabled person, his life expectancy, and his ability to benefit from home adaptations. It suggests that some authorities might follow a policy not to provide stairlifts for people with a deteriorating condition, because they will be unable to benefit safely or for very long from the lift. On the other hand, if a person is suffering from a terminal illness, an adaptation might be justified if it enables him or her to come home from a hospital or hospice in order to die.[29]

In practice, there is clearly fertile ground for dispute and for different and conflicting approaches to be taken by authorities. For example, some authorities decide as a matter of policy that only people in the highest priority category of need qualify for disabled facilities grants – whilst those coming into the second priority category might qualify for minor adaptations from social services departments.[30]

The wording of the legislation makes it quite clear that the final decision is for the housing authority, and not the social services department or the disabled person, to make.[31] Furthermore, because it is a question of whether the housing authority is *satisfied* (a subjective term), it is not generally for the courts to state in what circumstances an authority should or should not be satisfied. Even if the social services department refuses to make an assessment, or takes an unreasonably long time in doing so, the housing authority can presumably still proceed – since it will have carried out its duty to consult, even if the body consulted (ie social services) has not responded.

However, the guidance from the Department of Environment and Department of Health has stated that only *rarely* should housing authorities not follow any recommendations the social services department makes.[32] And, if a housing authority rejects recommendations for a grant – and does so on grounds other than *reasonableness and practicability* (ie the grounds laid down in legislation: see immediately above) – then it is acting unlawfully. For instance, when an authority refused to accept the social services department's recommendation of a shower-room adaptation for a severely disabled 18-year old, the ombudsman found maladministration. The authority had reached its decision by considering factors other than reasonableness and practicability – and therefore, by definition, those grounds necessarily represented irrelevant considerations.[33]

Once a housing authority is satisfied about the reasonableness, practicality, necessity and appropriateness of the adaptation, then it has a duty to approve the application.[34] This is a strong duty, which, once incurred, stands – irrespective of the financial position of the authority.

Distinction between approval of a grant application and actually getting a grant

From an applicant's point of view, the duty to approve applications is weakened to the extent that there are limits to the amount of grant. First, housing authorities operate a means-test, prescribed in legislation and similar to the test for housing benefit. This means that, depending on their means, applicants might receive all, some or none of the cost of the adaptation. One of the major criticisms of this means-test is that not only are the disabled applicant's means taken into account, but also the means of other members of the household in which he or she is living. The Department of Environment has announced its intention to alter this, so that the test will apply only to the disabled applicant and his or her partner.[35]

Second, even if applicants are eligible to receive the full amount of the cost of the adaptation, there is a ceiling on the amount of grant – currently £20,000 in England and £24,000 in Wales.[36] The process of means-testing has caused a number of problems, one of which is that people discontinue their applications for various reasons. For instance, if authorities send out assessment forms to be completed by applicants, the latter might find them so complicated that they simply do not pursue the application.[37]

In a case about renovation grants, the court held that an authority acted unlawfully when it modified the method, laid down in legislation, for calculating how much grant was payable (*R v Sunderland, ex parte Redezeus*). It had adopted a policy which, in its effect, restricted any grant to a maximum of 20% of the total cost of the adaptation. The authority had added an extra rule on top of those prescribed by legislation; it should not have done so, since the statutory formula was exhaustive.[38]

In addition, it is good practice for authorities to warn people not to start work on adaptations before grant approval has been given; they might endanger their eligibility for the grant. In one investigation, the ombudsman found maladministration when an authority failed to warn an applicant not to start work prematurely – though he also found that the latter had contributed to his own misfortune, having obtained and read a Department of Environment booklet which contained this very warning.[39]

Time taken to handle grant applications

Legislation places statutory time limits on the handling of applications; authorities must make decisions about them within six months.[40] In practice, this timescale is not always complied with and authorities employ various means in order to circumvent it. One such means is to operate an informal enquiry system, so that 'time does not start to run', even though the Department of Environment has stated that such systems should not be used to create unreasonable delay.[41]

However, the ombudsman's annual report has recognised that the pressure put upon authorities will inevitably force authorities to adopt policies of delay.[42] Indeed, in one particular investigation, the ombudsman directly criticised central government for placing authorities in an impossible position – ie one in which they were given only limited resources to provide unlimited, demand-led services. The ombudsman even doubted whether a court would censure the authority for breaching the statutory timescale – since the authority could do little about it.[43] And, investigating nine complaints of delay against one authority, the ombudsman found no maladministration, since central government had simply provided inadequate resources (in the form of credit approvals) and the authority had adopted a reasonable sequencing/queuing system.[44]

Nevertheless, even if the main reason for delay in providing home adaptations is financial restrictions, which are beyond the control of authorities to remedy, the ombudsman might still find maladministration – for example, because authorities have not adopted 'clear and comprehensive policies' and have failed to communicate the position clearly to the public.[45] Similarly, when an authority had imposed an embargo on processing renovation grant applications, the ombudsman found maladministration not on account of the embargo itself, but because of delay in handling an application submitted beforehand, which had consequently and unnecessarily fallen within the embargo. Adding insult to injury, the authority then failed to inform the applicants that there would be a delay of some 13–16 months; this too was maladministration. In this particular case, the ombudsman recommended the authority pay £3000 in compensation to reflect the cost of repairs the applicants had decided to carry out for themselves.[46]

The ombudsman has tried to reach balanced decisions in various ways. For example, she found an authority guilty of maladministration for failing to deal with an application in the prescribed six months. But, because the authority was in financial difficulties not of its own making, and because the particular complainant was only one of many others in the same position, the ombudsman found that the complainant had not suffered any 'individual injustice' – and thus the authority was not required to supply a remedy.[47] Equally, the ombudsman might not fault an authority which has considered the position carefully and in detail, if the funding is simply not adequate and the delay is therefore 'due to factors outside the council's direct control'.[48]

On the other hand, the ombudsman will sometimes find both maladministration and injustice when grant applications are not handled within the time limits. For example, one authority had expressly decided that limits were not to be exceeded, but delay still occurred – partly because of an apparent failure to re-train technical officers effectively. This was maladministration.[49] Of course, delay might not be connected with resources. A finding of maladministration followed, when an authority took 19 months to deal with an application for a renovation grant – and had simply failed to take any action for certain periods of time (eg it took six months to carry out a survey).[50]

It was maladministration when, on grounds that the screening of grant enquiries would cost too much, an authority did not publicise its priority system effectively, and there was no formal system for advising people that they could apply for priority. As a result, 'deserving' applicants were disadvantaged – and, there was a danger that priority might be awarded to those 'who shout loudest' rather than to the most needy. There were other flaws; for example, the priority criteria were neither adequately defined nor were they explained accurately on public enquiry forms. In addition, the criteria contained no allowance for exceptional or extenuating circumstances (see p.447), and the authority sometimes took account of other factors altogether (outside the criteria) when awarding priority, even if this meant overriding those very reasons that indicated (according to the criteria) that priority should have been given.[51]

For housing authorities, there are at least two major factors affecting speed of response. One concerns the long waiting lists for assessment by occupational therapists working in social services departments. The second concerns authorities' own limited resources to fund disabled facilities grants; they need to avoid passing more applications in a financial year than they have the money to pay for.

Minor works assistance (Home repair assistance)

Alternative or additional to disabled facilities grants has been minor works assistance (MWA). Housing authorities have the power, but not the duty, to provide this.[52] The Housing Grants, Construction and Regeneration Act 1996 replaces in December 1996 minor works assistance with a similar scheme – *home repair assistance.* This section should be read accordingly for the sake of completeness and as a pointer to the new scheme.

The MWA scheme has included assistance in the form of grants or materials for the following legally prescribed categories:[53]

- **staying put:** for elderly owners or tenants to carry out adaptations, improvements or repairs
- **elderly resident adaptation:** to enable an elderly person who is not an owner or tenant of the dwelling to move into the dwelling to be cared for
- **thermal insulation:** provision or improvement of thermal insulation;
- **patch and mend:** repairs (which must be in a designated 'clearance' area).

Applicants (or their spouses or the people they live with as spouse) for MWA must have been receiving certain State benefits in order to qualify. Landlords and council tenants have not qualified for MWA. In addition, the *staying put* and *elderly resident adaptation* assistance has been available only to people aged 60 or over. (This age-related restriction does not apply to the replacement scheme, home repair assistance: see above.) MWA has been limited to a maximum value of £1080 per application and £3240 in three years if several applications have been made.[54] In practice, it has been possible to make simultaneous applications for different items, in which case more substantial (ie above £1080, but still no more than £3240) work could be carried out at one time[55], although Circular guidance has suggested (but not insisted on) a normal gap of at least three months between applications.[56]

Guidance has also explained that MWA was designed to streamline assistance for improvements and repairs when only small scale work was required; sometimes MWA would be more appropriate as an interim measure in advance of major work. It was intended to 'provide much needed flexibility at the margins of the system'.[57] For smaller adaptations, MWA might have been more appropriate than a DFG (which involves an altogether more formal application procedure). Furthermore, people who have not qualified for a DFG might have done so for MWA; neither the DFG criteria concerning the purpose of the adaptation, nor the disability criterion, apply.

One weakness of the MWA scheme has lain in the fact it has been discretionary only. This has meant that in some authorities it has been generally not available at all; and, in others, it might have suffered unduly when budgets have been tight and local authorities have been reducing services.[58] However, any over-rigid policies excluding MWA have risked judicial review by the law courts on the grounds that the authority has been 'fettering its discretion' (see p.446).

Home improvement agencies

The strength of the MWA scheme lay in its flexibility, speed and ease of use (compared to disabled facilities grants), and in its effective operation in many areas by home improvement agencies on behalf of housing authorities. Typical work carried out by home improvement agencies includes door-answering systems, emergency alarms, heating, hoists, lifts, rails, ramps, showers and wider doorways.[59] Guidance from the Department of Environment encouraged local authorities to make use of home improvement agencies to deliver MWA – so long as authorities ensured that they fulfil their statutory responsibilities laid down in s.131 of the Local Government and Housing Act 1989.[60]

Agencies undertake a range of activities including advice, assessment, getting plans drawn up, checking specifications and costs, finding reliable and experienced builders, supervising work in progress, checking completed work, making follow-up visits.[61] The work of home improvement agencies has suffered also from the difficulty of obtaining timely assessments by local authority occupational therapists.[62] Although MWA might have been one channel of funding utilised by agencies, there are others – for instance, a health authority might even provide some funding for adaptations to enable people to be discharged from hospital promptly and so release hospital beds.[63]

Provision of home adaptations by social services departments

Social services departments have a duty under the s.2 of the CSDPA 1970 to make arrangements for the provision of adaptations (see p.158).

This overlap of responsibilities between social services and housing (or environmental health) departments creates the potential for confusion. In order to avoid this, housing authorities have generally undertaken major, structural adaptations, whilst minor, non-structural adaptations have fallen to social services departments. For example, a fixed ramp or hoist is structural, major and permanent, a portable ramp or hoist, non-structural, minor and temporary. Guidance from the Department of Health and Department of Environment suggests that strengthened joists or modified lintels to support a hoist is structural work (housing responsibility), but the hoisting equipment itself is non-structural (social services responsibility).[64] Stairlifts are sometimes regarded as adaptations, sometimes as equipment. Handrails and grab rails could be either structural (eg because they are screwed into walls) or non-structural (eg because they are easily installed and removed), whilst central heating would be major, but portable storage heaters, minor. In fact, central heating sometimes gives rise to particular confusion. Guidance states that it should not be installed in rooms the disabled person does not use – and that the replacement of other forms of heating by central heating should only be considered if the health of the disabled person is at risk.[65] In some areas, this last suggestion seems to have led to the refusal, by occupational therapists in social services departments, to assess applications for central heating only. They feel that the assessment should be carried out by a medical doctor.[66]

It can be seen that uncertainty could easily arise, as it has in fact done in the law of property more widely, about the difference between non-structural and structural features. This sort of question can lead to bitter disputes between the buyers and sellers of houses. For instance, one case which reached the Court of Appeal turned on whether pictures fitted into the recesses of wooden panelling, a statue, or a sundial were part of the property or not; ie had they become fixtures, or were they removable fittings or chattels? In the event, these were all held to be fittings.[67] To assist local authorities to agree on a division of responsibilities for grants for disabled people, Circular guidance issued in 1978, but now obsolete, contained an extensive list of examples of structural and non-structural adaptations.[68] The 1990 guidance, which replaced the 1978 Circular, expressed the same principle of division but without the long list of examples.[69]

Continuing duty and provision of major adaptations by social services departments

Despite the distinction between major and minor adaptations, social services departments sometimes incur legal responsibility for major adaptations as well.

This can happen when a social services department has made an assessment for an adaptation under s.2 of the Chronically Sick and Disabled Persons Act 1970 (CSDPA) and made a recommendation to the housing authority that a DFG application be approved. The housing authority might refuse the application because, for example, it considers that the applicant does not meet the statutory criteria in the housing legislation. For instance, the Department of Health and Department of Environment guidance has suggested that a housing authority might determine the required size of a disabled child's bedroom on the basis of basic *sleeping* needs; whereas the social services department might take account of the space the child needs *socially* to use the room as a bed/sitting room. Because this social need might not come within the statutory criteria governing mandatory DFGs (confined to disability/access questions: see above), the housing authority would anyway only be able to award a discretionary grant (see above) – and might, in fact, decide not to do so. In this situation, the social services department might have a continuing responsibility for the adaptation.[70]

Alternatively, the housing authority might approve the application for a DFG but assess, under the statutory means-test, that the applicant should contribute more of the cost than he or she actually can afford. In such circumstances, the social services department, operating its own, non-statutory means-test might judge that it should assist the person – for example, with an interest free loan or the placing of a charge on the property. This situation is envisaged by government guidance which, however, bafflingly goes on both to acknowledge and deny the consequence – namely that there are two different means-tests being applied.[71]

Sometimes when housing authorities fail to assist with a home adaptation, social services departments are slow to respond and to 'pick up' the continuing duty. In one such case, when the district council (housing authority) had not accepted the recommendation of the county council (social services department) for a shower-room extension, the latter did nothing for six months. This delay was maladministration.[72]

Social services departments sometimes 'top-up' a housing authority grant – ie make up the shortfall between what the housing authority gives and what the person can actually, reasonably afford. Government guidance has envisaged the existence of topping-up, but only in very limited circumstances.[73] In practice, topping-up policies are thought to vary between authorities; some have stopped them altogether as a matter of policy, whilst others continue to make generous provision. Blanket policies of not providing topping-up could be open to legal challenge (see p.446).

Provision of home adaptations by housing associations

Circular guidance has stated that both housing association tenants and housing associations themselves, on behalf of their tenants, can apply for disabled facilities grants. Housing association tenants can also apply for minor works assistance. In addition, grants are also available through the Housing Corporation in the form of housing association grant (HAG). However, the same guidance also suggests that housing associations should regard the DFG as the 'first line' of public funding.[74]

In practice, the situation is not so straightforward, since it is reported that some housing authorities take precisely the opposite view by insisting that HAG be used. Alternatively, housing associations might carry out minor adaptations from their rental income.[75] Whilst the existence of at least two routes (HAG and DFG) for major adaptations could work to the advantage of tenants, it might have the opposite effect by encouraging the jettisoning of responsibilities. In either case, local authority occupational therapists will be required to carry out assessments before major adaptations can be approved (even for HAG, the Housing Corporation Procedure Manual insists on OT assessment). Therefore, in the case of DFGs, any delay in assessment will reflect that generally experienced by applicants, whether or not they are housing association tenants. In the case of HAG, the delay could be even greater, because following assessment by an OT, separate approval by the Housing Corporation is required.[76]

3. MAINTENANCE OF ADAPTATIONS

Maintenance of some adaptations, such as lifts, pose problems of responsibility, especially because the sums of money involved can be substantial – whether to individual users who take out single contracts, or to authorities which agree block maintenance contracts. For example, maintenance charges for a through-floor lift could be as much as £200 per year, and for a stairlift £60. If loaned as equipment by the social services department, the equipment remains the property of the department; if obtained through a grant, then the lift is the property of the disabled person. However, ownership does not necessarily dictate the type of maintenance arrangements; people could be asked to pay their own maintenance charges, whether or not they own the equipment. Alternatively, social services departments might pay maintenance charges irrespective of ownership – or housing authorities offer to do so if people legally transfer ownership (of, for example, a stairlift obtained through a grant) to the authority.[77]

4. COMPLAINTS

If the complaint is about assessment by social services departments, then the social services complaints procedure should be used (see p.178).

If the complaint concerns the actions and decisions of the housing department, then complaints can be made to the local authority or a letter written to the Secretary of State. Under the terms of the Citizen's Charter, local authorities must have clear and well-publicised complaints procedures.[78]

In either case, the local ombudsman can be appealed to. The above sections in this chapter include a number of examples of investigations by the ombudsman, whilst the general principles on which the ombudsman operates have been explained elsewhere (see p.115).

Notes

1 Heywood, F. (1994). *Adaptations: finding ways to say yes.* Bristol: School for Advanced Urban Studies; Joseph Rowntree Foundation.

2 See eg Joseph Rowntree Foundation. *Lifetime home improvements* (brochure).

3 Millar, B. (1996). Staying power: a home-repair project which enables elderly people to return from hospital to improved living conditions faces an uncertain future. *Health Service Journal:* 11 January 1996, pp.14–15.

4 Statham, R.; Korczak, J.; Monagham, P. (Department of Environment) (1988). *House adaptations for people with physical disabilities: a guidance manual for practitioners.* London: HMSO, p.xiii. This book looks at a number of particular adaptations in great detail, examining all their aspects, including the social, architectural and financial, in text, plans and photographs.

5 Department of Health (1990). *Community care in the next decade and beyond: policy guidance.* London: DH, p.27.

6 *NHS and Community Care Act 1990,* s.47.

7 Doe 10/92; LAC(92)12. Department of Environment, Department of Health. *Housing and community care.* London: HMSO, 1992.

8 See eg Arnold, P.; Bochel, H.; Brodhurst, S.; Page, D. (1993). *Community care: the housing dimension.* York: Joseph Rowntree Foundation (in association with Community Care).

9 Social Services Inspectorate (Edwards, A. (1995). *Housing and community care: establishing a strategic framework.* London: Department of Health, para 2.9.

10 *Housing Act 1985,* ss.9–10.

11 See eg Heywood, F. (1994). *Adaptations: finding ways to say yes.* Bristol: School for Advanced Urban Studies; Joseph Rowntree Foundation, pp.50–52.

12 *Housing Grants, Construction and Regeneration Act 1996,* s.19.

13 Commission for Local Administration (93/A/3690). *Report on investigation into a complaint against London Borough of Hackney.* London: CLAE, 1995, pp.16–20.

14 Commission for Local Administration in England (94/C/2151 and 94/C/2783). *Report on investigation against Humberside County Council and East Yorkshire Borough Council.* York: CLAE, 1996.

15 Adams, J. (1996). Adapting for community care: part 1. *British Journal of Occupational Therapy:* March 1996; 59(3), pp.115–118.

16 *Housing Grants, Construction and Regeneration Act 1996,* s.19

17 Age Concern England (1996). *Age Concern briefing on the Housing Bills and their implications for older people.* London: ACE, p.5.

18 *Housing Grants, Construction and Regeneration Act 1996,* s.23

19 *Housing Grants, Construction and Regeneration Act 1996,* s.24

20 See: DoE 10/90; LAC(90)7. Department of Environment; Department of Health. *House adaptations for people with disabilities.* London: DoE, DH, paras 50–57.

21 See eg: Commission for Local Administration in England (92/C/2376). *Report on investigation against Manchester City Council.* York: CLAE, 1994, pp.2, 6, 9.

22 *Housing Grants, Construction and Regeneration Act 1996,* s.23

23 *R v Bristol City Council, ex parte Naqvi* [1994] 26 HLR 640 (QBD).

24 *Housing Grants, Construction and Regeneration Act 1996,* s.24

25 This distinction is actually suggested by government guidance: DoE 10/90; LAC (90)7. *Department of Environment; Department of Health. House adaptations for people with disabilities.* London: HMSO, para 45.

26 Department of Health (1994). *Housing and homelessness: report of the community care monitoring special study October 1993 – April 1994.* London: DH, p.20.

27 *Local Government and Housing Act 1989,* s.107. See Housing Act 1985, s.604 for definition of fitness which includes aspects of a dwelling such as repair, stability, damp, ventilation, lighting, water supply etc. Now see: *Housing Grants, Construction and Regeneration Act 1996,* s. 24

28 See eg Heywood, F. (1994). *Adaptations: finding ways to say yes.* Bristol: School for Advanced Urban Studies; Joseph Rowntree Foundation, pp.85–89.

29 DoE 10/90; LAC (90)7. *Department of Environment; Department of Health. House adaptations for people with disabilities.* London: HMSO, 1990, paras 36–43.

30 See eg: Commission for Local Administration in England (92/A/3898). *Report on investigation against London Borough of Newham.* London: CLAE, 1995, p.3.

31 See wording of *Housing Grants, Construction and Regeneration Act 1996,* s.24

32 DoE 10/90; LAC (90)7. Department of Environment; Department of Health. *House adaptations for people with disabilities.* London: HMSO, 1990, para 23.

33 Commission for Local Administration in England (93/B/3111 & 94/B/3146). *Report on investigation against South Bedfordshire District Council and Bedfordshire Council.* Coventry: CLAE, 1996, p.24.

34 *Housing Grants, Construction and Regeneration Act 1996,* s.24

35 Department of Environment (1994). *The future of private housing renewal programmes: explanatory paper linked to the Housing White Paper 'Our Future Homes'.* London: DoE, p.5.

36 SI 1994/648. *Housing Renovation etc Grants (Reduction of Grant) Regulations 1994.*

37 Pieda PLC (1993). *Monitoring the new renovation grant system: report for the period April 1990 – March 1991.* London: Department of Environment, p.5.
38 *R v Sunderland City Council, ex parte Redezeus* (1995) 27 HLR 477 (QBD).
39 Commission for Local Administration in England (93/C/3807). *Report on investigation into a complaint against Gateshead Metropolitan Borough Council.* York: CLAE, 1995, pp.9–10.
40 *Housing Grants, Construction and Regeneration Act 1996,* s.34.
41 DoE 12/90. Department of Environment. *Local Government and Housing Act 1989: house renovation grants.* London: DoE, para 15.
42 Commission for Local Administration (1994). *The local government ombudsman 1993/1994: annual report.* London: CLAE, p.24.
43 Commission for Local Administration (92/B/3013). *Report on investigation against Birmingham City Council.* Coventry: CLAE, 1995, pp.19–20.
44 Commission for Local Administration (92/C/2850, 93/C/0481, 1573, 2831, 3457, 4250, 94/C/1283, 1815, 4082). *Report on investigation into a complaint against Liverpool City Council.* York: CLAE, 1995, pp.32–35.
45 *Investigation into complaint 93/218 against Merthyr Tydfil Borough Council* (1994): reported in Local Government Review Reports: 26 August 1995; 159(673).
46 Commission for Local Administration in England (92/C/2864). *Report on investigation into a complaint against Liverpool City Council.* York: CLAE, 1996, pp.12–13.
47 Commission for Local Administration in England (94/C/0964 & 94/C/0965). *Report on investigation against Middlesbrough Borough Council and Cleveland County Council.* York: CLAE, 1996, pp.10–11.
48 Commission for Local Administration in Wales (93/465). *Investigation into complaint against Cyngor Dosbarth Dwyfor.* Reported in: Local Government Review Reports: 18 March 1995; 159, pp.207–212, 220.
49 Commission for Local Administration in England (93/C/2124). *Report on investigation against Liverpool City Council.* York: CLAE, 1995, p.14.
50 Commission for Local Administration in England (93/C/3877). *Report on investigation into complaint against Liverpool City Council.* York: CLAE, 1996, pp.8, 14.
51 Commission for Local Administration in England (92/C/4251). *Report on investigation into complaint against Liverpool City Council.* York: CLAE, 1996.
52 *Local Government and Housing Act 1989,* s.131.
53 *Local Government and Housing Act 1989,* s.131.
54 SI 1990/388. *Assistance for Minor Works to Dwellings Regulations 1990* (as amended).
55 Macintosh, S.; Leather, P. (1993). *Minor works: a major step: minor works assistance in practice.* Nottingham: Care & Repair, p.15.
56 DoE 4/90. Department of Environment. *Assistance with minor works to dwellings.* London: HMSO, para 10.
57 DoE 4/90. Department of Environment. *Assistance with minor works to dwellings.* London: HMSO, para 3.
58 Macintosh, S.; Leather, P. (1993). *Minor works: a major step: minor works assistance in practice.* Nottingham: Care & Repair, p.6.
59 Fielder, S.; MacIntosh, S.; Tremlett, A. (1994). *Review of the home improvement agency grant programme: report of associated studies.* London: DoE, p.9.
60 DoE 4/90. *Department of Environment. Assistance with minor works to dwellings.* London: HMSO, para 7.
61 See eg Heywood, F. (1994). *Adaptations: finding ways to say yes.* Bristol: School for Advanced Urban Studies; Joseph Rowntree Foundation, p.68.
62 Pitts, J. (1992). *A report on the interface between home improvement agencies and occupational therapists.* Nottingham: Care & Repair, pp.12–13.
63 Randall, B. (1995). *'Staying put: the best move I'll never make'.* Anchor Housing Association.
64 DoE 10/90; LAC (90)7. Department of Environment; Department of Health. *House adaptations for people with disabilities.* London: HMSO, para 19.
65 DoE 10/90; LAC (90)7. Department of Environment; Department of Health. *House adaptations for people with disabilities.* London: HMSO, para 54.

66 See eg Heywood, F. (1994). *Adaptations: finding ways to say yes.* Bristol: School for Advanced Urban Studies; Joseph Rowntree Foundation, p.90.

67 *Berkley v Poulett* (1976) 241 EG 911 (CA).

68 DoE 59/78; LAC (79)14; WOC 104/78. Department of Environment; Department of Health and Social Security; Welsh Office (1978). *Adaptations of housing for people who are physically handicapped.* London: HMSO, 1978.

69 DoE 10/90; LAC (90)7. Department of Environment; Department of Health. *House adaptations for people with disabilities.* London: HMSO, para 19.

70 DoE 10/90; LAC (90)7. Department of Environment; Department of Health. *House adaptations for people with disabilities.* London: HMSO, para 16.

71 DoE 10/90; LAC (90)7. Department of Environment; Department of Health. *House adaptations for people with disabilities.* London: HMSO, para 17.

72 Commission for Local Administration in England (93/B/3111 & 94/B/3146). *Report on investigation against South Bedfordshire District Council and Bedfordshire Council.* Coventry: CLAE, 1996, p.25.

73 DoE 10/90; LAC (90)7. Department of Environment; Department of Health. *House adaptations for people with disabilities.* London: HMSO, paras 18, 67.

74 DoE 10/90; LAC (90)7. Department of Environment; Department of Health. *House adaptations for people with disabilities.* London: HMSO, para 11.

75 An option discussed in: Housing Corporation, Housing Management and Research Division (1995). *Housing for older people: consultation paper, November 1995.* London: HC, p.6.

76 Heywood, F. (1994). *Adaptations: finding ways to say yes.* Bristol: School for Advanced Urban Studies; Joseph Rowntree Foundation, pp.47–50.

77 See eg Heywood, F. (1994). *Adaptations: finding ways to say yes.* Bristol: School for Advanced Urban Studies; Joseph Rowntree Foundation, pp.91–92. See also: Centre for Accessible Environments (1991). *Disabled facilities grants: stairlifts: proceedings of a seminar held at 35 Great Smith Street, London on 21 May 1991.* London: CAE.

78 *The Citizen's Charter: raising the standard.* London: HMSO, 1991 p.42.

CHAPTER 11

PROVISION OF EQUIPMENT FOR PUPILS AND STUDENTS WITH SPECIAL EDUCATIONAL NEEDS

COVERAGE

1. Type of equipment and practitioners involved
2. Provision of equipment in primary and secondary education
   - Overview of legislation: general and specific duties
   - Children with special educational needs
   - Assessing children's needs for equipment
   - Meeting children's needs for equipment
   - Educational, non-educational and other needs for equipment: division of responsibilities
   - Integrating children into ordinary schools: efficient use of resources
   - Uncertain provision and diverse funding of equipment
   - Special schools and independent schools: legislation and guidance
   - Assessment of pre-school children.
3. Complaints
   - Special Educational Needs Tribunal
   - Complaints to the Secretary of State
   - Local ombudsman
   - Judicial review.
4. Provision of equipment for children and young people leaving full-time education
5. Provision of equipment in further education
   - Role of Further Education Funding Council
   - Role of local education authorities.
6. Provision of equipment in higher education

Key points

This chapter deals with special educational provision selectively, focusing in detail on those aspects which are especially relevant to equipment provision. It summarises the legislation governing provision for children and young people in primary schools, secondary schools, colleges of further education, and students in higher education.

In particular, the significance of the distinction between a child's educational and non-educational needs is stressed. Also explained is the dilemma facing professionals who assess children's needs; should they record on a statutory statement of special educational needs what they consider a child really needs, or only what they know can be afforded?

Special education has proved generally to be an administrative and legal minefield. In contrast with, for example, community care legislation, the Education Act 1996 and associated Regulations put in place a detailed, statutory framework for assessment. Around this framework, an extensive body of case law has arisen, largely through the use of judicial review. The flow of judicial review cases is likely to be reduced by the workings of the Special Educational Needs Tribunal, a body created by the Education Act 1993. Even so, the Tribunal's decisions will no doubt continue to throw light on how children's needs should be met – including their needs for equipment and adaptations to school premises.

Questions people ask

- Is a wheelchair used by a child in a playground needed primarily for a medical, social or educational purpose?
- Why does it matter what the primary purpose of equipment is?
- Is a child's need for a lift at school, so that she can attend lessons on the first floor, an educational or a non-educational need?
- Why must an authority provide equipment which meets an educational need, but is not obliged to provide equipment which is categorised as non-educational?
- Does it make any difference to children's entitlement to equipment whether they are in a special or ordinary school – or whether they have a statutory statement of special educational needs?

1. TYPE OF EQUIPMENT AND PRACTITIONERS INVOLVED

Equipment which enables children, young people and older students with special educational needs (SEN) specifically to follow the curriculum includes, for instance, special desks and chairs, computer hardware and software, a wide range of specialist control devices, speech aids, reading and writing aids, hearing aids (such as radio microphones). Equipment needed might be ordinary or special. For example, a student with mobility problems in higher education might need an ordinary modem so that she can work more of the time from home by linking in to the university's computer facilities. And a student with dyslexia might need an ordinary spell-check facility on the computer. On the other hand, a student with visual impairment might benefit from equipment with speech output.[1]

Apart from being required by children or students to follow the curriculum directly, equipment might be needed to get by in school or college generally. Examples of this more general equipment includes adapted toilets and sinks, hydrotherapy pools, lifts, ramps, remedial splinting, special cutlery and crockery, special seating (including adapted, matrix and moulded seating), special wheelchairs and scooters, standing frames and boxes, widened doorways. For people with visual impairment an appropriately lighted, coloured and textured environment might be most important. For the purposes of the Education Act 1996, these two categories of equipment are distinguished from each other; the first is labelled *educational* (directly curriculum-related), the second *non-educational* (generally school-related). The legal and practical significance of the distinction is explained below.

Various staff and practitioners may be involved in different ways with the identification and assessment of children's needs, leading to the provision and use of equipment. These include teachers generally, headmasters, special educational needs advisory teachers, occupational therapists, speech and language therapists, physiotherapists, consultant paediatricians, psychologists, nurses and educational audiologists.

2. PROVISION OF EQUIPMENT IN PRIMARY AND SECONDARY EDUCATION

Overview of legislation: general and specific duties

Provision of equipment for pre-school children, children at school, and students in further and higher education is covered by various, and at times, detailed legislation.[2] A Code of Practice[3] on the identification and assessment of special educational needs offers guidance to education authorities and the governing bodies of all maintained schools. Equipment provision, though barely mentioned in legislation, is governed by it – and it is referred to specifically in the Code of Practice, to which education authorities and governing bodies must *have regard*.

The Education Act 1996 places general duties on education authorities to secure schools sufficient in 'number, character and equipment to provide for all pupils the opportunity of appropriate education…such variety of instruction and training as may be desirable in view of the pupils' different ages, abilities and aptitudes'. In particular, education authorities must 'have regard' to the need to secure special educational provision for children with special educational needs.[4]

The Education Act 1996, together with associated regulations, places specific duties on education authorities and school governing bodies. These duties include (i) the assessment of a child's special educational needs, (ii) the decision about whether the child needs a statement of special educational needs, and (iii) the meeting of those needs, whether or not a statement has been made. An education authority carries out this statutory assessment and makes a statement only if it thinks that a child's special educational needs cannot be met by the school and might require provision by the authority.[5] Such specific duties are 'strong' duties towards individual children and are to be contrasted with more general duties. The basic distinction between general and specific duties is referred to elsewhere (see p.137). In practice, the distinction means that legal actions about specific, rather than about general, duties are potentially easier for parents to win. For example, the duty to make the special educational provision listed in a statement of SEN is identifiable and absolute. The authority is bound to provide for every educational need identified in the statement of special educational needs. The strength of the duty has been confirmed in the law courts (*R v Secretary of State for Education, ex parte E*).[6] By contrast, the duty to provide sufficient schools etc under the 1996 Act is much more difficult to enforce in any particular instance – and is less likely to be the downfall of authorities in judicial review proceedings.[7]

However, even the strong duty under the Education Act 1996 to provide for every special educational need is subject to some qualification. For instance, the Court of Appeal stated in a later case (*Re L*) that the courts will only intervene if there is a *significant* mismatch between Part 2 of statements (educational needs) and Part 3 (provision). A challenge had been made to various aspects of a statement including the fact that reference to handwriting and note-taking appeared in Part 5 (non-educational provision) rather than Part 3 (educational) of the statement; and that, in any case, occupational therapy advice for such problems did not amount to a specification of provision to overcome those problems. The court pointed out, referring to the ex parte E case, that[8]:

> In explaining that the purpose of Part III is to make the provision intended by a local education authority to match the needs identified in Part II, the court was not inviting a line by line examination of the parts in order to gauge the degree of correspondence between them. Inelegant or even imperfect matching, whether or not the production of poor draftsmanship, would not be enough. Only if there were a clear failure to make provision for a significant need would the court be likely to conclude that there was such dereliction of duty' – as to warrant intervention.

Duties in relation to special educational needs are, in addition, replete with time limits and the rights of parents to make representations to the authority and to appeal to a Special Educational Needs Tribunal (see below). These duties have been thoroughly examined in the law courts over the years, mainly in connection with the Education Act 1981, a predecessor to the 1996 Act.

Children with special educational needs

Legislation states that a child has special educational needs if he or she has a *learning difficulty* which necessitates special educational provision. The child has a learning difficulty if he or she has 'significantly greater difficulty in learning than the majority of children of his age' – or if he or she is prevented or hindered through disability from using the educational facilities generally available to children of the same age in the area.[9]

A Code of Practice gives guidance to authorities and governing bodies about how to meet special educational needs. It explains that although up to 20% of children might have such needs at some time during their school life, only about 2% will need a statutory statement of special educational needs. This means that, in most instances, schools will meet the special educational needs of pupils from their own resources, without statements having been made. The code lists three stages or levels at which schools might do this, from 'giving special help' through to individual education plans which might include specific 'materials' and 'equipment'.[10]

An education authority might go on to make a statutory assessment, through its own initiative or by parental or school request. It has a duty to make an assessment if it thinks it is necessary, or probably necessary for it to determine the child's special educational provision.[11]

Assessing children's needs for equipment

When making the assessment, education authorities have a duty to seek parental, educational, medical, psychological and social services advice – as well as any other 'appropriate' advice.[12]

The Code of Practice states that, when an assessment is being carried out, consideration should be given to the use of information technology such as special keyboards and switch inputs, word processing facilities, software painting programmes, voice synthesizers linked to computers, and other communication software. Similarly, authorities should also enquire whether the school has explored the possibility of adaptations to the school – whether generally to improve physical access to the environment, or, for example, to assist children with a visual impairment by arranging for handrails, lighting and colour contrast.[13]

The Code also gives guidance on the criteria an authority might use when deciding whether or not to make a statement of special educational needs. Equipment is again mentioned. For instance, it suggests that a statement might not be necessary if a child needs access to specific equipment such as a portable word-processing device, electronic keyboard or tape-recorder; and similarly, if the need is only for minor adaptations such as doorway-widening or improvement of the acoustic environment. In such situations, the authority might think that 'the school could reasonably be expected to make such provision from within its own resources'.

On the other hand, the authority might conclude that the school could *not* reasonably be expected to make provision from its own resources if a child needs a 'significant' item of equipment such as a closed circuit television, a computer or CD-ROM equipment; or similarly if the need is for a major adaptation such as a lift.[14]

Meeting children's needs for equipment

If a child does not need a statement of special educational needs, then any special educational provision will be made under the specific duty imposed on school governing bodies, that they use their 'best endeavours' to meet the special educational needs of any child in the school.[15]

If, however, the assessment confirms that the authority needs to determine the child's special educational provision, then it must make a statement in a form prescribed by regulations.[16] The Regulations stipulate that the statement must be divided into sections about the:[17]

- child's **special educational needs**, 'in terms of the child's learning difficulties which call for special educational provision'
- **objectives** of the child's special educational provision
- the **educational provision** to meet the needs and objectives, including 'any appropriate facilities and equipment, staffing arrangements and curriculum'
- child's **non-educational needs**, 'for which the authority consider provision is appropriate if the child is to properly benefit from the special educational provision' already specified
- **non-educational provision:** the arrangements for provision, which either the education authority can provide, or which the education authority is 'satisfied' will be provided by the NHS, social services or some other body.

Guidance issued under the Education Act 1981 stated that education authorities should complete formal assessments within six months of announcing its intention to assess; whilst under the 1981 Act's successor, the Education Act 1996, a total of 26 weeks (subject to various exceptional circumstances) is laid down in Regulations – covering a period from the initial decision of an authority (or parental request) to make an assessment right through to a finalised statement.[18]

The local ombudsman has made a substantial number of investigations into delays in completing assessments. He has found maladministration when an authority took ten (rather than six) months to issue a draft statement.[19] And even if careful deliberation and a number of tests were required as part of the assessment process, a delay of two years in issuing the statement was maladministration.[20] When a statement was issued 15 months after the six-month deadline mainly because a headteacher had failed to provide educational advice within a reasonable time, the ombudsman censured the authority for not making a greater effort to obtain the advice more quickly.[21] And, even though a 16-month period taken to issue a statement was due to severe staffing problems in an authority's special needs section and psychology service – and even though the authority, whose staff were facing a difficult situation, had quite properly put in place a priority system – the ombudsman still found that the delay was 'unreasonable' and constituted maladministration.[22]

The bureaucratic delays surrounding the statutory assessment of children's special educational needs have long been known – and some authorities have offered alternative, simpler and quicker processes. However, if such schemes deny parents their statutory rights of appeal against authorities' decisions – and authorities fail to explain the difference between the two types of assessment process – then the ombudsman will find maladministration.[23] However, when an authority simply failed to inform parents of their rights to request an assessment, there was maladministration – but the ombudsman did not recommend compensation in this particular case because there had been no injustice, since the authority would probably have refused a request in any case.[24]

How much detail to include in a statement of needs?

Sometimes, concern arises about how much detail to include in the statement. Should provision be expressed, for example, in terms of 'information technology as appropriate to assist communication'; or should it specify instead the exact type and model of equipment required? On the one hand, a vague description allows for flexibility and might preclude the need for the statement to be constantly modified. On the other hand, it might mean that the appropriate equipment is not provided at all – if, for example, resources are scarce – and that it is then difficult to challenge the authority about the non-provision.[25] Managers might place pressure on professionals who contribute to statements, such as physiotherapists, to 'couch things in vague terms'.[26] Imprecise terms include 'regular', 'intensive', 'some help', from 'an adult' (who?), 'would benefit from' (is it or isn't it needed?), 'ideally' – and so on.[27]

The Code of Practice refers to this issue. Reference to provision for *educational needs* should normally be 'specific, detailed and quantified' (eg detailing the number of hours of special staff support needed) – although sometimes 'flexibility' should be retained precisely to allow for changing needs. Similarly, provision for *non-educational needs* should be described 'clearly and accurately' and be fully agreed as to nature and quantity.[28]

Taking one particular statement of special educational needs included in a report of the local ombudsman, both specific and non-specific provision is listed (eg specific equipment is mentioned, but is qualified by words such as 'appropriate' or 'if necessary'; whilst 'additional support' is listed without an indication of how much is required). The balance struck between inadequate and excessive detail illustrates how much depends on the will and resources of education authorities if the 'spirit' of such statements are to be realised. Under the educational provision, the following examples concerning equipment occur[29]:

- 'appropriate communication technology, such as the Touch Talker and appropriate information technology such as a lap-top computer. The technological equipment...will need to change with her development and changing needs'

- 'advice from the Local Educational Authority Special Needs Computer Centre regarding the provision and use of computer technology'
- 'staff tuition, as appropriate, from a suitably skilled person on...the use of communication technology'
- 'additional support from a Special Needs Assistant, working with the Class Teacher, to...assist in the use of technological aids, including monitoring...use of the equipment'.

And under non-educational provision:

- 'advice and provision of special seating as appropriate'
- 'consideration of wheelchair access and use on occasions'
- 'transport to and from school if necessary'.

In one case (*R v Cumbria CC, ex parte P*) which reached the High Court, a mother claimed that her child's statement of need was too general in its wording; speech therapy was referred to, but in a non-specific manner. There was further confusion about the distinction made in the statement between *educational provision* by a specialist speech and language teacher, and *non-educational provision* of speech therapy by the health authority. The judge stated that it would not be appropriate for the court to make a declaration that statements should generally specify the number and length of speech therapy sessions. He felt it would not be helpful and that such matters should instead be dealt with case-by-case with the help of appeal procedures. Otherwise, he implied, the search for specificity might be never-ending – since even a reference to 'a speech therapy session with a qualified therapist' has a degree of vagueness as to what is to be done in such a session. Nevertheless, in this particular case, the court did state that the authority ought to produce a new statement in a form which would make quite clear to the parents what their child would receive by way both of educational and non-educational provision.[30]

Educational, non-educational and other needs for equipment: division of responsibilities

The distinction between educational and non-educational needs is complex, sometimes troublesome and can affect equipment provision. For example, the status of special seating might be unclear, because although needed in school, it could be argued that it is not directly related to the curriculum; in which case, it becomes non-educational, rather than educational, equipment for the purposes of the Education Act 1996.

In summary, a child might have special educational needs for which equipment is required. If these needs are recorded in a statement of special educational needs, then they are sub-divided into educational and non-educational needs. Both types of need relate to the child's education, the former more specifically to following the curriculum, the latter more generally to managing at school. The term 'non-educational' is therefore somewhat misleading, since it does in fact refer to a child's needs at school.

Special educational needs and provision: educational or non-educational?

Sometimes, because of resource implications, disputes arise about whether provision for children's special educational needs should be designated educational or non-educational. This can affect which statutory body assumes responsibility.

If provision is deemed to be educational, then the education authority must make arrangements for that provision – this is a binding duty. In contrast, although education authorities may make non-educational provision themselves, they do not have an absolute duty to do so; they merely 'may arrange' provision 'in such manner as they consider appropriate'.[31]

The Code of Practice explains that a statutory statement must contain all the child's special educational needs, followed by all the special educational provision which the authority thinks is appropriate to meet *all* the child's learning difficulties. However, as far as non-educational provision goes, the statement need only refer to those needs and provision which the authority is satisfied will be met.[32]

The strong duty imposed on education authorities to meet children's special educational needs can mean that professionals, such as therapists, may find themselves aware of two types of need – the 'real' needs of the child and the needs which can be met within the resources available – and therefore face a dilemma about what to recommend.[33] This can lead to conflicts between good professional practice and duties to employers.[34] The issue has contributed toward the call for independent assessments – so that the functions of assessment and provision are separated and an authority, bearing in mind resources, is not judge in its own cause (see p.38).[35] In addition, the incentive for education authorities to define some types of provision as non-educational is clear, since it means that they can more easily tailor provision to resources. The resulting problem for children and their parents is equally obvious.

Further complication arises when other authorities such as the NHS agree to make provision – either as part of educational or of non-educational provision. In either case, there is no binding duty, and the health authority or NHS Trust could withdraw from provision, or refuse to make it in the first place. If they refuse to make a commitment to provide for a child's educational needs, the education authority still retains ultimate responsibility for making provision. However, if the refusal concerns provision for non-educational needs, then the education authority is under no duty, to ensure provision.[36] The longstanding tension between health and education authorities to which this situation leads, is reported in 1996 to be continuing – in respect, for example, of speech therapy.[37]

Disputes about distinguishing educational from non-educational needs have sometimes reached the law courts. Some have concerned the need for, and provision of, speech and language therapy (and thus, by implication, for example, communication aids). For instance, in *R v Oxfordshire CC, ex parte W*, it was held that speech therapy could be either educational or non-educational, but in this particular case, it was not unreasonable to categorise it as non-educational.[38] And in *R v Lancashire CC, ex parte M*, the authority claimed it had made an error by categorising speech therapy as educational provision, re-categorised it, and on that basis argued that it did not have to provide it all. In particular, it claimed that, as a matter of law, speech therapy could not be educational provision. The Court of Appeal ruled against the authority, stating that speech therapy can be classed as either educational or non-educational, depending on the health and development of the particular child. The court also pointed out that one of the judges in the Oxfordshire case:[39]

> 'appears to have accepted the argument for the education authority that the fact that speech therapists were employed by the NHS was a matter which the authority was entitled to take into account in its decision to treat speech therapy as non-educational provision in that case. For the reasons already given we respectfully disagree with that part of his judgement; speech therapy in a particular case may be non-educational provision, but whether it is cannot depend upon the identity of the speech therapist's employers.'

A more recent case (*R v Lambeth LBC, ex parte MBM*) determined that provision of a lift could not, as a matter of law, be educational – as opposed to non-educational – provision.[40] The ombudsman too has become entangled in this sort of issue; as illustrated by one investigation concerning speech therapy. The educational part of the statement of need specified that the child should have 'her language monitored and has access to regular sessions with a speech therapist'. But, the non-educational part of the statement also referred to 'regular speech therapy' – a common phrase in statements but one importing no agreement about how it was to be made available. In the event, neither the educational nor the non-educational provision was made adequately; the health authority, upon which the education authority had been relying, failed to deliver. The ombudsman, and the Secretary of State (to whom a separate appeal had been made) had to try to tease out the education authority's obligations – in the light of vague wording which, though contained in two different parts of the same statement of need, referred to the same service.[41]

Other statutory services: the NHS and social services departments

As already explained (see above) other authorities, such as the NHS and social services, might agree to make either educational or non-educational provision, but do not have a duty to provide either.

However, these other authorities do have a duty to 'help' education authorities in relation to special educational needs, though the duty is qualified. For example, in deciding whether or not to help, a health authority can consider whether its available resources make it 'reasonable to comply with the request'. Likewise, a social services department can consider whether the request is 'compatible' with its duties and whether the request 'unduly prejudices the discharge of any of their functions'[42] – as it might, if it was short of resources. A court case (*R v Northavon DC, ex parte Smith*) in a related field, child care, concerning similar duties of housing and social services departments, shows how flimsy such qualified duties can be.[43]

The practical consequences of this situation, and the resulting shortcomings in provision, have been frequently reported. Reliance by education authorities on other statutory services is problematic because there are no nationally defined levels of service which, for example, health authorities should provide for children with SEN.[44] The wide discretion which the NHS employs generally in providing services and equipment (see p.197) means that it might give a low priority to services for schools – for example, occupational therapy and speech and language therapy.[45] And the slow response of other statutory services might delay even the making of a statement of special educational needs; thus, in one investigation the local ombudsman did not criticise an education authority which took eight months to issue a draft statement (two months longer than recommended by government guidance) – because this was at least partly due to delay in receiving a report from an NHS clinical psychologist.[46]

Scope for uncertainty in categorising equipment

To sum up, the scope for uncertainties in equipment provision for special educational needs is considerable.

First, a decision needs to be made about whether the need for an item of equipment is anything to do with school at all. If it is not, then it might not feature in either the educational or non-educational part of a statement of needs. Even this decision could give rise to dispute; for example, calipers required by a child might be viewed as a straightforward health need and as irrelevant to the child's education. But, equally, Regulations define non-educational needs as those for which an 'authority considers provision is appropriate if the child is to properly benefit from the special educational provision'.[47] This is very broad and could, in principle, include almost anything. In the past, there has been some uncertainty, for example, about the provision of radio microphone hearing aids. On the one hand, they can be useful outside of school and education and so, arguably, should be funded by the NHS;[48] in practice, they are likely to be funded variously by the NHS, voluntary organisations, parents or sometimes education authorities.[49]

Second, if equipment is to feature in a statement of special educational needs because it is relevant to school, then it has to be characterised as either educational or non-educational. As already explained, this can lead to disputes about responsibilities. Precisely the same uncertainties, for the same reasons, apply when children do not have statutory statements of special educational needs – the main difference being that there are no statements to highlight the uncertainties.

Integrating children into ordinary schools: efficient use of resources

The duty of education authorities and schools to ensure that children with SEN are integrated in ordinary schools is a qualified duty. One of the qualifications is that the carrying out of the duty must be 'compatible with the efficient use of resources'.[50]

Adaptations to ordinary schools are sometimes needed to accommodate children with SEN – for instance, ramps, lifts, widened doorways. However, schools and authorities argue sometimes that particular adaptations are too costly and decline to provide them. In a recent High Court case, the judge ruled that an authority was justified in not providing a lift for a 10-year old girl with muscular dystrophy, who used a wheelchair and could not attend certain lessons which were held in classrooms on the first floor of the school. The judge held that the need for a lift was a question of mobility (ie a non-educational) and not an educational need. Therefore, there was no absolute duty on the education authority to provide it – and the authority could therefore take into account resources, costs and benefit.[51] In recognition of problems of access to ordinary schools, Regulations now place a duty on education authorities and schools to provide various information about special educational needs policies and arrangements, including (in the case of schools) access to facilities for disabled children.[52]

One study of the costs of ensuring access for disabled children to mainstream education, did identify adaptations to premises, rather than equipment, as one of the significant extra costs. This was because equipment was often personal to a child and so cost the same whether he or she attended an ordinary or a special school. Even so, extra costs are likely to be incurred when ordinary schools first build up general stocks of specialist equipment and spares, when they begin to take children with SEN.[53] In addition, special needs teachers in ordinary schools might need to spend on money experimenting with equipment, because it might be difficult to predict what will be suitable for particular pupils. Also adding to costs, is the considerable time spent by staff contacting useful sources of information and assistance, as well as the fact that certain types of equipment are liable to go missing.[54]

By contrast, special schools will already have a general pool of equipment – to such an extent that education authorities might not bother to specify equipment in the statements of special educational needs of children who are attending special schools. For instance, an authority might feel that a standing frame for a severely disabled child is a standard item in much the same way as a pencil.[55]

Uncertain provision and diverse funding of equipment

The consequences of the uncertainties described above are that it is not always clear what equipment or adaptations will be provided or who will pay for them and how quickly. Indeed, a recent report of the local ombudsman illustrates just how complicated matters can sometimes become. It concerned the provision of equipment for a severely physically and mentally disabled child (and also for her younger sister) and included the following aspects:[56]

- a mandatory reassessment under the Education Act 1981 of the child's needs which was never completed because various requested advice had not been forthcoming
- use of an adapted garden chair because the girl's wheelchair would not fit under the table
- disagreement between the mother and the occupational therapist, who both felt the garden chair was unsuitable, and the headteacher who stated that it was appropriate
- confusion because the standing frame which the girl had been using at school for limited periods belonged to the health authority and had actually been loaned to another pupil who was about to leave and take the frame with him
- omission by the education authority of the standing frame from the statement of special educational needs because it was assumed to be standard equipment which the special school would provide as a matter of course
- uncertainty and disagreement between the school, the education authority and the health authority about who should pay for the standing frame
- a standing frame used at home, funded jointly by the health authority and social services department – which, however, was too big and bulky to be transported easily and could not be used in school
- numerous assessments by various educational and health professionals
- the problem of the child, without the frame, being left lying on the floor at school for long periods
- the mother's wish for her daughter to have her own standing frame
- the mother's concern over one type of frame which raised the child 'almost head and shoulders' above the teachers and other pupils – and may have impeded eye contact and face-to-face communication
- the mother's concern that her daughter's posture deteriorated through using the garden chair for two years and that she was forced to use the wheelchair for lessons, when it really should have been used for mobility only.

The practices of NHS wheelchair services in relation to children's needs might vary and some services may provide three models – including one for school. However, a relevant factor might be the availability of education authority transport; rather than supply an extra wheelchair for school, a wheelchair service might feel that it is up to the education authority to ensure that the child has suitable transport to take the chair to and from school.[57] If a child requires an electric wheelchair for use in the playground, the wheelchair service might feel that the need is for social, rather than medical or health care, reasons – and decline to provide it. However, the education authority or school might also be reluctant to find the money. Some schools might allow children to take equipment home with them – others might not; not all equipment, anyway, will be easily or safely portable on a daily basis. The problems faced by children and their parents in obtaining suitable wheelchairs has been highlighted recently by a report on NHS wheelchair services; the following example, contained in the report, is referred to as a 'common scenario where the needs of many students are not being met':[58]

> 'Students whose needs are normally met by provision of a self propelling wheelchair are transferred to secondary school with long corridors, extensive grounds and an opportunity to use local facilities such as shops and library. Using local facilities is an essential part of the education programme and it is important in the development of social skills, self confidence and independence. The wheelchair service may not be prepared or financially able to meet the additional cost of an indoor-outdoor occupant controlled wheelchair which is essential if pupils are to take advantage of the full educational package and benefit from the opportunities available at the school.'

Funding for equipment can become diverse and unpredictable. Individual parents might be encouraged to buy equipment which their children require at home. Radio microphone aids might be supplied through private subscription[59], and wheelchairs through charities, fundraising events, golf clubs or parents.[60] Unexpected costs might arise which are difficult to meet, such as the maintenance of radio microphone hearing aids,[61] or the buying of batteries (£150) for a turbo-wheelchair which had been bought through fundraising – the fund could not be used on disposable items (such as batteries). Parents' support groups fund all manner of equipment including computers, televisions, video records and cookers.[62] Resort to diverse sources of funding is an established feature of providing equipment for disabled children and students from primary through to higher education; charitable trusts and voluntary organisations might assist by means of loans, grants, purchase or loan of equipment.[63]

Even when the responsibility for providing services and equipment is clearly identified in a statement of special educational needs, delay might affect actual provision. In such circumstances, the ombudsman finds maladministration – for example, if a specialist teacher is made available six months late,[64] or if speech therapy is denied to a child for the period of a school-term.[65] Maladministration occurs if the provision of a portable computer and associated software is delayed for months after the issue of the statement; the fact that the authority was attempting to meet provision without committing additional resources was no excuse, since it was clearly not possible and merely contributed to the delay.[66] Similarly, it is maladministration if, after a two year delay in making a statement, an authority delays further in making available the recommended special teaching. Also criticised was the authority's policy of not issuing final statements until the recommended provision was actually available – except to parents who demanded they be issued. This policy consequently put children, whose parents did not make such a request, at an unfair disadvantage.[67]

Special schools and independent schools: legislation and guidance

Regulations[68] govern the approval by the Secretary of State of *special* schools and *independent* schools which make provision for children with statements of special educational needs. Such schools include special schools maintained by the local educational authority, non-maintained schools (run by charities, which charge fees on a non-profit making basis) and independent schools. The Regulations refer to the health and welfare of pupils but do not mention equipment.

However, accompanying Circular guidance refers to the need for *special schools* to discuss with the NHS the need for nursing and therapy support (which could involve equipment).[69] In the case of *independent schools*, guidance makes explicit reference to the duty to ensure that children do not use wheelchairs which are too small for them or are in disrepair, calipers which they have outgrown, or 'inappropriate' hearing or mobility equipment. In addition, the suitability and location of fixed equipment should be reassessed regularly.[70]

Assessment of pre-school children

The Education Act 1996 stipulates that education authorities may assess the educational needs of children under the age of two years – and must do so when requested by parents – if they think that the child has special educational needs for which special provision needs to be determined.[71]

If health authorities think that children under five years old have special educational needs, then, after informing the children's parents and giving them the chance to discuss the matter, they have a duty to inform education authorities.[72]

3. COMPLAINTS

Special Educational Needs Tribunal

Various types of complaint can be made to the Special Educational Needs Tribunal, if the complaints procedure of the local authority or school has failed to resolve a dispute.[73] Appeals to the Tribunal can be made, for example, if an education authority refuses to assess a child's special educational needs, to make a statement, to maintain a statement or to make the provision in accordance with parents's wishes. There are other grounds of appeal.[74]

The Tribunal consists of three people including a legally qualified chairperson and two lay members with knowledge and experience of children and of local government. Various stages of the prescribed procedure have time limits attached – four or five months should be sufficient from the making of the appeal to the hearing. Indeed, the reported average length of time taken from the lodging to the hearing of an appeal is reported to be five months.[75] Decisions of the tribunal are binding on education authorities.[76] Although the Tribunal is intended to operate informally, parents can be accompanied by a lawyer but cannot claim legal aid. Education authorities are not expected to bring lawyers, unless parents do.[77]

One purpose of the Tribunal is to reduce the number of cases going to judicial review in the law courts, and to solve disputes more quickly and efficiently. However, an appeal can be made against a decision of the Tribunal to the High Court within six weeks of the decision – but only on points of law.[78] In its first year of operation, the Tribunal had to consider whether it would narrowly assess whether the authority had acted correctly, given the facts at the time – or whether it could take account of facts which had emerged since the original decision. It has decided to take the latter, broader option, since this could clearly be in the child's interests.[79] A broad approach has been confirmed by the Court of Appeal, which has held that the decisions of the Tribunal should be challenged in the law courts by way of *appeal*, rather than *judicial review*, procedure. In this way, the court has wider powers to hear new evidence and to make an order itself which the Tribunal should have made – rather than remit the case to the Tribunal to make the order.[80]

Complaints to the Secretary of State

Some complaints will not come within the remit of the Special Educational Needs Tribunal. In this situation, once school or education authority complaints procedures have been exhausted, it is possible to complain to the Secretary of State if duties are allegedly not being carried out or are being carried out unreasonably.[81]

The Secretary of State can be challenged by complainants who feel that she has not acted legally, fairly or reasonably – via judicial review in the law courts (see chapter 17). Alternatively, a complaint can be made to the Parliamentary ombudsman – for example, if the Secretary of State has dealt with a complaint slowly.[82]

Complaints to the local ombudsman

The general powers of the local ombudsmen have already been outlined (see p.115). In respect of education, they may investigate maladministration attaching to the actions and decisions of education authorities, but not to internal school matters. Over the years, there have been many investigations by the ombudsman in the field of special education about, for example, delay in making a statement of SEN, or failing to make the provision stipulated in a statement. A number of these investigations are referred to in this chapter.

Judicial review

In the past, many cases have been brought by parents seeking judicial review of the decisions and actions of education authorities. Few have been about equipment directly, but many have been about assessment and provision in general – and thus apply in principle as much to equipment as to any other service which a child needs. Some of these cases are referred to in this chapter, whilst others are cited in Chapter 17 on judicial review.

As already explained, it is expected that the Special Educational Needs Tribunal will now deal with most of the cases which formerly went to judicial review; indeed the courts were often at pains to point out that some of the disputes coming before them were not suitable for judicial review, but should better have been dealt with by appeal procedures within education authorities or involving the Secretary of State. For instance, appeal procedures (and now the Special Educational Needs Tribunal) can deal with questions of fact and professional judgements, whereas this is not the role of judicial review courts.[83]

4. PROVISION OF EQUIPMENT FOR CHILDREN AND YOUNG PEOPLE LEAVING FULL-TIME EDUCATION

The Disabled Persons (Services, Consultation and Representation) Act 1986 imposes certain duties of communication on education authorities, further education colleges, the further education funding council, and social services departments.

In essence, social services departments must be informed in advance when disabled pupils will be leaving school or full-time education. This is to establish whether (i) they are disabled in the view of the social services department and (ii) they require welfare services. If so, then before those children or young people leave full-time education, the education authority, college or funding council must inform the social services department when they will be leaving. The social services department must then make arrangements to assess the child or young person's needs. Circular guidance emphasises the importance of cooperation between the NHS, social services departments, voluntary organisations and the careers service.[84]

However, past reports on the operation of the Act and the provision of social services to young disabled people have found variable and sometimes unsatisfactory arrangements.[85] The significant role of occupational therapists has been recognised[86], as well as the need for advice about equipment and adaptations.[87] More recently, an SSI report noted continuing unevenness in the quality of services being provided to young people with disabilities, including significant delays in assessment for young people's equipment needs – although prompt initial responses to requests for home adaptations were common.[88]

5. PROVISION OF EQUIPMENT IN FURTHER EDUCATION

Role of further education funding council (FEFC)

The Further Education Funding Council (for England; there is also one for Wales) is responsible for providing funds to colleges of further education – that is for people over 16 but under 19 years of age. Under this general duty towards the population, the Council has a duty to ensure that sufficient further education facilities are provided, that they are of sufficient character and equipped sufficiently to meet the 'reasonable needs of all persons to whom the duty extends'. It must also 'take account of the different abilities and aptitudes' of people.[89] Toward people of 19 years of age or more, the Council has a duty to provide adequate facilities for a prescribed range of educational courses (eg leading to academic qualifications, leading to higher education, teaching basic skills, teaching independent living and communication skills to students with learning difficulties).[90]

Both these duties can clearly cover equipment and adaptations for disabled people, although they are qualified insofar as the council must make 'effective' use of its resources and not make any provision which might cause 'disproportionate' expenditure.[91]

In addition to the general duties just described, the Funding Council must specifically 'have regard' to people with learning difficulties (defined as under the Education Act 1996: see above). If the facilities available generally in further (or higher) education are not 'adequate' for any particular person with a learning difficulty, then the Council has a duty to make provision at a specialist institution, so long as this is in the person's best interests. This last duty applies to people with learning difficulties who are under 25 years old; for students who are older, only a power exists (ie the Council can make provision, but does not have to).[92] Again, both these duties might clearly be applied to the provision of suitable equipment and adaptations, such as computers, loop systems, ramps and lifts.

Most specialist colleges are registered charities and take students on a national, rather than a local basis.[93] The Council has the statutory power to provide financial support to such specialist facilities and placements.[94] Guidance issued by the Funding Council explains that amongst the criteria and factors which will be taken into account are the physical suitability of buildings and the availability of specialised personal or physical support.[95] In addition, mainstream colleges themselves have specific statutory powers to provide facilities for students with learning difficulties.[96]

Facilities in mainstream colleges

In practice, facilities in mainstream colleges are likely to vary. Some colleges run separate non-integrated courses for disabled people, whilst others try to enable disabled people to participate in mainstream courses.[97] Many colleges are without, for example, adequate lifts, appropriately designed and situated toilets, ramps, easily useable doors and accessible libraries and refectories. In addition, colleges may not exercise sufficient foresight and planning. For instance, a student using a wheelchair might have to attend all his classes in buildings *other* than the one with a suitable toilet – as well as being lifted up stairs by his fellow students. Apart from the difficulties for the student concerned, there is also a legal issue about the risk to the health and safety of the students doing the lifting.[98]

Role of local education authorities

Local education authorities have a duty to secure 'the provision for their area of adequate facilities for further education' – in the case of provision which it is not the duty of the FEFC to provide. This includes vocational, social, physical and recreational training and organised leisure-time occupation. In addition, in the case of part-time further education and full-time education for people 19 years of age or more (both of which the FEFC does have a duty to provide), authorities may still 'secure the provision of such facilities as appear to them to be appropriate' for meeting the needs of the local population – and they may do anything they consider 'expedient' or 'appropriate' in connection with such provision. In respect of both the duty and the power just described, authorities must 'have regard' to people with learning difficulties.[99] In a recent High Court case (*R v Islington LBC, ex parte Rixon*) about the duty of an education authority under this section, the judge ruled that an authority should conscientiously take into account Circular guidance from the Department for Education which urged that authorities ensure that 'adequate arrangements exist for assessing the needs of these students and identifying the provision that will be appropriate, and for the provision of such support services as are necessary.'[100]

Local education authorities are responsible for funding students who have statements of special educational needs who remain in a maintained school or in an independent, special school. (Otherwise, statements cease to have effect when children leave school and the FEFC becomes responsible for providing appropriate facilities). Dispute has arisen in the law courts when an education authority has attempted to jettison its duties (for financial reasons) laid down in a statement, by suggesting that when a child with severe speech and language problems reached 16, he would need less provision. The judge stated that an authority could not simply divest itself of responsibility for a pupil's schooling by failing to specify it in the statement – and then claim that it no longer had a duty because the pupil was no longer registered at a school appropriate to his needs.[101]

The duty of LEAs to make arrangements for the provision of free transport extends to students in the further education sector.[102]

6. PROVISION OF EQUIPMENT IN HIGHER EDUCATION

For disabled students in higher education, extra means-tested allowances are available if authorities are satisfied that students' disability is necessitating extra expenditure. The allowances are referred to as disabled students' allowances (DSAs). If people satisfy this condition, then they have a right to the allowances – although the actual amount they get (up to a maximum) is for authorities to decide.

The allowances available are up to £4975 per year for a non-medical personal helper, £3745 over the whole course for major items of specialist equipment, and £1245 per year for other costs.[103] A government guide suggests that these other costs could include minor items such as tapes and braille paper.[104]

Local education authorities award the allowances. Disability is not defined either in the Regulations which govern the allowances, nor in guidance which the Department for Education and Employment issues to authorities. Authorities differ in how they determine whether students are disabled and what their needs for assistance are. Practices vary from full, expensive assessments to acceptance of the student's word. Government guidance to LEAs states that the Regulations do not allow LEAs to pay for the costs of assessments to establish whether a person is disabled. If students cannot get free medical statements from the NHS, they might have to pay themselves; for example, it might cost dyslexic students up to £200 for a report from an educational psychologist. However, once disability has been established, education authorities can pay the costs of assessments to determine what needs a disabled student has – for example, an assessment by the National Federation of Access Centres to determine a student's need for specialist and general information technology.

Some students are thought to face particular problems within the present system of allowances. For instance, those with mobility problems may face major access problems, as well as incurring high travelling costs. Students with visual or hearing impairment might have to pay the high costs of employing personal helpers, as well as buy expensive equipment and large quantities of cassettes and other stationery. Students whose disabilities (eg dyslexia, epilepsy) are not readily visible might not be noticed – or even arouse the suspicions of authorities when they try to claim an allowance.

Payment of the allowance is sometimes direct to the student, who can then choose what to buy. Sometimes, the authority deals direct with the supplier of the equipment or services on behalf of the student. This might be quicker and result in a discount; the disadvantage is that sometimes the equipment supplied is inappropriate because the student has not been able to deal directly with the supplier. A third possibility is that some authorities ask the student to buy the equipment and then apply for reimbursement. This is perceived to be unreasonable and is contrary to guidance from the Department of Education and Employment.[105]

Under its general functions, the Higher Education Funding Council for England must, in the future, 'have regard to the requirements of disabled persons'.[106]

Notes

1 Examples from: SKILL (1995). *Specialist equipment in education: sources of help and information.* Factsheet no.20. London: SKILL, p.2.

2 *Education Act 1996; SI 1994/1047 Education (Special Educational Needs) Regulations 1994.*

3 Department for Education (1994). *Code of practice on the identification and assessment of special educational needs.* London: DFE.

4 *Education Act 1996,* s.14.

5 Department for Education (1994). *Code of practice on the identification and assessment of special educational needs.* London: DFE, p.79.

6 *R v Secretary of State for Education, ex parte E* [1992] 1 FLR 377 (CA)
7 See eg *R v Hereford Education Authority, ex parte Jones* [1981] 1 WLR 768 (QBD): although the authority lost this case because it had been making improper charges for music lessons, the judge noted that if, under s.8 of the Education Act 1944, the authority had stopped the music lessons altogether, the court would not have interfered.
8 *Re L* [1994] ELR 16 (CA).
9 *Education Act 1996,* s.312.
10 Department for Education (1994). *Code of practice on the identification and assessment of special educational needs.* London: DFE, pp.i, 25–31.
11 *Education Act 1996,* ss.321, 323, 324.
12 SI 1994/1047 *Education (Special Educational Needs) Regulations 1994,* r.6.
13 Department for Education (1994). *Code of practice on the identification and assessment of special educational needs.* London: DFE, pp.54–69.
14 Department for Education (1994). *Code of practice on the identification and assessment of special educational needs.* London: DFE, p.81.
15 *Education Act 1996,* s.317.
16 *Education Act 1996,* s.168.
17 SI 1994/1047 *Education (Special Educational Needs) Regulations 1994,* Schedule, Part B.
18 SI 1994/1047. *Education (Special Educational Needs) Regulations 1994.*
19 Commission for Local Administration in England (94/C/0743). *Report on investigation into a complaint against Manchester City Council.* York: CLAE, 1995, p.9.
20 Commission for Local Administration in England (93/C/3560). *Report on investigation into a complaint against Manchester City Council.* York: CLAE, 1995, pp.9–10.
21 Commission for Local Administration in England (94/A/0301). *Report on investigation into a complaint against London Borough of Newham.* London: CLAE, 1995, p.13.
22 Commission for Local Administration in England (94/A/3002). *Report on investigation into a complaint against London Borough of Wandsworth.* London: CLAE, 1996, p.17.
23 Commission for Local Administration in England (94/C/2021). *Report on investigation into a complaint against Cumbria City Council.* York: CLAE, 1995, pp.16–17.
24 Commission for Local Administration in England (94/A/1369). *Report on investigation into a complaint against the London Borough of Barnet.* London: CLAE, 1994, pp.16–17.
25 Audit Commission; Her Majesty Inspectorate of Schools (1992). *Getting on the act: provision for pupils with special educational needs: the national picture.* London: HMSO, p.24.
26 Call for changes in statementing. *Therapy Weekly:* 14 January 1993; 19(29), p.1: discussing the evidence put forward by the Chartered Society of Physiotherapy's paediatric special interest group to a House of Commons committee.
27 Bhuttacharji, S. (1992). Misleading statements: the art of 'statementing' for children with special needs is still much misunderstood. *Therapy Weekly:* 1992; 19(6), p.7.
28 Department for Education (1994). *Code of practice on the identification and assessment of special educational needs.* London: DFE, pp.87–88.
29 Commission for Local Administration in England (94/A/0732). *Report on investigation into a complaint against London Borough of Haringey.* London: CLAE, 1996, Appendix 1.
30 *R v Cumbria County Council, ex parte P* [1995] ELR 337 (QBD).
31 *Education Act 1996,* s.324(5).
32 Department for Education (1994). *Code of practice on the identification and assessment of special educational needs.* London: DFE, paras 4.28–4.35.
33 National Association of Health Authorities (1988). *Health authorities' concerns for children with special needs: a report on a survey of health authorities on the implementation of the Education Act 1981.* Birmingham: NAHA, 1981, p.8. Also a concern expressed in the minutes put before: the: House of Commons Education Committee (1993). *Meeting special educational needs: statements of needs and provision.* Volume 2. HC 287–II. London: HMSO, p.20 (Mr. Steinberg).
34 See eg Bhuttacharji, S. (1992). Misleading statements: the art of 'statementing' for children with special needs is still much misunderstood. *Therapy Weekly:* 1992; 19(6), p.7.
35 See eg *Hansard.* House of Commons Debates, Special Educational Needs, cols 1078–1979, Mrs Anne Campbell. And see the recommendations of: Leonard, A (1992). *A hard act to follow: a study of the experience of parent and children under the 1981 Education Act.* London: Spastics

Society, p.25. And see evidence submitted throughout: House of Commons Education Committee (1993). *Meeting special educational needs: statements of needs and provision.* Volume 2. HC 287–II. London: HMSO.

36 *House of Commons Education, Science and Art Committee* (1987). Special educational needs: implementation of the Education Act 1981. London: HMSO, vol 1, pxvii.

37 House of Commons Education Committee (1996). *Special educational needs: the working of the code of practice and the tribunal.* 2nd report. HC 205. London: HMSO, pp.18, 40 (memoranda submitted by the Association of County Councils and the Association of Metropolitan Authorities – and by the Council for Disabled Children).

38 *R v Oxfordshire County Council, ex parte W* [1987] 2 FLR 193 (QBD).

39 *R v Lancashire County Council, ex parte M* [1989] 2 FLR 279 (CA).

40 *R v London Borough of Lambeth, ex parte MBM* [1995] ELR 374 (QBD).

41 Commission for Local Administration in England (93/A/3128). *Report on investigation into a complaint against London Borough of Southwark.* London: CLAE, 1995.

42 *Education Act 1996,* s.322

43 *R v Northavon District Council, ex parte Smith* [1994] 3 WLR 403 (HL).

44 Touche Ross (1990). *Extending local management to special schools.* London: Touche Ross, p.19 (for the Department of Education and Science).

45 House of Commons Education, Science and Art Committee (1987). *Special educational needs: implementation of the Education Act 1981.* London: HMSO, vol 2, pp.19–21 (appendices to the minutes of evidence: memorandum from a district speech therapist. Mobley, P.M. (1996). A question of wants or needs. (Letter). *Therapy Weekly:* 7 March 1996, p.5.

46 Commission for Local Administration in England (93/C/3324). *Report on investigation into a complaint against Humberside County Council.* York: CLAE, 1995, pp.6–7.

47 SI 1994/1047. *Education (Special Educational Needs) Regulations 1994,* Schedule, Part B.

48 See eg: Scottish Home and Health Department (1989). *Management of ENT services in Scotland.* Edinburgh: HMSO, p.25.

49 See eg Scottish Education Department (1987). *The education of pupils with severe hearing impairment in special schools and units in Scotland.* Edinburgh: HMSO, p.11.

50 *Education Act 1996,* s.316.

51 *R v London Borough of Lambeth, ex parte M* [1995] ELR 374 (QBD).

52 Education Act 1996, s.317. SI 1994/1048. *Education (Special Educational Needs) (Information) Regulations 1994.* SI 1994/1421. *Education (School Information) (England) Regulations 1994.*

53 Coopers & Lybrand (1992). *Within reach: access for disabled children to mainstream education.* London: National Union Teachers in association with The Spastics Society, p.35.

54 National Foundation for Educational Research (1992). *OECD/CERI project: integration in the school: reports of the case studies undertaken in the UK.* Slough: NFER, p.36.

55 Commission for Local Administration in England (93/A/4314, 4432, 0377, 2210). *Report on investigation into complaints against East Sussex County Council.* London: CLAE, 1996, vol. 1 (p.19), vol.2 (p.13).

56 Commission for Local Administration in England (93/A/4314, 4432, 0377, 2210). *Report on investigation into complaints against East Sussex County Council.* London: CLAE, 1996, vol.2, case 93/A/4432.

57 See eg report of a survey which found wide variations in the transport provided: McMillen, P. (1992). Survey of transport for children in wheelchairs. *British Journal of Occupational Therapy:* 1992; 55(5), pp.179–182.

58 Aldersea, P. (1996). *National prosthetic and wheelchair services report 1993–1996.* London: College of Occupational Therapists, Part 2, p.11.

59 Scottish Home and Health Department (1989). *Management of ENT services in Scotland.* Edinburgh: HMSO, p.25.

60 Association of Paediatric Chartered Physiotherapists (1987). *Result of questionnaire into the provision and funding of equipment for children with special needs.* APCP.

61 Scottish Home and Health Department (1989). *Management of ENT services in Scotland.* Edinburgh: HMSO, p.25: annual maintenance of 70 such aids amounted to £4, 500.

62 National Foundation for Educational Research (1992). *OECD/CERI project: integration in the school: reports of the case studies undertaken in the UK.* Slough: NFER, pp.95, 131.

63 See eg Skill (1995). *Applying to trusts.* Information sheet 13. London: SKILL. Directory of Social Change (1995) *Educational grants directory.* London: DSC.

64 Commission for Local Administration in England (93/C/1811). *Report on investigation into a complaint against Manchester City Council.* York: CLAE, 1995, p.9.

65 Commission for Local Administration in England (93/A/1545). *Report on investigation into a complaint against London Borough of Sutton.* London: CLAE, 1995, pp.14, 21–22.

66 Commission for Local Administration in England (94/C/2021). *Report on investigation into a complaint against Cumbria City Council.* York: CLAE, 1995, pp.14, 18.

67 Commission for Local Administration in England (93/C/3560). *Report on investigation into a complaint against Manchester City Council.* York: CLAE, 1995, pp.7–10.

68 Both sets of regulations are made under the Education Act 1993 (now superseded by the 1996 Act). They are: SI 1994/651. *Education (Special Educational Needs) (Approval of Independent Schools) Regulations 1994;* and SI 1994/652. *Education (Special Schools) Regulations 1994.*

69 Department for Education. DFE 3/94. *Development of special schools.* London: DFE, para 117.

70 Department for Education. DFE 3/94. *Development of special schools.* London: DFE, paras 182–3.

71 *Education Act 1996,* s.331

72 *Education Act 1996,* s.332.

73 The operation of the Tribunal is governed specifically by SI 1995/3113 *Special Educational Needs Tribunal Regulations 1995 and by the Tribunals and Inquiries Act 1992.*

74 *Education Act 1996,* ss.333–336, schedule 10.

75 *Hansard,* House of Commons, 5 March 1996, Written Answers, col 174, Mrs Gillan.

76 SI 1994/3113 *Special Educational Needs Tribunal Regulations 1994.*

77 For a clear explanation of the Tribunal's workings see: Department for Education (1994). Special Educational Needs Tribunal: how to appeal. London: DFE.

78 For instance, a recent, unsuccessful, appeal was made against the Tribunal on the question of whether a child could appeal against a decision of the Tribunal (this had implications for legal aid availability): *S v Special Educational Needs Tribunal and Another* (1995) (CA), The Times, 18 December 1995.

79 Special Educational Needs Tribunal (1995). *Annual report 94–95.* London: SENT, p.15.

80 *R v Special Educational Needs Tribunal, ex parte South Glamorgan County Council* (1995) (CA), Times, 12 December 1995.

81 *Education Act 1996,* ss.496–497.

82 See eg: Parliamentary Commissioner for Administration (C.915/92). Delay in responding to a complaint about the exclusion of a child from school. In: *Fourth Report: session 1993–94: selected cases 1994: volume 2.* London: HMSO, 1994.

83 See eg: *R v London Borough of Newham, ex parte R* [1995] ELR 156 (QBD).

84 *Disabled Persons (Services, Consultation and Representation) Act 1986,* ss.5–6 (as amended by *Further Education Act 1992,* Schedule 8, paras 91–92). For explanation, see LAC(88)2. Department of Health and Social Security (1986). *Disabled Persons (Services, Consultation and Representation) Act 1986: implementation of sections 5 and 6.* See also: LAC(93)12. Department of Health (1993). *Further and Higher Education Act 1992: implications for sections 5 and 6 of the Disabled Persons (Services, Consultation and Representation) Act 1986.*

85 Social Services Inspectorate (Phillipson, J.) (1992). *Leaving special education: the next steps: report of a conference on the implementation of sections 5 & 6 of the Disabled Persons (Services, Consultation and Representation) Act 1986, held in London on 23rd April 1991.* London: Department of Health.

86 Social Services Inspectorate (Warburton, R.W.) (1990). *Developing services for disabled people: results of an inspection to monitor the operation of the Disabled Persons (Services, Consultation and Representation) Act 1986.* London: DH, p.13.

87 Social Services Inspectorate (1990). *Developing services for young people with disabilities: report on the progress of six local authorities towards implementing sections 5 and 6 of the Disabled Persons (Services, Consultation and Representation) Act 1986.* London: DH, p.29.

88 Social Services Inspectorate (1995). *Searching for service: an inspection of service responses made to the needs of disabled young adults and their carers.* London: DH, p.42.

89 *Further and Higher Education Act 1992,* s.2.

90 *Further and Higher Education Act 1993,* s.3, Schedule 2.

91 *Further and Higher Education Act 1992,* ss.2–3.
92 *Further and Higher Education Act 1992,* s.4.
93 McGinty, J. (1993). The contribution of the national specialist colleges. In: Hewitson-Ratcliffe, C. (editor) (1993). *Meeting the needs of students with learning difficulties and disabilities in specialist colleges.* London: Skill; Association of National Specialist Colleges.
94 *Further and Higher Education Act 1992,* ss.4–5.
95 FEFC 95/07. *Further Education Funding Council. Students with learning difficulties and/or disabilities.* Coventry: FEFC, p.18.
96 *Further and Higher Education Act 1992,* s.19.
97 Advisory Centre for Education (1994). *Special Education Handbook.* London: ACE, p.37.
98 Her Majesty's Inspectorate (1991). *Students with special needs in further education.* Education observed: 9. London: HMI, p.13.
99 *Education Act 1996,* s.15 as amended by Further and Higher Education Act 1992, s.11.
100 *R v Islington Borough Council, ex parte Rixon* (1996) (QBD), The Times, 17 April 1996. Referring to Circular no 1/93 issued by the DfE.
101 *R v Dorset County Council and Further Education Funding Council, ex parte Goddard* [1995] ELR 109.
102 DFE 1/93. Department for Education. The Further and Higher Education Act 1992. London: DFE, 1993. See also: SKILL (1995). *Financial assistance for students with disabilities in further education and training.* London: SKILL. Also: Advisory Centre for Education (1994). *Special Education Handbook.* London: ACE, chapter 5.
103 SI 1995/3321. *Education (Mandatory Awards) Regulations 1995,* Schedule 2, Part 2, para 10.
104 Department for Education; Welsh Office (1995). *Student grants and loans: a brief guide for higher education students 1995/96.* London: DFE, p.11.
105 See: Department for Education and Employment (1995). *Mandatory awards and the administration of disabled students allowances.* London: DfEE. Also: SKILL (1995). *Review of disabled students' allowances.* London: SKILL. And see general guidance leaflet: SKILL (1995). *Disabled students' allowances: evidence required by awarding authorities and guideline prices for support services: a guide for students, higher education staff and awarding authorities.* London: SKILL.
106 *Further and Higher Education Act 1992,* s.62(7A): as inserted by the *Disability Discrimination Act 1995,* s.30, and effective when s.30 comes into force, probably during 1996.

CHAPTER 12

PROVISION OF EQUIPMENT AND ADAPTATIONS FOR WORK

COVERAGE

1. Type of equipment and staff involved
2. Overview of legislation
3. Equipment and adaptations: Access to Work scheme
   - Who is eligible for assistance?
   - Value of assistance available
   - Requirement that equipment or adaptations meet an employment need
   - Financial eligibility for assistance
   - Ownership, maintenance and repair of equipment
   - Trends in provision of equipment and adaptations.
4. Blind homeworkers' scheme
5. Complaints about the Access to Work scheme
6. Disability Discrimination Act 1995: equipment and adaptations

Key points

A wide range of equipment and adaptations to premises and equipment is available which can assist disabled people to work. At the discretion of the Employment Service, this can be provided under the Access to Work scheme. The primary criteria underpinning provision are that the person must be disabled and that the equipment or adaptations should be *primarily* for the purpose of work.

This chapter outlines the legislative basis for provision and explains how the Access to Work scheme is applied in practice. Like other statutory services, the Employment Service has had to cope with striking a balance between people's needs and available resources. This has not been made any easier by the raising of people's expectations following the reorganisation, renaming and publicising of the service.

At the time of writing, the Access to Work scheme is in a state of transition. Demand outstripped resources in the year 1995–1996. As a result, the Employment Service announced at the end of 1995 that it would limit assistance to unemployed disabled people – although it would honour existing commitments. In March 1996, it relaxed this restriction for the year 1996–1997, whilst emphasising that the system of provision was not demand led and that similar restrictions might be reimposed in the future.[1] In addition, the Employment Service is revising the internal guidelines which govern how its staff administer the Access to Work scheme and make decisions about if and how to assist people.

Due to come into force at the end of 1996, is the part of the Disability Discrimination Act 1995 dealing with employment matters. Amongst various provisions, it places a duty on employers to make reasonable alterations (including equipment and adaptations) to the workplace, so that employees, or potential employees, are not discriminated against.

Questions people ask

- When will a wheelchair be provided by the Employment Service – and when by the NHS?
- Do people who are working from home qualify for equipment or adaptations to premises?
- Do employers have to contribute financially to adaptations made to equipment or premises for a disabled employee?
- Are people means-tested before the Employment Service provides equipment adaptations?

1. TYPE OF EQUIPMENT AND STAFF INVOLVED

Equipment and adaptations may be provided by the Employment Service if they are *primarily* for the purpose of work. The equipment need not be specially designed for disability but the person must need it for work as a result of his or her disability.

This chapter focuses on equipment and adaptations only. However, as emphasised elsewhere in this book, equipment might not be the answer. Thus, other assistance available through the Employment Service's Access to Work scheme includes, for instance, a human communicator (eg for everyday work or for interview), a part-time reader or assistant (eg for a blind or visually impaired person), a support worker (eg to give practical help at work, or going to and from work), assistance with taxi fares (eg if the person cannot use public transport).[2] However, the most common type of assistance received through the Access to Work scheme is in the form of special aids and equipment (SAE) (prior to 1994, the acronym 'SAE' referred to Special Aids to Employment).[3]

Enquiries and applications can be made at Jobcentres where disability employment advisers (DEAs) are based. They are part of specialist disability teams known as Placement, Assessment and Counselling Teams (PACTs) which offer further assessment and advice. In addition, the Employment Service makes use of technical consultants, regionally based, who can give specialist advice on equipment and adaptations if required.

The following list contains only examples of equipment and adaptations, and is not exhaustive of what might be available. It is drawn from both older and current information produced by the Employment Service; it should be stressed that equipment and adaptations are provided at the discretion of the Employment Service – it is not under a duty to do so.[4]

(i) Equipment for physically disabled people includes electrically powered wheelchairs with riser seats, stand-up wheelchairs, kerb-mounting wheelchairs, trolleys, electronic writing systems, special computer equipment and software packages, special telephones, page turning machines, special chairs (eg with extra back support), footstools and footrests, supportive cushions, workbenches and tools, special drawing boards, wrist supports, adjustable writing slopes, electronic staplers.

(ii) Equipment for people with visual impairment includes computers with enlarged screens, closed circuit television systems, voice activated computers, speech output computers, large print output devices, braille printers, colour printers, keyboard stickers, tape recorders, talking calculators, talking dictionaries, telephone switchboards with touch indicators, voice-activated switchboards, measuring devices with braille marking or audio output, special lighting, desk-lamps.

(iii) For people with hearing impairment, equipment includes amplifiers, loudspeaking telephone aids, minicom telephone equipment, induction loop systems, talking/communicating computers, paging or alarm systems, adaptations to switchboards.

(iv) Adaptations to premises or equipment include wheelchair ramps or lifts, hoists, stairlifts, handrails, adapted lavatories (with eg wide doors and grab rails), alarm systems with flashing lights, extra lighting, modified machinery (eg converting foot controls to hand controls), adapted cars (eg conversion to automatic transmission), adapted switchboards (eg for blind people).

2. OVERVIEW OF LEGISLATION

Equipment and adaptations have been provided under the Disabled Persons (Employment) Act 1944 and the Employment and Training Act 1973.

The 1944 Act does not create a duty but only a power: 'facilities may be provided'. It is for disabled people who, because of their disability, are unlikely to obtain employment or to work for themselves, either at all or for a long time. This may be because there is no work or because the person would not be able to compete, in terms of earnings and security, with non-disabled people doing the same work. The facilities may be provided so that the person can obtain employment or work under 'special conditions'; they can also be provided for training. Section 1 of the Act defines disability in terms of a person being 'substantially handicapped' in getting or keeping work because of injury, disease or congenital deformity.[5] The Disability Discrimination Act 1995, when in force, will make s.1 of the 1944 Act obsolete; already, in practice, the Employment Service does not insist that people be registered (see below).

The 1973 Act (as amended) empowers the Employment Service, an agency, to carry out certain functions of the Secretary of State. In particular, these functions include the general duty to make arrangements which will help people to get training, and to obtain or retain employment – and the power to make loans, grants or other payments either to people who under these arrangements promote or use facilities, or to other 'specified' people.[6]

Neither Act imposes explicit duties to provide equipment or adaptations; thus, all provision through the Employment Service would appear to be discretionary and to create no absolute 'rights' for disabled people.

3. EQUIPMENT AND ADAPTATIONS: ACCESS TO WORK SCHEME[7]

Who is eligible for assistance?

In practice the provision of both equipment and adaptations is made under what is now known as the Access to Work scheme operated by the Employment Service.

The scheme is open to people whether they work full-time or part-time (at least 8 hours per week), temporarily or permanently – and whether they are employed, self-employed or employed as 'remote workers' (ie employees who work from home). Since the scheme is to help people get work, keep work or make progress in their careers, it is also available to unemployed people. Assistance can be provided to unemployed disabled people not only when they are about to start a job, but also if they have an interview – or generally have a need for support, to enable them to compete for work on an equal basis with people who are not disabled. Assistance is not normally available to volunteers or people who are in receipt of benefits because they are unable to work.

For self-employed people, assistance is not available to pay for the standard equipment required when setting up a business – but may be available if any standard items need to be adapted.[8]

In order to benefit from the scheme, people do not have to be actually registered disabled under the 1944 Act – but must have a disability or health problem which affects their ability to work and which is likely to last at least 12 months. In other words, they must at least be *registrable* under the 1944 Act, if not actually registered. The disability and registration requirements under the 1944 Act will anyway be superseded by the Disability Discrimination Act 1995 when it comes into force; the register will be abolished and the 1995 definition take the place of the old definition in the 1944 Act.[9]

Restrictions imposed on Access to Work scheme, December 1995

The budget allocated for the entire Access to Work scheme (not just equipment adaptations) for the year 1995–1996 was £13.4 million. During the year it became evident that this was not adequate for the 10,000 people who had received assistance between April and November 1995. Accordingly, restrictions were imposed at the end of 1995, to the effect that funding would now be targeted only on disabled people who had been unemployed for at least four weeks – and on meeting existing commitments and renewing ongoing arrangements.[10]

In March 1996, it was announced that this restriction on assistance would be relaxed in 1996–1997. However, stating explicitly that Access to Work is not a 'demand-led programme', the Education and Employment Secretary pointed out that similar restrictions might be applied in the future, if demand again exceeds resources. Such restrictions are not portrayed as absolutely strict – if they were, the Employment Service might risk judicial review for 'fettering its discretion' (see p.446). The Service is likely to maintain that it considers every case on its merits, and that the policy is one of general priority rather than rigid exclusion.

The imposition of such priorities – whether intermittently or for longer periods – can impose on some people hardship, as well as anxiety caused by uncertainties and the delay which even short-term changes in policy can trigger. Thus, if assessment had been carried out and assistance agreed before December 1995, then commitments remained in place. But, otherwise, for example, a person might have been denied a £2000 upgrade to her computer – unless she left her job for at least four weeks, applied (now unemployed) for the upgrade and then tried to regain employment. Alternatively, the burden of paying for employees' equipment would simply fall on employers – not all of whom would be prepared, or able, to shoulder it.[11]

Value of assistance available

At the time of writing, various changes in policy are affecting the Access to Work scheme. From June 1996, the existing rules governing the value of assistance available – described in the following paragraphs – are due to change. From this date, the Employment Service will no longer meet the full costs of Access to Work assistance for disabled people who are already in employment. Assistance valued at no more than £300 will not be provided. Above that figure, the Service will meet 80% of the approved cost. However, for severely disabled people already in employment, assistance which costs in excess of £10,000 over three years will paid for in full.[12] The following paragraphs should therefore be read with these changes in mind.

Value of assistance with equipment

The maximum amount of assistance available (whether consisting solely of equipment or other types of assistance within the scheme as well) is £21,000 over five years. In exceptional circumstances, special consideration can be given to providing assistance above this value. In any case, a person can, if necessary, benefit from up to the same amount of assistance in another five year period once the first five year period has expired.

It should be emphasised that there is no absolute *right* either to the maximum amount or indeed to any amount of assistance. Provision is based on the Employment Service's assessment of people's needs. Some people's needs are met by providing assistance costing no more than a few hundred pounds; and most people's needs are met for less than £5000. Depending on the cost of the equipment or adaptations, authorisation is given at local level (up to £7000), general regional level (up to £12,000) or at regional director level (over £12,000). These figures are inclusive of VAT.[13]

Value of assistance with adaptations to premises and equipment

Payments by the Employment Service for adaptations to premises or to equipment cover the full cost of the adaptation (up to £21,000), unless the adaptation brings general benefits to the employer's business. For example, adaptations might make a building more accessible to other people, apart from the disabled employee in question. In this situation, the employer might be expected to contribute, up to, for example, 50% of the cost. Likewise, if the adaptation is for a longstanding employee who is of particular value, then the employer might be expected to contribute, for example, 25% of the cost. The Employment Service will not pay for adaptations for future, possible employment of disabled people – but only for current or new employees.

Assistance is not available for adaptations which employers have a statutory duty to provide under various legislation including the Factories Act 1961, the Offices, Shops and Railway Premises Act 1963, the Building (Fourth Amendment) Regulations 1985, and the Chronically Sick and Disabled Persons (Amendment) Act 1976. Exceptionally, assistance may be provided if the employee's job is at risk if such legal requirements are not complied with – but the employer clearly cannot afford the adaptation.[14]

Requirement that equipment or adaptations meet an employment need

Equipment or adaptations must be primarily needed for work, rather than daily living in general. In addition, the Employment Service does not normally provide equipment which non-disabled people, doing the same job, need. Even if special equipment is required, the Employment Service might first ask if the employer is prepared to provide the equipment at its own expense.[15]

It is sometimes advisable for equipment to be used for a trial period; and training might also be supplied by, for instance DEAs, technical consultants, suppliers, or manufacturers.

Examples of equipment and adaptations needed primarily for work

The following are examples only and are intended as a rough guide to decisions which the Employment Service might take.[16] The Service emphasises that every case is treated on its merits and that, ultimately, it has discretion – and the final word – in deciding what to provide:

Wheelchairs. A person who needs a wheelchair for general mobility both at home and at work would probably be expected to obtain it from the NHS. However, a special, stand-up wheelchair to do drawing-board work might be loaned through the Employment Service – as might a stair-climbing wheelchair.

User controlled, outdoor electric wheelchairs can be provided to enable people to get to work and for their mobility at work. If such wheelchairs are provided, they are not meant to be used for any other purpose – eg for going shopping. In the light of the Department of Health's recent announcement (see p.518) that such wheelchairs will be available through the NHS in England (as they are already are in Scotland), it remains to be seen whether the Employment Service will start to divert more requests to the NHS.

Lightweight wheelchairs can be provided, in principle at least, through NHS wheelchair services. Therefore, the Employment Service will not normally consider providing them – unless the NHS cannot provide a suitable model to meet the person's work needs.

Evacuation chairs. The Employment Service regards these chairs as primarily health and safety, rather than employment equipment – and thus not falling under the Access to Work scheme.

Adaptations to vehicles. These adaptations might be provided in order to enable people to travel to and from work or to undertake work for which driving is essential. Assistance will not be available for adaptations which a person could reasonably obtain through other sources – for example, through the Motability scheme (see p.478) for people receiving the mobility component of disability living allowance. However, if a car is being leased and the person incurs heavy mileage (over 12,000 miles per year) charges because of his or her employment, assistance might be provided.

Very exceptionally, people might be helped to purchase a vehicle – for example, if it was cheaper to provide a minibus for a group of disabled people working in supported employment, than to pay for their fares (eg taxi).

Car chair lifts. Car lifts, which either lift the wheelchair with occupant into a car, or the wheelchair alone on to the roof of a car, are not normally available through the Employment Service. This is because they are regarded as a mobility aid to everyday living in general, not employment in particular. However, they can be provided, exceptionally, if a person travels to various locations, as part of the job (ie not getting to and from the workplace) – and personal assistance for getting in and out of the car is not available.

Nevertheless, the Employment Service is likely to ask searching questions, such as whether the journeys are an essential part of the job, why personal assistance is not available, why – if the person is receiving it – the mobility component of disability living allowance is not used, how the person manages socially, and how extensively the person would use the lift outside work.

Low vision aids. Similarly, face-worn vision aids (eg spectacles and contact lenses) would normally be considered to be the responsibility of the NHS – but a special desk-attached magnifier, or closed circuit television (CCTV) system might fall to the Employment Service to provide. Applicants are referred for assessment for CCTVs to an NHS low vision clinic, the Royal National Institute for the Blind, or the Partially Sighted Society.

Hearing aids. Personal hearing aids are normally the responsibility of the NHS. However, the standard aids available on the NHS do not always meet people's hearing needs at work – and special, commercial aids will not be provided on the NHS, unless they are deemed to be clinically required. The Employment Service might consider providing assistance – and would hand over assessment and provision to an NHS hearing aid centre. The centre would invoice the Employment Service and provide a signed declaration to the effect that the NHS has no funds and that the hearing aid was required to meet an employment need.

Text telephones. This equipment, attached to telephone lines and consisting of keyboards and display panels, enables hearing impaired people to communicate by telephone. This equipment is often requested by people working for organisations for the deaf and hearing impaired; thus, the Employment Service will take care to ensure that the equipment is for the benefit of the applicant in particular, rather than the organisation in general.

Standard office/workplace equipment. Standard furniture will not be provided normally, since it is equipment which employers have to provide anyway, to both disabled and non-disabled employees. However, special or adapted items, required because of a person's disability – eg a workbench suitable for a wheelchair user – may be provided.

If a disabled person is a remote worker – ie an employee working from home – the Employment Service might provide any standard equipment which would not have been required had the person been working at the main workplace. For example, equipment normally shared between employees, might have to be duplicated especially for the remote worker; or extra equipment, such as a computer modem and fax, might be required because of the employee's remote location. These are additional costs and eligible for assistance. However, the employer would be expected to pay on-going costs, such as telephone line rental and calls, and 'consumables' such as paper and computer disks.

Financial eligibility for assistance

In principle, eligibility for the loan of equipment rests on an assumption that the person cannot afford to buy or hire the equipment. A formal means-test is not conducted, but the person is expected to indicate his or her financial position on the application form.

Ownership, maintenance and repair of equipment[17]

The Employment Service normally retains ownership of equipment and so remains responsible for maintenance, repair and replacement. If repair costs are less than £25, people in full-time employment are asked to pay for them. People using equipment (eg electric wheelchairs) in public places are advised to take out accident insurance. People can take equipment abroad in connection with their work but are responsible for any import and export charges, the safety of the equipment and repair costs. The Employment Service normally pays for an adaptation, notionally owns it (eg a stairlift), but might then make a gift of it to the employer – who is then responsible for its maintenance and repair.

Employers might need to bear in mind a number of tax considerations when contemplating adaptations to premises and equipment for disabled people. These include capital allowance tax relief on machinery and plant (the 'writing down allowance'), capital gains tax, and the increase in value for income tax and national insurance purposes of adapted company cars.

Trends in provision of equipment and adaptations

A survey published in 1990 included details about provision of equipment and adaptation through the Employment Service, under the Special Aids to Employment (SAE) and the Adaptations to Premises and Equipment (APE) schemes, which preceded the current Access to Work scheme. The main types of equipment provided included aids for visually impaired people, orthopaedic equipment and computer equipment. The main adaptations funded were lavatories – and improved access to buildings, lifts and stairlifts.[18] Figures for the first year, 1994–1995, of the Access to Work scheme show expenditure on equipment at £10.7 million and on adaptations at £659,000. These figures represent increased expenditure from the previous year, which was £7.2 million and £487,000 respectively.[19]

4. BLIND HOMEWORKERS' SCHEME

This scheme enables severely disabled people – not just those who are visually impaired – to set up businesses at home and to receive a subsidy to ensure a minimum income.

The scheme is administered by the social services departments of local authorities under s.29 of the National Assistance Act 1948. They provide the income subsidy and 25% of the capital setting-up costs – the Employment Service pays 75% of the setting-up costs. Voluntary organisations might act as agents for authorities. The setting-up costs can include equipment, but people benefiting are not now eligible for equipment and adaptations (under the Access to Work scheme[20]) – although they used to be (under SAE and APE: see above).[21] The scheme is little known and publicised and is used by no more than about two to three hundred people throughout Great Britain.

5. COMPLAINTS ABOUT THE ACCESS TO WORK SCHEME

The Employment Service appears not to offer a formal complaints or appeals system. Complaints can be made either to the local PACT manager or at regional level. Maladministration can be investigated by the Parliamentary ombudsman, since the Employment Service is a central government agency. The following is one example:[22]

> The ombudsman investigated one allegation that insufficient publicity had been given to a change in the equipment (SAE) scheme, when it was run by the Manpower Services Commission, part of the Department of Employment. He did not find maladministration; the level of publicity was justified because the change affected so few people. However, he did find that the Department's investigation into the same person's request for retrospective financial assistance was flawed. The person was claiming reimbursement for computer equipment he had bought – not realising that he might have been eligible for assistance at the time. The Department's own procedure guide was silent about such retrospective payments, although it did state that assistance was generally available for people who could not pay for equipment themselves without suffering hardship.
>
> In the event, the applicant had not provided evidence of such hardship – but nor had the Department asked for it. Accordingly, the ombudsman found that 'summary justice' had been dispensed; the Department offered its apologies and an ex gratia payment of £1419.70 by way of reimbursement.

6. DISABILITY AND DISCRIMINATION ACT 1995: EQUIPMENT AND ADAPTATIONS

Part 2 of the Disability Discrimination Act 1995 imposes a duty on employers to take various steps to ensure that employees or potential employees (ie job applicants) do not suffer discrimination. It is due to come into force at the end of 1996. The following summarises the duty in relation to equipment and adaptations.

Duty to take steps to prevent disadvantage: adjusting premises, and acquiring or modifying equipment

The main duty imposed on employers is to prevent either working arrangements, or physical features of the premises, from placing a disabled person at a 'substantial disadvantage in comparison with persons who are not disabled'. Employers must 'take such steps as it is reasonable, in all the circumstances of the case' to prevent such disadvantage. Amongst the steps specified which employers 'may have to take' are 'making adjustments to the premises' and 'acquiring or modifying equipment'.[23] However, the duty is not imposed on small businesses which have fewer than twenty employees.[24]

Of course much hinges on the word 'reasonable' and the legislation goes on to list relevant factors which should be had 'regard' to when determining whether it is reasonable to take a particular step:[25]

- the extent to which the step would be effective
- the extent to which the step is practicable for the employer
- the financial and other costs to the employer of the step and disruption to his activities
- the extent of the employer's financial and other resources
- the availability of financial or other assistance to the employer.

It will be noted that, in practice, assistance through the Access to Work scheme (see above) will be directly relevant to the last factor listed.[26]

In addition, the legislation enables the making of regulations about, for example, what physical features are and how they disadvantage disabled people, what steps it is reasonable for employers to take, the costs of taking steps (eg a ceiling).

Definition of disability

The Act defines a disabled person as one who 'has a physical or mental impairment which has a substantial and long-term adverse effect on his ability to carry out normal day-to-day activities'.[27]

The term 'long-term' is defined as an impairment which has lasted at least 12 months, is likely to last for at least 12 months, or is likely to be lifelong. The Act enables the making of regulations to determine what 'substantial adverse effects' are – and are not. It states that an impairment of severe disfigurement is to be treated as having a substantial adverse effects on the person's day-to-day activities.[28]

For an impairment to be treated as affecting normal day-to-day activities, it must affect at least one of the following: continence, eyesight, hearing, lifting/carrying/moving everyday objects, manual dexterity, memory or ability to concentrate/learn/understand, mobility, perception of risk of physical danger, physical coordination, or speech.[29]

The legislation goes on to stipulate that if a person is receiving medical treatment or is using equipment (eg a prosthesis), without which day-to-day activities would be substantially, adversely affected – then the person is to be taken as being affected in that way. (In other words, if equipment compensates for a disability, the person should still be regarded as disabled). However, spectacles and contact lenses are excluded from this particular provision.[30]

For people with progressive conditions, the position is more complicated. For example, the person might have an impairment which has an adverse effect on day-to-day activities, but not a substantial adverse effect. In this case, the impairment will be deemed to be having a substantial adverse effect, if it is likely that the condition will lead to such an impairment.[31] In practice, this means that people with, for example, HIV, will not be protected by the Act until they start to show symptoms.[32]

Notes

1 Department for Employment and Education (1996). *Shephard announces £6 million boost for disability programme.* London: DfEE (press release).
2 Employment Service (1994). *Access to work: practical help for disabled people and their employers: information for people with disabilities.* Sheffield: ES.
3 Beinart, S.; Smith, P.; Sproston, K. (1996). *The Access to Work Programme: a survey of recipients, employers, Employment Service Managers and Staff.* London: Social and Community Planning Research, p.19.
4. Employment Service:
   (1993). *Make it work: employment advice for people with disabilities.* Sheffield: ES;
   (1984) (1993 reprint). *Code of good practice on the employment of disabled people.* Sheffield: ES;
   (1988). *Employing people with disabilities: special aids to employment.* Sheffield: ES.
   (1988). *Employing people with disabilities: adaptations to premises and equipment.* Sheffield: ES.
   Some examples are also drawn from: Beinart, S.; Smith, P.; Sproston, K. (1996). *The Access to Work Programme: a survey of recipients, employers, Employment Service Managers and Staff.* London: Social and Community Planning Research, p.19.
5 *Disabled Persons (Employment) Act 1944,* ss.1, 15.
6 *Employment and Training Act 1973,* s.25.
7 The basic features of the Access to Work scheme are contained in: Employment Service (1994). *Access to work: practical help for disabled people and their employers.*
8 Employment Service (1994). *Access to work: draft procedures.* (April 1994). Sheffield: ES.
9 Ie the *Disability Discrimination Act 1995,* s.61 repeals s.1 of the 1944 Act (definition of disability), repeals ss.6–8 register of disabled people) and amends s.15 in various ways, including the definition of 'disabled person'.
10 Department for Education and Employment (1995). *New focus on access to work for disabled people: Shephard. (Press release: 14 December 1995).* London: DfEE.
11 See: Access to work squeezed. *Disability Now*: March 1996, pp.1–2.
12 Department for Education and Employment (1996). *Shephard announces £6 million boost for disability programme.* London: DfEE (press release).
13 Employment Service (1994). *Access to work: draft procedures.* (April 1994). Sheffield: ES.
14 Employment Service (1994). *Access to work: draft procedures.* (April 1994). Sheffield: ES.
15 Employment Service (1994). *Access to work: draft procedures.* (April 1994). Sheffield: ES.
16 The following are based mainly on: Employment Service (1994). *Access to work: draft procedures.* (April 1994). Sheffield: ES.
17 The following is based mainly on: Employment Service (1994). *Access to work: draft procedures.* (April 1994). Sheffield: ES.
18 Employment Service (1990). *Evaluation of special schemes for people with disabilities: summary paper.* Sheffield: ES, pp.25, 32.
19 Figures kindly provided by the Employment Service.
20 Employment Service (1994). *Access to work: draft procedures.* (April 1994). Sheffield: ES.
21 See eg: Parliamentary Commissioner for Administration (C552/88). Insufficient publicity to changes to special aids to employment scheme. In: *Fifth report: session 1989–1990: selected cases 1990: volume 3.* HC 548. London: HMSO.
22 Parliamentary Commissioner for Administration (C552/88). Insufficient publicity to changes to special aids to employment scheme. In: *Fifth report: session 1989–1990: selected cases 1990: volume 3.* HC 548. London: HMSO.
23 *Disability Discrimination Act 1995,* s.6.
24 *Disability Discrimination Act 1995,* s.7.
25 *Disability Discrimination Act 1995,* s.6.

26 See eg: Gooding, C. (1996). *Blackstone's guide to the Disability Discrimination Act 1995.* London: Blackstone Press, pp.22–23.

27 *Disability Discrimination Act 1995,* s.1.

28 *Disability Discrimination Act 1995,* schedule 1.

29 *Disability Discrimination Act 1995,* schedule 1.

30 *Disability Discrimination Act 1995,* schedule 1.

31 *Disability Discrimination Act 1995,* schedule 1.

32 See eg: Gooding, C. (1996). *Blackstone's guide to the Disability Discrimination Act 1995.* London: Blackstone Press, p.10.

CHAPTER 13

WAR PENSIONERS
PROVISION OF EQUIPMENT AND ADAPTATIONS

COVERAGE

1. Priority treatment for war pensioners
2. Special provision of equipment and adaptations
   - Background: from artificial limb and appliance centres to mainstream NHS
   - Special provision by the War Pensions Agency
   - Outdoor mobility needs: cars and war pensioner mobility supplement.

Key points

A number of special arrangements exist for war pensioners, some of which relate to the provision of equipment and home adaptations. For example, subject to some limitations, war pensioners have the right to priority NHS treatment; and, in addition, the Secretary of State has the power to pay for and provide equipment and home adaptations which statutory services cannot provide either at all or without excessive delay.

For the purposes of this book, the term *war pensioners* includes civilians as well as members of the armed forces. In addition, a number of other groups are also covered, including, coastguards, naval auxiliaries, merchant seamen[1], the Home Guard[2], Polish forces[3], and the Ulster Defence Regiment.[4] Formerly included were both Indian and Chinese seamen, but statutory schemes for these groups were revoked in 1988.[5]

1. PRIORITY TREATMENT FOR WAR PENSIONERS

War pensioners (ie who people who receive pensions for war injuries), have traditionally enjoyed priority access to NHS services. This stems from an undertaking given in a 1953 House of Commons paper.[6] However, Department of Health guidance continues to remind health authorities and NHS Trusts that this priority is limited to the extent that it is subject to emergency and other urgent cases of greater clinical priority. It is also only to be given to pensioners who need examination or treatment which relates primarily to the condition (ie the *accepted disablement*) for which they receive their pension.[7] Given the increasing demands on the NHS, and the flexible nature of a term such as 'clinical priority' (see p.201), the practical benefit of this special priority enjoyed by war pensioners is probably limited.

2. SPECIAL PROVISION OF EQUIPMENT AND HOME ADAPTATIONS

Background: from artificial limb and appliance centres to mainstream NHS

War pensioners traditionally had special access to equipment through artificial limb and appliance centres (ALACs), later known as disablement services centres (DSCs). Whilst the general population could obtain only artificial limbs and wheelchairs at these centres, war pensioners were able to obtain other equipment as well. This included, for example, orthopaedic footwear, hearing aids, spectacles, home nursing equipment, calipers, elastic hosiery, arm splints, cosmetic prostheses and wigs.[8]

Since the Disablement Services Authority ceased to exist on 31st March 1991, this 'one-stop' equipment service no longer exists in principle. Instead, war pensioners use ordinary NHS services to obtain the various equipment they might need.

Special provision by the War Pensions Agency

Despite the demise of the ALAC services, special provision of equipment is still possible. For example, if the local NHS or a social services department cannot provide a particular item of equipment either at all or without excessive delay, then, so long as the item is needed for the accepted disablement, it may be supplied by the War Pensions Agency.

The legal foundation for this special access to equipment lies generally in legislation passed during the First World War and specifically in more recent Regulations.[9] The latter state that the Secretary of State may meet the 'necessary expenses' of 'medical, surgical or rehabilitative treatment' and of 'appropriate aids and adaptations for disabled living'. The expenses must 'wholly or mainly' arise from the accepted disablement and the treatment or equipment should not be 'provided under legislation of the United Kingdom' (ie this is an 'anti-duplication' provision).

There are two main points to bear in mind. First, the Secretary of State (through the War Pensions Agency) has the power, but not a duty, to make this special provision. Second, the condition that the power apply only to equipment and treatment which cannot be provided under other legislation is difficult to put to the test. Does it refer to equipment which *in practice* a particular authority is not providing; or to services and equipment which are *in principle* never available from any authority? For instance, most types of wheelchair are available in principle through the NHS – but which types are available in a particular locality to a particular person at any one time is almost impossible to say.

Nevertheless, it appears that hitherto, the War Pensions Agency has taken the pragmatic view that if an authority does not supply an item of equipment at all, or if there is excessive delay, then it is empowered, under the Regulations, to provide the equipment. The problem for the Agency is that if NHS Trusts and social services departments know that the Agency is there to fill the gaps, then they might begin regularly to abdicate their responsibilities for war pensioners and pass the buck. The problem of giving meaning to legislative clauses which refer to what may or may not be provided under welfare legislation is discussed elsewhere (see p.74).

If home adaptations are required, a payment up to a value of £750 may be made. The payment may be made for one comprehensive adaptations, or in stages for several minor adaptations. The grant is a one-off and may only be paid a second time if a war pensioner is forced to leave his adapted house.

War pensioners who are amputees and whose disablement (including the prosthesis itself) causes wear and tear on clothing are entitled to a clothing allowance. The allowance is paid at two rates; the higher (£129 per annum at April 1995) for a tilting-table limb or more than one limb; the lower (£82) for a single limb which is not of the tilting-table variety.

Outdoor mobility needs: cars and war pensioner mobility supplement

Separate arrangements exist for the outdoor mobility needs of war pensioners arising from the accepted disablement.

In the past, invalid three-wheeled cars were provided under NHS legislation for war pensioners who needed them.[10] Such cars ceased to be issued to new applicants after 1975, but those still in use can be repaired and replaced whilst stocks last. The scheme is administered by central government and operated locally by approved repairers. To pensioners still within the scheme, a car maintenance grant is paid quarterly. Other, commercial, adapted cars, known as *loan cars,* were also formerly provided but are no longer issued, repaired or replaced.

New applicants, or war pensioners who no longer wish to use their old three-wheeled cars or loan cars, can apply for war pensioner mobility supplement (WPMS).[11] This is a sum of money payable to war pensioners, which they can use at their discretion (eg toward a car, outdoor electric wheelchair or taxi fares) to meet their needs for transport (see p.478).

Notes

1 The regulations are as follows: SR&O 1944/500. *War Pensions (Coastguards) Scheme 1944.* London: HMSO; SI 1964/1985; *War Pensions (Naval Auxiliary Personnel) Scheme 1964.* London: HMSO; SI 1964/2058. *War Pensions (Mercantile Marine) Scheme 1964.* London: HMSO. These

regulations were made under the Pensions *(Navy, Army, Air Forces and Mercantile Marine) Act 1939.* London: HMSO.

2 The Home Guard scheme is based on firstly: Cmnd 2663. Royal Warrant 1964. *Concerning pensions and other grants in respect of disablement or death due to service in the Home Guard.* London: HMSO. And secondly: Cmnd 2564. Order of Her Majesty 1964. *Concerning pensions and other grants in respect of disablement or death due to service in the Home Guard after 27th April 1952.* London: HMSO.

3 SI 1964/2007. P*ensions (Polish Forces) Scheme 1964.* London: HMSO. These regulations were made under the Polish Resettlement Act 1947. London: HMSO.

4 By an Order in Council of 4th January 1971 (Cmd 4567): *Pensions and other grants in respect of disablement and death due to service in the Ulster Defence Regiment.*

5 The following regulations were revoked in 1988: SR&O 1944/1083. *War Pensions (Indian Seamen etc) Scheme 1944.* London: HMSO; SR&O 1944/1186. *War Pensions (Chinese Seamen etc) Scheme 1944.* London: HMSO.

6 House of Commons (1953). Cmd 8842. *The Ministry of Pensions proposed transfer of functions.* London: HMSO, paras.12–13. This paper dealt with the proposed transfer of Ministry of Pension hospitals to the NHS.

7 HSG(94)28. NHS Executive. *Priority treatment for war pensioners.* London: Department of Health; EL(92)51. NHS Management Executive. *Priority treatment for war pensioners.* Leeds: DH, 1992 (now cancelled).

8 See, for example: Research Surveys of Great Britain (1984). *The supply of surgical appliances to war pensioners: report of a postal survey.* London: RSGB, p.10.

9 Naval and Military War Pensions etc. Act 1915. London: HMSO, s.3(1)(j). This refers to making provision for 'disabled officers and men after they have left the service, including provision for their health, training, and employment'. The regulations are firstly: SI 1983/883 *Naval and Air Forces etc (Disablement and Death) Services Pensions Order 1983.* London: HMSO, r.26 (made under the *Social Security (Miscellaneous Provisions) Act 1977,* s.12. And secondly: SI 1983/686. *Personal Injuries (Civilians) Scheme 1983/686.* London: HMSO, rr.25B, 48B (made under the *Personal Injuries (Emergency Provisions) Act 1939,* ss.1, 2).

10 The provision is now in: NHS Act 1977, s.5 and Schedule 2: giving the Secretary of State the power to provide 'invalid carriages' (defined as a 'mechanically propelled vehicle specially designed and constructed (and not merely adapted) for the use of a person suffering some physical defect or disability and used solely by such a person'); and to maintain, repair and provide a 'structure' in which to keep the vehicle.

11 Provided under: SI 1983/883. *Naval and Air Forces* etc. *(Disablement and Death) Services and Pensions Order 1983.* London: HMSO, s.26A; SI 1983/686. *Personal Injuries (Civilians) Scheme 1983/686.* London: HMSO, ss.25B, 48B.

PART III

14. Negligence
15. Product liability, safety and legislative requirements
16. Buying equipment and making consumer contracts
17. Challenging the decisions of statutory services about equipment provision: judicial review
18. Breach of duties in relation to equipment: criminal and civil liability

CHAPTER 14

NEGLIGENCE

COVERAGE

1. When do people have a duty of care?
   - Duty of care of statutory services and their staff
   - Duty of care of manufacturers, suppliers and distributors of equipment
   - Identifying who has a duty of care in any particular situation
   - Duty of care: failing to do something
   - Making statements or giving advice carelessly.
2. Breaching the duty of care
   - Reasonable standards of care
   - Knowing about a reasonable standard of care at the relevant time
   - Measuring the standard of care of professionals
   - Mistakes and inexperience.
3. Proving the cause of accidents, and types of harm
   - Which cause?
   - Losing a chance
   - Types of harm: physical, psychiatric, property, financial.
4. Type of damages awarded
5. Defences against allegations of negligence
   - Willingness of victim to run the risk of somebody else's negligence
   - Contributing to one's own misfortune
   - Bringing a legal action in time.

Key points

Basic rules of the law of negligence. The law courts find negligence when someone who has a *duty of care* towards a second person, *breaches* that duty – and, as a result of this, *causes harm* to the second person. For instance, a duty of care is owed by the manufacturer of a walking frame to try to ensure that it is not manufactured defectively – or by a therapist, who later prescribes the frame, to ensure that it is suitable for that particular patient. If, through sheer carelessness, the frame is defective or the frame is prescribed inappropriately – and the person falls and breaks a hip as a result – then negligence might be established.

This chapter outlines what is meant by a duty of care, covering situations in which it is a straightforward matter and those in which it is not. In principle, the duty of care is well-rooted in the NHS and private health care, although individual cases can still be difficult to win in practice. Negligence is also well-established in relation to manufacturers and defective products. However, the position is less clear in relation to local authorities and their staff; whilst there is also some uncertainty about the liability which follows from the negligence of independent contractors involved in the provision of equipment on behalf, for example, the NHS or social services departments.

Of considerable concern to professionals is to be able to distinguish negligent mistakes from those mere errors which we all make from time to time. But even if a person has breached the duty of care, there will be no legal finding of negligence unless it can be proved that the carelessness actually caused the harm complained of. It is the complexity of proving causation which often protects professionals and authorities from allegations of negligence. It needs to be stressed that no matter how careless somebody has been, no case in negligence will succeed unless causation can be proved.

The approach of the courts to the different categories of harm – personal injury, damage to property and financial loss – is described. Contributory negligence, which applies to situations in which people's own carelessness has contributed to the injury or loss which they have suffered, is also summarised.

Flexible application of the principles of negligence. The three key elements of negligence – *duty of care, breach of the duty* and *causation* – have to be argued and proved almost ritually in the law courts. But to some extent, the judges manipulate these concepts flexibly to reach the decisions they wish to reach – having regard both to fairness between the parties involved and to the social consequences of their decisions.

Take the case, for example, of a woman who has been using an electric riser chair loaned to her by a local authority, whose condition has now changed, who is 'stood up' by the chair and who falls and injures herself. She might bring an action alleging careless assessment and inappropriate provision of equipment. There are various pegs on which to hang the arguments on both sides. For instance, it could be argued that neither the therapist nor the authority owed the woman a *duty of care* in the first place – because they were performing the statutory function of assessment, which might exclude a common law duty of care. Less extremely, it might be argued that a duty of care did exist – but had been terminated when the woman's 'active' file was closed some weeks after provision of the chair.

Second, even if the duty of care did continue, it could be claimed that the therapist had *not been careless* – she had provided a chair in working order, in line with good practice, complete with written and oral instructions about how to use it. Third, it could be maintained that even if there was any carelessness, it was not the *cause* of the accident. Suppose the therapist had omitted to provide written information about what to do if the person's condition altered; if the woman had anyway thrown away all the other written instructions that she had been given without reading them, any additional information would have made no difference. The accident would still have occurred.

Thus, the principles of the law of negligence can be deployed flexibly by lawyers to argue for or against the imposition of liability in any particular case. For instance, when the House of Lords decided that local authority advisory teachers might owe a *duty of care* to children (whose parents they are advising), it pointed out that this did not in itself amount to finding liability – *carelessness* would still have to be proved and this could be difficult.

Negligence in society. The law of negligence reaches into much of daily life, is a major conduit for apparently increasing amounts of personal injury litigation in society – and, overall, can be viewed as a haphazard and inefficient system of compensation. On the one hand, it is a means by which service users or consumers can gain 'full compensation' for injury or loss caused by somebody else's carelessness – for example, the millions of pounds necessary to provide for a severely disabled person's lifelong need for care and equipment. And, if parties, or their insurance companies are willing to admit liability, then claims need not involve huge legal expenses. On the other hand, contested claims can result in lengthy proceedings, taking years, and involve large sums of money being spent on lawyers, expert witnesses, accident consultants, and adversarial procedures. In addition, success in negligence claims depends on proving fault; a claim might succeed if the doctor did it, but not if God or chance was to blame. Not only does this seem to create a socially unjust system, but it also encourages the development of a culture of blame.

(Note. **Defective products, the Consumer Protection Act 1987 and the law of contract.** The Consumer Protection Act 1987 is an obvious avenue for legal actions in respect of defective products (see Chapter 15). However, the Act does not replace the law of negligence in relation to defective products and, in any case, it is not always possible to use it. For example, the time limits for bringing an action under the Consumer Protection Act might have been exceeded or the product have been supplied before the 1st of March 1988 (the date on which the Act came into force). If a person has bought defective equipment, an action in contract (see chapter 16) could be brought either instead of, or in addition to, an action in negligence. The advantage in contract, is that neither resulting harm nor carelessness have to be proved against a supplier of equipment for certain defects – it is enough that the product is defective. On the other hand, the foreseeability of the various harmful consequences flowing from defective products is likely to be easier to prove in negligence than in contract: see p.414.)

Questions people ask

- What if an NHS wheelchair service loans a child an indoor, electric wheelchair, tells the parents that it can be used out of doors – but an injury then occurs, when the child tips out of it on uneven ground?
- What if a hospital patient is given a pair of crutches following a hip operation, but is given no advice about how to use them – and, as a result, the person slips, falls and breaks a leg?
- What if a walking frame has been manufactured defectively, breaks and causes an accident? And what if it has been designed badly?
- A woman weighing over 16 stone sits on a shower seat and is injured when it comes away from the wall. Might legal liability arise not only in relation to the

seat itself but also to how it is attached to the wall and to the therapist who recommended it? Might it attach to the manufacturer who has failed to provide clear instructions about the weight-bearing capacity of the seat?

- What is the difference, if any, between carelessness and a simple mistake on the part of a professional?
- What if somebody contributes to an accident himself?
- Is a social services department or an NHS Trust liable for the negligence of any independent contractors it uses – such as independent occupational therapists (to assess people) or private companies (eg to deliver and repair equipment)?

1. WHEN DO PEOPLE HAVE A DUTY OF CARE?

The person who is suing has to prove that he or she was owed a *duty of care* by the person being sued.[1] In the context of this book, this means showing that, for instance, a hospital, local authority, doctor, therapist, social worker or teacher owes a duty of care to the person who has suffered harm – or that the manufacturer or retailer of equipment owes a duty of care to the eventual user.

Negligence can arise out of a wide range of activities involving equipment – including manufacture, adaptation, installation, supply, selling, loan, repair, maintenance, assessment, advice-giving and prescription. In this way, negligence applies not just to the equipment hardware itself but to a number of services and activities surrounding its provision.

The law courts use a formula to decide whether or not a duty of care exists. The formula is expressed in slightly different ways from time to time but, at present, there are three main planks to it. First, the harm caused must have been foreseeable. Second, there must have been *proximity* or *neighbourhood* between the person who has been harmed and the person who caused the harm. Last, even if foreseeability and proximity are established, it must still be *fair, just* and *reasonable* for the courts to impose a duty of care.[2] These terms are useful handles with which to analyse sometimes complicated situations. They are also criteria with sufficient flexibility to allow judges to stretch or contract them to fit all manner of situation.

The law courts regularly have to consider when to impose a duty of care; some general examples relating to society at large may help the reader to appreciate how the concept is applied in practice. For example, a duty of care is owed by (i) a local authority to an employee to provide a work place sufficiently free of stressful conditions to ensure that employees do not suffer nervous breakdowns[3], (ii) a solicitor to a testator to draw up a will in time before the testator dies[4], (iii) an employer to an employee to write a reference carefully[5], (iv) the police to informants to keep confidential information securely[6], and (v) householders (to a vacuum cleaner engineer) to salt the steps leading up to their front door – to prevent the engineer slipping on black ice and sustaining an injury to his back.[7]

Equally, however, the courts have held that a duty of care is not owed by (i) the coastguard to mariners who die as a result of its carelessness[8], (ii) the

Ministry of Defence to its naval airmen to stop them drinking too much[9], (iii) an unemployment benefit adjudication officer to an applicant whose claim he negligently fails to determine correctly[10], and (iv) the police to motorists to warn them of dangers on the road following an accident.[11]

Duty of care of statutory services and their staff

Duty of care of health care practitioners

The existence of a duty of care between doctor and patient has been long-accepted – in fact assumed – in the context of health care. This has been so, whether the patient is paying privately or being treated on the NHS.[12] Thus, doctors, nurses, therapists, chiropodists and other healthcare practitioners owe their patients a duty to be careful. For example, there is *proximity* or *neighbourhood* between a therapist and the patient because the patient is relying, in a one-to-one situation, on the special skill and knowledge claimed by the therapist.[13] And it is *foreseeable* that if a physiotherapist carelessly gives heat treatment, the patient might suffer burns (*Clarke v Adams*).[14] It is also foreseeable that if a person is not instructed to use crutches properly, he may fall and break a bone (*Brushett v Cowan*).[15]

However, the courts will draw limits to the duty of care. For example, when a man had a vasectomy which later reversed itself, the pregnancy advisory service which had arranged the operation owed no duty of care to a future sexual partner. This was because she was 'a member of an indeterminately large class of females' who might have associated in the future with the man. To impose such an open-ended duty of care on the advisory service would have been an excessive burden.[16]

Duty of care to provide equipment carefully – but not necessarily just to provide equipment. Though negligence is well-established in the health care field, the courts have baulked at finding it when resources and policy decisions are in issue. Thus, there is no problem, in principle, about finding negligence if a doctor carelessly amputates the wrong limb. But the approach of the courts is likely to be different if a person loses the leg owing to a shortage of facilities in the local hospital – which meant that the operation was not performed in time. This is because such a situation generally concerns local policies, priorities and resource allocation, rather than the negligent actions of individual practitioners. Similarly, the courts are more likely to intervene if an NHS Trust supplies a wheelchair in poor repair than if it fails to supply the chair at all because of a budgetary shortfall – even though injury might result in both cases.

Health authorities have been found negligent for lack of adequate systems – for instance, for failing to make available obstetricians in an emergency[17], to ensure supervision of inexperienced staff[18] or to check the safety of beds.[19] And it does seem to be accepted by the courts that if health authorities – or even the Secretary of State for Health – are fulfilling their statutory functions 'wholly unreasonably' then liability in negligence is not necessarily ruled out. However, it would be very difficult to prove, because the courts would take into account the discretion of authorities (or the Secretary of State) to make policies, decide priorities and allocate resources.[20]

The duty of care of social services departments and their staff

Negligence in the local authority field is confused. The courts are prepared to find councils negligent for muddy roads[21] or ill-maintained pavements which cause accidents. And local authorities might be prepared to settle out of court when an accident occurs on a section of road, affected by black ice, which they have failed to grit.[22] However, in cases involving social services departments, the courts sometimes experience considerable difficulty in deciding whether to impose liability. As the House of Lords put it in 1995 (*X v Bedfordshire CC*), 'the courts should hesitate long before imposing a common law duty of care [on authorities] in the exercise of discretionary powers or duties conferred by Parliament for social welfare purposes'.[23]

One of the major concerns of the courts is not to extend, or create new, liabilities for fear of opening the floodgates of litigation – which could lead to over-defensive practices by social services departments.[24] Besides, the courts might feel that the resources authorities consume in preventing and contesting litigation could be better spent on providing public services.[25] Nevertheless, there are some circumstances in which social services departments and their staff could, in principle, be liable for carelessly providing, or for giving advice about, equipment.

In the light of the uncertainty which exists, the obvious answer might be for social services departments and their staff simply to be careful in everything they do. This, however, is an unhelpful suggestion, since, (i) negligence is anyway not deliberate and (ii) in a complicated area of care, made more difficult by a lack of resources, it is not always clear what amounts to negligence and how to avoid it.

The following paragraphs are necessarily tentative – reflecting the uncertainty in this area of law and the fact that the reported cases have not concerned the provision of disability equipment. After summarising the practical implications for equipment provision, they deal with the principles underlying the approach of the courts, discussed at length by the House of Lords in a 1995 case about negligent assessment and advice-giving in the local authority child care and education fields (*X v Bedfordshire CC*).

Liability in relation to equipment provision by social services departments: summary. On the question of negligence for the provision of equipment by social services departments, the suggested position in summary is as follows.

At one extreme, the careless installation of equipment (eg grab rails) which causes accident and injury, is more likely to attract a successful negligence claim on the basis that a common law duty of care exists (and that carelessness and causation might in principle be easily proven in this sort of case).

At the other extreme, a failure to assess a person who is on a long waiting list (for eg grab rails) and who falls and has an accident, is unlikely to attract liability. There is no shortage of reasons why. It could be argued that in these circumstances a duty of care has not even arisen (there has been no direct contact). Waiting lists are closely connected to local policies and resources – issues which the courts will not directly interfere with. And, even if a duty of care did exist, causation would be difficult to prove – how could it be shown that the woman would not have fallen anyway, even with grab rails? And so on.

Somewhere in the middle come more difficult situations. For example, following assessment, allegedly inappropriate equipment might be provided, equipment might be inappropriately withheld, or a therapist might give bad advice to a person about what equipment to buy. In any of these circumstances, an accident might subsequently occur. What might arguments denying negligence liability sound like?

First, it could be argued that assessment is a statutory function (ie one explicitly imposed by legislation such as the NHS and Community Care Act 1990) with which a 'superimposed' a common law *duty of care* would conflict. For instance, a decision not to provide a stairlift might be made on the basis of an authority's criteria of eligibility and priority categories; these are, in turn, an expression of an authority's policy; and, a policy is an exercise of an authority's discretion in carrying out its statutory functions. Therefore, in this situation a superimposed common law of duty of care would severely impede an authority's ability to carry out those functions.

If this argument fails, it could be maintained that the assessment decision was a reasonable one which other occupational therapists might have made, and so did not amount to *carelessness* (ie a breach of the duty of care). If this argument, too, failed, then causation might prove an adequate defence – ie that the carelessness did not cause the accident. For example, the person might have fallen down the stairs after tripping on the top landing, before reaching the position where the stairlift would have been. Therefore, it could be argued that the accident would have occurred in any event, stairlift or no stairlift.

The situation is made more complex still, because irrespective of such arguments and of the likelihood of negligence being proved, authorities might choose to settle rather than to contest some cases. The settlement might be in order to save money (ie legal costs), avoid bad publicity, spare the distress of staff involved – and, in any case, it might carry no admission of liability.

Duty of care: NHS and social services departments compared. The courts clearly maintain a distinction between local authority staff such as social workers – and NHS staff.[26] As already explained, principles of negligence are well-established in the NHS but not in social services. Thus, the courts are prepared to find health care professionals negligent for careless assessments – for example (*Maynard v West Midlands RHA*), when a woman had to have an unnecessary, diagnostic operation (attended with certain risks and which resulted in paralysis of her left vocal cord), after both a physician and a surgeon had failed to heed the strong medical indications that she had tuberculosis.[27] Similarly, a trainee general practitioner has been held liable for failing to diagnose pneumonia in a patient who subsequently died.[28]

As explained at some length below, the position can be far less clear when it comes to finding professionals (such as social workers) in social services departments liable for negligent assessments. But, as community care policies develop, with increased emphasis on the delivery of health and social care in people's own homes, it could become increasingly difficult for the courts to distinguish between, for example, the negligent assessments of therapists employed by the NHS and those of therapists employed by social services departments. This difficulty would be further underlined in situations where NHS therapists formally carry out assessments on behalf of social services departments – as they do in a number of geographical areas. Indeed, in Northern Ireland, both health and social care is delivered by unified bodies known as health and social boards (and health and social services trusts); thus, occupational therapists, whether delivering 'health' or 'social' services, work for the same employer, and are generally regarded as 'health care' professionals.

The difference between making and implementing decisions. One helpful distinction is between carelessness in making decisions and carelessness in implementing them. Sometimes the former are referred to as policy, the latter as operational, matters.

Policy matters involve use of an authority's *discretion*, when it *makes decisions* in the course of carrying out its *statutory functions*. For instance, assessing a person's needs for community care is a statutory function (ie expressed in legislation) and involves decision-making; whereas operational matters follow, but are not part of, the decision-making. For example, having assessed a person's community care needs in terms of a raised toilet seat, the delivery and installation of the seat might be operational.

The House of Lords (*X v Bedfordshire CC*) recently gave an example from the education field; the decision to close a school is a policy decision, whilst taking care of the physical well-being of pupils is an operational matter which involves a common law duty of care.[29] Similarly, an authority may owe a duty of care in operational matters in respect of firefighting – for example, when a fire brigade is called out to a house on fire, takes action, leaves – but has to be recalled when it becomes clear that the fire has not been extinguished. By this time, the fire cannot be controlled and the house cannot be saved; the court imposed liability.[30] The same conclusion was reached when an authority was held liable for the negligence of one of its fire brigade officers who ordered that a sprinkler system in a burning building be turned off.[31] However, the uncertainty attaching to the outcome of judicial decisions in the local authority field is illustrated by a third recent case involving an authority whose fire brigade had failed to ensure the provision of an adequate supply of water at a fire. This too, might seem to be an operational matter – but the court held in this case that to superimpose common law liability in negligence would be to impede the performance of statutory duties.[32]

If the matter involves policy, the courts will not impose a duty of care. The courts have stated that authorities will not be liable in negligence for carelessly performing functions which involve policy. Therefore, if a social services department formally categorises a person's need as 'low priority' and on that account fails to assess her for a long time – and she has an accident which arguably could have been prevented (had she been assessed) – the courts are unlikely to interfere. This is because priorities and waiting lists are policy matters.

There is a proviso. If an authority is making decisions which involve policy, but is behaving very waywardly, then the courts might, exceptionally, intervene. However, they would do so on the basis that the behaviour is so wayward, that the authority is not, *in fact*, carrying out its statutory functions at all.[33] Assessing that only people with green hair have community care needs might be an example of this, since such behaviour could be no part of the NHS and Community Care Act 1990, s.47 which imposes a duty on authorities to assess people who appear to be in need as a result, for example, of disability, age, or mental health problems – not green hair.

If the matter does not involve policy, then it is possible that a duty of care will be imposed, so long as statutory functions are not impeded by doing so. The House of Lords has stated that if there is no policy aspect, then a decision or action of an authority might give rise to a common law duty of care – existing quite independently of the statutory functions of an authority. Such a duty of care could only exist if it does not interfere, or is not in conflict with, statutory functions (*X v Bedfordshire CC*).[34]

For example, the High Court (*Vicar of Writtle v Essex CC*) has found a local authority negligent when one of its social workers failed to warn the staff of a children's home about the fire-raising tendencies of a particular child. This finding was made on the basis that the failure to warn was unconnected with policy – and that a common law duty of care applied.[35] And some years ago the Court of Appeal (*Wyatt v Hillingdon LBC*) suggested that a successful action in negligence might be possible if a local authority supplied a person with a defective bed which collapsed and caused injury.[36] In the light of such examples, it would follow that if a therapist carries out an assessment and recommends the installation of grab rails – which were then installed carelessly by the authority's technical officer – the courts might be ready to find the authority liable for the negligent installation.

Making the distinctions: policy, operations and discretion. One of the difficulties about the distinction between policy and operational matters is knowing when and how to apply it.

The courts (*X v Bedfordshire LBC*) have stated that anything affecting an authority's policies and use of resources relates to its discretion to make decisions.[37] This is potentially wide. Suppose that, after a person has been assessed as urgently needing grab rails and a raised toilet seat, there is a delay in their provision. The person becomes progressively more frail and at risk and finally falls – an accident which her family claim could have been avoided. Apart from the fact that causation would be difficult to prove (see below), is this a policy or an operational matter? For instance, the delay could have been caused by sheer careless oversight (operational) – or by a deliberate policy not to employ more technical officers, in the light of a shortage of money (policy).

Recognising the difficulties involved in making these sometimes fine distinctions, the courts have shied away from imposing a rigid rule. Instead, they have explained that much will depend on the facts of each case and of each type of case. For instance, the House of Lords (*X v Bedfordshire CC*) has kept its options open by explaining that failure to allocate a suitable social worker, to make proper investigations and to remove children – all activities associated with assessment – do not necessarily involve policy, but could do in some circumstances.[38]

Assessment and advice: duty of care? In the light of the distinction between policy matters which exclude, and operational matters which do not exclude, the possibility of negligence, the pressing question remains about whether social services staff can be held liable for the consequences of careless assessments. In 1995, the House of Lords (*X v Bedfordshire CC*) attempted to answer this question in relation to assessment and advice-giving in the local authority child care and education fields.[39]

It decided that the careless assessments of children by social workers and a psychiatrist did not give rise to liability in negligence, either on the part of authorities or their staff. The authority could not be *directly liable* (see p.319) because to impose a duty of care would 'cut across the whole statutory framework set up for the protection of children at risk' (including police, educational bodies, doctors). In addition, 'the task of the local authority and its servants in dealing with children is extraordinarily delicate'; whilst imposition of liability might lead authorities to adopt a 'more cautious and defensive approach to their duties'. Furthermore, the frequent conflict between social workers and children's parents means that there is often:

> 'fertile ground in which to breed ill feeling and litigation, often hopeless, the cost of which both in terms of money and human resources will be diverted from the performance of the social service for which they were provided'.

Finally, the court pointed out that 'novel categories of negligence' should be developed cautiously; and that in this case, the court was being asked to 'erect a common law duty of care in relation to the administration of a statutory social welfare scheme' for the first time.[40]

The social workers and psychiatrist were not liable (and thus the authority was not *vicariously liable*: see p.318) because they owed a duty of care *to the authority* (their employer) – but *not to the children*. The court drew the analogy with a doctor writing a medical report for an insurance company – his duty of care is to the company, not to the applicant for insurance. It also pointed out that unlike housebuyers who might rely on the report of a surveyor (who has a contract with the building society but not with the housebuyers), the children and parents being assessed did not rely on the assessment – ie they would not 'regulate their conduct' as a result. The court also stated that, even if a duty of care were not precluded in this way, it would anyway not be just and reasonable to impose it – for the same reasons as for not imposing direct liability on the authority (see immediately above).[41] The judges were therefore making plain that although social services functions which contain policy aspects preclude negligence liability, it by no means follows that even purely operational functions will therefore automatically give rise to a duty of care.

The court also considered cases in the local authority education field. The same result was reached in relation to the direct liability of authorities for the assessment of children; the court would not superimpose a common law duty of care on top of the statutory functions. It stated that other remedies were more suitable than litigation – and that even if the statutory mechanisms for consultation and appeals (contained in education legislation) failed in any particular case, an investigation by the ombudsman into administrative failures would be the appropriate avenue.[42] However, the court found that staff such as educational psychologists, headmasters or advisory teachers (and thus authorities also, vicariously) could, in principle, owe a duty of care when assessing children or giving advice to parents. Nevertheless, in any particular set of circumstances, a duty of care would not be imposed if to do so would result in a conflict with the authority's statutory functions. The essential difference drawn between the role of such educational staff giving advice – and the role of the social workers and the psychiatrists in the child care cases – was explained to be twofold. First, any conflict between the staff's duty of care to the authority and their common law duty to give careful advice is not so obvious in the context of an education advisory service. Second – in the education, but not in the social services, context – it is clear that parents will rely and act on what professionals say, just as NHS patients do when given advice by doctors.[43]

Nevertheless, the House of Lords emphasised that even if a duty of care existed, this did not necessarily amount to establishing liability; and thus implied that it was not opening the floodgates. This was to emphasise that a court would still have to decide whether, for example, a head teacher or advisory teacher had exercised reasonable care and skill 'in accord with the views that might have been entertained at the time by reasonable members of the teaching profession.'[44] Thus, even if the first element of negligence, the duty of care, was present – the second, the breach of the duty, might not be.

Negligent statements? The outcome of the House of Lords case involving child care and education matters could suggest that the courts are more likely to find negligence if careless advice has been given – but not for the more concrete actions, omissions, assessments and decisions directly related to statutory functions.[45] Indeed, in another case heard in 1994 (*T v Surrey CC*), a child was injured in the care of a childminder known by the authority to be unsuitable. The authority was held not liable in negligence for having failed previously to cancel the registration of the childminder. However, it was held liable for a negligent statement because one of its officers had explicitly informed the child's mother that there was no reason why her child should not be left with that childminder.[46]

Duty of care in education?

In the local authority education field, the House of Lords (*X v Bedfordshire CC*) recently accepted that authorities and schools generally have a common law duty of care to look after the *physical well-being* of pupils – and that breach of this duty can give rise to findings of negligence.[47] A number of previous cases support this view, involving, for example, a 12-year old girl who put her hand through the non-reinforced glass panel of a door in a corridor[48] – or a 7-year-old girl whose hand was seriously injured by a powerful spring-door.[49] The Court of Appeal (*Van Oppen v Bedford Charity Trustees*) too has confirmed that a 'school is under a duty to take reasonable care for the health and safety of the pupils in its charge'.[50] These cases clearly suggest that schools and education authorities owe a duty of care not to provide equipment or adaptations carelessly. On a similar basis (*Fowles v Bedfordshire CC*), a local authority has been held liable by the Court of Appeal when it failed to supervise young people doing gymnastics at a youth centre.[51]

As already mentioned, the House of Lords (*X v Bedfordshire CC*) has also ruled that an education authority is not directly liable for negligent assessment of children or negligent advice-giving – but that it might bear vicarious liability for the negligence of its staff in some circumstances (see immediately above).

Duty of care in residential or nursing homes

Home owners and staff clearly owe a duty of care to residents of independent residential and nursing homes. Apart from ordinary common law negligence, homes could be liable too under the Occupiers Liability Act 1957 – which imposes a similar duty of care in respect of 'visitors' (including eg residents, visitors) using the premises. In addition, if individual residents are paying for themselves and have a contract with the home, then they might be able to bring an action in contract as well as negligence. For instance, the courts are unlikely to be sympathetic to home owners if accidents occur in those nursing homes where (it is reported that) residents use wheelchairs with punctures (or without tyres altogether), with split seats and back canvases, without brakes or footplates (or waist straps), and with unstable bases (eg because they are being used by bilateral amputees).[52]

Liability in some circumstances extends also to homes run directly by social services departments, since the basic care of vulnerable people is generally a straightforward operational matter – and not a policy issue which the courts would fight shy of. It may perhaps be likened to the duty of care education authorities and schools owe to children in respect of their physical well-being in schools (see above). Hence, no doubt the readiness, for example, of an authority to settle out of court with the family of a resident, a woman with learning disabilities, who died after getting into an excessively hot bath and being severely scalded.[53] And, in early 1996, substantial damages were awarded against Leicestershire County Council in respect of two women, who as children, were subjected to persistent physical, sexual and emotional abuse in one of the council's children's homes.[54]

When an authority arranges for people to be cared for in a home run by an independent organisation, the position might differ. The authority might not be liable for negligence of the staff of a home, unless it has chosen the home carelessly or failed to monitor it (evidence of this might be, for example, failure to carry out its statutory duties relating to the monitoring, registration and inspection of homes[55]). Even then, it might still have to be proved that the authority retained an explicit duty of care in relation to the health and welfare of each individual resident in the independent home – because such a duty does not follow necessarily from the statutory duty to assess people and to make arrangements for accommodation.[56]

When does the duty of care begin and end?

As explained below, if a hospital closes its doors altogether, a duty of care might not arise (see p.322). But, if they are open, it might be a little uncertain not only when the duty actually begins, but also how long it endures. Given, for example, the inability of some authorities to provide reliable follow-up services – such as review, monitoring, reassessment, collection and replacement of equipment – this is an important question. For example, community care guidance itself acknowledges the difficulties facing authorities in reviewing people's needs[57]; whilst orthopaedic surgeons have in the past been criticised for failing to follow up patients after an operation and initial prescription of an orthotic appliance.[58]

One finding of negligence involved lack of arrangements for a person who had gone home following an eye-lid operation performed by a plastic surgeon in private practice; the surgeon failed to ensure that there was adequate telephone cover and that he would be informed of any messages left by the patient.[59] In another, Canadian, case (*Brushett v Cowan*), the court pointed out that there is a clear duty on a surgeon to provide post-operative care for a patient – including advice on the use of crutches.[60] And, in a more recent English case, when a person was discharged home following an operation, the court found a lack of reasonable care in the lack of a clear procedure for him to return to hospital in case of problems with the stitching.[61]

A continuing duty of care might apply to the loan of equipment by statutory services. Thus, social services departments normally ensure that maintenance contracts are taken out for major items of equipment such as lifts or hoists. In addition, they will review the use of equipment from time to time – to establish that it is still safe to use. It might be necessary for the NHS to reassess people's needs for wheelchair cushions – since if their needs alter or cushions become worn, people become vulnerable to pressure sores. Furthermore, it is certainly good practice to check that, once equipment has been ordered, delivered and installed, everything has gone as planned, and the person knows how to use the equipment or adaptation. This might involve visits and the giving of instructions and advice by occupational therapists – for example, when bathing aids have been supplied. At least two problems arise; first, therapists sometimes have insufficient time to make all the visits demanded by good practice. Second, with both safety and legal liability in mind, there is sometimes a question about a) what constitutes adequate training and instruction for various groups of users with differing cognitive abilities, and b) how one proves that suitable instruction has been given (eg perhaps asking users to sign a form to that effect).

One way of diluting the duty of care is for an authority to explain to equipment users that they, too, have responsibility for maintaining equipment – and for informing the authority when the equipment is no longer suitable, is worn or is in disrepair. Another might be for an authority to close the file of people who have been given simpler equipment (not requiring maintenance) within three weeks of assessment; any future contact beyond a six-month period would be viewed as a new referral and assessment.[62] However, though this might bring to an end the duty of care in some respects, the matter remains complicated by the fact that if equipment has been loaned, then it remains the property of the local authority. To that extent the authority retains an interest; and in the absence of the regular review and formal maintenance (eg as happens with major items of equipment), it is difficult to say how far the duty of care of authorities extends in the case of smaller items of equipment. Certainly in practice, authorities do not have the resources to review regularly, or even at all, every last item of equipment they issue; for instance, a single local authority might have as many as 50,000 items of equipment on loan at any one time.

A recent report on NHS wheelchair services has indicated some of the factors and complications affecting wheelchair maintenance. For example, powered chairs generally need an annual maintenance check, non-powered chairs a triennial one – whilst some users are not able to care for wheelchairs or to request and arrange maintenance visits from NHS repairers. Thus, a 'blanket' maintenance policy will not suffice. In addition, some manufacturers recommend when maintenance checks is needed, but the problem with such recommendation is that (i) it is usage rather than length of ownership which is significant, and (ii) unnecessarily frequent checks are costly. On the other hand, not to follow the recommendation might absolve the manufacturer from responsibility if a fault (and accident) occurs.[63]

Duty of care of manufacturers, suppliers and distributors of equipment

The duty of care owed by manufacturers of products in general was firmly established in two cases heard in the 1930s. They revolved around a ginger beer bottle containing a decomposed snail[64] and underpants suffused with chemicals which badly irritated the skin of the wearer.[65]

In some circumstances, the duty of care of manufacturers falls away. After it has left the manufacturer, the product might be tampered with, badly treated, adapted, or have its instructions for use removed. A wheelchair might be adapted and made defective by a hospital's bio-engineering department. A car might be adapted for a disabled person, by removing the strut between front and rear doors – without the approval of the manufacturer, since the strut aids the car's 'crumple-resistance' in a crash.[66] Similarly, if the product should clearly have been inspected by somebody else before it was used – eg if instructions to hospitals or retailers are that the brakes of a wheelchair should always be tested first – then the manufacturer's duty of care may be discharged, partly or wholly. For instance, in one case a chemist's shop was successfully sued by a schoolgirl (through her father), after it had disregarded the manufacturer's warning to check chemicals before selling them on.[67] However, in a contract law case, when a boy lost an eye through using a defective catapult, it was argued for the importer that the defect could have been discovered before use, had the two prongs been squeezed together, or the catapult held down under one's foot and the elastic then tested. The court was unimpressed, pointing out that the potential customer could also have[68]:

> 'tried biting the catapult, or hitting it with a hammer, or applying a lighted match to ensure its non-flammability, experiments which, with all respect are but slightly more bizarre than those suggested...none of these tests is called for by a process of "reasonable examination", as that phrase would be understood by the common-sense standards of everyday life.'

All sorts of people can have a duty of care. Suppliers of parts, retailers, repairers and distributors have a duty to take care; for instance, suppliers of windscreens for cars[69], lift repairers[70], motor repairers[71] or chemists supplying doctors with drugs.[72] Secondhand car dealers (and by implication, therefore, wheelchair dealers) should check that a vehicle is reasonably safe to use.[73]

Identifying who has a duty of care in any particular situation

Who is liable: manufacturer, supplier, a local authority, the staff of the local authority, a subcontractor?

People who have been negligent (and their employers) can be sued because they have breached their duty of care. The latter may be liable *vicariously* or *directly* (see below). It is often important to sue the employer rather than the employee, because it is the employer who is more likely to have the *deep pocket* – ie be able to afford to pay any damages.

In any one situation, there could be several people who owe a duty of care and thus several parties to sue – especially if it is not clear precisely what or who caused the accident, or which party is in the best position to pay damages. The question of whom to sue becomes even more important, given, for example, the prevalent 'contract culture' engulfing the NHS and social services departments.

For instance, following a wheelchair accident, relevant parties to sue could be any, or all, of the manufacturer, the retailer, the NHS Trust staff (and therefore the NHS Trust itself) who prescribed and adapted the wheelchair – and the independent contractor who had recently repaired the chair for the NHS Trust. Similarly, if a patient is injured when being transferred by nurses from a hospital bed to an easy chair, the picture might be many-sided. Were the nurses careless? Was the system of nursing adequate – were there enough staff on the ward? Had the staff received training in lifting and handling? Did the brakes of the wheeled bed fail? Was the floor surface appropriate and non-slip, was the right type of polish used, was the polish applied properly by the cleaners? In order to amass evidence it might be necessary even for solicitors to employ specialist accident investigators or consultants to compile a report which takes many months to complete.

And, for example, in a case brought in the Republic of Ireland concerning diphtheria vaccine which allegedly caused brain damage to a child who had eczema, there were several defendants. These were the Wellcome Foundation (in relation to the vaccine testing), a doctor (question of knowledge of child's eczema, and of whether eczema was a contra-indication), the Southern Health Board (issue of vicarious liability for a nurse involved), and the Irish Minister for Health (in relation to any constitutional obligation it might have to compensate children).[74]

Vicarious liability: employer's liability on behalf of its staff. If NHS doctors, nurses or therapists negligently prescribe an item of equipment, the NHS Trust for which they are working can be sued as well. Similarly, if a manufacturer's employee negligently installs a piece of equipment, the employer will be vicariously liable. However, if the employee is doing something quite outside the definition of his or her job, then the employer might escape vicarious liability. For instance, in one case a bus company escaped vicarious liability after one of its bus conductors, rather than the driver, turned the bus around at the end of the route and caused an accident – because conductors are not employed to drive buses.[75] This rule will apply whether the employee is acting deliberately or inadvertently outside her job – and whether the employer is in the independent or public sector. For instance, in one case the House of Lords stated that the Home Office could be vicariously liable for the acts of prison officers who had deliberately broken Prison Rules by confining a prisoner to a strip cell; the officers' actions were not so far removed from their authorised duties as to fall outside the their course of employment.[76] What might be the attitude of the courts to a physiotherapist, working in the outpatient department of a hospital, who starts to practise acupuncture (not part of physiotherapy training) without the agreement or knowledge of her managers? Though, in a narrow sense it is outside of the definition of her job, her actions would still fall within a broader definition of, for example, 'treating patients'.

When employers are found vicariously liable for the negligence of their staff, it is open to them, in principle, to sue those staff (ie their own employees) to recover some of the money they have had to pay by way of compensation. It has been reported that this has been happening to some extent in, ironically, solicitors' firms – although only when staff have sufficient assets to make them worth suing.[77]

Independent contractors. As far as independent contractors are concerned, an employer is not normally liable for the carelessness of the contractor. However, the employer might be liable if, for example, he chose the contractor carelessly or failed to check the work. For example, in a 1916 case (*Pinn v Rew*), the defendant (through his agent), employed a drover to drive a cow and a calf to the his farm. Along the way, a dog was tossed and the plaintiff injured; the court held that not only was the drover negligent, but so too was the defendant for employing only one man on a dangerous task for which his powers would be inadequate. The defendant would be negligent whether or not the drover was regarded as an employee or independent contractor.[78]

An employer will not, however, be liable for what is called 'collateral negligence' of the contractor – that is carelessness not connected with the specific contracted task. Collateral negligence is, however, a vague term. For example, in a 1912 case, the court heard how a tool was dropped into the street by a workman (an independent subcontractor) who was installing window casements on the third floor of a building in Fenchurch Street, London; a commercial traveller from Birmingham selling horseshoes was hit. The Court of Appeal held that the defendants, who had been employed to erect the building, were not liable for the act of the workman, because it amounted to collateral negligence.[79]

Direct liability. People or organisations might have an overriding, direct duty to be careful. This means that not only are they vicariously liable for the negligence of any employees – but are liable in their own right as well. This means that they cannot get rid of their ultimate responsibility to somebody else.[80] For example, employers are directly liable for providing competent workers, proper equipment and safe systems of work[81], as well as safe premises. The distinction between direct and vicarious liability can be important – in the child care and education case already discussed above, the House of Lords considered separately the duty of care of authorities and of their staff.[82]

Uncertainties about the liability of statutory services for independent contractors. The liability of statutory services for independent contractors is slightly uncertain. The question seems to be whether authorities, even if they choose contractors and monitor them carefully, are still liable for the negligence of contractors. Such liability would clearly go beyond the normal rule about independent contractors (see immediately above) and would do so on the basis of 'non-delegable duties' – ie duties for which ultimate responsibility cannot be shifted.

In summary, and whatever the answer to this question, victims of negligence could anyway sue independent contractors for negligence. If authorities have not chosen and monitored contractors carefully, they, too, could be sued; and, in some situations (ie where a non-delegable duty is held to exist), they could be sued even if they have chosen and monitored carefully. From the standpoint of authorities, they might already be contractually indemnified by the independent contractors for any liability arising from the negligence of the latter. If they are not indemnified, then even if sued by the victim, the authority could in turn sue the contractors for breach of contract (ie for failure to deliver services with reasonable care and skill: see p.411).

The following are a few examples of situations in which the extent of liability might be uncertain in relation to equipment provision:

(i) **Practice in the NHS.** In practice, health authorities in the past, and now NHS Trusts, indemnify healthcare practitioners. Some NHS Trusts have joined the *Clinical Negligence Scheme for Trusts* (CNST), which is, in effect, a contributory NHS insurance scheme.[83] For claims relating to incidents which occurred before April 1995, health authorities and NHS Trusts are covered by the Existing Liabilities Scheme. The NHS Executive and NHS Litigation Authority organise and manage these schemes.[84] NHS Trusts which do not join the CNST are likely to meet compensation claims out of their own resources rather than seek alternative insurance – since insurance policies might be unsatisfactory and demand very high annual contributions.

So long as NHS clinical treatment is at issue, this indemnity covers both employees and independent contractors (eg a visiting medical consultant). However, this practical state of affairs is determined by Department of Health policy, which would not necessarily define the legal position in respect of NHS services – if, for instance, the policy were to be changed.[85]

Furthermore, the limits of even the NHS scheme might not always be obvious. Liability for visiting medical consultants is one thing, but what about other contractors, not involved in clinical treatment – including those involved in equipment provision? Imposition of direct liability on the NHS might even be influenced by how clearly it is indicated to patients that independent contractors are indeed 'independent' and not really part of the NHS. For instance, private sector prosthetists or orthotists, contracted to the NHS, often work on hospital premises, measuring, making and fitting artificial limbs. They might appear to patients to be just one more member of the 'NHS team'. In contrast, NHS wheelchair maintenance and repairs might be carried out by a local garage (an NHS-approved repairer) entirely removed from NHS premises. Although wheelchair users are still receiving, in principle, an NHS service, it is possible that this situation might be less likely to attract direct NHS liability – given the obviously independent role of repairers.

(ii) **Private hospital treatment.** In the case of private hospitals, or private treatment in NHS hospitals – neither case covered by the NHS scheme – the position is not wholly clear.

If the patient is paying a consultant directly, he will have a case in contract against the consultant – and the hospital will probably be liable in negligence only for the careful choice and monitoring of the consultant. The Court of Appeal (*Cassidy v Ministry of Health*) has stated that if a 'patient himself selects and employs the doctor or surgeon...the hospital authorities are if course not liable for his negligence, because he is not employed by them'.[86]

If the patient pays the hospital directly, it might be less easy to determine whether the duty of the hospital (contractual or in negligence) extends beyond careful choice and monitoring of the consultant to direct liability (on the basis of a non-delegable duty) for the negligence of the consultant.[87] The courts (*Roe v Ministry of Health*) have suggested that the hospital would be liable for all staff: whether 'permanent or temporary, resident or visiting, whole-time or part-time. The hospital authorities are responsible for all of them'.[88] However, a more recent and major case (*Yepremian v Scarborough General Hospital*) in the Canadian law courts has held that a hospital does not have a non-delegable duty of care (ie beyond careful choice, regular review of performance of staff etc) to patients.[89]

(iii) **Contracting out equipment services by social services departments.** Local authorities are empowered to make arrangements with other organisations for the provision of social services. Thus, if they contract out the delivery, maintenance, collection and recycling of equipment, it might be uncertain whether they remain directly liable for the negligence of contractors, or only liable for their careful selection and monitoring. The language of s.30 of the National Assistance Act 1948, under which such arrangements are made, might suggest that authorities will remain directly liable, since it states that authorities may 'employ as their agent' an independent sector organisation – and principals are normally liable for the acts of their agents.

(iv) Distinction between referral and delegation. Liability might sometimes depend on the narrow dividing line between the *referral* and *delegation* of service users.

For instance, doctors sometimes delegate and sometimes refer patients to therapists practising complementary medicine. What is the difference? Delegation, but not referral, means the doctor remains directly liable since the patient remains under his care. But such direct liability can be avoided if doctors refer patients, so long as they choose with reasonable care therapists who are professionally qualified.[90] Thus, a general practitioner might purchase the services of a physiotherapist – either an independent one, or in an NHS hospital – to treat one of his patients and provide her with a walking aid. Is he delegating or referring? And what if his group practice directly employs a physiotherapist and he passes the patient on to her?

Duty of care: failing to do something

In general, the courts are wary about finding negligence simply because a person has failed to do something.

For example, an NHS Trust could avoid a duty of care if it literally closes its doors and refuses to provide treatment because it does not have sufficient resources. However, once a person has been accepted as a patient, the duty arises. It might therefore legally be safer for authorities to give no treatment at all – ie decide to close their doors – than to give inadequate treatment. However, once the doors are open and a person has entered, then a duty of care is owed (*Barnett v Chelsea and Kensington Hospital*); and a failure to diagnose or treat carefully could breach that duty.[91] When people are turned away then, failing a negligence action, a judicial review case might be brought; but, as explained elsewhere in this book, patients who challenge such rationing decisions are unlikely to succeed (see p.428).

Clearly, there are omissions and there are omissions. Once a special relationship has arisen between, for example, a health care practitioner and a patient, then an omission can be as drastic as an action. Absence of explanation about how to use a walking frame could be as harmful as a poor explanation; the former is an omission, the latter is not, but either could cause an accident. Thus, where a special relationship has arisen, the courts may elide the distinction between actions and omissions, since, either way, a duty of care has arisen to prevent harm. Recently, for example, the House of Lords held a solicitor negligent for failing to draw up a will in good time.[92] And a general practitioner was held liable when a person suffering from manic depression threw himself off a balcony and was severely injured; the doctor had failed to carry out an adequate mental examination and to refer him to the community mental health team.[93]

In the case of the hospital that closes its doors, the special relationship might never arise. Similar perhaps, is the situation of a person who has been waiting two years for an assessment by social services; it could be argued that a duty of care has been denied the opportunity to come into being. And, in a recent case, when a local authority failed carelessly to deregister a childminder suspected of violence towards children, the court held that it was not liable in negligence when another child was subsequently injured. This was because the judge was loath to impose liability on the authority for an *omission*, as a result of which a third party (ie the childminder, but not the authority or its staff) caused injury.[94]

Making statements or giving advice carelessly

Negligent statements and financial loss

The courts have developed a separate test for establishing a duty of care in relation to negligent statements which cause financial loss. Negligent statements apply to advice-giving by professionals in a wide range of contexts – though the doctrine of negligent statements has developed particularly in the context of the giving of financial and business advice – as a result of which financial loss is incurred.[95]

Under this doctrine, the courts have in the past only awarded damages for 'pure' financial loss if it has been caused by negligent words rather than actions (see below). Thus, where the loss is only financial, then an action for negligent words (sometimes called negligent misstatement or negligent statement) has been more likely to succeed than an action in ordinary negligence (ie involving negligent actions). However, recently the House of Lords has found negligence even where pure financial loss was caused by an act rather than words – when a solicitor failed to make a client's will in time.[96] Indeed, it might be difficult to distinguish between negligent actions and negligent words, and both might be present in many instances.

The formula adopted by the courts is basically as follows. A person, who claims to have special expertise, makes a statement to a second person, knowing that it is likely to be relied on. The second person does in fact rely on it and suffers detriment.[97] Special expertise is not confined to the business or financial world, and public authorities can be liable for negligent statements causing financial loss in respect of, for example, land registration[98] or land planning.[99] However, the advice given probably needs to be of a formal or professional nature – for example (*Tidman v Reading BC*), if minimal information is given in response to an informal planning enquiry made to a local authority, the courts will not find negligence.[100]

Accordingly, there might be a distinction between advice given in a formal assessment by an occupational therapist and a few words uttered on the telephone by a reception officer of a social services department. Furthermore, the courts (*Tidman v Reading BC*) will be keen not to impose swingeing liability on authorities – since to do so would not be in the public interest if it resulted in authorities ceasing to give advice altogether.[101] As already explained, the courts might be especially reluctant to impose liability on social services departments. Even so, the decisions of the courts cannot always be predicted and it would be good practice for authorities to ensure that their staff do not give advice carelessly.[102] For instance, under the forthcoming scheme of NHS wheelchair vouchers, therapists will be advising about which wheelchair to buy. If people then purchase an inappropriate wheelchair, having added their own money to the NHS voucher, they might allege that the therapists gave bad advice.

Nevertheless, even in the NHS field, it might not be easy to win a case on the basis of an alleged negligent statement. For instance, in one case a woman had signed a sterilisation consent form which included the statement, 'we understand that this means we can have no more children'. Subsequently she became pregnant, but failed in an action alleging that the form amounted to a negligent statement – ie that she would not become pregnant if she had the operation.[103]

If physical injury (rather than just financial loss) results from a statement, then the courts might be quite ready to impose negligence liability. The judge made this point in the case already mentioned (*T v Surrey CC*) concerning the parent who was given negligent advice about a childminder by the local authority officer.[104] But, reliance and causation still has to be proved – ie that the person would still have acted in the same way and sustained injury, even if the negligent statement had not been made. For example, if the authority could have shown that the mother would anyway have chosen the childminder, even if the statement had not been carelessly made, then the negligence action would have failed.

Equipment provision: examples of distinction between words and actions in relation to financial loss

The distinction between actions and words, which has, in the past, determined whether people can recover in negligence for pure financial loss, can lead to odd consequences if pursued to an extreme. These consequences can be avoided when the courts are prepared to blur the divide between words and actions. The following examples are purely hypothetical; they are also tentative, since, as already explained, the doctrine of negligent statement is strongest in the area of financial advice and transactions.

(i) A hoist, totally inappropriate for a particular person's needs, is loaned by the NHS and causes injury and financial loss. There is no problem, in principle, about recovering for both the injury and the financial loss;

(ii) No injury is caused by the fall from the hoist, but there is financial loss; for example, the person cannot get out and about, cannot obtain a replacement, and loses several weeks of earnings. The loss cannot be claimed for, if the negligence is regarded as a negligent action;

(iii) The person, relying on explicit and formal advice from, for example, an independent therapist, goes out and buys an inappropriate hoist and suffers financial loss (eg she has wasted her money, and loses earnings because she cannot get out and about). It is possible that a claim could made by alleging a negligent statement made by a specialist professional.

2. BREACHING THE DUTY OF CARE

The law of negligence requires that the person who is being sued should have been careless. In one sense, this implies moral fault in so far as people are held responsible for their actions; in another, however, moral fault is absent because the notion of negligence implies that the consequences – ie the accident – were neither desired nor foreseen by the careless person. Without intention or actual foreseeability, it is difficult to identify moral fault.[105] Indeed, it is notable that when the courts ask whether an incident was 'foreseeable', they are not asking whether it was actually foreseen by the individual defendant but whether it was foreseeable by the 'reasonable man'. In any case, when deciding how to place 'the blame' and who should pay damages, the courts sometimes consider explicitly not just who is at fault but also who can afford to bear the loss. For instance, surveyors (normally insured) can better bear the loss of their own negligent surveys than the housebuyers who have relied on them.[106]

Carelessness can apply to all manner of actions and statements involving, for example, the manufacture and supply of defective products, the inappropriate supply of equipment by statutory services, lack of communication between practitioner and patient and poor instructions about how to use equipment.

Reasonable standards of care

The benchmark of carelessness is based on the concept of *reasonableness*. Thus, a doctor or therapist acts carelessly if he or she does something which a reasonably competent doctor or therapist would not have done.[107] The same applies to, for example, carpenters – with different standards though for the amateur and the professional.[108]

It might be careless for an NHS physiotherapist to prescribe a wheelchair in a particular situation, if other reasonably competent therapists would not have done so. For instance, the user of the wheelchair might be an amputee for whom the wheelbase of the chair needs to be adjusted if he or she is not to be at risk of overbalancing and tipping out. It might well be careless to supply the chair unadjusted. And, negligence might be imposed on a doctor or therapist who fails to explain to a person how to use crutches, with the result that the person falls and breaks a limb (*Brushett v Cowan*).[109] Yet just because serious consequences flow from the actions of a health care professional does not mean that negligence will be established. For instance, when an anaesthetist registrar pierced the dura mater at a caesarian birth causing a leakage of cerebrospinal fluid and subsequent severe spinal headaches, the court found that reasonable care had been taken even though the needle had been inserted slightly too far and caused a puncture.[110]

Indeed, alleged breaches of carelessness may be all-embracing. For example, in one Australian negligence case involving various staff such as doctors, therapists and nurses, a number of points were alleged (*Elli Andjelkovic v Capital Territory Health Commission*). These concerned an over-polished floor and failure to give warning about it, unsafe crutches, a worn crutch tip, failure to assist the person, failure to train the person how to use the crutches, failure to take reasonable steps to prevent the person slipping, and failure to supervise the person properly.[111]

A manufacturer might be careless if it supplies equipment without adequate labelling, instructions or warnings – for example, when a bottle of corn solvent, sealed only by a cork, is supplied with no warning that special precautions should be taken. The plaintiff suffered injuries to his leg and genitals which had to be repaired by plastic surgery.[112] For example, lift repairers might be liable for failing to replace a fractured gland, as a consequence of which the lift falls to the bottom of the shaft[113]; as might motor repairers for failing to replace the flange of a wheel[114], or car dealers for omitting to check the brakes of a secondhand car.[115] Similarly, if a chemist is held liable for carelessly providing a patient or doctor with the wrong drug (belladonna instead of dandelion extract)[116], so could a pharmacist or surgical appliance fitter be liable for supplying carelessly the wrong type of appliance which subsequently causes harm.

In one case (*Haley v LEB*), the House of Lords examined the duty of care owed to disabled people in the street. An electricity board was held to be negligent for protecting a hole in the street with barriers sufficient for sighted, but not for blind, people. The court pointed out that, given the statistical evidence that one in every five hundred people is blind, it was 'quite impossible to say that it is not reasonably foreseeable that a blind person may pass along a particular pavement on a particular day'.[117]

Knowing about a reasonable standard of care at the relevant time

The identification of a reasonable standard of behaviour is based on knowledge at the time of the incident in question. This is particularly relevant when a case comes to court many years after the harm has occurred. The courts will try to be careful not to use the benefit of hindsight but to analyse what was known at the time of the accident. For example, one case involved Nupercaine ampoules contaminated by phenol which had percolated through invisible cracks in the ampoules. In 1954, the court held that at the relevant time (1947), competent anaesthetists were not negligent in being unaware of this risk of the percolation.[118]

The Department of Health issues safety notices about equipment, based on the reporting of accidents or adverse incidents. The present arrangement (from August 1995) is that the Medical Devices Agency (MDA) or NHS Estates issue hazard notices in urgent cases, and safety notices or device bulletins for the less urgent.[119] For example, in 1995, the MDA issued a notice about the danger of people's scrotum becoming trapped between the frame and the plastic seat insert of a particular make of bath-lift chair. It recommended that seat inserts should be inspected and certain types withdrawn and returned to the manufacturer.[120] Similarly, another notice recommended that the footplates and bearings of a particular make of 'swivel walker' should be inspected at least once a week, following an injury to a child after a walker had tipped backwards.[121] The supply of equipment with a hidden fault or inherent danger before the distribution of such a notice might not amount to negligence, because the average manufacturer, supplier or local authority could not have known about it. However, to continue supply of the equipment after the dangers are known might well constitute negligence. Recently, for example, it became clear that the use of wooden tongue depressors to splint the arms of premature babies led to a risk of fungal infection which could result in death (in two cases) and amputation of part of the arm (in a third case). The MDA promptly issued a hazard notice.[122] In some circumstances, unsafe products are anyway recalled, although present recall systems are thought to be of limited effectiveness.[123]

In the case of equipment manufacturers, a defect in the actual manufacturing process will strongly indicate negligence.[124] This is because there is limited room for debate – assuming the products have not been interfered with after leaving the manufacturer – if, for example, kettles explode, bottles of beer contain snails, or underpants are full of harmful chemicals. However, the courts are more reluctant to impose liability if the fault is one of *design* rather than actual *manufacture* – since at the time of design, the defect might well have been unknown. There are complex issues of public policy to weigh up about the costs and risks to society associated with research and development.[125] However, this reluctance would be unlikely to continue if a manufacturer continued to produce the defective equipment, once the design defect had become known – for instance, if a tyre manufacturer were to fail to act in the case of tyres known to be faulty and to cause accidents.[126]

It has been suggested that developments such as the Internet, which result in knowledge becoming available quickly to the population at large, could pose problems for the courts; for instance, patients might gain access to information about best practice which some doctors were not yet aware of.[127]

Measuring the standard of care of professionals

How is the standard of care measured? What is reasonable? One method is for the courts to accept expert evidence from other professionals. If there is conflicting expert evidence which both supports and does not support the actions of the person accused of negligence, then the courts are likely to find that the person has not acted negligently. This is because they do not consider it appropriate to be the arbiters between differing or rival professional opinions or schools of thought.[128]

Although expert evidence from members of the relevant profession is influential and persuasive in legal actions, it is for the courts ultimately to decide what constitutes reasonable practice.[129] Accordingly, just because it is common practice for hospital wheelchairs to be maintained poorly, a court will not necessarily accept that the practice is reasonable. This has been long recognised as a problem[130], and the Department of Health has been so concerned that it has issued notices on more than one occasion about how wheelchairs should be maintained.[131] Indeed, one case (*Clarke v Adams*) concerned the warning given by a physiotherapist to a person during electrical treatment. She instructed the patient to tell her if she experienced anything more than comfortable warmth. Despite the fact that the chief examiner of the Chartered Society of Physiotherapy gave expert evidence that the warning was entirely proper, the therapist was nevertheless held to have been negligent for the burns which the patient suffered and which led to amputation of part of his leg.[132] On the other hand (*McKay v Royal Inland Hospital*), just because a patient with multiple sclerosis falls out of a bed which had no side boards, negligence will not necessarily be established. The boards had not been used because of the psychologically detrimental effects – and the exercise which the patient was performing when she fell had been carefully taught by the physiotherapist. The action was dismissed because the treatment had been delivered by qualified staff according to established practice.[133]

Even if practitioners were to act against all orthodox practice, the court will, in principle, not *automatically* find negligence. Instead, it would listen to the reasons given by the defendant and decide whether the action could still be justified in the particular circumstances.[134] Along the same lines, the Court of Appeal stated that just because a step, 'designed to avert or minimise or avert a risk', is omittted, this does not mean that negligence (carelessness) is thus established.[135] For instance, generally speaking, occupational therapists in social services departments might not provide stairlifts for people who suffer from serious epilepsy. If an OT did recommend one, and an accident occurred, the court would at least hear the reasons, before 'condemning' her.

Whose reasonableness: that of the professional or service user?

The courts look at the standard of the reasonably competent professional – and not at what the reasonable patient or client might expect.[136]

For instance, some cases in the NHS context concern the adequacy of information given by doctors to patients. The courts have made it clear that they will look at what other reasonable doctors would have said – and not what reasonable patients think should have been said.[137] For example, a person might undergo an operation – to make walking easier and remove the need for calipers

– which entails a minimal chance of creating further damage that would necessitate the use of a wheelchair. The point at which the doctor should say something might be hard to identify – for example, he might judge that the chance of something going wrong is so remote that it would, on balance, be more detrimental and anxiety-making to the patient to mention such a minute risk, than to remain silent.

If at least some other doctors would have withheld such information, as the defendant did, the courts are likely to accept that a professional has not been negligent. This is because, as already pointed out, the courts will not decide against a defendant on the basis of differences of professional expert opinion.

Mistakes and inexperience

The practising professional might very well worry about knowing when a mistake – which of course everybody makes from time to time – amounts to negligence. There is probably no answer (*Whitehouse v Jordan*), since it will depend on the mistake and whether the courts think that it was an error which a reasonably competent professional would have made.[138] This suggests that the courts are prepared to state that a mistake was a *mere error* – and *not negligence* – but only in some circumstances. However, since those circumstances are difficult to predict, the legal position remains a worrying one for professionals – who are understandably concerned not only that mere errors should be distinguished from negligence, but that *bad decisions* should be differentiated from *decisions which happen to turn out badly*.[139]

However, the courts have indicated that they will take account of the pressures put upon, for example, NHS staff:[140]

> 'full allowance must be made for the fact that certain aspects of treatment may have to be carried out in what one witness (dealing with the use of a machine to analyse the sample) called 'battle conditions'. An emergency may overburden the available resources, and, if an individual is forced by circumstances to do too many things at once, the fact that he does one of them incorrectly should not lightly be taken as negligence.'

Even so, when a doctor in a hospital casualty department failed to spot a depressed fracture of the skull (with a hole in it of between a quarter and half an inch), the court made a finding of negligence, even though the doctor was young, dealing with 60 cases a day, and that the judge was[141]:

> 'satisfied that that the casualty officer was both a most competent and a very careful doctor. He was now a general practitioner...and it would be the greatest possible injustice to him if any other view was taken of him as a result of this case. No man could honestly say that he had never fallen below the standard of taking reasonable care at some time or other in his life. Moreover, the burden of work put upon the casualty department...was such that it was not surprising that a young doctor failed on occasion to measure up to the standard of care.'

Two further examples illustrate the difficulties of pinpointing suitable standards of care. First, a therapist might visit a man in his own home to conduct a review of his needs, and conclude that continued use of the walking frame which has been loaned previously is unsafe. The man agrees not to use it – and to use his wheelchair instead – and the therapist arranges for the frame to be collected in a week's time, rather than taking it away at once. In the interim, the man does use it and has an accident. Second, a therapist visits a disabled child who has been supplied with a special wheelchair. She notices that the brakes are not working properly, suggests that the wheelchair should not be used until it is repaired – and that the child should use his other wheelchair. The therapist also offers to contact the NHS wheelchair repairer, but the parents reassure her that they will do so themselves. They fail to do so. Some time afterwards, the child is transferring himself out of the chair without assistance (it has been recommended to the parents that they should assist in transfers), the wheelchair moves, the child falls and is injured. In both these cases the therapist has relied on what the service users said to her, and in the second case parental supervision is also in issue. Both cases also raise questions about the degree to which people are responsible for what happens in their own homes – clearly the degree of supervision which professionals are able to exercise in the community is substantially less than in the institutional (eg hospital) setting.

Assumption of negligence?

Sometimes, the circumstances of an accident might so clearly suggest negligence that what is called the *evidential burden* shifts from the alleged victim to the defendant. This is known as *res ipsa loquitur*, 'the thing speaks for itself'. Although the victim still has ultimately to prove that the defendant was negligent, it is the defendant who has to bring evidence to show that he or she was not negligent.

Thus, if a person goes into hospital with two fingers in contraction, has an operation and a splint applied – but then emerges with his whole hand disabled, there is strong evidence of negligence.[142] Similarly, a hospital might have a hard task in denying negligence if a patient is burnt on the buttock when being given electrical coagulation treatment and permanent muscle injury is caused[143] – or if a patient under an anaesthetic is burnt by a hot water bottle provided by a nurse.[144] And the law concerning defectively manufactured products has developed to such an extent that there might be almost an assumption of negligence in many cases.[145]

Inexperienced staff and lack of resources?

It might seem reasonable to allow a newly qualified doctor or therapist to perform to a lower standard than an experienced practitioner. However, the courts insist that the standard remain the same for both the experienced and inexperienced professional, on the grounds that a high standard of patient care could otherwise not be maintained. For instance, if a newly qualified physiotherapist loaned a walking frame – against accepted practice – to a person with dementia who then had a serious accident, her inexperience would be no defence.

Nevertheless, when an inexperienced professional has been careless, but was under supervision, then it might be the supervisor (eg senior therapist or doctor) who is found to be negligent instead of, or as well as, the inexperienced practitioner.[146]

Record-keeping

From the point of view of authorities, good record-keeping is important in order to contest allegations of carelessness, since service users now have rights to see their own records (see p.128). Indeed, without good records, it might be impossible to contest negligence actions; it is reported that hospitals in the United States are unable to defend between 35% and 40% of such actions because of problems with documents.[147]

Good record-keeping concerns not only the making of the record itself (eg clarity, neatness, legibility, up-to-dateness, logical structure) – but also ensuring that the record does not go missing and deciding how long to keep it.[148] Department of Health guidance refers to the various legal considerations affecting the length of time various types of record need to be kept – bearing in mind, for example, personal injury claims, product liability, people of 'unsound mind', children or obstetrics.[149] However, better standards of documentation might carry with them some negative aspects – for example, when staff are taught 'defensive' record-keeping in terms of what is written down and how – with a view to minimising the risk of legal liability at a later date.

3. PROVING THE CAUSE OF ACCIDENTS, AND TYPES OF HARM

It has to be shown, assuming that there has been a breach of the duty of care, that the breach *caused* the harm complained of. Causation can be difficult to prove and is the rock on which many negligence cases founder.

A clear example of this concerned a workman who drank tea laced with arsenic (*Barnett v Chelsea and Kensington*). He went to a hospital casualty department which, instead of diagnosing the problem and treating it, sent him home. He died. The court had no difficulty finding carelessness – but the man's widow did not win the case, because evidence suggested that he would have died anyway, whether or not the hospital had treated him.[150]

Likewise, a hospital nurse might carelessly fail to provide a pressure relief mattress for a person who then goes on to develop such serious pressure sores that he dies. Assuming that carelessness was established, causation might not be proved if it could be shown that, even on entry to hospital, the person's skin was so fundamentally damaged that serious pressure sores would have developed *in any case.*

Indeed, the health service ombudsman has acknowledged the difficulty of attributing blame in the case of pressure sores, since they develop so easily when elderly people are confined to bed for any length of time. Although he investigates maladministration and failure in services, and not negligence, nevertheless the question of causation arises all the same. Sometimes he can pinpoint poor practice – as when, for example, a patient with a sore which was beginning to heal was sent on a long ambulance trip home, precautions (such as dressings and a special cushion) were not taken, and the sore deteriorated on the journey.[151] In another case, he investigated the development of pressure sores in hospital, due to the allegedly inadequate provision of special equipment including a ripple mattress and sheepskin rug. Although the patient might have been occasionally without the rug (when it was being washed), and the ripple mattress might not have been available all the time (there was only one on the ward and would have been in demand from other patients) – nevertheless the nurses' evidence was that the mattress was not needed at the relevant times, whilst the consultants confirmed that the development of the sore was inevitable given the generally poor condition of the patient.[152]

Which cause?

There are other types of case in which causation is difficult to prove. If several causes exist, it is sometimes hard to say which of them actually caused the harm. For example, a hospital might discharge a person home without the appropriate equipment, such as a walking frame, grabrails in the bathroom and a raised lavatory seat. If the person then falls and sustains broken bones, it might be difficult to prove whether the main cause was the lack of equipment, the slippery bath rug in the bathroom, a dizzy spell or an indeterminate blend of all of these.

It is not just the law courts which might face such problems. The insurance ombudsman has expressed his disquiet over the acrimony which sometimes flares up between claimant and insurance company about causation. For example, the company might claim that the disability being claimed for stems not from a shoulder injury received at work, for which it would be bound to pay benefits – but from an underlying arthritic condition and a recent stroke, for which it would not be bound to pay. In which case, the disputing parties might argue about whether there is a sole cause – and, if not, about the proportion that each factor has contributed to the overall disability.[153]

Material contribution to an accident

If there are several causes, it might be difficult to analyse exactly to what degree each contributed to the accident. However (*Bonnington Castings Ltd v Wardlaw*), so long as a particular cause can be proved to have at least *materially contributed*, then the test of causation might be satisfied.[154] For example, if a person falls when using a walking frame with worn tips on a slippery floor, it might be impossible for a court to establish in what proportion the floor or the tips each contributed to the accident – but nevertheless easier to decide that, in any event, the worn tips made a material contribution.

Several causes of unknown relevance to an accident

On the other hand, where there are several possible causes of the damage, each of which could have solely caused the damage, then it might be impossible to establish causation in respect of any one of those causes.[155] The following example explains:

> An elderly and frail woman lives at home has diabetes and a controlled heart condition. She accidentally takes an excessive quantity of her prescribed drug, suffers a hypotensive attack, collapses and remains lying on the floor of her draughty hallway for eight hours. She is eventually found and taken to hospital with hypothermia. She is examined, a developing pressure sore noted and a pressure relief mattress recommended. Put in a hospital bed, the mattress is not provided as a result of an oversight. Within two days a serious pressure sore has developed and the skin broken down. Despite treatment, a bacteria-resistant infection sets in, septicaemia results and the woman dies. An allegation of negligence is brought by the family to the effect that, had the pressure relief mattress been supplied as recommended, then the sore would not have broken down and she would not have died.
>
> The hospital puts forward a number of alternative causes, each of which, it argues, could also have been the sole cause. First, it argues that the fall and eight hour lie in the hallway were sufficient to cause the pressure sore subsequently to break down. Second and separately, the sore might anyway have broken down solely on account of the woman's diabetes – which put her at increased risk of tissue breakdown. Third, again separately, the sore could have broken down solely on account of the woman's heart failure and associated circulatory problems – also factors affecting tissue breakdown. Finally, the woman was clearly very depressed, and responded neither to pain nor to the advice of the hospital staff. This meant that she caused the breakdown of tissue by not moving/shifting her position in bed at all; thus, the sore would have deteriorated even had the mattress been available, and even had the nursing staff turned her more than they actually did.

An intervening cause

Negligence liability is sometimes denied successfully by showing that something else happened between the negligent action and the harm which was caused. For example, if a doctor fails to diagnose diabetes but a second doctor, having identified the diabetes, operates and kills the patient, the first doctor is not liable for his carelessness.[156] And, if the user of a defective walking frame becomes aware that it is damaged, but continues to use it, then this may break the chain of causation – in which case the manufacturer would not be liable in negligence. For example (*Lambert v Lewis*), in a case in which a farmer was sued for causing an accident, he in turn sought an indemnity from the supplier of the faulty Landrover trailer coupling which had caused the accident. The court held that he could no longer claim the indemnity (ie that the coupling was fit for its purpose), because his knowledge of the defect had intervened.[157]

Harm too unlikely or remote

Causation can also be disputed by admitting that the negligent action physically caused the harm – but that the type of harm was so unlikely that it was too remote for the law courts to find causation. Thus, the courts have had to decide about whether the destruction of a ship was foreseeable, given that it was caused by a plank of wood dropped into the hold, striking something, and giving off a spark that ignited petrol vapour. Liability was established.[158]

And in a 1963 House of Lords case, a boy knocked a paraffin lamp down a manhole, over which a tarpaulin had not been properly closed (when the Post Office workers left for their teabreak). An explosion occurred and the boy was badly burnt; liability was established because the type of injury – ie from lamp burns – was foreseeable, even if the explosion and the extent of the burns were not.[159]

For instance, using a hoist to transfer a man from bed to chair, a district nurse might carelessly allow him to fall to the floor and sustain injury. The injury to the man is certainly not too remote; but the injury to his wife who hearing the commotion, hurried up the stairs in a panic, slipped, fell and was injured, might be. One test of remoteness is that the injury should at least be of a foreseeable type. Thus, it could be argued that an injury to the wife when helping the nurse to lift the husband would have been foreseeable – but that the accident on the stairs was not. But, once it is accepted that the type of injury was foreseeable, then the extent of the injury is irrelevant. For instance, if it was foreseeable that the frail husband might suffer some broken bones from being dropped, then the fact that the injuries consisted of unusually severe fracturing would be no defence. Another way of denying liability to the wife might be to say that, in the circumstances – since the wife's injury was not foreseeable, and it was the husband who was the patient – no duty of care to the wife arose in the first place.

Injuries and thin skulls

The 'eggshell skull' rule means that somebody who has been careless cannot plead that the victim was particularly vulnerable to the injury he or she has suffered; the negligent person has to 'take his victim as he finds him'.

For instance, if a person with particularly weak bones suffers unusually severe injuries after an accident in a badly maintained wheelchair, it is no defence to claim that her injuries were out of the ordinary for that type of accident. For instance, in one case a factory worker was burnt on the lip by molten metal. The burn healed, but because of a premalignant condition, he went on to develop and die of a cancer triggered by the burn. The employer was liable.[160] Therefore, it cannot be argued that, really, the injuries were caused by the victim's own vulnerability, rather than the defendant's carelessness.

Losing a chance

Sometimes people wish to claim that they have 'lost a chance' of something because of somebody else's negligence. For instance, when a boy fell out of a tree and broke his leg, he claimed that the negligent failure of the hospital to diagnose and to treat the fracture deprived him of a 25% chance of avoiding avascular necrosis (*Hotson v East Berkshire*). The courts found it difficult to decide the case. The judge at first instance, and then the Court of Appeal, awarded 25% of what the full liability would have been. However, the House of Lords awarded nothing because it felt that since there was a 75% chance of the disability arising anyway, it had been caused, on the balance (at least 51%) of probabilities, by the accident itself rather than the hospital's negligence.[161] And, in the Canadian Supreme Court, a doctors' failure to tell a patient about cancer and to follow up the diagnosis, did not result in damages being awarded – although the Court of Appeal had awarded them for loss of a chance.[162] Thus, the law is not wholly clear in this area – and even the House of Lords did not rule out loss of a chance in medical negligence cases generally.[163]

There are anyway other cases in which the courts have been prepared to award damages for loss of a reasonable chance to do or avoid something. For example, if an employer writes a negligent letter of reference, the employee does not have to show that there was at least a 51% chance that he or she would otherwise have got the job – but merely that there was a reasonable chance of getting it.[164] Or, a bank which receives negligent advice from chartered accountants and loses the chance to sell land at a more favourable price, might be entitled to damages for loss of a chance – so long as the chance was substantial rather than speculative. For example, the bank would have to show that if it had received good advice, there was a substantial chance (i) that it would have relied on it and sold the land, and (ii) that, having done so, it would have received the more favourable price.[165] And, when the holder of a beauty contest gave one competitor no opportunity to attend the final selection process (the letter of invitation was sent too late), the woman won damages even though, statistically, she had only a one-in-four chance of winning one of the twelve 'prizes' (three year theatrical engagements).[166]

The issue seems to reduce to whether the courts regard the harm as consisting of the overall loss (ie the disability) or the loss of the chance.[167] Clearly, had the House of Lords applied in the *Hotson* case the balance of probabilities test to the loss of the chance – rather than to the overall disability – there would have been little problem in finding negligence (as, indeed, the lower courts did). This seems to be a difficult area of law. In any event, in the field of disability equipment, examples of 'lost chances' are not hard to find. For example, if therapists and nurses allow some people who have had a stroke to use a wheelchair on a hospital ward – and attempt no rehabilitation – the person might miss an irrevocable opportunity of regaining walking ability.

Types of harm: physical, psychiatric, property, financial

Harm or damage can comprise personal injury, physical or mental, damage to property, or purely financial loss.

The law of negligence has not been applied to these different types of harm in uniform manner. Negligence seems to be most developed in the sphere of physical injury and damage to property. And, if a person is physically injured and also suffers financial loss or medically recognised psychiatric harm, then that person's claim for all three different types of harm is likely to be recognised. However, if a person suffers psychiatric harm *only* or financial loss *only* – ie with no accompanying physical injury, then, traditionally, it has been more difficult to win damages.

It should be emphasised that the position, even in principle (let alone practice) is not entirely predictable, since the law of negligence continually evolves as the law courts refine and modify their approach.

Financial loss

In the case of financial loss only (known sometimes as *pure financial or economic loss*), the courts have been reluctant to impose liability. The much-quoted reason for this is that the courts have feared to impose liability 'in an indeterminate amount for an indeterminate time to an indeterminate class'.[168] As explained above, the courts have been more ready to award damages in respect of pure financial loss on account of negligent *statements* or *words* than of *acts* – but there is some evidence that this is now changing and that negligent acts, too, sometimes give rise to liability for financial loss.[169]

Psychiatric harm

If a person suffers psychiatric injury only, sometimes referred to as *nervous shock*, for example, by witnessing an accident, the courts show considerable reluctance in imposing liability. However, if the shock accompanies physical injury, or sometimes damage to property[170], then there is not this problem in principle. For instance, if a defective wheelchair causes a traffic accident and an onlooker suffers psychiatric injury only, the courts might be most reluctant to impose liability. On the other hand, if the same person is caught up in the accident and is physically injured, the reluctance (other things being equal) would disappear.

A major reason for this is that the courts appear to be afraid of opening the floodgates to a large number of claims. However, liability *is* imposed in some circumstances. This depends on the relationship of the claimant to the person involved in the accident, on the claimant's proximity in space and time to the accident, and on the way in which the mental harm was caused.[171] For instance, in one case a woman who saw her family members dead and severely injured in hospital shortly after a car accident, did win damages.[172] In another, a man who claimed damages for psychiatric illness arising from watching his son dying in hospital after a motor bike accident failed. Having assumed (for the purposes of the case) the alleged negligence of the hospital in failing to diagnose the damage to the son's left kidney to be true, the court found that because the process was a continuing one over time, and the son's death was expected when it came, there was no sudden 'shock'. There could therefore be no damages for nervous shock.[173]

In a third case, however, the parents of a child who died two days after birth because of negligence, claimed successfully for damages for psychiatric illness incurred during the chaos and pandemonium of the delivery in the hospital (in which the husband had helped at the request of the staff).[174] And in 1995, the House of Lords was prepared to award damages to a person in a car accident who suffered nervous shock but no physical injury. This was because the person had actually been in one of the cars involved in the accident – and so personal injury was *foreseeable*, even if it had not actually resulted.[175]

The psychiatric injury must be a recognised medical condition ('normal' mental suffering or grief does not count, unless physical injury occurs as well). Post-traumatic stress disorder is one such condition. The person who suffers the condition must be a person of reasonable fortitude and not unduly vulnerable to such an injury. For instance, in one case (*Bourhill v Young*) a bystander (a 'fishwife'), 8 months pregnant, witnessed an accident involving a tramcar and a motor cycle. The motor cyclist died and she suffered a miscarriage. The court discussed whether she had a peculiar susceptibility to nervous shock. It concluded that the motor cyclist could not have foreseen the injury which she suffered.[176]

Damage to property

In practice, damage to property is often covered by first party insurance and so might often not involve litigation unless the victim or his insurance company insists on legal action.[177]

A confusing distinction has to be made in the case of defective equipment. First, damage to the *equipment itself*, such as damage done to a wheelchair as a result of defective tyres is not regarded as property damage – but as financial loss. In this case, a person might succeed in suing under contract (assuming there was one), but not in negligence. This reflects the fact that the law of negligence covers defective products which *cause harm*, not products which are *merely defective*.[178]

Second, and in contrast, damage to *other property* is regarded as property damage; for example, the damage done to clothing in the accident caused by the wheelchair with the defective tyres. However, and confusingly, if the tyres had been replacements and thus not supplied with the original wheelchair, then a claim could be made for damage to the wheelchair as well as the clothing – because it now has become 'other property' in relation to the tyres.[179]

Home adaptations. Confusing and sometimes frustrating consequences can follow if, for example, a builder constructs, an architect designs, or a surveyor approves, a defective adaptation (eg a downstairs extension).

If the adaptation can be regarded as a distinct item in itself, rather than an integral part of the dwelling structure, then subsequent damage to the structure or other parts of the house could be claimed for. For instance, the courts have stated that if a central heating boiler exploded and caused damage to the house, it would have damaged other property.[180] Electrical wiring might be regarded as non-structural and as separate from the rest of the house which might be damaged in event of a fire. A steel frame supporting walls and floors could be integral if supplied by the same builder who built the rest of the house – but non-integral if supplied by a separate contractor.[181] Likewise if a vertical, home lift, installed as a home adaptation, malfunctioned and damaged a ceiling.

If a defect is discovered before it has caused either damage to other property or personal injury, a negligence action against a builder will not succeed – because no damage or loss has been caused. (A legal action in contract might succeed – but this could only be brought by the original owner who had made the contract with the builder.) Once the defect has been identified before harm has resulted, the courts view it as a defect of quality but not a dangerous defect – and therefore a matter of contract, not of negligence.[182] However, *if there is personal, physical injury* involved and the defect was not known about previously, then the distinction does not matter; a negligence claim can be made in respect of the injury and damage to other property.

The courts have softened this hard-line position by holding that if a person knows about the defect and then suffers injury, he or she can still claim, so long as he could not reasonably have removed the defect or avoided running the risk posed by it (as in the case of a council tenant who had little choice but to continue using the unlit and unrailed steps leading to the house).[183] And it is also possible that, in the future, the courts might change their approach to this problem and make builders liable for financial loss to subsequent purchasers – who currently stand to suffer substantial injustice.[184]

Lastly, builders, architects, surveyors and subcontractors are strictly liable under the Defective Premise Act 1972 for building work, including construction, enlargement and conversion – but only if a new dwelling is being provided and, when completed, it is not fit for habitation. Therefore, the Act would seem not to apply to adaptations to existing dwellings.[185]

4. TYPE OF DAMAGES AWARDED

The law courts calculate damages under a number of different headings, such as pain and suffering, loss of faculty (eg a limb) and amenity (eg consequent inability to play cricket), loss of earnings, damage to property – and so on. If serious injury has been sustained, equipment and adaptations may be required. Increasingly, occupational therapists are being asked to provide solicitors with assessments on what people's needs are going to be.[186] Such assessments might cover not only people's immediate and short-term, but also their longer term, needs. This means predicting not only how often equipment might need to be replaced, but also people's changing or even escalating needs as they grow older and their physical condition alters.

5. DEFENCES AGAINST ALLEGATIONS OF NEGLIGENCE

Liability for death or personal injury cannot be excluded

Under the Unfair Contract Terms Act 1977, anybody engaged in a course of business (including public authorities and government departments) cannot exclude liability in negligence for personal injury or death. Thus, no manufacturer, retailer, social services department or NHS Trust can exclude such liability for the negligent provision of equipment. For example, it would not be possible for a company which hires out wheelchairs to exclude liability for death or injury to a person caused by the company's negligence (eg not maintaining the brakes). Nor, for example, can the NHS or a social services department exclude such liability, since the Act applies to 'notices' as well as to contract terms – and thus applies even though statutory services do not make legally enforceable contracts with service users (see p.391). In addition, liability cannot be excluded under the Act for other damage (eg damage to property) unless it is *reasonable* to do so but cannot be excluded for defective consumer products anyway.[187]

The extent to which this legislation covers voluntary organisations seems to be unclear; the meaning of business in the context of voluntary organisations is discussed elsewhere (see p.358).[188]

Willingness of victim to run the risk of somebody else's negligence

In principle, there is a defence to negligence, if a person willingly runs the risk of another person's negligence.[189] In general, this defence is not well-established; however, it may have some application to this book.

The defence could perhaps be argued if, for example, an NHS therapist loans an indoor electric wheelchair, stating that it could be used out-of-doors, but warning of the dangers (such as instability on rough ground). Or, similarly, if she loans a wheelchair in poor repair, pointing out the possible dangers, but stating that it is 'better than nothing'. In both cases, the user of the equipment hears what is said and decides to use the wheelchair all the same. However, depending on the circumstances, such a defence might well fail, since acceptance of the risk might have to entail both awareness of the dangers involved and also some sort of agreement to waive any legal claims if an accident occurs.[190] In any case, an agreement which supposedly exempts a person from liability could fall foul of the Unfair Contract Terms Act 1977 (see above) – which does not allow anybody acting in the course of a business to exclude liability for personal injury or death caused by negligence.[191]

Concern about this legal principle might be one of the reasons why, in a case investigated by the local ombudsman, the local authority would not authorise installation of a stairlift for a person with motor neurone disease. Provision of the stairlift had been denied because it would have breached safety standards laid down in the authority's *Design Guide on Housing for People with Disabilities* – even though the person was prepared to sign a letter absolving the authority from the possible legal consequences of an accident. Still, the authority would not provide the lift.[192] On the other hand, in another ombudsman case, it became clear that the authority had provided a shower only on condition that the user sign an agreement absolving it from responsibility should he suffer a spasm in the chair and suffer injury.[193]

Contributing to one's own misfortune

Arguing contributory negligence is not really a complete defence, but a way of redistributing some of the blame.[194] For example, if a person uses an NHS-supplied walking frame even though he becomes immediately aware that it was broken, then the court might state that he was at least partially to blame – and reduce the damages awarded against the NHS Trust which had supplied the frame. Thus, a person who is given crutches but fails to ask the doctor how to use them properly, might be held 20% to blame for the subsequent injury suffered (*Brushett v Cowan*).[195]

Bringing a legal action in time

There are time limits for bringing negligence actions. If the action concerns personal injury or death, it must be brought within three years. This is either from the date of the accident – or from the date that the plaintiff first knows (i) that the injury was significant, (ii) that it was caused by negligence and (iii) the identity of the person allegedly responsible – or could reasonably have acquired this knowledge. The courts have the discretion to waive the time limits.[196]

If the action concerns damage to property, the action must be brought within six years of the date of the accident.[197] If the property damage is *latent* (ie concealed) and not discovered within the six years, then an action must be brought within three years of the time when the plaintiff first knows or ought to have known about the damage. In any event, the action cannot be brought more than 15 years after the alleged negligence.[198]

In some circumstances, personal injury cases can be brought a very long time after an accident has occurred – if knowledge of the requisite factors is not gained for many years. In addition, the limitation period does not begin to run for children, until they are 18 – or in the case of a mentally disabled person, until he or she has become mentally capable.[199] Thus, towards the end of 1995, 33 years after being severely brain-damaged at birth, a person won £1.25 million in compensation.[200]

Notes

1 The modern conception of a duty of care is normally traced to the case involving a ginger beer bottle containing a decomposed snail: *Donoghue v Stevenson* [1932] AC 562 (HL).

2 See eg *Caparo Industries PLC v Dickman and others* [1989] 1 All ER 798 (at 801 to 803) (HL): company auditor's duty to the shareholders.

3 *Walker v Northumberland County Council* [1995] 1 All ER 737 (QBD).

4 *White v Jones* [1995] 1 All ER 69 (HL).

5 *Spring v Guardian Assurance* [1994] 3 All ER 129 (HL).

6 *Swinney and Another v Chief Constable of Northumbria Police* (1996) (CA), Times, 28 March 1996.

7 Frost, B. (1995). Man who fell on icy step wins £100,000 payout. *The Times:* 24 February 1995.

8 *Skinner v Secretary of State for Transport* (1994) (QBD), Times, 3 January 1995: alleged negligence in failing to respond to a distress signal from a fishing vessel, which subsequently sank with four men, including the plaintiff's husband.

9 *Barrett v Ministry of Defence* (1994) (CA), Independent, 3 January 1995: joint 30th birthday party and promotion celebrations at a naval base in Norway involving very heavy drinking.

10 *Jones v Department of Employment* [1988] 2 WLR 493 (CA): the court stated that although such a government officer owed no duty of care in negligence, his decision could be challenged by way of the appeals procedure in the legislation or by means of judicial review.

11 *Ancell and Ancell v McDermott and Others* (1995) 159 LGRevR 389 (CA).

12 See eg *R v Bateman* (1925) 94 KB 791 (CA)

13 *R v Bateman* [1925] 94 KB 791: a case involving a panel doctor's appeal against a manslaughter conviction, in which Lord Hewart, CJ, made a general summary about the doctor's duty to a patient.

14 See eg *Clarke v Adams* (1950) SJ 599.

15 A Canadian case: *Brushett v Cowan* (1987) 40 DLR (4) 488

16 *Goodwill v British Pregnancy Advisory Service* (1996) 146 NLJ 173 (CA).

17 *See eg Bull v Devon Area Health Authority* [1993] 4 Med LR 117 (CA).

18 *Jones v Manchester Corporation* [1952] 2 QB 852 (CA): anaesthetic, pentothal, given by inexperienced doctor.

19 *Denton v South West Thames Regional Health Authority* (1980) (QBD): unreported, referred to in Jones, M. (1991). *Medical negligence.* Sweet & Maxwell, p.91.

20 See eg *Re HIV Haemophiliac Litigation* [1990] NLJ 1349 (CA): concerning contaminated blood supplies.

21 *Misell v Essex County Council* (1994) (QBD), Independent, 7 December 1994. The council had failed to take reasonable steps to ensure that a country road, persistently muddy, was safe – by, for example, putting up warning signs and requiring lorries to be washed before emerging from a quarry.

22 Victim of icy road wins £300, 000. *The Times:* 16 March 1995.

23 *X (minors) v Bedfordshire County Council* [1995] 3 All ER 355 (HL) (at 392).

24 For example, in September 1994, it was reported that over 70 compensation claims were in the process of being brought by children and young people who were alleging that they had been abused whilst they were in the care of local authorities: Strong, S. (1994). Claiming to care. *Community Care:* 8–14 September 1994, pp.14–15.

25 See: conclusions of following article, which provides a manageable summary of the latest House of Lords rulings in this field: Baker, C. (1995). Tort: when are local authorities liable. *Solicitors Journal:* 21 July 1995, pp.706–707.

26 See: *X (minors) v Bedfordshire County Council* [1995] 3 All ER 355 (HL).

27 *Maynard v West Midlands Regional Health Authority* [1985] 1 All ER 635 (HL).

28 *Bova v Spring* [1994] 5 Med LR 120 (QBD).

29 *X (minors) v Bedfordshire County Council* [1995] 3 All ER 355 (HL) at 368.

30 *Duff v Highland and Islands Fire Board* (1995), Times, 3 November 1995 (Outer House of the Court of Session, Scotland).

31 *Capital Counties plc and Another v Hampshire County Council* (1996), The Times, 26 April 1996.

32 *Church of Jesus Christ of Latter-Day Saints (Great Britain) v Yorkshire Fire and Civil Defence Authority* (1996), The Times, 9 May 1996 (QBD).

33 *X (Minors) v Bedfordshire County Council* [1995] 3 All ER 353 (HL) at 369–370.
34 *X (minors) v Bedfordshire County Council* [1995] 3 All ER 355 (HL).
35 *Vicar of Writtle and Others v Essex County Council* (1979) 77 LGR 656
36 *Wyatt v Hillingdon Borough Council* (1978) 76 LGR 727, CA
37 *X (minors) v Bedfordshire County Council* [1995] 3 All ER 355 (HL).
38 *X (minors) v Bedfordshire County Council* [1995] 3 All ER 355 (HL) (at 380).
39 *X (minors) v Bedfordshire County Council* [1995] 3 All ER 355 (HL).
40 *X (minors) v Bedfordshire County Council* [1995] 3 All ER 355 (HL) (at 380–382).
41 *X (minors) v Bedfordshire County Council* [1995] 3 All ER 355 (HL) (at 382–384).
42 *X (minors) v Bedfordshire County Council* [1995] 3 All ER 355 (HL) (at 395–396).
43 *X (minors) v Bedfordshire County Council* [1995] 3 All ER 355 (HL) (at 389–400).
44 *X (minors) v Bedfordshire County Council* [1995] 3 All ER 355 (HL) (at 396).
45 See discussion of the child care and education cases *(Newham, Bedfordshire, Dorset* etc) as dealt with in the Court of Appeal: Dugdale, T. (1994). Negligence liability and public service professionals. *Professional Negligence:* 1994;10(3), pp.82–85.
46 *T (a minor) v Surrey County Council and others* [1994] 4 All ER 577 (QBD).
47 *X (minors) v Bedfordshire County Council* [1995] 3 All ER 355 (HL) (at 368).
48 *Reffell v Surrey County Council* [1964] 1 All ER 743 (QBD).
49 *Morris v Carnarvon County Council* [1910] 1 KB 159 (KBD).
50 *Van Oppen v Clerk to the Bedford Charity Trustees* [1989] 3 All ER 389 (CA).
51 *Fowles v Bedfordshire County Council* [1996] ELR 51 (CA).
52 Aldersea, P. (1996). *National prosthetic and wheelchair services report 1993–1996.* London: College of Occupational Therapists, Part 2, p.22.
53 Bath tragedy parents compensated. *Care Weekly:* 1 December 1994, p.5.
54 Dyer, C. (1996). £225, 000 for 'tortured' women. *Guardian,* 3 April 1996.
55 One county council admitted that it had failed to meet the legal requirements to inspect private residential homes at least twice a year – homes, at which it was alleged serious abuse of mentally handicapped residents had taken place: Kelsey, T. (1994). Council broke the law over homes for handicapped. *Independent:* 21 September 1994.
56 See eg a case about sexual abuse concerning the placement of children by an education authority in an independent boarding school; although in this case, the authority had no powers of inspection: *P and Others v Harrow London Borough Council* [1993] 2 FCR 341 (QBD).
57 Social Services Inspectorate, Department of Health; Social Work Services Group, Scottish Office (1991). *Care management and assessment: practitioners' guide.* London: DH, p.83.
58 See eg NHS Management Consultancy Services (1988). *Study of the orthotic services.* London: Department of Health, p.16. Also: Bowker, P. *et al.* (1992). *A study of the organisation of the orthotic services in England and Wales.* Salford: Salford Health Authority Physiotherapy Service, University of Salford; Department of Orthopaedic Mechanics, North Western Orthotic Unit, p.88.
59 *Corder v Banks* (1960) Times, 9 April 1960 (QBD).
60 *Brushett v Cowan* (1988) 40 DLR (4) 488 (Newfoundland Supreme Court).
61 *Joyce v Merton, Sutton and Wandsworth Health Authority* [1996] 7 Med LR 1 (CA): however, the patient failed to win his case, because he could not prove that his problems would have been identified even if a proper procedure had been in place.
62 Social Services Inspectorate (Booth, L.; Strettle, T.). *Inspection of community services for physically disabled people in the London Borough of Wandsworth: 28 June – 12 July 1995.* London: Department of Health, p.35.
63 Aldersea, P. (1996). *National Prosthetic & Wheelchair Services Report 1993–1996.* London: College of Occupational Therapists, Part 2, pp.30–31.
64 *Donoghue v Stevenson* [1932] AC 562 (HL).
65 *Grant v Australian Knitting Mills* [1936] AC 85 (PC).
66 Car adaptation fears. *Disability Now,* February 1996, pp.1, 3.
67 Eg *Kubach v Holland* [1937] 3 All ER 970 (KBD).
68 *Godley v Perry* [1960] 1 All ER 36 (QBD).
69 *Evans v Triplex Glass* [1936] 1 All ER 283 (KBD): in which a manufacturer of a windscreen was not found liable when it shattered, because there could have been reasons for this other

than a manufacturing defect. One of these could have been that the windscren was strained when it was screwed into place by the Vauxhall Motor Co.

70 *Haseldine v Daw* [1941] 2 KB 343 (KBD): concerning the negligent repair of a lift in a block of flats; an engineer failed to replace a gland properly, which caused the gland to fracture, the lift to fall to the bottom of the well and injury to the plaintiff.

71 *Stennet v Hancock and Peters* [1939] 2 KBD 578 (KBD): negligent replacement of the flange of a wheel by motor repairer.

72 *Thomas v Winchester* 6 NY 397 (1852)

73 *Andrews v Hopkinson* [1957] 1 QB 229 (QBD): a longstanding defect in the drag-link of the steering should have been detected by a competent mechanic – and the secondhand motor dealer should have instigated the examination of a well-known 'danger spot' in old cars: the steering mechanism.

74 *Best v Wellcome Foundation & Others* [1994] 5 Med LR (Irish Supreme Court).

75 *Beard v London General Omnibus Company* [1900] 2 QB 530 (CA).

76 See eg *Racz v Home Office* [1994] 2 WLR 23 (HL).

77 MacErlean (1994). Legal firms sue for losses. *Independent on Sunday:* 18 September 1994. See also: Hilborne, N. (1996). Model clause to indemnify staff. *Law Society Gazette:* 21 February 1996; 97(7), p.64.

78 *Pinn v Rew* (1916) 32 TLR 451 (KBD).

79 See eg: *Padbury v Holliday & Greenwood Ltd* (1912) 28 TLR 492 (CA).

80 *Cassidy v Ministry of Health* [1951] 2 KB 343 (CA).

81 *Wilsons and Clyde Coal Co v English* [1938] AC 57 (HL).

82 *X (minors) v Bedfordshire County Council* [1995] 3 All ER 355 (HL).

83 The scheme was brought into force by: SI 1996/251. *National Health Service (Clinical Negligence Scheme) Regulations 1996.*

84 See: EL(96)11. NHS Executive. *Clinical negligence and personal injury litigation: claims handling.* Leeds: Department of Health, 1996. Also: FDL(95)56. *NHS Executive. Clinical negligence funding: new arrangements for claims incurred before 1 April 1995.* Leeds: Department of Health.

85 HC(89)34. Department of Health. *Claims of medical negligence against NHS hospital and community doctors and dentists.* London: DH, Annex A, para 5: but junior doctors involved in private care might still be acting under their NHS contract, and so might still be indemnified by the NHS.

86 *Cassidy v Ministry of Health* [1951] 2 KB 343 (CA). In which Lord Denning refers to *Hillyer v Governors of St Bartholomew's Hospital* [1909] 2 KB 820.

87 A parallel duty, to choose independent contractors carefully, was illustrated recently in a contract case, when a tour operator (the first defendant) was held to be in breach of its contractual duty to take care of a tourist's safety – when the second defendant (a tour guide) failed negligently to ensure that a speedboat driver (an employee of the third defendant) was reasonably competent and qualified. The tourist was killed; the first defendant was liable in contract: *Wong Mee Wan v Kwan Kin Travel Services Ltd* (1995) Solicitor's Journal, 8 December 1995; 139(47), p.245 (LB).

88 See eg: *Roe v Ministry of Health* [1954] 2 All ER 131 (CA).

89 *Yepremian v Scarborough General Hospital* (1980) 110 DLR (3d) (Ontario CA) (Canadian case in which hospital staff provided emergency services negligently failed to diagnose diabetes in a man who subsequently suffered a heart attack and brain damage.

90 Stone, J. (1996). Complements slip: when patients are referred to complementary therapists, who remains responsible for their care. *Health Service Journal:* 25 January 1996, pp.26–27.

91 *Barnett v Chelsea and Kensington Hospital Management Committee* [1969] 1 QB 428 (QBD). And see: Brazier, M. (1992). *Medicine, patients and the law.* London: Penguin, p.23.

92 *White v Jones* [1995] 1 All ER 69 (HL).

93 *Mahmood v Siggins* [1996] 7 Med LR 76 (QBD).

94 *T (a minor) v Surrey County Council and others* [1994] 4 All ER 577 (QBD).

95 *Hedley Byrne & Co Ltd v Heller & Partners Ltd* [1964] AC 465: involving reliance by one company on a careless statement made by a bank about the financial health of another company.

96 *White v Jones* [1995] 1 All ER 69 (HL).

97 *Caparo v Dickman* [1990] 2 AC 605 (HL). In which it was decided that the auditor of a public company owed a duty of care to individual shareholders (since it was reasonably foreseeable that they might rely on the auditor's report when dealing with the company's shares) – but not to potential investors or people who might be preparing takeover bids.

98 *Ministry of Housing and Local Government v Sharp* [1970] 2 QB 223 (CA).

99 *Shaddock v Parramatta City Council* (1981) 36 ALR 385 (High Court of Australia). Involving the purchase of property for redevelopment, after the local council had failed to inform the buyer of a road widening scheme.

100 *Tidman v Reading Borough Council* (1994), Times, 10 November 1994 (QBD).

101 *Tidman v Reading Borough Council* (1994), Times, 10 November 1994 (QBD).

102 Discussion of the Tidman case: Murphy, G.; Rutherford, L. (1995). Advising the advisers. *Solicitors Journal:* 10 February 1995, pp.112–113.

103 *Worster v City and Hackney Health Authority* (1987) (QBD), The Times, 22 June 1987.

104 *T (a minor) v Surrey County Council and others* [1994] 4 All ER 577 (QBD).

105 Cane, P. (1987). *Atiyah's accidents, compensation and the law.* 4th edition. London: Weidenfeld and Nicholson, p.417.

106 *Smith v Eric S Bush* [1990] 1 AC 831 (HL).

107 *Bolam v Friern Hospital Management Committee* [1957] 2 All ER 118 (QBD): a case about the giving of electro-convulsive therapy and the risk of fractures. The evidence suggested that the risk was one in ten thousand, and no warning was given to the patient. He suffered severe physical injuries including dislocation of the hip joints and fractures of the pelvis.

108 *Wells v Cooper* [1958] 2 QB 265 (CA).

109 A Canadian case: *Brushett v Cowan* (1987) 40 DLR (4) 488

110 *Muzio v North West Herts Health Authority* [1995] 6 Med LR 184 (QBD).

111 An Australian case: *Elli Andjelkovic v Capital Territory Health Commission 1987* (Supreme Court of the Australian Capital Territory Canberra, 25th August 1987) (reported on LEXIS).

112 *Devilez v Boots* (1962) 106 Sol J 552.

113 *Haseldine v Daw* [1941] 2 KB 343.

114 *Stennet v Hancock* [1939] 2 All ER 578 (KBD).

115 *Andrews v Hopkinson* [1957] 1 QB 229 (QBD).

116 *Thomas v Winchester* (1852) 6 NY 397.

117 *Haley v London Electricity Board* [1964] 3 All ER 185 (HL) (Lord Reid).

118 *Roe v Minister of Health* [1954] 2 QB 66 (CA).

119 The system of issuing hazard notices, safety notices and device bulletins – to the NHS, social services departments, voluntary bodies and private organisations is explained in: LASSL (95)7. Department of Health. *Notification by the Department of Health of hazard and safety information which may affect the personal social services.* London: DH, 1995.

120 *MDA SN 9513* June 1995. *Arjo hygiene chairs: risk of patient entrapment.* Medical Devices Agency Adverse Incident Centre. London: Department of Health.

121 *MDA SN 9507* May 1995. *Salford swivel walkers: regular inspection and maintenance.* Medical Devices Agency Adverse Incident Centre. London: Department of Health.

122 Tonks, A. (1996). Fatal outbreak traced to wooden tongue depressors. *British Medical Journal:* 11 May 1996; 312, p.1186.

123 National Consumer Council (1995). *Unsafe products: how to use the Consumer Protection works for consumers.* London: NCC, p.12.

124 Fleming, J. (1992). *The law of torts.* 4th edition. Sydney: Law Book Company, p.485.

125 See eg *Wyngrove's Curator v Scottish Omnibuses* [1966] SC 47 (HL): a case concerning the design and safety of the platforms of buses of which some 600 were in operation, each of which might carry 200,000 passengers a year. The financial consequences of finding the buses unsafe would have been great. (See: Weir, T. (1992). *A casebook on tort.* 7th edition. London: Sweet & Maxwell, p.142.

126 Victor, P. (1996). Dunlop in 'faulty tyres cover-up'. *Independent:* 5 March 1996.

127 Coiera, E. (1996). The Internet's challenge to health care provision: a free market in information will conflict with a controlled market in health care. *British Medical Journal:* 6 January 1996; 312, pp. 3–4.

128 *Bolam v Friern Hospital Management Committee* [1957] 2 All ER 118 (QBD). And see: See eg *Hughes v Waltham Forest Health Authority* [1991] 2 Med LR 155 (CA) (differing opinions of specialist surgeons: applying the House of Lords case: *Maynard v West Midlands Regional Health Authority* [1984] 1 WLR 634 (failure to diagnose tuberculosis)).
129 *Sidaway v Bethlem Royal Hospital Governors* [1985] 1 All ER 643: about the failure of the surgeon to give a warning of the small risk involved in an operation on cervical vertebrae of the patient.
130 Crewe, R. (1989). Wheelchairs by design: how Stoke Mandeville drew up a policy to improve its wheelchairs. *Nursing Standard:* 16 December 1989, pp.4–6.
131 SIB(95)18. Department of Health and Social Security; Scottish Home and Health Department; Welsh Office; Department of Health and Social Services (Northern Ireland). *Regular inspection and maintenance of wheelchairs.* London: DHSS. This guidance was reproduced in SAB(91)32. Department of Health; Scottish Home and Health Department; Welsh Office; Department of Health and Social Services (Northern Ireland). *Wheelchairs: inspection and maintenance.* London: DH.
132 *Clarke v Adams* (1950) 94 Solicitors Journal 599.
133 *McKay v Royal Inland Hospital* (1965) 48 DLR 2d 665 (British Colombia Supreme Court).
134 *Clark v MacLennan* [1983] 1 All ER 416 (QBD): about the timing of an operation to relieve stress incontinence in a woman who had just had a baby. See also: *Hunter v Hanley* [1955] SC 200 (Scottish case: Court of Session, Inner House). About injury suffered when a hypodermic needle broke: in which it was held that a deviation from approved practice did not itself constitute negligence: it would still have to be proved that no 'professional man of ordinary skill' would have done the same.
135 *Wilsher v Essex Area Health Authority* [1986] 3 All ER 801 (CA) (at 814).
136 See eg *Bolam v Friern Hospital Management Committee* [1957] 2 All ER 118.
137 *Sidaway v Bethlem Royal Hospital Governors* [1985] AC 871. However, in Canada, for instance, the courts have taken into account what the reasonable patient might expect to be told, see eg *Reibl v Hughes* [1980] 2 SCR 880.
138 See: *Whitehouse v Jordan* [1980] 1 All ER 650 (CA) and [1981] 1 All ER 267 (HL): involving brain damage to a child and trial by forceps, to see whether a forceps delivery rather than a Caesarean section would be possible.
139 See eg: Fleming, J.G. (1992). *The law of torts.* Sydney: Law Book Company, p.109.
140 *Wilsher v Essex Area Health Authority* [1986] 3 All ER 801 (CA) (at 812).
141 *McCormack v Redpath Brown and Co and Another,* Times, 24 March 1961 (QBD).
142 *Cassidy v Ministry of Health* [1951] 2 KB 343 (CA).
143 *Clarke v Worboys,* Current Law Year Book 1952, no.2443 (CA).
144 *Hall v Lees* [1904] 2 KB 602 (KBD).
145 Fleming, J.G. (1992). *Law of torts.* 8th edition. Sydney: Law Book Company, p.485.
146 See the discussion in *Wilsher v Essex Area Health Authority* [1986] 3 All ER 801 (CA). Also: *Jones v Manchester Corporation* [1952] 2 All ER 125 (CA): although one of the three judges dissented from the decision that the hospital board be vicariously liable for failing to ensure that the doctor received advice and instruction about the use of pentothal.
147 Audit Commission (1995). *Setting the records straight: a study of hospital medical records.* London: HMSO, p.16 (referring to figures produced by the St. Paul International Insurance Company).
148 *Ibid,* p.9 and generally.
149 HC(89)20. Department of Health. *Preservation, retention and destruction of records: responsibilitiess f health authorities under the Public Records Acts.*
150 *Barnett v Chelsea and Kensington Hospital Management Committee* [1969] [1968] 2 WLR 422
151 Health Service Commissioner (SW.28/84–85). *Care of an elderly patient. 1st report for session 1985–86. HC 27.* London: HMSO, 1985.
152 Health Service Commissioner (W.298/85–86). *Aspects of nursing care.* 1st report for session 1986–87. HC 111. London: HMSO, 1987.
153 Insurance Ombudsman (1995). *Insurance ombudsman: annual report and case review 1994.* London: Insurance Ombudsman Bureau, pp.35–36.
154 See eg *Bonnington Castings Ltd v Wardlaw* [1956] AC 613 (HL): a case about pneumoconiosis and silicon dust in which it was held that the defendant was liable because the dust materially

contributed to the disease – even though nobody knew how much (in percentage terms) it had contributed.

155 *Wilsher v Essex Area Health Authority* [1988] 1 All ER 871 (HL): a case concerning the possible causes of blindness in a premature baby and whether it had been caused by the excessive administration of oxygen.

156 *Yepremian v Scarborough General Hospital* (1980) 110 DLR (3d) 513 (Ontario CA)

157 See eg *Lambert and another v Lewis and others* [1981] 1 All ER (HL): concerning continued use of trailer coupling on a Landrover, even though the owner was aware of the defect.

158 *Re Polemis and Furness, Withy & Co* [1921] 3 KB 560 (CA).

159 *Hughes v Lord Advocate* [1963] 1 All ER 705 (HL).

160 *Smith v Leech Brain & Co Ltd* [1962] 2 QB 405 (QBD).

161 *Hotson v East Berkshire Area Health Authority* [1987] AC 750 (HL).

162 *LaFerriere v Lawson* [1994] 5 Med LR 185 (Supreme Court of Canada).

163 See: Foster, C. (1995). A plea for a lost chance: Hotson reconsidered. *New Law Journal:* 17 February 1995, pp.228–229 (Part 1); 24 February 1995, pp.228, 281 (Part 2).

164 *Spring v Guardian Assurance PLC* [1994] 3 All ER 129 (HL) (at 154).

165 *First Interstate Bank of California v Cohen Arnold & Co* (1995) (CA), 11 December 1995.

166 *Chaplin v Hicks* [1911] 2 KB 786 (CA).

167 For a summary of the law about lost chances, see: Wilkinson, H.W (1996). The loss of a 'chance' in conveyancing transactions. *New Law Journal:* 26 January 1996, pp.88–89. Noble, M (1996). A second chance. *New Law Journal:* 1 March 1996; 146(6733), pp.310–311.

168 A much cited quote of Cardozo CJ from a United States case: *Ultramares Corporation v Touche* (1931) 174 NE 441.

169 *White v Jones* [1995] 1 All ER 69 (HL): a solicitor, failing to make a will in time, caused loss to the intended beneficiaries and was held negligent.

170 Eg *Attia v British Gas PLC* [1988] QB 304 (CA): when a house burnt down through the negligence of the defendants.

171 Eg *Alcock v Chief Constable of South Yorkshire* [1992] 1 AC 310 (HL): in which the House of Lords rejected the claims of 10 people who had suffered psychiatric harm when witnessing the Hillsborough football ground disaster.

172 *McLoughlin v O'Brian* [1983] 1 AC 410 (HL).

173 *Sion v Hampstead Health Authority* [1994] 5 Med LR (CA).

174 *Tredget and Tredget v Bexley Health Authority* [1994] 5 Med LR (County Court).

175 *Page v Smith* (1995) (HL), The Times, 12 May 1995.

176 *Hay or Bourhill v Young* [1943] AC 92 (HL).

177 Rogers, W.V.H. (1994). *Winfield & Jolowicz on tort.* 14th edition. London: Sweet & Maxwell, pp.19–22.

178 *Murphy v Brentwood District Council* [1990] 2 All ER 908 (HL) (Lord Keith at 918).

179 This would is on the basis of the 'complex structure' theory, outlined in: *Murphy v Brentwood District Council* [1990] 2 All ER 908 (HL).

180 See eg *D & F Estates Ltd v Church Commissioners for England* [1988] 2 All ER 992 (HL); *Murphy v Brentwood District Council* [1990] 2 All ER 908 (HL).

181 *Murphy v Brentwood District Council* [1990] 2 All ER 908 (HL).

182 *Murphy v Brentwood District Council* [1990] 2 All ER 908 (HL) (Lord Bridge).

183 *Targett v Torfaen Borough Council* [1992] 3 All ER 27 (CA).

184 See eg: Martin, R. (1996). Defective premises: the empire strikes back. *Modern Law Review:* January 1996; 59(1), pp.116–124. And see: *Invercargill City Council v Hamlin,* The Times, 15 February 1996 (PC), in which the Privy Council found that a New Zealand local authority was liable in negligence for economic loss resulting from its negligence inspection of house foundations.

185 See eg: Justice (1996). *Protecting the householder against defective building work.* London: JUSTICE, pp.48–49. Liability only arises if work is not carried out in a professional or workmanlike manner, or comprises improper materials – and the consequence of this is that the dwelling is unfit for habitation. The duty is owed not just to the present owner but to anybody else who later has an interest in the property. The duty is owed under the Defective Premises Act 1972 and applies to defects – whether or not injury or damage has occurred. The drawback is that

there is an absolute time limit of six years from when the building was complete – whether or not the defect could have been discovered then. In addition, the Act does not apply if the owner of the dwelling has an alternative remedy under an approved scheme.

186 Hoare, R. (1995). Rehabilitation experts: what they do and where to find them. *Solicitors Journal:* 30 June 1995, pp.18–22 (Supplement).

187 *Unfair Contract Terms Act 1977,* s.2, and Consumer Protection Act 1987, s.7.

188 Jones, M.A. (1993). *Textbook on torts.* 4th edition. London: Blackstone Press, p.196.

189 Known as: *volenti non fit injuria.*

190 See eg *Nettleship v Weston* [1971] 2 QB 691 (CA): an inexperienced driver, known to be so by the plaintiff who was giving her driving lessons and was injured, could not plead that he knew he consented to the risk of being injured.

191 See generally: Rogers, W.V.H. (1994). *Winfield & Jolowicz on Tort.* 14th edition. London: Sweet & Maxwell, pp.728–736.

192 Commission for Local Administration in England (88/A/303). *Complaint against the London Borough of Islington.* London: CLAE, 1988.

193 Commission for Local Administration (93/C/2475). *Report on investigation against Leeds City Council.* York: CLAE, 1995, p.9.

194 *Law Reform (Contributory Negligence) Act 1945,* s.1.

195 *Brushett v Cowan et al.* (1987) 40 DLR 488 (Newfoundland Supreme Court) (Canadian case).

196 *Limitation Act 1980,* s.11

197 *Limitation Act 1980,* s.2.

198 *Limitation Act 1980,* ss.14A, 14B

199 *Limitation Act 1980,* s.28.

200 Laurance, J. (1995). Man handicapped as a baby 33 years ago wins £1.25 million. *The Times:* 15 November 1995.

CHAPTER 15

PRODUCT LIABILITY, SAFETY AND LEGISLATIVE REQUIREMENTS

COVERAGE

1. How European directives become United Kingdom law.
2. Product liability and the Consumer Protection Act 1987 (Part 1)
    - What makes equipment defective legally?
    - Who is liable for defective products?
    - Causing harm
    - Categories of damages which can be claimed
    - Defences to liability for allegedly defective products.
3. Consumer safety requirements and standards: new approach directives
    - European directives generally: aims, approach, implementation and the CE mark.
4. Medical Devices Regulations: duties, equipment covered, organisations affected
    - Duty to ensure that medical devices conform to essential requirements
    - What does it mean to place equipment on the market or put it into service?
    - Essential requirements for medical devices
    - CE mark: the mark of conformity
    - What is a medical device?
    - What happens if duties are breached?
    - Reporting problems with products.
5. Unsafe products: General Product Safety Regulations 1994
    - Duty not to place unsafe products on the market
    - What if other legislation already applies to particular types of product?
    - Duty to provide information
    - What happens if duties are breached?

6. Health and safety at work: lifting and handling people
   - Health and safety at work: general provisions affecting equipment use in relation to service users
   - Lifting and handling people in hospital and in their homes.

Key points

Product liability, medical devices, general product safety – and lifting and handling of loads. This chapter covers various legislation affecting consumer protection and safety, the technical specifications of products, and health and safety at work. The legislation affects manufacturers, suppliers, retailers, statutory services and voluntary organisations alike.

Because of its size, even a summary of this whole area of law is far beyond the scope of the book; instead, this chapter focuses on several aspects which are particularly relevant. These concern *product liability, medical devices, general product safety, and the manual handling and lifting of loads* (including people). A brief explanation of the relationship between European Community Directives and English legislation is provided at the beginning of the chapter – since all the legislation covered in this chapter stems from such Directives.

(1) The *Consumer Protection Act 1987* (Part 1) provides people with a route to compensation if defective products cause harm or damage.

(2) The *Medical Devices Regulations 1994* stipulate that if medical devices are placed on the market, they must conform to certain safety and performance requirements.

(3) As a fallback or catch-all, the *General Product Safety Regulations 1994* apply to products not already covered by other, specific legislation, and stipulate that unsafe products must not be placed on the market. Also, s.10 of the *Consumer Protection Act 1987* (Part 2), states that unsafe consumer products should not be supplied; however, this general safety requirement has been largely replaced by the General Product Safety Regulations, but will still apply in some limited circumstances.

(4) The *Manual of Handling of Loads Regulations 1992* place duties on employers in relation to the lifting and handling of people – with consequences for the use of lifting, handling and turning equipment, and for the training of staff. Breach of the Regulations can give rise to both civil and criminal liability. Also mentioned briefly are sections 3 and 7 of the *Health and Safety at Work Act 1974* under which employers have a duty not to put at risk the health and safety of non-employees (eg service users or consumers), and employees must take reasonable care for the health and safety of themselves and other people who might be affected by what they do.

Physical properties, performance, instructions, labelling etc. Important to note is that legislation applies to various aspects of the safety and performance of products – not just basic physical properties. For instance, the Consumer Protection Act refers to instructions, warnings, the 'get-up' of products and how they are marketed, marks – and ultimately defines defective products in terms of people's expectations. The General Product Safety Regulations refer to packaging, instructions (for use, assembly, and maintenance), labelling and information. And the Medical Devices Regulations refer to, for example, information, labelling and instructions.

Summary of potential liabilities *Manufacturers* (including statutory services and voluntary organisations) of equipment might, depending on particular product type and other circumstances, incur criminal liability under the Medical Devices Regulations for placing on the market, products which do not meet essential requirements or are without a CE mark. Civil liability might also arise. They might incur criminal liability under the General Product Safety Regulations for placing unsafe products on the market. And manufacturers might incur civil liability under Part 1 of the Consumer Protection Act 1987 for supplying defective products that cause harm or damage.

Suppliers of equipment (including statutory services and voluntary organisations) might 'become manufacturers' for the purpose of liability under legislation if, for example, they adapt equipment, or otherwise interfere with it, so as to affect its safety qualities.

Suppliers (as 'suppliers') might incur criminal liability under the General Product Safety Regulations by knowingly supplying dangerous products. If these Regulations do not apply, suppliers might instead be criminally liable under s.10 of the Consumer Protection Act 1987. Suppliers (again in their capacity as 'suppliers') might incur civil liability under Part 1 of the Consumer Protection Act if they cannot identify, when asked, the original producer (ie manufacturer, 'own-brander' or importer) from whom they originally obtained the defective product. And employers who make available dangerous equipment (eg wheelchairs used by hospital patients) might incur criminal liability under their duties towards non-employees under s.3 of the Health and Safety at Work Act 1974.

Finally, alternatively or in addition, *manufacturers and suppliers* might simply incur civil liability under the common law of negligence if they supply unsafe products (see Chapter 14).

General characteristics and implications of the legislation covered. The legislation dealt with in this chapter is in some respects quite specific. It puts in place reasonably detailed frameworks for regulating products in terms of health, safety and performance. It imposes apparently firm and straightforward duties, and so contrasts with the vagueness of some of the welfare legislation dealt with in Part II of this book. However, the legislation stops short of excessive detail. For example, rather than prescribe impossibly detailed statutory standards for products, the Directives set out a number of broad 'essential requirements' which products must meet – leaving detailed technical specification to be set out in European 'harmonised' standards, which do not in themselves carry the force of law.

There are perhaps less helpful aspects. For instance, doubt remains about whether some of the UK legislation (eg the Consumer Protection Act 1987) correctly interprets the original EC Directives on which it is based. In addition, not only is the meaning of some of the terms in the legislation unclear (eg 'medical device')', but the process of interpretation can be made more difficult because it requires scrutiny of both the UK legislation and the European directives – as well as of guidance produced by the European Commission and UK government departments respectively. It should be emphasised that some of the explanation in this chapter, particularly of the Medical Devices Regulations 1994 and the General Product Safety Regulations 1994, is to some extent speculative. Both contain language which is not necessarily easily understood; and it is notable that guidance from the Department of Trade and Industry stresses in bold print that it is guidance only, that it has no legal force, and that 'in case of doubt legal advice should be sought on questions of interpretation'.[1]

The various duties imposed by this legislation are generally qualified so as to avoid imposing absolutely strict liability. For example, safe products are defined under the Consumer Protection Act 1987 (Part 1) in terms of people's expectations – and in terms of 'minimum risk' (rather than 'no' risk) under the General Product Safety Regulations. Employers have a duty under the Manual Handling of Loads Regulations to minimise lifting and handling by their staff which might cause injury – but only to a reasonably practicable extent. And people who place medical devices on the market in contravention of the Medical Devices Regulations have a defence that they employed 'due diligence'. It is easy to criticise such defences and qualifications on the grounds that they give too many escape routes for manufacturers and employers. However, looked at on the basis of fault, it is easy to sympathise with manufacturers and others, since otherwise they stand to be made strictly liable even if they have been careful. The consumer point of view is that liability should nevertheless be strict, since manufacturers and employers can better bear the cost (eg through insurance) of unsafe products than consumers. And, the consumer argues, the extra cost of the insurance or of conformity to legislation is anyway reflected in prices, and therefore passed on to consumers.

Questions people ask

- What is a medical device under the Medical Devices Regulations – does it cover 'social care' daily living equipment as well as healthcare products?
- What is a CE mark – is it a guarantee of safety?
- What is the definition of a defective product under the Consumer Protection Act?
- What is an unsafe product under the General Product Safety Regulations?
- How long do suppliers of equipment have to keep records to avoid potential liability under the Consumer Protection Act?
- When do suppliers, including statutory services and voluntary organisations, become liable for defective and unsafe products?

1. HOW EUROPEAN DIRECTIVES BECOME UNITED KINGDOM LAW

Most of the legislation referred to in this chapter stems from European Community directives published in the *Official Journal of the European Communities*. Implementation dates are included. By those dates, each country must make and bring into force its own legislation which reflects what the Directives say. For instance, the United Kingdom has enacted the Consumer Protection Act 1987, the Medical Devices Regulations 1994, the General Product Safety Regulations 1994, and the Lifting and Manual Handling of Loads Regulations 1992.

This legislation creates various tensions. The government seems keen to reduce regulation in order to minimise the burdens on business; yet, the directives represent even more regulation and entail extra costs associated with compliance.[2] However, in the long term, the overall purpose of these European Directives is to break down trade barriers within Europe, caused by diverse legislation. Thus, on a Europe-wide scale, these Directives would seem to be about fewer, rather than more, barriers to business. Furthermore, for example, compliance with the lifting and handling legislation might cost money in terms of providing training and equipment (such as hoists) – but will surely save money in reducing back injuries to staff.[3] Even so, the costs of compliance generally might place a significant burden on some companies. For example, depending on the type of medical device which a company produces, the quality systems required (eg ISO 9000) to ensure compliance with the Medical Devices Regulations will vary.[4]

If directives are implemented late or incorrectly, there are various possibilities:

(i) **Late implementation of directives.** If a directive is implemented late by a Member State (eg the United Kingdom), then it might be possible for a person to take direct legal action against a public body (deemed to be an 'emanation' of the State: eg a health authority by relying on the original directive. However, if a *private body* (eg a private employer) is involved, this is not possible[5] – but the person might instead be able to bring a case against central government for failing to implement the directive.

For example, if the UK government had not implemented the Manual Handling of Loads Directive in time, then a nurse working in the NHS who had been forced to lift heavy loads and injured her back – might have been able to bring an action against the health authority or NHS Trust (a public body) that employed her. Alternatively, had she been working in a privately-run hospital, she might have been able to bring an action against central government for non-implementation. In the event, the Directive was implemented on time: 1st January 1993.

(ii) **Incorrect implementation of directives.** Similarly, if a directive *is* implemented – but is not implemented *properly* – then it might be possible to pursue a legal action on the basis of what the directive, as well as the United Kingdom's implementing legislation, says. Faced with discrepancies in wording between the two, the UK courts are sometimes prepared to strain the meaning of UK legislation, or even read in extra words, so that it conforms to the meaning of the EC directive it is supposed to reflect.[6] For example, there is a view that both the Manual Handling of Loads Regulations 1992 and the Consumer Protection Act 1987 do not mirror their parent directives. And, at an extreme, the courts are prepared simply to overrule altogether UK legislation which is clearly in conflict with European Union legislation.[7]

(iii) **Compensation in damages.** An award of compensatory damages to individuals against central government for failure to implement a directive will, at the least, be limited to those circumstances in which a directive confers clear rights on individuals in relation to their health, safety or economic welfare – and in which the breach is a serious one and is the direct cause of damage to the injured party. An example in early 1996 confirmed that damages were payable; it involved the United Kingdom and Spanish fishermen – whose livelihood had been affected in the 1980s by discriminating provisions in the Merchant Shipping Act 1988, which were contrary to (and, in effect, non-implementation of) European legislation.[8] Damages might also be available to individuals who sue central government for incorrect implementation of a directive along the same lines as for non-implementation.[9]

(iv) **Actions by the European Commission.** In addition, the European Commission itself sometimes pursues legal actions against Member States. For example, it has commenced an action against the United Kingdom in relation to the Consumer Protection Act – which, it is claimed, does not reflect adequately the original Directive's 'development defence risks' defence afforded to the manufacturers of products.

2. PRODUCT LIABILITY AND THE CONSUMER PROTECTION ACT 1987 (PART I)

The Consumer Protection Act 1987 (Part 1) creates 'strict liability' for defective products, including equipment. A product is defective if its safety is not what people are generally entitled to expect. In deciding about such expectations, all circumstances should be taken into account (eg not just the physical properties of a product) – including instructions, warnings, markings, 'get-up' etc.

If defective equipment is supplied and harm or damage results from the defect, then the manufacturer is, in principle at least, strictly liable. For consumers, this is a distinct advantage because carelessness on the part of the manufacturer does not have to be proved – whereas it does in negligence. Fortunately, from the point of view of manufacturers, there are a number of defences which have the effect of making liability less than strict. In addition, there will be circumstances in which the Act will not apply in any case. For instance, a claim might involve equipment supplied before the Act came into force (1st March 1988). Nor will the Act apply if an action is brought outside of the overall time limit (ie 10 years from when the equipment was supplied).

Suppliers, too, are liable under the Act if they cannot identify the original producer of the product when asked to (hence the need for good record-keeping). In addition, suppliers who substantially adapt a product so as to affect its safety properties might become a manufacturer for the purposes of the Act – in effect they have manufactured a new product.

A recent report by the National Consumer Council confirms that nobody seems to know quite how the Act is working out in practice. There appear to be very few reported court judgements dealing either with Part 1 of the Consumer Protection Act 1987 in the United Kingdom, or with equivalent legislation in other European Community countries.[10] (The Act implements a European Directive[11]; thus there is equivalent legislation in other member states of the Community). The identified total up to 1994 was three – involving a mountain bike in Italy, and candles and paint in Germany.[12] The fact that liability is strict and that carelessness does not have to be proved could mean that defendants – or their insurance companies – will in practice settle claims quickly out of court. For example, one case involving a thumb injury and a sharp locker in a sports club was settled in six months. But another, concerning surgical scissors which broke during an operation because of inadequate heat treatment, still took three years.[13]

What makes equipment defective legally?

The Consumer Protection Act 1987 (Part 1) defines a defective product in some detail. The scope of the Act is very broad since it covers many products and many types of damage. At the same time, certain types of damage are excluded, and some doubts remain about the practical application of the definition, essentially circular, of a defective product.

Recognising a defective product ought to be simple – when, for example, a new wheelchair falls to pieces, a stair lift doesn't work, the jaws of a helping hand stick do not close, or a hair drier catches fire. However, the position is not always so straightforward, since the defectiveness might depend not on the hardware itself, but how it is meant to be used and what instructions are supplied with it. For instance, a spring-loaded riser chair, the tension of which has to be set according to the weight of the sitter, might be deemed defective if it comes with no instructions or warnings – even though the chair itself is in perfect condition. In addition, the Act resorts to defining defective products ultimately in terms of what consumers expect.

(i) **Component parts: eg the backrest of a wheelchair.** The definition supplied by the Act of what constitutes a product is broad, covering all manner of product and including component parts. The definition extends to goods and electricity but does not cover land or buildings.[14] For example, the footrest of a wheelchair is covered.

(ii) **Damage.** The Act states that liability only arises if damage is caused wholly or partly by a defective product.[15] The meaning of *damage* includes death, personal injury or damage or loss to property. In turn, personal injury includes 'disease and any other impairment of a person's physical or mental condition' – also a wide definition.[16] Any damaged property must normally be for private, domestic use – so that damage to business premises would not be covered; and the claimant must have intended the damaged property 'mainly for his own private use, occupation or consumption'.[17]

(iii) **Damage to the product itself.** The Act states that damage to property does not include damage to the product itself or to the larger product of which the defective product is a part.[18]

For example, if the defective tyre of an electric wheelchair bursts, no claim can be made either for the tyre or for damage done to the wheelchair in the resulting accident. However, confusingly, if the tyre was a replacement, or supplied separately from the rest of the wheelchair, then damage to the wheelchair (but still not to the tyre) could be claimed under the Act.[19] (In the law of contract, this difficulty does not exist and damages can be claimed for a defective product itself: see chapter 16).

(iv) **Reasonable expectations of safety and use, information, instructions etc.** The Act states that a product is only defective if its safety 'is not such as persons generally are entitled to expect'. What people expect hinges on 'all the circumstances' including: how a product has been marketed, the purposes for which it has been marketed, its 'get-up', the use of any mark in relation to the product, instructions and warnings. Also to be taken into account is what 'might reasonably be expected to be done with or in relation to the product' – as well as the time the product was supplied.[20]

For example, a successful claim has been made under the Act on the basis of inadequate instructions for a self-assembly clothes-dryer.[21] But an indoor electric wheelchair, sold with clear instructions and with warnings against its use out-of-doors, might not be regarded as defective if the user drives it down the High Street, tips out and is hurt. However, if no indication had been given that the wheelchair was for indoor use only, then it might be regarded as defective under the Act.

Although grounded ultimately in people's expectations, the test of defectiveness *appears* to be reasonably objective because it is about the expectations of people generally, not of the particular person making the claim or of the producer denying it.[22] However, although reasonable expectations might be easy to identify in some cases, in others they will not be.[23] Furthermore, the test has been criticised on the grounds that it is circular. What is a safe product? What people expect. What do people expect? A safe product. It has been argued that to use consumer expectations as a test of safety is anyway unsatisfactory, since people's expectations can be affected by the particular type of transaction. On this view, the test would better refer to a general, objective and reasonable view of a product's safety, irrespective of 'expectations' stemming from the particular contractual situations in which consumers find themselves.[24] For instance, the lower price of an item might affect expectations – and so, under the Act as it stands, a poor quality product would not automatically be considered defective.[25]

(v) **Comparing other products.** The Act states that no assumption will be made that just because other products of the same type, but supplied at a later date, were safer, the product in question was unsafe.[26] For example, just because one hoist sling which was involved in an accident was not as safe as one marketed 12 months later, does not mean that the former will held by a court to be defective.

Claims under the Act have been brought in the United Kingdom in relation to a wide range of products, including heart pacemakers, lap seat belts, faulty studs on football boots, surgical scissors, supermarket trolleys, a folding aluminum ladder and many kitchen appliances.[27]

Just because a product causes an injury, it does not follow *automatically* that it will be held to be defective under the Act. Thus, if a walking frame collapsed, the court might still wish to hear evidence which pointed to a defective aspect of the frame – such as poor welding. For instance, in an Italian case (brought under legislation equivalent to the Consumer Protection Act 1987), the court did not decide that a bicycle was defective just because its frame collapsed, but on the basis of a technical report which showed faulty welding.[28] Against this approach, is the view that if a new kitchen appliance bursts into flame, it must be defective – further evidence is surely unnecessary; no consumer expects this to happen.[29] However, a Dutch case illustrates some of the complication[30]:

> Involving the rules established by the EC directive on product liability, it concerned a person who sustained serious injuries when opening a Pepsi-Cola bottle. In the first court, the person was unable to prove that it was a Pepsi-Cola bottle which caused the injury. On appeal, the court accepted that it was a Pepsi-Cola bottle which had caused the injury, but found that the plaintiff could not prove that there was a defect. On further appeal, the Supreme Court disagreed with the Court of Appeal, holding that it had wrongly not accepted the consumer's offer to furnish evidence; had the consumer been able to produce the evidence, he would have established that the bottle was defective and that he had been opening it in the normal manner. The Supreme Court also stated that the manufacturer could have rebutted the claim either by showing that the bottle was not defective when it was put into circulation, or that the defect was apparent or capable of being discovered before the bottle was opened.

Who is liable for defective products?

Producers and manufacturers

The Act specifies that the following are liable for supplying defective products[31]:

- 'the producer of the product' (ie the manufacturer)
- 'any person who, by putting his name on the product or using a trade mark or other distinguishing mark in relation to the product, has held himself out to be the producer of the product' (ie an own-brander)
- 'any person who has imported the product into a member State from a place outside the member States in order, in the course of any business of his, to supply to it another' (ie an importer).

For example statutory services and voluntary organisations could clearly be producers when they manufacture products; whilst a supplier could be an own-brander when it places its own trademark on equipment manufactured by somebody else. And an English company which imported wheelchairs from the Far East, and then supplied them to a French company, would be liable as importer (the French company would not be).

Suppliers

Failure of a supplier to identify original producer of a defective product. The Act imposes liability on *suppliers* (as opposed to producers: see above) if they are unable to identify, when asked and within a reasonable time, the original producer of a defective product.[32] For instance, if a physiotherapist loans a defective walking frame which causes an accident, the injured person can ask for the identity of the manufacturer of the frame. If the physiotherapist cannot supply it (eg perhaps because of an absence of records), then she, or her employer, could be liable. On this basis, liability could attach to statutory bodies (eg local authorities), private bodies (commercial firms), self-employed practitioners and voluntary bodies – whether selling, hiring out or loaning equipment.

The liability of suppliers in this respect is strict – much stricter in fact than in ordinary negligence – where carelessness would have to be proved. It is therefore imperative that suppliers keep good records. Generally, this will be financially worthwhile (balanced against the costs of liability), although sometimes it might be expensive, or even too expensive. In addition, it might not always be possible to keep records; for example, charity shops selling second-hand goods face insuperable difficulty.[33] And record-keeping does not enter the picture in the case of the unmonitored but widely acknowledged 'migration' of wheelchairs or walking frames from one statutory service to another and thence to a voluntary organisation.

There are many practices and procedures which staff in statutory services can follow to avoid liability as supplier – whether under the Consumer Protection Act, or in ordinary negligence. For instance, physiotherapists might check crutches for wear or stress – and discard, rather than mend them. Walking aids might be clearly marked with the name of the manufacturer, the name of the hospital department and the date of purchase. It might not be practicable to keep records of individual walking aid ferrules (ie the rubber tips), but batch records could be kept instead. Similarly, rather than tamper with artificial limbs, therapists might refer patients back to the limb centre.[34]

Liability of suppliers who affect the safety of products. Any supplier who repairs, reconditions, adapts, refurbishes etc a product – to the extent that he affects the original design and safety specifications – is likely to be held to be the producer of a product for the purposes of the Consumer Protection Act. In effect, a new product has been created. However, the Act does not deal with this point explicitly – so that to some extent this is conjecture, although it is the view expressed by, for example, the Department of Health.[35] What is not conjecture, because the Act says as much, is that the original manufacturer will cease to be liable if somebody else affects the safety of a product – since the manufacturer is only responsible for a defective product if it was defective when he supplied it (eg to the retailer).[36] For example, amidst general concern that adaptations to cars for disabled people are not always safe, a car manufacturer has expressed disquiet about a particular adaptation to one of its models. It involves the removal of the upright strut between the front and rear doors. This strut gives the car some crumple-resistance in collisions – and Peugeot has not approved or sanctioned such adaptations.[37] Clearly, faced with a claim involving this aspect of the car, the manufacturer would seek to deny liability.

This aspect of liability is of particular concern to those working in the disability field (eg rehabilitation engineers, therapists) who adapt various items of equipment to suit individual disabled people's needs. However, the point at which a court might rule that a new product has come into being could be difficult to predict. A minor alteration might suffice; for example, the cutting or bending of an orthopaedic insert for an individual patient or the bending of a needle prior to use – especially if this is not in accordance with the manufacturer's instructions.[38] In this respect, the General Product Safety Regulations are more explicit and state that professionals in the supply chain who 'affect the safety properties of a product' become the producer for the purposes of the Regulations (see: p.375). If this type of approach were to be adopted by the courts in respect of the Consumer Protection Act, then suppliers might be liable as 'producers' not only if they adapt, recondition or repair equipment – but also if they affect its safety (eg by carelessly storing walking frames, by continuing to loan worn equipment, or by removing crucial instructions and warnings). On the other hand, if in such circumstances suppliers are not regarded legally as having become producers, then advantage could not be taken of the Act.[39] Instead, consumers might still be able to bring legal actions in contract or in ordinary negligence.

Defective products must be supplied by people engaged in the course of business

Products must be supplied in the *course of business* for liability to arise under the Act.[40] Thus, if in a private capacity, a person lends a defective bath lift to a friend or acquaintance, the Act could not apply. On the other hand, business is defined to include a trade or profession, the activities of trade or professional associations, and the activities of local or other public authorities.[41] This would seem to embrace statutory services – both as producers when they manufacture or adapt equipment, or as suppliers when they loan equipment which somebody else has manufactured.

However, the definition of 'business' does not specifically mention voluntary bodies and there is some uncertainty how far the Act applies to their various activities. It is generally thought that liability would not apply to cakes sold at a garden party and sale held by a charity, or to homemade toys sold at the occasional church bazaar.[42] However, at the other extreme, the Act might apply with full rigour to a voluntary organisation which sells disability equipment regularly and formally, whether by mail order or through a shop. The line between liability and non-liability is probably vague, and how UK courts would deal with difficult cases is uncertain.[43] Guidance issued by the Department of

Trade and Industry suggests that a voluntary organisation which exists *solely* to provide equipment (or other services) free of charge to people in need will escape the reach of the Act. However, if it provides equipment free of charge, but is engaged also in other commercial activities, then the Act will apply even to the free equipment provision.[44]

There is also a defence against liability if the product was supplied by a manufacturer, own-brander or importer but this was not in the course of business and there was no view to a profit.[45]

What does it mean to supply equipment?

A producer is not liable if he did not actually supply the product in question – but the definition of supply is wide. It includes selling, hire, loan and making a gift.[46] Should there be any doubt, the original wording of the Directive might indicate an even wider meaning: 'put into circulation'.[47] Thus, it has been suggested that because, in English law, the word 'supply' requires a transfer of ownership or temporary possession, it might not cover some situations, such as the use of supermarket trolleys or of transit wheelchairs in a hospital. But the broader wording of the Directive probably would cover such transactions.

It has been suggested also that the breadth of the term, 'put into circulation', removes doubt about whether what is being supplied is predominantly a product or a service. This is a significant distinction because it is only to the former that the Act applies. On this view, even if the product is not a predominant part of a transaction, the Act might still apply. For example, the transit wheelchair used to take a person from the ward to a rehabilitation room or to the operating theatre is only a small, incidental part of a service – ie hospital treatment – but it could still be a defective product which has been put into circulation.[48]

(Nevertheless, more recently, another European Community directive and its associated UK regulations have defined a similar term, 'putting into service' rather more narrowly. It is defined as making a product 'ready for use on the Community market for the first time for its intended purpose'.[49] This definition would not embrace, for example, the repeated loan of an item).

Causing harm. Just as causation has to be proved in contract and negligence cases, so too does it have to be under the Consumer Protection Act. If it cannot be shown that the product was defective and that it caused the damage, then there will be no liability. The Act is probably strongest when the defect is alleged to stem from the manufacturing process, since it is difficult for a manufacturer to argue that a product is not defective, when it does not conform with the manufacturer's own design.[50] However, even then causation needs to be shown – ie that it was the defective product that caused the accident.

For example, an insurance company might quickly settle a claim about an exploding hair dryer on the basis that it is almost, by definition, defective and likely to cause an accident.[51] It might be less likely to concede liability if the dispute revolves around, for example, the adequacy of the instructions for the maintenance of an electric wheelchair.

Categories of damages which can be claimed

The *categories of damages* which can be claimed are the same as in ordinary negligence cases (see p.338) and include, for example, pain and suffering, loss of amenity, loss of earnings, medical expenses etc.

Defences to liability for allegedly defective products

In principle, the liability of producers is strict if defective products are supplied.[52] Carelessness does not have to be shown – it is enough if the product is defective for whatever reason. However, the Consumer Protection Act lists explicitly a number of defences which mean that liability is in fact less than strict. Indeed, to some extent these reintroduce the principles used to assess liability in ordinary negligence – such as the state of knowledge at the time a product is supplied (see p.326).

(i) **Compliance with legal obligations.** If the defect was present because the producer had conformed with other legal obligations (for example, a safety requirement stemming from a European directive), then the producer will escape liability under the Act.[53]

(ii) **Supplying products in the course of business.** A person will not be liable under the Act either if he or she simply did not actually supply the product, or if it was not supplied in the course of business (see above).[54]

(iii) **Defect present when originally supplied.** If the defect was introduced after the product was supplied by the producer, then the producer will not be liable under the Act.[55]

For example, if a supplier, such as a hospital bio-engineering department, adapts a high seat chair and introduces a defect, then the producer will not be liable for any harm occurring as a result of the defect. Similarly, if a social services department has stored its small stock of walking frames so badly that they have been weakened.

(iv) **Knowledge when the product was supplied.** Liability might not be established under the Act if, when the product was supplied, the general state of scientific or technical knowledge was such that a (not the) producer of that type of product could not have been expected to discover the defect.[56]

This sort of defence might be an effective defence if it is alleged that the *design* of the product was defective – or that the manufacturing defect could not reasonably have been avoided or detected. Such a test is similar to that applied in ordinary negligence cases. It is sometimes known as the *development risks defence* and is intended to protect manufacturers from liability for products, whose defectiveness could only reasonably be known in hindsight but not at the time they were designed and manufactured. It has been pointed out many times that this test lets manufacturers 'off the hook' too easily. It means that they can say 'not that they could not have discovered the defect, but that they could not have been expected to take the steps necessary to discover the defect'. The argument continues that, since they can insure against liability (and pass the insurance costs on to consumers), manufacturers should be made strictly liable – rather than leaving consumers to bear the loss.[57] On the other hand, regarded from a fault-based or moral point of view, manufacturers might understandably bridle at the imposition of such strict liability – which could be imposed no matter how careful they had been.

There has long been a view that the United Kingdom has not properly implemented the EC Directive in this respect, in so far as the development risks defence in the Consumer Protection Act is wider than that stated in the Directive.[58]

(v) **Defects of component parts.** If a producer provides an allegedly defective component part, he will not be liable under the Act, if the following can be shown. The relevant defect must be a defect in the whole product and have been caused either by the *defective design of the whole product* – or by the *instructions given* by the producer of the whole product to the producer of the component.[59]

For example, the producer of a supposedly defective wheelchair footplate would not be liable if the defective function was due to the overall wheelchair design or the instructions it had received from the wheelchair manufacturer about how to make the footplate.

(vi) **Excluding liability.** Liability under the Act cannot be excluded by any term in a contract or in any other way.[60]

(vii) **Bringing an action in time.** Under the Act, an action must be brought within three years of when the damage (ie personal injury or damage to property) occurred or of when the person first became aware of (or should reasonably have become aware of) the damage (and that it was caused by the defect) and of the identity of the person to be sued. However, overall, actions can only be brought up to ten years after a producer or supplier has supplied a product.[61]

Thus, the importance of good record-keeping by both producers and suppliers is again demonstrated; it could provide a complete defence to any actions by showing that the product in question had been supplied over 10 years ago.[62] In fact, Department of Health guidance recommends that records be kept for at least 11 years, to cover the extra time allowed for the serving of a writ.[63]

The Consumer Protection Act came into force on 1st March 1988, and so cannot apply to products supplied before that date.[64]

(viii) **Amount of damages.** A court cannot award damages under the Consumer Protection Act 1987 unless they exceed £275.[65]

3. CONSUMER SAFETY REQUIREMENTS AND STANDARDS: NEW APPROACH DIRECTIVES

In addition to Part 1 of the Consumer Protection Act, which imposes civil liability for defective products, various other pieces of legislation place various duties on manufacturers and suppliers of equipment in respect of the safety and performance of products.

European directives generally: aims, approach, implementation and the CE mark

A number of European Community directives affecting the safety and performance aspects of products have either become, or are in the process of becoming, United Kingdom law.

Some of the directives are expressed to concern safety only; others take account of other aspects. For example, the Medical Devices Directive refers to *safety, protection of health and performance*[66]; whereas the Safety of Toys Directive refers to *safety characteristics* only.[67] In addition to Directives such as these which are aimed at specific types of product, the General Product Safety Directive is a catch-all. It is aimed generally at the safety aspects of products not already covered by other, more specific directives, such as, for example, those covering medical devices, toys, low voltage equipment[68], and lifts (forthcoming).

Nevertheless, it needs to be borne in mind that the *overall, primary* purpose of the European directives is not safety. Instead, the preamble of directives generally explains that if product safety and performance is governed from country to country by different legislation and administrative rules, then disparities arise which can impede trade, create unequal competition, and deny consumers a common market. Indeed, the first sentence of the Medical Devices Directive refers to article 100a of the Treaty of Rome (1957: establishing the European Economic Community), which concerns harmonisation of the internal European market.[69]

In some respects, it is therefore misleading to regard this legislation in terms solely of consumer safety, even though the derivative English regulations might be classed under the general heading of 'consumer protection'. In this respect, there is a potential for conflict between legislation which protects consumers and that which facilitates trade.[70] For example, the creation of harmonised European standards – not in themselves legal requirements, but compliance with which is assumed to equate with conformity to the legislation – does not necessarily mean the raising of standards. Harmonised standards need to meet the 'essential requirements' laid down in legislation but no more; otherwise they would in effect become a barrier to trade – and in any case would not be a clear benchmark to aim for in complying with legislation. Thus, the harmonisation process can lower, as well as raise, the level of pre-existing national standards – as pointed out by a manufacturer of medical lifting equipment in relation to a draft European standard.[71]

Even so, the importance of consumer protection has been recognised in its own right over the years in a number of European Community resolutions.[72] And, for example, the Medical Devices Directive also states in its preamble that 'medical devices should provide patients, users and third parties with a high level of protection and attain the performance levels attributed to them by manufacturers'.

Essential requirements, standards and the CE mark

Recent Directives place duties on manufacturers to place a CE Mark on products.[73] Such a mark indicates that a product conforms to *essential requirements* laid down in legislation.

The current approach of the European Community deliberately avoids including detailed product standards in legislation. This new approach is in contrast to that taken early in the 1980s which tended toward more detailed legislation.[74] Instead, recent directives impose essential requirements only. The detailed working out and application of technical standards is left to national standards bodies (eg the British Standards Institution) which work together in the European Committee for Standardisation (CEN) and the European Committee for Electrotechnical Standardisation (CENELEC). Once European standards have been developed, and the European Commission has 'mandated' and accepted them as meeting the essential requirements of a particular directive, then they are known as *harmonised standards*. A legal presumption can then be made that any products conforming to those harmonised standards comply also with the relevant essential requirements laid down in the directive.[75]

In fact, even this more general approach, which represents a retreat from more detailed and prescriptive legislation, is itself said to be under review, because of the administrative and legal burdens it is placing on individual countries.

To some degree – for example, in the case of low risk medical devices – the CE Mark represents self-certification by manufacturers that their equipment conforms to the essential requirements imposed by legislation. Although quality control measures are stipulated in Directives, it is important to note that the CE Mark is not a cast-iron guarantee of safety.[76] Rather than a safety mark it is a 'passport' which entitles products to free circulation within the European Community.[77] Nevertheless, in the case of some products, such as medium or high-risk medical devices, compliance does have to be checked independently (see below).

Which Directive and which set of regulations applies?

Often products are subject to one directive only, but sometimes more than one might apply. For instance, the Toy Safety Directive covers all safety aspects of toys.[78] But this is not the whole picture, because, for example, the electro-magnetic properties of toys (mostly unconnected with safety) are not covered by the Directive – and instead will come under the Electromagnetic Compatibility (EMC) Directive and associated UK Regulations.[79] Thus, both Directives might apply to toys (although only one CE mark would be required). However, in contrast, for example, the EMC legislation will not, after 13 June 1998, apply to medical devices (although until that date, manufacturers of relevant products can choose to comply with either the EMC legislation or the medical devices legislation).[80]

Again, it might be unclear under what directive a particular type of equipment comes; for example, there has been uncertainty about whether domestic stairlifts and domestic through-floor lifts will be covered by directives affecting machinery, medical devices or lifts. In the event, it is likely that they will fall under the first of these – machinery. And, in the absence of clear indication in the legislation or authoritative guidance from a government department, it might be for manufacturers to decide (for commercial/financial reasons) about which directive to conform to. For instance, electronic speech aids might conceivably come under either the Medical Devices Directive or the Low Voltage Directive; however, from the point of view of the consumer, if equipment is safe under one Directive it is probably going to be safe also under the other.

Alternatively, it could be that an item of equipment (or at least specific aspects of it) are not covered at all by any of these specific directives and regulations. In which case, the General Product Safety Regulations 1994 apply either to the item as a whole, or to those specific aspects not otherwise covered. These Regulations in effect catch anything that slips through the net by supplying a general safety requirement.[81]

4. MEDICAL DEVICES REGULATIONS: DUTIES, EQUIPMENT COVERED, ORGANISATIONS AFFECTED

The Medical Devices Regulations 1994, together with the European Directive[82] on which they are based, are of potentially extensive application to much of the equipment dealt with in this book.

In summary, the Regulations impose essential requirements which must be met before medical devices are placed on the market and stipulate that a CE mark must be placed on products to indicate such conformity. The requirements relate to, for example, safety (including information, instructions, labelling), performance, specification, design, manufacturing process and packaging. Medical devices are classified in terms of risk; and the classification determines the degree of checking and verification that takes place. Failure to ensure that products conform to essential requirements or to place a CE Mark on products entails breach of the Regulations and criminal liability (and, in some circumstances, potential civil liability).[83] In particular, manufacturers need, for example, to ascertain the class of device their products come under, check that those products meet the relevant essential requirements, prepare and make available the technical documentation required, draw up a declaration of conformity before applying a CE mark (the badge of conformity), operate corrective and vigilance procedures, and register with the Medical Devices Agency.[84]

The Regulations, which cross-reference to the original Directive, are quite detailed and the following is an outline only, summarising the main duties imposed, the range of equipment covered and the type of organisation affected. The precise practical effect of the Regulations is not yet known, since there is some uncertainty about the meaning of some of the terms, how statutory services are affected, and what range of equipment is going to be covered in practice by the definition of the term 'medical device'.

The Regulations came into force in January 1995 and so apply potentially to devices placed on the market for the first time from that date. However, there is no obligation on manufacturers to comply until after the 13th June 1988 (the end of the transitional period). Up to that date, manufacturers can choose instead to adhere to existing regulatory controls, such as the Department of Health's Manufacturer Registration Scheme (MRS). After the 13th June 1998, devices placed on the market for the first time must carry the CE marking.

Duty to ensure that medical devices conform to essential requirements

The Regulations state that 'all devices placed on the market or put into service must comply with all the relevant essential requirements'. Manufacturers must ensure that any of their products which are medical devices meet those requirements and that the devices carry a CE mark (an indication of conformity).[85]

The legal definition of manufacturer extends to anybody who fully refurbishes, assembles, packages, processes and/or labels ready-made devices, and/or 'assigns to them their intended purpose' – with a 'view to their being placed on the market under his own name'. If a supplier buys a device and then places his own brand name on a product before selling it, the supplier has become the manufacturer – since when he sells it on to a consumer he is in effect placing a 'new' product on the market. The term, assigning to intended purpose, seems to refer, for example, to a product put to a use, or into a context of use, not intended by its original manufacturer.

However, this liability does not apply to people who assemble or adapt devices, already on their market, 'to their intended purpose' for individual patients.[86] Examples of this last activity to which liability does not apply are given by guidance from the Medical Devices Agency: assembling an orthopaedic implant, fitting a dental appliance, or making a plaster cast.[87]

What does it mean to place equipment on the market or put it into service?

Equipment is 'placed on the market' when a new or 'fully refurbished' device (which is not to be used for clinical investigation) is first made available, for payment or free of charge, for distribution or use within the European Community.[88]

Devices might be first made available by manufacturers either to suppliers or direct to consumers. Thus, when a supplier sells a device on to a consumer, the device is not being placed on the market; it was placed on the market when the manufacturer sold it to the supplier. The Regulations define 'placed on the market' as extending to the situation in which devices are provided free.[89] They might be provided as part of a promotion; for example, companies sometimes make available diabetes injection pens at hospital clinics. The meaning of fully refurbished is not made clear by the legislation; a reasonable interpretation might be that it should apply to major reconstruction and upgrading, rather than the regular servicing and maintenance, of equipment.[90]

The Regulations also apply to products which are 'put into service'. This means the 'making it [a medical device] ready for use on the Community market for the first time for its intended purpose'.[91] European Commission guidance explains the difference; 'placing on the market' does not necessarily mean supplying the equipment to a consumer (ie it might be placed on the market when the manufacturer sells it to a supplier); whereas putting it into service means use 'first use...by the end user'.[92]

The application of the term 'put into service' remains unclear; the Medical Devices Agency has hitherto not published a detailed explanation. For instance, the term might apply to the situation in which a supplier installs a medical device made up of several readymade parts he had previously bought from manufacturers. However, complications might rapidly arise in analysing the transaction and applying the terms of the Directive and Regulations to it; for example, are the parts themselves medical devices, does their original labelling remain or has the supplier put on his trademark, are they 'accessories' as defined in the Regulations and Directive – and so on. Published advice from the European Commission and Medical Devices Agency is awaited.

Do statutory services place products on the market?

Generally speaking, statutory services will not be affected by these Regulations. Most of the time, they loan equipment which has already been placed on the market by manufacturers when it is first sold to the NHS or to a social services department or to intermediary suppliers. However, equipment is sometimes manufactured by staff such as rehabilitation engineers, occupational therapists or chiropodists. Alternatively, pre-existing products might be adapted or repaired by NHS staff to the extent that they become 'fully refurbished'.

In either of these two cases, it is not wholly clear in what circumstances the duty regarding the CE mark and essential requirements arises for statutory services. Advice from the Medical Devices Agency (MDA) suggests that if a device is manufactured or refurbished by a healthcare establishment and is used only within that establishment, by or under the direction of staff, then the Regulations do not apply. Healthcare establishments include, at least, NHS hospitals, private hospitals, general practices, clinics, rehabilitation centres and occupational therapy centres.

Second, the advice suggests, if such a device is transferred from one NHS establishment to another (ie one under different management), then the device is placed on the market and the Regulations do apply.

Third, if the device is loaned or given to the patient to take home, then the Regulations do not apply because the activity should be regarded as still internal to the hospital. This principle could apply to provision of equipment by disablement services departments, occupational therapists and general practitioners. Examples given by MDA advice are the fabricating by GPs of arm slings from bandages, rubber tubing and polyurethane foam, and the making of splints and supports by physiotherapists.[93] The argument in support of the MDA view seems to rest on the assumption that health care is a 'special case' – not just inside hospitals, but also in community units, general practices and patients' homes. Otherwise, without such a special case being made out for health care, first loan to a service user of a manufactured device would seem to come within the Regulations – given that the broad definition of what it is to place a product on the market includes, according to European Commission guidance, the loan and gift of products.[94]

Whether a similarly special case could also be made out for social services departments if they manufacture or refurbish rehabilitation equipment is probably a moot point.

Do voluntary organisations place products on the market?

It seems reasonable to suppose that voluntary organisations are covered by the Regulations, since, for example, there is no stipulation that the person placing the product on the market should be acting in the course of business or commercial activities. This is in contrast both to Part 1 of the Consumer Protection Act 1987 and the General Product Safety Regulations which do refer to business activities and so raise some doubts about the extent of their application to voluntary organisations.

Essential requirements for medical devices

The essential requirements of devices are stated at some length in the Directive[95] and consist of a series of broad statements. These encompass, for example, the chemical, physical, biological, environmental and construction properties of devices. They also deal with information about, and the labelling of, devices. Rather than repeat these requirements, the Medical Devices Regulations 1994 refer to, and so must be read with, the Medical Devices Directive.

These essential requirements are not detailed statements of technical standards, but there is a presumption that if a device conforms to a 'harmonised' European standard, then it conforms also to the essential requirements.[96] However, if, as is often the case, no harmonised European standard exists, then there is no presumption that conformity with a British standard implies conformity with the essential requirements. This principle was demonstrated in a High Court case (*Balding v Lew Ways Ltd*), involving a children's tricycle which did not meet the essential requirements of the Toys Safety Regulations 1989 (implementing a European directive) but did conform to the relevant British standard. The manufacturer tried to defend itself by arguing that it had taken all reasonable steps and acted with all due diligence to conform to the requirements. However, the court held that this argument would not succeed, since the manufacturer should have confirmed with its analysts whether or not the tricycle conformed to the Regulations – not just whether it conformed to a British standard.[97]

The explicit obligation placed on manufacturers is to ensure that their medical devices conform to the essential requirements, not to harmonised standards. Therefore, they could instead attempt to ensure that the essential requirements were met in some other way. However, conformity to harmonised European standards (if they exist) will normally be the surest and easiest way of ensuring that essential requirements are met; to attempt another route is 'not for the faint-hearted'.[98] Apart from anything else, the manufacturer would be forgoing the legal presumption of conformity that accompanies adherence to harmonised standards.

CE Mark: the mark of conformity

Manufacturers (or their authorised representatives in the Community) have an obligation to place a CE mark on a device to show that it conforms to the essential requirements. If, however, the device is *custom-made* (or intended for clinical investigation), then although it must still conform to the essential requirements, a CE mark must not be placed on it.

The CE mark must be visible, legible and indelible and be applied to the device (if practicable and appropriate), on the instructions for use, and on the sales packaging (where applicable).[99]

In order to place the CE mark on their devices, manufacturers have to follow certain procedures, which vary depending on the class (see below) of a device. These procedures consist essentially of certification by the manufacturer, backed up by more or less (depending on the class of device) independent inspection and assessment by a 'Notified Body' (ie an organisation designated by the Medical Devices Agency).[100] Briefly, the duties placed on manufacturers are as follows[101]

- **Class 1 devices:** declaration of conformity with the essential requirements stipulated in legislation
- **Class IIa devices:** declaration of conformity and assessment of conformity by a Notified Body
- **Class IIb devices:** audit by Notified Body of quality assurance or type-testing, and of production audit or sampling

- **Class III devices:** audit similar to Class IIb, but, in addition, manufacturer must submit design dossier to the Notified Body.

Some anxiety exists about the costs manufacturers of equipment will incur by complying with the Regulations. Changes to administration, quality systems, assessment of products, design, manufacture, labelling, packaging and documentation might all be required. The Medical Devices Agency has estimated that gross compliance costs for private industry would be about £50 million, with benefits of £12 million because of lowered trade barriers. A conservative estimate of the costs to the NHS in respect of in-house manufacturing of devices was £3.5 million.[102] One of the anticipated problems for manufacturers is knowing exactly what they must do to comply with the Regulations. Indeed, apart from any changes to the actual manufacturing process, the cost might lie in analysing what they already do, and organising or reorganising existing quality procedures and paperwork. In one sense, the costs to companies might be as much about *demonstrating* that their products are up to standard, as *actually making them so.*

CE mark and technical documentation

In order to place a CE mark on Class 1 devices, for example, manufacturers must follow the 'declaration of conformity procedure' (set out an Annex 1 of the Directive). This involves preparing the relevant technical documentation, having in place corrective action and vigilance procedures (see below), and actually declaring that a device meets the essential requirements. The technical documentation is thus an important part of what is essentially a self-regulation process for this class of device. The documentation needs to cover, the description of the product, raw materials and components, intermediate product/sub-assembly, final product, packaging and labelling, design verification, risk analysis, reference to relevant harmonised standards, and (if relevant) clinical data.[103]

What is a medical device?

A medical device is defined as an apparatus, appliance, instrument, material or other article. It must be intended by the manufacturer to be used for[104]:

- 'diagnosis, prevention, monitoring, treatment or alleviation of disease'; or
- 'diagnosis, monitoring, treatment, alleviation of, or compensation for, an injury or handicap'; or
- 'investigation, replacement or modification of the anatomy or of a physiological process'; or
- 'control of conception'; AND the device must 'not achieve its principal intended action in or on the human body by pharmacological, immunological or metabolic means, even if it is assisted in its function by such means'.

The Regulations also cover accessories – ie 'an article which, whilst not being a device, is intended by its manufacturer to be used together with a device to enable it to be used in accordance with the use of the device intended by the manufacturer of the device'.[105] The Directive states that 'accessories shall be treated as medical devices in their own right'.[106]

The following points examine in detail what a medical device might look like in practice. However, other than the legal definition, the scope of the term 'medical device' is likely to remain somewhat vague until cases come before the law courts. Nevertheless, the definition is potentially wide, embracing many types of product:

(i) **Are medical devices 'daily living' products?** Does the definition of medical device apply to the array of what one might call simple daily living equipment – for example, long-handled pickup sticks, special cutlery? Such an application would certainly seem to be possible, given the above definition – even though such items of equipment would not normally be called 'medical devices' in ordinary language. For instance, much equipment provided by social services departments, or by private mail order companies, 'compensates for a handicap' – but is hardly thought of in the health care context (eg special cutlery). Furthermore, the legal test of whether a product is a medical device seems to rest on the intention of the manufacturer. This might be ascertained by assessing, for example, design, patent, publicity/ advertising, and both where and how the product is sold. Does this mean that taking, for example, two similar walking sticks, one might be a medical device and the other not, depending on the intention of the manufacturer (eg disability item or fashion accessory)?

Certainly, a literal interpretation of the legal definition would mean that medical devices extend far beyond the health care field. Even so, draft guidance produced by the European Commission contains many examples taken from the health care, not the social care, field. Thus, the low risk, Class I devices (see below) are categorised, for example, as those which immobilise the body (eg surgical collars), provide external patient support (eg wheelchairs), or collect liquid (eg incontinence pads).[107]

(ii) **Examples of medical devices.** Guidance notes produced for trading standards officers by the Medical Devices Agency (MDA) give an idea of the scope of equipment covered. Although such guidance is not a statement of the law, it might well be relied on by the law courts were a case to be brought which questioned the ambit of the term medical device.

The guidance suggests that medical devices include items such as dressings and bandages, products for the care of contact lenses, ready-made spectacles, incontinence pads, bath lifts, hoists and other transfer equipment, colostomy and urine bags, pain-relief equipment such as massagers and electrical stimulators, pressure relief equipment, postural support equipment, elastic hosiery and trusses, wheelchairs (and specially adapted scooters and buggies), walking sticks, walking frames and crutches.

Limits to the definition of *medical device* are also suggested. Exclusions include protectors such as ear-defenders and ear-plugs, cyclists' helmets, protective sportswear such as shin-pads and helmets, sunglasses (unless medically prescribed), motor vehicles including those adapted for disabled drivers – and walking sticks for use by 'hikers' or as a dress accessory.[108]

Another publication of the Medical Devices Agency includes the following within a long list of examples of medical devices: equipment for disabled people (generally), artificial limbs, artificial eyes, buggies for disabled people, condoms, contact lenses, dialysers, dressings and wound healing devices, examination gloves, hearing aids and inserts, hospital beds, incontinence appliances and pads, infusion pumps and controllers, intra-uterine devices, intravascular catheters and cannulae, mattresses and covers, nebulisers, orthoses, ostomy appliances, oxygen equipment, patient hoists and lifting equipment, physiotherapy equipment, prescribable footwear, pressure relief equipment, scooters for disabled people, special support seating, suction devices, syringes and needles, urinary catheters and drainage bags, vehicles for disabled people, ventilators, walking aids and wheelchairs.[109]

(iii) Examples of custom-made devices. The legislation states that a custom-made device refers to a device prescribed by a medical practitioner or 'professional user' and intended for the sole use of an individual 'patient'. It excludes specifically mass-produced devices which need to be adapted to meet the needs of the medical practitioner or professional user.[110]

Guidance gives examples of custom-made devices. They include artificial eyes (made for individual patients), dental appliances (eg braces), dental prostheses (dentures, crowns, bridges), hearing aids inserts, made-to-measure footwear, joint replacement implants.[111]

(iv) Manufacturer's intention. As already mentioned, the status of products hinges on the manufacturer's intention. However, although a medical device must have been intended for use in relation to disease, injury or disability, *it need not have been intended solely for such use.* For instance, a manufacturer of walking sticks might intend that the same model be used for both 'disabled' people and other people as well. In which case, the sticks could still come, in principle, under the definition of medical device. But discerning the manufacturer's intention might itself be difficult. This sort of problem is well-rehearsed in the area of VAT legislation, which, though, applies zero-rating generally only to equipment solely intended for disabled people – but not to equipment intended for the use of other people as well (see p.66). Given the large, shifting grey area between what is clearly 'disability' equipment and what is equally clearly 'ordinary' equipment, there are no easy answers.

(v) Classes of device. Further clues to the definition of a medical device are afforded by the broad classification of devices by the Directive into *low risk* (non-invasive), *medium risk* and *high risk* devices. The class into which a particular device fits is governed by factors relating to whether, for instance, the device is invasive or active (in the sense of exchanging or administering energy). However, the Directive does not provide specific examples of devices falling into each category.

Though not having the force of law, European Commission guidance does give some indication about what sort of devices might come into each class. This is important for all concerned to know, since the class determines the type and scale of conformity procedure. Devices which do not, or at least do no more than, touch people's skin fall into Class I; for example, hospital beds, hoists, walking aids, wheelchairs, stretchers, elastic hosiery, ostomy pouches, incontinence pads and urine bottles. Thus, most of the equipment dealt with this in book fits into this, the lowest risk, class.

Products belonging to other, higher risk, classes demand more rigorous compliance procedures. For instance, urinary catheters, contact lenses, tracheal tubes attached to a ventilator, and perineal re-education devices fall into Class IIa – as do syringe needles, lances, dental bridges, dental crowns, TENS devices and hearing aids. Insulin pens, dialysis equipment and ventilators come under Class IIb.[112]

(vi) **Who defines medical devices in practice?** Despite the examples of medical devices given by the Medical Devices Agency and the European Commission, the situation would seem to be vague and unclear. Whilst the examples might clarify the situation in relation to some equipment, a wide range of products might lie on the border; should they carry a CE mark or not?

In the absence of authoritative statements from the law courts, it could be for manufacturers to make decisions about whether or not to define border products as medical devices. For instance, a manufacturer might see a commercial advantage in placing the CE Mark on a reaching stick; the stick might thereby seem to gain in status. Commercial competitors might themselves respond by placing their own CE mark on their sticks – or, alternatively, claim that the first manufacturer has breached the Regulations because the reaching stick is in fact not a medical device at all.

A voluntary organisation could similarly make an impact. For instance, it might believe that substandard reaching sticks are being sold – but not as medical devices and therefore with no CE Mark. In the hope of improving quality, it might, for example, complain to trading standards officers that the sticks were medical devices, ought to bear the CE mark, and therefore conform to the essential requirements.

What happens if duties are breached?

Breach of the regulations is a *criminal* offence.[113] Depending on the type of device, this can lead to prosecution of a manufacturer or supplier either by the Medical Devices Agency or by trading standards officers. For example, a manufacturer might fail to place a CE Mark on a product, or alternatively place the Mark on a product which does not conform to the essential requirements.

Manufacturers can use the defence of *due diligence*, by showing that they 'took all reasonable steps and exercised all due diligence to avoid committing the offence'. If they claim that they relied on information provided by somebody else, they have to show that it was reasonable for them to have relied on it.[114]

As explained elsewhere (see p.461), the agencies charged with enforcing this type of legislation have a certain amount of discretion. Thus, for example, if a product is found not to conform to the essential requirements, a company which efficiently recalled the product and withdrew it immediately from the market might avoid prosecution – it might anyway be able to invoke the defence that it had acted with due diligence, and that the defect in the product was not foreseeable. On the other hand, if a company did not have the paperwork either demonstrating that it had shown due diligence in manufacturing the product, or enabling it to recall the product efficiently, then it might well stand to be prosecuted. Similarly, enforcement authorities might take a dim view of manufacturers who, seeking a commercial advantage, place the CE mark on their products, without being able to demonstrate specific compliance with the legal requirements.

Before initiating criminal prosecution, various notices can be served on manufacturers – including *compliance* notices, suspension notices, prohibition notices and notices to warn.[115]

It could be open to individuals to bring a civil action for breach of the Regulations (see p.463), since the Consumer Protection Act 1987 expressly allows this[116] – for example, if a device which was unsafe because it did not conform to the essential requirements caused an accident. However, the victim would still have to prove that the accident was caused as a result of the equipment not conforming to the essential requirements.

Reporting problems with products

Under the Regulations, manufacturers are under a duty to report to the competent authority (the Medical Devices Agency) the malfunctioning or deterioration of products, or inadequate labelling or instructions, which led, or might lead, to the death or harm of the user. They must also report any connected technical or medical reasons for such problems which lead to a systematic recall of a particular type of device.[117]

The Medical Devices Agency has established an Adverse Incident Centre, from which hazard warnings and safety notices are issued to statutory services, the private sector and voluntary organisations. For example, health care employees should (irrespective of the Medical Devices Regulations) report safety-related incidents – as explained in 1993 guidance from the Department of Health.[118] The agency explains that the incidents which should be reported include (i) safety-related incidents, (ii) problems arising from incorrect use, or inappropriate modification, adjustment or maintenance, (iii) minor accidents or anomalies which might reflect inadequate quality assurance or instructions.[119]

5. UNSAFE PRODUCTS: GENERAL PRODUCT SAFETY REGULATIONS

Apart from dealing with the safety aspects of particular product types, such as toys, medical devices, low voltage electrical equipment and furniture, legislation imposes a general safety requirement in relation to products in general. This requirement is mainly contained in the General Product Safety Regulations 1994 which came into force on 3rd October 1994.[120]

The Regulations are based on a European Directive.[121] To a large extent, they have replaced the operation of s.10 of the Consumer Protection Act 1987 which previously imposed the general safety requirement.[122] The Regulations apply only to products (or aspects of products), which are not already covered by other European Community law.[123] For example, if there were ten safety aspects to a particular product, only nine of which were covered by a specific directive, then the general safety requirement would apply to the tenth. Thus, the Regulations will not apply to medical devices, which are already covered by the Medical Devices Regulations 1994; however, as already pointed out above, there is uncertainty about how far the term 'medical device' is applicable to everyday consumer products which might be useful for disabled people. Otherwise coverage is wide; examples given by Department of Trade and Industry guidance include DIY tools and equipment, fireworks for consumers, food and drink, household goods, nursery goods, motor vehicles.[124] The Regulations state that for their purpose a product is one that is 'intended for consumers or likely to be used by consumers'.[125]

The Regulations apply potentially not only to manufacturers, but also to suppliers of equipment – including statutory services and voluntary organisations. However, there is room for uncertainty because the Regulations only apply to people and organisations engaged in commercial activity – and it is not made clear whether statutory services and voluntary organisations are engaged in commercial activity.

Duty not to place unsafe products on the market

The central duty imposed by the Regulations is that producers must not place unsafe products on the market. In addition, separate duties are placed on distributors of products.[126]

Safe products

A safe product is defined to mean a product which under normal or reasonably foreseeable conditions of use does not present any risk – or at least no more risk than is consistent with a high level of health and safety. This 'minimum risk' test is a vague one, the outcome of which might be difficult to predict in many cases.[127] Guidance from the Department of Trade and Industry points out that not every risk can be eliminated, since some products carry some risk by their very nature – for example, scissors and knives – although labelling and packaging can lessen some risks.[128]

Under the Regulations, relevant aspects of products are wide-ranging and include composition of products, packaging, instructions for assembly and maintenance, their effect on other products, presentation, labelling, instructions for use and disposal, other indications, and information. In addition, the types of consumer, especially children, who are at serious risk when using the product, must be taken into account. Lastly, even if other products of the same type involve less risk than the product under consideration, it does not mean that the latter will automatically be deemed unsafe.[129]

Whose duty is it not to place unsafe products on the market?

The duty applies to producers and distributors who are engaged in a 'commercial activity' in relation to the particular product in question.[130]

The extent to which statutory services and voluntary organisations are affected by the Regulations seems somewhat unclear; it depends on the meaning both of the terms 'commercial activity' and 'placed on the market'. These are discussed below.

Producers. Under the Regulations, *producers* of products must not place unsafe products on the market. Any of the following are considered to be producers.

First, the *original manufacturer, own-brander* (ie supplier who affixes a name, trade mark or other distinctive mark) or *person who reconditions* a product. Second, a *representative*, established in the European Community, of a manufacturer who is not based in the Community; if no representative is established, then the *importer* is considered to be the producer. Third, *other professionals in the supply chain*, to the extent that they affect the safety of products already placed on the market.[131]

Therefore, a supplier who repaired, adapted, interfered with packaging or labelling, or did anything else that affected the product's safety, would be liable. (If these activities amounted to reconditioning, then they could be liable as *manufacturer*, rather than as *professional in the supply chain*). Thus, in such circumstances, if local authorities or voluntary organisations are (i) deemed to be engaged in commercial activity, (ii) placing products on the market (see below), and (iii) the products were not medical devices (for the purpose of the Medical Devices Regulations) and did not come under any other European directive – then they could be liable as producers.

Distributors. Liability under the Regulations attaches not only to *producers* but also to *distributors*. A distributor is defined as a professional in the supply chain who does not affect the safety of the original product (compare with the professional in the supply chain who does affect product safety and so is defined as a producer: see immediately above).[132]

Under the Regulations, distributors also have a duty to help ensure compliance with the requirement that producers must not place unsafe products on the market. A distributor commits an offence by supplying products which he knows, or should have presumed, are dangerous – given the information available to him and his expertise.[133] Thus, a statutory service or voluntary body could easily be liable on this basis – but again only if it were deemed to be engaged in commercial activity (see below) and the products were not medical devices.

It might not always be clear whether people are producers or suppliers when they affect the safety of products. For example, retailers who assemble equipment, or even food shops, are normally thought of as distributors, but might be categorised as producers under the Regulations because they affect product safety.[134]

People must be engaged in a commercial activity

A product must be intended for, or likely to be used by, consumers – whether supplied free of charge or for payment. This applies to products whether they are new, used or reconditioned. However, the product must also be supplied in the course of a 'commercial activity'.

It is the definition of the term *commercial activity* which throws doubts on how far the Regulations apply to statutory services and voluntary bodies which supply equipment. Commercial activity is defined to include 'business' or 'trade' and it does not have to be for profit.[135] So it would include, for example, free gifts given away by private sector retailers companies – but it is not immediately obvious whether it would cover the free loan or other supply of equipment by statutory services and voluntary bodies.

Unlike the Consumer Protection Act 1987, which defines 'business' explicitly to include the activities of statutory services, the Regulations do not define business in this way. It is therefore not necessarily clear whether the supply of equipment to individual service users by statutory services is a commercial activity or not. A further question arises over voluntary organisations, since neither the Regulations (nor indeed the Consumer Protection Act) indicate expressly whether business includes the activities of voluntary organisations.

In the absence of express definitions, the following might be the situation. As far as statutory services go, the courts might adopt the definition of business similar to that given in the Consumer Protection Act – and so embrace statutory services, but still leave open the issue of voluntary organisations.

Alternatively, the courts could decide what constitutes business activity under the Regulations on the facts of particular cases. Some activities are more likely to be classed as commercial than others. For instance, the making of hire charges or selling of equipment by a social services department or voluntary organisation might be deemed more clearly commercial than the free loan of equipment. The large scale, mail order selling by a large voluntary organisation of equipment might be more commercial than the occasional hire charge made by a small, local organisation run by volunteers. It is conceivable even that the courts might find more commercial elements present if statutory services have contracted out their equipment delivery and maintenance services to private companies – than if they make direct provision themselves.

Tentative and cautious guidance produced by the Department of Trade and Industry suggests that voluntary organisations 'which exist *solely* to provide goods free of charge' are probably not engaged in commercial activities and so escape the Regulations. However, if a voluntary organisation were loaning equipment free of charge to some people, but selling services and goods to others, then even the free loan would be regarded as commercial activity. The guidance stresses that, in its view, all the circumstances of the operations of an organisation have to be taken into account in deciding whether it is engaged in commercial activity.[136]

Equipment used exclusively in commercial activity. Despite the requirement of commercial activity (see immediately above), the General Product Safety Regulations state that they do not apply to any product 'used exclusively in the context of a commercial activity' – even if it is 'used for or by a consumer'. They only apply if the product is actually supplied to a consumer.[137]

For example, shampoo used in a hairdresser's shop to wash a customer's hair is not covered by the Regulations; but if the customer takes the shampoo home (whether paid for or as a gift), a *supply* has taken place and the Regulations will apply. Department of Trade and Industry guidance gives other examples including shopping trolleys used in supermarkets, escalators in a shopping centre, and cleaning products used for car valet services. (It points out that such products would though be covered by health and safety at work legislation). It suggests that once a product is supplied to consumers to take away 'for private use' then the product falls within the Regulations.[138]

Secondhand equipment etc. The Regulations do not apply to secondhand products which are antiques, or to products which the seller has told the purchaser need to be repaired or reconditioned.[139] Guidance from the Department of Trade and Industry suggests that traders must make this very clear – for example, by displaying both a prominent general notice and by displaying those products in a separate area of the premises.[140]

What does it mean to place a product on the market?

Under the Regulations, a producer (but not a distributor), is liable if it places an unsafe product on the market. But what does it mean for a product to be placed on the market? This is not defined in the Regulations. However, guidance produced by the European Commission gives a broad definition; a product is placed on the market when it is first made available on the Community market through sale, lease, loan, hire, gift (or any other legal instrument).[141] And, the Medical Devices Regulations define it as 'the first making available in return for payment or free of charge'.[142]

Guidance from the Department of Trade and Industry states that when a product has been reconditioned, or where its safety aspects have been affected, wittingly or otherwise, by a professional in the supply chain (eg retailer or supplier), a product can be placed on the market more than once – since it is no longer the same product for the purpose of the Regulations.[143] For example, if a car manufacturer sells a car to a supplier, the product has been placed on the market. When the supplier then hires out the car regularly, he is not placing it on the market on each occasion. However, if at some point, the supplier reconditions or otherwise affects its safety, and hires it out again, it would have been placed on the market for a second time. But subsequent hiring episodes would again not be placing the car on the market.

Nevertheless, even if the company does not place the car on the market each time it is hired out, it could still be liable for hiring out an unsafe product – but liable as *distributor*, rather than *producer* (see above).

What if other, specific legislation already applies to particular products?

The General Product Safety Regulations do not apply to products which already have all of their safety aspects covered by other European legislation – for example, toys or medical devices. However, where a product has some, but not all, safety aspects covered, then those aspects not covered will still come under the Regulations.

When the Regulations do apply, the safety of a product is gauged with reference to a 'pecking order'. First, if either some, or all, aspects of a product are not covered by specific European legislation, then if instead the product (or those particular aspects) conforms with relevant UK domestic legislation, it (or they) will be presumed to be safe.

Second, in the absence both of relevant European and UK legislation, the safety of the product will be assessed taking account of, in order of priority, European standards (which have not yet been mandated under a Directive), European technical specifications, national standards, accepted industry codes of good practice, the state of the art and technology. However, even if a product meets any of these criteria, it must also satisfy the level of safety consumers reasonably expect.[144]

Continuing application of s.10 of the Consumer Protection Act 1987

Prior to the 1994 Regulations, the general product safety requirement in United Kingdom law was supplied by s.10 of the Consumer Protection Act 1987. It states that it is an offence to supply consumer goods which fail to comply with the general safety requirement, which is outlined in the rest of the section. The operation of this section has been largely superseded by the Regulations.

However, there are some situations in which it will still apply – for example, where (i) the supply by distributors/suppliers of a particular type of unsafe product is not caught by a specific-product directive (ie a directive does exist but penalises only manufacturers) – and (ii) such supply cannot be caught by the General Product Safety Regulations (because they only apply to products, or aspects of products, not covered at all by a directive). Department of Trade and Industry guidance explains that, for example, personal protective equipment is one such example, since the Personal Protective Equipment Directive places obligations on manufacturers only.[145]

Duty to provide information

In addition to the duties already outlined, the Regulations stipulate that producers have a duty to provide relevant information for consumers to assess the risks involved. They must also implement measures so that they themselves are well-informed about the risks of their own products. These measures could include marking products or batches of products, sampling marketed products, investigating complaints and informing distributors about such monitoring.[146]

Distributors also have a duty to participate in the monitoring of the safety of products by informing others of risks (eg consumers and producers) and co-operating in action to avoid the risks.[147]

What happens if duties are breached?

If the duties imposed on producers not to place unsafe products on the market – and on distributors not to supply unsafe products – are not adhered to, then there is a breach of statutory duty.[148] Criminal prosecutions by trading standards officers can be brought. However, breach of the duties to supply information and carry out monitoring (see above) is not a criminal offence *in itself* under the Regulations.

Producers and distributors can argue a *defence of due diligence*; ie that they took all reasonable steps to avoid committing the offence. They can also argue that they acted in reliance on information given by somebody else or that the offence itself was due to the act or omission of somebody else – although they must show that it was reasonable to have relied on the information.[149]

It is not clear how the courts would view a civil claim for breach of statutory duty (see p.463) under these Regulations which are silent on this point.

4. HEALTH AND SAFETY AT WORK: LIFTING AND HANDLING PEOPLE

The subject of health and safety at work generally is beyond the scope of this book, not least because the subject, even in relation to equipment alone, is large. However, one set of regulations, based on a European Directive, are particularly topical in relation to this book. The Manual Handling Operations Regulations 1992, have implications for equipment manufacturers and retailers, health and social care practitioners and their employers – and older people and disabled people themselves.

Health and safety at work: general provisions affecting equipment use in relation to service users

The Health and Safety at Work 1974 (s.3) places a general duty on *employers* 'to conduct his undertaking in such a way as to ensure, so far as is reasonably practicable, that persons not in his employment who may be affected thereby are not thereby exposed to risks to their health and safety'. Whilst this might apply to independent contractors (ie they are not employees), it might equally apply to hospital patients, the residents of nursing homes or even people in their own homes who are being visited by health and social care staff. For example, this section could apply to the use in hospitals or nursing homes of dangerously ill-maintained wheelchairs.

In addition, s.7 of the Health and Safety at Work 1974 places a duty on *employees* 'to take reasonable care for the health and safety of himself and of other persons who may be affected by his acts or omissions at work'. This, too, could cover unreasonably careless acts by staff in relation to equipment use by service users. Under the Act, breach of these duties gives rise to criminal, but not to civil, liability[150]; though an action in common law negligence could always be pursued instead.

Lifting and handling people in hospital and in their homes

The Manual Handling Operations Regulations 1992 place a duty on employers to ensure, so far as is reasonably practicable, that employees do not have to risk injury by manually handling or lifting people or things. The Regulations impose duties on a self-employed person in relation to him- or herself. If it is not reasonably practicable to eliminate this risk, the employer has to do a number of things. First, it must make a 'suitable and sufficient' assessment of the manual handling operations which are being undertaken. The assessment must take account of a number of legally prescribed factors, including the following:

- **nature of handling tasks:** for example, holding loads at a distance from the trunk, twisting, stooping, reaching, sudden movements, excessive lifting, excessive pulling, prolonged physical effort etc
- **loads** which may be heavy, bulky, difficult to grasp or unstable
- **working environment:** does limited space prevent good posture, are floors slippery or uneven, is the lighting poor?
- **does the job** require unusual strength or height, is it hazardous to those with a health problem, does its safe performance depend on special information or training?

If circumstances have changed since the assessment was made or there is anyway reason to suppose that the assessment is no longer valid, then the employer must review it and make any required changes. Second, he must take 'appropriate steps' to reduce the risk of injury to the 'lowest level reasonably practicable'. Third, he must give employees general indications or more precise information about the weight of loads. An obligation is placed on the employee too; he or she must 'make full and proper use of any system of work' which the employer has provided to comply with the Regulations.[151]

The Regulations derive from a European Directive, but there is some doubt whether they reflect the Directive accurately in all respects. The Directive states that manual handling should only take place if it cannot be avoided – it says nothing about whether it is 'reasonably practicable' to avoid it.[152] This means that it is possible that some legal actions could be brought not just on the basis of breach of the UK Regulations, but alternatively of breach of the Directive.[153] The possibilities of relying directly on a European directive, rather than its manifestation in UK legislation, are summarised elsewhere (see p.352).

Implication of Regulations

The Regulations have an obvious application to practitioners such as nurses, physiotherapists, occupational therapists and personal care assistants – some of whom are at constant risk of serious back injury. The implications are that employers such as NHS Trusts and social services departments might have to provide their staff with more lifting, turning and handling equipment (see p.497 for examples).

The Regulations threaten to give a sharper edge to legal actions against employers for back injuries to staff. Employers such as the NHS clearly stand in some jeopardy of legal action, given the sometimes chronic shortage of staff and equipment which can lead to nurses and therapists handling, sometimes singly, very heavy or awkward patients. Even when two or more staff are present, unexpected injury can easily occur. For instance, a person being helped out of bed might suddenly slip – causing injury to the back of at least one of the staff.

Some employers are taking the new legislation seriously. For example, NHS Trusts now employ lifting and handling advisers and provide increased quantities of lifting equipment, setting aside, for example, tens of thousands of pounds per annum in order to implement a policy of 'minimal lifting' in, ideally, a 'no-lifting' culture.[154] In practice, if they are unable to deny that they have breached their duty, employers might defend themselves by denying that the breach actually caused the injury complained of (for causation, see: p.465).

Difficult decisions?

The practical benefits of safer handling and increased use of assistive lifting and turning equipment seem obvious; injury and chronic back problems are a serious occupational hazard for practitioners such as nurses and therapists. However, the situation is not without some complications and conflicts. The work of some professionals necessitates lifting and handling; for example, rehabilitation therapists transfer people from bed to chair, in order to assist them regain physical function, and lifting via means of a hoist might not aid rehabilitation in such circumstances. There are in fact various types of other lifting and handling equipment (eg turning discs, transfer boards) short of hoists which might both protect staff and serve rehabilitation purposes.

Conflict might also arise between disabled people and those who are lifting them. In some situations, use of hoists might cause discomfort to a disabled person and be awkward and time-consuming.[155] Discomfort might be caused by use of inappropriate slings.[156] Hoists might seem undignified to some people who would prefer to be lifted out of bed by their carers or helpers.[157] Further tension might arise, if, for example, health and social care practitioners refuse to lift people in their own homes, suitable equipment is not available, and carers are left to do the lifting; carers are not covered by the Regulations, which apply as between employers and employees.

The Health Services Advisory Committee has illustrated the possible complexity of decision-making. An 83-year-old, mentally confused, abusive and aggressive woman was discharged home. Two community nurses visited, and were helping the woman out of bed when she lifted both her feet so as to increase the weight on the nurses. Both nurses experienced back pain. Continued visiting by the two nurses was ruled out and three alternatives considered: provision of a hoist, readmission to hospital, and provision of an adjustable height bed which the woman could get in and out of herself. The hoist was ruled out on safety grounds, since the woman might be uncooperative and thrash around; the family opposed readmission to hospital; so, after a delay, a suitable bed was provided.[158]

Notes

1 Department of Trade and Industry (1995). *The General Product Safety Regulations: guidance for businesses, consumers and enforcement authorities.* London: DTI, Foreword.

2 See eg report on progress with the Deregulation and Contracting Out Act 1994 – and the guidelines issued to government departments to ensure that compliance costs are rigorously examined before new legislation is accepted: *Hansard,* House of Commons, Oral answers, 26 February 1996, cols 571–577.

3 Williams, K. (1996). Handle with care. *Nursing Standard:* 3 April 1996; 10(28), pp.26–27: in which it is claimed that one NHS Trust reduced staff absence for back injury to the tune of £400, 000 saved in a year.

4 Tremaine, B. (1996). Quality systems and the CE mark: the options for SMEs. *In Focus:* April 1995. (*In Focus* is the executive summary of Health-Care Focus, the journal of the Association of British Health-Care Industries).

5 Eg *Marshall v Southampton Area Health Authority (Teaching)* (152/84) [1986] ECR 723: about differing retiring ages for men and women.

6 *Litster v Forth Dry Dock & Engineering Co Ltd* [1990] 1 AC 546 (HL): an employment case about the transfer of undertakings, in which the House of Lords read in extra words to UK regulations.

7 *Factortame v Secretary of State for Transport* [1989] 2 All ER 692 (HL).

8 *Francovich v Italian State* (C 6/90 & C 9/90) [1992] IRLR 84: about an employer's insolvency and payment of arrears to employees. Also: *R v Secretary of State for Transport, ex parte Factortame and others* (joined with: *Brasserie du Pecheur SA v Federal Republic of Germany*) (Cases C-46/93 and C48/93), The Times, 7 March 1996 (ECJ). See: Geddes, A. (1996). Claims for damages against the state. *New Law Journal:* 29 March 1996; 146(6737), pp.451–452: the Spanish fishermen/Factortame case.

9 *R v HM Treasury, ex parte British Telecommunications plc* (Case C-392/93), The Times, 16 April 1996 (ECJ).

10 85/374/EEC. *Council Directive of 25 July 1985 on the approximation of the laws, regulations and administrative provisions of the Member States concerning liability for defective products.*

11 Ibid.

12 Hodges, C. (1995). Product liability. *Solicitors Journal:* 15 December 1995, p.1262.

13 National Consumer Council (1995). *Unsafe products: how the Consumer Protection Act works for consumers.* London: NCC, pp.13–14.

14 *Consumer Protection Act 1987,* ss.1, 45.

15 *Consumer Protection Act 1987,* s.2.

16 *Consumer Protection Act 1987,* ss.5, 45.

17 *Consumer Protection Act 1987,* s.5.

18 *Consumer Protection Act 1987,* s.5(2).

19 See list of examples of defective goods, examining liability in negligence, under the Consumer Protection Act 1987 and in contract: Atiyah, P.S; Adams, J. (1995). *The sale of goods.* 9th edition. London: Pitman Publishing, pp.243–247.

20 *Consumer Protection Act 1987,* s.3.

21 National Consumer Council (1995). *Unsafe products: how the Consumer Protection Act works for consumers.* London: NCC, p.20.

22 Department of Trade and Industry, Consumer Safety Unit (1993). *Guide to the Consumer Protection Act 1987: product liability and safety provisions.* London: DoTI, p.5.

23 Atiyah, P.S. (1995). *The sale of goods.* 9th edition. London: Pitman Publishing, p.238.

24 Stapleton, J. (1994). *Product liability.* Law in Context (series). London: Butterworths, pp.234–236.

25 Department of Trade and Industry (1995). *Guide to the Consumer Protection Act 1987: product liability and safety provisions.* London: DTI, pp.3–4.

26 *Consumer Protection Act 1987,* s.3.

27 National Consumer Council (1995). *Unsafe products: how the Consumer Protection Act works for consumers.* London: NCC, pp.9–10.

28 Hodges, C. (1995). Product liability. *Solicitors Journal:* 15 December 1995, p.1262.

29 National Consumer Council (1995). *Unsafe products: how the Consumer Protection Act works for consumers.* London: NCC, pp.16–17.

30 See summary: Joustra, C. (1994). *Consumer Law Journal:* 1994, CS 55.

31 *Consumer Protection Act 1987,* s.2.

32 *Consumer Protection Act 1987,* s.2.

33 Stapleton, J. (1994). *Product liability.* Law in Context (series). London: Butterworths, pp.293, 312: eg it might be expensive to keep exhaustive records of generic NHS prescriptions of drugs to patients.

34 *Consumer Protection Act 1987*: implications for physiotherapists. *Physiotherapy:* 1988; 74(4), pp.175–176.

35 See eg HN(88)3. Department of Health and Social Security. *Procurement: product liability.* London: DHSS, para 3.

36 *Consumer Protection Act 1987,* s.4(2).

37 Car adaptation fears. *Disability Now,* February 1996, pp.1, 3.

38 Examples suggested in: Saunders, M.T. (1989). Product liability. *Journal of the Medical Defence Union:* Summer 1989, pp.38–39.

39 See eg: Stapleton, J. (1994). *Product liability.* Law in Context (series). London: Butterworths, pp.313–314.

40 *Consumer Protection Act 1987,* s.4.

41 *Consumer Protection Act 1987,* s.45.

42 Department of Trade and Industry (1995). *Guide to the Consumer Protection Act 1987: product liability and safety provisions.* London: DTI, p.5.

43 Stapleton, J. (1994). *Product liability.* Law in Context (series). London: Butterworths, p.315.

44 Department of Trade and Industry (1995). *The General Product Safety Regulations: guidance for businesses, consumers and enforcement authorities.* London: DTI, p.11.

45 *Consumer Protection Act 1987,* s.4.

46 *Consumer Protection Act 1987,* s.46.

47 85/374/EEC, a.7.

48 Stapleton, J. (1994). *Product liability.* Law in Context (series). London: Butterworths, pp.317–323.
49 SI 1994/3017. *Medical Devices Regulations 1994,* r.2.
50 Atiyah, P.S. (1995). *The sale of goods.* 9th edition. London: Pitman Publishing, p.237.
51 National Consumer Council (1995). *Unsafe products: how the Consumer Protection Act works for consumers.* London: NCC, pp.13–14.
52 *Consumer Protection Act 1987,* s.2.
53 *Consumer Protection Act 1987,* s.4.
54 *Consumer Protection Act 1987,* s.4.
55 *Consumer Protection Act 1987,* s.4.
56 *Consumer Protection Act 1987,* s.4.
57 National Consumer Council (1995). *Unsafe products: how the Consumer Protection Act works for consumers.* London: NCC, pp.22–23.
58 85/374/EEC, a.7: 'that the state of scientific and technical knowledge at the time when he put the product into circulation was not such as to enable the existence of the defect to be discovered'.
59 *Consumer Protection Act 1987,* s.4.
60 *Consumer Protection Act 1987,* s.7.
61 *Consumer Protection Act 1987,* s.11A.
62 *Limitation Act 1980,* s.11.
63 HC(89)20. Department of Health. *Health services management: preservation, retention and destruction of records: responsibilities of health authorities under the Public Records Acts.* London: DH, Appendix C, para 11.
64 *Consumer Protection Act 1987,* s.50(7).
65 *Consumer Protection Act 1987,* s.5.
66 93/42/EEC. *Council Directive of 14 June 1993* concerning medical devices.
67 88/378/EEC. *Council Directive of 3 May 1988 on the approximation of the laws of the Member States concerning the safety of toys.*
68 73/23/EEC. An 'old approach' directive, later modified so as to incorporate the CE mark – implemented in: SI 1994/3260. *Electrical Equipment (Safety) Regulations 1994.*
69 See generally eg Burrows, N. (1990). Harmonisation of technical standards: reculer pour mieux sauter? *Modern Law Review:* September 1990; 53(5), pp.597–603.
70 McGee, A.; Weatherill, S. (1990). The evolution of the Single Market: harmonisation or liberalisation. *Modern Law Review:* September 1990; 53(5), pp.578–596.
71 Clark, N. (1996). Sorting out the standards. *Hospital Equipment Supplies:* March 1996, p.27.
72 Summarised in: Hodges, C. (1995). Development of consumer safety policy in the European Community. *Consumer Law Journal:* 1995, pp.51–55.
73 93/68/EEC: the CE Marking Directive, the purpose of which was to introduce a harmonised set of rules relating to the operation of CE marking.
74 See eg: European Commission (1994). *Guide to the implementation of Community harmonisation directives based on the new approach and the global approach.* Brussels: EC.
75 For summaries of the situation in relation to medical/health equipment, see eg: Feneley, R.; Ludgate, S. (1994). The European Directives: safeguarding the patient and staff. *Health Trends:* 1994; 26(4), pp.109–112.
76 Medical Devices Agency (1995). *Doing no harm.* London: MDA, p.8.
77 Medical Devices Agency (1994). *The Medical Devices Regulations 1994: guidance notes for trading standards officers.* London: MDA, p.9.
78 Department of Trade and Industry, Consumer Safety Unit (1995). *General Product Safety Regulations 1994: guidance for businesses, consumers and enforcement authorities.* London: DoTI, para 14.
79 SI 1992/2372. *Electromagnetic Compatibility Regulations 1992.*
80 Medical Devices Agency (1995). *The Medical Devices, Electromagnetic Compatibility and Low Voltage Directives. Bulletin no. 15.* London: Department of Health.
81 SI 1994/2328. *General Product Safety Regulations 1994,* r.3.
82 *Council Directive 93/42/EEC concerning medical devices.* OJ No. L.169, 12.7.93

83 Medical Devices Agency (undated). *Guidance notes for manufacturers of class 1 medical devices.* London: Department of Health, p.3.
84 Medical Devices Agency (undated). *Guidance notes for manufacturers of class 1 medical devices.* London: Department of Health, pp.4–5.
85 SI 1994/3017. *Medical Devices Regulations 1994,* rr.5, 6.
86 SI 1994/3017. *Medical Devices Regulations 1994,* r.13.
87 Medical Devices Agency (1995). *Activities of health establishments (in-house manufacture) in the UK.* Directives Bulletin no. 18. London: MDA.
88 SI 1994/3017. *Medical Devices Regulations 1994,* r.2.
89 SI 1994/3017. *Medical Devices Regulations 1994,* r.2.
90 Cutler, I.R. (1996) Amendments to the Medical Device Directive. *Medical Device Technology:* January/February 1996, pp.24–27.
91 SI 1994/3017. *Medical Devices Regulations 1994,* r.2.
92 See eg: European Commission (1994). *Guide to the implementation of Community harmonisation directives based on the new approach and the global approach.* First version. Brussels: EC, p.21.
93 Medical Devices Agency (1995). *Activities of health establishments (in-house manufacture) in the UK.* Directives Bulletin no. 18. London: MDA.
94 See eg: European Commission (1994). *Guide to the implementation of Community harmonisation directives based on the new approach and the global approach.* First version. Brussels: EC, p.20.
95 93/42/EEC *Council Directive concerning medical devices.* OJ No. L.169, 12.7.93
96 SI 1994/3017. *Medical Devices Regulations 1994,* rr.2, 5(7).
97 *Balding v Lew Ways Ltd* (1995) (QBD), The Times, 9 March 1995
98 Clark, N. (1996). Sorting out the standards. *Hospital Equipment Supplies:* March 1996, p.27.
99 SI 1994/3017. *Medical Devices Regulations 1994,* r.6.
100 SI 1994/3017. *Medical Devices Regulations 1994,* rr. 7–17.
101 SI 1994/3017. *Medical Devices Regulations 1994,* rr.7–10 referring to the original Directive. For a summary see: Medical Devices Agency (1995). *Conformity assessment procedures.* Directives Bulletin no 4. London: MDA.
102 Medical Devices Agency (1994). *Compliance costs assessment.* Directives Bulletin no 14. London: MDA.
103 Summary from: Medical Devices Agency (undated). *Guidance notes for manufacturers of class 1 medical devices.* London: Department of Health, pp.6–7.
104 SI 1994/3017. *Medical Devices Regulations 1994,* r.2.
105 SI 1994/3017. *Medical Devices Regulations 1994,* r.2.
106 93/42/EEC. *Council directive concerning medical devices,* a.1.
107 See European Commission (1994). *Guidelines to the classification of medical devices.* 4th draft. Brussels: EC.
108 Medical Devices Agency (1994). *The Medical Devices Regulations 1994: guidance notes for trading standards officers.* London: MDA, p.18–19.
109 Medical Devices Agency (1995). *Doing no harm.* London: Department of Health (back cover).
110 SI 1994/3017. *Medical Devices Regulations 1994,* r.2.
111 Medical Devices Agency (1994). *The Medical Devices Regulations 1994: guidance notes for trading standards officers.* London: MDA, p.21.
112 See European Commission (1994). *Guidelines to the classification of medical devices.* 4th draft. Brussels: EC.
113 The Regulations are enforced through the machinery of the *Consumer Protection Act 1987.*
114 *Consumer Protection Act 1987,* s.39: which applies to safety regulations made under s.11 of the 1987 Act.
115 SI 1994/3017. *Medical Devices Regulations 1994,* r.19; referring also to enforcement procedures in the Consumer Protection Act 1987.
116 The Regulations are made under the *Consumer Protection Act 1987,* which states at s.41 that civil actions for breach of statutory duty are possible so long as specific sets of regulations do not forbid such actions.
117 Part of the essential requirements in the annexes of the Directive: 93/43/EEC. *Council Directive concerning medical devices* – the implementing regulations (SI 1994/3017. *Medical Devices Regulations)* refer to these annexes.

118 HSG(93)13. *Reporting on adverse incidents and reactions, and defective products relating to medical and non-medical equipment and supplies, food, buildings and plant, and medicinal products.* London: Department of Health, 1993.
119 Medical Devices Agency (1995). *Doing no harm.* London: MDA, p.4.
120 SI 1994/2328. *General Product Safety Regulations.*
121 92/59/EEC. *Council Directive of 29 June 1992 on general product safety.*
122 Although these may still be relevant in certain circumstances: for example, where the safety aspects of a product were covered by other EC legislation, but only in respect of persons who first place the product on the market, but not to subsequent distributors (as in the case of the Personal Protective Equipment Directive): Department of Trade and Industry, Consumer Safety Unit (1995). *General Product Safety Regulations 1994: guidance for businesses, consumers and enforcement authorities.* London: DoTI, para 8.
123 SI 1994/2328. *General Product Safety Regulations,* r.3.
124 Department of Trade and Industry (1995). *The General Product Safety Regulations 1994: guidance for businesses, consumers and enforcement authorities.* London: DTI, para 10.
125 SI 1994/2328. *General Product Safety Regulations,* r.2.
126 SI 1994/2328. *General Product Safety Regulations,* rr.7, 9.
127 Cartwright, P. (1995). Product safety and consumer protection. *Modern Law Review:* March 1995; 58, pp.222–231.
128 Department of Trade and Industry (1995). *The General Product Safety Regulations 1994: guidance for businesses, consumers and enforcement authorities.* London: DTI, p.12.
129 SI 1994/2328. *General Product Safety Regulations,* r.2.
130 SI 1994/2328. *General Product Safety Regulations,* r.2: which defines a relevant product as one which is intended or likely to be used in the course of a commercial activity.
131 SI 1994/2328. *General Product Safety Regulations,* r.2.
132 SI 1994/2328. *General Product Safety Regulations,* r.2.
133 SI 1994/2328. *General Product Safety Regulations,* r.9.
134 Cartwright, P. (1995). Product safety and consumer protection. *Modern Law Review:* March 1995; 58, pp.222–231.
135 SI 1994/2328. *General Product Safety Regulations,* r.2.
136 See discussion of the meaning of 'commercial activity' in: Department of Trade and Industry, Consumer Safety Unit (1995). *General Product Safety Regulations 1994: guidance for businesses, consumers and enforcement authorities.* London: DoTI, annex.
137 SI 1994/2328. *General Product Safety Regulations,* r.2.
138 Department of Trade and Industry, Consumer Safety Unit (1995). *General Product Safety Regulations 1994: guidance for businesses, consumers and enforcement authorities.* London: DoTI, paras 11–12.
139 SI 1994/2328. *General Product Safety Regulations,* r.3.
140 Department of Trade and Industry, Consumer Safety Unit (1995). *General Product Safety Regulations 1994: guidance for businesses, consumers and enforcement authorities.* London: DoTI, para 16.
141 European Commission (1994). *Guide to the implementation of Community harmonisation directives based on the new approach and the global approach.* First version. Brussels: EC, p.20.There is in fact a distinction between the General Product Safety Regulations and the Medical Devices Regulations; the former refer to products being placed on the market, but the latter add the words 'for the first time'. However, the significance of the distinction is not clear because EEC guidance about Directives states anyway that 'placing on the market' refers only to when a product is first made available.
142 SI 1994/3017. *Medical Devices Regulations 1994,* r.2.
143 Department of Trade and Industry, Consumer Safety Unit (1995). *General Product Safety Regulations 1994: guidance for businesses, consumers and enforcement authorities.* London: DoTI, para 24.
144 SI 1994/2328. *General Product Safety Regulations,* r.10.
145 89/686 EEC and 93/95/EEC. And: SI 1992/3139. *Personal Protective Equipment Regulations 1992.*
146 SI 1994/2328. *General Product Safety Regulations,* r.8.

147 SI 1994/2328. *General Product Safety Regulations,* r.9.
148 SI 1994/2328. *General Product Safety Regulations,* r.12.
149 SI 1994/2328. *General Product Safety Regulations,* r.14.
150 *Health and Safety at Work Act 1974,* s.47.
151 SI 1992/2793. *Manual Handling Operations Regulations 1992,* rr.2, 4–5, schedule 1.
152 20/269/EEC. *Council Directive of 29 May 1990 on the minimum health and safety requirements for the manual handling of loads where there is a risk particularly of back injury to workers, a.4.*
153 Austin, J. (1994). A lift in the law. *Therapy Weekly:* 23 June 1994, pp. 7–8.
154 Snell, J. (1995). Raising awareness. *Nursing Times:* 2 August 1995; 91(31), pp.20–21.
155 See eg a detailed letter from a person who suffered a brainstem stroke – on the implications of using lifting and turning equipment: Grant, C.F. (1995). Lifting aids: the patient's opinion. *British Journal of Therapy and Rehabilitation:* June 1995; 2(6), p.331. And see reply by Nicola Stacey of the Disabled Living Foundation who points to the complexity of moving and handling practice and to the importance of training and of getting used to equipment.
156 Love, C. (1996). Economic considerations when choosing a hoist and slings. *British Journal of Therapy and Rehabilitation:* April 1996; 3(4), pp.189–1988.
157 Social Services Inspectorate (Cope, C., Watson, A., Tweedale, L.) (1995). *Inspection of community services for physically disabled people in Wirral, 9–20 October 1995,* p.41.
158 Health Services Advisory Committee (1992). *Guidance on manual handling of loads in the health services.* Sudbury: Health and Safety Executive, p.20.

CHAPTER 16

BUYING EQUIPMENT AND MAKING CONSUMER CONTRACTS

COVERAGE

1. When do people make contracts to buy equipment or adaptations?
    - Loan of equipment by statutory services: is there a contract?
    - Legal relations are necessary for a contract to exist
    - Entering contracts freely: unfair contracts, undue pressure and influence, mental capacity
    - Offering equipment and accepting the offer
    - Giving payment or consideration for equipment
    - Effect of guarantees
    - Providing aftersales services
    - Contracts for private medical treatment and the provision of equipment
    - Who can enforce a contract?
    - Equipment damaged or destroyed before delivery: who is responsible
    - Equipment damaged before delivery and mail order: who bears the loss.
2. Equipment which is of unsatisfactory quality
    - Sellers are strictly liable for breach of contract
    - Things that can be wrong with equipment
    - Supply of services and equipment together.
3. What to do when equipment is unsatisfactory
    - Harm caused by defective or unsatisfactory equipment
    - Rejecting equipment altogether
    - Can sellers of equipment exclude or restrict liability?
    - Categories of damages
    - Time within which a legal action must be brought
    - Mitigation and contributory negligence.

Key points

Basic rules of contract. This chapter cannot even begin to cover comprehensively the law of contract; there are many other books which do so. Instead, it selects issues and examples which are particularly relevant, such as how fit a walking frame is for its intended purpose, how the durability of a wheelchair is measured in legal terms, and how the courts might decide that contracts of sale are unfair to the consumer.

The law of contract applies when people make a bargain together – for example, when they buy equipment from a shop or voluntary organisation (maybe by mail order), or pay a builder to widen a doorway for wheelchair access. It also applies to private health care and social care. For example, equipment might be provided as part of agreed services, such as a hospital operation or nursing home care. Contracts are made not just when equipment is sold, but also when it is hired or supplied on a hire-purchase basis.

One advantage of using the law of contract to gain redress is that when goods are sold and are not, legally, of satisfactory quality, then liability for breach of contract is strict – that is, carelessness or unreasonableness on the part of the supplier does not have to be proved. In other words, if people buy equipment which is clearly defective, they do not have to prove that the retailer was at 'fault'. Furthermore, the law of contract, unlike the law of negligence or the Consumer Protection Act 1987 does not insist that injury or damage must have resulted. It is enough that the product is unsatisfactory and that the buyer has therefore been deprived of his bargain.

The disadvantage of the law of contract, is that, generally speaking, only the person who has made the contract can sue. This is known as *privity of contract.* For example, if a woman buys a defective stairlift which, as a result, injures a friend, the latter cannot sue in contract for her own injuries but would have to do so in negligence or under the Consumer Protection Act 1987.

In relation to the supply of goods, the rules and concepts of contract law are well-established and relatively clear – compared, for example, to the developing law of judicial review (Chapter 17). Even so, the certainty of contract law (applied to the sale of goods) begins to fray sometimes at the edges when the courts consider, for example, how durable products should be, what length of time a buyer reasonably needs to discover whether a product is unsatisfactory, and what an unreasonable term in a contract is. In addition, modern legislation has introduced new elements to the law of contract by imposing rules which protect consumers – for example, from *unfair* contractual terms. Such has been the effect of consumer protection legislation, that it has been suggested that there are now almost 'two laws' of contract – one extending to purely commercial agreements, the other to agreements involving consumers.[1] This chapter concentrates on this second area of contract law – ie agreements between two parties, one of whom is a consumer.

Provision of equipment by statutory services. The position is not so straightforward when statutory services provide equipment for individual service users. There is almost certainly no legally enforceable contract when statutory services loan equipment to service users, even if a financial charge is made. If, for example, statutory services delegate equipment provision to an independent organisation, a voluntary body or private company, there is still no contract with service users. The contract is between the independent organisation and the NHS Trust or social services department.

Application of contract law to equipment provision. In the context of this book contractual issues are becoming increasingly important. For instance, some social services departments and NHS Trusts are urging people to buy their own equipment. Whereas previously these people might have had a non-contractual loan arrangement with the local authority, now they will be making contractual purchasing arrangements with private sector retailers. On the whole, many people buying their own disability equipment are likely to be ill-informed and be at risk of making bad bargains; this might be due, for example, to people's general unfamiliarity with disability equipment (see p.70). It might also be coupled with, for instance, anxiety about the unexpected bodily changes they (eg older people) are undergoing, which makes them vulnerable to making over-hasty and inappropriate purchases.

Settling disputes. In practice, consumer litigation in relation to the sale of goods is not widespread. A major reason for this is that often the amounts of money at stake are unlikely to encourage legal action.[2] Another reason is good will and business sense; for example, many retailers will repair and replace faulty goods or refund the purchase price – although there is generally no legal obligation to do so. Many manufacturers offer guarantees, although the legal status of these is somewhat uncertain. Similarly, disputes can sometimes be solved informally through trade associations – for instance, by means of their complaints, conciliation or arbitration procedures.

Nevertheless, there are good reasons to know about the law of contract. For consumers, the knowledge might be useful as a last resort if they are clearly getting nowhere in informal negotiation. For suppliers, it can be useful when they are faced with unreasonable complainants who are insisting on their 'rights'. Furthermore, not all equipment and adaptations are cheap. Electric wheelchairs can cost thousands of pounds; and home adaptations tens of thousands.

Questions people ask

- What if a new wheelchair has scratched paintwork?
- What does a retailer do if a person buys a riser chair, and months later complains that she has changed her mind?
- What if a hoist or stairlift has been installed badly and causes injury to a person and damage to the house?
- What does a shop do when, 6 months after an elderly lady bought a stairlift which she has barely used, but really wanted at the time of purchase, relatives angrily complain that she was pressured into buying it?
- What effect does a guarantee on an electric scooter have?
- What happens when a person states specifically, when buying a wheelchair, that it must be able to climb kerbs of up to 4 inches – but it turns out that the wheelchair cannot do so?
- What can be done about a sub-contractor who has carried out a poor home adaptation?
- Does an excessively high price for an adapted car mean that the contract is legally unfair?
- How is reasonable durability of equipment such as wheelchairs or walking aids measured legally?

1. WHEN DO PEOPLE MAKE CONTRACTS TO BUY EQUIPMENT OR ADAPTATIONS?

The ability to sue, or at least to threaten to sue, in contract, obviously depends on the existence of a contract in the first place. For a contract to exist, an offer has to be made by one person and accepted by another. Both people must intend to be legally bound by the agreement. In addition, each must be giving up something; in a contract for the sale of equipment, the seller gives up the product, the buyer money.

However, before explaining these rules, the section immediately below explains the position when statutory services loan equipment to service users.

Loan of equipment by statutory services: is there a contract?

When *statutory services* supply equipment to individuals, the courts are unlikely to hold that contracts exist. For example, this was the approach of the House of Lords in a case about the prescription of drugs by the NHS[3]:

> 'Sale is a consensual contract requiring agreement, express or implied. In the present case there appears to me to be no need for any agreement. The patient has a statutory right to demand the drug on payment of 2s. The hospital has a statutory obligation to supply it on such payment. And if the prescription is presented to a chemist he appears to be bound by his contract with the appropriate authority to supply the drug on receipt of such payment. There is no need for any agreement between the patient and either the hospital or the chemist, and there is certainly no room for bargaining. Moreover the 2s. is not in any sense the price; the drug may cost much more and the chemist has a right under his contract with the authority to receive the balance from them. It appears to me that any resemblance between this transaction and a true sale is only superficial.'

The Royal Commission on Civil Liability for Personal Injury also assumed that no contract exists between the NHS doctor and the patient.[4] Although this is about supply by the NHS, it seems reasonable to suppose that the same principle applies to the other statutory services covered in this book. Indeed, the principle was applied in a case involving a different type of public service altogether, when a court found that the relationship between a poultry farmer and a public utility company (an electricity board), was non-contractual. The farmer had lost a certain quantity of the poultry he was rearing because of fluctuations in the power supply: the judge treated[5]:

> 'the supply of electricity by the Board not as the acceptance of an offer...to take and pay for a supply, so as to create a contract, but as given in pursuance of the Board's statutory duty to give a supply to a consumer who, being entitled, demands it'.

Therefore, the courts will not recognise the existence of contracts when the information and policy documents of statutory services apparently offer people certain 'entitlements' (eg so many hours of home help a week) if they come forward and can meet certain conditions (eg demonstrate particular needs). The same applies to statements made in charters – they are not contractual (see p.145). And even an individual letter sent by a local authority to a user of services setting out what is available under what conditions, is unlikely to be held to be contractual.[6]

Legal relations are necessary for a contract to exist

In order for a contract to exist, there must be an agreement creating *legal relations* between the buyer and the seller. If the agreement is a formal commercial or business one, as opposed to a domestic or informal social agreement, then there is a strong presumption that legal relations – and therefore a contract – exist. This presumption can be overturned if there are very clear words in the agreement stating that legal relations are not intended. Thus, in one case involving Vernons Pools, the court accepted the statement made on the back of the coupons that the relationship between company and participant amounted to a gentleman's agreement, not to a legally enforceable contract.[7] Nevertheless, even then a court might analyse the contract and decide that the words do not *in fact* exclude legal relations.[8]

If the agreement is domestic or social in nature, then the courts will examine it to determine whether or not legal relations are intended. For example, the courts have held that an agreement between husband and wife is normally not enforceable, because no legal relations were intended when it was made[9] – but it might be enforceable if made when they were about to separate.[10] However, three women who shared a house, jointly entered a newspaper fashion competition in the Sunday Empire News, and agreed to share any winnings, were held to have intended to create legal relations.[11]

Thus, a person might give a walking stick to a friend, in return for a long-coveted orthopaedic pillow, only for the stick to break or the pillow to sag. Or, an older woman might ask a family friend to put up grab rails (which subsequently come away from the wall, causing damage and injury) in the bathroom – in return, say, for a traditional Sunday lunch. These are probably, but not necessarily, domestic or informal social agreements which are not legally enforceable.

Entering contracts freely: unfair contracts, undue pressure and influence, mental capacity

An agreement must be entered into freely by both parties, ie buyer and seller. Once this fact is established, there are a few circumstances in which a court might hold that a contract is unfair and overturn it; but, basically, the courts are reluctant to interfere, because of the well-known rule, buyer beware (caveat emptor). This rule is likely to predominate even if an excessively high price has been charged. However, there are a number of situations in which the validity of a contract can be attacked. These are summarised immediately below.

Unfair contracts: plain language, good faith, unequal bargaining power
The courts are loath to overturn contracts on the sole grounds that two people have unequal bargaining power, as a result of which one person has made a bad bargain.[12] Nevertheless, recent Regulations[13], deriving from a European Community Directive[14], do make inroads into the ability of sellers to impose unreasonable terms on consumers.

The Unfair Terms in Consumer Contracts Regulations 1994 state that the terms of a consumer contract could be unfair if they have not been made in good faith, and if they cause a significant and detrimental imbalance in the rights and obligations of the consumer. The Regulations only apply to terms which have not been individually negotiated. This means that they will apply to the many transactions in which the seller's terms have been drafted and fixed in advance.

Factors relevant to unfairness include, for example, inequality of bargaining position, the plainness and intelligibility of the language used in the contract, and whether the seller or supplier has dealt fairly and equitably with the consumer.[15] Other considerations suggested by the Regulations, indicatively but not exhaustively (ie suggesting but not prescribing), include manipulation by the seller of the final price to be paid and restriction of a consumer's right to take legal action. Various others are listed.[16]

The Regulations do not allow terms dealing with the 'main subject-matter' of the contract or the price to be questioned directly – unless they are expressed in language which is not plain and intelligible.[17] This seems to mean that consumers cannot complain simply because they have made a bad bargain in relation to what they have bought or what they have paid for it. However, the original Directive explains that price and subject matter can be taken account of when assessing other terms in the contract.[18] Whilst the Regulations might invalidate a particular term, the rest of the contract will stand unless this has become impossible by the removal of the unfair term.[19]

The Regulations overlap with another piece of legislation – the Unfair Contract Terms Act 1977 (see p.415) – though the latter deal only with unfair terms excluding or limiting the liability of a party when things go wrong.

Office of Fair Trading: examples of unfair terms. Under the Unfair Terms in Consumer Contracts Regulations, the Office of Fair Trading (OFT) can consider 'any complaint' and has the power to take legal action against sellers or suppliers using unfair contract terms. When deciding what to do about complaints, the OFT can take into account undertakings by sellers, suppliers or trade associations that they will not use the unfair term(s) in the future.[20] This system means that (i) consumers do not have to take direct legal action and (ii) that sellers and suppliers might well agree to change their contracts by abandoning certain terms – rather than become involved in litigation. However, there is no appeal procedure included.[21]

In the first six months after the Regulations came into force in July 1994, the OFT received over 300 complaints about alleged unfair contract terms – of which about one half were potentially unfair in the OFT's judgement. The OFT has stated that companies should not consider their contract terms, even if they have used them for many years, as necessarily 'bullet-proof'; whilst unreadable small print is 'totally indefensible'. In response to the concern of the OFT, some companies moved quickly to excise from their standard contracts terms which, for example[22]:

- exclude all liability for personal injury, loss or damage on a football training course
- exclude a travel agent's liability for breaches of contract and negligence
- exclude liability totally by stating that a car wash was 'used entirely at owner's risk
- limit the commitment of car dealers to take back cars from dissatisfied consumers – by excluding any vehicles which had suffered, in the opinion of the dealer, over £150's worth of damage.

Quite apart from the Unfair Contract Terms Regulations, the courts might anyway intervene if people try to impose unfair contractual terms. They might hold that if there was a particularly unusual contractual term, printed amongst the normal conditions on the back of a contract, it should be made conspicuous – for example, in red ink. This rule was applied in one case when the contractual term, imposed by a picture library, stipulated unusually high overdue charges on the transparencies it loaned.[23]

Sometimes the courts find that supposed contractual terms only come to the attention of the consumer after the contract has been made – and so are not part of the contract at all. This happened, for example, when a motorist paid to get into a multi-storey car park and obtained a ticket, which referred him to conditions printed on notices inside the car park. These attempted to exclude all liability – but the court suggested that the contract was made when the motorist put his money into the machine at the entrance and received a ticket.[24] If so, the terms of the notice could not possibly have been part of the contract, however fair or unfair they were. Similarly, if people hire deckchairs[25] or take hotel rooms[26], terms introduced respectively by the receipt for the chair (ie after payment) or by a notice in the room (ie after having booked in) come too late to be part of the contract.

Threatening, unduly influencing or misleading people, doorstep selling and mental incapacity

There is sometimes a fine line between good salesmanship and pressurised selling. In addition, feelings can run high when elderly, sometimes vulnerable, people appear to be 'persuaded' by a 'hard-selling' technique to buy inappropriate equipment which they can ill afford. Equally, however, retailers might themselves come under unfair pressure from relatives who are angry that £3000 of their potential inheritance has been spent on an electric wheelchair that is not being used. This might be in spite of the fact that their mother took a definite decision that she wanted the chair – and that she was fully supported by her husband. He foresaw that, even if the chair were not used a great deal, it would still have psychological value in offering the potential for mobility and independence. Even when pressurised selling does occur, there might be little legal redress available except possibly in the following types of situation.

Duress and threatening people. The courts are prepared sometimes to overturn contracts because of *duress*. Traditionally, duress has been defined very narrowly. Generally speaking, it must involve serious, illegal threats towards life or limb or property.[27] Clearly, this is unlikely to apply to sales of equipment, other than in extreme cases. For instance, it would not apply to a 'pushy' salesman who visited an elderly person at home, persuaded her to buy an electric scooter she did not really need, refused to take a cheque and drove her to the bank to withdraw cash.

However, more recently, the courts have expanded the concept of duress to include what has been called 'economic duress'. This involves one party placing excessive pressure – that is, more than legitimate, commercial pressure – on another party who, in the circumstances, has no option but to accede.[28] This doctrine has been developed in commercial cases; it is perhaps not clear how it might be applied in the consumer context. To give a hypothetical example, economic duress might be present if the supplier of a complex, custom-made wheelchair asked the consumer to pay more than had originally been agreed – simply because he knew that the latter needed the wheelchair urgently, and had no viable alternative.[29]

There is of course a distinction between this narrow, judicial definition and use of the word duress in other contexts where it is employed more loosely. For instance, the health service ombudsman has made a finding of duress against a health authority which failed to inform the wife of a severely brain-damaged man about the fees she would have to pay to a private nursing home – the hospital was refusing to care for her husband any longer. He concluded that although she had 'acquiesced in the need for her to pay the nursing home fees, in my opinion that was inequitable in the circumstances'. She had been placed under 'duress' because of a 'failure to inform her of all the relevant considerations she should have had placed before her'.[30]

Unduly influencing people. Second, it is possible in some circumstances that the courts might find that *undue influence* had been used to make an *unconscionable bargain*, if – to use the language of the courts – the exploited person is poor, ignorant, or weak-minded, or in need of special protection.[31] The range of contexts in which the courts might apply this principle is not clear – it seems to have been most commonly considered in relation to the selling of property at an undervalue. For instance[32]:

A 'frail old man of 80' had agreed by mistake to sell his bungalow for £2950 instead of for £29,500. The judge found that there was no binding contract, either because a 'unilateral mistake' had been made or because there had never been a proper agreement on the subject matter of the contract. However, he said that in any case he would have set the contract aside as an 'unconscionable bargain'; the desire for a quick sale, and old age with accompanying diminution of capacity and judgement, amounted to the traditional requirement of the courts that 'poverty and ignorance' be present.

Misrepresenting what equipment is capable of. Third, if a salesman persuades a person to buy equipment by saying something, whether deliberately or carelessly, which was untrue, then the courts might find that *misrepresentation* had occurred.[33] For instance, the salesman might state explicitly that the wheelchair requires no maintenance (eg tyre pumping or battery recharging). If the woman relies on this to the extent that she would not have bought the wheelchair had she known the truth, then misrepresentation might have occurred – the misrepresentation caused her to make an agreement she would not otherwise have made.[34] In these circumstances, it might be possible to have the contract 'rescinded', in which case she would get her money back. However, the type of redress available depends to some extent on what type of misrepresentation has taken place – ie whether it was innocent, negligent or fraudulent. The legal rules governing the law of misrepresentation are complex and not explained here.

Alternatively, if the courts held that the statement was actually part of the contract, then the woman would be able to sue for breach of contract. A third possibility is that the woman might be able to sue in negligence on the grounds that a negligent statement had been made (see p.336).

Doorstep selling. If salespeople pursue *doorstep selling* by visiting, unsolicited, the homes or places of work of consumers, then any contract of sale made during the visit can be cancelled within the next seven days. The position is similar if the visit was requested, but the contract eventually concluded involves goods or services which the consumer didn't know, or could not reasonably have known, the seller was involved with. However, the relevant legislation[35], deriving from a European Community directive[36], lists a number of types of contract to which it does not apply – including those involving £35 or less. Accordingly, if a person telephones a supplier of electric wheelchairs after seeing an advertisement in the Sunday newspaper, receives a visit and buys a chair, the legislation could not apply. But they would apply if the 'wheelchair' salesman was unexpectedly selling stairlifts as well. And if the same salesman made an unannounced visit to, for example, sheltered housing, they would also apply.

Buying 'necessary' equipment and being mentally incapable.

Under the general, common law, if a person is *mentally incapable* at the time a contract is made, the contract is voidable (ie can be cancelled) if the other person (eg the seller) knew, or should have known, that the buyer was mentally incapable. If the seller did not know this, the contract cannot be cancelled in this way.[37]

When 'necessary' *goods* are sold, and the seller does not know of the buyer's mental incapacity, then the same rules apply – the contract is still enforceable. However, if the seller is aware of the buyer's incapacity, then the Sale of Goods Act 1979 states that the buyer still has to pay a reasonable price for the goods.[38] Traditionally, 'necessary' goods have been taken to include food, drink and clothing needed for everyday living and suitable people's ordinary circumstances in life.

In the context of this book, the scope of the meaning of 'necessaries' is unclear, but it might embrace more than what is needed for bare, physical survival. When considering necessaries for minors – also, in principle, incapable of making contracts[39] – the courts have held, for example, that a racing bicycle for an apprentice was a 'necessary'[40] – but that extravagant clothing for a Cambridge undergraduate was not.[41] So, if a person bought five walking frames, the requirement that they all be paid for might not apply – because although a person might need one frame, he would not need five. They, or least four of them, would not then be 'necessaries' and the Act would not apply to them.[42]

Disability Discrimination Act 1995

Part 3 of the Disability Discrimination Act 1995, coming into force gradually from the end of 1996 onwards, places a duty on suppliers of goods and services not to discriminate against disabled people. Steps to be taken by suppliers include changes to practices, policies, procedures and physical features – and the provision of auxiliary aids to enable disabled people to use services. However, the steps only have to be taken if they are reasonable.[43]

Suppliers cannot pass on the costs of taking such reasonable steps to disabled people. However, apart from this, if a supplier is providing a special service, then a disabled person can be charged a higher price than would be charged to a non-disabled person. For instance, a customised shoe made to an unusual pattern or from unusual material, or a special order, might justify a higher price.[44] Presumably, domiciliary visits to housebound people to demonstrate and sell equipment would be another example justifying a higher price.

Any legal action for damages brought in connection with discrimination under this part of the Act has to be brought in tort and might, for example, include a claim of damages for injured feelings. However, any term of a contract for the provision of goods, services or facilities which contravenes the legislation is anyway void – ie has no effect.[45]

Offering equipment and accepting the offer

The law courts have tended to identify the making of an agreement by looking for *offer* and *acceptance* – ie an offer by, for example, a seller of a commode and the acceptance of that offer by a buyer. This might seem to be quite straightforward but is not always so – even in normal transactions in the shops. For instance, when a pharmacy displays disability equipment on its self-service shelves, it is not offering the equipment for sale. This principle was established in a case (*Pharmaceutical Society v Boots*) when a court held that, instead, the pharmacy is merely inviting the customer to make an offer – which the staff at the till are then free to accept or reject:[46]

> The case involved a Boots branch in Edgware and the sale of syrup medicines containing small quantities of strychnine and codeine. The decision of the court meant that Boots was complying with the Pharmacy and Poisons Act 1933, which required that certain items be sold only under the supervision of a pharmacist. However, had placing the items on the shelf amounted to an offer, then the pharmacist would not have been free to bar the sale, which would have been complete when the customer accepted the 'offer' by taking the medicines to the till.

Similarly, if a seller of stairlifts places advertisements in a local newspaper, he is not making a contractual offer to sell the stairlifts, but merely inviting consumers to make an offer – which the seller is free to accept or reject.

On the other hand, a retailer who places an advertisement in the local newspaper – offering an electric riser chair for £1.00 to the first customer to arrive next Monday morning – could probably not claim that the advertisement was simply a sales ploy and nothing more. The firm would be bound in contract to supply the chair. This example is based on an American case about an offer of fur coats for $1 each to the first three customers into the shop on a Saturday morning.[47] Likewise, in a much cited case heard in 1893 in this country (*Carlill v Carbolic Smoke Ball Co*), a manufacturer was bound when it offered £100 'reward' for anybody who used its protective, carbolic smoke ball but still contracted influenza – and stated also that it had deposited £1000 in the bank to show its 'sincerity' in the matter. The court held that the advertisement was not a 'mere puff' but a contractual offer which could be accepted by anybody meeting the conditions – that is, buying the smokeball, using it and contracting influenza.[48]

A much more recent case in 1995 (*Bowerman v Association of British Travel Agents*) concerned a notice displayed in a tour operator's office that ABTA would protect any customers from the consequences of the insolvency of tour operators. The Court of Appeal held that the notice amounted to a 'unilateral' contract which contained legally enforceable promises. ABTA could easily have indicated on the notice that it was not 'really' making promises – though of course, for commercial reasons, it had not in fact done this.[49] To take a comparable example: a notice in the window of a supplier of electric wheelchairs might advertise a scheme (implemented and guaranteed by a trade association) – to the effect that spare parts would be available for any chair, for up to five years from purchase. Such a notice might be held to be contractual and enforceable against the trade association, even though it was not formally part of the contract between the consumer and the retailer.

Giving payment or consideration for equipment

Another essential element of a contract for equipment provision is that the parties, ie the supplier and the recipient, give *consideration.*

This means that both parties give something up – for example, the exchange of goods and money which takes place between seller and buyer. The consideration does not necessarily have to be *adequate,* in the sense of the going market rate.[50] Therefore, if a company was offering, for example, kettle tippers, at a knockdown price – even as little as £0.25 – the consideration would still be *sufficient* to support a contract.

Free loan of equipment by statutory services and voluntary bodies

If, for example, voluntary organisations loan equipment free of charge, then there is, in an obvious sense, a lack of consideration; the user of the equipment is not paying anything. And, in any case, as already explained, whether or not payment is made, the supply of equipment by statutory services to service users is unlikely to be seen by the courts as a contractual activity (see p.391).

However, it has been pointed out that the courts are ingenious at finding consideration – even when there is none very apparent.[51] For example, in the case of the smoke ball, already mentioned above, the buyer had paid the *retailer,* but it was the *manufacturer* who was offering the reward in the event that anybody should catch influenza. Therefore, it seemed unclear what consideration or payment the buyer of the smoke ball was offering the manufacturer, in return for the offer of the reward. Recognising this potential difficulty, the court held that the consideration could consist of the unpleasant activity of using the smoke ball.[52]

Thus, it has been suggested that, even though the courts do not in practice recognise contracts between statutory services and the users of those services, there is in fact consideration present. For instance, even if users are not paying for equipment, the statutory service might still be getting a bargain, because it is taking the opportunity to do its statutory duty.[53] And, it is even conceivable that a user of equipment is giving consideration by agreeing to maintain it (eg by cleaning, or recharging the batteries of, a wheelchair).

Free loan of equipment: bailment. When statutory services and voluntary organisations loan equipment free of charge, the principle of bailment might apply.[54] Quite apart from any 'agreements' (eg about the maintenance and return of the equipment) the borrower might sign, the common law of *bailment* anyway imposes an obligation on the borrower (the *bailee*) to return the equipment in good condition at the appropriate time. If the equipment is damaged because of carelessness, the voluntary body or statutory service could, in principle, sue the person for damages.[55] Similarly, the law of bailment would also apply when, for example, social services departments make charges for equipment – for example, £2.00 per week for the use of a high seat chair.

Given that the whole transaction between, for example, a social services department and a user is non-contractual, what is the effect of 'indemnity clauses' signed by users? For instance, a user might undertake that he will 'be responsible for any damage to the equipment/adaptations however caused and will make good such damage'.[56] This undertaking might do no more than to confirm the liability the borrower anyway incurs under the law of bailment, or simply in negligence (ie common law duty of care). However, this particular undertaking, taken literally, is rather more harsh, since it would cover damage caused not just by the borrower's carelessness or fault, but also by factors beyond his control. Thus, given that the agreement is non-contractual, and that it imposes greater liability than is imposed by the common law of bailment or negligence, it may be unclear how enforceable the agreement would be in some circumstances.

In addition – quite apart from the law of bailment – the NHS has the power under the NHS Act 1977 to make charges for the repair or replacement of any equipment (even if normally provided free of charge), if it is necessitated by an act or omission of the user.[57]

Conversely, if the equipment is defective when it is loaned and causes an accident, the user (borrower) is not short of potential remedies; apart from a possible action under the law of bailment against the lender, he could, depending on the circumstances, rely on the law of negligence or the Consumer Protection Act 1987.

Effect of guarantees

In practice, the guarantees of manufacturers are a commonplace part of consumer sales and normally work quite straightforwardly.

Nevertheless, the *legal status* of manufacturers' guarantees is apparently *not* straightforward. First, guarantees do not apply between the consumer and the supplier or retailer of the goods, since the offer of the guarantee is made by the manufacturer. Second, guarantees might have no *legal* effect even between consumer and manufacturer, because purchasers are not giving extra payment, or consideration (see above). However, it is thought that the courts might hold that the guarantee forms part of a *collateral contract* – ie the manufacturer's offer of a guarantee induces the customer to enter into the main contract to buy the goods from the retailer. Last, this legal uncertainty would not apply to an *extended guarantee*, of the type now in vogue, for which the customer pays extra. In this case, there is a straightforward contract between the consumer and the dealer or the insurance company – the extra payment being the consideration for the extended cover.[58] However, extended warranties have recently attracted criticism, since there is evidence that retailers provide inadequate information about them in terms of prices, terms and conditions. The Office of Fair Trading has called for voluntary action on the part of retailers but, failing this, has threatened regulation.[59]

It has been pointed out that the absence of 'legal guarantees' – ie guarantees regulated by legislation – creates uncertainty about their effect.[60] Nevertheless, it has also been suggested that the present system allows informal negotiation, whereas legal guarantees might encourage confrontation and evasion.[61]

Providing aftersales services

There is no automatic legal obligation placed on suppliers to repair or replace faulty goods, although many will do so in practice. Similarly, there is no legal obligation on suppliers to carry spare parts or provide aftersales services[62] – it has been pointed out that such an obligation would be costly to small shopkeepers. There are also difficult questions about how long parts should be kept, and what the position is if the manufacturer goes out of business.[63] Nor are manufacturers legally obliged to continue to make spare parts, although any particular contract might in fact stipulate this. Alternatively, the guarantees provided by manufacturers of, for example, bathroom equipment might state that spare parts will be available for at least ten years from the date of purchase.

Some suppliers or retailers might fail to offer aftersales support at all, in an attempt to keep down their own running costs – and so undercut rivals. Some commentators have even suggested that the absence of the availability of spare parts amounts almost to a defect in a product – and that if this situation is unsatisfactory nationally, it will become even worse as goods begin to flow more freely across Europe.[64]

Access to aftersales services can be important, all the more so, if people have bought expensive equipment for which they need maintenance, continuing advice and spare parts. Sometimes manufacturers go out of business; this has been a feature of the disability equipment market, particularly when small scale development of a specialist product has taken place, but the developer cannot sustain commercial activity over time. If commonly available electrical parts have not been used, then the users of, for example, electric wheelchairs – which have been specially modified or which users cannot afford to replace (or both) – might face considerable difficulties and anxiety. They might even consider buying and hoarding spare parts for the future.[65]

With these concerns in mind, the codes of practice of trade associations might insist that members offer aftersales services. For example, the British Association of Wheelchair Distributors (a section of BSTA: the British Surgical Trades Association), states that its members should have an 'existing and comprehensive "in house" and after sales service', and, specifically, 'hold adequate stocks of components related to the various products which it distributes'.[66]

Contracts for private medical treatment and the provision of equipment

Equipment is sometimes provided for paying patients in private or in NHS hospitals. In either case, clear written agreement is desirable about what is being provided and what it will cost.

For example, Department of Health guidance states that before the NHS provides services, the private patient must sign an undertaking to pay, having been fully informed about the costs. It notes that supplementary charges to inpatients should not be made for 'implants, aids and appliances', so long as they are prescribed for the medical condition of the person while he is a private inpatient. In other words, the costs of any equipment should be included in the original charges.

Sometimes a person enters an NHS hospital privately for a minor condition, only to have a more serious complication diagnosed. He can then revert to NHS status, but might have to go on to a waiting list and, in any case, would still have to pay for the treatment and equipment received whilst a private patient.[67]

Who can enforce a contract?

Generally speaking, a contract can be enforced only by somebody who is a party to the agreement.[68] Therefore, for instance, if a defective, domestic vertical lift causes an accident, injuring both the woman who purchased the lift and her husband, then only the woman (ie the purchaser and one party to the contract) can sue in contract for replacement of the defective item and for her injuries. The husband could not sue – although his wife might be able to sue for his injuries if she suffered loss because of them; for example, she might be paying for their treatment.[69] The husband might, however, be able to sue in negligence or under the Consumer Protection Act 1987. Similarly, a person might receive a disabled facilities grant from a housing authority, and make a contract with a builder to carry out an adaptation. The builder, in turn, might arrange for a subcontractor to undertake some of the work, including the installation of a concrete ramp. The ramp is badly defective and crumbles within a few months. The person cannot sue the subcontractor *in contract* because he only ever had a contract with the original builder – and it is the latter he would have to sue. (The builder could, in turn, sue the subcontractor). However, if personal injury was caused by the defective ramp, then an action in negligence might succeed against the subcontractor (see p.338).

Equipment damaged before delivery: who is responsible

It is sometimes important to know when the *ownership* of equipment changes from that of seller to buyer. For instance, when a person pays for a reclining chair in a shop, does it belong to her straightaway – even though it will not be delivered for a week? If it does belong to her – does she, rather than the shop, then bear *the risk* if it is lost or damaged accidentally whilst it is being delivered?

Common sense might prevail. If retailers follow good business practice, they are unlikely to let customers bear the loss; they are also better-placed to take out insurance. Furthermore, in such situations, retailers have become bailees (ie they are looking after the goods for customers) and would be liable for *careless* damage to, or destruction of, the equipment. However, if the equipment was accidentally harmed, was expensive, and retailers felt that they could bear the loss, they might not accept responsibility.

The terms of the contract can deal with this problem, by stating exactly when ownership is transferred and where the risk lies. For instance, from the point of view of a consumer, the contract should state that the risk remains with the seller until the equipment is safely delivered into the hands of the buyer. If the contract is clear about ownership and risk, then the rules below do not apply.[70]

If the contract is silent about ownership and risk, then the legislation states that the risk passes when ownership is transferred.[71] But when is ownership transferred? First, if a consumer pays for a *specific* item (eg the reclining chair she tries out in the shop), then ownership is transferred from the seller to the buyer there and then – even though the chair has not yet been delivered. Therefore, if the chair was damaged later that day (eg on the seller's premises), it would be the buyer's loss, unless the seller was at fault.

Second, if a consumer orders a particular model of chair – but not, for example, the actual one she saw in the shop – then, the rule is different, because the item paid for in the shop is *non-specific*. In this case, ownership only passes when the chair is packed, labelled and delivered either to the buyer or to an independent carrier (at either of which points, the seller gives up control over the item) – but not before.[72] So, if the chair was damaged on the seller's premises, it would be the seller's loss.

Third, if goods are damaged once they have been delivered to an independent carrier, then the loss is the buyer's, unless the arrangements the seller has made with the carrier for delivery are unreasonable.[73]

Finally, if an item is delivered on approval, then ownership is only transferred when the buyer (i) indicates acceptance or (ii) keeps the goods beyond the time limit for their return – without indicating that they are being rejected.[74] If the goods meet with a genuine accident before ownership has been transferred according to these rules, then the buyer is not liable. If, however, damage is caused by the buyer's carelessness, then he would have failed in his duty as a bailee (see above).

Mail order selling of equipment

Mail order selling can be very important to disabled people who are housebound and cannot get out to the shops – not only to buy disability equipment but also quite ordinary products. Evidence of this is afforded by recent joint ventures between voluntary organisations and commercial companies to produce and distribute mail order catalogues of specialist equipment. Nevertheless, mail order does increase the risk of people buying the wrong equipment – as suggested some years ago by a survey of a voluntary organisation's postal sales of disability equipment to people with rheumatism.[75]

An offer is made when the buyer sends in an order; the offer is accepted, and the contract therefore entered into, when the seller sends a receipt, an acknowledgement of the order or the product itself.[76] If the goods are sent on approval, as they often are, then the rule already explained above applies. However, it seems to be unclear when ownership, and therefore the risk relating to the goods, passes to the consumer who has already paid for them. For example, if the goods never arrive, what is the legal position – even if, as a matter of good practice, the mail order company might replace them? In one commercial case, the House of Lords ruled that ownership passed when the goods were posted, thus placing the risk on the buyer.[77]

The code of practice of the Mail Order Traders' Association, whose members include some of the very large mail order firms, deals with these issues in the following way. Goods might be sent on approval (see above) – in which case ownership does not pass until the buyer indicates acceptance. Alternatively, if customers have already paid for the goods, they have at least 14 days to return the goods and get their money back. However, if goods are damaged in the post, customers can return them, get a replacement (or their money back if no replacement is available) and reimbursement of carriage costs in some circumstances.[78] More particularly, the 'Chester-care' catalogue (produced by Homecraft Supplies), an established mail order catalogue of daily living (disability) equipment, states that products can be returned within 14 days of receipt if they are damaged, faulty or 'even unsuitable for your purpose'. In this event, they can be replaced or payment refunded – and the return postage costs refunded also.

2. EQUIPMENT WHICH IS OF UNSATISFACTORY QUALITY

Sellers are strictly liable for breach of contract

If a contract is for the supply of goods, then it is not necessary to show that the seller has been careless, if the contract has been breached, for example, in terms of the quality of the goods. This contrasts with the law of negligence, which requires that carelessness be shown before a person is held liable for breach of a duty of care. However, if the contract includes the provision of services as well as equipment, the position is not so straightforward (see below).

Things that can be wrong with equipment

Whether or not a contract states explicitly that equipment should conform to certain standards, these are anyway assumed to exist – ie they are implied – by legislation which covers the selling,[79] hire-purchase,[80] and hire of goods.[81] The assumption also extends to goods which are supplied as part of services (eg measuring, making and fitting an artificial limb, or installing a ceiling-fixed hoist).[82] In particular, there are terms which imply that equipment must *correspond with its description* and that it will be of *satisfactory quality*. These are explained immediately below.

Equipment should correspond with how it is described
It is implied by legislation that goods will correspond with their *description*.[83] For example, a walking frame, described in a brochure as made of lightweight metal, would not correspond with its description if it was in fact made of a heavy metal. Even though it might still be of good quality, its functionality could be crucially different for the particular person using it; he or she might be unable to manage the weight. Of course, short of specifying a weight in the brochure, or even if a weight was given, arguments might arise about the meaning of 'lightweight' – since such a term is elastic depending on view point. Similarly, equipment will not correspond to its description if a mail order catalogue is simply wrong about the dimensions of, for instance, the seat height of a chair or of a perching stool.

Equipment should be of satisfactory quality
Legislation states that goods should be of satisfactory quality. The term *satisfactory* is explained as what a reasonable person would regard as satisfactory – in the light of how the goods are described, their price and other relevant circumstances. The *quality* of goods includes their state and condition, and aspects of quality include fitness for purpose, appearance and finish, freedom from minor defects, and safety and durability.[84] It is noteworthy that people's 'regard' (ie expectations) – one of the themes central to this book (see p.21) – determine what is satisfactory. This illustrates the principle that when people make contracts, they are making bargains, part of which relates not only to the physical constitution of goods, but also, for example, to the price being paid. Thus, it might be that the reasonable person would expect that a 'helping hand' (ie a reaching stick with jaws) costing £25 should be more durable than one costing £3.99; in which case, when both break after twelve months of reasonably heavy use, only the former, but not the latter, might be deemed legally unsatisfactory.

In contrast, however, there would be no such distinction if both purchasers reached home and found that the jaws of the helping hands did not work from the outset. Both items, the cheap and the expensive, would clearly be of unsatisfactory quality. In such an instance, it would seem unnecessary even to refer to people's regard or expectations – since both helping hands would be clearly defective and not fit for their purpose. Nevertheless, the logic of measuring quality in terms of expectation would still hold good, in the sense that nobody would regard as satisfactory a helping hand whose jaws did not work.

It should be noted that the implied term of satisfactory quality only applies to goods sold by a seller in the course of business. This calls into question the meaning of a 'business' (eg does it apply to a Saturday afternoon church bazaar), already discussed elsewhere in this book in relation to other legislation (see p.358).

Fitness for purpose. Legislation states that equipment is fit for its purpose, if it is fit 'for all the purposes for which goods of that kind are commonly supplied'.[85]

For example, a special teapot tipper for people with shaky hands should be able not only to hold the teapot securely in an upright position but be able to tip it effectively as well. If it could not tip, it would not be fit for the purpose. Similarly, a court has held that dentures are unfit for their purpose if they do not fit a person's mouth and so cannot be used for 'eating and talking in the ordinary way'.[86] A product could be unfit if labels, information and instructions are missing or inadequate.[87] For example, a lack of instruction about setting the tension of a riser chair in relation to the weight of the user, could cause an accident by throwing him or her across the room. And failure to provide information about maintaining an electric scooter could result in damage both to the batteries and the scooter.

Clearly, there is a difference in principle, between an item which is genuinely not fit for its purpose – and a simple *change of mind* by the buyer. For instance, a person might buy a special type of bath, with a hinged, walk-in side. She might be perfectly physically capable of using it, but does not in fact do so because she remains fearful of bathing alone, and getting stuck or having an accident. Months later, she – or perhaps relatives – claim it is not fit for its purpose. This is simply a change of mind – there is nothing wrong with the bath.

Fitness for purpose: disability equipment and special considerations. Special considerations and difficulties apply to the sale of disability equipment; and what does seem to emerge from the following examples is the importance of the availability of expert information and advice when (or before) people buy equipment. Clearly, salesmen – as opposed to, for example, NHS therapists – cannot be expected to give disabled people a comprehensive 'assessment' in relation to their physical abilities or to their home or work environment. This could not be a part of ensuring that a product was legally 'fit for its purpose'. But, it is equally certain that people can very easily buy equipment that is practically of little use.

In recognition of the special field in which its members operate, the code of practice of the British Association of Wheelchair Distributors, a section of BSTA, acknowledges the extra difficulties of selling to disabled people by including, under the heading, 'Sales Function', the statement that it 'is the responsibility of the member to ensure, so far as is possible, that a product sold to an individual user is suitable for that person's ability'. It also states that before the conclusion of a sale, the purchaser should be 'given reasonable and fair tuition in its use under the conditions which the purchaser best describes as "normal" for his purposes'.[88] Similarly, the code of practice of the Rehabilitation Products Section of BSTA states firmly: 'Products shall only be supplied which fulfil a genuine need'.[89] And, the code of practice of the Hearing Aid Council states that 'dispensers shall, where appropriate, make it known to their clients that a hearing aid may not necessarily be of benefit'.[90]

Examples of practical complications in buying suitable equipment. A man might buy an electric wheelchair which, at the time of purchase, is suitable for his use. But, at the end of eight months, his disabling condition has progressed and the wheelchair is no longer suitable. The man – or his relatives – might claim that the supplier should have known that this would happen. Equally, the supplier could argue that the wheelchair was more than fit for its purpose at the time it was sold, and had at least 8 months' usage. In such situations, there might be no clear 'right' or 'wrong' (legal or moral) involved.

Similarly, a physically frail woman with some sensory loss in her hands and a balance disorder might hear about triangular, wheeled walking frames, with handles and bicycle-type brakes. She goes with a friend to a specialist shop and buys one, paying over £200. After using the frame for a few weeks, she is having difficulty in using it; because of her sensory loss, she cannot grip the brakes evenly and this makes the walker difficult and sometimes dangerous to use. In addition, a series of steps lead up to her house, up and down which she has to carry the (heavy) walker whenever she goes out. When she bought the walker, she did not explain to the staff about the sensory loss or the steps; but, equally, the staff who clearly knew little about the walker, made no attempt to discuss how she might use the product. The question then remains about how far sales staff should provide advice and information; indeed in this last sort of example, where is the line to be drawn between giving sales advice about equipment and advising about particular disabilities (a task for which staff are neither qualified nor paid)? In practice, some retailers are likely to give more advice than others – for instance, the Keep Able superstores (which have employed occupational therapists amongst their sales staff) seem to provide plentiful advice to customers – amounting sometimes almost to 'assessments'.

The importance of buying carefully is suggested by the 1993 General Household Survey, carried out by the Office of Population Censuses and Surveys. Surveying the use of mobility aids, it found that only 54% of items bought by relatives or friends were actually being used, compared to over 70% of items bought by users (or their spouses) themselves and 83% provided by social services departments or the NHS.[91] Thus, carers might have to return electric wheelchairs they have bought for their relatives, but who are unable to operate them.[92] Elsewhere, it has been pointed out that it is not just private provision of wheelchairs which it is difficult to get right:[93]

> 'With more than 600 types of wheelchair to choose from and an almost infinite number of adjustments and extras to suit individuals or specific tasks, making an appropriate assessment for an individual is no mean feat. A wheelchair is a complex

set of compromises between critical (or "loaded") and desirable features which can only be proven for an individual in practice. In the circumstances, it is not surprising that many assessments for state and private provision are less than satisfactory.'

In similar vein, a most useful guide produced by the Medical Devices Directorate (based on work carried out by Banstead Mobility Centre and analysed by the Research Institute for Consumer Affairs) listed a number of the social and environmental factors affecting powered wheelchair use. These included dwelling type, access to it, storage space and facilities, facilities for charging the batteries, terrain (eg hills, bumps, traffic density, pavement widths, kerb heights), length of period regular use (with seating needs in mind) – and so on.[94] And special wheelchair seating needs, for example, to provide body support, encourage good bladder function, make breathing easier for those with cardio-pulmonary disorders, enable good eye contact, provide comfort, be 'user-friendly' for carers and provide optimum positioning for function, education, swallowing, eating/drinking and communication.[95]

Not only might such matters be of enormous importance to people's daily lives, but they might relate specifically to safety as well. For instance, the necessity for suitable facilities for, and an understanding of, charging wheelchair batteries is underlined by the potential danger of leaking gas, leaking acid, inadvertent short-circuiting of batteries, and of trailing leads when wheelchairs are charged out-of-doors etc.[96] And in the case of stairlifts, occupational therapists can point to a number of 'contra-indications' including anxiety, balance or spatial disorders, other people in household (eg young children) severe epilepsy, or progressive/deteriorating conditions.[97]

Equipment not fit for purpose? There are some examples which begin to suggest that, even in the legal sense, some equipment is not fit for its purpose and so of unsatisfactory quality. For example, a guide to prescribing wheelchairs noted that wheelchairs, describing themselves as climbing kerbs to certain heights, might be literally capable of doing so. However, it pointed out that even experienced wheelchair users rarely attain those heights – because, for instance, of pain, impaired balance, reduced strength, lessened fine co-ordination of control, and lack of ability to transfer weight/balance at just the right moment. In addition, fear might 'also be a factor but, having observed many groups of able-bodied therapists during wheelchair study days, it could be said that fear of kerb climbing is not confined to disabled users'.[98]

Thus, it might be argued that the reasonable user will be disappointed by a wheelchair which cannot in practice climb as described – and that in such circumstances he will regard it as being of unsatisfactory quality. Similar considerations might apply to manufacturers' claims about the portability, foldability, transportability or pushability of wheelchairs; for example, if a wheelchair that describes itself as portable can be carried easily by a young, strong person – but not by most carers who are elderly – then arguably, the chair is of unsatisfactory quality in the light of how it has been presented by the manufacturer.[99]

Fitness for a special purpose. If the buyer explains to the seller the *particular purpose* for which he or she is buying the equipment, the position is a little different.

For instance, a person might buy a kerb-climbing wheelchair not just to negotiate normal kerbs generally, but the particularly high one (eg 6 inches) outside her house. In this case, when she 'makes known' the purpose to the seller, there is a condition implied by legislation that the equipment should be up to the job. However, the buyer must make the purpose known to the seller and she must also rely – or it must be reasonable for her to rely – on the skill or judgement of the seller.[100]

When a woman bought a Harris tweed coat, to which she was allergic, she had not informed the seller of her unusual allergy and so had no remedy – the seller could not have been expected to anticipate the 'abnormal'.[101] And, if a physiotherapist who regularly loans walking aids to patients, buys a walking stick privately for her father, she might not be able to rely on the implied condition that the stick be fit for the special purpose she made known to the salesman. (For instance, the optimum height of a stick might depend on whether it is needed for support or balance, the type of handle on the father's gripping ability, and the robustness on how long the stick is likely to be used for). The courts might hold that it was not reasonable for her to rely on the seller's judgement – because she was herself an expert.

Appearance, finish and minor defects of equipment. Appearance, finish and minor defects are specified by legislation as 'in appropriate cases' aspects of the quality of goods.[102]

For example, appearance and finish might be blemished by poor paintwork on a wheelchair. Likewise, a computer keyboard with one key not working properly, which occasionally fails to communicate with the computer, and with persistently stiff keys, is suffering from a number of minor defects. These might amount to legally unsatisfactory quality – just like, as the courts have put it, 'an army of minor, unconnected defects' in a motor car.[103] In any case, even a single defect, apparently minor, such as a loose screw, could cause a major problem – as a court ruled when a loose bit of sealant entered the lubrication system of a car, causing serious damage when the camshaft was deprived of its lubrication.[104] In addition, even if minor defects do not prevent a product from fulfilling its main function (eg a car being roadworthy), defects might still make it of unsatisfactory quality. As the court pointed out in another case, the buyers of a new Range Rover would have the expectation also of an 'appropriate degree of comfort, ease of handling and reliability and, one may add, of pride in the vehicle's outward and interior appearance'.[105]

Durability of equipment. There is no easy way of predicting the decisions of the courts about the durability of products. They have commented on durability in a case about a defective Landrover trailer coupling; the House of Lords stated that goods should remain fit for their purpose for a reasonable time – and that a reasonable time depended 'on the nature of the goods'.[106] This is no doubt a sensible, though not necessarily an informative, approach – other than to confirm that the courts will take each case on its facts.

In the case of disability equipment, durability is sometimes a pertinent issue. For instance, NHS wheelchair services incur large repair and replacement costs in respect of their wheelchair stocks. But it might be unclear in what circumstances the wheelchairs lack durability in a legal sense. It is possible that the manufacturers are indeed supplying poor quality wheelchairs. But, equa'ly, it could be argued that if the NHS insists on buying wheelchairs cheaply, tnen, inevitably, they will be to some extent less durable than more expensive, robust models. (Thereby, the NHS is of course also providing an incentive for manufacturers to produce cheap wheelchairs.) And the courts will take account of price in deciding whether goods are satisfactory (see above). For example, the NHS might sometimes try to save costs by loaning, to people who are very heavy, wheelchairs which are safe to use, but not as robust as more expensive models. It is not too surprising if the life of the chairs is shortened.

It might be difficult to assess the durability of some types of equipment, since not only the weight, but also the intensity and type of use of equipment can vary enormously. Take the brake cables of a walker (a wheeled walking frame) which break prematurely because of repeated gripping by the user – could it be argued that they were not legally durable? The manufacturer might claim that the brake cables were not intended to withstand such usage; but surely there is a question mark against durability if repeated gripping by disabled users is foreseeable, and the instructions fail to indicate that the brakes should not be used in such a way.[107]

Similarly, the fact that the average life of an artificial limb is reported in Parliament to be five years, does not necessarily provide legal answers about what the durability of a particular limb used by a particular person should be.[108] On the other hand, for instance, reasonable durability of a stairlift, designed for light daily use by people between a minimum and maximum weight, might be more easily assessed.

A comparable issue faces national and international standards-setting bodies when they develop technical specifications in relation to the 'essential requirements' stipulated by European Community legislation such as the Medical Devices Directive 1994 (see p.365). For example, should hoists and pulleys be designed for the heaviest patient conceivable; if not, what weight should be decided upon, and what will be the consequences for the design, materials, construction and cost of the equipment?[109]

Knowledge of unsatisfactory quality of equipment

Legislation states that if the unsatisfactory aspects of a product have been pointed out, or if the buyer has examined the equipment to an extent that should have enabled him to spot them, then there will be no implied term that the equipment is of satisfactory quality.[110]

For example, a seller might explain that the fold-up platform of a secondhand stairlift needs replacing. Alternatively, the buyer might look at the stairlift and see quite clearly for himself that the platform is not working or is missing altogether.

Secondhand equipment

The implied contractual term that goods will be of satisfactory quality applies to secondhand items as well as to new; however, the courts will take account of the fact that the goods are secondhand. So, a secondhand stairlift which had some defects would not necessarily be of unsatisfactory quality – compare a case involving a Jaguar car with a defective clutch.[111] But, if it was 'clapped out' and broke down after a short while, it might be unsatisfactory – as the court ruled in another case involving a 1964 secondhand Jaguar with an engine which failed after 2300 miles, nearly 17,000 miles short of what, on the dealer's own evidence, was to be expected.[112]

Supply of services and equipment together

A transaction involving equipment can be one of three types for the purposes of contract law; supply of the equipment alone, supply and related work (eg the work of installation or repair of equipment), or supply as part of a broader service. The category into which a particular equipment transaction comes affects the standard of liability relevant to a breach of contract.

First, the straightforward sale of equipment has already been dealt with. It is a strict term of consumer contracts that equipment should be, for example, of satisfactory quality and correspond to how it is described.[113]

Second, if goods or equipment are supplied as part of a contract for work and materials, such as the repair of a wheelchair or bicycle, or the installation of a central heating system, then the liability is also strict.[114] For example, if as part of a wheelchair repair, new but defective tyres were supplied, there would be strict liability for breach of the implied term that the tyres be of satisfactory quality.[115]

Third, a contract might be for professional services – for example, assessment and treatment by a physiotherapist, of which provision of equipment is an incidental part (eg supply of a cushion as part of an overall treatment programme for a neck strain). Contracts for services bear an implied term that the services will be carried out with *reasonable care and skill*.[116] This does not amount to strict liability if things go wrong; rather, it is relying on a notion of fault and reasonableness – thus resembling the law of negligence in this respect. This, then, differs from the strict liability applying to the two categories of contract described immediately above. Because there is no strict liability, 'success', in relation to what a person wants or expects from a service, is not necessarily guaranteed. For instance, in contracts for private medical treatment, the courts have held that there is no automatic implied term that operations, such as those for vasectomy, will be successful; what the surgeon is doing is contracting to carry out the operation with reasonable care and skill.[117] So, if a private physiotherapist provides a person with assessment and advice about what equipment to buy, she is contracting to provide these services with reasonable care and skill.

However, if the provider of the service promises explicitly a successful outcome, then failure to deliver this outcome might amount to a breach of contract – as occurred when a plastic surgeon failed to warn a patient about the risk of scarring and said to the patient: 'no problem. You will be very happy'.[118] And in one vasectomy case, the court held that the nature of the particular contract (eg it contained no warning that the operation might not be successful) meant that the surgeon had not just agreed to carry out the operation with reasonable care and skill, but also to 'make the male plaintiff irreversibly sterile'.[119] Similarly, it is thought that a stricter form of liability does sometimes apply to architects. The court explained this in one case (*Greaves v Baynham Meikle*) on the grounds that design contracts are sometimes drawn up so that, as a matter of fact rather than law, a term can be implied that the outcome will be fit for the purpose – not just that the architect will exercise reasonable care and skill. In this particular case, a warehouse had been designed without taking account of the use of forklift trucks which subsequently damaged the floor.[120] A comparable example might involve an architect designing a new bathroom for a disabled person in a wheelchair, which turned out to be inappropriate and unusable, because all its features were the wrong height for the wheelchair. Even suppose the architect were able to prove (which, anyway, he might not be able to) that, in the circumstances, he had exercised reasonable care and skill – he might still be held strictly liable.

Supply of equipment and services

Possible complication about liability can arise precisely because of these different standards of liability: *strict liability* for the supply of goods, but only *fault liability* for the supply of services.[121] What happens then, if it is unclear whether the contract is primarily for the supply of equipment (or at least equipment as part of a work/materials contract) – or primarily a contract of services? For instance, persistent discomfort and pain sometimes affect people who have artificial limbs. Is the discomfort caused by the limb itself or by the fitting of it? And, whatever the cause of the discomfort, is the contract to be regarded as, overall, one for the supply of goods or of services?

The Sale of Goods and Services Act 1982 (s.1(3)) appears to provide the answer by stating that strict liability attaches to goods even if services are also being provided under the contract. This reflects the approach taken by the courts in older cases – for example, when a dentist supplied ill-fitting dentures (*Samuels v Davis*)[122], and a hairdresser used a hair dye containing a 10% (instead of a 4%) acid solution which gave the customer dermatitis (*Watson v Buckley*).[123] In both cases the products (the dentures and the dye) were provided as part of a contract for services; in both, the court imposed strict liability for the faulty products. In the context of this book, therefore, it would seem that strict liability would be imposed for equipment, even when supplied as part of a broader contract of services. Of course, even applying strict liability, the aggrieved person would have to show that the product actually was of unsatisfactory quality. Thus, the maker of an artificial limb, deprived of the opportunity to argue that he had used reasonable care and skill, might argue that, given a particular patient's complex needs, the limb was still of satisfactory quality even if it caused discomfort.

3. WHAT TO DO WHEN EQUIPMENT IS UNSATISFACTORY

Harm caused by defective or unsatisfactory equipment

Apart from suing in respect of the cost of defective equipment itself, people can sue for personal injury or harm to other property caused by defective equipment. For instance, when a six-year old boy lost an eye using a cheap, polystyrene catapult which was clearly unfit for its purpose, he gained damages for pain and suffering, the loss of the eye and the discomfort of removing the eye daily.[124]

And, in contrast to negligence, there is no problem in principle about suing for financial loss alone – ie even when there has been no physical injury or damage to other property (see p.336). This ability to sue comes with the proviso that the person suing must be a party to the contract (see p.402).

Suing for medically recognised psychiatric harm, might, as in negligence, be more difficult if there is no accompanying physical injury (see p.336). However, the courts do sometimes make awards in contract for *mental distress*, which can include ordinary feelings such as disappointment and inconvenience. Mental distress covers such feelings of 'mental suffering' but stops short of recognised psychiatric harm. However, the circumstances in which the courts will award such damages are limited.[125] They might occasionally do so if the object of the contract was clearly to provide peace of mind (eg on a luxury holiday) or if there has been physical inconvenience (eg living in a house whilst it is being extensively repaired).[126]

A further distinction between suing in contract and in negligence is that, in contract, damages aim to put people in the position they would have been in *after* the contract had been successfully carried out. In negligence, damages aim to restore people to the position they were in *before* the accident – ie had the accident never occurred. This can be explained by the following example, based on an American case in which a skin grafting operation on somebody's burnt hand made things worse – and the court debated how to assess the damages:[127]

A person might be unable to walk except with crutches and undergo a routine operation to restore full, unaided, walking ability. The operation is performed carelessly and the person has permanently to use a wheelchair.

If the operation were performed on the NHS and the person were to sue in negligence (because there is no contract), the damages would be assessed by comparing the effects on the person of using a wheelchair (his *current situation*) compared with using crutches (ie his situation *before the operation*). But, if the operation were private and a contract existed (explicitly promising success: see above), then the damages would be assessed differently by comparing the use of the wheelchair (*current situation*) to walking (ie the anticipated outcome *after the operation*). In these circumstances, damages for breach of contract could, in principle, be greater than in negligence – were the loss of unassisted walking ability valued more highly by the court than crutch-assisted walking.

Did the defective equipment cause the harm?

Compensation might be sought not just for the cost of replacing equipment, but also for other, *consequential loss* – ie personal injury, damage to property or other financial loss caused by the defective equipment. It is necessary to prove that the breach of contract (ie the supply of defective equipment) actually *caused* the harm for which the claim is being made. This can sometimes be difficult to do – some of the common problems in proving causation are outlined elsewhere in this book (see p.331).

It has to be proved that the harm or loss must have been a *direct* and *natural* result of the breach of the contract – or at least within the *reasonable contemplation* of the parties. For example, in a case concerning the delay in carrying a broken crank shaft of a mill, the carrier was not liable for loss of profits to the mill, because it could not reasonably know that the delay would cause the loss of profits.[128] And, in a second case, a firm which delivered a commercial laundry's boiler several months late was liable for the loss of *ordinary* profits the laundry would have made – but not for the extra profits expected from a special contract; the latter could not be foreseen.[129] A third and more recent case decided that for losses to have been contemplated by the parties when the contract was made, the foreseeabilty of the losses must be greater than the foreseeability of harm or loss required in negligence.[130] This is one reason why, given a choice, it might be preferable to sue in negligence rather than contract.

If, for example, a defective car hoist collapses and causes a person serious injury, the broken limb and bruising obviously stem directly and naturally from the defective equipment. Further, it might be argued that the person's consequent inability to use his car for work was within the reasonable contemplation of both parties to the contract. This argument might well be contested by the supplier of the hoist; alternatively it might be strengthened if the supplier knew, at the time the contract was made, exactly why the car hoist was needed (ie that it was essential to the person's job as a salesman). Depending on the detailed circumstances, a claim might therefore be made for compensation in respect not only of replacing the defective hoist and the injuries – but also loss of earnings.[131]

Rejecting equipment altogether

If a breach of contract is serious, then goods can be rejected altogether (on the grounds that the contract has been *repudiated* by the seller), the purchase value claimed back, and any additional damages claimed as well.[132] For example, if the contract stated that it was essential that a braille reading machine be delivered and installed by a certain date – and it was not, then the buyer could treat the contract as ended. This is because *time had been made of the essence*; it was crucial to the contract. By not adhering to this stipulation, the seller has repudiated the contract. It is not always clear when the courts will view a breach of contract as serious enough to terminate the contract altogether. If the breach is perceived as less serious, then, for example, the buyer might have to keep the equipment and sue for damages.

However, in a *consumer contract*, if any of the implied terms about quality or description are breached, then the buyer has the right (but is not obliged) to terminate the contract altogether and reject the equipment.[133] But, if the consumer keeps the equipment and treats it as his own, or does not inform the seller within a reasonable time that he is going to reject it, then he can no longer reject it – although he could still sue for damages.[134] What is a reasonable time might relate to the complexity of the equipment. Thus, it will not be the same for a bicycle as for a nuclear submarine – as pointed out by the court in a case concerning a new Nissan car which the purchaser had owned for three weeks and driven 140 miles. This meant that when it broke down, he could not reject it – but was able to claim damages for the cost of getting home, the full tank of petrol lost, a spoilt day and five days' loss of use of the car.[135] This issue might be particularly important in relation to some disability equipment, including, for example, wheelchairs and the increasingly sophisticated computer equipment for people with speech difficulties.

Can sellers of equipment exclude or restrict liability?

Consumers are protected by the Unfair Contract Terms Act (UCTA) 1977. This deals with *unfair* terms in contracts which attempt to *exclude* or *restrict the liability* of people acting in the course of business. This Act overlaps to some extent with the recently implemented Unfair Terms in Consumer Contracts Regulations (see above).

Very broadly, in the context of this book, the Act means that people contracting to supply equipment (or supplying equipment non-contractually: see p.391) in the course of a business can never exclude their liability for death or personal injury caused by their negligence. Therefore, for example, a contract term is ineffective if it states that the seller of a through-floor lift is not liable under any circumstances (including negligence) for injury or death.

If the contract instead attempts to restrict liability in negligence for other damage, then the term is only effective if it is *reasonable* (see below).[136] Thus, the courts have held that it is unreasonable for surveyors – who are reporting to building societies or local authorities – to exclude their liability in negligence to house buyers who are relying on their findings.[137] But, whilst it might not seem unreasonable for a supplier of an electric wheelchair to try to exclude liability for damage to other property (eg clothing) caused by batteries which leak – he could not do so because the Consumer Protection Act 1987 (s.7) would prevent such exclusion for a consumer product.

The Act makes it quite clear that just because a person is aware of a term in a contract which excludes or restricts liability in negligence, this does not mean that he voluntarily accepts the risk.[138]

Apart from liability in negligence, the Act also states that in a consumer contract, the party dealing on its standard terms (eg the seller of equipment) cannot exclude liability for breach of contract. Nor, unless it is reasonable, can he claim to be entitled either to deliver something different than had been reasonably expected, or not to perform at all part of or all of the contract.[139] And, in any case, liability cannot be excluded or restricted in relation to the quality, fitness for purpose or description of goods in consumer contracts (see above).[140]

Where the Act does not impose an absolute bar on excluding or limiting liability, then much depends on this pervasive concept of reasonableness. The Act states that a term must be 'fair and reasonable' in the light of the circumstances which were known, or should have been known, to both parties when the contract was made. In addition, a number of relevant matters are listed as to whether a term is reasonable[141]:

(i) The **relative bargaining strengths** of the two parties.

For example, a frail, slightly confused elderly woman has less bargaining strength than the multi-national supplier who sells her an electric riser chair.

(ii) Has the consumer received an **extra inducement** to agree to the particular contract term – or could he have entered into a similar contract without having to agree to such a term?

Either could weaken the consumer's claim, because it would suggest that the consumer had the reasonable choice of not making the agreement.

(iii) If the consumer did not **know about the term**, or could not reasonably have known about it, then the term might be held to be unfair.

For example, a contract term which was in very small print or difficult to understand, might be unreasonable. Printed 'microscopically' in a maintenance agreement (eg for a stairlift), the term might state that, in the event of breakdown, the consumer is responsible for delivery, and the costs of delivery, of the item back to the manufacturer for examination and repair. This could be held to be unfair because the term was 'concealed', and was unusual or could not be easily complied with. In a commercial shipping case ('*The Zinnia*'), the judge was minded to hold contractual conditions unreasonable and unfair because of the barely readable small print and the 'convoluted and prolix draftsmanship', which meant that a law degree was almost required to understand it. (However, this argument was not put before him, so he did not actually make the ruling.)[142]

(iv) If it was reasonable at the time of the contract to expect that the consumer could have **complied with a particular term**, then the supplier might succeed in excluding liability.

For instance, if a hire agreement makes it clear that electric wheelchair batteries have to be looked after and recharged, then if they are not, the supplier might be able to exclude liability for any resulting damage to the wheelchair. However, this example illustrates some of the complexity relating to the selling of disability equipment. It might be reasonable for NHS occupational therapists to investigate thoroughly a person's disability, home environment and capacity to look after equipment – but how far should sales staff be expected to do this in each individual case?

This aspect of compliance with a term, refers to the time when the contract was made – not at a later date with the benefit of retrospect.[143] For instance, take the example given in (iii) above; it could be claimed that when the contract was made, a frail, elderly woman could not reasonably be expected to arrange for the return of the stairlift. Thus, in the same shipping case also referred to above ('*The Zinnia*'), the judge would have held a repair clause unreasonable, had it meant that the owner of a ship would only have a remedy if he returned the ship to the repairer's yard. This was a 'capricious' clause since its effectiveness would have depended on where the problem occurred – and even at the time the contract was made, it would have been clear that the clause could not have been complied with in many circumstances.[144]

(v) If the equipment has been manufactured, processed or adapted to **special order**, then this might affect whether attempts to exclude liability are reasonable.

For example, if the manufacturer warned of certain disadvantages pertaining to the specially adapted wheelchair ordered by the consumer, then the latter might have little complaint when those disadvantages in performance become apparent.

Categories of damages

Generally speaking, the categories of damages that can be claimed in contract are similar to those in negligence (see p.338). These include, for instance, pain and suffering, loss of faculty and amenity, loss of earnings, damage to property – and so on. It should be borne in mind that although actions for personal injury can be bought in contract (and thus damages cover eg pain and suffering, loss of amenity), most personal injury claims are brought in negligence or breach of statutory duty.[145]

Time within which a legal action must be brought

Actions for breach of contract must be brought within six years of the breach.[146] However, if personal injury is involved, the period is three years.[147]

The rules about latent damage to property (ie where the defect does not become apparent for some time but claims can still be made) which apply in negligence cases (see p.340), seem not to apply to claims in contract.[148]

Mitigation and contributory negligence

Mitigation is not a complete defence, but is a way of reducing the damages awarded against a person for a breach of contract. For instance, if a person sues for loss of earnings caused by late delivery of a defective wheelchair, then if it had been reasonably possible to hire one for that period instead – the failure to do so could result in a reduction of the damages.[149] For example, in one case, a person who had been injured refused to have an operation which might have restored his previous earning ability. The court held that he should have chosen to have the operation; because he did not, the damages awarded were limited. (The labourer concerned had a disability in his hand resulting from two separate accidents at work. The operation would have given a 90% chance of restoring mass action of the fingers, and a 35% chance of fine finger movement).[150]

It is unclear whether the partial defence of contributory negligence (see p.340) – ie where damages can be reduced because somebody has contributed to his own loss – can be used in contract cases.[151]

Notes

1 Brownsword, R. The philosophy of welfarism and its emergence in the modern English law of contract. In: Brownsword, R.; Howells, G.; Wilhelmsson, T. (eds.) (1994). *Welfarism in contract law.* Aldershot: Dartmouth Publishing Company.

2 Atiyah, P.S., Adams, J. (1995). *The sale of goods.* 9th edition. London: Pitman Publishing, p.xii.

3 *Pfizer Corporation v Ministry of Health* [1965] AC 512 (HL) (at 535–536).

4 Lord Pearson (Chair) (1978). *Royal Commission on Civil Liability and Compensation for Personal Injury.* Cmnd 7054. London: HMSO, para 1313.

5 *Willmore and Willmore (Trading as Lissenden Poultry) v South Eastern Electricity Board* [1957] 2 Lloyds Rep 375 (QBD).

6 *R v Knowsley Metropolitan Borough Council, ex parte Maguire and Others* (1990) 90 LGR 653 (QBD): refusal of taxi licenses.

7 *Jones v Vernon's Pools Ltd* [1938] 2 All ER 626 (KBD).

8 *Rose & Frank Co v JR Crompton Bros* [1924] All ER Rep 245 (CA): at the end of a document drawing up a commercial agreement between two firms, it was expressly stated that the 'arrangement' was not a legal agreement. The judge at first instance interpreted the document as a whole, and stated that it was in fact a legal agreement because of the way in which the rest of the document had been written. The Court of Appeal disagreed.

9 *Balfour v Balfour* [1919] 2 KB 571 (CA): about a financial agreement between a husband working in Ceylon who agreed to pay his wife regular sums of money following her return to England on medical grounds. After she had obtained a decree nisi (he was consorting with another woman), she attempted, unsuccessfully, to enforce the agreement.

10 *Merrit v Merrit* [1970] 1 WLR 1211 (CA). A wife agreed with her husband, who had gone off with another woman, that if she met all the costs of the house, he would transfer ownership

of the house to her once the mortgage repayments were complete. The husband refused, but the agreement was held to be enforceable.

11 *Simpkins v Pays* [1955] 1 WLR 975 (Chester Assizes).

12 Treitel, G.H. (1995). *Law of contract.* 9th edition. London: Sweet & Maxwell/Stevens, p.382–4.

13 SI 1994/3159. *Unfair Terms in Consumer Contracts Regulations 1995.*

14 Directive 93/13/EEC.

15 SI 1994/3159. *Unfair Terms in Consumer Contracts Regulations 1995,* rr.4, 6., Schedule 2.

16 SI 1994/3159. *Unfair Terms in Consumer Contracts Regulations 1995,* Schedule 3.

17 SI 1994/3159. *Unfair Terms in Consumer Contracts Regulations 1994,* r.3(2).

18 Directive 93/13/EEC.

19 SI 1994/3159. *Unfair Terms in Consumer Contracts Regulations 1994,* r.5.

20 SI 1994/3159. *Unfair Terms in Consumer Contracts Regulations 1994,* r.8.

21 Lockett, N.; Egan, M. (1995). *Unfair terms in consumer agreements.* Chichester: Wiley, pp.59–60.

22 Office of Fair Trading (1995). *The OFT targets unfair contract terms.* Press release 53/95, 15 December 1995.

23 *Interfoto Picture Library v Stileto Visual Programmes* [1988] 1 All ER 348 (CA).

24 *Thornton v Shoe Lane Parking* [1971] 2 QB 163 (CA).

25 *Chapelton v Barry Urban District Council* [1940] 1 All ER 356 (CA).

26 *Olley v Marlborough Court Hotel* [1949] 1 All ER 127 (CA).

27 Eg *Barton v Armstrong* [1975] 2 All ER 465 (PC): involving transactions which the managing director of an Australian company executed under threat of death from the chairman.

28 See eg Adams, J.; Brownsword, R. (1995). *Key issues in contract.* London: Butterworths, pp.31–33.

29 See: *North Ocean Shipping Co Ltd v Hyundai Construction Co Ltd (The Atlantic Baron)* [1979] QB 705 (QBD). Involved the building of a tanker by a South Korean company for a Monrovian shipping company for a fixed in price in US dollars. Following a devaluation in the dollar the construction company demanded 10% extra on the price. For commercial reasons, the shipping company was not in a position to resist. The court held that, in principle, this amounted to economic duress – although the shipping company lost the case for other reasons – namely its lack of protest when the extra was paid, and the delay in making its claim to get the money back.

30 Health Service Commissioner (E.62/93–94). *Failure to provide long term NHS care for a brain damaged patient.* 2nd report 1993–1994. HC 197. London: HMSO, 1994.

31 Eg: *Evans v Llewellin* (1787) 1 Cox CC 333 (poor person exploited into selling share in an estate at great undervalue). See also *Creswell v Potter* [1978] 1 WLR 255 (when, during divorce proceedings, a wife transferred her share in the home at great undervalue and with no independent advice).

32 *Watkin v Watson-Smith* (1986), Times, 3 July 1986 (Chancery Division).

33 Under the *Misrepresentation Act 1967.*

34 Eg *Dick Bentley Productions v Harold Smith (Motors) Ltd* [1965] 1 WLR 623 (CA): sale of a Bentley car on the basis of an untrue statement about its mileage.

35 SI 1987/2117. *Consumer Protection (Cancellation of Contracts Concluded away from Business Premises) Regulations 1987.*

36 Directive 85/577/EEC.

37 *Hart v O'Connor* [1985] 2 All ER 880 (PC): an agreement for sale of farmland in New Zealand. The seller, unknown to the buyer, as of 'unsound mind' when he signed the agreement. The Privy Council held that the contract should stand.

38 *Sale of Goods Act 1979,* s.3(2).

39 But see eg: *Minors' (Contracts) Act 1987* (s.3) which, basically, ensures that children cannot get away with simply refusing to pay for goods they have received, or taking goods back, claiming there is no contract.

40 *Clyde Cycle Co. v Hargreaves* (1898) 78 LT 296. A 19-year old apprentice to a scientific instrument maker who used the bike for races rather than work and refused to pay money owing on it. By holding that the bike was a necessary, the court ensured that he would have to pay the debt.

41 *Nash v Inman* [1908] 2 KB 1 (CA): thus the tailor could not enforce the contract and obtain his money.
42 See example of pairs of shoes in: British Medical Association; Law Society (1995). *Assessment of mental capacity: guidance for doctors and lawyers.* London: BMA, Law Society, p.49.
43 *Disability Discrimination Act 1995,* ss.20–21.
44 Gooding, C. (1996). *Blackstone's Guide to the Disability Discrimination Act 1995.* London: Blackstone, p.38.
45 *Disability Discrimination Act 1995,* ss.25–26.
46 *Pharmaceutical Society of Great Britain v Boots Cash Chemists (Southern) Ltd* [1952] 2 QB 795.
47 *Lefkowitz v Great Minneapolis Surplus Store* 251 Minn 188 (1957).
48 *Carlill v Carbolic Smoke Ball Co* [1893] 1 QB 256 (CA).
49 *Bowerman and Another v Association of British Travel Agents Ltd* (1995) (CA), Times 23 November 1995.
50 *Mountford v Scott* [1975] 1 All ER 198 (CA): where £1 a year for the option to buy a house was held to be sufficient consideration, even though it was obviously merely a 'token'.
51 Adams, J.; Brownsword, R. (1987). *Understanding contract law.* London: Fontana, p.85.
52 *Carlill v Carbolic Smoke Ball Co* [1893] 1 QB 256 (CA).
53 See generally: Kennedy, I.; Grubb, A. (1994). *Medical law: text with materials.* 2nd edition. London: Butterworths, pp.52–53.
54 See generally: Palmer, N. (1991). *Bailment.* 2nd edition. London: Sweet & Maxwell.
55 Eg under the *Torts (Interference with Goods) Act 1977.*
56 Taken from example clause in: London Boroughs Occupational Therapy Managers' Group (1992). *Occupational therapists' criteria for the loan of equipment to people with disabilities.* London: LBOTMG, Appendix II.
57 *NHS Act 1977,* s.82. And: SI 1974/284. *NHS (Charges for Appliances) Regulations 1974.*
58 See discussion in: Lowe, R.; Woodroffe, G. (1995). *Consumer law and practice.* 4th edition. London: Sweet & Maxwell, pp.58–59. And: Atiyah, P.S; Adams, J. (1995). *The sale of goods.* London: Pitman Publishing, pp.247–251.
59 Office of Fair Trading (1994). *Extended warranties on electrical goods: a report by the Office of Fair Trading.* London: OFT.
60 Terreiro, M. (1995). Guarantees and after-sales service: brief analysis of the Green Paper presented by the European Commission. *Consumer Law Journal:* 1995; 3(3), pp.79–93.
61 Bradgate, R. (1995). Harmonisation of legal guarantees: a common law perspective. *Consumer Law Journal:* 1995; 3(3), pp.94–109.
62 *L Gent & Sons v Eastman Machine Co Ltd* (1985) (CA): an unreported case referred to in: the Law Commission (1987). *The sale and supply of goods.* No. 160. London: HMSO, para 3.66.
63 Law Commission (1987). *The sale and supply of goods.* No. 160. London: HMSO, para 3.66.
64 Terreiro, M. (1995). Guarantees and after-sales service: brief analysis of the Green Paper presented by the European Commission. *Consumer Law Journal:* 1995; 3(3), pp.79–93.
65 See eg: Carman, A.J. (1991). Rearguard action for spare parts. *Therapy Weekly:* 20 June 1991, p.5.
66 British Association of Wheelchair Distributors (1995). *Code of practice.* Paras 2.01, 4.03.
67 Department of Health and Social Security (1986). *Management of private practice in health service hospitals in England and Wales.* London: DHSS.
68 *Dunlop Pneumatic Tyre Co. Ltd v Selfridge and Co Ltd* [1915] AC 847 (HL).
69 Eg *Preist v Last* [1903] KB 148 (CA): a case in which the husband, who had bought the hot water bottle, and not his wife who had been scalded by it, could sue in contract for the cost of the treatment of her injuries – which he was paying for.
70 *Sale of Goods Act 1979,* s.17.
71 *Sale of Goods Act 1979,* s.20.
72 *Sale of Goods Act 1979,* s.18.
73 *Sale of Goods Act 1979,* s.32(2).
74 *Sale of Goods Act 1979,* s.18, Rule 4.
75 See eg Stowe, J.; Chamberlain, A. (1980). Aids for arthritics: report of a survey on aids supplied postally by the British Rheumatism Association. *Occupational Therapy:* March 1980; 43(3), pp.80–84.

76 Wilkinson, S.; Schofield, P. (1995). *Good housekeeping consumer guide: you and your rights.* London: Ebury Press, p.37. This is on the basis of the so-called 'postal rule', where a contract is made when the acceptance of an offer is posted – even if it never arrives: eg *Household Fire and Carriage Accident Insurance Co Ltd v Grant* (1879) 4 Ex D 216 (CA).
77 Lowe, R.; Woodroffe, G. (1995). *Consumer law and practice.* 4th edition. London: Sweet & Maxwell, p.87: referring to an old commercial case: *Badische Anilin und Soda Fabrik v Basle Chemical Works* [1898] AC 200 (HL).
78 Mail Order Traders' Association (1995). *Catalogue mail order code of practice.* MOTA.
79 *Supply of Goods Act 1979.*
80 *Supply of Goods (Implied Terms) Act 1973*
81 *Supply of Goods and Services Act 1982.*
82 *Supply of Goods and Services Act 1982.*
83 *Sale of Goods Act 1979, s.13; Supply of Goods and Services Act 1982, ss.3, 8; Supply of Goods (Implied Terms) Act 1973,* s.9.
84 *Sale of Goods Act 1979, s.14; Supply of Goods and Services Act 1982, ss.4, 9; Supply of Goods (Implied Terms) Act 1973,* s.10.
85 *Sale of Goods Act 1979, s.14; Supply of Goods and Services Act 1982, ss.4, 9, 18(3); Supply of Goods (Implied Terms) Act 1973,* s.10.
86 *Samuels v Davis* [1943] 1 KB 526 (CA).
87 Eg *Wormell v RHM Agriculture (East) Ltd* [1987] 1 WLR 1091 (CA): a case about herbicide for wild oats, in which the Court of Appeal held that the warnings on cannisters were, in fact, adequate.
88 British Association of Wheelchair Distributors (1995). *Code of practice.* Paras 3.01, 3.04.
89 British Surgical Trades Association (1996). *Rehabilitation Products Section code of practice.* Sevenoaks: BSTA, 1996.
90 Hearing Aid Council (1995). *Code of practice, examinations and registration.* London: HAC.
91 Foster, K.; Jackson, B.; Thomas, M.; Hunter, P.; Bennett, N. (Office of Population Censuses and Surveys) (1995). *1993 General Household Survey.* London: HMSO, p.83.
92 Campbell, F.; Ross, F. (1990). Dealing with wheels: factors to consider when patients need a wheelchair. *Community Outlook:* October 1990, pp.23–26.
93 Bradshaw, S. (1995). Where there's a wheel... *Therapy Weekly:* 23 February 1995, pp.7–8.
94 Medical Devices Directorate (1993). *Which one should they buy? A powered vehicle prescription guide for therapists.* London: Department of Health, pp.24–27.
95 British Society of Rehabilitation Medicine (1995). *Seating needs for complex disabilities: a working party report.* London: BSRM, p.4.
96 Medical Devices Directorate (1993). *Which one should they buy? A powered vehicle prescription guide for therapists.* London: Department of Health, Appendix 2.
97 London Boroughs Occupational Therapy Managers Group (1988). *Occupational therapists' criteria for the provision of home adaptations in the homes of people with disabilities.* London: LBOTMG (section 6: Lifts).
98 Medical Devices Directorate (1993). *Which one should they buy? A powered vehicle prescription guide for therapists.* London: Department of Health, p.26.
99 Medical Devices Directorate (1993). *Which one should they buy? A powered vehicle prescription guide for therapists.* London: Department of Health, p.26.
100 *Sale of Goods Act 1979,* s.14.
101 *Griffiths v Peter Conway Ltd* [1939] 1 All ER 685 (CA).
102 *Sale of Goods Act 1979,* s.14; *Supply of Goods and Services Act 1982,* ss.4, 9, 18(2); *Supply of Goods (Implied Terms) Act 1973,* s.10.
103 *Bernstein v Pamson Motors (Golders Green) Ltd* [1987] 2 All ER 220 (QBD).
104 *Bernstein v Pamson Motors (Golders Green) Ltd* [1987] 2 All ER 220 (QBD).
105 *Rogers v Parish (Scarborough) Ltd* [1987] QB 933 (CA): about a Range Rover, purchased as new, but with various defects: the purchaser was trying to reject the car after driving over 5000 miles – and succeeded in the Court of Appeal.
106 *Lambert v Lewis* [1981] 1 All ER 1185 (HL).
107 RICA (1996). Consumer clinic: is this walking frame defective? *Disability Now:* March 1996, p.12.

108 Average length of life of a limb given in answer in: *Hansard,* House of Commons, Written Answers, 16 July 1991, col 141, Mr Dorrell.
109 Clark, N. (1996). Sorting out the standards. *Hospital Equipment Supplies:* March 1996, p.27.
110 *Sale of Goods Act 1979,* s.14; *Supply of Goods and Services Act 1982,* ss.4, 9, 18(2); *Supply of Goods (Implied Terms) Act 1973,* s.10.
111 *Bartlett v Sidney Marcus* [1965] 1 WLR 1013 (CA).
112 *Crowther v Shannon Motor Company* [1975] 1 WLR.
113 *Sale of Goods Act 1979,* s.14.
114 *Supply of Goods and Services Act 1982,* s.1(3).
115 *Supply of Goods and Services Act 1982,* s.4.
116 *Supply of Goods and Services Act 1982,* s.13.
117 *Eyre v Measday* [1986] 1 All ER 488 (CA).
118 *La Fleur v Cornelis* (1979) 28 NBR (2d) 569 (Canadian case).
119 *Thake v Maurice* [1986] 1 All ER 497 (QBD).
120 *Greaves v Baynham Meikle* [1975] 1 WLR 1095 (CA). Although the case was decided in negligence, the court stated that some design contracts carry an implied term (of fact, not of law) of strict liability of reasonable fitness for purpose.
121 See discussion in: Atiyah, P.S.; Adams, J. (1995). *The sale of goods.* 9th edition. London: Pitman Publishing, pp.19–25.
122 *Samuels v Davis* [1943] 1 KB 526 (CA).
123 *Watson v Buckley, Osborne Garrett & Co Ltd and Wyrovoys Products Ltd* [1940] 1 KBD 174 (Manchester Michaelmas Assizes).
124 *Godley v Perry* [1960] 1 All ER 36 (QBD).
125 *Hayes v James & Charles Dodd* [1990] 2 All ER 815 (CA): concerning purchase of a car repair business on the basis of unsound advice which caused anxiety and vexation. This case referred to a previous one involving breach of a consultant orthopaedic surgeon's contract by a health authority on mental health grounds (ie forcing him to undergo a psychiatric examination on the basis of a breakdown of working relationships): *Bliss v South East Thames Regional Health Authority* [1987] ICR 700. In both cases, the Court of Appeal rejected the award by the original trial judges of damages for mental distress. In the latter, damages were awarded for breach of the contract of employment, but not for mental distress, frustration, injured feelings and annoyance.
126 Humphries, M. (1996). Contractual damages for mental distress. *Solicitors Journal:* 23 February 1996; 140(7), pp.182–183.
127 *Hawkins v McGee* 84 NH 114, 146 A 641 (1929). Described in: Burrows, A (1994). R*emedies for torts and breach of contract.* 2nd edition. London: Butterworths, p.18.
128 *Hadley v Blaxendale* (1854) 9 Exch 341.
129 *Victoria Laundry (Windsor) Ltd v Newman Industries Ltd* [1949] 2 KB 528 (CA).
130 *Koufos v C. Czernikow* 'The Heron II' [1969 1 AC 350 (HL) (at 385–387).
131 See eg *Victoria Laundry (Windsor) Ltd v Newman Industries Ltd* [1949] 2 KB 528 (the supplier of the faulty boiler knew that if it broke down the laundry's business would be adversely affected – it was aware of the nature of the business and, in addition, had been informed by the laundry (by letter) that it intended/needed to put the boiler to use as soon as possible.
132 *Sale of Goods Act 1979,* s.11.
133 *Unfair Contract Terms Act 1977,* ss.6, 7
134 *Sale of Goods Act 1979,* ss.11, 35.
135 *Bernstein v Pamson Motors (Golders Green) Ltd* [1987] 2 All ER 220 (QBD).
136 *Unfair Contract Terms Act 1977,* s.2.
137 *Smith v Eric S Bush, Harris v Wyre Forest DC* [1990] 1 AC 831 (HL).
138 *Unfair Contract Terms Act 1977,* s.2.
139 *Unfair Contract Terms Act 1977,* s.3.
140 *Unfair Contract Terms Act 1977,* ss.6, 7
141 *Unfair Contract Terms Act 1977,* s.11, Schedule 2. Strictly speaking, the following considerations are stated to apply only to ss.6 and 7 of the Act – ie to the description and quality of goods – but, in practice, they may be applied by the courts to make sense of the occurrences of the

concept of reasonableness in ss.2 and 3, ie in case of terms limiting liability for negligence or breach of contract.

142 See eg *Stag Line Ltd v Tyne Repair Group Ltd 'The Zinnia'* [1984] 2 Lloyd's Rep 211 (QBD).

143 Obviously, this prospective, rather than retrospective, approach will be favoured by commercial interests, see eg: Adams, J.; Brownsword, R. (1988). The Unfair Contract Terms Act: a decade of discretion. *Law Quarterly Review:* January 1988; 104, pp.94–119.

144 *Stag Line Ltd v Tyne Repair Group Ltd 'The Zinnia'* [1984] 2 Lloyd's Rep 211 (QBD).

145 Burrows, A. (1994). *Remedies for torts and breach of contract.* 2nd edition. London: Butterworths, pp.186–187.

146 *Limitation Act 1980,* s.5.

147 *Limitation Act 1980,* s.11.

148 *Limitation Act 1980,* s.14A.

149 Eg *British Westinghouse Co. v Underground Electric Railways Co. of London* [1912] AC 673 (HL): involving the original supply of below-standard turbines which the plaintiff replaced in order to mitigate losses – some of which were recoverable, but others were not because of the effectiveness of the mitigating action (the new turbines were superior and so savings were made which would not have been if the original turbines had been up to standard).

150 *McAuley v London Transport Executive* [1957] 2 Lloyds Reports 500 (CA).

151 See discussion in: Burrows, A. (1994). *Remedies for torts and breach of contract.* 2nd edition. London: Butterworths, pp.80–87.

CHAPTER 17

CHALLENGING THE DECISIONS OF STATUTORY SERVICES ABOUT EQUIPMENT PROVISION

JUDICIAL REVIEW

COVERAGE

1. Supervision of *how* authorities decide to provide equipment, not what they decide
   - Judicial review in the NHS, social services and education fields.
2. Making decisions unreasonably, illegally or unfairly
   - Making decisions about equipment unreasonably
   - Making decisions about equipment illegally
   - Making unfair decisions about equipment.
3. Judicial review: solutions and obstacles
   - Solutions which the courts can impose
   - Forcing people to seek other solutions
   - Obstacles to success in judicial review.

Key points

Principles of judicial review. As has been made clear in Parts I and II of this book, statutory services have substantial discretion to decide what services and equipment to provide. They make decisions about who will receive equipment at all, what type, in what circumstances, and how quickly. When making these decisions, they are supposed to act within the framework of the powers and duties they are given by legislation (see Chapter 6). Although authorities possess this wide discretion to make policies and priorities, to allocate resources and to ration services – it is not untrammelled discretion. This is because the law courts have the power to intervene by *judicially reviewing* the decisions and actions of public bodies, including all the statutory services relevant to this book. If the courts find that an authority has made a decision which is *unreasonable*, *illegal* or *unfair*, then they can rule that the authority must re-take its decision – this time in the proper manner.

Judicial review differs in a fundamental respect from civil legal actions brought in negligence, contract or breach of statutory duty (see Chapters 15, 16 and 18). The latter three are primarily about enforcing people's *private law* rights and can involve claims for damages. By contrast, judicial review is a *public law* procedure and is primarily about ensuring that public bodies are not abusing their powers. Damages are not generally available to individual complainants. Therefore, put simply, the judicial review courts are not concerned if authorities refuse to provide equipment, but only that they should refuse *in the proper manner*. In other words, first and foremost, the courts have to pay more attention to procedure than to the consequences for people's welfare.

Use of judicial review to challenge decisions about equipment. For equipment providers, judicial review is significant because it can be used to challenge their decisions about priorities and rationing of services. For example, judicial review applications have been used many times to challenge the decisions taken by education authorities about children's special education – and are now being made increasingly to oppose decisions about the provision of community care and sometimes about the provision of health services.

More generally, judicial review is a developing and influential area of law, even though it cannot deliver compensatory damages to complainants. For example, it is the means by which a number of decisions made by central government – such as those made by the Home Office about immigrants and prisoners – are regularly overturned. The expanding influence of judicial review is one of the grounds on which the judiciary is sometimes criticised and which reportedly enrages some government ministers. Indeed, a civil service booklet on the subject, entitled the *Judge over your shoulder*, advises civil servants how to avoid adverse findings by the courts.[1] At a time of increased pressure on the budgets and functions of statutory services, moderate use of judicial review is probably a socially useful tool to curb the worst excesses of poor decision-making by public bodies. And even some of the critics of the judiciary recognise that carelessly and loosely drafted legislation gives rise to uncertainty which then has to be dealt with in the law courts.[2]

Judicial review has been used extensively – and sometimes successfully – in the fields of homelessness and *special education*; the Education Act 1993 (and the Housing Act 1985) both contained provisions precise enough to provide grounds on which to challenge local authorities. In the *NHS context*, challenges to the rationing of services generally fail – a reflection perhaps of the vagueness and generality of duties imposed by the NHS Act 1977. The number of cases brought in the *social services field*, in respect of the provision of welfare services (including equipment) have generally been few and far between. However, with the implementation of the NHS and Community Care Act 1990, disputes about community care have multiplied and are increasingly reaching the law courts. A number of these have revolved around s.2 of the Chronically Sick and Disabled Persons Act 1970. Although these cases have not been about equipment in particular, there are direct implications since equipment is provided under s.2. Furthermore, hypothetical examples of equipment – such as stairlifts, televisions and chairs – have been a feature of submission and discussion in court. The 1970 Act is at the centre of a much wider legal and policy community care debate; and judicial review is being used to test for the existence of disabled people's 'rights', as well as for the coherence of the mass of community care legislation and guidance.

Questions people ask

- Can a social services department adopt a policy of never providing high seat chairs, no matter what a person's need is?
- What can a person do if he or she has been waiting for two years for an assessment by the social services department for equipment?
- Similarly, what if a person is assessed as needing a stairlift, but told that there is a 12-month wait before one can be supplied and installed?
- Can an authority insist that a woman go into a residential home because the equipment and the care which she would need in her own home, would cost too much?
- Can powered nebulisers loaned by the NHS for three months be withdrawn and users told to buy, or otherwise obtain, their own?
- Can an NHS wheelchair service state that it will only supply wheelchairs to people who need them 'permanently' or for a long period (for example, more than six months)? Can it therefore deny a wheelchair to a person who has a terminal illness and will be dead within six months?

1. SUPERVISION OF HOW AUTHORITIES DECIDE TO PROVIDE EQUIPMENT, NOT WHAT THEY DECIDE

Judicial review is used primarily to supervise the decisions of public bodies, to ensure that they are not acting *unreasonably*, *unfairly* or *illegally* (see below). As a consequence, individual service users might benefit when, for example, an authority has to re-take decisions, following judicial review. However, it is important to keep in mind – and this will be reiterated several times – that the courts are enforcing only *indirectly* the legal rights of individuals.

Primarily, the courts are ensuring that public bodies make their decisions properly and lawfully, not whether they arrive at the correct decision; an authority can make a mistake without acting improperly or illegally.[3] This is why the courts will not interfere directly with a professional judgement, so long as it is not tinged with procedural irregularity. They have sometimes been at pains to point this out, particularly when faced with a profusion of cases about special education (square brackets added)[4]:

> Having heard the argument, I shall deal shortly with the points raised but I do urge those who specialise in this branch of the law, and their names appear again and again in this type of proceedings, and those who grant legal aid, to bear in mind that in general the court is reluctant to grant judicial review in cases which are essentially concerned with professional judgements with a number of variables in play and that it may well be in the better interest of the child to appeal to the Secretary of State [this would now be the Special Educational Needs Tribunal] and have all relevant points considered than to go to the court which cannot come to any ultimate decision as to what is to be done with the child.

Thus, if a court finds that a public body has made an improper decision by denying services or equipment to a person, it will not award damages. Nor, in principle, will it even directly order that the person must receive the services or equipment. Instead, the court will order that the authority should re-take the decision about provision, this time in a proper manner. For instance, an authority might assess a person for services under s.2 of the Chronically Sick and Disabled Persons Act 1970, which imposes an explicit duty to consider people's needs for, amongst other things, home adaptations. If it makes the assessment without considering them, then it has acted illegally – because it has not followed the wording of the legislation. However, the court would not order directly that the authority provide the adaptations. Instead, it would tell the authority to carry out another assessment, this time in conformity with the legislation – ie taking account of a possible need for home adaptations. Following the reassessment, it would still be for the authority to decide whether or not to provide them.

At the same time a court will be wary of interfering with decisions about policy, priorities and resources, since it is not a 'general investigator of social policy and of allocation of resources' – even when a baby with a 'hole in the heart' is being denied treatment. Indeed, the courts (*R v Central Birmingham HA, ex parte Collier*) might be so wary that, even if an authority was breaching its public law duties blatantly, they might exercise their discretion not to intervene.[5] For instance (*R v Central Birmingham HA, ex parte Walker*), they might not wish to precipitate, by ruling against authorities, an increase in litigation which will divert the resources of statutory services into meeting complaints and away from service users.[6]

The supervisory and 'mediating' function of judicial review courts, their primary concern with procedure rather than substance (ie how authorities provide services, not what they provide) and a reluctance to interfere with the policies of authorities – means that the decisions of the courts and their consequences are not always clear cut. The High Court decision (*R v Gloucestershire CC, ex parte Mahfood*) in 1995 that an authority could not suddenly withdraw home help services provided under s.2 of the CSDPA is a good example.[7] What the court granted in one statement, it countermanded in another when it proceeded to rule that the council could withdraw services if it first reassessed people's needs according to its new, more restrictive policy. Though the decision seemed fairly logical, it caused uncertainty. After all, the basic question seemed to be – could vulnerable people continue to receive home helps or not? The court had seemed to say both 'yes' and 'no'. This was reflected in the newspaper headlines of the following day:

- 'Care cut unlawful but councils can tailor provision to resources'[8]
- 'Disabled pensioners win community care battle'[9]
- 'Council's cuts in care for disabled are ruled illegal'[10]
- 'Crude council wins right to scrap care'.[11]

All these are accurate but give very different impressions – compare, for example, the second with the fourth. In fact, it is the first which best sums up the judgement. In the event, the uncertainty is set to continue, because nearly a year later in June 1996, the Court of Appeal (*R v Gloucestershire CC, ex parte Barry*) overruled the High Court, stating that resources could not be taken into account when assessing people's needs.[12] The Court of Appeal decision is itself likely to be contested in the House of Lords.

Nevertheless, in one sense, the courts' supervisory function which puts them at one remove from directly enforcing the rights of service users, can be seen as an advantage – namely, that the courts are invested with a neutrality and impartiality which adds to their authority.

Judicial review in the NHS, social services and education fields

The courts have interfered little in decisions about the provision of *NHS services and equipment*. Cases do reach the law courts fairly regularly, and fail just as regularly – whether they are about non-provision for babies with heart problems, waiting times for orthopaedic patients, treatment for children with leukaemia, or treatment for infertility in women over 35 years old. These cases have not concerned the provision of disability equipment – but the principles argued apply equally to any services or equipment provided under the NHS Act 1977 (sections 1 and 3). The courts have expressed themselves extremely reluctant to interfere with the policy decisions which health authorities make – not least because the NHS Act 1977 imposes such vague duties (see p.197); indeed, as suggested elsewhere in this book, these duties seem in practice to be as much policy statements as enforceable law, and (in respect of any one specific service) to resemble powers rather than duties.

Since the passing of the Education Act 1981, judicial review has been used extensively to challenge decisions in the *field of special education*. Although the reported cases have generally not highlighted equipment, many of the principles are as relevant to equipment provision, as to any other special educational service. For example, the issue of whether services such as speech therapy are 'educational' or 'non-educational' has long been debated and has reached the law courts on occasion (see p.269). Sure enough, a recent case concerning equipment and involving the same question reached the High Court – about a schoolgirl's need for a lift (which would enable her to attend classes on the first floor of the school). Such has been the flood of judicial review cases in special education generally, the Education Act 1993 created a Special Educational Needs Tribunal, designed to channel grievances away from the law courts.

The use of judicial review to challenge the provision by social services departments of equipment and related welfare services (including residential care) has, on the whole, been sparing. A trickle of cases – mostly unsuccessful from the applicants' point of view – did reach the law courts in the 1970s and 1980s, some of them concerning s.2 of the CSDPA. However, since the implementation of the NHS and Community Care Act 1990, this situation has changed. The number of cases reaching the High Court, the Court of Appeal and even the House of Lords is growing. They have been about, for example, disputes over a person's choice of residential home (*R v Avon CC, ex parte M*)[13], the nature of respite care to be provided by an authority (*R v North Yorkshire CC, ex parte Hargreaves*)[14], the closure of local authority residential homes (*R v Wandsworth LBC, ex parte Beckwith*)[15], the wish of an elderly woman to remain supported in her own home rather than a nursing home (*R v Lancashire CC, ex parte Ingham*)[16], the provision of education and recreation services (*R v Islington LBC, ex parte Rixon*)[17], and the withdrawal of home help services (*R v Gloucester CC, ex parte Mahfood*).[18]

None of these have been about, but most are relevant to, equipment. This is because some relate to s.2 of the CSDPA (which explicitly governs equipment provision amongst other services) – and even those which do not, have nevertheless been about community care services, assessment, legislation and guidance – within which framework, equipment provision under the CSDPA firmly sits. Also, the courts have been prepared to compensate for the brevity of community care legislation governing assessment – by turning to the copious quantities of community care guidance issued by the Department of Health (see p.173).

Nevertheless, as one of the judges observed during the recent Court of Appeal case concerning the withdrawal of home help on the ground of resources, the issues are by no means black and white. He pointed out that, even if the services users won the case (ie if the court were to rule that authorities could not take account of resources when assessing need and what is necessary to meet that need under s.2 of the CSDPA 1970) it might be a distinctly Pyrrhic victory. All that might happen is that in the future authorities would act very much more defensively, and avoid being legally 'pinned down' by the CSDPA.[19]

2. MAKING DECISIONS UNREASONABLY, ILLEGALLY OR UNFAIRLY

When hearing judicial review cases, the law courts employ an array of conceptual tools to analyse the actions and decisions of statutory bodies, whether central or local government or any other public bodies. The main concepts are *unreasonableness, illegality* and *unfairness.*

Such a threefold, conceptual division is an over-simplification and there are other ways of categorising the grounds of judicial review. Indeed, the grounds 'for intervention are fluid and overlap, making rigid categorisation impossible'.[20] Not only do the concepts overlap, but beneath and around them lie a large number of other subordinate and related concepts. For instance, in one case (*R v Ealing LBC, ex parte Leaman*) brought under s.2 of the CSDPA about assistance with holidays, the authority was accused of breaching its statutory duty, fettering its discretion, taking account of an irrelevant consideration, and making a decision which was so unreasonable that no authority could have taken it. The judge shied away from dealing with each of these grounds in turn – instead he simply concluded that the authority had acted in a way which was 'quite wrong'.[21] Nevertheless this conceptual division will serve the purpose of this book.

Making decisions about equipment unreasonably

One longstanding definition of *unreasonableness* is unhelpfully circular, since it states that an authority acts unreasonably by coming 'to a conclusion so unreasonable that no reasonable authority could ever have come to it.'[22] A more recent and slightly more useful definition is that an unreasonable decision is one that is 'so outrageous in its defiance of logic or accepted moral standards that no sensible person who had applied his mind to the question to be decided could have arrived at it'.[23] A literal application of such an extreme definition would mean that, only rarely, if ever, would the courts find that a statutory body was behaving unreasonably. However, in practice, the courts do make many findings of unreasonableness, not because authorities are acting outrageously, but because the definition is relaxed.[24]

In one case (*R v DHSS, ex parte Bruce*) concerning services provided under s.2 of the CSDPA, the judge did suggest just how difficult proving unreasonableness might be. The applicant would have had to show that 'no local authority, properly discharging their duty and having regard to the facts before them, would have declined that request'.[25] And it is not irrational for an authority to decide that a woman must enter a residential home, because it can no longer afford to support her in own home – even though the latter was the preferable option and had previously been accepted by the authority.[26]

Contrastingly, in a case (*R v Gloucestershire CC, ex parte Mahfood*) about home help provision under s.2 of the CSDPA, the High Court suggested that if a social services department were to deny services to people who would otherwise be at severe physical risk, it would be acting unreasonably.[27] And, in a homelessness case (*R v Wandsworth LBC, ex parte Banbury*), which revolved around a man with epilepsy and whether he was so 'vulnerable' as to be included within a priority group, the court seemed to take a similar view. It found that the decision of the authority, that the man was not vulnerable, was not so unreasonable that no reasonable local authority could have taken it. However, if the attacks of epilepsy had been 'taking place with intense regularity, vulnerability would be established, and to contend otherwise would be flying in the face of reality'.[28] And, when a local authority proposed sudden alterations to its contractual terms with local, private residential homes, the court held that it was acting unreasonably (*R v Cleveland CC, ex parte Cleveland Care Homes*). This was because the swift introduction of these new terms, without consultation, would have had the effect of causing many of the homes to close and thereby frustrate the purpose of the NHS and Community Care Act 1990 – which was to ensure that care was available for people who needed it.[29]

People's reasonable needs for equipment under the CSDPA

The application of a reasonableness test to the assessment of people's needs, suggested in the *Mahfood* case (above) attempts to introduce a modicum of objectivity. It is saying that if a person is in such need that the average occupational therapist or local authority would say that it is necessary to provide services, then an authority has to do so.

However, such a reasonableness test appears to rest on a steep and slippery slope; for example, how can the courts, or for that matter anybody else, begin to assess how reasonable it is to deprive elderly people of the ability to bathe or shower for years? Yet it is common practice for local authorities to relegate bathing and washing needs to just such a low priority. Indeed, it is interesting to note – with objectivity of need in mind – that occupational therapists from countries such as Australia, who hold hygiene in higher regard than their counterparts in England (perhaps because of climatic differences), have been known to bridle against the priorities to which they have to work in English social services departments. In any case, as resources become more constricted and authorities provide ever-less generously, so too is the notion of reasonable provision likely to slip towards the less generous. If a stand is not taken at some point, any idea of the 'right' to services that the CSDPA was apparently intended to establish[30], slips quickly out of sight.

It was with this sort of concern in mind that the barristers representing service users in the same case (under a different name: *R v Gloucestershire CC, ex parte Barry*) in the Court of Appeal argued that the assessment of people's needs – and the meeting of those needs – represented a basic safety net or floor. They suggested that even if reasonableness and resources can be taken account of when assessing for, and providing, other community care services – they cannot be a factor when people's needs, and what is necessary to meet those needs, are being assessed under s.2 of the CSDPA 1970. When the Court of Appeal delivered its judgement against Gloucestershire County Council, one of the judges pointed out that the logical consequence of allowing people's needs to be defined by available resources would be that a complete lack of resources would mean that a disabled person could not have any needs. This would be a nonsense.[31]

Making decisions about equipment illegally

In its broadest sense, illegality would cover the concepts of unreasonableness and unfairness, since if a court rules against an authority on any of these grounds, it follows that the authority has acted illegally. However, in a narrower sense, adopted in this chapter, illegality occurs if an authority has failed to follow legislation – for example, by failing to follow the statutory wording in its entirety, or, equally, by introducing 'extra' irrelevant factors not contained in the legislation. Sometimes the courts will intervene if a person's right to be considered for services depends on a 'pre-condition' (eg being an 'ordinary resident' within the area of a local authority). And though they are reluctant to interfere with the assessment decisions of authorities, the courts might take a hand if it is clear that authorities have not followed proper assessment procedures clearly entailed by the legislation or guidance.

Failing to follow legislation: examples

The High Court has stated that a social services department acts illegally if it fails at least to consider providing assistance with privately arranged holidays under s.2 of the CSDPA 1970 (*R v Ealing LBC, ex parte Leaman*). This section states explicitly that an authority has a duty at least to consider a person's need not only for holidays arranged by the authority itself, but also for holidays arranged by somebody else.[32] Similarly if the authority failed altogether to consider adaptations or facilities (ie equipment) for safety, comfort or convenience – also referred to in the same section of the CSDPA – it might also be acting illegally.

In another case involving s.2 of the CSDPA (*R v Gloucestershire CC, ex parte Mahfood*), a social services department had suddenly withdrawn or reduced home help services from a number of people, because it was short of money. The court found that it was not acting in accordance with its duty to provide home help; and, although it could have discharged this duty by reassessing service users according to new criteria, it had failed to do so. The duty was absolute and the authority had not adhered to it.[33] Likewise, in another case (*R v Secretary of State for Education and Science, ex parte E*), neither the local education authority nor the Secretary of State had ensured that provision was made for all of the needs of a child which had been recorded in a statement of special educational needs. The court held that the duty was absolute, and so the authority was acting illegally.[34] But, when a health authority sets priorities, rations resources and thereby forces elderly people and children to wait years for orthopaedic surgery – the courts will not find illegality, because s.3 of the NHS Act 1977 precisely fails to impose such absolute duties (see p.199).[35]

Sometimes, if legislation is sparse in detail, the courts refer to guidance when deciding whether an authority has taken into account relevant factors. Following a community care assessment for the provision of respite care, the court (*R v North Yorkshire CC, ex parte Hargreaves*) held that when an authority had taken account of the wishes of a relative, but not those of the service user herself, it had acted unlawfully because this failure breached Department of Health policy guidance.[36] Similarly, in yet another community care case (*R v Avon CC, ex parte M*), the judge referred to guidance which stated that authorities, when carrying out assessments, should take into account the individual needs of people with learning disabilities (ie a mental handicap). Indeed, the court found that the local authority had not given enough weight to the decision of a complaints procedure review panel of a social services department – either because of unintentional perversity or lack of understanding of the legal status of the decision.[37]

A decision of an authority which denied a person accommodation under homelessness legislation was 'bad in law', because, when concluding whether the person was vulnerable, the authority took account only of a medical report, and not other factors. But, under the legislation, vulnerability can be caused by non-medical factors also; the assessment should have reflected this.[38] Likewise, an authority made a flawed decision when it denied that its offer – of rehousing a married woman (who had left her violent husband) with two children – was unsuitable. The court found that although the authority had on this occasion considered both medical and social factors, it had made two separate decisions – instead of the one composite, final decision which was required.[39]

Going beyond the legislation: examples

An authority acts illegally, when it considers not only too few, but also too many, factors. For instance, a housing authority, suffering from budgetary pressures, introduced a policy, not based on the legislation[40], when assessing how much mandatory renovation grant to give people. In effect, this new policy stated that the authority would pay no more than 20% of the total cost of the renovation. This was unlawful: it fell 'outside the council's statutory powers'.[41] The courts would also doubtless find illegality – or perhaps unreasonableness (see above) – if an authority were to assess people's needs for equipment, not by assessing their disability, but by the colour of their hair. This would be because the legislation, the National Assistance Act 1948, states that arrangements are to be made for disabled people, not for people with green hair. Thus, in one education case about the allocation of school places, the court stated[42]:

> 'to allocate boys to particular schools according to the colour of their hair or, for that matter, the colour of their skin...would be so unreasonable, so capricious, so irrelevant to any proper system of education that it would be ultra vires altogether, and the court would strike it down at once.'

Similarly, authorities cannot legally provide services or equipment beyond those sanctioned by legislation; in other words, though many disputes concern 'under-provision', cases are sometimes brought in which authorities are accused of 'over-provision'. For instance (*R v Ealing LBC, ex parte Jennifer Lewis*), a council tenant who was concerned about rent increases brought a claim that the provision of welfare services by councils was illegal in so far as they were being paid for out of the Housing Revenue Account. The Court of Appeal ruled against the authority, since the legislative wording, 'management of houses or other property' did not cover the provision of such services. The authority was therefore acting beyond its powers.[43]

On the same principle, it is possible that a disgruntled local taxpayer could bring a case against an authority if there was substantial evidence that large quantities of equipment were being provided – but, unused, were being left in people's homes, rather than collected and loaned to other people. For example, under s.2 of the CSDPA 1970 authorities are empowered only to make arrangements for provision if it is *necessary* for them to meet the *needs* of a disabled person. If an authority reassesses a person, decides on a reduction or withdrawal of services or equipment previously being provided – on the basis that the previous level of provision was not strictly 'necessary' but merely generosity on the part of the authority – it might have to show that the previous provision was not wholly based on s.2 of the CSDPA. Otherwise, the authority would be open to an allegation that it had acted illegally, since s.2 provides for necessary, but not for desirable or extra-generous provision.

Is an authority in breach of its duty if it delays in performing it?

Statutory services sometimes take a long time to get things done. Older people can wait years to receive an assessment from social services departments; and children can wait for similar periods for their statements of special educational needs to be finalised. The question, generally unanswered, is at what point an authority does its duty so slowly, that the law courts will find that it is failing to do it altogether. For example, it is arguable that if a person waits two or three years for an assessment by a social services department, the authority is clearly in breach of its duties to assess people who appear to be in need or who are disabled – under, respectively, s.47 of the NHS and Community Care Act 1990 and s.4 of the Disabled Persons (Services, Consultation and Representation) Act 1986.

The publicity leaflet of a social services department might state that people are welcome to join the waiting list for an assessment for equipment – but warn that they might have to wait not only months, but even years. Even following an assessment, there might be a further wait for the actual loan of a major piece of equipment such as a stairlift (for example, until another user dies). The leaflet points out that if people were to buy their own equipment, they would not have to wait – but that they would be without the benefit of an expert assessment (implying that they might be at risk of making an inappropriate purchase?). In such circumstances, it is possible but unlikely that the courts would find that authorities were failing to do their duty and therefore acting illegally.

If legislation imposes a precise time scale, within which an authority must act, then it should be reasonably clear that the authority is breaching its duty. On the other hand, if the authority is doing its best in the face of lack of money and resources, it is not certain quite what the courts would order as a remedy. As pointed out elsewhere, the courts are not obliged to make orders against authorities which are acting illegally (see p.452). For example, the local ombudsmen have acknowledged that, faced with a lack of money, authorities have had little choice but to devise ways around the 6-month time limit for approving applications for renovation grants (including disabled facilities grants).[44] They have even doubted whether the courts would criticise an authority which was operating a fair priority system within the resources it had available.[45]

If there is no statutory time scale imposed, the courts will probably be even more reluctant to intervene. For instance, under homelessness legislation, authorities have a duty to secure permanent accommodation for people in priority need, who are unintentionally homeless. In one case (*R v Brent LBC, ex parte Macwan*), the authority decided to place somebody in temporary, rather than permanent accommodation, for three years – after which permanent accommodation would be found. The court held that, although this was not totally consistent with the *Code of Guidance for Local Authorities on Homelessness*, it was not so unreasonable or in such conflict with the Code that it was illegal. The authority was still carrying out its duty – even if it was not doing it straight away.[46] In a case about delay in making a statement of special educational needs, the legislation did not impose a time limit, although Circular guidance did suggest 6 months. The court was asked to consider whether the delay amounted to breach of statutory duty or to unreasonable delay. It found that there was no breach of duty, and that the delay was not unreasonable, because the authority's actions had been affected by the intention of the parents to appeal to the Secretary of State.[47]

Is a person entitled to services?

As already explained, judicial review courts do not normally make decisions for authorities, but merely ensure that authorities make them properly. The courts are reluctant to interfere with questions of policy and resources which impact, for example, on whether seriously ill babies should receive treatment[48], or an elderly woman should be supported in her own home rather than forced into a nursing home.[49] Similarly, they will not normally question professional, 'clinical' judgements (except, for instance, through the use of expert witnesses in negligence cases). For example, in one case, the Court of Appeal stated[50]:

> 'No doctor can be required to treat a child, whether by the court in the exercise of its wardship jurisdiction, by the parents, by the child or by anybody else. The decision whether to treat is dependent upon an exercise of his own professional judgement...'

However, people's entitlement to services sometimes depends on factors other than resources and specialist professional judgements. For example, a pre-condition even of the possibility of equipment provision under s.2 of the CSDPA is that the person be an 'ordinary resident' within the area of an authority. A similar pre-condition to the right to an assessment for equipment is that the person be disabled.[51] Having established this pre-condition of entitlement in terms of a person's status, authorities then go on to decide, through assessment, whether the main condition of entitlement to services is met – ie basically whether they 'need' those services. The courts might sometimes intervene to greater or lesser degree when pre-conditions are in issue; and there is a suggestion that such conditions involve an objective state of affairs, rather than the subjective view of an authority. For example, either a person is, or is not, a local resident – it is surely not a matter of opinion. In addition, even if pre-conditions are not at stake, the courts might still interfere with local authority decision-making, if it is clearly flawed procedurally.

Pre-condition to entitlement: defining a term and applying it to particular people. The courts sometimes intervene when disputes arise about ordinary residence – ie where people are deemed to be living. They might state not only what the definition of an ordinary resident is, but also rule *whether particular people are ordinary residents* or not. What they have not gone on to do is rule whether, therefore, services must be provided – that is still for authorities to decide. The courts have ruled on ordinary residence in the fields of, for example, education grants[52], or residential accommodation for mentally handicapped children[53] and adults.[54]

If the status of a person is objectively certain, and a duty in respect of that type of person is clearly expressed, then the courts can more confidently state what an authority ought to be doing. For instance, if a person has been given a conditional discharge from hospital by the mental health review tribunal, then a health authority automatically has a duty to provide aftercare services under s.117 of the Mental Health Act 1983. The authority cannot make a subjective decision about whether it considers such provision appropriate – the status of the person, discharged under s.73 of the MHA 1973, triggers a strict duty.[55] After all, either a person has been discharged from hospital or he has not; it is not a matter of opinion.

Under s.4 of the Disabled Persons (Services, Consultation and Representation) Act 1986, a similarly clear pre-condition would appear to govern a person's entitlement to an assessment if he requests it – he must be 'disabled'. The legislation states not that he must be disabled *in the opinion* of the authority, but simply disabled. This suggests an objective status and one which the courts could, in principle (though so far they have not) rule upon, as they do ordinary residence. In practice, the courts are likely to do little more than ensure that authorities adhere to the legislative definition contained in s.29 of the National Assistance Act 1948 – and at least have regard to the Department of Health guidance on the subject. Indeed, this guidance maintains that it is for authorities to decide whether people are disabled, asking them to be generous rather than narrow in their decisions.[56]

Along similar lines, the courts have found that an immigration's officer's decision was flawed, because it could only be made on the basis that the person was an 'illegal entrant' – and there was insufficient evidence to this effect. Therefore, the decision could not stand.[57] This was seen to utilise the doctrine of 'precedent fact'; ie a fact which had to be objectively established, before an authority could use its discretion to make decisions about a person. However, this doctrine has been used only in very limited circumstances.[58]

Pre-condition to entitlement: defining a term, but leaving it to authorities to apply it to particular people. Sometimes the courts will define what a term means but then leave it up to an authority to decide whether a particular applicant comes within the definition. For example, in the field of homelessness, the House of Lords has stated that 'applicants' for housing accommodation cannot be people so mentally incapacitated that they are unable to make an application or authorise an agent to do so. The court held that it was implicit in the Housing Act 1985 that an applicant should have the capacity to understand and respond to an offer of accommodation – and undertake the ensuing responsibilities.[59] The courts have also held that people known as 'New Age Travellers' are not gypsies, even though they recognise that the definition of gypsy in legislation is imprecise.[60] However, whilst they might be prepared to pronounce and elaborate upon legislative definitions, the courts will try to avoid deciding whether any particular applicants are gypsies – that is for the local authority to do.[61]

In social security appeal cases, the courts sometimes intervene in this manner. Thus, one case, about the registration of a residential home, hinged on whether two residents with epilepsy were receiving 'personal care' – even though they did not need assistance with bodily functions. The court interpreted the Registered Homes Act 1984 to mean that personal care could include other assistance, as well as assistance with bodily functions; any such residents were therefore receiving personal care.[62] The Court of Appeal has held that a deaf person who requires frequent attention from another person – so that she can lead a normal social life – is entitled to disability living allowance. The question turned on whether a person who 'required' attention needed only attention which was necessary in order to maintain life itself. The court held that attention could be required for more than this – including 'a reasonable level of social activity'.[63] Similarly, the House of Lords has decided that if a blind person needs help when walking in unfamiliar surroundings, then (i) it was in connection with his 'bodily functions', (ii) it was 'attention' and (iii) such a person was therefore entitled to attendance allowance.[64]

When reading this type of case, it becomes clear that the courts tread a fine line (once they have defined the meaning of a term) between deciding themselves on the status of a particular person or leaving it up to the authority. This is because in some circumstances, a decision about the meaning of a term will afford the authority little room for manoeuvre when it re-takes its decision. Indeed, it is not always clear quite which option the courts are taking.

Interfering with the judgments of authorities about disabled people's needs? As already explained, the courts are reluctant to interfere with the decisions of authorities and the professional judgement of their staff – especially, when decisions or assessments are made about the needs which people's medical or disabling conditions give rise to.[65]

The reticence of the courts in this respect normally applies throughout the assessment and decision-making process. For instance, under the NHS and Community Care Act 1990, it is for social services departments to decide whether to assess a person at all, to decide what level of assessment to provide, to draw conclusions about the person's needs and to decide what services to provide. Courts are likely to intervene rarely. And whether a child has special educational needs to the extent that an education authority, rather than a school, should meet them, is a matter for the education authority, not the courts.[66] Similarly, when deciding how to meet the special educational needs of a child, the courts would be slow to interfere with the 'substantive merits of a decision honestly and carefully taken in purported exercise of a duty which involves a substantial measure of judgement'.[67]

Indeed, the courts are quite prepared to accept that an authority might come to different conclusions about the same person at different times. For example (*R v Gloucestershire CC, ex parte Mahfood*), the High Court has explicitly accepted that an authority might reassess people's needs for services or equipment under s.2 of the CSDPA – and come up with different, harsher, conclusions on the second assessment in the light of reduced resources.[68] Similarly, when a child's special educational needs were assessed and then assessed again by the Secretary of State, the findings differed (*R v Secretary of State for Education, ex parte C*). On the first occasion, the child was deemed to have special educational needs, on the second not. The court found that different assessment results, even emanating from the same assessor's examination of the same facts, would not necessarily be irrational.[69]

Sometimes, it is true, the courts will, or at least threaten to, intervene. In the *Mahfood* case, the judge suggested that he would find that an authority was acting unreasonably if it denied services to people at severe physical risk.[70] However, this can be viewed not as challenging professional judgements, but as supporting them; that is, the average occupational therapist would judge that people at serious risk need services – thus an authority which denied them would be acting unreasonably because its decision would not be reflecting reasonable professional judgements. Similarly, the court might agree with an expert report that, when assessing a person's needs for residential care, a local authority should take account of psychological, as well as physical, 'needs'.[71]

The courts have also became entangled in the argument about whether speech therapy for children with special educational needs should be classed as 'educational' or 'non-educational' provision (see p.269 for the significance of this distinction). In one case (*R v Lancashire CC, ex parte M*), the court referred to the 1972 report of a government committee chaired by Professor Quirk, and endorsed the position of speech therapy as one situated between education and medicine. On this basis, the court found against the education authority which was claiming that speech therapy could not be regarded as educational provision.[72] This 'interference' by the courts was, however, again based, at least partly, on expert professional opinion (ie in the form of the Quirk report). Likewise (*R v Wiltshire CC, ex parte D*), a court ruled against an authority because it had failed to act on the 'unchallenged and uncontradicted evidence' of the Director of the Dyslexic Institute as to the provision of special support needed by the child. The authority had failed to discharge its statutory duty and had behaved unreasonably.[73]

Questioning procedures surrounding the assessment of people's needs. Though the courts avoid challenging professional judgements, they are sometimes ready to question the procedures which surround them and to pronounce upon factors which should, or should not, be taken into account. For instance, if an authority's internal guidelines state that a decision should be made by staff at a particular level – for example, an occupational therapist (assessing for equipment) – the court might strike down the decision, if it is made by subordinate staff. Thus (*R v Islington LBC, ex parte Aldabbagh*), when a decision about housing transfer was taken by a local authority neighbourhood officer, instead of a neighbourhood manager (as the authority's own policy stipulated), the court overturned the decision.[74] Similarly (*R v Wiltshire CC, ex parte D*), a court ruled against a local education authority because the statement of special educational needs which it drew up did not reflect the uncontested report of a doctor which had specified what provision the child required. This was 'unreasonable' – and the failure of the authority to give a second report to their special needs panel, when it was considering the case, meant that the decision of the panel was flawed for lack of relevant evidence.[75]

If authorities have quite clearly failed to follow legislation or guidance, the courts will intervene. They might bluntly tell authorities, for example (*R v Waveney District Council, ex parte Bowers*), that there 'can be no question but that the applicant is vulnerable' under homelessness legislation – of a man who had suffered a serious head injury. The mistake the authority had made was to apply wrongly a test of 'substantial' disability and substantial need, based on the Homelessness Code of Guidance – instead of working primarily from the legislation's test of 'vulnerability' based on 'handicap or physical disability'.[76]

Authorities which have attempted to adopt a blinkered approach have sometimes been admonished by the courts – not necessarily because of clear contravention of legislation or guidance, but perhaps as much out of common sense. For instance, in one homelessness case, when the authority had a duty in legislation to assess whether dependent children are likely to live with an applicant, the court ruled that the duty extended to assessment not just of past and present, but also future, arrangements.[77] Similarly (*R v Mid Glamorgan CC, ex parte Miles*), when an authority refused to give a community care assessment to a prisoner, because his possible needs existed only at some unspecified time in the future, a judicial review hearing was granted. Just before the hearing, an agreement was reached that the assessment would be made – the court confirmed the agreement, ruling that an assessment be undertaken and that the prisoner was entitled to have his application for an assessment considered by the authority.[78] This was particularly important since otherwise a vicious circle could not be broken; parole would not be granted without the community care assessment and vice versa.

In a case (*R v Avon CC, ex parte M*) about residential care for a person with a mental handicap (learning disability), the court gave short shrift to an authority which was claiming that his psychological needs were, in fact, mere preferences or whims which it did not have a duty to meet. The court supported this finding not only with reference to expert professional opinion, but also to Department of Health guidance which emphasised the importance of the individual basis on which services should be planned.[79] In another community care case (*R v Gloucestershire, ex parte RADAR*), the court stated that when an authority knew of people who appeared to be in need – and therefore incurred a duty to assess them – it was not discharging its duty by simply sending them a letter offering an assessment on condition that they responded to the letter. This was because it would follow that assessment would only be triggered by request (ie by those who responded) – whereas the duty in legislation expressly did not hinge on request but on apparent need.[80] In the last three cases mentioned, the courts were not themselves actually determining when a person is or isn't in need, but were ruling upon procedural aspects of, or factors in, assessing need – respectively, taking account of future needs, acknowledging psychological needs, responding to an appearance of need – in line with legislation, guidance, expert opinion and common sense.

Making unfair decisions about equipment

The concept of fairness is broad and is sometimes referred to as *natural justice*; whilst unfairness is sometimes also termed *procedural impropriety*. Fairness embraces many other concepts which the courts are prepared to invoke to safeguard people's rights to reasonable treatment by public bodies. These include giving people a *fair hearing*, avoiding *bias* (including any appearance of bias), *consulting* with people, and taking account of people's *expectations*. The courts emphasise continually that the extent to which they will apply these concepts is very much dependent on context.[81] This can make it difficult to predict how the courts will react in particular situations.

Generally speaking, the more a person's property and personal rights are affected, the greater might be the judicial insistence on fairness. For example, questions of fairness form an important part of the extensive use of judicial review in relation to prisoners, immigration and homelessness – all obviously related to fundamental aspects of people's lives.

Fair hearing

Giving a *fair hearing* means that authorities must allow people to make themselves heard. For example, this might involve being given the opportunity to contribute to a community care assessment. Indeed, the fact that this is precisely what is recommended by Department of Health guidance might strengthen such an argument in court.[82] Enabling a person to participate and contribute to an assessment could presumably involve giving people literally the ability to speak – for instance, through a human, or electronic, communicator.

People cannot receive a fair hearing if a biased decision is made; *bias* is another ground for judicial review of decisions. It means that not only must the decisions of public bodies be unbiased but they must also be *seen to be unbiased* or at least not involve a *real danger of bias.* Thus, for instance, if a community nurse manager was deciding on the priority of home-based patients – one of whom was her relative – then she might be accused of bias.

Sometimes it is alleged that local authority officers cannot give fair assessments or fair hearings – because they are influenced by their awareness of resources or by prior knowledge and opinion about the people they are assessing. For instance, in one homelessness case (*R v Tower Hamlets LBC, ex parte Khatun*), it was alleged that a local authority officer, who was aware of the local housing shortage, could not conduct a fair interview – and that the interviewer should come from outside the authority. The Court of Appeal found in favour of the authority which, it said, had finite resources and had to decide 'who should conduct the interviews and what questions should be asked to enable the authority to carry out its statutory functions'.[83] Similarly (*R v Avon CC, ex parte Crabtree*), a childminder protested that it was unfair that a panel, which had decided that he should be deregistered, had included social workers against whom he had previously registered complaints. The Court of Appeal accepted that the procedure might seem unfair, but held that the panel could still reach a fair decision. Furthermore, the interests of the child came first – and, anyway, the decisions of many administrative bodies are inevitably taken by people who have a prior knowledge of the facts in question.[84] In another case (*R v Mid-Glamorgan CC, ex parte B*), it was alleged that the members of a local authority education committee had betrayed their bias (see below) by using terminology such as 'our authority' and 'our officers' – and because one of the members became very hostile to a solicitor at the hearing before being brought under control by the clerk. The court ruled that although the use of the terminology was unfortunate and gave the impression of bias, it did not in fact amount to a 'real danger' of bias; nor did the 10–15 second outburst at the end of the proceedings.[85]

It is anxiety about the effect of lack of resources on authorities' judgements about people's needs – including their needs for equipment – which has prompted calls for truly independent assessments (see p.38).

Consulting with people

Sometimes the duty to consult is contained in legislation – thus, a health authority's failure to consult a community health council about the closure of a bone marrow unit was unlawful, irrespective of any issues of fairness.[86]

However, where legislation does not impose duties to consult, the courts might intervene by employing the concept of fairness. They have ruled in some cases against local authorities which had not consulted with the residents of the residential homes which they were proposing to close. The courts do not say that the authorities cannot close homes – but that, if they wish to do so, they must first go through a proper consultation process. Again therefore, it is not the decision itself which the courts are looking at, but the way in which it is reached.

The courts might declare not only that there is a duty to consult, but also stipulate what the essentials of that consultation should be. Thus (*R v Devon CC, ex parte Baker*), authorities might have to give residents knowledge of the closure plans for their residential home, to allow reasonable time for them to object, and to consider their objections.[87] Accordingly (*R v Wandsworth LBC, ex parte Beckwith*), it was unfair when a council held consultations about only some, but not all, of the issues surrounding the closure of residential homes in Wandsworth.[88] On the other hand, education authorities are not obliged to provide interpreters when they arrange consultative meetings for parents.[89] And, if an authority is proposing to close a nursery, its decision is valid even though the early stages of the process might have been unfair – so long as proper consultation then supersedes the initial unfairness.[90] However, if an authority were to produce a consultation paper which was fundamentally misleading, then the courts will find fault with it.[91] By way of contrast, if a consultation document is *explicitly* devious and contains obvious inconsistencies and contradictions, the court will not interfere – since its shortcomings are visible to all(!).[92]

Giving reasons for decisions

It has been pointed out that 'listen means tell'.[93] In other words, it is of limited use to give a person a fair hearing if he or she doesn't know why an authority has made an adverse decision. For example, if people are denied equipment and services, it is quite natural that they should wish to know the reasons why. However, it does not follow that authorities have a duty to provide such reasons, nor are the arguments, for and against the giving of reasons, necessarily straightforward.

Sometimes legislation contains a specific duty to give reasons; for example, the Education Act 1996 imposes a duty on education authorities, when deciding to assess a children's special educational needs, to give parents the reasons.[94] However, legislation is often silent about the giving of reasons, and there is no mention of it in any of the community care or health service legislation which applies to this book. Consequently, it is left to the courts to make judgements about what fairness requires in particular situations. Whilst the giving of reasons instinctively seems to be good practice and desirable, the courts are, at the same time, concerned to protect authorities from excessive burdens. For example, in a case about treatment for a child with leukaemia (*R v Cambridge HA, ex parte B*), the High Court ruled that the health authority should produce a detailed account of how it had rationed its resources and why it had decided not to provide treatment. However, later the same day, the Court of Appeal overturned this ruling, explaining that this requirement would place too great a load on the authority.[95]

In English law, there is no universal duty to give reasons for administrative decisions[96] and so, again, much depends on the context.[97] The fact that it might be, in the main, good practice to give reasons, does not mean that the courts will always state that there is a legal duty to do so. Thus, there are contexts in which the giving of reasons would normally be required, and others in which it would not. And in those contexts where there is no general rule, one way or another, reasons might sometimes be required, depending on the circumstances.[98] In a recent case (*R v Bristol CC, ex parte Bailey*), concerning an application for a renovation grant (of which a disabled facilities grant is one type), the court found that there was no duty to give reasons.[99] Similarly, a local authority's appeals unit does not have to give reasons when it decides about a person's housing priority.[100] And, the High Court has held that a committee of the English Nursing Board had no duty to give reasons to the original complainant when it decided to discontinue the investigation – in this, it differed from an industrial tribunal.[101]

Even in a context where reasons might normally be required, circumstances might still dictate whether or not they should be given in any particular case. In a dispute about a child's special educational needs (*R v Secretary of State for Education, ex parte S*), the Court of Appeal ruled that the Secretary of State did not have to disclose the advice which he had received about the case, since the advice did not contain any new material which the parents and education authority did not already know about. The advice amounted to no more than a 'critical analysis of the quality of the evidence as well its content'.[102]

The information sources on which reasons are based might also be in issue. For instance, a person might need to know on what information an authority has based its reasoning. If an authority has taken account of gossip – for example, from a neighbour, to the effect that an applicant for a stairlift can climb the stairs perfectly well – then the courts might rule that the authority should disclose the gossip and its source.[103] Reasons also need to be comprehensible and informative in order to explain why a particular decision has been made. For instance, if a case goes to appeal, the court has to identify what the reasons for the original decision were.[104] It will not suffice for a housing authority simply to recite the wording of homelessness legislation in giving its reasons for refusing an application (*R v Islington LBC, ex parte Trail*).[105] For instance, a social services department has a duty to provide equipment when it thinks it 'necessary' (s.2 of the CSPDA). It would be inadequate reasoning if the authority stated (assuming that it was obliged to give reasons at all) that it would not provide equipment 'because it was not necessary'. The authority would have to explain why it was not necessary. Similarly (*R v Islington LBC, ex *parte Hinds*), a court might fault an authority for giving reasons (demanded by homelessness legislation) that mix up findings of fact, other factual considerations and conclusions/value-judgements – leaving the reader puzzled about the reasoning process.[106]

However, in contrast (*R v Lancashire CC, ex parte M*), standard-form decision letters, with variations to reflect different outcomes of decisions, do not necessarily mean that an authority is failing to consider people's cases properly.[107] And, although a duty to give the *grounds* for a decision might be imposed by legislation, it does not follow that detailed reasons must be given of the decision of an authority's education appeal committee: there 'is a distinction between grounds and reasons'.[108]

Development of the law in relation to reasons. The judicial review courts seem, in any case, still to be 'exploring' the extent of, and limits to, the duty of public bodies to give reasons. For example, in a homelessness case (*R v Lambeth LBC, ex parte Walters*), which revolved around whether the applicant's son had a medical need for central heating, the applicant obtained the support of her GP. However, the authority denied that central heating was needed and refused to provide the applicant with the authority's medical assessment. The court held that this was unfair – and that there was a general duty in English Law to provide reasons whenever the 'statutorily impregnated administrative process is infused with the concept of fair treatment to those potentially affected by administrative action'.[109] Nevertheless, the Court of Appeal (*R v Kensington and Chelsea RBC, ex parte Grillo*) has since ruled that, in homelessness cases, local authorities are under no such general duty to give reasons for their decisions.[110] (Apart from this absence of a general duty, the homelessness legislation does in fact place a statutory duty on authorities to give reasons at certain points of the assessment procedure.)

People's legitimate expectations and changing policies

Legitimate expectation is a developing concept. Basically, it refers to the expectations which are generated – and then disappointed – when a public body makes 'promises' or statements of policy but does not keep to them.

For example, an authority might state in its policy documents that any person who meets certain assessment criteria will be able to have a telephone. If the person meets the criteria, but the authority then goes back on its policy and refuses to provide the telephone, then the person could argue that his legitimate expectations have been dashed. There has been some uncertainty about whether, in such circumstances, the courts would be able to order that the person should receive the telephone which has been denied – or merely order that the authority should talk or consult with the person first – before denying it. Generally speaking, since the purpose of judicial review is not to enable the courts to take decisions for authorities, but to ensure that authorities make decisions properly, the courts might tend to take the latter, 'hands-off' approach. Thus, rather than order that the person be given the telephone, the court might order that the authority 'go away', and consult with the person properly, giving him or her an opportunity to object to the change in policy. However, it has been suggested in another context (*R v Ministry of Agriculture, ex parte Hamble*) that in some circumstances, legitimate expectation could be *substantive* (ie provision of the telephone) rather than merely *procedural* (ie consultation only).[111]

In a case about the provision of a lift for a disabled school pupil (*R v Lambeth LBC, ex parte MBM*), the child's mother felt that the child's statement of special educational needs implied that a lift would be provided. The judge decided that the statement did not carry this implication, but that, in any event, the child had received the sympathetic and informed decision she had been entitled to by way of legitimate expectation.[112] And, when an authority had failed to apply its own policy to a homelessness application, the court held that it did not have a duty to do so, since legitimate expectation was procedural only. However, judicial review was still granted because, even so, the council had not given enough consideration to its own policy.[113]

Consistency and changing policy? It might be good practice to act consistently and to follow policies, but authorities also need to be free to alter them according to fluctuating resources and changing local needs. To be forced to adhere everlastingly to a particular policy would make no sense – and, inevitably, a certain proportion of people are bound to be 'caught out' when policies are changed.

Nevertheless, whilst on one level it is perfectly understandable and rational that policies should change, individual disabled people can be badly affected. For example, a parent of a boy with cerebral palsy and visual impairment might go to an NHS wheelchair clinic, 'armed' with information about which wheelchair is needed and supported by physiotherapists and occupational therapists. The request might be refused because, although other children with similar needs had succeeded in obtaining that type of wheelchair, the policy has now changed. Instead, a basic chair which is too large and seems not to meet the boy's needs might be offered – on a 'take it or leave it' basis.[114]

The decisions of the courts represent a balancing act. A court might not approve if an authority departs arbitrarily and informally from its stated policy.[115] Thus, an authority should at least state officially that it is changing its policy.[116] But, on the other hand, even if the authority's policy is set out in an individual letter and appears to specify conditions – which the particular applicant (say for a taxi licence) takes steps to meet – the letter should not be regarded as a binding contract. It is merely an accurate representation of the authority's policy at the time.[117] Similarly, a council's written undertaking to a tenant about eviction gave rise to no legal relations – there was no right, contractual or equitable, which she could enforce.[118] And, even if the court were to find that a person had a legitimate expectation that the council would do something (eg sell a property to her) – it might rule that this expectation had been satisfied, if the council changed its mind but gave her the opportunity (even though at short notice) to speak and to write to councillors.[119] An authority might not change its policy generally, but still decide not to apply it to a particular person, and thus to deny the services that she had been expecting. For example, in a homelessness case, an authority failed to make the normal two offers of accommodation, making only one instead. The court ruled that the authority was perfectly entitled to do this, since 'what it cannot do is bind itself, in advance of considering each application on its merits'.[120]

Nevertheless, conversely, in an immigration case (*R v Secretary of State, ex parte Asif Khan*), the court stated that a Minister could not withdraw from a statement or undertaking made to an individual in a Circular letter without providing a fair hearing and in any case only if overriding public interest required the withdrawal.[121] More recently, a court ruled that if the Secretary of State does not conform to his own policy guidance on immigration (which he should at least have regard to, even though it is not law), then he has acted unfairly if no reasons are given for the decision.[122] However (*R v Ministry of Agriculture, ex parte Hamble*), overriding policy interests might justify sudden changes in policy – for example, a change in licensing policy for trawlers could be justified by the pressing need to limit trawling in the North Sea.[123]

Building flexibility into policies. However the courts might deal with legitimate expectation in any particular case, public bodies can minimise the risk of adverse judicial review. For instance, although community care guidance urges authorities to produce and disseminate a plethora of information about their services and people's eligibility for them, authorities can attempt to avoid making rash and unqualified promises.

Thus, authorities can temper their information about who is eligible for equipment and other services by including phrases such as 'resources allowing', or 'subject to regular reviews of policy', or 'in 90% of cases' – which make it plain from the outset that no absolute, open-ended promises are being made. In addition, although the courts are unlikely to conclude that authorities are entering into contracts when they provide, or promise to provide, services (see p.391) – authorities could even state clearly that no contractual obligations are being entered into.

Over-rigid policies: the fettering of discretion

Whilst authorities have to act consistently by following their own policies, they must, paradoxically, also ensure that they do not behave too consistently. An authority should not take over-rigid decisions; if it does so, it might be *fettering its discretion*; this is unlawful because an authority cannot 'slavishly follow a policy without regard to individual cases'.[124]

The concept of fettering discretion is used to prevent authorities from adopting blanket policies which they are not prepared to modify, even in exceptional circumstances. For instance, a social services department might adopt a policy that it will not provide people with non-slip bath mats or special cutlery. Likewise, a health authority might state that it will only provide chiropody services and equipment for people in priority groups, or that it will not supply incontinence pads to people in residential homes.

There is nothing to prevent authorities adopting such policies. Indeed, the courts recognise that in order to deal with large numbers of people, authorities need to evolve policies and rules – for example, to avoid 'fruitless applications involving expense and expenditure of time'.[125] However, authorities should always be prepared to consider individual cases in order to see whether exceptional needs constitute an exception to the policy. As the House of Lords put it in a case about the handling by the Secretary of State of a complaint about milk price fixing (*Padfield v Ministry of Agriculture*) – there is a balancing act to be performed between always following a prescribed policy and the freedom to depart from the policy at will. It was not a question of one or the other, 'all or nothing'.[126] For example, the London Boroughs Occupational Therapy Managers Group issued some years ago guidelines on criteria for the provision of home adaptations.[127] It helpfully lists a number of contra-indications in relation to the provision of stairlifts, including 'progressive conditions'. Such a guideline adopted by a local authority is legally and administratively permissible, so long as it does not become a rigid policy.[128]

The NHS has long had priorities and rationing in place – for instance, priority groups for chiropody services have been advocated in Department of Health guidance for many years.[129] However, if authorities are not to fetter their discretion, other people who are not in the priority groups should have the opportunity, in exceptional circumstances, to gain access to chiropody services. In practice, it is not clear how easy this would be, since if everybody were to present a special case, an excessive amount of time might be spent on individual assessments. Under similarly broad legislation governing the provision of schools by local education authorities, the courts (*Smith v ILEA*) held in the 1970s that an authority can implement a general policy (to make schools comprehensive), so long as it listens to objections and considers whether its policy should be applied in particular cases.[130]

In a recent case about infertility treatment (*R v Sheffield HA, ex parte Seale*), a health authority had adopted a blanket policy of denying treatment to people 35 years of age and above. The judge admitted that, clinically, it would be desirable to investigate each patient according to a range of factors and criteria – not just age. But, in practice, the authority had to take account of resources and it was not unreasonable that it should adopt age as an appropriate criterion.[131] However, the practical complications of applying and justifying such policies have been pointed out; first, age might indeed be an appropriate criterion, but not the only one – and be of varying importance depending on the individual. Second, in this particular case, it seems that the infertility treatment could have had the effect of curing the painful condition of endometriosis from which the woman suffered – and that there were thus additional, clinical reasons for providing the treatment.[132]

The care authorities need to take to demonstrate that they are not following rigid policies was suggested in an education case (*R v Hampshire CC, ex parte W*); the authority was accused of refusing to make a statement of special educational needs, because of a policy of keeping the authority's level of statementing to the 2% national average – a figure indicated in the draft code of practice presaging the introduction of new legislation (the Education Act 1993). In fact, the court found no evidence to support this accusation, nor was it prepared to infer it; however, it stated that had it thought that such a policy lay behind the decision, it would have not hesitated to intervene.[133]

Fettering of discretion in the case of powers rather than duties. It should be noted that even in the case of powers, as opposed to duties, authorities still need to take care not to fetter their discretion. For instance, authorities have a power, but not a duty to provide home repair assistance (HRA) to enable people to remain in their own homes (see p.242). As a consequence, it is reported that a number of authorities do not provide the assistance at all – because there is no duty to do so. However, even though authorities are entitled to adopt such a policy not to provide HRA, they must always be prepared to consider provision in exceptional, individual circumstances. It would be unlawful if authorities decided never to provide it under any circumstances, since it would be a fettering of their discretion – a number of court cases concerning discretionary educational grants have illustrated this.[134] The position would be similar in the case of discretionary disabled facilities grants,[135] or services and equipment provided for older people under 1968 legislation.[136]

It might not be enough for an authority to go through the motions of taking account of exceptions. For example, a court accepted that a review and appeal procedure would save from unlawfulness a policy which meant that every application for a (student) grant was initially refused. However, if after 3 years, 300 appeals had been made – all of which were unsuccessful – then, as a matter of both common sense and law, the policy was clearly too rigid. In addition, if the exceptions for which the appeal procedure was meant to cater were limited to 'most extraordinary' circumstances, then the authority would be coming very close to a blanket policy which in theory admitted of exceptions, but in reality prevented proper consideration of each application.[137] And, in a case about a grant for a student's degree course in medicine, the court held that the authority had fettered its discretion because the policy had not provided for any exceptions. Even if the authority had, in fact, been prepared to make an exception, it did not explain this to the applicant – so denying her the chance to make representations to the authority. Furthermore, if an authority does not have a procedure for gathering and considering extra information about individual applications, then it cannot be operating an effective exceptions policy – because it is preventing itself from identifying the individual circumstances which might turn out to be exceptional.[138]

Fettering of discretion: writing letters to applicants. In one case (*R v Cumbria CC, ex parte 'NAB'*), an education authority's policy not to maintain statements of special educational needs for children with a developmental quotient between 70 and 85 was challenged. The court found that the policy itself was not irrational, and that there was no evidence that the authority was fettering its discretion by 'shutting its ears'. Indeed, the authority's letter to the child's mother had offered to give further consideration to the decision if requested.[139] On the other hand (*R v Harrow LBC, ex parte Carter*), when a housing authority had a policy, in itself reasonable, about homelessness and 'local connection' (a test establishing which authority should take responsibility for a person), the authority had fettered itself because officers could only depart from the policy with difficulty. On the evidence of the letters sent by the authority in the case, the judge was not satisfied that it recognised that there could be exceptions. For instance, when deciding to refer an applicant back to another authority, it had not acknowledged the need to take account of how the circumstances in that second authority might affect the applicant.[140]

Authorities need to be careful, for example, when they write letters to individual applicants, refusing services, on the basis of priorities. A court (*R v Bristol CC, ex parte Bailey*) observed that such a letter – which stated bluntly that renovation grants were only available if houses were unfit for human habitation (ie the criterion for mandatory grants) – would have been a fettering of discretion, had not council policy, *in fact*, been to consider also discretionary applications on their merits.[141]

3. JUDICIAL REVIEW: SOLUTIONS AND OBSTACLES

Solutions which the courts can impose

The courts can make a number of different types of ruling. Basically, they can overturn (*certiorari*), prevent (*prohibition*), or force authorities to take (*mandamus*), decisions or actions. *Injunctions*, similar to the last of these, are seldom used in judicial review. Finally, the courts can make *declarations* about how the law applies to a particular, or particular type of, situation.

Declarations do not order an authority to do something, but state what the court's view of a situation is. Applications for declarations can be made in *private law*, as well as by means of judicial review (*public law*). For instance (*Re S*), in 1995 the Court of Appeal decided that it could give a declaration in private law on behalf of the close friend of a man who had suffered a stroke. The friend was resisting the attempts of the man's family to move him.[142]

One way of looking at some declarations is that they are 'advisory' and apply to hypothetical cases – albeit cases which might in future be in issue.[143] On the other hand (*Airedale NHS Trust v Bland*), they might explicitly apply to very real situations of life and death – in which, for instance, decisions have to be made about whether patients in a persistent vegetative state should be allowed to die.[144] A declaration might be sought about whether it was lawful for NHS occupational therapy departments to sell particular types of equipment needed for people's daily living, but not their clinical, needs. For instance (*R v Hereford and Worcester LEA, ex parte Jones*), some years ago a declaration was successfully sought stating that an education authority would be acting illegally, under s.61 of the Education Act 1944, if it went ahead with proposed charges for individual tuition in music.[145] A declaration might still be granted in some circumstances even if the dispute is actually resolved during the hearing.[146] In other circumstances, it might not be granted at all if it is being sought for reasons which the courts consider are without merit – for example, simply to support a future action in negligence.[147]

Declarations might be resorted to when it is too late to do anything else – as when regulations were issued by a government department without proper consultation, in breach of duties laid down in legislation. By the time the case had come to court, the regulations had already been brought into force, and the protestor anyway agreed with their main substance.[148] Similarly (*R v Ealing LBC, ex parte Leaman*), a court found that an authority had improperly refused to consider assisting a person with a holiday under s.2 of the CSDPA; but, by the time the case came to court, it was all too late – the holiday was long gone. The court observed that it could not award damages anyway, nor could it not see what to quash (even had it been minded to make such an order). Instead, a declaration was made that the authority had been in the wrong.[149] And in the Court of Appeal case (about community care home support services and the CSDPA: *R v Gloucestershire CC, ex parte Barry*), declarations were virtually all that could be asked for. The first applicant had since obtained the services he had been seeking, whilst the original second applicant (Mrs Ingham) was dead (the Court of Appeal allowed her daughter and the voluntary organisation, RADAR, to step in).[150]

Forcing people to seek other solutions

The courts sometimes state that other avenues of redress, or *alternative remedies*, should be used instead of, or at least before, judicial review. For instance, the Education Act 1996 provides for complaints to be made to the Secretary of State[151]; whilst the Special Educational Needs Tribunal is designed to channel many complaints made under the Education Act 1996 away from the law courts. And, even before the creation of the Tribunal, the courts would sometimes rule against judicial review applicants who had not exhausted the various appeals procedures afforded by education legislation.[152]

The Local Authority Social Services Act 1970 gives the Secretary of State powers to intervene if social services departments are failing unreasonably to carry out their statutory duties – ie powers to declare that they are in 'default' of their duty.[153] On occasion, the courts have stated that these default powers are the appropriate channel for enforcing duties to provide services under s.2 of the CSDPA (*Wyatt v Hillingdon LBC*)[154], or residential accommodation under the National Assistance Act 1948 (*Southwark LBC v Williams*).[155] The same Act sets up statutory complaints procedures. When the courts apply such a restrictive test, then they are likely to state that only in exceptional circumstances could judicial review be resorted to before the appeal procedures, provided in legislation, had been exhausted.[156]

All these are reasons why the courts might not *give leave* (see below) to people to bring judicial review cases. Nevertheless, it does not follow automatically that the courts will insist that other avenues be used. For example, it might be unclear whether the Secretary of State's default powers (see immediately above) can be appealed to when a local authority fails to consult the residents of homes it is proposing to close. This is because those powers can only be applied in relation to social services duties, and consultation is not obviously one of those. Furthermore, if the issue is entirely connected with law (as opposed to disputed facts) and is within a developing field of law – then it might anyway be more appropriate for the courts to deal with it than the Secretary of State; the Court of Appeal (*R v Devon CC, ex parte Baker*) took this view in a case about the closure of residential homes.[157] This latter point was taken up in a recent case concerning the withdrawal and reduction of services under s.2 of the CSDPA (*R v Gloucestershire CC, ex parte RADAR*). Responding to the local authority's argument that its statutory complaints procedure should have been used rather than the law courts, the judge stated that judicial review was the appropriate method to deal with general issues of principle as to the legal obligations of the authority.[158]

Because the Education Act 1996 provides the Secretary of State with powers of intervention, it does not exclude altogether the jurisdiction of a judicial review court.[159] Similarly, although magistrates can hear appeals against the refusal of a local authority to grant taxi licenses, the question of whether the authority has acted outside its powers is for the judicial review courts, not the magistrates.[160]

Obstacles to success in judicial review

There are a number of obstacles in the way of bringing, and succeeding in, an action for judicial review. These include knowing when judicial review is appropriate, gaining permission to bring a case, and acting within the time limits. In addition, even if authorities have acted improperly, judicial review courts are not obliged to impose a solution or remedy. Moreover, financial damages are not generally available through the judicial review procedure.

First, it is important to make the correct decision about whether the action should be brought as a private law action (eg for negligence or breach of statutory duty) or as a judicial review case. The division in English law, between private and public law is not always clear. However, if the wrong decision is made, the consequences can be unfortunate; if a private law action is brought and the court finds that it should have been brought in public law, the action will be dismissed. It cannot be 'converted' automatically into a public law action – and the very short time limit for applying for judicial review will probably have expired anyway. Therefore, sound advice to people might be that, if in doubt, they should bring a judicial review application – this can be converted later into a private law action if necessary.[161]

Second, when a person begins a private law action – for example, for negligence or breach of statutory duty – he can simply issue a writ. But, in order to bring a judicial review case, permission has to be given by the courts. This means that there has to be a preliminary hearing before a High Court judge.[162] The courts have explained that the purpose of this permission, or giving of leave, is to protect both the courts from inappropriate applications and public bodies from undue uncertainty.[163] In the community care field, for example, the Press fairly regularly report that applicants have been given leave to apply for a judicial review. However, it does not follow that all of these will progress to a full hearing. Applicants might withdraw if they reach an agreement with authorities in the mean time – since gaining leave for judicial review is a good bargaining counter and might catalyse a settlement. Generally speaking, nobody wants to go to court if it can be avoided. For example, at the time of writing (April 1996), it is reported that a man has been granted leave for a judicial review of an authority which, allegedly, has delayed in providing an assessment of his need for central heating. Whether a full hearing will take place, and join the growing list of reported community care cases, is unknown. The judge himself has urged the council to act before a full court hearing.[164] Similarly, an expedited (ie speeded up) judicial review hearing has been granted to a disabled couple, who have been on a waiting list for a disabled facilities grant for over a year – even though their needs have been judged to be of some urgency.[165]

Third, the time limit for bringing judicial review is very short – three months from the date of the occurrence of the decision or action being contested. The limit can be waived if there are good reasons for the delay in bringing the case.

Fourth, judicial review courts do not have to provide a remedy – and might not do so for a number of reasons. For example, the applicant might not have provided full information to the court[166], the authority might be doing all it can to remedy its breach of duty[167], or it might be too late to do anything about the problem.[168] In addition, the court might feel that the outcome of a dispute anyway would be the same – even if the authority were to make its decision properly. For instance, obliged under homelessness legislation to give reasons, and informed by guidance about what the reasons might be, an authority failed to provide them in an adequate or intelligible sense. However, no remedy or relief was given, because the applicant would have fared little better even had they been given.[169]

Fifth, except where a claim for damages (which could have been awarded in a private law action) has been linked to the application for judicial review, damages are not awarded in judicial review.[170]

Notes

1 Treasury Solicitor's Department. *Judge over your shoulder: judicial review: balancing the scales.* London: Treasury Solicitor's Department.
2 Toynbee, P. (1995). Judicial review is a mere elastoplast. *Independent:* 2 August 1995.
3 See eg: *Re L* [1994] ELR 16 (CA) (at 26): discussing a child's statement of special educational needs and whether Part 3 (provision for needs) reflected Part 2 (needs).
4 *R v London Borough of Newham, ex parte R* [1995] ELR 156 (QBD).
5 *R v Central Birmingham Health Authority, ex parte Collier* (1988) (CA) (Transcript, 6 January 1988).
6 *R v Central Birmingham Health Authority, ex parte Walker* (1987) 3 BMLR 32 (CA).
7 *R v Gloucestershire County Council, ex parte Mahfood and Others, R v Islington London Borough Council, ex parte McMillan* (1996) 160 LGRevR 321 (QBD).
8 Waterhouse, R. (1995). *Independent:* 17 June 1995.
9 Murray, I. (1995). *Times:* 17 June 1995.
10 Pallot, P. (1995). *Daily Telegraph:* 17 June 1995.
11 Brindle, D. (1995). *Guardian:* 17 June 1995.
12 *R v Gloucestershire County Council, ex parte Barry; R v Lancashire County Council, ex parte Gilpin and RADAR* (1996) (CA) (7–10 May 1996, CO/95/1779, CO/95/1134, transcript)
13 *R v Avon County Council, ex parte M* [1994] 2 FCR 259 (QBD).
14 *R v North Yorkshire County Council, ex parte Hargreaves* (1994) 26 BMLR 121 (QBD).
15 *R v Wandsworth London Borough Council, ex parte Beckwith* (1995) (HL), Times, 14 December 1995.
16 *R v Lancashire County Council, ex parte Ingham and Whalley* (1995) (QBD) (5 July 1995, CO/774/95, CO/108/95, transcript).
17 *R v Islington Borough Council, ex parte Rixon* (QBD), The Times, 17 April 1996.
18 *R v Gloucestershire County Council, ex parte Mahfood and Others, R v Islington London Borough Council, ex parte McMillan* (1996) 160 LGRevR 321 (QBD).
19 *R v Gloucestershire County Council, ex parte Barry; R v Lancashire County Council, ex parte Gilpin and RADAR* (heard in the Court of Appeal, 7–10 May 1996). From the author's own notes of the case.
20 Fordham, M. (1994). *Judicial review handbook.* Chichester: Wiley, p.263.
21 *R v London Borough of Ealing, ex parte Leaman* (1984) (QBD), Times 10 February 1984 (LEXIS, 6 February 1994).
22 *Associated Provincial Picture Houses Ltd v Wednesbury Corporation* [1947] 2 All ER 680 (CA).
23 *Council of Civil Service Unions v Minister for the Civil Service* [1985] AC 374 at 410 (HL).
24 Wade, H.W.R.; Forsyth, C.F. (1994). *Administrative Law.* 7th edition. Oxford: Clarendon Press, p.401.
25 *R v Department of Health and Social Security, ex parte Bruce* (1986) (QBD), Times, 8 February 1986 (and LEXIS, 5 February 1986).
26 *R v Lancashire County Council, ex parte Ingham* (1995) (QBD), 5 July 1995 (transcript).
27 *R v Gloucestershire County Council, ex parte Mahfood and Others, R v Islington London Borough Council, ex parte McMillan* (1996) 160 LGRevR 321 (QBD).
28 *R v Wandsworth Borough Council, ex parte Banbury* (1986) 19 HLR 76.
29 *R v Cleveland County Council, ex parte Cleveland Care Homes Association and Others* (1994) LGRR 641 (QBD)
30 *Hansard,* House of Lords, 9th April 1970, col.241, Earl of Longford.
31 Richard Gordon, Cherie Booth in: *R v Gloucestershire County Council, ex parte Barry; R v Lancashire County Council, ex parte Gilpin and RADAR* (1996) (CA) (7–10 May 1996, CO/95/1779, CO/95/1134): from the author's own notes of the case.

32 *R v London Borough of Ealing, ex parte Leaman* (1984), Times 10 February 1984 (LEXIS, 6 February 1984).
33 *R v Gloucestershire County Council, ex parte Mahfood and Others, R v Islington London Borough Council, ex parte McMillan* (1996) 160 LGRevR 321 (QBD).
34 *R v Secretary of State for Education and Science, ex parte E* [1992] 1 FLR 377 (CA).
35 *R v Secretary of State for Social Services, ex parte Hincks* (1980) 1 BMLR 93 (CA).
36 *R v North Yorkshire County Council, ex parte Hargreaves* (1994) 26 BMLR 121 (QBD).
37 *R v Avon County Council, ex parte M* [1994] 2 FCR 259 (QBD).
38 *R v London Borough of Lambeth, ex parte Carroll* (1987) 20 HLR 142 (QBD).
39 *R v Lewisham London Borough Council, ex parte D* [1993] 2 FCR 772 (QBD).
40 *Local Government and Housing Act 1989*, s.116.
41 *R v Sunderland City Council, ex parte Redezeus* (1995) 27 HLR 477 (QBD).
42 *Cumings v Birkenhead Corporation* [1972] 1 Ch 12 (CA).
43 *R v London Borough of Ealing, ex parte Jennifer Lewis* [1992] 24 HLR 484 (CA).
44 Commission for Local Administration (1994). *The local government ombudsman 1993/1994: annual report.* London: CLAE, p.24.
45 Commission for Local Administration (92/B/3013). *Report on investigation against Birmingham City Council.* Coventry: CLAE, 1995, pp.19–20.
46 *R v Brent London Borough, ex parte Macwan* [1994] 2 FCR 604 (CA).
47 *R v Gloucestershire County Council, ex parte P* [1994] ELR 334 (QBD).
48 *R v Central Birmingham Health Authority, ex parte Collier* (1988), Times 6 January 1988 (Lexis 6 January 1988) (CA). *R v Central Birmingham Health Authority, ex parte Walker* (1987) 3 BMLR 32 (QBD and CA).
49 *R v Lancashire County Council, ex parte Ingham and Walley* (5 July 1995, Transcript, CO/774/95, CO/108/95) (QBD).
50 *Re J (A Minor) (Wardship: Medical Treatment)* [1991] Fam 33 (CA).
51 *Disabled Persons (Services, Consultation and Representation) Act 1986*, s.4.
52 *R v Barnet London Borough Council, ex parte Shah* [1983] 2 AC 309 (HL).
53 *R v London Borough of Redbridge, ex parte East Sussex County Council* [1993] COD 168 (QBD).
54 *R v Waltham Forest London Borough Council, ex parte Vale* (1985) (QBD), Times 25 February 1985.
55 *R v Ealing District Health Authority, ex parte Fox* [1993] 1 WLR 373 (QBD).
56 LAC(93)10. Department of Health. *Approvals and directions for arrangements from 1 April 1993 made under schedule 8 of the National Health Service Act 1977 and sections 21 and 29 of the National Assistance Act 1948.* Appendix 4 (reiterating guidance on disability, registration etc previously contained in local authority circulars 25/61 and 17/74).
57 *R v Home Secretary, ex parte Khawaja* [1984] 1 AC 74 (HL).
58 *Re S (Minors)* [1995] ELR 98 (CA): limited use of 'precedent fact' indicated by the court in this special education case about the 'objective suitability' of a school.
59 *Garlick v Oldham Metropolitan Borough Council (and related appeals)* [1993] 2 All ER 65 (HL).
60 *R v Dorset County Council, ex parte Rolls and Another* (1993) 26 HLR 381 (QBD).
61 *R v South Hams District Council, ex parte Gibb* (1993) 26 HLR 307 (QBD).
62 *Harrison v Cornwall County Council* (1992) 156 LGR 703 (CA).
63 *Secretary of State for Social Security v Fairey* (1995) (CA), Times, 22 June 1995.
64 *Mallinson v Secretary of State for Social Security* [1994] 1 WLR 630 (HL).
65 *Re J* [1992] 4 All ER 614 (CA).
66 *R v Secretary of State for Education and Science and Another, ex parte Lashford* [1988] 1 FLR 73 (CA).
67 *R v Mid-Glamorgan County Council, ex parte Greig* (1988) (QBD), Independent 1 June 1988.
68 *R v Gloucestershire County Council, ex parte Mahfood and Others, R v Islington London Borough Council, ex parte McMillan* (1996) 160 LGRevR 321 (QBD).
69 *R v Secretary of State for Education, ex parte C* [1996] ELR 93 (QBD).
70 *R v Gloucestershire County Council, ex parte Mahfood and Others, R v Islington London Borough Council, ex parte McMillan* (1996) 160 LGRevR 321 (QBD).
71 *R v Avon County Council, ex parte M* [1994] 2 FCR 259 (QBD).
72 *R v Lancashire County Council, ex parte M* [1989] 2 FLR 279 (QBD).
73 *R v Wiltshire County Council, ex parte D* [1994] 1 FCR 172 (QBD).
74 *R v London Borough of Islington, ex parte Aldabbagh* (1995) 27 HLR 271 (QBD).

75 *R v Wiltshire County Council, ex parte D* [1994] 1 FCR 172 (QBD).
76 *R v Waveney District Council, ex parte Bowers* (1982) 4 HLR 120 (CA).
77 *R v Kingswood Borough Council, ex parte Andrew Smith-Morse* (1994) 159 LGRevR 469 (QBD).
78 *R v Mid Glamorgan County Council, ex parte Miles* (1993) (QBD). Summarised: Clements (1994). Community care: definition of 'need'. Legal Action: January 1994, p.21.
79 *R v Avon County Council, ex parte M* [1994] 2 FCR 259 (QBD).
80 *R v Gloucestershire County Council, ex parte Royal Association for Disability and Rehabilitation* (21 December 1995, Transcript, CO/2764/95).
81 *Lloyd v McMahon* [1987] AC 625 (HL).
82 See eg: Social Services Inspectorate, Department of Health; Social Work Services Group, Scottish Office (1991). *Care management and assessment: practitioners' guide.* London: HMSO, pp.51–52.
83 *R v Tower Hamlets London Borough Council, ex parte Khatun* [1995] 27 HLR 465 (CA).
84 *R v Avon County Council, ex parte Crabtree* (1995) (CA), Independent, 29 November 1995.
85 *R v Mid-Glamorgan County Council, ex parte B* [1995] ELR 168.
86 This was contravention of Community Health Council Regulations (SI 1985/304). *R v North West Thames Regional Health Authority and Others, ex parte Daniels* (1993) (QBD), Independent, 18 June 1993.
87 *R v Devon County Council, ex parte Baker and Johns and R v Durham County Council, ex parte Curtis and Broxson* (1994) LGRevR 241 (CA).
88 *R v London Borough of Wandsworth, ex parte Beckwith* (1995) LGRevR 929 (QBD): the second Beckwith case, heard on 24 May 1995.
89 *R v Birmingham City Council, ex parte Darshan Kaur* (1990) (QBD), Times, 11 July 1990.
90 *R v London Borough of Barnet, ex parte B* [1994] ELR 357 (QBD).
91 *R v Secretary of State for Transport, ex parte Richmond upon Thames London Borough Council* (No 2) [1995] COD 188 (QBD): concerning night-flying restrictions: the consultation paper was misleading and so could not amount to full and fair consultation.
92 *R v Secretary of State for Transport, ex parte Richmond upon Thames London Borough Council* (No 3) (1995), Times, 11 May 1995 (QBD): continuing dispute about night-flying restrictions.
93 Fordham, M. (1994). *Judicial review handbook.* Chichester: Wiley, p.346.
94 *Education Act 1996*, s.323(4).
95 *R v Cambridge Health Authority, ex parte B* [1995] 1 FLR 1055 (QBD and CA).
96 *R v Secretary of State for the Home Department, ex parte Doody* [1993] 3 WLR 154 (HL): concerning prisoners, mandatory life sentences and the Secretary of State's duties.
97 *Lloyd v McMahon* [1987] 1 All ER 1118 at 1161 (HL): requirements of fairness depend on the character of the decision-making body, the type of decision, the statutory framework and what other procedural safeguards may be necessary for fairness. These requirements were recited in: *R v Civil Service Appeal Board, ex parte Cunningham* [1991] 4 All ER 310.
98 *R v Higher Education Funding Council, ex parte Institute of Dental Surgery* [1994] 1 WLR 242 (QBD): whether reasons should be given for academic decisions.
99 *R v Bristol City Council, ex parte Karelene Bailey and Dennis Bailey* (1995) 159 LGRevR 221 (QBD).
100 *R v London Borough of Newham, ex parte Dawson* (1994) 26 HLR 747 (QBD).
101 *R v English Nursing Board, ex parte Roberts* [1994] COD 223 (QBD).
102 *R v Secretary of State for Education, ex parte S* [1995] 2 FCR 225 (CA).
103 *R v Poole Borough Council, ex parte Cooper* (1994) (QBD), Independent, 13 October 1994: a homelessness case where an authority wrote to the tenant's landlord seeking information. Unfavourable information was duly supplied in strict confidence and not disclosed by the authority to the applicant: this was held to be unfair to the applicant.
104 *R v Lancashire County Council, ex parte Maycock* (1995) 159 LGRR 201 (QBD): school admission appeals.
105 See a homelessness case: *R v Islington London Borough Council, ex parte Trail* [1994] 2 FCR 1261 (QBD).
106 *R v London Borough of Islington, ex parte Hinds* [1994] COD 494 (QBD).
107 *R v Lancashire County Council, ex parte Maycock* (1995) 159 LGRevR 201 (QBD): school admission appeals.

108 *R v Lancashire County Council, ex parte M* [1995] ELR 136 (QBD).
109 *R v London Borough of Lambeth, ex parte Walters* (1994) 26 HLR 170 (QBD).
110 *R v Kensington and Chelsea Royal Borough Council, ex parte Grillo* (1995) (CA), Times, 15 May 1995: a homelessness case.
111 *R v Ministry of Agriculture Fisheries and Food, ex parte Hamble (Offshore) Fisheries Ltd* [1995] 2 All ER 714 (QBD): in which the concept of legitimate expectation was thoroughly reviewed.
112 *R v London Borough of Lambeth, ex parte MBM* [1995] ELR 374 (QBD).
113 *R v London Borough of Newham, ex parte Campbell* (1994) 26 HLR 183 (QBD).
114 Sinfield, C. (1996). 'Having to fight for something as basic as a decent wheelchair is a disgrace. *Disability Now:* February 1996, p.13.
115 *R v Leeds City Council, ex parte Hendry* (1994) LGRevR 621 (QBD): a local authority informally departed from its policy in relation to taxi licences: this was unlawful (except the applicant did not succeed because of a failure to disclose full information about his case).
116 *R v Secretary of State for Transport, ex parte Richmond upon Thames London Borough Council* (No 2) [1995] COD 188 (QBD): concerning night-flying restrictions: the Secretary of State, having suggested the need to reduce noise, proceeded to do the opposite.
117 *R v Knowsley Metropolitan Borough Council, ex parte Maguire and Others* (1990) 90 LGR 653 (QBD): refusal of taxi licenses.
118 *Southwark London Borough Council v Logan* (1995) (CA), Times, 3 November 1995.
119 *R v London Borough of Camden, ex parte Hughes* [1994] COD 253 (QBD).
120 *R v London Borough of Newham, ex parte Campbell* (1994) 26 HLR 183 (QBD).
121 *R v Secretary of State for the Home Department, ex parte Asif Khan* [1984] 1 WLR 1337 (CA).
122 *R v Secretary of State for the Home Department, ex parte Benjamin Yaw Amankwah* [1994] Imm AR 240 (QBD).
123 *R v Ministry of Agriculture Fisheries and Food, ex parte Hamble (Offshore) Fisheries Ltd* [1995] 2 All ER 714 (QBD).
124 *R v London Borough of Bexley, ex parte Jones* [1995] ELR 42 (QBD).
125 *British Oxygen Co Ltd v Board of Trade* [1971] AC 610 (HL) (at 631).
126 *Padfield v Minister of Agriculture* [1968] AC 997 (HL).
127 London Boroughs Occupational Therapy Managers Group (1988). *Occupational therapists' criteria for the provision of adaptations in the homes of people with disabilities.* London: LBOTMG.
128 Commission for Local Administration (94/C/1563). R*eport on an investigation into complaint against Sheffield City Council.* York: CLAE, 1996, p.12. In this case, the local ombudsman found that the policy in relation to stairlifts was not in fact inflexible or 'blanket'.
129 HRC(74)33. Department of Health and Social Security. *Chiropody.* London: DHSS, 1974.
130 *Smith and Others v Inner London Education Authority* [1978] 1 All ER 411 (CA).
131 *R v Sheffield Health Authority, ex parte Seale* (1994) 25 BMLR 1 (QBD).
132 Elliston, S.; Britton, A. (1995). Is infertility an illness? *New Law Journal:* 11th November 1994, pp.1152–1553.
133 *R v Hampshire County Council, ex parte W* [1994] ELR 460 (QBD).
134 See eg cases about discretionary student grants: *R v Warwickshire County Council, ex parte Williams* (1995) (QBD), Independent, 15 February 1995: policy not to give grants if students had alternative financial sources. And: *R v Southwark London Borough Council, ex parte Udu,* Times, 30 November 1995: policy not to assist students attending postgraduate courses or private colleges.
135 *R v Bristol City Council ex parte Karelene Bailey and Dennis Bailey* (1995) 159 LGRR 221 (QBD). This case hinged on whether or not a local authority had adopted a rigid policy of never awarding discretionary renovation grants under s.115 of the Local Government and Housing Act 1989. In the event, the court found no such policy but made clear that had there been, the authority would have been fettering its discretion.
136 *Health Service and Public Health Act 1968,* s.45.
137 *R v Warwickshire County Council, ex parte Collymore* [1995] ELR 217.
138 *R v London Borough of Bexley, ex parte Jones* [1995] ELR 42 (QBD).
139 *R v Cumbria County Council, ex parte 'NAB'* (1995) 159 LGRevR 729 (QBD).
140 *R v Harrow London Borough Council, ex parte Carter* (1994) 158 LGRevR 601 (QBD).
141 *R v Bristol City Council, ex parte Karelene Bailey and Dennis Bailey* (1995) 159 LGRR 221 (QBD).

142 *Re S* (1995) (CA), Independent, 7 March 1995. The family was trying to take him back to Norway by private aeroplane.

143 For summary of these remedies, see: Public Law Project (1995). *The applicant's guide to judicial review.* London: Sweet & Maxwell, pp.23–29.

144 *Airedale National Health Service Trust v Bland* [1993] 1 All ER 821 (HL).

145 *R v Hereford and Worcester Local Education Authority, ex parte Jones* [1981] 1 WLR 768 (QBD).

146 *R v London Borough of Lambeth, ex parte G* [1994] ELR 207 (QBD): a dispute about grants for school pupils: the Council agreed to make the award during the hearing.

147 *R v Gloucestershire Council, ex parte P* [1994] ELR 334: dispute about the issuing of a statement of special educational needs: a draft statement was issued during the proceedings.

148 *R v Secretary of State for Social Services, ex parte Association of Metropolitan Authorities* [1986] 1 WLR 1 (QBD).

149 *R v London Borough of Ealing, ex parte Leaman* (1984) (QBD), Times, 10 February 1984 (LEXIS, 6 February 1984).

150 *R v Gloucestershire County Council, ex parte Barry; R v Lancashire County Council, ex parte Gilpin and RADAR* (1996) (CA) (7–10 May 1996, CO/95/1779, CO/95/1134).

151 Eg *Cumings and Others v Birkenhead Corporation* [1972] 1 Ch 12 (CA): about choice of schools open to Roman Catholic children.

152 Eg: *Re S (a minor)* [1995] COD 132 (CA).

153 *Local Authority Social Services Act 1970,* s.7D.

154 *Wyatt v Hillingdon Borough Council* (1978) 76 LGR 727 (CA).

155 *Southwark London Borough Council v Williams* [1971] 1 Ch 734 (CA).

156 *Re S (Minor)* [1995] COD 132 (CA): challenge to an amended statement of a child's special educational needs.

157 *R v Devon County Council, ex parte Baker and Johns and R v Durham County Council, ex parte Curtis and Broxson* (1994) LGRevR 241 (CA).

158 *R v Gloucestershire County Council, ex parte Royal Association for Disability and Rehabilitation* (21 December 1995, Transcript, CO/2764/95).

159 *R v Inner London Education Authority, ex parte Ali and Murshid* [1990] COD 305–387 (QBD).

160 *R v Leeds City Council, ex parte Hendry* (1994) 158 LGRevR 621 (QBD).

161 *Rules of the Supreme Court,* Order 53, r.9(5).

162 *Supreme Court Act 1981,* s.31.

163 *Inland Revenue Commissioners v National Federation of Self-Employed and Small Businesses Ltd (NFSESB)* [1982] AC 617 (HL).

164 Court orders council to assess man's need. *Community Care:* 22–28 February 1996, p.4.

165 (News item). Waiting list challenged. *Community care:* 21–27 March 1996, p.5.

166 *R v Leeds City Council, ex parte Hendry* (1994) 158 LGRevR 621: taxi licence case.

167 See comments in: *R v Inner London Education Authority, ex parte Ali and Murshid* [1990] COD 305–387 (QBD): concerning whether sufficient school places were being provided by the ILEA under s.8 of the Education Act 1944.

168 *R v London Borough of Ealing, ex parte Leaman* (1984) (QBD), Times, 10 February 1984 (LEXIS, 6 February 1984): assistance with holidays under s.2 of the CSDPA.

169 *R v London Borough of Islington, ex parte Hinds* [1994] COD 494 (QBD).

170 *Rules of the Supreme Court,* Order 53, Rule 7.

CHAPTER 18

BREACH OF DUTIES IN RELATION TO EQUIPMENT

CRIMINAL AND CIVIL LIABILITY

COVERAGE

1. Criminal liability for breach of statutory duty
   - Breach of duties: examples
   - Power of the criminal courts to award compensation
   - Strictness of liability
   - Regulation, persuasion, notices and prosecution.
2. Civil liability for breach of statutory duty
   - Identifying duties in legislation
   - Can breach of a duty give rise to a civil action for damages?
   - Causing harm, type of harm, damages and defences.

Key points

This chapter gives a very brief outline of what the consequences are when organisations or individuals – in their capacity, for example, of manufacturers, suppliers, public bodies or employers – breach statutory duties.

Criminal liability. Breach of statutory duty occurs when a body or person, upon whom legislation places a duty, fails to carry out that duty. Criminal prosecutions can be brought for breaches of statutory duty under, for example, the health and safety and consumer safety legislation dealt with in chapter 14 of this book.

Thus, a manufacturer who continues to produce and sell defective walking frames, even after the defect was well-known, could be prosecuted under, for instance, the Medical Devices Regulations. Such prosecutions are brought by the appropriate body, such as a local authority trading standards department, the Health and Safety Executive, or the Medical Devices Agency of the Department of Health. Prosecution is likely to be a last resort, since enforcement bodies also have the power to issue various types of notice, and to coax as well as to employ a 'sledge-hammer' approach.

Civil liability. In addition, civil legal actions for damages can sometimes be brought by individuals who have suffered harm or loss because of the breach of duty. However, though reasonably well-established in principle in the health and safety field, such actions are much less so in the field of welfare law. Indeed, the courts are, not surprisingly, most reluctant to allow people to sue public authorities for damages, simply because those bodies have failed in their duty to provide a public service. To recognise such a right would be akin to granting contractual rights – which are markedly absent when statutory welfare services are provided for individuals (see p.391). Nevertheless, civil actions for breach of statutory duty can be, in principle, easier to win than actions for negligence, because sometimes the duty is so strict that a person can be found liable even if he or she was not careless. However, not all duties are that strict, in which case it might still be necessary to show some form of unreasonable or careless behaviour.

To make things more complicated, legislation sometimes expressly *excludes*, or *includes*, the possibility of civil legal action. Alternatively, if the legislation does not say one way or another, then it is up to the courts to decide whether damages may be awarded for breach of duty. In the health and safety field, the courts might be ready to recognise a right of individuals to sue for damages for breach of duty. However, in other fields, such as welfare provision by statutory services, the courts generally find the reverse and decide that Parliament did not intend to give people such a right.

Questions people ask

- Are damages available when people breach duties laid down in legislation?
- When can both criminal and civil actions be brought if manufacturers, suppliers, statutory services, voluntary organisations breach their statutory duty?
- What happens if employers breach their duty by not minimising, or removing altogether, the need for staff to lift patients and clients?
- What if a social services department assesses formally that a person needs a stairlift, but then doesn't provide it?
- What if a residential home fails to provide adequate equipment for residents?

1. CRIMINAL LIABILITY FOR BREACH OF STATUTORY DUTY

Where legislation creates a criminal offence for breach of statutory duty, the primary legal action which can be taken is criminal prosecution by, for example, local authority trading standards officers, local authorities in their capacity as registration authorities for residential homes, the Health and Safety Executive, or the Medical Devices Agency.

Breach of duties: examples

There are countless examples of breach of statutory duty affecting equipment which could be given. For example, the General Product Safety Regulations 1994 prohibits the placing of unsafe products on the market, and provides for penalties of a fine or imprisonment.[1] The Medical Devices Regulations 1994 impose penalties for failure of manufacturers to conform to essential requirements affecting the safety and performance of medical devices (see Chapter 15).

Health and safety legislation imposes general duties on employers, not only towards employees but also towards other people, including, for example, hospital patients or residents of nursing and residential homes.[2] Thus, a residential care home might be fined £20,000 for failing to safeguard the health and safety of a resident who died when she was scalded in a bath – as a result of the failure of the home to ensure that water temperature was regulated.[3] Such an incident could typically be a breach of duty under s.3 of the Health and Safety at Work Act 1974 to ensure that people who are not employees (ie residents) are not exposed to risks to their health and safety. A further offence, of failure to undertake a risk assessment, would come under the Management of Health and Safety Regulations 1992.[4] And, the registration and inspection units of local authorities and health authorities are responsible for registering and inspecting independent residential and nursing homes – and for issuing notices, cancelling registration, or bringing prosecutions for breach of Regulations.[5] For example, it would be an offence if adequate facilities and adaptations for physically disabled people were not provided in residential homes.[6]

Power of the criminal courts to award compensation

In addition to imposing criminal penalties, the criminal law courts have the power to award compensation orders in favour of the victim of the breach of duty.[7] Such compensation orders seem to be reasonably well-established, for example, in cases involving the Trade Descriptions Act 1968.[8] However, such orders are not intended to be made in complicated cases – and the standard of proof needed in a criminal, is greater than in a civil, court of law.[9] However, since applications for compensation are made in what are mostly relatively straightforward cases, the success rate is reported to be high – 80% in magistrates' courts and 58% in Crown Courts.[10] Although prosecutions are brought by enforcement agencies, such as trading standards departments, it is of course open to private individuals to report incidents and provide information to enforcement bodies.[11]

Strictness of liability

Depending on the legislation and the duty in question, strictness of liability for breach of the duty varies. For example, a manufacturer or employer may only have to adhere to a duty so far as it is *reasonably practicable* to do so. This qualification applies, for example, to the duty of employers to minimise the need for employees to undertake manual handling which involves a risk of injury.[12] Thus, an employer might have a defence if, despite clear guidelines and a system of training and supervision, an unforeseeable emergency leads to a physiotherapist injuring herself whilst lifting a patient. Once duties are qualified in this way, then liability begins to shift away from strictness back to the notion of carelessness as a necessary part of liability, characteristic of the law of negligence. Furthermore, the duties are not all one way, since, for example, staff also have a duty – to 'make full and proper use' of any system which the employer provides to reduce the risk of injury.[13]

Apart from qualifying some duties, legislation also provides for explicit defences. For instance, the defence of *due diligence* is that the accused has taken all reasonable steps to avoid committing the offence. This defence is available to, for example, people who have placed unsafe products on the market[14], or who have placed on the market medical devices which do not conform to the statutory 'essential requirements'.[15] By contrast, other legislation imposes much stricter liability; for instance, the Employers' Liability (Defective Equipment) Act 1969 imposes liability on employers for the injuries caused to employees by defective equipment – even if the defect stems from the fault of a third party (eg the supplier of the equipment) and even though the employer has taken reasonable care to choose a reputable supplier.[16]

Regulation, persuasion, notices and prosecution

Not all breaches of safety legislation will result in criminal prosecution, either straightaway or at all. Enforcement bodies have powers to issue notices of various types – for example, *prohibition, suspension, compliance, improvement* or *warning* notices – in order to protect the public or employees and to persuade or force offending organisations to comply. Less serious breaches of legislation could result in notices requiring compliance; more serious ones could attract notices which prohibit the organisation from continuing to supply the product. A warning notice may, for example, relate to products already supplied in the past, but now considered to be unsafe.[17]

Safety legislation is not a straightforward area of the law; though it imposes criminal penalties, it is sometimes regarded as only 'quasi-criminal' – viewed a little like minor motoring offences. Enforcement authorities exercise considerable discretion in deciding whether to prosecute or not. One view is that they will act in order to ensure the greatest compliance with the legislation. Thus, if it is effective, a 'softly-softly' approach may be pursued. For example, in one case, a trading standards department agreed not to prosecute the manufacturer of an over-concentrated oven cleaner which had burned 70 consumers. This was on the basis that a compensation fund would be set up by the company and the product reformulated.[18]

If, on the other hand, the same type of positively dangerous offence is persistently committed, prosecution may follow not only to deter the particular offender, but also to warn other potential offenders. For instance, an NHS hospital was recently fined £15,000 when a disposal container full of used syringes was left near a toy box: a child, waiting to see a specialist, had started to play with them.[19] This type of hazard is a perennial one in hospitals; so there was an added incentive to prosecute. Similarly, the size of a fine will not necessarily be in proportion to any injury actually inflicted by a dangerous product. When a woman ate a chocolate nut crunch which contained a knife blade, she suffered a cut tongue, which remained sore for two days. A fine of £25,000, imposed by the Crown Court, was upheld by the Court of Appeal – it would keep manufacturers on their toes to ensure that such dangerous foreign bodies did not get into their products.[20]

An actual consumer transaction might not be necessary to found a prosecution. For instance, the High Court has found that a retailer can be guilty of giving misleading price indications under s.20 of the Consumer Protection Act 1987 (about bedroom and kitchen furniture), even if the indication had not actually been given to any particular consumer.[21]

2. CIVIL LIABILITY FOR BREACH OF STATUTORY DUTY

In addition to criminal prosecution, it is sometimes possible for people to win civil actions for damages for breach of statutory duty. Such civil actions are reasonably well-established within the health and safety at work field, less so in the field of consumer protection, and very difficult to win against public bodies providing welfare services and equipment.

Identifying duties in legislation

In order even to consider an action for breach of statutory duty, a duty needs to be identified in legislation. If there is no duty, there can be no breach. Thus, if the function involved is only a power – that is the authority can, but does not have to, do something – then an action for breach of statutory duty is not relevant.[22]

If there is a duty, it has to be a reasonably clear one, since otherwise the courts may be unable to say whether it has been breached. Not all duties are as clearly stated as, for instance, the duty concerning unsafe products: 'No producer shall place a product on the market unless the product is a safe product'.[23] In contrast, many of the duties relevant to the provision of equipment by statutory services are couched in very different language. The duties hinge on whether authorities are 'satisfied'[24], or whether, in the eyes of the authority, it 'appears'[25] that a person is in need. Or, the duties may explicitly be 'general'[26], or towards the local population[27], rather than towards individuals. The law courts are likely to state that the generality and vagueness of such duties are evidence that Parliament could not have intended that authorities be strictly liable in damages.[28]

Responsibility for performing statutory duties cannot generally be delegated, so that even if an independent contractor is used – for example, to implement a lifting and handling system in a hospital – the employer (eg the NHS Trust) may remain directly liable for any breach of the Manual Handling of Loads Regulations.[29]

Can breach of a duty give rise to a civil action for damages?

When considering a civil claim for damages for breach of statutory duty, the courts have to ascertain whether the duty can, in principle, give rise to civil liability at all.

Legislation sometimes expressly includes, expressly excludes – or is silent about – the possibility of civil action. For example, legislation expressly states that breach of the duty of employers – to take reasonable care of the health and safety of non-employees (eg hospital patients) – cannot give rise to a civil action.[30] On the other hand, legislation which stipulates that medical devices must conform to essential requirements allows civil actions in principle[31], as does legislation which requires employers (including social services departments and the NHS) to minimise the lifting and manual handling which employees have to undertake.[32] But, under the General Product Safety Regulations, it is not clear whether the courts would entertain civil actions for breach of statutory duty – since the Regulations are silent on this point.[33]

Even if the courts are satisfied that the legislation is clearly intended for the benefit or protection of a particular class of individuals (ie each disabled person to whom a duty applies)[34], they might insist that the legislation, in addition, must be explicit in conferring the private law right to sue for, and win, damages.[35]

Welfare legislation: comforts for the 'sick and disabled'

Welfare legislation – such as the CSDPA 1970, the NHS and Community Care Act 1990 and the Education Act 1996 – is silent about whether damages are obtainable for breach of statutory duty.

As already explained above, the courts might anyway find that duties are too general or too vague to give private legal rights to individuals, for infringement of which damages are payable. But there are also other arguments which the courts use to block actions for breach of statutory duty. They may simply say that the very *nature* of such legislation does not give people rights to pursue legal actions, since – as the Court of Appeal put it in a case about services provided under the CSDPA 1970 – it is concerned with 'comforts to the sick and disabled'.[36] Cases brought under the process of judicial review (see Chapter 17) sometimes revolve around whether a public authority has breached its duty. However, the significance of bringing a case for breach for statutory duty is that, in principle, damages are available – whereas in judicial review they are not. For example, in a recent judicial review case about provision of home help services under s.2 of the CSDPA, the High Court decided that there had been a breach of statutory duty – but there was no question of damages being awarded.[37]

Solutions other than legal actions for breach of statutory duty

Sometimes the courts rule that if other methods of redress – *alternative remedies* – are available, then they should be used to solve disputes, instead of legal actions for breach of statutory duty.

For example, the courts have stated that special education legislation provides such a comprehensive framework for the participation of parents and for appeals procedures, that Parliament could not possibly have intended to give aggrieved parents the right to win damages.[38] Similarly, the courts might cite the existence of the default powers of the Secretary of State (see p.450) for use against social services departments as a reason why an action for breach of duty is not appropriate.[39] Furthermore, even if the relevant legislation does not provide such alternative procedures, it still does not follow that the courts will allow an action for breach of statutory duty – even, for example, if an authority has failed to meet its obligations when it omitted to cancel or suspend the registration of a suspect childminder who went on to injure another child.[40] Nevertheless, conversely, just because there *is* another method of redress, it does not necessarily follow that the courts will never allow a civil action for breach of statutory duty. This was established by a case at the end of the last century involving health and safety legislation and the duty to fence off machinery. Despite the existence of a criminal penalty – ie an alternative remedy – the court held the injured workman could still sue for damages.[41]

Breach of duty in respect of operational or executive activities

Despite the difficulty of succeeding with actions for breach of statutory duty in providing welfare services, a few cases have been successful in the housing and education fields. Some of the reasoning of the courts has emphasised the distinction between the *policy* decisions and the *operational* actions of authorities. The approach of the courts has been that actions for breach of statutory duty cannot succeed in respect of the *decision-making* (policy) functions of authorities – but that they may succeed in relation to the *executive* (operational) functions.[42]

For example, the refusal to provide a bath lift under s.2 of the CSDPA 1970 is a policy matter and calls for decision-making (ie an assessment) by an authority. The courts will not interfere with such a decision by countenancing actions for breach of statutory duty. However, once the decision has been made that the lift is needed and that the authority has a duty to provide it, then it is arguable that arrangements for the actual supply and installation are an operational or executive matter. They no longer involve statutory decision-making. Failure to make these operational arrangements could possibly give rise to a successful action for breach of statutory duty.

However, recent decisions of the law courts have leaned away from finding breach of statutory duty in the welfare field; and the House of Lords (*X v Bedfordshire CC*) has even thrown doubt on a number of past cases which apparently supported findings of breach.[43] One such was a homelessness case heard in 1979 which suggested that a housing authority could be in breach of its duty, and liable in damages, even if decision-making was involved.[44] Other cases, from the education field, which apparently gave people remedies for breach of statutory duty, have also been explained away. Either they have been characterised as cases in which the court granted injunctions or declarations (ie telling somebody what to do, see p.449) but not damages. These cases would now be brought under judicial review proceedings (which did not exist in their present form before 1977) – not breach of statutory duty. Or, they have been explained as cases which were used erroneously to support the doctrine of breach of statutory duty. For example, one case decided in 1910[45], involving a child's injury in a school playground, has now been held to have been about negligence, not breach of statutory duty.[46]

Nevertheless, the courts seem to have preserved the possibility of finding authorities in breach of private law duties – and of awarding damages – when the breach of duty does not concern decision-making. Instead, the breach would relate solely to operational matters (after any decision-making was over) – such as the non-provision of housing for homeless people who have been assessed as requiring it under the legislation. In a recent homelessness case (*R v Northavon DC, ex parte Palmer*), the Court of Appeal explained that the applicant could 'not recover damages save for breach of a private law duty' and that she could not 'establish a private law duty until the local authority's public law decision-making function has been concluded…'.[47] Thus in principle, the non-provision of equipment – once an authority has accepted that it is necessary for it to provide the equipment – could also give rise to an action for breach of statutory duty. In practice, it would be difficult to win damages in such a case; and the courts might rule that judicial review proceedings were more appropriate.

Causing harm, type of harm, damages and defences

Plaintiffs have to show that the alleged breach of duty caused the harm or damage which they are seeking compensation for. The same, general principles, already explained in relation to negligence, apply – including the difficulty of proving causation (see p.331). In addition, the courts adopt other ways of limiting the ambit of actions for breach of statutory duty.

For example, in the last century, a number of sheep were washed off a ship's deck because they had not been penned in. Although the shipowner had thereby breached his statutory duty, no damages were payable because the purpose of the legislation was to prevent the spread of contagious diseases, not to prevent animals being washed overboard.[48] Therefore, although the breach of duty caused the damage, there was no remedy. In another case, it was held that legislation, which placed duties on race tracks in relation to bookmakers, had been passed for the benefit of the public – and not for the bookmakers. Therefore, an aggrieved bookmaker could not win damages for breach of statutory duty, even though the breach had caused him loss.[49] A similar example from the equipment field could be a breach of an NHS Trust's duty to minimise the lifting of patients by its staff. If the Trust breached its duty but the staff concerned did not suffer injury but instead had their clothes torn or soiled, they could probably not claim damages. The purpose of the Regulations is to safeguard staff from injury, not clothes from damage.[50]

In order to pursue a civil action, some harm or damage must have occurred – as in negligence.[51] For example, an employee could not sue an employer before any injury had occurred from unsafe lifting practices – although, of course, the Health and Safety Executive could threaten a criminal prosecution in such circumstances. Damages will be awarded on the same lines as for negligence. The time within which an action for breach of statutory duty must be brought will differ, as in negligence, depending on the type of damage being claimed for (see p.340). The principle of contributory negligence applies to breach of statutory duty as it does to ordinary negligence (see p.340).[52]

Notes

1 SI 1994/2328. *General Product Safety Regulations 1994,* rr.12, 13, 17.
2 *Health and Safety at Work 1974,* s.3.
3 Summarised briefly in: *Community Care:* 14 December – 4 January 1996, p.4.
4 SI 1992/2041. *Management of Health and Safety at Work Regulations 1992.*
5 *Registered Homes Act 1984,* s.49.
6 SI 1984/1345. *Residential Homes Care Regulations 1984,* r.10.
7 *Powers of the Criminal Courts Act 1973,* s.35.
8 Atiyah, P.S.; Adams, J. (1995). *The sale of goods.* 9th edition. London: Pitman Publishing, pp.254–258.
9 In civil courts the standard of proof is required is the 'balance of probabilities' (ie at least a 51% likelihood); in criminal courts it is 'beyond reasonable doubt' – a higher standard.
10 National Consumer Council (1995). *Unsafe products: how the Consumer Protection Act works for consumers.* London: NCC, p.28: reporting the findings of a LACOTS (Local Authorities Coordinating Body on Food and Trading Standards) report, Criminal law compensation.
11 *R v Milton Keynes Magistrates' Court and Others, ex parte Roberts* (1994) (QBD), Independent, 26 October 1994. A case in which trading standards officers acted on a plan provided by the Ford Motor Company to uncover a trade in counterfeit spare parts.
12 SI 1992/2793. *Manual Handling Operations Regulations 1992,* r.4.
13 SI 1992/2793. *Manual Handling Operations Regulations 1992,* r.5.
14 SI 1994/2328. *General Product Safety Regulations 1994,* r.14.
15 *Consumer Protection Act 1987,* s.39.
16 *Employers' Liability (Defective Equipment) Act 1969.*
17 See eg *Consumer Protection Act 1987,* ss.13–14; *Health and Safety at Work 1974,* ss.21–22; SI 1994/3017. *Medical Devices Regulations,* r.19.
18 National Consumer Council (1995). *Unsafe products: how the Consumer Protection Act works for consumers.* London: NCC, p.12.
19 Wilkinson, P. (1996). Hospital fined for syringe negligence. *The Times:* 20 February 1996.
20 *R v F & M Dobson Ltd,* The Times, 8 March 1995 (CA).
21 *MFI Furniture v Hibbert* [1996] COD 100 (QBD).
22 Stanton, K.M. (1986). *Breach of statutory duty in tort.* London: Sweet & Maxwell, p.4.
23 SI 1994/2328. *General Product Safety Regulations 1994,* r.7.
24 This word governs provision of services and equipment under s.2 of the CSDPA.
25 Governs duty of authorities to make community care assessments under s.47 of the NHS and Community Care Act 1990.
26 A general duty governs the provision of services for children in need: *Children Act 1989,* s.17.
27 As is the duty to provide home help services under Schedule 8 of the *NHS Act 1977.*
28 *X and others (minors) v Bedfordshire County Council* (and other appeals) [1995] 3 All ER 353 (HL) (at 378–9).
29 See eg: Mackay, I. (1996). Corporate liability for the health and safety of others. *New Law Journal:* 29 March 1996; 146(6737), pp.438–440: discussing the reluctance of the courts to

allow delegation of responsibility of the duty under s.3 of the Health and Safety at Work Act 1974 (see above).

30 *Health and Safety at Work Act 1974,* ss.3, 47.

31 SI 1994/3017. *Medical Devices Regulations 1994.* And see Consumer Protection Act 1987 under which the Regulations are partly made, s.41.

32 SI 1992/2793. *Manual Handling Operations Regulations 1992;* see *Health and Safety at Work Act 1974,* s.47(2).

33 SI 1994/2328. *General Product Safety Regulations 1994.*

34 Part of the twofold test laid down in: *Lonrho Ltd v Shell Petroleum Co Ltd* [1982] AC 173. A case concerning alleged breach of sanctions against Southern Rhodesia following the Unilateral Declaration of Independence – in respect of petrol supply.

35 *Hague v Deputy Governor of Parkhurst Prison* [1991] 3 All ER 733: an action brought by two prisoners who were seeking damages for breach of statutory duty: they had been unlawfully segregated. The action failed.

36 *Wyatt v Hillingdon LBC* [1979] 76 LGR 727 (CA).

37 *R v Gloucestershire County Council and Others, R v Islington London Borough Council, ex parte McMillan* (1995) (QBD), Times Law Reports, June 21 1995.

38 *X and others (minors) v Bedfordshire County Council (and other appeals)* [1995] 3 All ER 353 at 398–9.

39 *Wyatt v Hillingdon BC* [1979] 76 LGR 727 (CA).

40 *T v Surrey County Council and Others* [1994] 4 All ER 577 (QBD) at 597.

41 *Groves v Lord Wimborne* [1898] 2 QB 402.

42 *Cocks v Thanet District Council* [1983] 2 AC 286 (HL): about duties under homelessness legislation.

43 *X and others (minors) v Bedfordshire County Council* [1995] 3 All ER 353 at 378–9.

44 *Thornton v Kirklees Metropolitan Borough Council* [1979] QB 626 (CA).

45 *Ching v Surrey County Council* [1910] 1 KB 736 (CA).

46 By the House of Lords in: *X and others (minors) v Bedfordshire County Council (and other appeals)* [1995] 3 All ER 353). It referred back to the Court of Appeal's dismissal of these cases: *E (A minor) v Dorset County Council and other appeals* [1994] 4 All ER 640.

47 *R v Northavon District Council, ex parte Palmer* (1995) 27 HLR 576 (CA).

48 *Gorris v Scott* (1874) LR 9 Ex 125.

49 *Cutler v Wandsworth Stadium Ltd* [1949] AC 398 (HL).

50 SI 1992/2793. *Manual Handling Operations Regulations 1992,* r.4.

51 Although at least one case has suggested that it is not always necessary: *Simmonds v Newport Abercarn Black Vein Steam Coal Company Limited* [1921] 1 KB 616 (CA): breach of the duty to pay wages to a collier's boy.

52 *Law Reform (Contributory Negligence) Act 1945,* s.4.

PART IV

A–Z LIST OF EQUIPMENT AND ITS AVAILABILITY THROUGH STATUTORY SERVICES

The following list indicates what equipment and adaptations are available, what they are for, and (with some provisos indicated immediately below) how to get them.

Exhaustiveness of list

The list is not intended to be exhaustive, but aims to give the reader a reasonably detailed idea of the types of equipment available. For example, different types of wheelchair are mentioned, but not every type. In addition, it is difficult to know where to draw the boundaries around what is included. On one side, there are many products not thought of as specialist or as particularly for older or disabled people – for instance, automatically operated car windows, letter cages, television remote controls. Many of these are not listed below (though some are), but this does not mean that they are any the less useful. In addition, medical products such as breast implants, dental products, heart pacemakers, suction devices are omitted – whilst stoma care devices, and oxygen therapy equipment are included.

For exhaustive listings and details about available equipment, the reader is referred, for example, (1) to the Disabled Living Foundation's four volume, continually updated: *DLF Hamilton Index* (also available on CD ROM) – and (2) to the series of books produced by the Disability Information Trust (based at the Nuffield Orthopaedic Centre in Oxford). Other organisations produce catalogues, booklets or leaflets about equipment – for example, the Royal National Institute for the Blind, the Royal National Institute for Deaf People, the Partially Sighted Society.

Explanation of key to statutory services: explanation

Each entry in the list is followed in brackets by one or more abbreviations. These refer to the statutory service(s) which may be able to provide the equipment. *It must be stressed that this is intended to be a very broad indication only because, as this book has repeatedly explained, it is not possible to state what equipment a particular service will provide to a particular person under particular conditions in any particular locality at any particular point in time.* Thus, the list acts as a general prompt to how equipment might be available; but actual provision for any individual person will hinge on the person's actual needs – and local criteria of eligibility, budgets, priorities and agreed divisions of responsibility between statutory services.

The reference to statutory services against each entry in the list is based on a hybrid approach – with an eye both to legislation and what goes on in practice. The disdvantage of this approach cuts two ways; professionals in statutory services might look at some of the entries and regard them as misleading because they suggest that provision is possible – even though in practice it is never made. But, conversely, a failure to indicate the possibility of theoretical provision panders to local practices (which might be overly restrictive and even illegal in some circumstances) and does not reflect the potential scope of the underlying legislation. And, in any case, even the availability of equipment provided frequently is subject to whether people meet criteria of eligibility. However, in the author's view, this approach to the list is inevitable because of the difficulty of disentangling the legislation from the practice; for instance, as chapter 8 points out, the vague duty to provide a comprehensive health service embraces, in theory, 'all and nothing'; in practice, what is actually provided falls somewhere between the two extremes. For example:

(1) **Social services and the NHS.** Social services departments have a duty to make arrangements in relation to 'facilities' for disabled people's 'greater safety, comfort or convenience'. This is a wide duty and so the abbreviation 'ssd' is attached to many of the entries in the list below. However, this does not mean that in practice any particular social services department will provide all those types of equipment – for example, gardening equipment is likely to be very low on the list of priorities, even though the legislation enables its provision in theory. An NHS Trust might provide incontinence pads to one person, but not to another who does not meet the local criteria of eligibility for provision. Furthermore, a statutory service might be involved in assessing people for, and advising them about, particular types of equipment – without necessarily going on to make provision. For instance, social services departments might assist people to make applications to voluntary organisations for items such as electric wheelchairs or electronic communication aids.

(2) **Social Fund.** Similarly, the Social Fund (for example, in the form of community care grants) can in particular circumstances, be used for all manner of equipment – for instance, beds and mattresses, electric wheelchairs, incontinence pads, washing machines. In practice of course the Fund is not a major source of wheelchair or incontinence pad provision (compared to the NHS) – but nevertheless, in principle, the abbreviation 'sf' could have been placed against many more of the products listed below than it actually has been.

(3) **NHS occupational therapists.** It is difficult to reflect in the list practices such as the following: for example, NHS hospital occupational therapy departments provide daily living equipment (notionally the responsibility of social services departments, not the NHS) by means of selling it, providing it free (either from their own funds or by financial arrangement with social services), or advising and assisting people to buy equipment

mail order (eg there might be a demonstration/display collection of equipment and a set of mail order catalogues from which to order it).

The fact that many of the items on the list have more than one abbreviation set against them reflects the fact that the same type of equipment can be provided in principle by different agencies depending on how its *primary purpose* is viewed – for health care (NHS), social care (social services department) or employment (Employment Service) – and so on.

Key to statutory services

ba	Benefits Agency (agency of the DSS, responsible for paying, for example, the mobility supplement of disability living allowance)
dh	Department of Health
dss	Department of Social Security
edu	Education authorities/schools
emp	Employment Service
hou	Housing/Environmental Health Departments
nhs	NHS (hospital or community health services)
nhs/dt	NHS (on Drug Tariff carrying prescription charge)
nhs/fh	NHS fundholding general practitioners: equipment which fundholding GPs can provide for their patients free of charge
nhs/sa	NHS (specified appliances for which outpatients can be charged by hospitals)
ssd	Social Services Departments
wpa	War Pensions Agency

Private purchase and assistance from voluntary organisations

Of course, all the products listed below could be privately purchased – and many, in principle at least, obtained with assistance from voluntary organisations.

Clearly, private purchase will be more relevant to products which are widely advertised in the Press, available from pharmacies, and of the cheaper variety – than to sophisticated environmental controls or communication aids costing many thousands of pounds. Even so, electric wheelchairs or scooters, advertised regularly in Sunday newspapers can cost £2000–£3000.

Practical advice and assistance about equipment

Disabled living centres, already referred to, provide expert advice and assistance about many types of equipment – and can be visited in order to view and try out various types of equipment. The Keep Able superstores, too, offer a wide selection of equipment for sale that can be viewed and tried out. In addition, many specialist voluntary organisations can give detailed advice on particular types of equipment – lists of such organisations can be found in various directories.

A–Z LIST OF EQUIPMENT

Abdominal supports (nhs/sa). Abdominal supports are one of the few items NHS Trusts can lawfully make a financial charge for (£28.30 at the time of writing), although exemption or reduction is possible, based on age, income or medical status.[1]

Abduction equipment (nhs,ssd,edu). Eg equipment, especially for children, to keep legs apart, such as belts, cushions, seats, toys.

Acoustic insulation (hou,ssd). Eg for a household with an exceptionally noisy child.

Air beds (nhs). Eg for pressure relief: see *Pressure relief equipment.*

Alarms (ssd,hou). There are various types of alarm.

Community alarms allow elderly and disabled people to call for help at the touch of a button. They might be hard-wired (for example, in sheltered, or other type of, housing scheme) or 'dispersed' in individual dwellings from where a call is transmitted by telephone either to friends and relatives, or to a control centre. The transmitter might be fixed (eg ceiling cord) or portable (eg bodyworn device). Alarm services are provided by local authorities (social services and housing departments), housing associations, voluntary organisations and commercial companies. Apart from the cost of the alarm unit, weekly charges vary – in 1994, between £0.50 and £3.00 a week. The users of alarm systems might or might not have a legal contract with the agency running the service.[2]

Arm orthoses: see *Orthoses.*

Artificial arms: see *Artificial limbs.*

Artificial breasts (nhs,nhs/fh). Available free of charge through the NHS, following an operation. If the operation is performed privately, the prosthesis must be bought privately. The fitter is usually an employee of a commercial supplier contracted by the NHS – but might be a surgical appliance officer or breast care nurse. A temporary prosthesis is provided before the permanent one is supplied following post-operative reviews. Good practice has been identified as including cooperation between the breast care nurse and surgical appliance officer, holding of a range of bras available for fitting purposes (supplied free of charge by a High Street shop), the holding of a wide range of stock, same-day fitting, and an advisory service (eg about clothing and swimwear).[3]

In 1988, the Breast Care and Mastectomy Association identified various concerns: limited choice, hurried fitting procedures, inadequate premises, lack of privacy, lack of mirrors, male fitters, and the attitude of the fitter.[4] A more recent study found that all fitting was carried out by females but that there was a lack of choice in some areas – for example, because of a reluctance to spend money on holding stock or a lack of storage of space.[5]

Artificial eyes (nhs). Available through sixteen centres (and 56 associated clinics) in England and Wales, staffed by orbital prosthetists. Services provided include facial prostheses (where necessary to support the eye), checks, polishing (including a postal service), repair, replacement, advice and occasional domiciliary visits.[6]

Artificial hands: see *Artificial limbs.*

Artificial larynxes (nhs). Ie electronic equipment (for people with no voice, rather than a weak voice) held to throat to detect movement and produce electronic speech.

Artificial limbs (nhs). Artificial limb provision includes upper and lower limbs, parts of limbs and a range of accessories. Modern lower limbs are made of plastic and modular, although older models of rigid limbs made of metal or tin are still maintained for older users who want them. Accessories include anti-perspirant lotion, gloves, mittens, special cutlery, stump socks, stout gloves, suspender belts, thigh stockings. A number of items are used in the post-operation period, including stump shrinkers/supports, wheelchair stump boards, pneumatic post amputation mobility (PPAM) aids (plastic air bags in a frame with a rocker end, to encourage early walking under supervision).[7]

Stress is laid on the importance of treating the various stages of the amputation process as a single process, to be planned carefully with the amputee by a multi-disciplinary team.[8] Rehabilitation should, in effect be started before, not after, the amputation operation.[9] These stages include the decision to amputate, amputation, post-amputation recovery, rehabilitation and review. Key members of the team include consultants in rehabilitation medicine, rehabilitation engineers, prosthetists (usually contracted from the private sector), nurses, physiotherapists, occupational therapists, clinical psychologists, hospital social workers.[10]

Adaptations to the home environment, as well as other, equipment might be needed. For instance, people with artificial lower limbs might require also bath hoists, bath seats, rails, raised toilet seats, showers, trolleys walking aids, wheelchair ramps and wheelchairs.[11]

Artificial limbs: background. The DHSS used to provide artificial limbs through artificial limb and appliance centres (ALACs) before the Disablement Services Authority (DSA) took over responsibility in 1987. In 1991, the DSA ceased to exist and responsibility for provision was devolved to individual health authorities.

Like wheelchair provision, the former centralised system of limb provision run by the DHSS and the DSA provided a clearer national picture of how, and how well, the service was being run. For example, the 1986 McColl report made a number of criticisms of artificial limb provision. Too many 'ill-fitting' limbs which caused 'unnecessary pain and suffering' were provided; an ill-managed service meant that patients experienced 'serious delays' and other difficulties; the contractual arrangements between the DHSS and private firms were unsatisfactory.[12] A 1989 report found discomfort or pain the most common perceived problem amongst limb users surveyed in Scotland.[13] In the same year, the Monopolies and Mergers Commission reported on limb provision and recommended change, having concluded that it was against the public interest for one of the firms involved to hold a 70% share of the market.[14] One of the matters referred to in the report was that prosthetists, working contractually for the NHS, tended to provide limbs manufactured by their own, rather than by other firms.

It is thought that a certain amount of poor assessment, restricted choice and uncomfortable fitting persists.[15] However, its extent is probably unclear and difficult to measure given the non-use of many limbs and the low expectations of some, particularly elderly, users.

Artificial limbs: current provision. The devolvement of services by the Disablement Services Authority has not had quite the disruptive effect on limb services it has on wheelchair services. This is largely because the limb services have tended to remain concentrated at regional level, providing contractual services to purchasing health authorities in the region; multi-disciplinary assessment and rehabilitation procedures survived relatively well. Furthermore, it appears that the funding available for limb services is more adequate than that for wheelchair services.[16] Nevertheless, when services were devolved from the Disablement Services Authority, regional budgets were 'ring-fenced'. The government optimistically pointed out that there was nothing to stop health authorities exceeding their ring-fenced amounts by adding resources from elsewhere.[17] In fact, since that ring-fencing no longer exists, there is a danger that limb services will lose status and have their budgets reduced or restricted accordingly.

The reorganisation of limb services has resulted in the dilution of specialist services for smaller groups of people – such as those with artificial upper limbs or congenital limb deficiencies. In particular, the availability of expert occupational therapists has diminished. One consequence is that when staff with little or no appropriate knowledge fit electric components, users do not receive proper instruction and training and so reject the limbs. There are concerns also that NHS Trust managers are not always aware of the importance of consultants in rehabilitation medicine. The retrograde consequence of this is that inadequately trained consultants might run limb services.[18]

The contractual system now in place within the NHS has meant that prosthetic services are delivered on the basis of three year contracts, divided into service contracts (between NHS Trust and health authority) and prosthetic contracts (between NHS Trust and prosthetic company/firm). Prosthetic contracts might be awarded primarily on financial, rather than clinical, grounds.[19] This can interrupt continuity of care and services for users, thus eroding their confidence and the quality of care they receive. The successful rehabilitation of children and young people in particular can be hindered.[20] Also affected is team cohesion, the morale of prosthetists and sometimes the organisation of accommodation within the centre. A further, and potentially detrimental consequence, is when a smaller centre without adequate professional expertise, but competing for contracts and patients, is reluctant to refer a child to another centre which does possess special expertise.[21]

Transport of amputees to limb centres has long been a problem.[22] In some areas, the problem might have lessened through devolvement of the limb services. Waiting times for both appointments and provision of limbs are likely to vary.[23]

Artificial limbs: use. Over 70% of lower limb amputees are over 60 years old. The major causes of amputation are peripheral vascular disease and diabetes; trauma (accidents) and tumours are also causes. It has long been suspected that many amputees do not use their limbs, instead using wheelchairs, with which many of them are also provided.[24] Hence the letter sent by the Disablement Services Authority in 1989 – possibly quite reasonable, but one which nevertheless excited controversy – to the effect that amputees should not be routinely issued with a spare or second limb.[25] A further reason for non-issue of spare limbs is the ease and speed with which modern modular limbs can be repaired.[26] However, lack of use of limbs might be avoidable if people receive appropriate rehabilitation, advice and support – though the subject seems to be much disputed.[27]

Bags. Eg carrying/shopping bags for use on *Walking frames* or *Wheelchairs*, or drainage bags for *Catheters*.

Bath boards (ssd,nhs). Fit across the bath to aid getting in and out. See also *Bath equipment.*

Bath cushions (ssd,nhs). Eg for support or pressure relief. See also *Bath equipment.*

Bath equipment (ssd,nhs). Eg bath boards, lifts, mats, rails, seats. Although such equipment could be regarded as either daily living or nursing equipment, it is probably more usually regarded as the former – and thus the responsibility of social services departments. However, if, for instance, a bath lift is needed because the person had to bathe daily for a medical (eg a skin) condition, then the NHS might take responsibility. Confusingly, social services departments might regard people's needs for bath equipment as a low priority – unless there is a medical condition, in which case they might make more urgent provision. However, if bathing is viewed as a low priority, the result can be very long waits for assessment, or possibly even no assessment at all. Alternatively, some authorities introduce *fast-track assessment* for people with such needs – by, for example, contracting with independent occupational therapists or disabled living centres to clear waiting lists. In addition, authorities might suggest that people buy their own products, such as bath mats. See also *Baths.*

Bath lifts (ssd,nhs). Bath lifts/seats for transferring the user in and out of the bath (electric or manually operated). See also *Bath equipment.*

Bath mats: see *Bath equipment.*

Bath rails (ssd,nhs). Eg short grab rails, longer hand rails: see *Bath equipment.*

Bathrooms (hou,ssd). Eg a downstairs bathroom extension/conversion: see also *Bath equipment.*

Baths (hou,ssd). Eg adjustable-height, built-in seat, shallow, transfer-seat (ie moves up and down and swings out), walk-in (with hinged side). Although showers are often a suitable and cheaper solution, there might be particular reasons for providing a specialist bath – eg medical reasons (such as skin condition, double incontinence, stoma), or the need of other family members to have a bath.[28] See also *Bath equipment.*

Bath seats (ssd,nhs). For example, built-in, insert seats, electric lifter. See *Bath equipment.*

Batteries see eg *Hearing aid batteries, Wheelchair batteries.*

Battery chargers: see *Wheelchair accessories and associated equipment.*

Bed backrests (nhs,ssd). Eg adjustable angle. See *Bed equipment.*

Bed boards: see *Bed equipment.*

Bed cot sides: see *Bed equipment.*

Bed cradles (nhs,ssd). Frame to keep bedclothes aloft from person's legs: see *Bed equipment.*

Bed equipment (nhs,ssd). Eg backrests, boards, cradles, cot sides, overbed tables, rails, raising blocks, rope ladders. Responsibility might vary between the NHS and social services departments, depending on whether the need for equipment is defined as health or social care. See also *Beds.*

Bed overtables (nhs,ssd). For eating, reading, other activities in bed. See *Bed equipment.*

Bed pads: see *Incontinence equipment, Bed equipment.*

Bed pans: see *Incontinence equipment, Bed equipment.*

Bed rails (nhs,ssd). Eg side rails to prevent person falling out of bed. See *Bed equipment.*

Bed raising blocks (nhs,ssd). To raise the level height of the bed or to raise the height of one end only. See *Bed equipment.*

Bed rope ladders (nhs,ssd). Eg for person to pull themselves up in bed by. See *Bed equipment.*

Bed sides: see *Cots, Bed equipment.*

Bedrooms (hou,ssd). Eg downstairs extension/conversion.

Beds (nhs,nhs/fh,ssd,sf). For example, adjustable height, air, high, multi-adjustable/adjustable posture, pressure relief, rocking, stand-up, tilting, water. See also *Bed equipment, Mattresses.*

Bibs (ssd,nhs). Eg plastic, trough-type.

Bidets (hou,ssd).

Bookrests, book stands (ssd,edu,emp). For example, attachable to table or bed, free-standing. See also *Page turners.*

Books (edu,emp,ssd). Eg talking books/books on tape: see *Reading equipment.*

Boots (surgical) (nhs). Eg orthopaedic boots: see *Footwear.*

Bottle holders (ssd). For example, frames, handles, stands and tippers for bottles (eg milk, soft drinks, alcohol, hot water).

Bottle openers (ssd).

Bottom wipers (ssd,nhs). Stick-type devices which assist people with limited reach or grip. See *WC equipment.*

Bowls: see *Crockery.*

Brace supports (nhs). Eg orthotic support for limbs or trunk of body (see *Orthoses*).

Braille equipment (edu,emp,ssd). For example, braille writing machines and frames, computer braille outputs, braille markings (eg cooker knobs, electrical equipment controls, measuring jugs, playing cards). See *Reading equipment, Visual impairment equipment.*

Brassieres (surgical) (nhs/sa). Surgical brassieres are one of the few items NHS Trusts can lawfully make a financial charge for (£19.25 at the time of writing), although exemption or reduction is possible, based on age, income or medical status.[29]

Breast prostheses: see *Artificial breasts*

Brushes (ssd). Eg long-handled.

Buggies (edu,nhs,ssd). Special children's pushchairs or wheelchairs: see *Wheelchairs.*

Calculators (edu,emp,ssd). Eg tactile, talking – for people with a visual impairment.

Calipers (nhs). Rod-like limb supports: see *Orthoses.*

Can openers (ssd).

Cantilever tables: see *Overbed tables.*

Car adaptations and accessories (emp,ssd). For example, adjustable height seats, adjusted foot controls (eg position or height of pedals), converting foot to hand controls (eg clutch), driver-in-wheelchair, high roofs, infra-red switching systems, insert seats (eg to attach/detach from existing seat for disabled children, for people with back problems), long seat runners (to make more space for getting in and out), low floors, ramps, safety belts and harnesses, steering wheel balls, swivel seats and cushions, wheelchair clamping systems (eg in vans), wheelchair rear access, wheelchair winches/hoists, wide rear-view mirrors.[30]

Generally speaking, arrangements through the Motability scheme to hire or buy cars (see *Cars*) do not cover adaptations; they have to be paid for separately. However, Motability does administer or run various funds through which assistance with adaptations might be obtainable. The cost can be considerable; for example, adaptations allowing people to remain in their wheelchairs as a passenger or driver (requiring eg high roofs, low floors, ramped/lift access) can cost from £2000 to over £12,000.[31]

In principle, car adaptations could be regarded as daily living equipment or minor adaptations which social services departments could provide; in practice, few are likely to. However, some might, in some circumstances, provide belts, harnesses or seats for disabled children. If adaptations are required primarily for work, the Employment Service might assist through the Access to Work scheme.

Thus, various adaptations can be made to cars. In addition, commercial, non-adapted cars have a variety of different dimensions and features, some of which may be useful (albeit 'accidentally') to disabled people.[32]

Car safety belts, harnesses: see *Car adaptations and accessories.*

Car seats: see *Car adaptations and accessories.*

Carpet sweepers (ssd). Eg lightweight: see *Cleaning equipment.*

Carpets (ssd). Eg easily cleanable, hardwearing, short-pile (considering wheelchair use), slip-resistant, stain-resistant, waterproof.

Cars (ba,dh,wpa,emp).

Cars: old statutory loan scheme. A number of three-wheeler cars and a few four-wheeler (adapted, commercial cars) are still on loan to people through a scheme administered still by central government (Department of Health) – although most people now receive a weekly payment to use for their mobility needs (see below).

The car loan scheme is operated centrally from Blackpool, although repairs and maintenance are carried out locally by approved repairers. Three-wheeled cars can be maintained and repaired – and, whilst stocks last, replaced. Four-wheeled cars can be maintained and repaired (for which a special allowance is payable) but not replaced. For both three- and four-wheeled cars, a petrol tax allowance is payable.

Cars: mobility State benefits/allowances. Since the mid-1970s, new, eligible claimants have not been able to obtain the loan of cars – but instead have claimed *mobility allowance* (up to 1992) and now the mobility component of the disability living allowance (DLA). In summary, eligibility for the mobility component of DLA is established if a person is over four years old and under 66 when he first claims, and if he is likely to benefit from 'facilities for enhanced locomotion'. The higher rate can be claimed if the person is unable, or virtually unable to walk, deaf and blind, born without feet, a double amputee, or is severely mentally impaired and has severe behavioural problems. The lower rate can be claimed if the person can walk but is so severely physically or mentally disabled that he needs guidance or supervision most of the time. Eligibility has to have existed for three months before application and be likely to continue for at least six months.[33] War pensioners claim war *pensioners' mobility supplement* (WPMS) (see Chapter 13). People already loaning a car are free to transfer to receipt of these weekly payments.

There are a number of schemes which assist people to use their (higher rate) mobility benefit to contract hire (lease) or hire-purchase mobility equipment, such as cars or powered wheelchairs (which have not been generally available on the NHS). Over a million people are in receipt of the higher rate of DLA mobility component, and so form a substantial market for cars; evidence of this is the widespread local advertising by local garages and car dealers about their involvement with, for example, Motability – the best known of the finance schemes. Private companies also offer their own finance schemes. Nevertheless, people can spend their mobility benefit in any way they please – whether on taxi fares or on anything else, related or not to mobility.

Cars: driving assessment centres. A number of specialist driving assessment centres assess people's ability to use powered pavement vehicles, their driving ability, and their needs for adaptations. The centres make various charges for these services.

Catheters: see *Incontinence equipment.*

Ceilings (hou,ssd). Eg reinforced to take hoist track.

Central heating: see *Heating.*

Cervical collars: see *Orthoses.*

Chair raising blocks (ssd). Raise the height of the chair to make getting in and out easier. See also: *Chairs.*

Chairs (ssd,emp,edu,sf). Eg electric riser, high seat, reclining. Sometimes loaned by social services departments. For children there are multi-adjustable or modular products with, for example, footrests, head/neck supports, leg dividers, pommels, detachable trays, wings.

Chairs are expensive items and so will not be provided in profusion. For example, high seat chairs (literally a chair with a high seat to make sitting down and standing up easier) might be subject to waiting times, loan charges, restricted provision and perhaps non-provision in some areas. A local authority's policy might state that the primary need for the chair must be on the grounds of reduced mobility rather than 'comfort' (though this word appears in s.2 of the CSDPA 1970: see p.165), and that it must not be provided to furnish the home (on the grounds that if clients do not have a chair at all, they would have to obtain one anyway). Of course, the possibility of raising the height of an existing chair would normally be considered first in any case.[34] Chairs might also be provided by the Employment Service if they are needed primarily for work.

Channel ramps (ssd,edu,emp). Eg portable pair of narrow ramps can be transported by wheelchair user.

Chemical commodes/toilets (ssd,nhs). Eg might be provided by the NHS for shorter term, and by social services for longer term, use. Social services departments might charge (eg for supplies of the fluid), or ask the user to pay a firm directly for regularly collecting the waste (eg on a weekly basis). See *Commodes.*

Cleaning equipment (ssd). Eg lightweight carpet sweepers, vacuum cleaners. Vacuum cleaning systems built into walls of house. Long-handled brushes, dusters, dustpans.

Children's equipment for development, therapy and play (nhs,ssd,edu variously). Eg balls, blocks, car seats, cylinders, play environments, hammocks, play shapes, roundabouts/swings (eg for wheelchairs).

Click/count syringes: see *Diabetes equipment.*

Clocks (ssd,emp). For example, flashing, tactile, talking or vibrating (for people with hearing loss).

Closed circuit television systems (emp,edu,nhs): magnifies text on screen for people with visual impairment, sometimes available through the Employment Service following specialist NHS assessment.

Clothes-hanging rails (hou,ssd). Eg relocation of rails to make them more accessible.

Cochlear implants (nhs). Electronic hearing aid which stimulates nerve endings in the inner ear to introduce or restore a perception of sound. It can be effective for profoundly deaf people even when other external, high-powered hearing aids are not. The potential benefits are immense, the cost to the NHS per implant (including operation, training, speech therapy etc) great.[35] Thus, the structure, level and quantity of NHS implant services – including criteria of 'need' and patient selections – are unsettled.[36] The use of cochlear implants for children (the optimum age for implantation is at the age of two or three) excites substantial division of opinion within the deaf community. In part at least, this reflects a wider debate (see p.61) about whether to accept a disability as normal (and eg regard deaf people who use sign language as a 'linguistic minority'), or treat it as a medical condition to be cured.[37] See also: *Hearing equipment.*

Cold pads (nhs). Eg supplied by physiotherapists for treatment/pain relief.

Collars (surgical): see *Orthoses.*

Commodes (nhs,ssd). Eg chemical, metal, upholstered (ie with removable cushion, so that it is more acceptable as an item of furniture in the home), wheeled, wood (including cane). Might be provided by the NHS for shorter term, and by a social services department for longer term, use.

The use of commodes illustrate some of the points made elsewhere in this book. Sometimes when money is short (see p.36), they might be recommended by statutory services – instead of, for example, a stairlift. This raises questions about how people's needs are assessed by statutory services – in terms of basic physical needs, or of people's dignity, privacy and social needs. Similarly, money is likely to dictate the provision of a basic metal commode, instead of upholstered models which can actually act as pieces of furniture in their own right; for instance, in the last century they were made out of mahogany, beech, cane, wicker and leather. Appropriate provision is important; people might have difficulty getting on and off commodes of the wrong height, and might fall. Supplied with a commode on discharge from hospital, people might have received no instructions about use, maintenance and what to do if problems arise (eg splitting bowls). Carers might be even more negative than the users of commodes, for various reasons from the unpleasant task of regular cleaning to the fact that the commode is a constant reminder of (for example) a spouse's medical condition or disability.[38]

See also *Chemical commodes/toilets.*

Communication equipment (nhs,nhs/fh,edu,emp,ssd). Equipment to enable people to communicate both in speech and writing. It ranges from the cheap and simple to expensive, high technology. It includes, for example, *electronic communicators* (eg with keyboard and speech synthesiser, pocket-sized and portable, or larger), *electronic scanning boards* (light moves around options until user chooses desired one), *personal computer equipment* with special software, *eye transfer/scanning frames* (communication by looking at letters, numbers, symbols or pictures in different parts of a frame or board), *picture/word/letter charts* (or cards, booklets), *voice amplifiers.* There is now a range of sophisticated and complex computer *hardware and software* to augment communication – as well as many *specialist switches* to operate it (eg joystick, puff/suck, pressure mat, eye control, foot-operated).

Communication equipment can assist a range of people, including those with a progressive neurological disorder (such as motor neurone disease or muscular dystrophy), cerebral vascular accident (stroke), cerebral palsy, head injuries, laryngectomy or learning disabilities. People who have a high dependency on nursing and medical care can sometimes benefit greatly; an ability to communicate might assist their psychological well-being as well as enable them to discuss and contribute to their care.[39]

Communication equipment: specialist centres and assessment. Both in price and complexity communication equipment varies enormously. Speech and language therapists working for the health service often assess people for such equipment – although particular expertise is concentrated in a number of communication aids centres (CACs) scattered across the country.[40] Some speech and language therapy departments of NHS Trusts might use smaller collections of equipment for assessment and short, trial periods of loan. CACs provide expert information, advice and assessment – and they also sometimes loan equipment on a short-term, trial basis. There are other specialist centres which assess people's needs for communication equipment for educational needs. For instance, the Aids to Communication in Education (ACE) Centre in Oxford (there is also one in Oldham) assesses children or people in further education whom it thinks it can help. It also loans equipment for trial periods. The Centre for Micro-Assisted Communication (CENMAC) fulfils a similar role in London.

The assessment and use of equipment can be a complex process, particularly for children. Provision of communication aids without support and training for the user is a false economy if the equipment is not used, or used to no effect, as a result. Yet, it is thought that users of complex communication equipment might need up to 100 hours of training.[41] One specialist centre concluded that, because the development of communication ability is complex, it might not be enough to train the child in the technical workings of equipment. In addition, intervention needs to deal with 'social competence' for example, appropriate participation in conversations and interactions, to be varied according to the situation. Only then might the child use the equipment effectively.[42]

Assessment might be carried out by a number of different professionals, if the overall needs of the child are to be understood and equipment made best use of. These might include, for example, speech and language therapists, occupational therapists and teachers – with support, as necessary, from bio-engineers, educational psychologists, physiotherapists, specialist advisory teachers, school doctors, paediatricians, neurologists, social workers etc.[43]

The availability of short-term loan equipment can meet a number of needs including use of an aid for trial purposes, whilst a more permanent aid is on order/awaited, whilst an aid is being repaired, or when a person's condition is changing rapidly and necessitates change of aids at short intervals of time.[44]

Communication equipment: funding. Funding of communication equipment has been prone to uncertainty. Reasons for this include low profile (both the general public and many professionals know little about communication aids) and expense (which can be exacerbated as people's needs change – as a child develops, or an adult's neurological condition progresses). Trial loan of the more complex equipment is particularly important, so that people have time to learn how to exploit it and find out whether it is suitable.

In addition, communication aids illustrate well how equipment can fall between different statutory services, all of which might be reluctant to formally take policy decisions about responsibility – for fear of the resource implications. How the primary purpose of the equipment is viewed might determine, for example, whether funding will come from the NHS, an education authority or school, the Employment Service, a social services department or a voluntary organisation.[45] An additional possible channel of funding exists from April 1996, when fundholding general practitioners may purchase communication aids for their patients. Alternatively, school parents' groups might help, or people might purchase aids privately. Although communication aids centres carry out assessments and sometimes loan equipment for trial periods, they do not generally make longer term loans. Failure to resolve uncertainties about responsibility can lead not just to delay in the provision of expensive products but also the less costly.

In order to minimise the disappointed expectations of people who are assessed for equipment but can obtain no statutory funding, some CACs will not accept people for assessment unless a source of funding has been identified first. Even if people without such a source do eventually find funding – for example, a year later – their needs might have changed and they might require a complete reassessment.[46] When communication aids centres were first formally set up in 1983, a DHSS Circular referred to the need for NHS consultants, who referred their patients to CACs, subsequently to prescribe any equipment which was recommended.[47] Nevertheless, nationally, no clear channel for funding communication equipment has emerged[48] – although arrangements might be better organised in some areas than others. For example, the proportion of aids funded by the NHS in some localities is rising as the needs of people with communication impairments are being increasingly recognised.[49]

And, in some areas, joint funding arrangements are made between the NHS, the education authority and social services department. The size of such joint funds might vary from a few thousand pounds to £20,000. However, it is thought that a realistic *average figure* for a local authority's area – varying in particular cases according to population size –would be £100,000 annually for an assessment and long-term loan service.[50] There is also concern that when education authorities loan equipment to children or young people, it remains the property of the authority – so, for example, on leaving a further education college, a person might be deprived of the equipment on which they have come to rely.[51]

Nevertheless, a confused situation persists generally – and private fund-raising is resorted to by many parents of children. Teachers and other professionals might have to spend valuable time going unsuccessfully from pillar to post to identify funding – before, perhaps, having to fundraise themselves. People might die before health authorities, having recommended provision, actually make it.[52] Sometimes education authorities are prepared to fund equipment for writing purposes – whereas, they regard equipment for speech output as the responsibility of the NHS. This might reflect the longstanding uncertainty and sometimes disputes about who should provide speech and language therapy for children with special educational needs – the education authority or the NHS. However, the distinction between speech and writing aids is less tenable than it once might have been, since a range of computer equipment now fulfils both functions. Nevertheless, a survey conducted in 1994 showed that education authorities were providing the bulk (84%) of communication aid services for children. This was mostly through use of Grants for Educational Support and Training (GEST).[53]

Communication equipment: costs. The costs of equipment can be high – for example, in 1993–1994, one CAC recommended equipment for 71 patients, 4 of whom required items costing over £5,000 each. In addition, there are maintenance, insurance and modification costs. On the other hand, 10 patients were recommended items at virtually no cost, such as alphabet/picture charts. Although equipment might be expensive, it is increasingly sophisticated and adaptable. This can mean that people with changing needs might be able to continue using the same product modified – rather than have to use several different items over a period of months or years. This could offset the cost of providing expensive equipment in the first place – it also means that the user does not have to learn how to use new equipment and to undergo the associated psychological disruption.[54] Even so, a child might need a 'system' of communication equipment for different situations, for example, computers for education, small portable devices for written messages, a letter board or symbol reference book when out and about, and a speaking device for home, friends and school.[55]

Community alarms: see *Alarms.*

Computer equipment (edu,emp,ssd). Eg specialist hardware, software, large screens, adapted keyboards, special switches etc.

Cooker hob guards (ssd). To prevent saucepans falling off cooker: see *Kitchen equipment.*

Cookers (ssd,hou). Eg with suitable features, such as low-level grills, side-opening oven doors. See: *Kitchen equipment.*

Cooking equipment see: *Food and drink preparation equipment.*

Corner seats (ssd,edu). Eg floor-level seats for children.

Corsets (nhs/sa). As 'spinal' or 'abdominal' supports, corsets are one of the few items NHS Trusts can lawfully make a financial charge for (£28.30 at the time of writing), although exemption or reduction is possible, based on age, income or medical status.[56]

Cots (nhs,ssd). Including cot/bed sides for both adults and children. See also *Beds.*

Crockery (ssd). For example, plates or bowls which are deep, sloped, perhaps with curved edges. See *Eating and drinking equipment.*

Crutches: see *Walking aids.*

Cups (also glasses, mugs) (ssd,nhs). For example, large- or two-handled, lidded (to prevent spillage), moulded (for grip), spouted (to assist drinking). Cup/glass holders with special handles, moulding etc also available. See *Eating and drinking equipment.*

Cushions (ssd,nhs). Eg pressure relief cushions for *Chairs, Wheelchairs.*

Cutlery (ssd). Eg angle-handled, combined (eg spoon and fork in one), easy-grip, large-handled, plate-fixed (clamped) rocking blade, swivel handle cutlery. See *Eating and drinking equipment.*

Cutting/chopping boards (ssd). Eg frame (for holding bread), non-slip, with spikes (for vegetables).

Cycles (nhs). Eg battery-assisted cycles, four-wheeled cycles, hand-propelled cycles, tricycles, wheelchair bicycles (tandem style, with wheelchair replacing front wheel and rider pedalling behind). Provision, in principle, is possible by the NHS – eg for children.

Diabetes equipment (nhs/dt,nhs). For people with diabetes who require insulin injections, a variety of equipment is available – some is available on prescription and some not. Equipment listed in the Drug Tariff and therefore available on prescription by general practitioners includes: reusable glass syringes, reusable needles, disposable plastic syringes, disposable needles, disposable injection pens, pre-set syringes and click-count syringes (both for visually impaired people), syringe carrying cases, most blood glucose testing strips, most lancets, equipment and strips (or tablets) for urine testing for glucose, tablets and strips for urine testing for ketones, needle clipping/chopping device (to remove needle from hub and incorporating receptacle from which needles cannot be retrieved with capacity of 1,200 needles).[57] People with diabetes (which cannot be treated by diet alone) are exempt from paying prescription charges.[58]

Other equipment, not listed on the Drug Tariff includes reusable pen-type syringes and needles for them[59], some types of lancet, jet injectors, location trays, syringe and strip guides, syringe magnifiers, centre point funnels, blood testing machines/meters. Hospital consultants have the power to prescribe equipment which they think is clinically necessary, whether or not it is on the Drug Tariff. In practice, resources are likely to constrain such prescription. In addition, manufacturers supply some equipment, such as reusable pen-type syringes, free of charge to patients through hospital diabetes clinics.

As emphasised in the introduction to this book, the use of equipment might be part only of a wider picture. For example, education and prevention are important aspects of the treatment and management of diabetes.[60] NHS diabetes centres and teams, including specialist nurses and consultants, carry out this function. Because diabetes can affect people's kidneys, eyes and feet, a number of other professionals are involved including, ophthalmologists, dieticians and chiropodists.[61] The level and standard of diabetes services is likely to vary depending on locality.[62]

Door bells (hou,ssd). Eg loud, vibrating, visual.

Door knob turners (ssd).

Doors and doorways (hou,ssd,emp,edu). Eg doors which are automatically operated, foldable, intercom-operated, re-hung, reverse-opening (eg for emergency access), sliding. Doorways which are widened. Door accessories/parts include large or easy-grip handles, portable handles.

Dressing equipment (ssd). Eg longhandled shoehorns, stocking aids.

Drinking equipment (ssd,nhs): see *Eating and drinking equipment*, also *Cups*.

Dusters (ssd). Eg long-handled.

Dustpans and brush (ssd). Eg long-handled.

Eating and drinking equipment (ssd,nhs). Eg non-slip mats, plate guards, special crockery, special cutlery. Probably more usually regarded as daily living equipment to be provided by social services departments, but could be seen as meeting a nursing or medical need – and thus to be provided under the NHS (eg by dietician, community nurses).

Ejector chairs/seats see: *Riser chairs*.

Elastic shoe laces (ssd).

Elastic hosiery (nhs/dt,nhs/sa). Elastic hosiery (compression support stockings), listed on the Drug Tariff, can be prescribed by NHS Trusts and GPs (at £5.50 per item, £11.00 per pair, from April 1996), although exemption is possible, based on age, income or medical status.[63]

Elbow orthoses: see *Orthoses*.

Electric plugs (ssd). Eg plugs with handles, night-light plugs, in various colours.

Electric sockets (hou,ssd,emp). Eg extended, illuminated or raised sockets.

Electric riser chairs (ssd,emp,edu): see *Riser chairs*.

Electric tin openers (ssd).

Electric toothbrushes: see *Toothbrushes*.

Electric wheelchairs: see *Wheelchairs*.

Emergency call systems: see *Alarms*.

Enuresis alarms (nhs). Eg to break bedwetting habits in children: see *Incontinence equipment*.

Environmental control equipment (nhs,ssd,edu,emp). Environmental control equipment can enable severely disabled people to control their environment – for example, front door, alarm, television, computer, curtains, tilting bed, loudspeaking telephone, speech synthesiser. Equipment varies from sizeable visual display units on plinths, hard-wired into the home and fixed – to lightweight remote control boxes, able to 'learn' up to 232 infra-red channels, mounted on wheelchairs.[64] In a sense, even a television remote control unit is a simple environmental control.

Environmental control systems are of particular benefit to people with a high-level spinal injury, who perhaps have only head, suck/blow, eyebrow movement. A range of controls can allow people even with such minimal movement to operate equipment. In addition, people with multiple sclerosis, motor neurone disease, end-stage respiratory disease, poliomyelitis, severe rheumatoid arthritis or osteo-arthritis can also benefit.

For the future, there is talk of fully automated houses for disabled people, geared to the use of multi-functional infra-red controls – as well as multi-purpose 'smart cards', and 'set-top' boxes to enhance the television as an information and communication vehicle. Television links to surgeries and hospitals could make possible a certain amount of remote care and 'telemedicine', including home diagnosis (eg the transmitting of pictures of heartbeats to cardiologists). However, such developments might carry with them legal and ethical problems, especially if electronic surveillance is involved.[65] The development of infra-red control boxes – small, mobile and lightweight – has been a welcome advance for those who can use them; since the larger, hard-wired systems sometimes necessitated considerable installation work, disruption and cost. In addition, this development will presumably facilitate the use of such equipment in the workplace and in education.

Environmental control equipment: provision. In the past, severely disabled people who met the Department of Health's criteria of eligibility, could be provided either with a comprehensive system, (the PSU6, marketed by Possum Controls) or the SEC1B (marketed by Hugh Steeper). The criteria stated that in order to qualify for provision, people had to be so disabled that they could not do simple tasks like ringing bells for attention or switching on lights. In addition, other people might qualify who were a little less disabled – if they had the ability and will to use the equipment, and could not be assisted so effectively by cheaper or simpler equipment. A broader approach to eligibility was also possible, if there was clinical necessity – for example, bearing in mind imminent physical deterioration in the light of a progressive neurological condition.

Local medical assessors and coordinators would make the necessary arrangements, but the system remained controlled and funded by the Department of Health on a national basis (ie for England). If additional adaptations were needed to the home, such as electrical wiring or joinery, social services departments were expected to arrange and to fund them. In April 1995, the central budget for England was devolved to NHS regions, where it was ring-fenced for a year.

If people do not meet the criteria for NHS provision, then social services departments can provide environmental control equipment – usually, smaller, cheaper items than those provided by the NHS, with a more limited range of functions. However, in principle there is nothing to stop social services departments from providing more sophisticated, expensive equipment (which the NHS won't provide) – just as they provide a range of other daily living equipment and home adaptations.[66]

Environmental control equipment: issues about provision. Devolvement of the budget for environmental controls from the Department of Health to NHS regions might allow more flexible prescription of equipment in terms of the range of equipment available and the criteria of eligibility governing provision. In the past, the Department of Health placed contracts with only two companies and offered only a very limited range of equipment – basically only two models. This situation is now changing; the two companies have over the last few years diversified their products, whilst other companies are being invited to submit tenders. With a wider range of models to choose from, prescription could become more modular and precise (rather than one large expensive system or nothing at all), and in some cases cheaper.

On the other hand, once devolved, budgets become vulnerable and might be lost or removed altogether. Severely disabled people are seriously disadvantaged from speaking up for themselves – especially if they do not have the equipment which would enable them to do so. There are no more than about three thousand people who use equipment prescribed in the past by the Department of Health.[67] Substantially larger numbers of people could almost certainly benefit significantly from environmental controls (even without relaxing the eligibility criteria used in the past), but the Department of Health was caught in a cleft stick – greater publicity would have meant greater demand which it did not wish to meet. Indeed, in the financial year 1990–1991, the Department wrote a letter to medical assessors, asking them to exercise restraint in prescription, since demand was exceeding resources (the constraints implied in this letter were lifted the following year).[68] In Scotland, the devolvement some years ago of budgets on the basis of population, had the reported consequence that some local budgets were inadequate to meet people's needs. For example, one particular area might have exceeded its allocation in a particular year, if it had more applicants than planned for – even though another area might have had fewer. Whilst a central budget could have coped with such fluctuations, the local budgets could not.

Concern has been expressed in the past that assessors were not always sufficiently expert in the field of disability. In addition, assessment for environmental controls has often been carried out in isolation from the other needs, including those for equipment such as wheelchair and communication aids, of the person.[69]

Repair, support and maintenance services reportedly took up 33% of the entire Department of Health budget for environmental control systems.[70] Given the high dependency of users, such services are obviously of the utmost importance and will be a major consideration for the NHS when it makes contracts with companies to supply and maintain equipment. All sorts of faults can occur, such as flooding a keyboard with orange juice, failure of a hand control, suck/blow switch failure, erasure of telephone numbers and failure of the mains circuit breaker. In the past, manufacturers might have only provided a 48-hour emergency breakdown service – whereas, realistically, far more rapid response might be needed in some situations.[71]

Environmental control equipment: aspects of use. Environmental control systems are used in institutions as well as people's homes – for example, in spinal injury units. This can be helpful as a way of introducing people to such technology in advance of a formal assessment when they are ready to go home. Some people might reject the equipment, at least initially, since it emphasises the loss of independence. For seriously ill patients, whether in hospital or at home, the equipment cannot be used as a complete 'minder service', since switches might fail or the person be unable to use the equipment if suffering cardiac or respiratory distress. If there is a chance of rehabilitation, the equipment needs to be seen to be part of that process, rather than as a lazy shortcut.[72] Some studies in the United States have investigated whether the costs of medical or nursing attendance can be reduced by the use of environmental controls. If so, then insurance companies might consider funding provision of the equipment, based on a cost/benefit analysis.[73]

In the early 1980s, a study of environmental control users in Scotland concluded that, for effective use of such equipment, greater attention needed to be paid to human factors. For example, it found unsuccessful use of the equipment in 14 out of 41 patients – 33%. It identified four main problems: (1) the difficulty of assessing accurately, not just people's physical abilities, but also their circumstances and attitudes – and changes in all of these; (2) lack of training and encouragement; (3) unfavourable attitude towards the installation of the equipment by the user or carer; (4) lack of clarity amongst professionals about who was responsible for training and supporting users.[74]

Eye prostheses (nhs): see *Artificial eyes.*

Fencing (ssd,hou). Eg garden fencing for protection of a vulnerable people.

Ferrules (nhs,ssd). To attach to the legs of crutches, walking sticks, walking frames: see *Walking aids.*

Finger orthoses: see *Orthoses.*

Fire alarms (hou,ssd,emp). Eg flashing alarms for people with a hearing impairment.

Fireguards (ssd). Eg might be supplied if required by a child beyond the 'normal' age.

Floor wedges (nhs,ssd,edu). To support children.

Food and drink preparation equipment (ssd,nhs,emp). Eg blenders, choppers, food processors, graters, peelers. If considered at all by statutory services, this equipment could be provided as daily living equipment by social services departments. Items such as liquidisers could possibly be supplied by the NHS if required for a particular medical condition. If such equipment were required primarily for work, the Employment Service might provide assistance. See also: *Eating and drinking equipment.*

Foot stools (ssd,nhs). Could be provided by either social services or the NHS, depending on the purpose of the stool; ie is it for a daily living need (eg comfort) or for a medical need (eg fluid drainage)? See *Stools.*

Footwear (nhs,nhs/fh). Footwear ranges from the simple and straightforward to be found in any shoe shop, to the specialist orthopaedic footwear made to order in a hospital. For example, ordinary slip-on shoes might help somebody with difficulty in bending down or with swollen feet, outsize footwear people with particularly large feet, and velcro fastenings people who find tying difficult because of arthritis in the hands. Some shops and mail order services specialise in footwear for extra-large feet or for feet which are otherwise unusual and difficult to fit.

Orthopaedic footwear includes both bespoke and ready-made shoes and boots. In addition, adaptations and additions to footwear include palliative insoles, corrective insoles, digital orthoses, toe blocks, bed boots, night splints for in-toeing, heel cups, cast sandals, hallux valgus orthoses, ankle-foot orthoses.[75]

Most orthotic footwear supplied by the NHS is authorised and prescribed, at least in principle, by orthopaedic consultants. Orthotists, usually employees of private companies working on NHS premises, make and fit orthoses to the prescription of consultants. However, foot orthoses are also assessed for, recommended and made by chiropodists and sometimes by physiotherapists. Supply arrangements are administered day-to-day by surgical appliance officers. From April 1996, fundholding general practitioners are empowered to purchase directly orthopaedic footwear for their patients.

Footwear provision: general organisation as part of the orthotic service. The orthotic service generally has attracted considerable criticism over the years and continues to do so. Since two thirds of orthoses relate to footwear, this criticism relates equally to footwear (see below: *Orthoses*).

Footwear provision: particular problems. As usual, good practice can be found at specialist centres. However, various criticisms have been made about the system of orthotic footwear provision, relating to, for example, ill-fitting footwear, old-fashioned and unattractive styles, outdated methods of manufacture, colour and weight. People might be unable to put on or take off the footwear unaided, have not received a full assessment before prescription, have inadequate time to identify problems at the fitting and delivery stage, and have not benefited from followup and review services. They might simply not wear the shoes because they are 'humiliatingly ugly or painfully uncomfortable'.[76]

In recognition of these problems, a 1991 report recommended substantial change, including the expansion of consumer choice, provision of better services and improvement of the actual footwear.[77]

Footwear: charges. All footwear, actual shoes or boots, or adaptations, should be provided free of charge under s.1 of the NHS Act 1977. However, it is thought that NHS Trusts sometimes make unlawful charges for footwear (see p.213).

Footwear: rules about when it can be provided by the NHS. The provision of orthotic appliances has been governed by guidelines laid down by the Department of Health in a long-lived publication (*MHM 50*) produced by the North West Thames Regional Health Authority. The guidelines are now officially obsolete, but they will no doubt continue to be used by surgical appliance officers for some time to come – until individual health authorities or NHS Trusts draw up replacements.[78] The following are some of the provisions contained in the guidelines:[79]

> Special bootees can be provided for children with gross sensory disturbance of the feet. People should have a choice of colours, at least black, blue, brown, maroon and mushroom. Two pairs of shoes should normally be supplied, and three if clinically necessary. A third pair might also be justified if the wearer walks a lot in the course of work, excessive wear and tear is incurred, or the wearer is a young person pursuing active, recreational activities. Safety surgical footwear can be provided if a person would anyway require safety footwear at work. People with

large or odd-sized feet will not normally qualify for NHS provision, unless additional, built-in surgical features are needed, or the person has an allergic condition.

If people need adaptations to ordinary shoes, then they must buy the shoes first; the NHS adaptation will then be free. They will probably be advised by orthotists or surgical appliance officers about what to buy, and advised to ask the shoe shop whether they can take a couple of pairs on approval for inspection at the hospital. No time scale is given for the frequency of replacement, but it is made clear that people should not have to wait until their current footwear is totally worn out. Repairs are free, unless the footwear has been damaged intentionally or carelessly. For adapted shoes, repairs have to be carried out and paid for privately, if they do not affect the NHS-supplied adaptation.

It is thought that these guidelines are variably applied, with the result that some people receive less than is recommended. For instance, children might be issued routinely with only one pair of shoes at a time, and thus have no shoes to wear if repairs are required. Choice of colour might be restricted or non-existent, indoor shoes or slippers are rarely provided.[80]

Footwear: role of chiropodists. The absence of suitable treatment and footwear can result in reduced mobility or even immobility with all the attendant problems – and expense for other services – which such disability can cause. Even within the priority groups, there are likely to be variable waiting times both for the first full treatment and then repeat treatments. Chiropodists make and supply orthotic devices, including a variety of insoles and inserts, though such provision is likely to vary in scale and in the way it is organised.[81] The provision of NHS chiropody services is likely to be variable, not only for people in their own homes, but also for those in residential and nursing homes (see p.238).

Priority groups for NHS chiropody services, recommended by DHSS guidance in the 1970s, have long been in place; the groups are older people, younger adults with physical or mental disabilities, children, and expectant mothers.[82] Even so, a 1986 report found that NHS chiropodists spent 7% of their time treating non-priority group patients.[83] Whatever the reason for this, such statistics might constitute a defence to any charges that a health authority was 'fettering its discretion' by operating rigid priorities and not taking account of exceptional needs outside the priority groups (see p.446).

Flowtron equipment (nhs). Electrical equipment used for treatment of oedema (bodily fluid build-up) by simulating the pump action of muscles. Sometimes loaned for short-term use by physiotherapists.

Forks (ssd): see *Cutlery*.

Fracture boards (nhs). Eg to support limb horizontally from wheelchair seat.

Games (ssd,edu). Eg large/large-display playing cards, playing card holders, tactile playing cards, magnetic chess sets.

Garage doors (hou,ssd,emp). Eg automatic garage doors.

Garden/front paths (hou,ssd). For example, widened, levelled for wheelchair use or for people who have difficulty walking.

Gardening equipment (ssd,emp). For example, long-handled tools. Could be provided by social services departments but is likely to be viewed as low priority. This is because although gardening can be of enormous psychological importance to people and can contribute to both their mental and physical health, the inability to garden is not viewed as a threat to life or independence. Nevertheless, arguably such equipment falls within the wording of s.2 of the CSDPA: facilities for greater safety, comfort or convenience. If a disabled person worked as a gardener, he or she might be eligible for equipment through the Employment Service.

Glass (hou,ssd). Eg strengthened door or window glass to protect particular groups of people at risk.

Glasses: see *Cups, Spectacles.*

Grab rails: see *Rails.*

Groundfloor conversions/extensions (hou,ssd). Eg groundfloor bathrooms, lavatories, bedrooms.

Hair prostheses: see *Wigs.*

Handgrip materials (ssd,edu,emp). Eg foam tubing to attach to various everyday items such as cutlery or writing utensils. See also *Turners.*

Handrails: see *Rails.*

Head sticks (ssd,edu,emp). Eg for page-turning, operating switches, operating light-pointer (eg with communication board or chart) – held in place by head band or strap.

Hearing aid batteries: see *Hearing equipment.*

Hearing aids: see *Hearing equipment.*

Hearing equipment (nhs,ssd,edu,emp). Personal hearing aids include in-the-ear aids, behind-the-ear aids, bodyworn aids, spectacle hearing aids, ear trumpets, conversation tubes, tinnitus maskers, hearing protectors (muffs, ear plugs), cochlear implants (discussed under their own heading).

Environmental hearing aids include, for example, induction loops (for use with personal hearing aids), flashing alarms or doorbells, vibrating or flashing smoke detectors, vibrating clocks.[84] Also, telephone aids include inductive couplers for use with personal hearing aids, amplified handsets, extra bells, extra hearing piece (for other ear), flashing lights, visual display/text telephones.[85]

As pointed out throughout this book, equipment is not always 'the answer'. For example, in the context of deafness, 'human aids to communication' might be necessary and include interpreters, communicators, lipspeakers and notetakers. Thus, for a person to receive (legally) a 'fair' assessment – for example, a fair 'hearing' for equipment provision under community care and disability legislation (see p.440) – it is arguable that an interpreter is a necessity.[86]

Personal hearing aids are available through the NHS, whilst environmental equipment can sometimes be obtained through social services departments, education authorities and schools, and the Employment Service.

Hearing equipment: NHS provision of personal hearing aids. Most people's clinical needs for a hearing aid are capable of meeting met by the mainstream range provided by the NHS. If a consultant believes that, exceptionally, a person needs a commercial model not normally supplied by the NHS, he or she can prescribe it – if allowed to by the NHS Trust managers who control the relevant budget. Practice is therefore likely to vary. The main NHS range covers behind-the-ear, in-the-ear, and bodyworn aids.

Draft guidance issued by the Department of Health in 1995 tries to answer some of the recurring questions which have affected NHS provision of hearing aids. The position seems straightforward but, in practice, has sometimes given rise to uncertainties[87]:

> In summary, hearing aids, batteries and other accessories are provided free of charge, although prescription is a matter of clinical judgement. Spare hearing aids and spare accessories can be provided, but only exceptionally – for example, if a person is both visually and hearing impaired. Repair or replacement cannot be charged for, unless damage or loss has occurred as a result of carelessness or misuse. Because hearing aids remain the property of the NHS, patients should not be asked to insure them – unless they wish to insure themselves against the possibility of having to pay the NHS for repair or replacement. If people buy hearing aids privately, they have to expect to pay for the cost of batteries, maintenance and repairs. However, if they are attending on NHS hearing aid clinic, but already have a privately-bought aid of a type which the NHS would have prescribed, then the NHS can provide batteries or repair and replace the aid.

Relevant to the question of insurance, is the fact that some NHS Trusts might operate harsher policies than others, when deciding whether to penalise children who damage expensive hearing aids.[88] For this reason, some parents have insured against the costs of paying the NHS for repair or replacement – through, for example, an addition to their household contents policy.[89] There is also a view that spare aids should be issued more routinely to children, since otherwise the malfunction or loss of the aid affects the child adversely until a replacement is obtained.[90]

In some localities, the NHS might replace batteries for hearing aids which people have purchased privately – if, for example, they would have qualified for provision of a similar aid on the NHS. However, this practice is likely to vary, and has led to confusion in the past. For example, one investigation by the Parliamentary ombudsman in the 1970s referred to the Scottish Office's claim that there were no powers in the NHS legislation enabling health districts to provide batteries for privately purchased aids. In the event, the NHS supplied another aid (with batteries).[91] There has also been uncertainty in the past about where statutory responsibility lies for providing radio microphones in school (ie the child has a receiver, the teacher a microphone and transmitter). Both education authorities and the NHS might provide them – practice has varied locally.

Long waiting times can occur when GPs refer patients to a hospital consultant, who in turn refers them on to hearing aid centres.[92] In order to avoid such delay, direct referral from GP to hearing aid centre is sometimes possible – although this might increase the risk that a few serious conditions remain undiagnosed.[93] Furthermore, unless the capacity of hearing aid clinics is adequate to manage an increased workload and range of tasks, there is some danger that waiting times will simply be transferred from one part of the chain to another.[94] A letter sent in 1994 by the NHS Executive to health authorities and NHS Trusts asked them to 'consider' the merits of a direct referral system.[95] Some NHS Trusts employ hearing therapists who are able to give advice and assistance with the use of hearing aids – both personal and environmental. However, hearing therapists remain in short supply, despite the fact that their value in providing audiological rehabilitation services was recognised in a Department of Health 'health notice' issued in 1988.[96]

Hearing equipment: private purchase of personal hearing aids. There is a thriving private market for hearing aids. The advantages of buying privately are increased choice and greater speed. The main disadvantage is that expensive mistakes can be made; hearing aids can range in price from £250 to £1,200.[97] Repairs can also be costly. Given that aids are expensive, there has been concern that consumers should not be taken unfair advantage of – and hearing aid dispensers are required to be registered with the Hearing Aid Council and to adhere to a code of practice (see p.407).[98] Nevertheless, fears persist that some private dispensing is pursued to the disadvantage of consumers[99], whilst regulation of mail order selling is thought to be desirable.

Sometimes commercial dispensers work under contract to the NHS but also have a private business, or hearing aid shops are located actually on NHS premises. Department of Health guidance reminds authorities that if the NHS is selling hearing aids by way of income generation, then it must be made quite clear that such selling is a private service, quite distinct from normal NHS provision. Patients must be given the opportunity to see what NHS aids are available and not be subjected to pressure to buy privately.[100] Not only is the potential for abuse very clear, but an extensive grey area exists, in which the distinction between pressure and persuading people to 'exercise choice' is fragile. Aware of this, the National Committee for Professionals in Audiology has issued its own ethical guidelines. For example, it notes that the promise of shorter waiting times could constitute pressure being put on patients to switch from NHS to private provision and should be avoided; and states that advertising within a hospital should be balanced, promoting both private and NHS provision.[101]

Hearing equipment: management of hearing loss. It is thought that about four million people suffer some degree of hearing impairment, and that this figure rises to 60% of people over the age of 70. Various problems have affected the recognition and management of people's hearing problems. For instance, people might be embarrassed about losing their hearing, believing that it is a stigma to be concealed. Sometimes GPs, ill-informed about the latest technology, might say to older people that hearing loss 'is only to be expected'. Hospital, residential home and nursing home staff might not bother to check whether people's hearing aids are working, or to consider that somebody's confused behaviour might be due to a hearing problem rather than mental deterioration. In addition, it is thought that many people use their hearing aids not at all, seldom or incorrectly; the small numbers of hearing therapists in the NHS does not ameliorate this situation.[102]

Hearing equipment: environmental hearing aids. A number of factors have affected the provision of specialist hearing equipment by social services departments – such as low priority, the lack of ring-fenced budgets[103] and the lack of specialist staff who know about the equipment.[104] Sometimes, in order to promote awareness and use of environmental equipment by hearing impaired people, social services departments fund the display and provision of equipment through hospital audiology departments.[105]

Apart from the equipment itself, installation costs such as wiring can be expensive and might not always be included in local budgets.[106] However, the costs can be prohibitive to users.

Hearing induction loops (ssd,edu,emp). For use with personal hearing aids. Might be regarded as a non-structural or minor adaptations which could be provided by social services departments.[107] See *Hearing equipment.*

Heating (hou,ssd). Eg central heating provided as a home adaptation usually has to be argued for on health grounds such as respiratory problems or the ill-effects of damp. Doctor's letters are often required. The application might need to show why heating is needed in every room – instead of, for example, a storage heater in one or two rooms. More minor adaptation could involve, for instance, relocation of heating controls.

Helmets (nhs). Eg to protect child: see *Orthoses.*

Helping hands (ssd,emp,edu). Ie reaching sticks with jaws on end.

High seat chairs (ssd,emp): see *Chairs.*

Hip orthoses (nhs): see *Orthoses.*

Hoist tracks (hou,ssd,emp). Eg ceiling fixed tracks.

Hoists (nhs,nhs/fh,ssd,hou,emp,edu). Eg bath, car, ceiling-fixed, ceiling-tracked, electric, floor-fixed, hydraulic operation, mobile, wall-fixed, wheelchair, with slings, with seats/chairs. Hoists are used to transfer people, for example, from chair to bed, or from wheelchair to bath, from car to wheelchair. They have become a centre of attention since the passing of health and safety regulations which place a duty on employers to minimise the lifting and handling of loads by employees. One obvious way of doing this is to increase the use of hoists. From the point of view of nurses and therapists who are at high risk of back injury, this is to be welcomed. However, there are other considerations; the Manual Handling of Loads Regulations and their implications are discussed in Chapter 15.

Hoists might be provided by community nursing services (sometimes for use only by nurses when they visit), social services departments – and from April 1996, fundholding general practitioners also have the power to provide them.

Hot pads/packs (nhs). Eg supplied for physiotherapists for treatment and pain relief.

Illuminated switches (ssd). Can be seen in the dark.

Immersion heaters (hou,ssd).

Incontinence equipment (nhs,nhs/dt,nhs/fh,ssd,sf). A range of equipment is available for the management of incontinence. Some, listed on the Drug Tariff, is prescribable by general practitioners. This includes catheter bags, catheters, drainage dribbling appliances, leg bags with belts (but not leg bag garments), male urinals, night drainage bags, penile sheaths, tubing and accessories. Prescription charges apply, although there are exemptions depending on age, financial and medical status (see p.212). Apart from pharmacists who dispense NHS prescriptions of appliances, a number of specialist dispensing appliance centres (run by private companies) also do so under contract to the NHS. Services provided are provision (including home delivery), advice (and sometimes free-phone helplines), fitting and customisation of appliances.[108]

Incontinence pads, sheets and other materials are not prescribable on the Drug Tariff, except in Scotland, where a restricted range of pads can be prescribed. However, community nursing services can provide such incontinence materials free of charge; from April 1996, fundholding general practitioners are also able to (see p.211).

NHS continence advisers have played an increasingly important role – providing services directly to the public, as well as advising and training other professionals to deal with incontinence. The services offered by continence advisers vary from place to place in terms of the balance between a training/educational role and personal caseload (the latter varying from substantial to minimal), telephone advice service, accessible office, referral procedures (eg direct or only through other professionals), monitoring of product supplies, and introduction of assessment forms for other nurses.[109] An indicator of the prevalence of incontinence in society is that continence advisers might promote continence in factories.[110]

The Department of Health has stated that *residents of nursing homes* should receive incontinence materials within the basic fees charged by nursing homes – whoever is paying those fees.[111] However, as explained elsewhere in this book (see p.237), the legislation which governs the provision of services and equipment in nursing homes is vague[112], and the range of pads which a nursing home is prepared to provide might be limited. Thus, if the resident needs or wants another type, he or she might have to pay extra. *People in residential homes* could, according to the guidance, have incontinence pads supplied by the NHS – not by the home. However, the language of the guidance makes it clear that the NHS is not obliged to provide pads – and is silent about what is supposed to happen when it does not.[113] In the past, social services departments have sometimes provided and funded incontinence materials in their own residential homes.

For people living at home, social services departments are empowered under the NHS Act 1977 to provide 'laundry facilities'.[114] These might include linen-washing, linen-loan and pad collection services, as well as, for example, the provision of washing machines. In some areas, the NHS, already providing special collection services for people with a stoma, might also provide laundry services. Pad disposal services are sometimes run jointly by the NHS and social services department – or by neither. Where collection services do not exist, the pads have to be disposed of as normal rubbish, a clearly unsatisfactory arrangement.

Incontinence equipment: effects of incontinence and solutions. There are a number of key points which make the management of incontinence and the provision of equipment and materials difficult. About three million adults and half a million children in the United Kingdom are thought to suffer from incontinence of urine, of faeces or of both. Incontinence is thought to affect up to 50% of nursing home residents and 15% of elderly people living at home.[115] It is a sensitive and emotive issue; people might be reluctant to seek help from professionals – perhaps out of embarrassment or in ignorance of possible solutions.[116] Incontinence is sometimes the trigger which leads to judgements being made about whether older people can continue to manage in their own homes – or if they can remain even in a residential home – since, in principle, incontinence is one of the criteria of demarcation between residential and nursing home care. At the same time, incontinence is reported no longer to be a sufficient criterion for the admission to hospital of elderly patients.[117] In summary, the Royal College of Physicians pointed out that:

> 'Incontinence can have a devastating effect on the life of sufferers and their families and can be of enormous cost to the nation. Children, men and women may be ostracised and old people institutionalised because of incontinence. The lifestyle of all may be diminished. Nocturnal enuresis can be a traumatic experience for children leading to a sense of humiliation, alienation and to vulnerability to verbal and physical abuse'.[118]

Incontinence itself is only a symptom, underlain by various causes, physical or mental. Consequently, the solution might be, for example, surgical, psychological or a question of 're-training' the bladder and controlling people's sometimes unnecessary urges to go the lavatory. So sometimes the use of equipment might be highly inappropriate – for example, catheterising residents of homes or hospital patients because of staff's unwillingness or inability to re-establish continence.[119] At worst, residents of homes might be left sitting in their own urine – in lino-covered rooms and on water-resistant chair covers for easy cleaning.

Solutions might be environmental, since some people's incontinence is little to do with their bladder, but more to do with limitations in mobility. For instance, if people are sitting in chairs which they find it difficult to get out of, they might not get to the lavatory in time. And similarly, if a person can walk only slowly, but the lavatory is not within easy reach – it might take the person 10 minutes to get up the stairs. And lavatories which are not well sign-posted in residential or nursing homes, might contribute to people's supposed 'incontinence'. The outdoor environment, too, should offer adequate numbers of public lavatories which, for example, have extended opening hours, are accessible, and have high standards of design, maintenance and hygiene. A campaigning group – All Mod Cons – works towards such ends.[120] The attempt by some local authorities to close down, or to restrict the opening hours of public lavatories has detrimental consequences for many people – those who are 'incontinent', those who need to use lavatories fairly frequently, and to lesser extent everybody else as well.

Sufferers are often embarrassed to talk about incontinence – but the consequences can be devastating. People might become housebound, fearful of ever going out, and lose their confidence and self-respect. Professionals too might not know what to say or do. In the face of this great silence, ignorance and suffering, attempts have been made in the last 15 years to bring the subject out into the open. This means that particular sensitivity is required in publicising services and advice; for example, placing leaflets in the lavatories of an advice centre, rather than by the front door (where people are embarrassed to pick them up), providing discreet laundry and pad collection services – or naming a clinic a 'pop-in', rather than an incontinence, centre.[121] Various voluntary organisations have been active and the Department of Health has also promoted awareness. Many areas now have *continence advisers* who work in the NHS (see above).

Incontinence equipment: assessment, priorities and rationing. The stories of inappropriate provision of incontinence pads are many – including attics full of unused pads, and their use for budgerigar cages or car windscreens. For instance, some people receiving incontinence pads might not need them because there are other solutions; whilst regular review and reassessment can identify changes in people's needs.[122] Proper assessment of needs can save nursing homes, health authorities and NHS Trusts considerable sums of money which would otherwise be spent inappropriately.[123]

However, this should not obscure the very real issue of rationing which affects people in their own homes, and residents of residential and nursing homes. Incontinence pads are sometimes seen as an easy target by NHS managers seeking to reduce expenditure; and provision for people is thought to vary widely.[124] From time to time, protests reach the House of Commons and the Press at large about proposed, or actual, blanket rationing of pads – for example, the proposal in 1990 to withdraw incontinence pads from 400–500 residents of residential care homes in Leicestershire.[125] Recognising the distress which this can cause, the Department of Health did issue guidance to the NHS in 1991, warning against withdrawal which could cause distress and before alternative arrangements were in place[126]; The guidance, which did not suggest what the 'alternative arrangements' might be, was in addition to a previous Department of Health 'health notice' issued in 1988, which stated that health authorities should consider the provision of a district-wide incontinence service.[127] A report produced by the Department in 1991 recognised the many problems affecting the provision of continence services and the need for improvement.[128] Nevertheless, in the same breath, the Department has reiterated time and again – albeit not as explicitly and helpfully as it might have – that the NHS is under no absolute obligation to provide pads at all.[129] The nature of such statements, made not just for incontinence pads, but for many types of equipment and services, has been discussed elsewhere (see p.25). Hence the ability of health authorities to write to users of incontinence aids letters to the effect that:[130]

> 'You will be aware that, in a modern NHS, each health authority has to look carefully at costs and expenditure. After careful thought I have therefore decided that the free supply of incontinence aids can no longer be sustained.'

The Continence Foundation has produced guidance for NHS purchasers and drawn attention to many aspects of provision. For example, it recommends that criteria of eligibility (based on eg a lower age limit, diagnosis or severity of incontinence) should be consistently applied to people living in their own homes or in residential homes. Reassessment of need should occur regularly; decisions about whether and how to run a home delivery service need to be taken; and laundry services should be provided discreetly, regularly and reliably. Many other aspects of assessment and provision are dealt with.[131]

Incontinence pads, sheets: see *Incontinence equipment.*

In-shoe orthoses: see *Footwear.*

Insoles: see *Footwear.*

Insulin cartridges: see *Diabetes equipment.*

Intercom systems (nhs,ssd,hou). Eg door-entry system.

Ironing boards (ssd). Eg portable (eg for use on chair or table), wall-fixed (fold-down) can be used by people in chair or wheelchair.

Jar openers (ssd). Eg fixed, gripping jaws, rubber grip.

Kerb-climbing wheelchairs: see *Wheelchairs.*

Kettle tippers (ssd). Ie tipping frame holds kettle for pouring.

Key turners (ssd).

Key wrist attachments (ssd). Eg so that visually impaired people will not mislay their front door key.

Keyboards (edu,emp). Eg braille, large, moulded, small, with delayed key response.

Kidney dialysis equipment: see *Renal dialysis equipment.*

Kitchen equipment (ssd,hou variously). Eg cookers with special features, jar openers, pull-out drawers/surfaces (eg for wheelchair user), talking weigh scales, tap turners, tin openers, work surfaces (adjustable height, operated electrically or manually).

Knee orthoses: see *Orthoses.*

Kneeling frames (nhs,ssd,edu). For children.

Knitting equipment (ssd,emp,edu). Eg frames, machines, knitting needle holders.

Knives: see *Cutlery.*

Ladderback chairs (ssd,edu). For children.

Lancets (nhs). For blood samples: see *Diabetes equipment.*

Laundry equipment (ssd,hou). Eg washing machines and driers.

Lavatories: see *WCs.*

Leg bags: see *Incontinence equipment.*

Leg orthoses: see *Orthoses.*

Leg raisers (ssd,nhs). Platforms to raise legs level with bed height, to assist people to get in and out. Electrically operated.

Leisure equipment (ssd). Unlikely to be provided by many social services departments, though advice might be given.

Letter cages (ssd,hou). Eg for those who have difficulty bending down.

Lever taps (hou,edu). See *Tap turners.*

Lifting and handling equipment (nhs,ssd,hou,edu,emp). Eg hoists, lifting belts, transfer boards, transfer discs, turning/rolling/sliding sheets. See *Hoists, Lifts.*

Lifts (nhs,ssd,hou,edu,emp): see *Bath lifts, Short-rise platform lifts, Stairlifts, Through-floor lifts.*

Light switches (hou,ssd,emp). Eg easy-to-use switches (eg automatically programmed, large, light-touch, remote control, rocker-type).

Lighting (hou,ssd,edu,emp). Eg to assist people with visual impairment.

Liquid level indicators (ssd). Give auditory signal when a vessel (eg coffee mug) is nearly full: eg for visually impaired person.

Liquidisers (nhs,ssd). Eg could be appropriate for the NHS to provide for people with a specific medical condition which prevents them otherwise eating: eg on the recommendation of a dietician.

Locating equipment (ssd,emp,edu). Eg electronic equipment to assist visually impaired people avoid obstacles.

Long-handled brushes (ssd). Also long-handled combs.

Long-handled dustpans and brush (ssd).

Long-handled shoehorns: see *Dressing aids.*

Long-handled toothbrushes: see *Toothbrushes.*

Loudspeaking telephones: see *Telephones.*

Low vision equipment: see *Visual impairment equipment.*

Magnifiers (nhs,ssd,edu,emp). Eg bar (eg for placing on lines of page), floor-standing, handheld, illuminated, spectacles-attached.

Mats (ssd). Eg bath, non-slip.

Mattress covers (nhs). Eg to assist management of incontinence.

Mattress variators (ssd,nhs). Placed under mattress to sit person up: electrically powered.

Mattresses (nhs,nhs/fh). Eg pressure relief, variable posture, waterproof.

Monkey poles (nhs,ssd). Pole at head of bed with suspended handle to enable person to pull himself up.

Moon script writing equipment (ssd,edu,emp): see *Visual impairment equipment* and also *Writing equipment.*

Motor vehicles: see *Cars.*

Mouth sticks (ssd,edu,emp). For example, used as page turners. See also *Head sticks.*

Mugs: see *Cups.*

Musical potties (nhs,ssd). To assist toilet-training.

Myo-electric hands (nhs). Electric, artificial hands which respond to nervous impulses: see: *Artificial limbs.*

Nasal cannulae (NHS). Eg for use with respiratory equipment.

Nebulisers (nhs,nhs/dt,nhs/sf). Nebulisers allow drugs to be taken in solution in a mist or fine spray; they are sometimes also used to deliver moist air through a saline solution to enhance sputum clearance.[132]

Powered nebulisers (with air compression units) are available on loan through the mainstream NHS; however, people are often asked to buy their own, either straight-away, or after a limited loan period. Practice varies, and if people have difficulty in affording nebulisers, assistance from a voluntary organisation might be available. Occasionally NHS Trusts might consider longer term loan. From April 1996, fundholding general practitioners have the power to provide powered nebulisers free of charge, as well as the handheld nebulisers they anyway prescribe under the Drug Tariff for the standard prescription charge (with the usual possible exemptions: see p.212).

Disquiet has surfaced over the last few years about the provision of powered nebulisers, especially in those areas where it has been suspected that the NHS has been making illegal charges. Heated Parliamentary exchanges took place and guidance was issued by both the Department of Health and the Welsh Office, reiterating the legal position. This was that (1) the NHS can ask people to buy their own equipment, (2) it cannot sell equipment to patients, unless it is equipment specified in legislation (which powered nebulisers are not), (3) general practitioners have no powers to prescribe powered nebulisers (but this has now changed for fundholding practitioners: see above), and (4) that health authorities have no powers to reimburse patients who buy machines privately (see p.213).[133]

Neck orthoses: see *Orthoses.*

Needle threaders (ssd,emp,edu).

Night drainage bags: see *Incontinence equipment.*

Non-slip materials (ssd,edu,emp). More accurately, 'anti-slip'. Eg non-slip materials for floors, tabletops.

Office furniture (emp). Eg chairs (eg multi-adjustable, split seat for arthrodesis, with special supports and rests), tables (eg multi-adjustable).

One way sheets (nhs,sf). Eg for incontinence management. See *Sheets.*

Openers (ssd). Eg can, jar, tin.

Orthopaedic footwear: see *Footwear.*

Orthoses (nhs,nhs/fh). Orthoses have been defined as externally applied devices which modify the structure or function of the neuro-musculo-skeletal system.[134] They include calipers, collars, elastic hosiery/fabric supports, elastic joint supports, foot-wear, heel cups/pads, insoles, jackets, splints, trusses. Other miscellaneous items include protective helmets, harnesses and restraints.

Most orthotic equipment supplied by the NHS is authorised and prescribed, at least in principle, by orthopaedic consultants. Orthotists, usually employees of private companies working on NHS premises, make and fit orthoses to the prescription of consultants. However, orthoses are also assessed for, recommended, fitted and made by physiotherapists, chiropodists, occupational therapists and bio-engineers. The provision of orthotic equipment in NHS hospitals is administered day-to-day by surgical appliance officers. From April 1996, fundholding general practitioners can provide free of charge orthotic appliances to patients, as well as the elastic hosiery and trusses they have anyway prescribed under the Drug Tariff (for the standard prescription charge).

Orthoses: issues about provision. The orthotic services have suffered substantial criticism in the last decade, through at least two major reports which have found extensive shortcomings. The second of these begins its summary as follows[135]:

> Our study shows the orthotic service to be a large, costly service providing annually, across the UK, an estimated one million items costing seventy million pounds... Yet, the picture which emerges...is of an uncoordinated and rudder-less service in which informed management, service audit and strategic planning appear to have little place.

The report confirms many of the criticisms which have long been levelled at the orthotic service. The following points, unless otherwise indicated, are drawn from it.

Surgical appliance officers (SAOs) administer the provision of appliances in hospitals. Their role varies from little direct contact with patients or appliances, to heavy involvement including the fitting of simple appliances. But SAOs often have had no formal training and might be unduly influenced by the commercial orthotists with whom they are in constant contact. Many consultants who prescribe orthoses 'have virtually no knowledge of functional biomechanics'. The necessity for GPs and other professionals such as therapists and chiropodists to refer patients to consultants before an appliance can be supplied often wastes a great deal of time. The patient might wait many months for a 10 minute-long appointment, only for the consultant to rubber-stamp the original recommendation of the therapist or chiropodist. In fact, Department of Health guidance recognises this problem and does suggest that referral to, and authorisation by, consultants is not always necessary.[136]

Although particular groups of people who have been prescribed orthoses, such as children or people with diabetes, are followed up – most people who have been prescribed appliances by orthopaedic surgeons are not. And, even if a review does take place, it might not include review of the appliance. It seems also that the checking of decisions about what precise appliance will be suitable, whether the prescription has been adhered to, and if the supplied appliance is satisfactory or has even been supplied at all – is a haphazard affair. The checking might even be left to commercial orthotists who, attached to manufacturers, are in a position to abuse the system. In fact, Department of Health guidance has formally adverted to the pitfalls of placing contracts with orthotic companies which both supply and manufacture appliances. Not only might resulting bias limit patient choice, but it will not necessarily represent value for money either, since orthotists might recommend one of their own custom-made devices, instead of another company's cheaper, ready-made appliance.[137]

Orthoses: current Department of Health guidance about contracting. Somewhat belatedly, the Department of Health has issued guidance about contracting for orthotic services. The guidance deals with many issues under the main headings of meeting patients' needs, effectiveness of contracting arrangements, managing the quality of services, staffing and value for money.[138] However, the guidance is only by way of 'encouragement' to purchasers and providers – and the annexes are more in the way of general guidelines than prescription for change. They are laid down largely in the form of lists of questions about different aspects of contracting and service provision.

Orthoses: previous detailed guidelines and rules affecting provision. The provision of orthotic appliances has been governed in the past by Department of Health policy guidelines contained in a long-lived, looseleaf publication produced by the North West Thames Regional Health Authority and known as 'MHM 50'. The guidelines set out in the first part of the publication have now been rendered officially obsolete by guidance issued in September 1995 (see immediately above). However, the old guidelines will no doubt continue to be used by surgical appliance officers for some time to come – since the new guidance does not carry the same type of prescriptive, detailed rules.[139] The old guidelines carried, for example, the following rules (comments have been added in square brackets)[140]:

> It is for consultants to decide whether stock or non-stock items are required. When deciding with which contractor to place an order, account should be taken of the advantage of placing it with a firm with whom the patient has dealt before. For example, the firm might have detailed measurements and knowledge of the patient's condition. Surgical brassieres should not be supplied automatically with breast prostheses; patients are expected to supply their own for adaptation, unless a commercial stock size is unsuitable. Again, it is for the consultant to decide whether to authorise the provision of a custom-made brassiere.
>
> Consultants are supposed to ensure that appliances are satisfactory in terms of function, fit and manufacture. [This is thought to seldom happen.] Various standards are suggested for delivery times; new appliances (ie first prescription for a person) and children's appliances should be given priority. Most appliances should be delivered within four weeks of being ordered (not spinal braces, full-length calipers, hip appliances and surgical footwear, which should be delivered for rough fitting within six weeks and final fitting within eight).
>
> Repeat prescriptions can be authorised by consultants for up to five years after the initial prescription, if the condition of the patient is reasonably stable. If there is doubt about such stability during the five years, re-referral and reassessment should take place. [Advantages to the wearer are that appliances can be replaced with a minimum of fuss; disadvantages are that replacement may continue even though the person's condition has changed or more appropriate appliances have become available.][141]
>
> Appliances can be repaired free of charge unless the wearer is to blame through an act or omission. Patients should be encouraged to carry out repairs to fabric supports themselves. If substantial repair is needed, a new item should be ordered and a prescription charge made. On the other hand, if the manufacturer offers to replace the item, the offer should be accepted and no charge made to the patient. If adapted items need repair, patients should make their own arrangements, unless the NHS adaptations are affected – in which the case the NHS will carry out the adaptations free of charge.
>
> Decisions about when appliances need to be replaced depend on 'serviceability of the appliance' and the clinical needs of patients. Duplicate appliances may be

provided on the basis of a person's needs at work, hardship, medical grounds and hygienic grounds.

Orthoses: charges. Abdominal and spinal supports can be charged for by hospitals, elastic hosiery and trusses by both hospitals and GPs – although the usual exemptions and reductions apply (see p.212). Elastic hosiery is charged for at the standard prescription charge (per leg); abdominal supports and spinal supports command higher charges. Otherwise, all orthoses provided as part of NHS treatment should be free of charge under s.1 of the NHS Act 1977.

Orthotic appliances: see *Orthoses.*

Overbed tables (ssd,nhs). Eg cantilever type.

Oxygen cylinder trolleys: see *Respiratory equipment.*

Oxygen cylinders: see *Respiratory equipment.*

Oxygen equipment: see *Respiratory equipment.*

Oxygen masks: see *Respiratory equipment.*

Page turners (ssd,edu,emp). Eg book, electrically operated, manually operated (eg by foot), newspaper.

Penile sheaths: see *Incontinence equipment.*

Personal care equipment (ssd). Eg adjustable mirrors, electric driers, long-handled holders (for sponges, flannels, brushes, combs), portable hair washing basins, long-handled/angled toe nail cutting scissors.

Pickup sticks (ssd). Ie long-handled stick with jaws on end.

Pill dispensers (ssd). Eg for organising daily doses of pills. Available with braille markings.

Pillows (nhs,ssd). Eg for sleeping/neck problems.

Plastic sheets: see *Sheets.*

Plate guards (ssd). Eg to stop food spilling over edge of plate: see *Eating and drinking equipment.*

Plates (ssd). Eg plates with deep end and high rim: see *Eating and drinking equipment.*

Play equipment (nhs,ssd,edu). Eg play environments, shapes, toys, wheelchair swings/roundabouts.

Plugs (ssd). Eg plugs (electric, sink) with handles.

Potties (nhs,ssd). Eg musical potties for training children.

Pressure relief cushions: see *Pressure relief equipment.*

Pressure relief equipment (nhs,ssd). Eg various types of bed, cushion, mattress, seating including air, alternating-pressure, fluidised bead flotation, foam, gel, low air loss, mixed filling, ring, ripple, turning (eg motorised beds) or water.

The treatment of pressure sores costs the NHS anything from between £60 million to £200 million per year; the costs of treating a patient with a severe pressure sore have been estimated at about £25,000; and various surveys have indicated a high prevalence of pressure sores – for example, 42% in traumatic orthoapaedic wards,

16% of all patients in a hospital, 6.7% of patients in the community, 7.3% of patients in a nursing home. The Department of Health commissioned a report which suggested that the prevention of pressure sores could be more costly than treatment – though this calculation could be offset by other complications such as longer hospital stay, the need for plastic surgery and litigation. And, of course, the scope of the report excluded quality of life issues.[142] Equipment can be an important and effective means of preventing/treating pressure sores, although the comparative effectiveness of different types of pressure relief equipment has not been well-researched.[143]

Shorter hospital stays and community care policies means that the proportion of people at risk of pressure sores in the community is likely to increase. However, pressure relief equipment available in the community through NHS community nursing services might contrast unfavourably with the standard of products available in hospital.[144]

Pressure relief mattresses: see *Pressure relief equipment.*

Pressure relief seating: see *Pressure relief equipment.*

Prone boards (nhs,ssd,edu). Boards on which children lie on their fronts, for example, with abduction blocks, adjustability (from horizontal to vertical position), supports, wheels. See also: *Supine boards, Side-lying boards.*

Protective equipment (nhs,ssd). Eg helmets, pads for children.

Puzzles (edu). Eg puzzle pieces with knobs for easy handling.

Quadrupod walking aids: see *Walking aids.*

Radio microphone aids: see *Hearing equipment.*

Rails (ssd,hou,emp,edu). Eg bath, floor-fixed, grab, hand, stair, wall-fixed, WC-surround.

Raised plug sockets: see *Electric sockets.*

Raised toilet seats (ssd,nhs,edu,emp).

Raising blocks: see *Bed raising blocks, Chair raising blocks.*

Ramps (hou,ssd,edu,emp). Eg fixed or portable ramps to allow access to people who use wheelchairs or can use steps only with difficulty.

Reaching sticks (ssd,emp,edu): Ie reaching sticks with jaws on end.

Reading equipment (nhs,ssd,edu,emp). Eg bookrests, bookstands, low vision aids (from NHS low vision clinics), page turners, reading frames, reading scanners/machines, recumbent spectacles, talking equipment (eg books, calculators, weighing scales), talking computer terminals. See *Visual impairment equipment.*

Reading frames (ssd,emp,edu). Eg magnifying or isolating sections of text.

Reading scanners/machines (emp,edu,ssd). Eg scans printed text to produce either magnified image on screen or speech output. See *Reading equipment.*

Reclining chairs: see *Chairs.*

Recumbent spectacles (ssd,edu,emp). Allows person lying flat to look around the room, read, watch television. See: *Reading equipment.*

Renal dialysis equipment (nhs). Depending on the type of dialysis, equipment and adaptations required include the dialyser machine, catheter, bag, separate dialysing room or transportable cabin unit, heating appliances if necessary, and an electrical generator for emergency use. If a person has *haemodialysis* at home, then guidance states that the NHS is responsible for[145]:

- necessary adaptations to the home (eg separate room and direct water supply)
- the provision and maintenance of equipment; the provision of drugs and dressings (dialysis patients are exempt from prescription charges because they have a 'permanent fistula requiring a surgical dressing')
- the cost of running machines
- the cost of installation and rental of a telephone if one is not already available
- provision of heating appliances if necessary and in any case the cost of heating the dialysis room to the necessary temperature (though no contribution should be made to the cost of pre-existing central heating)
- provision of an emergency generator if during a power cut the person could not be taken back into hospital.

The guidance provides further detail about requirements for flooring, standard of decoration, sink and drainage board size, positioning of the telephone point, the setting up of a cold water supply direct from the mains, separate metering of the electricity supply – and so on. Patients who require any items listed on the Drug Tariff and prescribed by general practitioners are exempt from prescription charges, since they have a 'permanent fistula'.[146]

The equipment and adaptation needs of people having *continual ambulatory peritoneal dialysis* (CAPD) – the most common form of home dialysis[147] – are less. This method involves pouring, via a catheter, dialysate solution into the abdomen from a raised bag – and draining it back into the bag then positioned at a low level. However, though an easier method, the changing of the bag must take place in clean surroundings to prevent infection. If adaptations to improve bathing arrangements are needed, then it might be unclear whether the responsibility falls to the NHS, the social services department or housing authority. (There are two other methods of home dialysis used by relatively few people; *continuous cycling peritoneal dialysis* (CCPD) and *intermittent peritoneal dialysis* (IPD)).

The NHS will not provide all adaptations which might be required – but only those which it considers necessary and directly associated with the treatment. Indeed, guidance from the Department of Environment and Department of Health states that discretionary disabled facilities grants (see Chapter 10) might be given for the 'sterile facilities' required for peritoneal dialysis.[148] In some areas, NHS dialysis services might be contracted out to private sector providers.[149]

Respiratory equipment (nhs,nhs/dt). Respiratory equipment used at home includes oxygen cylinders, oxygen concentrators and ventilators. Powered nebulisers are sometimes used to aid breathing (see above).

Respiratory equipment: oxygen cylinders. Oxygen cylinders may be regularly prescribed by general practitioners. Initial prescription might be made by a hospital consultant when a patient leaves hospital. Prescription charges apply as usual, but GPs sometimes prescribe two or three cylinders together on the same prescription form and for a single standard charge. Cylinders can either be collected and returned by the patient's friends or relatives, or by the pharmacist or other contractor. Oxygen cylinders are generally prescribed for people's intermittent oxygen needs, to fill small cylinders for use after exercise, or as backup in case of a fault in an oxygen concentrator (see below). The cost to health authorities of oxygen cylinder services can be substantial; in 1989, the average annual cost to each family health services authority was £140,000.[150]

Oxygen cylinder stands are loaned free of charge to patients if there would otherwise be a risk of accident.[151]

Respiratory equipment: oxygen concentrators. If a person requires concentrated long-term oxygen therapy, then *oxygen concentrators* can be prescribed. These machines separate a high proportion of nitrogen from ordinary, ambient air and thus deliver oxygen-enriched gases to the patient. Though fairly heavy and thus kept in a single position in the house, connecting tubes allow use in several rooms. The Drug Tariff now advises in detail about prescription, reflecting the concern that, as the use of concentrators grew from the late 1980s, prescription was not always being made appropriately.[152] The Drug Tariff states that:[153]

> Concentrators are cost-effective if a person uses at least 21 cylinders per month (the equivalent of about 8 hours' use a day), that normally the need should be for at least 15 hours' therapy a day – but that in 'no circumstances' should they be prescribed for people who require oxygen for less than 8 hours each day.
>
> It is suggested that concentrators may be provided, for example, when there is an absolute indication of need (eg chronic obstructive airways disease), a palliative need (eg for people dying with fibrosing alveolitis, emphysema) and various other conditions (eg severe kyphoscoliosis, gross obesity or the end stages of peripheral neuropathies and muscle disorders). A number of companies contract with health authorities to provide oxygen concentrator services including supply, installation, instructing the patient, maintenance, emergency call-out (within 10 hours) and removal when the equipment is no longer needed. If interruption of the supply is likely to be detrimental, general practitioners can also prescribe 'backup' oxgyen cylinders in anticipation of breakdown of the concentrator.

From April 1992, oxygen concentrators have not attracted a prescription charge in England.[154]

Respiratory equipment; ventilators. For people who cannot breathe unassisted, ventilators, traditionally, a hospital-based treatment, might also be loaned by to people in their own homes. For people who would otherwise have remained in hospital, discharge home with a ventilator can have a 'knock-on' effect in terms of need for other equipment and changes to the environment. For instance, there might be a need for extra power points, a ceiling-fixed hoist for people who are immobile, a trolley for equipment, perhaps an environmental control system or a wheelchair adapted to hold the ventilator.[155] For people who suffer from nocturnal hypoventilation, a ventilator system can be prescribed which delivers *continuous positive applied pressure* via a breathing circuit with a nasal or full-face mask.[156]

Ring cushions: see *Pressure relief equipment.*

Ripple beds/mattresses: see *Pressure relief equipment.*

Riser chairs (ssd,emp,edu). Chair with rising seat which can stand somebody up; eg electrically powered, or spring-operated. Sometimes needs careful adjustment in relation to the user's weight, so that the user is not 'catapulted' out of the chair by the spring-setting. See *Chairs, Riser seats.*

Riser seats (ssd,emp,edu). Eg portable seats for use in any chair: spring- or lever-operated. See *Riser chairs.*

Robots: see *Environmental control systems.*

Rocking beds (nhs,ssd). To assist breathing (eg using body weight to assist function of diaphragm): see *Beds.*

Roho cushions. Well-known brand name of air cushion with linked cells/pockets. See *Pressure relief equipment.*

Rollators (nhs,ssd). Wheeled walking frames. See: *Walking aids.*

Safety belts: see eg *Car adaptations and accessories, Wheelchair accessories and associated equipment.*

Safety harnesses: see eg *Car adaptations and accessories, Wheelchair accessories and associated equipment.*

Sanitary chairs (nhs,ssd). Chairs with cutout seat which can be used over WCs; might be wheeled.

School desks (edu). Eg suitable for wheelchair use.

School furniture (edu).

Scissors (ssd,emp,edu). Eg electric, large-handled, left-handed, lightweight, spring-operated.

Scooters: see *Wheelchairs.*

Seating (ssd,nhs,edu,emp variously). Eg bath seats, car seats, raised toilet seats, riser seats, shower seats, special wheelchair seating.

Seating support systems (ssd,nhs). Eg for wheelchair, or other chair.

Self-lift chairs (ssd,emp): see *Riser chairs.*

Self-pasting toothbrushes (nhs,) see *Toothbrushes.*

Sewing equipment (ssd,edu,emp). Eg sewing machines (eg foot-operated), needle threaders.

Sheepskins (nhs). Eg covers, fleeces for pressure relief. See: *Pressure relief equipment.*

Sheets (nhs,sf). Eg 'one-way' absorbent sheets for incontinence.

Shoe adaptations (nhs): see *Footwear.*

Shoe inserts (nhs): see *Footwear.*

Shoes (nhs): see *Footwear.*

Short-rise platform lifts (hou,ssd,emp,edu). Eg might be appropriate for negotiating outside steps when a ramp is not feasible. See also *Stair lifts, Through-floor lifts.*

Showers (hou,ssd). Eg built-in swing-out/transfer seat, built-in WC, low threshold access, ramped. There are also fixed but foldable shower seats, shower stools, mobile shower chairs, shower stretchers and trolleys.

Side-lying boards (nhs,ssd,edu). Eg for children to lie on their sides, for example, with abduction blocks, adjustability (from horizontal to vertical position), supports, wheels. See also: *Supine boards, Prone boards.*

Sinks (hou,ssd). Eg insulated, low-level, shallow (for wheelchair use).

Slippers (nhs): see *Footwear.*

Smoke detectors (ssd,hou).

Software (edu,emp). Eg braille translation, large display, predictive (finishes words automatically).

Spectacle-attached vision aids: see *Visual impairment equipment.*

Spectacles: see *Visual impairment equipment.*

Speech equipment: see *Communication equipment.*

Speech synthesizers: see *Communication equipment.*

Spinal supports (nhs/sa). Spinal supports are one of the few items which NHS Trusts can lawfully make a financial charge for (£19.00 at the time of writing), although exemption or reduction is possible, based on age, income or medical status (see p.212).

Sponges (ssd). Eg long-handled.

Spoons: see *Cutlery.*

Sports equipment (nhs,ssd,edu,emp). Likely to be regarded as low priority by social services departments and not provided. In principle, the NHS might exceptionally provide sports wheelchairs. Education authorities or schools might provide sports equipment – as might the Employment Service if it is required for work.

Stair gates (ssd,hou). Eg provided for children who have a need for such safety equipment beyond the age a normal child needs it.

Stairlifts (ssd,hou,emp,edu). Attach to rail which runs up the side of the stairs. Different models allow perching, sitting or standing – and larger versions (normally in public places) will take wheelchairs. Curved rails can be used to negotiate bends. More than one stairlift might be required if there is more than one flight of stairs. Stairlifts are provided by statutory services according to a variety of arrangements. They are increasingly advertised in the national press – for example, in Sunday newspapers – as well as on non-prime-time television. Staff of statutory services normally work to a list of 'contra-indications' suggesting that a stairlift is not appropriate – for example, for people with poor balance, epilepsy, or progressive/deteriorating conditions.

Stand-up beds (ssd,nhs). Stand person up.

Standing boxes (ssd,nhs,edu). Support children in standing position.

Standing frames (ssd,nhs,edu,emp). Support children (and sometimes adults) in standing position.

Sticks: eg *Pickup sticks, Reaching sticks, Walking aids, White sticks.*

Stocking aids: see *Dressing aids.*

Stoma care equipment (nhs,nhs/dt). Stoma care equipment is standardly prescribed by general practitioners – following initial provision by the hospital after an operation. In a few areas, nurses are allowed to prescribe certain Drug Tariff items including stoma care appliances (see p.210). Various stoma care appliances are listed on the Drug Tariff, including adhesive discs/rings/pads/plasters, bags, bag closures and covers, belts, deodorants, filters/bridges, flanges, irrigation appliances, pressure plates/shields, stoma caps and tubing.[157] People with a stoma are exempt from prescription charges (see p.212). Some pharmacists who dispense stoma care equipment can also offer advice – and dispensing appliance centres (DACs) provide specialist dispensing and fitting services.

Stoma care nurses provide services not only for patients, but also advise general practitioners about the care and appliances required by patients. Some disquiet continues to be expressed about those stoma care nurses whose posts are paid for by private companies; they might not be sufficiently impartial when recommending appliances and therefore not necessarily act in the best interests of patients. A recent article points out that the problems of such 'linked deals' generally between commercial companies and the NHS have been recognised by the National Audit Office as widespread.[158] In addition, the Department of Health has issued guidance warning against agreements which stipulate that the NHS will buy particular products in a certain quantity.[159] The article points out that such deals might fall outside normal commercial or financial evaluation, by-pass competitive tendering procedures, and subject NHS staff to pressure from companies.[160]

The needs of people with a stoma can be complex, and relate to biophysical matters (nutrition, hygiene), psychology (self-concept, self-esteem, self-expression), information, education, and socio-cultural matters (eg need to maintain normal relationships and to resume social roles).[161]

Stools: (ssd,edu,emp). Eg footstools, legstools, kitchen perching stools, step stools with vertical/horizontal rails or frame.

Storage units (hou,ssd). Eg accessible kitchen or bedroom units.

Straws (ssd,nhs). Eg for drinking: with one way valve to prevent flow back, or wider diameter to enable more/thicker intake.

Supine boards (nhs,ssd,edu). For children to lie on their backs, for example, with abduction blocks, adjustability (from horizontal to vertical position), supports, wheels. See also: *Side-lying boards, Prone boards.*

Support systems (ssd,edu) Eg foam support systems for children.

Surgical footwear: see *Footwear.*

Switchboards: see *Telephones.*

Switches. Eg for computer/electronic equipment: combination switches giving multiple options, eyebrow control, foot-operated, joystick, suck/puff.

Syringe needles/sharps: see *Diabetes equipment.*

Syringes: see *Diabetes equipment.*

Tables (ssd,edu,emp,sf). Eg adjustable height (for wheelchair use).

Talking books: see *Reading equipment.*

Talking calculators: see *Reading equipment.*

Talking weighing scales (ssd,edu,emp). Eg kitchen weighing scales. See: *Kitchen equipment.*

Talking newspapers: see *Reading equipment.*

Tap turners (ssd). To fit over existing taps. See also *Taps.*

Taps (ssd,hou). For example, foot-operated, knee-operated, lever, shut-off taps (ie shut themselves off after a period).

Telephone aids: see *Telephones.*

Telephones (ssd,emp). Telephones and aids to assist use of the telephone including adapted switchboards, amplifiers (including portable ones), built-in loudspeakers (for handless use), cordless telephones, inductive couplers, large buttons/dials, large print dialling discs, text telephone units (eg Minicom), visual display units etc.

Televisions (ssd). Televisions and aids for watching television. Eg adapted to receive Oracle subtitles, to record subtitles on video, television sound receiver (ie no pictures), earphones/amplifiers.

TENS machines (nhs). Transcutaneous electrical nerve stimulators for pain relief. Sometimes available on loan from the NHS (eg from physiotherapists); for longer term use, people often have to obtain their own.

Thermometers (ssd,emp,edu). Eg talking thermometers for visually impaired people.

Through-floor lifts (hou,ssd,emp,edu). With or without a lift shaft – although the latter is simpler in people's homes. Advantages of these lifts are, for example, that they can take a wheelchair – unlike a standard stairlift. Disadvantages are that they take up a lot of space. Sometimes occupational therapists will recommend through-floor lifts, if a disabled person has a deteriorating condition such as multiple sclerosis or suffers from epileptic fits which raises doubts about the safety of stairlift use. See also: *Stairlifts.*

Tin openers (ssd). Eg electric.

Toilet equipment: see *WC equipment.*

Toothbrush holders (ssd,nhs).

Toothbrushes (nhs). Eg double-headed, long-handled, electric, self-pasting. People normally buy for themselves; might be supplied through NHS if there is a special need.

Toothpaste tube holders/squeezers (ssd).

Toys (nhs,ssd,edu). Developmental equipment might be available through statutory services; toy libraries exist for such purposes (see p.83).

Transcutaneous electrical nerve stimulators: see *TENS machines.*

Transfer boards (nhs). Eg for transfer from wheelchair to car, chair or bed.

Transfer sheets (nhs).

Transfer slings/belts (nhs). With handles; placed around a person, they aid movement and transfer by others (eg from wheelchair to bed, from car to wheelchair).

Trolleys: (ssd). Shopping trolleys (act also as walking support and might have seat), walking trolleys (eg combined tea trolley and walking aid which might be adjustable in height).

Trusses (nhs,nhs/dt). Available on prescription as a Drug Tariff item through the NHS: the usual exemptions apply depending on age, medical condition, financial status (see p.212).

Turners (ssd). Eg door handle, key, tap.

Turning equipment (nhs). Eg turning discs (for swivel transfer), electric turning aids, mattress-turning aids, rolling/turning sheets.

Urinals: see *Incontinence equipment.*

Vacuum cleaners (ssd). Eg lightweight. Or vacuum cleaning system built-in to walls of house.

Vehicles: see *Cars.*

Vertical lifts: see *Through-floor lifts.*

Visual alarms: see *Visual impairment equipment, Alarms.*

Visual impairment equipment (nhs,ssd,edu,emp). Equipment for people with visual impairment, like hearing aids, breaks down into two main categories: personal appliances and environmental equipment.

Personal optical appliances include, apart from spectacles and contact lenses, a variety of low vision aids. Magnifiers are, for example, illuminated, handheld, stand-based, headband-attached or spectacle-mounted. Telescopes (ie multi-lens system, rather than simple lens) are handheld or spectacle-mounted. Closed circuit television systems, complete with scanner, can provide people with large print displays of documents which they would otherwise be unable to read. See also *Reading equipment.*

Environmental equipment (not directly enhancing vision), is wide ranging. Tactile (including braille) markings and controls, or auditory indicators, can enable people with poor, or no, vision to operate a range of ordinary equipment, from cookers to televisions and from central heating controls to lifts. To give but a few examples: braille (or moon script) writing machines, bread-cutting frames, cooking equipment, electronic location aids (detects obstacles), liquid level indicators, self-threading needles, telephones with large-number key pads, television sound receivers (ie no television necessary), white canes/sticks, writing guide frames.

In addition to equipment, the environment can be modified with stronger lighting, colour contrasts, or the arrangement of furniture.

Visual impairment equipment: spectacles, contact lenses and low vision aids. Sight tests can be given by registered optometrists, ophthalmologists, ophthalmic medical practitioners or the hospital eye service (HES). Tests have to be paid for, although they are free or provided at reduced cost for certain categories of people, depending on financial, medical and age status.[162] If people are housebound, domiciliary sight tests are possible; they also have to be paid for, although again exemptions and reductions apply. Sight tests carried out by the HES are free of charge.

Spectacles and contact lenses are provided through an NHS voucher scheme. Cash vouchers to cover the full cost of spectacles are available to children under-16, people under-19 in full-time education, and people getting income support or family credit. Vouchers to cover part of the cost of spectacles are issued to people who need complex lenses, whose needs are changing frequently or who have a low income. In addition, there are special supplements for other clinically necessary features such as small frames, custom-made frames, prisms and tints, and special lenses. Vouchers for contact lenses are available only through the HES and for clinical reasons, although people can put their spectacle vouchers towards contact lenses, and pay the difference themselves. Similarly, they can choose to pay the difference to obtain more expensive pairs of spectacles.[163]

Once spectacles or contact lenses have been prescribed they can be dispensed either direct by the HES or through dispensing opticians. However, not all dispensing opticians are registered with the General Optical Council. Those who are not can dispense reading spectacles (technically defined) and magnifiers, but cannot dispense to children under the age of 16 years or to people who are registered as partially sighted – nor can they dispense contact lenses or give sight tests.[164] Following deregulation of the market in spectacles, readymade reading glasses are available in the High Street generally but are unlikely to provide their wearers with a long-term solution, since two eyes rarely need the same amount of magnification – and they can sometimes cause headaches and eyestrain.[165]

Low vision aids can be loaned through the HES free of charge. Occasionally, the HES contracts out the administration of its low vision aid service to High Street optometrists. Some High Street practitioners do stock low vision aids, but, unless people go through the HES, such aids have to be purchased privately. Children might be able to obtain or use low vision aids such as magnifiers and closed circuit televisions through education authorities.[166] The Employment Service sometimes provides low vision aids needed primarily for work, including closed circuit television systems – following assessment at an NHS low vision clinic.

Visual impairment equipment: registration of people who are blind or partially sighted. Hospital consultants certify that people are blind or partially sighted. Once people are certified, social services departments are informed so that they can then register them. Registration enables people to take advantage of a few benefits such as additional income tax relief, a small reduction on a television licence, small concessions in relation to benefits (income support, housing benefit, council tax benefit) and car parking concessions.[167] Furthermore, although registration is not necessary in order to receive services from social services, it helps because people are at least then known to the local authority.[168]

The registration process does not work effectively, with long delays between certification and registration. In addition, assessment by social services is sometimes delayed if a person is not regarded as a high priority.[169] Attempts have been made to improve the coordination of services; in 1990 the certification form (BD8) was revised and a Circular issued with various recommendations. These included improved collaboration between services and prompt, organised action by social services departments.[170] Consultants are thought to take different approaches to certification of people as blind – and the RNIB estimates that 77% of those eligible are not registered.[171] Complications surrounding certification and registration appear to persist; both service users and professionals sometimes fail to understand the distinction between the two. Registration with the local authority need not follow from certification by the NHS, if service users do not consent; indeed, some may find it very distressing to be told that they are being registered blind. Furthermore, the label is misleading, since most people registered blind are not totally sightless.[172]

Visual impairment equipment: environmental aids. Staff of social services departments involved with providing equipment (and other services) for visually impaired people include social workers, occupational therapists, mobility officers, technical officers, or home teachers.[173] Who is involved will depend on what expertise is available locally. It has been pointed out it does not matter if users of services are confused about who provides what, so long as they receive a good quality of service. If, however, people do not know that information and assistance is available at all, then there is cause for concern.[174]

Local authorities sometimes contract out the delivery of srevices to local voluntary bodies; and in some areas the voluntary bodies themselves might make subcontracts.[175] Conversely, a local authority might act as a local agent for a national voluntary organisation, distributing equipment free of charge – for example, for the British Wireless Fund for the Blind.[176]

Voluntary activity for visually impaired people is long-established and continues.[177] The Royal National Institute for the Blind sells a wide range of equipment and provides a talking book service, The British Wireless for the Blind Fund provides radios for blind people, and local voluntary groups may provide local talking newspaper services. Resource centres can now be found in many areas, run by voluntary organisations or social services departments. Equipment is on display and can be tried out, advice and information obtained – and items sometimes purchased.[178]

Major surveys carried out by the RNIB provided detailed information about the use of equipment by visually impaired people. For instance, the survey of adults showed that 80% of visually impaired people under 60 years of age use tape players, falling to 38% of people over the age of 75. About 12% of all visually impaired people possessed an RNIB Talking Book machine. About 60,000 telephones were provided with assistance from local authorities and voluntary organisations – this represents 11% of all telephones possessed by visually impaired people. The survey showed that people under 75 years old were very much more aware of daily living equipment/gadgets than those over 75 – and also more likely to make use of them, once they had obtained them. People who were registered with the local authority were more likely to be aware of what was available. It was thought that the lack of awareness and use of equipment amongst people over 75 might be due to the adoption of coping strategies which obviate the need for equipment, other disabilities which deflect attention away from visual needs, and problems of dexterity in using equipment (eg timer devices). Radios are not listened to by 19%, although televisions are used by 90%, of visually impaired people.[179]

Voice amplifiers: see *Communication equipment.*

Voice synthesizers: see *Communication equipment.*

Walking aid ferrules: see *Walking aids.*

Walking aids (nhs,nhs/fh,ssd). Eg crutches, walking frames, walking sticks, children's training walking frames (eg the child stands, supported, inside wheeled frame) – and ferrules (often rubber) to fit on the bottom of walking aids. *Walking frames* are of various types such as foldable, forearm-support (gutter-type), hinged (so each side of the frame can move independently), one-handed use, triangular, wheeled (eg 'rollator', two- or four-wheeled), with brakes, with seats, zimmer (or pulpit-type). Accessories include bags, baskets, ferrules and spikes. *Crutches* might be axilla (armpit support), elbow (with handgrip on crutch and 'cuff' at elbow), forearm (forearms, lying in 'gutter' armrests, take the weight), lightweight, metal, wooden. *Walking sticks* include four-legged-base (quadrupod), three-legged-base (tripod), various handled (eg contoured, crook, right-angled, swan-neck), with seat.

Normally supplied by the NHS (particularly physiotherapists), walking aids are sometimes supplied by other NHS staff, social services departments (eg for people with simple problems or a need for standard equipment), general practitioners, the Red Cross, and, when a specialist aid is needed primarily for work, possibly by the Employment Service. From April 1996, fundholding general practitioners can purchase walking aids for their patients). Of course many people buy their own walking sticks, although physiotherapists in particular are aware of how frequently inappropriate walking aids (eg of the wrong height) are bought and used incorrectly. For instance, surveys have found a high proportion of people using unsuitable walking aids – in relation, for instance, to height, weight, comfort of the handle, and mental ability to cope.[180]

Walking frames: see *Walking aids.*

Walking sticks: see *Walking aids.*

Wash basins (hou,ssd,edu,emp). Eg adjustable-height (manual or electric operation), contoured for arm support, cut-out/concave front, wall-fixed (allowing easier wheelchair access).

Washing machines (ssd,sf). Social services departments might occasionally provide washing machines (eg for people with HIV/AIDS out of a special budget, or with heavy incontinence). Sometimes voluntary organisations might be able to help: for instance, the Joseph Rowntree Foundation Family Fund sometimes assists with washing machines if a child's disability causes constant bedwetting or dirty clothes.

Watches (emp,edu,ssd). Eg large display, tactile, talking, vibrating.

Water beds: see *Beds, Pressure relief equipment.*

WCs (water closets) (hou,ssd,emp,edu). Eg adjustable height (eg electrically or lever operated), chemical, high seat (for people with difficulty bending down), low seat (eg for wheelchair transfer), macerating, waterless and without chemicals (electric), washing WCs (ie automatically wash and dry the user's bottom), WC plinths (to raise height). Support frames and rails can be installed around WCs, and raised seats or self-lift seats attached.

WC equipment (ssd,hou,nhs,edu,emp): eg bidet-type WCs, plinths, rails, raised seats, support frames, toilet paper dispensers. See also *WCs.*

WC rails: see *WC equipment.*

Wedges: see *Floor wedges.*

Weighted cuffs (edu,emp,ssd). Eg to steady the hand whilst writing: see *Writing equipment.*

Wheelchair accessories and associated equipment (nhs,edu,emp,sf,ssd,hou variously). A wide range of wheelchair accessories (and other associated equipment), includes backrest covers, bags/baskets, battery chargers, belts, capes, car hoist/winches, clamping systems (for vans), covers, cushions (eg pressure relief), gloves, harnesses, hoists (eg car), lapstraps, lifts, pumps, ramps (eg portable, 'channel' ramps), seat covers, special seating systems, spoke guards, stairlifts (eg with large platform), storage facilities (eg for electric wheelchairs). Some of these might be available through NHS wheelchair services.

Wheelchair cushions: see *Wheelchairs.*

Wheelchair ramps: see *Ramps.*

Wheelchair seating: see *Wheelchairs.*

Wheelchairs (nhs,edu,emp,sf,ssd). The many wheelchairs available on the market include amputee (eg with extended wheel base to prevent tipping), attendant-propelled, children's buggies, elevating-seat (raises seated height of user), foot-propelled (eg chair with castor wheels), heavy duty (ie high weight capacity), lever-propelled, lightweight, manual (ie non-electric), kerb-climbing, lever-operated, one-hand propelled, reclining, spinal carriages, sports, stair-climbing, standup, trolley-type (eg hand-propelled, low-level trolley with backrest, legs horizontal out in front of the child), user-propelled – and so on. Some people's needs for wheelchairs are complex and require a careful choice of the right model, parts and accessories (see p.407).

Included under the general term wheelchairs are larger wheelchairs, electric scooters, and car-shaped electric vehicles. If such vehicles can travel over four, but not more than eight, miles per hour, then they are known as Class 3 vehicles.[181] They can be used at not more four mph on pavements, and at not more than the eight mph on roads; their use is subject to various conditions including the age of the driver (must be at least 14 years old), and the existence of a speed-limiting switch or switches, together with lights, mirrors, horn etc.

There is a wide choice of wheelchair parts, depending on the model, including armrests (eg adjustable-height, desk-type to fit under desk, detachable), backrests (eg adjustable-angle, adjustable-tension), footrests (eg detachable, swing-away), seats (eg adjustable-tension, angled) tyres (pneumatic, solid), wheels (eg angled, quick-release, with various handrims). Many accessories are also available (see *Wheelchair accessories and associated equipment*). The profusion of parts and accessories means that a wheelchair can be supplied in 'modular' fashion, built up with various parts to meet the needs of the user. This is one of the limitations, however, on the functioning of a secondhand market in wheelchairs; what was built up to suit one person might not be appropriate for another.

Many different groups of people use wheelchairs, from disabled children who cannot walk at all and use several different models (for different activities), to older people who can walk indoors but need a wheelchair for occasional outings.

Wheelchairs: summary of provision. There are various ways in which people obtain wheelchairs. NHS wheelchair services loan a wide range but are inevitably constricted by resources; nevertheless, quality and levels of provision vary from authority to authority, depending on local policies, priorities and resources. Wheelchairs are loaned free of charge. In the past, they had to be prescribed by doctors, consultants and general practitioners, many of whom lacked sufficient expertise.[182] Now, specially accredited occupational therapists and physiotherapists undertake much of the prescribing. However, concern remains about the lack of nationally recognised standards and training for wheelchair-prescribing therapists.[183]

Education authorities and schools sometimes provide wheelchairs which are needed primarily for a child's educational needs. Similarly, the Employment Service might loan wheelchairs which are deemed to be necessary for people's needs at work. Social services departments sometimes still provide basic wheelchairs and apparently did, in the past (the 1970s), supply outdoor electric models on occasion. People in receipt of the mobility component of the disability living allowance (see *Cars*) might decide to use it on a wheelchair, whilst financial assistance for an electric wheelchair is sometimes obtainable through the Social Fund.

Voluntary organisations and local fundraising are frequently resorted to, in order to assist people who require specialist wheelchairs which they cannot obtain through statutory services. For example, hitherto, user controlled, electric wheelchairs for outdoor use have not been available widely in England – although this is set to change shortly, following an announcement by the Department of Health in February 1996. The activity of voluntary organisations is by no means negligible. For instance, Whizz Kidz funded nearly 700 new, adapted, powered, manual and sports wheelchairs in five years.[184] Local branches of the British Red Cross also make hundreds and sometimes thousands of loans of basic, manual wheelchairs each year to people who have short-term need – whether for an outing, holiday, or for a recovery period following hospital day surgery.

Wheelchairs: background to NHS provision. The wheelchair service was formerly run centrally by the Department of Health and Social Security (DHSS). Following the McColl review of the service and the highly critical report which emerged in 1986[185], a special health authority was set up in 1987. Known as the Disablement Services Authority (DSA), it presided over a period of change, which culminated in devolvement of the service to individual district health authorities in 1991. These authorities now purchase wheelchair services from NHS Trusts. The McColl report was scathing about various matters, including the standard of assessment of people's needs, the restricted choice of models available, the unsuitability of many prescriptions and the poor standards of repair services.

When the wheelchair service was run centrally by the DHSS, the procedures and practices of the local wheelchair centres (then known as ALACs: artificial limb and appliance centres) were regulated in considerable detail by the *ALAC Manual*: a looseleaf set of 'rules' produced and updated centrally. There were also fewer wheelchair centres than there are now. The DSA too, during its short lifetime, continued to issue national guidance on provision. As a result, it was possible, at least until 1991, to form a picture of how provision was working across the country. Because the service is now so fragmented, it is very much more difficult to find out what is going on, a problem exacerbated by the reluctance of some NHS Trusts to divulge information. Indeed, it was reported recently that the Department of Health was unable to provide a list of English wheelchair providers for a research project which the Department was itself funding.[186] The adequacy of funding of wheelchair services varies[187], different eligibility criteria are used to decide who can get what sort of chair, and standards of service are diverse.

Some of the longstanding problems which have affected NHS provision of wheelchairs include the quality of assessment of people's needs (including their psychological needs), the range of chairs available, repair, delivery times, and whether to provide cash or vouchers so that people can then buy their own. These and some other aspects of provision are covered below.

Wheelchairs: assessment. Assessment is not just about the physical suitability of wheelchairs, but also about people's aspirations, life style, attitudes, social and work needs – and, crucially, their environment. The expectations of users revolve around the improvement of health, well-being, comfort, mobility, social interaction and general role in life. Thus, a wheelchair is not just about physical mobility but the self-identity and worth of a person.[188] And assessment is not just about whether a person 'fits' into a wheelchair, but about the ease of folding, lifting, pushing or propelling it. The last two factors relate in part to the weight of the user and quality of the engineering.

There is little point in providing a wheelchair in an unsuitable environment – for example, one without ramps for access to the house, or with narrow doorways through which the chair will not fit.[189] Similarly, electric wheelchairs need a storage place – not only for the sake of convenience, but also safety. Until the environment is made suitable, provision of (and benefit from) a wheelchair can be delayed or obstructed; and whilst the NHS might still be quite happy to provide the chair, social services departments might take months to assess the need for adaptations. Even then, financial assistance might not be available towards a grant for adaptations, or further delay be experienced (see Chapter 12).

Assessment needs to take account also of the needs of carers who may well be involved in assisting users in and out of wheelchairs, as well as pushing, folding, lifting, and storing wheelchairs. Their health needs can easily deteriorate, especially when wheelchairs are too heavy or awkward to manage. One survey conducted in 1993 found that over 50% of carers of wheelchair users felt that their needs were not being met.[190]

Wheelchairs: special seating. The assessment and provision of special seating is an important area in its own right. Depending on their disabilities, people might require special supportive or rehabilitation seating. For example, 6% of NHS wheelchair users in a health authority might have special seating needs.[191] If people with progressive neurological diseases do not have suitable seating support, the resulting pressure, instability and imbalance can cause pressure sores, spasm, spasticity, deformity and contractures.[192] Special seating includes fixed format seating, modular seating, matrix (ie multi-adjustable) seats, customised seats.[193]

Apart from special seating support systems, all users of wheelchairs who spend long periods of time during the day in their wheelchairs are likely to need cushions – for comfort and to avoid the danger of pressure sores. For example, in 1991 it was estimated that between 70,000 and 100,000 wheelchair users were at risk of developing pressure sores.[194] Some of these cushions are basic – others are sophisticated and expensive pressure relief items, such as the Roho.[195]

Administrative and financial responsibility for special seating systems – as opposed to cushions – is not always clear. For instance, the Disablement Services Authority, when it administered the wheelchair service, was reported as stating that it was in the business of mobility, not special seating.[196] Nevertheless, it has been more recently reported that the NHS (though not necessarily NHS wheelchair services) funds 94% of special seating, with private purchasers, social services departments and voluntary organisations making up the rest. The average cost of providing wheelchair users with special seating is about £480.[197]

A report by the British Society for Rehabilitation Medicine identified some of the problems affecting the provision of special seating, including delayed or inappropriate referral, delays in assessment and provision, assessment in 'artificial' environments, inability to meet the changing needs of users, under-funding, delays in obtaining funding, restrictions on funding of trial use of equipment, cross-boundary funding, wide variety of funding arrangements, repair and replacement delays, transport difficulties, provision for children in special schools – and 'the compromises that have to be made between support, comfort, function and aesthetics'.[198] These problems tend to reflect those affecting the provision of wheelchairs in general (see below).

Wheelchairs: range available and resources. The standard NHS range of NHS wheelchairs is thought to be good value and satisfactory for most people.[199] Indeed, 65% of NHS wheelchair users are 'part-time' or occasional users; of these, 80% have the standard transit, attendant propelled wheelchair. Most of these chairs have puncture proof tyres and require no maintenance during their average loan period of 20 months. However, the standard range does not meet everybody's needs, and the weight of the standard chair can be a problem for carers.[200] Since the NHS wheelchair service was devolved a greater range of wheelchairs has been available; although a standard range remains, wheelchair services are prepared to step outside it in order to meet special needs. Furthermore, the existence of local services has led, in principle, to more flexible provision suited to local needs.

To be weighed against this welcome development, is the fact that many wheelchair services face a lack of resources which can restrict or delay the provision of both standard and non-standard chairs. Resources might vary from service to service, reflecting not only differing local needs but also arbitrary distribution of funding. Furthermore, the expertise and adequate staffing levels previously available in fewer, supra-district, centres, are now spread thinly.[201] Demand has increased as a result of greater local publicity when services were devolved, and as a consequence of community care policy. Increased demand can be measured not only in numbers of people and greater expectations, but also complex needs which can, for example, require expensive wheelchairs and special seating. Funding problems also arise when people are receiving care, treatment or education in one area but have to seek funding from another. The rules about residency for the purposes of social services and NHS are not wholly consistent, and anyway do not address equipment specifically.[202]

Thus, whilst one authority might provide well-designed, lightweight, self-propelling wheelchairs for 'active' users, another might insist that it will no longer provide any type of chair to people who retain some walking ability indoors. One authority might assess people very quickly and deliver a chair within a week or two – another might keep people waiting for three years. The fragmentation of the wheelchair service has had a detrimental on efficient use of resources, since local services are unable to take advantage of bulk buying.[203] In some localities, it appears that wheelchair services achieve a reasonably high profile amongst NHS Trust managers and health authorities (ie the purchasers of services). In others, services remain peripheral, ill-funded and low priority; for instance, the provision of expensive, sophisticated wheelchairs does not generally attract the same attention or funding commanded by hip replacements, heart transplants or finished 'consultant episodes'.[204]

Wheelchairs: user controlled, indoor/outdoor electric wheelchairs. Generally speaking, user controlled electric wheelchairs for outdoor use have not been available in England, Wales or Northern Ireland.[205] Exceptional provision has sometimes taken place in individual cases, whilst some areas, such as Manchester, Newcastle and Bradford have piloted provision on a small scale. Since 1992, such electric wheelchairs have been available throughout Scotland.

The Department of Health announced in February 1996 that it is making extra money available to allow provision of these chairs to about 3% of wheelchair users ('severely disabled people') in England. This is something of an 'about-face'. Previously the government insisted either the scheme would cost too much (£30–£40 million per year, instead of the £6.4 million now costed) or that it was up to local health authorities to decide whether to make extra resources available.[206] However, the decision comes after a decade of constant criticism that a basic requirement for independence – mobility – was being denied to disabled people.[207] Guidelines to NHS wheelchair services state that health authorities should formulate their own local criteria of eligibility; however, these should be within a national framework of eligibility based on (1) inability to propel a manual wheelchair out-of-doors, (2) ability to benefit from the chair (through increased mobility) by way of an improved quality of life, and (3) ability to use the wheelchair safely.[208]

Criteria imposed on Scottish health boards by the Scottish Office, when it decided to make such chairs available in 1992,[209] included:

> severe and permanent restricted mobility for medical reasons, inability to walk, inability to propel a manual wheelchair, ability of users to operate the chairs without endangering themselves or others, compliance with DVLC requirements in relation to epilepsy and loss of consciousness, having the required visual acuity, suitable residential environment including storage area with power supply for a battery charger, ability to ensure that the chair will be maintained adequately, ability to derive significant improvement in independence and quality of life.

Wheelchairs: repair services. The need for reliable, responsive repair services has long been recognised. National guidelines for wheelchair services indicate the range of tasks and functions expected of repairers; they include storage of wheelchairs and associated equipment, delivery and collection, refurbishment, modification, repair and maintenance, achieving appropriate response times, providing appropriate facilities for clients, establishment of good working practices/systems.[210]

Contracts made by NHS wheelchair services with independent repairers might specify response times such as 5 days, 3 days and same day for non-urgent, urgent and emergency repairs respectively. However, such response times might not be adhered to, especially in the case of non-standard wheelchairs – for which the spares might not be to hand.[211] Repairers sometimes deliver wheelchairs for occasional users direct, and are then expected to provide basic instructions to both the user and the carer; however, many users might not receive either demonstration or instruction.[212]

Wheelchair delivery times. Continuing criticism of delivery times, following assessment, has led to guidance from the Department of Health setting target delivery times for non-powered wheelchairs (4 days) and powered chairs (16 days).[213] This followed adverse findings published by the National Audit Office in 1992, that delivery times for non-powered chair ranged from 3 to 28 days and for powered chairs from 13 to 143 days.[214] Standard chairs are normally supplied fairly swiftly, but special chairs and special seating might be delayed because they have to be ordered from the manufacturer.[215] A short-term shortage of money might also cause delay.

Wheelchairs: safety. Safety issues continue to be of concern, given the longstanding recognition of the dangers posed by wheelchairs kept in poor repair. The importance of safety procedures and of adequate instructions has been discussed in Chapter 2.

Wheelchairs: insurance. Wheelchairs remain generally the property of the NHS, so that users should not be asked to insure their chairs against damage; except in cases of deliberate mistreatment (see p.213), the NHS will replace them. However, the government has stated that users 'may be advised' to take out third party insurance in case of accidents and injury to other people.[216] Scottish Office guidance on the same issue stated rather more forcibly that patients and carers 'should be advised strongly' to take out third party insurance, perhaps within a comprehensive scheme covering theft, fire, liability and 'get you home' cover.[217]

Wheelchairs: NHS wheelchair vouchers. For many years, debate has continued about whether the NHS should make available vouchers or cash, so that people could buy their own wheelchairs – topping up the voucher/NHS cash with their own money, in order to buy the model of their choice. Early in 1996 the Department of Health has announced that it will be introducing an NHS voucher scheme.

Guidelines are due to be issued, and will have to deal with a number of difficult questions. Will the value of the vouchers be flat-rate or varied depending on needs? After what period of time will a person be able to obtain a second voucher? Some people might need a new chair every five years, but others – because of changing medical condition or heavy use of the chair – will need one much sooner. Some users, especially children, require more than one chair – will they receive more than one voucher? Who will own the wheelchair – the NHS or the user? Will the NHS maintain and repair the chair; and what if a person has bought such a powerful chair, that the NHS will baulk at the costs of maintenance, including battery replacement? What is the position if an NHS therapist recommends a particular type of chair, but the user decides to buy another, adding his or her own money? In these circumstances, would the NHS still maintain and repair it; and what if the chair purchased is inappropriate – will the NHS still assist the user?

Since disabled people often have little money, it is questionable how many people will be able to take advantage of the new scheme by adding significant sums of their own money to the voucher. The voucher scheme might even perpetuate, or even encourage, a two tier service. Furthermore, there might be restrictions on which suppliers will exchange vouchers, thus limiting choice. Indeed, there is an informed view that service users would benefit more from better funding of NHS wheelchair services, than from the introduction of a voucher scheme.

Wheelchairs: responsibilities of statutory services and criteria of eligibility for provision. Traditionally, NHS wheelchair services have had a continual struggle to set rational criteria of eligibility which will ensure the equitable delivery of services within budget. Other statutory services, such as education authorities and schools, the Employment Service and the Social Fund, have tried to do the same. Due to limited resources all round, such criteria can strike a negative note, often seeking to identify what does not have to be provided and to pass the buck to other authorities. The situation is exacerbated when, in addition, 'cross-boundary' disputes arise for a 'small but significant group of people of all ages' who might be in schools, residential homes or nursing homes; disagreement between authorities results in long delays and sometimes non-provision of wheelchairs.[218] The following summarises some of the key issues:

(1) Wheelchairs: permanent, long-term loan. Traditionally, the NHS has only loaned a wheelchair to people who have a permanent, or at least a longer term need for it. This has meant that in practice, people whose need for a wheelchair is for six months or less have had to obtain it from elsewhere. For example, NHS Trust community nursing services and the British Red Cross might loan wheelchairs for short-term periods; and, in the past at least, social services departments have sometimes done so. The position at present is unclear: it is thought that in most areas, the short-term/long-term loan distinction persists – whereas in a few areas the main NHS wheelchair service covers all provision, irrespective of the length of loan. One glaring, and sometimes scandalous, deficiency in this approach is that NHS wheelchair services are reported sometimes to deny the loan of a wheelchair to terminally ill people who are expected to die within six months.[219] Even on the harsh logic of this criterion of eligibility, surely those people's needs are permanent?

A general consequence of this approach is that people with short-term needs – for example, following a short hospital stay or day surgery – are routinely referred to the local British Red Cross, or other local voluntary organisation. The Red Cross reports that demand for wheelchairs has increased to such an extent that it is seeking some assistance from the NHS in order to meet it. Since the local Red Cross branches are voluntary organisations and not delivering NHS services directly, they can make hire and deposit charges for the loan of wheelchairs – for example, £4.00 per week and £5 respectively. (The NHS would not be able to make such charges.)

(2) **Wheelchairs: occasional users.** Some NHS wheelchair services will not provide wheelchairs for people who are occasional users. For instance, people who require an attendant-propelled wheelchair a few times a year are occasional users – and short-term loan from the Red Cross is the obvious solution. However, the definition of occasional user sometimes moves into more controversial territory when it is extended to embrace regular but 'part-time' users. Such users might be ambulant at home, but need the chair once a week to do their shopping. Notwithstanding the existence of Shopmobility schemes (see below), some people could be seriously disadvantaged by the application of such a criterion.

(3) **Wheelchairs: users in nursing homes.** Standard attendant-propelled wheelchairs have sometimes been supplied, with little discrimination, to people in nursing homes. However, chairs often go into a 'pool' used for general transit purposes – for example, to move residents from the lounge to the dining room. Many NHS wheelchair services will no longer supply chairs in this way, but continue to provide them on an individual basis for residents who can benefit from greater independence. Alternatively, some NHS wheelchair services might still supply a fixed number of chairs to nursing homes as a general resource. A proportion of NHS wheelchairs used in nursing homes are thought to be unsafe, either because they are in a state of disrepair, or because they are being used inappropriately (eg when bilateral amputees use unstable wheelchairs).[220]

(4) **Wheelchairs: more than one.** Some people, especially children, need more than one wheelchair. Different wheelchair services are likely to employ different criteria. Sometimes the availability of suitable transport between a child's home and school can affect whether a wheelchair is transportable, and thus whether a second chair is needed.[221]

(5) **Wheelchairs: division of responsibility between statutory services.** In principle, the criteria which statutory services use to determine whether they will fund wheelchairs, depend on the primary purpose for which they are required. Is a child's need for an electric wheelchair in the school playground or in long corridors, an educational, health or social need? Depending on which, it could be argued that responsibility should fall to the education authority or school, the NHS or social services.[222] Sometimes joint funding is agreed, in order to circumvent such administrative obstacles.

(6) **Wheelchairs: consistent application of criteria of eligibility.** Given the widespread fragmentation of NHS wheelchair services, there is no 'national' wheelchair service. Accordingly, and with evidence of variable provision, it would be difficult to maintain that there is an equitable service nationally. Even more disturbing perhaps is that faced with limited resources, increasing and sometimes unpredictable demand, local services fail to apply their own policies and criteria consistently over a period of

time. Alternatively, services might adhere consistently but rigidly to policies which allow for provision of standard chairs only.[223]

Wheelchairs: non-statutory provision. Outside of statutory services, the role of the British Red Cross, and that of voluntary organisations which provide financial assistance, has already been mentioned.

A relatively recent development has been the proliferation of Shopmobility schemes, basically shopping centre schemes which loan electric wheelchairs and scooters for use around town centres. By March 1995, there were about 120 in the United Kingdom. Schemes are run by local councils or voluntary organisations and make deposit, hire or annual membership charges. A report by the Automobile Association has pointed out the success of the schemes, not only in assisting disabled people, but also in bringing significant income to shopping centres.[224] In addition, private voluntary and commercial organisations hire out wheelchairs, charging a wide range of deposit, daily and weekly charges. Deposit charges might range from £10 to £100 and weekly charges from, on average £10 to £15.[225]

White canes: see *Visual impairment equipment.*

White sticks: see *Visual impairment equipment.*

Widened doorways (hou,ssd,emp,edu). Eg for wheelchair access.

Wigs (nhs/sa). Wigs are one of the few items which NHS Trusts can lawfully make a financial charge for, although exemption or reduction is possible, based on age, income or medical status (see p.212). From April 1996, charges are £46 for a stock modacrylic wig, £120 for a wig made partly of human hair and £175 for a bespoke wig made wholly of human hair.[226]

Department of Health guidelines, now obsolete, contained criteria governing the prescription of wigs. These listed a number of conditions/causes: congenital dystrophy of the skin, alopecia (total or partial but severe/longstanding), extensive scarring, prolonged (if not permanent) baldness through illness or treatment (including drugs). The guidelines went on to emphasise that the NHS should not be providing wigs either for male baldness or for elderly women whose hair is thinning through age.[227]

Wigs are prescribed by hospital consultants. Surgical appliance officers handle administration and finance, whilst the practical fitting services and instructions are supplied by 'wig agents' – normally trained hairdressers who attend hospital regularly. Alternatively, some hospitals give patients vouchers to take to selected hairdressers. Patients sometimes experience a lack of privacy in hospital when they try on wigs.[228] When hospital administrators change the contracted suppliers in order to reduce costs, they might not foresee the problems which result – for example, increased delivery times and patient complaints (since changing wig suppliers/cleaners/dressers is comparable to forcing people to change their longstanding, favourite hairdresser).[229]

Windows (hou,ssd). Eg electrically operated. Also window openers (eg reaching sticks with attachments on end).

Workbenches (emp,edu). Eg multi-adjustable.

Work surfaces (hou,ssd). Eg adjustable-height kitchen units/surfaces.

Writing frames/guides: see *Writing equipment.*

Writing equipment (ssd,edu,emp). Eg computer software, writing frames/guides, weighted cuffs.

Notes

1 SI 1989/419. *NHS (Charges for Drugs and Appliances) Regulations 1989.* Also: SI 1988/551. *NHS (Travelling Expenses and Remission of Charges) Regulations 1988.*

2 Calling for Help! Group (1994). *Community alarm systems: a national survey.* London: Anchor; Help the Aged; National Housing and Town Planning Council; Research Institute for Consumer Affairs. And for a review of policy, practice, impact and relevance of community alarms to community care, see: Thornton, P.; Mountain, G. (1992). *A positive response: developing community alarm systems for older people.* York: Joseph Rowntree Foundation; Community Care.

3 Bowker, P.; Rocca, L.; Arnell, P.; Powell, E. (1992). *A study of the organisation of the orthotic services in England and Wales: report to the Department of Health.* Salford: Salford Health Authority Physiotherapy Service; University of Salford, Department of Orthopaedic Mechanics; North Western Orthotic Unit, p.90.

4 Lee, J. (1991). Breast prostheses. *British Medical Journal:* 5 January 1991; 302, pp.43–44.

5 Bowker, P.; Rocca, L.; Arnell, P.; Powell, E. (1992). *A study of the organisation of the orthotic services in England and Wales: report to the Department of Health.* Salford: Salford Health Authority Physiotherapy Service; University of Salford, Department of Orthopaedic Mechanics; North Western Orthotic Unit, p.90.

6 National Artificial Eye Service. *The National Artificial Eye Service: a guide.* (undated booklet, obtained 1995).

7 See generally: Amputee Medical Rehabilitation Society (1992). *Amputee rehabilitation: recommended standards and guidelines.* London: AMRS, pp.12–13. Also: Lambert, A.; Johnson, J. (1995). Stump shrinkers: a survey of their use. *Physiotherapy:* April 1995; 81(4), pp.234–236. Also: White, E.A. (1992). Wheelchair stump boards and their use with lower limb amputees. *British Journal of Occupational Therapy:* May 1992; 55(5), pp.174–178. Also: Lein, S. (1992). How are physiotherapists using the Vessa pneumatic post-amputation mobility aid? *Physiotherapy:* May 1992; 78(5), pp.318–32.

8 Eg Ham, R.; Regan, J.M.; Roberts, V.C. (1987). Evaluation of introducing the team approach to the care of the amputee: the Dulwich approach. *Prosthetics and Orthotics International:* 1987; 11, pp.25–30.

9 Lindsay, J.A. (1992). Rehabilitation of amputees. *British Medical Journal:* 28 March 1992; 304, p.842.

10 Amputee Medical Rehabilitation Society (1992). *Amputee rehabilitation: recommended standards and guidelines.* London: AMRS, pp.8–9.

11 Knight, P.; Urquhart (1989). *Outcomes of artificial lower limb fitting in Scotland.* Edinburgh: ISD Publications, pp.40–43.

12 McColl, I. (Chair) (1986). *Review of artificial limb and appliance centre services: the report of an independent working party under the chairmanship of Professor Ian McColl.* 2 vols. London: Department of Health and Social Security, vol.1, p.15.

13 Knight, P.; Urquhart, J. (1989). *Outcomes of artificial lower limb fitting in Scotland: a survey of new patients referred to the limb fitting service.* Edinburgh: Common Services Agency, p.85.

14 Monopolies and Mergers Commission. *Artificial lower limbs: a report on the supply of artificial lower limbs in the United Kingdom.* London: HMSO, pp.1–2.

15 Limb, M.; Calnan, M. (1991). Artificial limbs: a real need. *Health Service Journal:* 15 November 1990, pp.1696–1697.

16 Aldersea, P. (1996). *National prosthetic and wheelchair services report 1993–1996.* London: College of Occupational Therapists, pp.iii–iv.

17 *Hansard,* House of Commons, 22 March 1990, Written Answers, Mr. Freeman.

18 Aldersea, P. (1996). *National prosthetic and wheelchair services report 1993–1996.* London: College of Occupational Therapists, Part 1, pp.xiii, 3.

19 Aldersea, P. (1996). *National prosthetic and wheelchair services report 1993–1996.* London: College of Occupational Therapists, Part 1, pp.11–12.

20 See eg: Aldersea, P. (1996). *National prosthetic and wheelchair services report 1993–1996.* London: College of Occupational Therapists, Part 1, pp.11–13. Also: Amputee Medical Rehabilitation Society (1992). *Amputee rehabilitation: recommended standards and guidelines.* London: AMRS, p.27.

21 Aldersea, P. (1996). *National prosthetic and wheelchair services report 1993–1996.* London: College of Occupational Therapists, Part 1, p.4.

22 McColl, I. (Chair) (1986). *Review of artificial limb and appliance centre services: the report of an independent working party under the chairmanship of Professor Ian McColl.* 2 vols. London: Department of Health and Social Security, vol.1, p.26. Also: Monopolies and Mergers Commission. *Artificial lower limbs: a report on the supply of artificial lower limbs in the United Kingdom.* London: HMSO, pp.11, 70–73.

23 Eg National Audit Office (1992). *Health services for physically disabled people aged 16 to 64.* London: HMSO, p.20. Also: Edwards, F.C.; Warren, M.D. (1990). *Health services for adults with physical disabilities.* London: Royal College of Physicians, p.66.

24 Aldersea, P. (1996). op cit, Part I, p.2.

25 Storm over DSA advice on limbs and wheelchairs. *Therapy Weekly:* 6 April 1989; 15(37), p.1.

26 Keetarut, S. (1989). Spare artificial legs. *British Medical Journal:* 18 November 1989; 299, p.1260.

27 Eg Kulkarni, J.R. (1995). Mobility after amputation of a lower limb. (Letter). *British Medical Journal:* 16 December 1995, pp.1643–1644. Also: Walker, C.R.C.; Ingram, R.R.; Hullin, M.G.; McCreath, S.W. (1994). Lower limb amputation following injury: a survey of long-term functional outcome. *Injury: International Journal of the Care of the Injured:* 1994; 25(6), pp.387–391. Also: Lachmann, S.M. (1993). The mobility outcome for amputees with rheumatoid arthritis is poor. *British Journal of Rheumatology:* 1993; 32, pp.1083–1088. Also: Datta, D.; Nair, P.N.; Payne, J. (1992). Outcome of prosthetic management of bilateral lower-limb amputees. *Disability and Rehabilitation:* 1992; 14(2), pp.98–102. Also: Collin, C. (1991). Rehabilitation of elderly people with prostheses. (Letter). *British Medical Journal:* 1 June 1991; 302, p.1336.

28 London Boroughs Occupational Therapy Managers Group (1988). *Occupational therapists' criteria for the provision of home adaptations in the homes of people with disabilities.* London: LBOTMG (section 2).

29 SI 1989/419. *National Health Service (Charges for Drugs and Appliances) Regulations 1989.* Also: *SI 1988/551. National Health Service (Travelling Expenses and Remission of Charges) Regulations 1988.*

30 See eg Cornwell, M. (1996). The role of the car in the mobility chain. *British Journal of Therapy and Rehabilitation:* May 1996; 3(5), pp.247–252.

31 Research Institute for Consumer Affairs (1995). *Ability car guide.* London: RICA, p.15.

32 See eg: Research Institute for Consumer Affairs (1995). *Ability car guide.* London: RICA (publication has a number of accompanying, detailed fact sheets about individual car models.)

33 *Social Security Contributions and Benefits Act 1992,* s.73.

34 See eg: London Borough Occupational Therapy Managers' Group (1992). *Occupational therapists' criteria for the loan of equipment to people with disabilities.* London: LBOTMG, p.22.

35 See variously: National Deaf Children's Society (1992). *Cochlear implants and deaf children.* London: NDCS, pp.19–21. Worsfold, S. (1994). The 'bionic ear' controversy. *Therapy Weekly:* 20 October 1994, p.5. And: Ramsden, R.; Graham, J. (1995). Cochlear implantation: a safe and cost effective treatment for profoundly deaf adults and children. *British Medical Journal:* 16 December 1995; 311, p.1588.

36 Haggard, M. (1993). *Research in the development of effective services for hearing-impaired people.* London: Nuffield Provincial Hospitals Trust, pp.118–132.

37 See eg: Kennedy, D. (1996). Deaf minority tells campaigning peer to abandon fight: Ashley's support for 'bionic ear' attacked by critics who fear threat to language and community. *Times:* 5 June 1996.

38 The above points drawn from: Naylor, J.; Mulley, G. (1993). Commodes: inconvenient conveniences. *British Medical Journal:* 13 November 1993; 307, pp.1258–1260.

39 Most examples from: Easton, J. (1994). *Twelfth annual report of the assistive communication aid centre, Frenchay Hospital, Bristol.* Bristol: ACAC, pp.5–6.

40 For an assessment of their function and effectiveness, see: Chamberlain, A.; Rowley, C.; Stowe, J.; Hennessy, S.; Leese, B.; Tolley, K.; Wright, K. (1993). Evaluation of Communication Aid Centres in England and Wales. *Health Trends:* 1993; 25(2), pp.75–79.

41 Initiative on Communication Aids for Children (1994). *Communication aids for children: a briefing for purchasers and managers.* London: ICAC, p.7.

42 Jolleff, N.; McConachie, H.; Winyard, S.; Jones, S.; Wisbeach, A.; Clayton, C. (1992). Communication aids for children: procedures and problems. *Developmental Medicine and Child Neurology:* 1992; 34, pp.719–730.

43 Initiative on Communication Aids for Children (1994). *Communication aids for children: guidelines to good practice.* London: ICAC, p.13.

44 For an assessment of their function and effectiveness, see: Chamberlain, A.; Rowley, C.; Stowe, J.; Hennessy, S.; Leese, B.; Tolley, K.; Wright, K. (1993). Evaluation of Communication Aid Centres in England and Wales. *Health Trends:* 1993; 25(2), pp.75–79.

45 See eg: Rowley, C.; Stowe, J.; Bryant, J.; Chamberlain, M.A. (1986). *Communication aids provision.* Leeds: University of Leeds, Rheumatology and Rehabilitation Research Unit, 1986, pp.41–46.

46 Easton, J. (1994). *Twelfth annual report of the assistive communication aid centre, Frenchay Hospital, Bristol.* Bristol: ACAC, p.8.

47 HN(84)12. Department of Health and Social Security. *Communication aids centres (CACs): procedures for out of district referrals.* London: DHSS.

48 Rowley, C.; Stowe, J.; Bryant, J.; Chamberlain, M.A. (1986). *Communication aids provision.* Leeds: University of Leeds, Rheumatology and Rehabilitation Research Unit, 1986, p.43.

49 Easton, J. (1994). *Twelfth annual report of the assistive communication aid centre, Frenchay Hospital, Bristol.* Bristol: ACAC, pp.9.

50 Initiative on Communication Aids for Children (1994). *Communication aids for children: guidelines to good practice.* London: ICAC, p.22.

51 Initiative on Communication Aids for Children (1994). *Communication aids for children: guidelines to good practice.* London: ICAC, p.23.

52 Larcher, J. (1996). Speak up and make yourself heard: your GP may now purchase communication aids. *Disability Now:* April 1996, p.20.

53 Initiative on Communication Aids for Children (1994). *Communication aids for children: guidelines to good practice.* London: ICAC, pp.21–24.

54 Examples from: Easton, J. (1994). *Twelfth annual report of the assistive communication aid centre, Frenchay Hospital, Bristol.* Bristol: ACAC, pp.6, 11.

55 Jolleff, N.; McConachie, H.; Winyard, S.; Jones, S.; Wisbeach, A.; Clayton, C. (1992). Communication aids for children: procedures and problems. *Developmental Medicine and Child Neurology:* 1992; 34, pp.719–730.

56 SI 1989/419. *NHS (Charges for Drugs and Appliances) Regulations 1989.* Also: SI 1988/551. *NHS (Travelling Expenses and Remission of Charges) Regulations 1988.*

57 Based on: Department of Health; Welsh Office (1995). *Drug Tariff: March 1995.* London: HMSO. Also list kindly provided by the British Diabetic Association.

58 SI 1989/419. *National Health Service (Charges for Drugs and Appliances) Regulations 1989,* r.6.

59 *Hansard,* House of Commons, 7 November 1995, Written answers, col 678, Mr Malone.

60 British Diabetic Association (1993). *Recommendations for the management of diabetes in primary care.* London: BDA, pp.2–6.

61 British Diabetic Association (1988). *Diabetes in the United Kingdom – 1988.* London: BDA, pp.15–16. Sheffield Health Authority (1993). *People with diabetes mellitus: a strategy for health services.* Sheffield: SHA, pp.14–18.

62 Clinical Standards Advisory Group (1994). *Standards of clinical care for people with diabetes.* London: HMSO, p.5.

63 SI 1989/419. *NHS (Charges for Drugs and Appliances) Regulations 1989.* Also: SI 1988/551. *NHS (Travelling Expenses and Remission of Charges) Regulations 1988.*

64 Curtin, M. (1994). Technology for people with tetraplegia: part 2: environmental control units. *British Journal of Occupational Therapy:* November 1994; 57(11), pp.419–424.

65 Gann, D.; Iwashita, S. (with Barlow, J.; Mandeville, L.) (1995). *Housing and home automation for the elderly and disabled.* Sussex: Science Policy Research Unit, University of Sussex; Electrical Contractors' Association, pp.19–20. See also: Doughty, K.; Costa, J. (1995). Automated care

in the community: an engineer's dream, a health professional's dilemma? *British Journal of Occupational Therapy:* February 1995; 2(2), pp.83–86.

66 See generally: Department of Health (1993). *Environmental control systems funded by the Department of Health.* London: DH. (No longer extant, since the devolution of the budget to the NHS).

67 Barnes, M.P. (1994). Switching devices and independence of disabled people. *British Medical Journal:* 5 November 1994; 309, pp.1181–1182.

68 Mandelstam, M. (1992). *Environmental control systems: investigating provision.* London: Disabled Living Foundation, pp.6, 10.

69 British Society of Rehabilitation Medicine (1994). *'Prescription for independence': a working party report of the BSRM Environmental Control Special Interest Group.* London: BSRM.

70 See generally: British Society of Rehabilitation Medicine (1994). *'Prescription for independence': a working party report of the BSRM Environmental Control Special Interest Group.* London: BSRM, p.13.

71 For a detailed appraisal, see: West Midlands Regional Health Authority (1990). *Pilot scheme to aid and monitor patients relying on environmental control equipment: the report of a working party.* Birmingham: WMRHA.

72 Woods, B.M.; Jones, R.D. (1990). Environmental control systems in a spinal injuries unit: a review of 10 years' experience. *International Disability Studies:* 1990; 12, pp.137–140.

73 McDonald, D.W. (1989). Environmental control unit utilisation by high-level spinal cord injured patients. *Archives of Physical Medicine and Rehabilitation:* August 1989; 70, pp.621–623. Symington, D.C. (1986). Environmental control systems in chronic care hospitals and nursing homes. *Archives of Physical Medicine and Rehabilitation:* May 1989; 67, pp.322–325.

74 Bell, F.; Whitfield, E.; Rollett, P. (1987). Investigation of Possum users in Scotland. *International Rehabilitation Medicine:* 1987; 8(3), pp.105–112.

75 Bowker, P.; Rocca, L.; Arnell, P.; Powell, E. (1992). *A study of the organisation of the orthotic services in England and Wales: report to the Department of Health.* Salford: Salford Health Authority Physiotherapy Service; University of Salford, Department of Orthopaedic Mechanics; North Western Orthotic Unit, pp.64–65.

76 See variously: Newson, F.; Robinson, N.; Smith, S. (1992). Orthopaedic footwear: a quality initiative to find out what patients think. *Physiotherapy:* January 1992; 78(1), pp.12–14. Also: Michaelson, P. (1992). Supply of orthopaedic bespoke footwear in the UK. *Physiotherapy:* February 1992; 78(2), p.117. Also: Tomlin, Z. (1991). Putting the boot in footwear. *Therapy Weekly:* 12 December 1991; 18(24), p.1. Also: Platts, R.G.S. (1989). The NHS boot. *British Medical Journal:* 14 October 1989; 299, pp.932–933. Also: Costigan, P.S.; Miller, G.; Elliot, C.; Angus Wallace, W.A. (1989). Are surgical shoes providing value for money? *British Medical Journal:* 14 October 1989; 299, p.950.

77 Disabled Living Foundation; Chartered Society of Physiotherapy; King's Fund; Society of Chiropodists (1991). *Footwear: a quality issue: provision of prescribed footwear within the National Health Service.* London: Disabled Living Foundation, p.viii.

78 The guidelines have been replaced by the less detailed and prescriptive advice in: HSG(95)47. NHS Executive. *Contracting for orthotic services.* London: Department of Health, 1995, para 7.

79 North West Thames Regional Health Authority. *MHM 50: provision of medical and surgical appliances.* (Looseleaf: now obsolete).

80 Disabled Living Foundation; Chartered Society of Physiotherapy; King's Fund; Society of Chiropodists (1991). *Footwear: a quality issue: provision of prescribed footwear within the National Health Service.* London: Disabled Living Foundation, pp.34–38.

81 See eg. Cartwright, A.; Henderson, G. (1986). *More trouble with feet: a survey of foot problems and chiropody needs of the elderly.* London: HMSO, p.68.

82 HRC(74)33. Department of Health and Social Security. *Reorganisation of National Health Service and of local government: operation and development of services: chiropody.* London: DHSS, 1974. Also: HC(77)9. Department of Health and Social Security. *Organisation of chiropody services.* London: DHSS, 1977.

83 See eg. Cartwright, A.; Henderson, G. (1986). *More trouble with feet: a survey of foot problems and chiropody needs of the elderly.* London: HMSO, p.62.

84 A series of helpful factsheets are available from the Royal National Institute for Deaf People.

85 Information about telephones and telephone accessories is available from the Royal National Institute for Deaf People and also from British Telecom.

86 Commission of enquiry into human aids to communication (1992). *Communication is your responsibility: the report of the Commission of Enquiry into Human Aids to Communication.* London: British Association of the Hard of Hearing; British Deaf Association; National Deaf Children's Society; Royal National Institute for the Deaf, p.9.

87 Department of Health (1995). *Hearing aid services provided by audiology departments.* Draft. London: DH.

88 National Deaf Children's Society (1990). *Audiological services for children: recommended practice.* London: NDCS, p.18.

89 National Deaf Children's Society (1993). *Insurance of children's hearing aids.* (Information sheet). Wakefield: NDCS.

90 National Deaf Children's Society (1990). *Audiological services for children: recommended practice.* London: NDCS, p.18.

91 Parliamentary Commissioner for Administration (5/325/77). *Provision of batteries for a hearing aid. 3rd report for session 1977–78.* London: HMSO, 1978.

92 Eg Reeves, D.; Mason, L.; Prosser, H.; Kiernan, C. (1994). *Direct referral systems for hearing aid provision.* Manchester: University of Manchester, pp.21–27. Also: Royal National Institute for the Deaf (1988). *Hearing aids: the case for change.* London: RNID.

93 Reeves, D. (1994). *Direct referral systems for hearing aid provision: summary report.* Manchester: University of Manchester, p.16

94 Fox, G.C.; Sharp, J.F. (1994). Direct hearing aid referral: the effect upon outpatient waiting times in a district general hospital. *Journal of the Royal Society of Medicine:* April 1994; 87, pp.215–216.

95 EL(94)35. NHS Executive. *Audiology services: direct referral projects.* Leeds: Department of Health, 1994.

96 HN(88)26. Department of Health. *Development of services for people with physical or sensory disabilities.* London: DH, 1988, Annex A.

97 Royal National Institute for the Deaf (1994). *Hearing aids: questions and answers.* London: RNID, p.8.

98 *Hearing Aid Council Act 1968.*

99 Royal National Institute for the Deaf (1988). *Hearing aids: the case for change.* London: RNID, pp.9–11.

100 Department of Health (1995). *Hearing aid services provided by audiology departments.* Draft. London: DH.

101 National Committee for Professionals in Audiology (1994). *Ethical guidelines for commercial dispensing of hearing aids in association with NHS.* NCPA.

102 See: Corrado, O. (1988). Hearing aids. *British Medical Journal:* 2 January 1988; 296, pp. 33–35. Also: Pedley, K. (1988). Earlier referral of adult patients with hearing loss. *Update:* March 1988; 36(15), pp.1837–1843. Also: Anand, J.K.; Court, I. (1989). Hearing loss leading to impaired ability to communicate in residents of homes for the elderly. *British Medical Journal:* 27 May 1989; 298, pp.1429–1430. Rye, S. (1990). A confusion of sound. *Nursing Times:* 12 September 1990; 86(37), pp.43–44.

103 Department of Health (1995). *Think dual sensory: draft good practice guidelines for older people with dual sensory loss.* London: DH, p.24: points out that ringfenced budgets can be 'useful', not only for hearing or visual impairment equipment but also for equipment for deaf–blind people (making three ringfenced budgets).

104 Eg Social Services Inspectorate (Munro, P.) (1990). *'A secret service': an evaluation of personal social services for people with a hearing impairment in Tameside.* London: Department of Health, p.15.

105 Social Services Inspectorate (1989). *Sign posts: leading to better services for deaf–blind people.* London: Department of Health, p.25.

106 National Deaf Children's Society (1989). *A good deal for deaf children? A report on provision of aids and adaptations by social services departments under the 1970 Chronically Sick and Disabled Persons Act.* London: NDCS, 1989.

107 See DoE 59/78. Department of Environment; Department of Health and Social Security; Welsh Office (1978). *Adaptations of housing for people who are physically handicapped.* [Now obsolete].

108 Touche Ross (1994). *Department of Health reimbursement and remuneration of appliances report.* London: Touche Ross, pp.21–28. See also, for example, company booklet describing activities: Thackraycare. A guide to services for the healthcare professional.

109 Rhodes, P.; Parker, G. (1993). *The role of continence advisers in England and Wales.* York: University of York, Social Policy Research Unit.

110 See eg: Pomfret, I.; Steele, W. (1991). A working service. *Nursing Times:* 24 April 1991; 87(17), pp.46–48.

111 HSG(92)50. NHS Management Executive. *Local authority contracts for residential and nursing home care: NHS related aspects.* London: Department of Health, 1992. And see: HSG(95)8. Department of Health. *NHS responsibilities for meeting continuing health care needs.* London: DH, Annex A, para G.

112 SI 1984/1578. *Nursing Home and Mental Nursing Homes Regulations 1984,* r.12.

113 HSG(92)50. NHS Management Executive. *Local authority contracts for residential and nursing home care: NHS related aspects.* London: Department of Health, 1992.

114 *NHS Act 1977,* s.21 and Schedule 8.

115 Figures referred to in: Nazarko, L. (1994). Drugs, continence, elderly people. *Primary Health Care:* January 1994; 4(1), pp.19–22.

116 Eg: Henry, T. (1996). Survey shows hidden problem. *Nursing Times:* 14 February 1996; 92(7), p.62–66.

117 Rhodes, P. (1993). The sound of silence: no-one wants to be responsible for the provision of continence services. *Health Service Journal:* 21 October 1993, pp.28–29.

118 Royal College of Physcicians (1995). *Incontinence: causes, management and provision of services.* London: RCP, p.4.

119 Eg: Cassidy, J. (1995). Home sick. *Nursing Times:* 17 May 1995; 91(20), pp.20–21.

120 Cunningham, S. (1995). Toilets out of order. *Nursing Times:* 13 December 1995; 91(50), pp.55–58.

121 Brown, C. (1994). Community centre: a clinic that aims to attract people who may otherwise fall through the net of traditional continence services. *Nursing Times:* 26 January 1994; 90(4), pp.86–89.

122 Eg: Sanderson, J. (1991). *An agenda for action on continence services.* London: Department of Health, pp.5–7.

123 Nazarko, L. (1993). Incontinence through incompetence. *Nursing Standard:* 28 April 1993; 7(32), pp.52–53. Also: Nazarko, L. (1993). Solving incontinence through assessment. *Nursing Standard:* 27 October 1993; 8(6), pp.25–27.

124 Eg Rooker, J. (1992). *Community continence services: a survey of the policy and practice of district health authorities in England with respect to the provision of continence services and aids to those patients outside hospital.* London: Labour Party, p.13.

125 Eg *Hansard:* Written Answers, 20th December 1990, cols 347–348, Mr. Dorrell.

126 EL(91)28. NHS Management Executive. *Continence services and the supply of incontinence aids.* London: DH, para 3.

127 HN(88)26; HN(FP)(88)25; LASSL(88)8. Department of Health. *The development of services for people with physical disabilities.* London: Department of Health, Annex A, para xx.

128 Sanderson, J. (1991). *An agenda for action on continence services.* London: Department of Health.

129 The repetitive answers to the persistent questions about incontinence pads can be found year after year in Hansard. Most recently, see, for example: *Hansard,* House of Commons, Written Answers, 17 January 1996, col 595, Mr Bowis.

130 Quoted in Parliamentary debate: *Hansard,* House of Commons Debates, National Health Service, 21 October 1991, National Health Service, col 676, Mr. Cook (referring to Scarborough health authority).

131 Norton, C. (1995). *Commissioning comprehensive continence services: guidance for purchasers, May 1995.* London: Continence Foundation, pp.16–20.

132 O'Driscoll, R. (1991). Home nebulized therapy – is it effective? *Respiratory Medicine:* 1991; 85, pp.1–3.

133 *Hansard*, House of Commons Debates, National Health Service, 21 October 1991, col 662, Mr Rhodri Morgan and Mr William Waldegrave. See also: FHSL(W)115/91. Welsh Office. *Charging NHS patients.* Cardiff: Welsh Office, 1991. Also: FHSL(W)21/92. Welsh Office. *The provision of powered nebulisers under the National Health Service.* Cardiff: Welsh Office, 1992. And: EL(92)20. NHS Management Executive. *Provision of equipment by the NHS.* London: Department of Health, 1992. The general position was reiterated again in 1995: *Hansard*, House of Commons, Written Answers, 13 March 1995, col 395, Mr Sackville.

134 Paraphrase of the definition used by the International Standards Organisation.

135 Bowker, P.; Rocca, L.; Arnell, P.; Powell, E. (1992). *A study of the organisation of the orthotic services in England and Wales: report to the Department of Health.* Salford: Salford Health Authority Physiotherapy Service; University of Salford, Department of Orthopaedic Mechanics; North Western Orthotic Unit, p.95. See also: NHS Management Consultancy Services (1988). *Study of the orthotic services.* London: Department of Health.

136 HSG(95)47. NHS Executive. *Contracting for orthotic services.* London: Department of Health, 1995, Annex A, paras 7–8.

137 HSG(95)47. NHS Executive. *Contracting for orthotic services.* London: Department of Health, 1995, para 6.

138 HSG(95)47. NHS Executive. *Contracting for orthotic services.* London: Department of Health, 1995.

139 The guidelines have been replaced by the less detailed and prescriptive advice in: HSG(95)47. NHS Executive. *Contracting for orthotic services.* London: Department of Health, 1995.

140 North West Thames Regional Health Authority. *MHM 50: provision of medical and surgical appliances.* (Looseleaf: now obsolete).

141 Bowker, P.; Rocca, L.; Arnell, P.; Powell, E. (1992). *A study of the organisation of the orthotic services in England and Wales: report to the Department of Health.* Salford: Salford Health Authority Physiotherapy Service; University of Salford, Department of Orthopaedic Mechanics; North Western Orthotic Unit, p.89.

142 Department of Health (1993). *Pressure sores: a key quality indicator: a guide for NHS purchasers and providers.* London: DH, pp.4–6.

143 Nuffield Institute for Health, University of Leeds; NHS Centre for Reviews and Dissemination (1995). The prevention and treatment of pressure sores. *Effective Health Care:* October 1995; 2(1).

144 See eg: James, H. (1995). Preventing pressure sores in patients' homes. *Professional Nurse:* July 1995; 10(10), pp.649–652.

145 HSC(IS)11 (March 1974). Department of Health and Social Security. *Services for chronic renal failure.* London: DHSS.

146 HSC(IS)11 (March 1974). Department of Health and Social Security. *Services for chronic renal failure.* London: DHSS.

147 Renal Services Working Party (1991). *Provision of services for adult patients with renal disease in the United Kingdom.* Renal Association, p.25.

148 DoE 10/90; LAC (90)7. Department of Environment; Department of Health. *House adaptations for people with disabilities.* London: HMSO, para 57.

149 Bennett-Jones, D. (1996). NHS will be left with high risk, low profit services under private finance initiative. (Letter). *British Medical Journal:* 23 March 1996; 312, p.780.

150 Williams, B.; Nicholl, J. (1991). Recent trends in the use of domiciliary oxygen in England and Wales. *Health Trends:* 1991; 23(4), pp.166–167.

151 Department of Health; Welsh Office. *Drug Tariff:* March 1995. London: HMSO, p.326.

152 Williams, B.; Nicholl, J. (1991). Recent trends in the use of domiciliary oxygen in England and Wales. *Health Trends:* 1991; 23(4), pp.166–167.

153 Department of Health; Welsh Office. *Drug Tariff:* March 1995. London: HMSO, pp.323–329.

154 See: HSG(92)10. NHS Management Executive. *Charges for drugs, appliances, oxygen concentrators and wigs and fabric supports.* London: Department of Health, 1992.

155 *Nursing Standard:* 12 July 1995; 9(42), pp.38–39. Also: Branthwaite, M.A. (1989). Mechanical ventilation at home. *British Medical Journal:* 27 May 1989; 298, p.1409.

156 Jones, S. (1995). Applying nasal intermittent positive pressure ventilation. *Nursing Times:* 1 November 1995; 91(44), pp.32–33. Hendrick, A.; Wiltshire, N. (1995). Sleep apnoea. *Professional Nurse:* July 1995; 10(10), pp.624–627.

157 Department of Health; Welsh Office (1995). *Drug Tariff:* March 1995. London: HMSO, p.187.

158 National Audit Office (1991). *National Health Service supplies in England.* London: HMSO.

159 NHS Management Executive (1993). *Standards of business conduct for NHS staff.* Leeds: Department of Health. Also: NHS Executive (1994). *Commercial approaches to the NHS regarding disease management packages.* Leeds: Department of Health.

160 Black, P. (1996). Choice cuts: the growth of sponsored stoma-care nurses is proving an increasing threat to services offered by the NHS. *Nursing Times:* 21 February 1996; 92(8), pp.28–30.

161 Deeny, P.; McCrea, H. (1991). Stoma care: the patient's perspective. *Journal of Advanced Nursing:* 1991; 16, pp.39–46.

162 SI 1986/975. *NHS (General Ophthalmic Services) Regulations 1986* (as amended).

163 The voucher scheme is based on the following: the *NHS Act 1977* as amended by the *Health and Medicines Act 1988,* s.13; SI 1986/975. *The NHS (General Ophthalmic Services) Regulations 1986.* And, SI 1989/396. *NHS (Optical Charges and Payments) Regulations 1989.*

164 Opticians Act 1989, s.27. And see: HC(89)12. Department of Health. Contains: FPN 473; HC(FP)(89)6. *Arrangements for General Ophthalmic Services from 1 April 1989.* (Appendix 6, para 24).

165 Help the Aged (1994). *Better sight.* London: Help the Aged, p.7.

166 Lane, A. (1993). Blind and partially sighted children in Britain: the RNIB survey, volume 2: a summary. *British Journal of Visual Impairment:* 1993; 11(1), pp.9–11: commenting on the RNIB survey.

167 Summarised in: Ford, M.; Heshel, T. (1994). *In Touch 1994/5 handbook.* London: Broadcasting Support Services, pp.115–116.

168 Bruce, I.; McKennell, A.; Walker, E. (1991). B*lind and partially sighted adults in Britain: the RNIB survey.* Volume 1. London: HMSO, 1991, p.272.

169 Lovelock, R.; Powell, J.; Craggs, S. (1995). *Shared territory: assessing the social support needs of visually impaired people.* York: Joseph Rowntree Foundation; Community Care, pp.19–26. Social Services Inspectorate (1988). *A wider vision: the management and organisation of services for people who are blind or visually handicapped.* London: Department of Health, p.20.

170 HN(90)5; HN(FP)(90)1; LASSL(90)1. *Department of Health. Certification of blind and partially sighted people: revised form BD8 and procedures.* London: DH. The recommendations were taken from: Department of Health (1989). *Co-ordinating services for visually handicapped people: report to the Minister for the Disabled.* London: HMSO.

171 George, M. (1994). Guiding light. *Community Care:* 13–19 October 1994.

172 See: Lovelock, R.; Powell, J.; Craggs, S. (1995). *Shared territory: assessing the social support needs of visually impaired people.* York: Joseph Rowntree Foundation; Community Care, pp.19–26.

173 Social Services Inspectorate (1988). *A wider vision: the management and organisation of services for people who are blind or visually handicapped.* London: Department of Health, p.15.

174 Jobbins, M. (1992). Can the RNIB Needs Survey turn the tide for people with visual impairment or will more be said than done? *British Journal of Visual Impairment:* 1992; 10(1), pp.7–9.

175 Summarised in: Ford, M.; Heshel, T. (1994). *In Touch 1994/5 handbook.* London: Broadcasting Support Services, p.92.

176 Ford, M.; Heshel, T. (1994). *In Touch 1994/5 handbook.* London: Broadcasting Support Services, p.343.

177 See: Lovelock, R.; Powell, J.; Craggs, S. (1995). *Shared territory: assessing the social support needs of visually impaired people.* York: Joseph Rowntree Foundation; Community Care, p.35.

178 See generally: Ford, M.; Heshel, T. (1994). *In Touch 1994/5 handbook.* London: Broadcasting Support Services.

179 Bruce, I.; McKennell, A.; Walker, E. (1991). *Blind and partially sighted adults in Britain: the RNIB survey.* Volume 1. London: HMSO, 1991, pp.88–90, 139–140, 207–210, 212–214.

180 Simpson, C.; Pirrie, L. (1991). Walking aids: a survey of suitability and supply. *Physiotherapy:* March 1991; 77(3), pp.231–234.

181 SI 1988/2268. *Use of Invalid Carriages on Highways Regulations 1988. Made under s.20 of the Chronically Sick and Disabled Persons Act 1970.*

182 See eg: McMahon, M.; Dudley, N.J. (1992). General practitioners and wheelchair prescribing. *British Journal of Occupational Therapy*: May 1992; 55(5), pp.183–185.

183 See eg: Silcox, L. (1995). Assessment for the prescription of wheelchairs: what training is available to therapists. *British Journal of Occupational Therapy:* March 1995; 58(3), pp.115–118.

184 Godsmark, C. (1995). Whizz kidz on wheels: on a charity that calls itself 'the movement for non-mobile children'. *Therapy Weekly:* 2 March 1995, p.8.

185 McColl, I. (Chair) (1986). *Review of artificial limb and appliance centre services: the report of an independent working party under the chairmanship of Professor Ian McColl.* 2 vols. London: Department of Health and Social Security.

186 Hodges, C. (1996). The fragmented services. *Therapy Weekly:* 28 March 1996, p.7.

187 Smith, S.; Goddard, T. (1994). *Wheel power? Case studies from users and providers of the NHS wheelchair services.* London: Spastics Society, p.18

188 Smith, C.; McCreadie, M.; Unsworth, J. (1995). Prescribing wheelchairs: the opinions of wheelchair users and their carers. *Clinical Rehabilitation:* 1995; 9, pp.74–80.

189 See eg Kettle, M.; Rowley, C.; Chamberlain, A. (1992). A national survey of wheelchair users. *Clinical Rehabilitation:* 1992; 6, pp.67–73.

190 Smith, C.; McCreadie, M. (1994). A heavy load. *Health Service Journal:* 28 April 1994, p.27.

191 Lachmann, S.M.; Greenfield, E.; Wrench, A. (1993). Assessment of special seating and/or electronic control systems for wheelchairs among people with severe physical disabilities. *Clinical Rehabilitation*: 1993; 7, p.151–156.

192 Leonard Cheshire Foundation (1990). *Report on the wheelchair and seating project carried out in residential homes of the Leonard Cheshire Foundation for physically disabled people.* London: LCF, p.5.

193 British Society for Rehabilitation Medicine (1995). *Seating needs for complex disabilities: a working party report of the British Society of Rehabilitation Medicine.* London: BSRM, p.ii.

194 National Audit Office (1992). *Health services for physically disabled people aged 16 to 64.* London: NAO, p.20. Referring to findings of the National Consumer Council reported in 1991.

195 Aldersea, P. (1991). Under pressure: provision of pressure cushions to wheelchair users has now been devolved to local level. *Therapy Weekly:* 27 June 1991, p.9.

196 Leonard Cheshire Foundation (1990). *Report on the wheelchair and seating project carried out in residential homes of the Leonard Cheshire Foundation for physically disabled people.* London: LCF, p.13.

197 British Society for Rehabilitation Medicine (1995). *Seating needs for complex disabilities: a working party report of the British Society of Rehabilitation Medicine.* London: BSRM, pp.18–19.

198 British Society for Rehabilitation Medicine (1995). *Seating needs for complex disabilities: a working party report of the British Society of Rehabilitation Medicine.* London: BSRM, pp.i–ii.

199 Glasman, D. (1993). Deals on wheels: the wheelchair service in England is fragmented and users are not treated according to their needs. *Health Service Journal:* 16 September 1993, p.14. See also: Harris, C. (1991). Standard chair 'meets most needs'. *Therapy Weekly:* 11 July 1991, p.3.

200 Aldersea, P. (1996). *National prosthetic and wheelchair services report 1993–1996.* London: College of Occupational Therapists, Part 2, pp.15–21.

201 Smith, S.; Goddard, T. (1994). *Wheel power? Case studies from users and providers of the NHS wheelchair services.* London: Spastics Society, p.18

202 Aldersea, P. (1996). *National prosthetic and wheelchair services report 1993–1996.* London: College of Occupational Therapists, Part 2, pp.6–7.

203 Aldersea, P. (1996). *National prosthetic and wheelchair services report 1993–1996.* London: College of Occupational Therapists, p.iii, Part 2 (p.16).

204 Wise, J. (1995). Fashionable wheelchair madam? Forget it. *Therapy Weekly:* 16 November 1995, p.4. (Article by Rehabilitation Services Manager).

205 See eg: Muscular Dystrophy Group (1994). *Batteries not included: wheelchair service survey.* London: MDG.

206 Eg: *Hansard,* House of Commons, 14 June 1994, Written Answers, col 382, Mr. Bowis.

207 See eg: Kerridge, A. (1995). Batteries not included: the campaign for state funding for indoor/outdoor powered wheelchairs. *British Journal of Therapy and Rehabilitation*: February 1995; 2(2), pp.75–82. George, M. (1992). Wheel lock: a survey shows disabled people are

not being given appropriate wheelchairs owing to lack of funds. *Nursing Times:* 1 January 1992; 88(1), p.17. Segal, A. (1986). Push for power: powered wheelchairs are essential for thousands of the disabled, but the government is not providing them. *New Society:* 25 April 1986, pp.16–17.

208 HSG(96)34. *NHS Executive. Powered indoor/outdoor wheelchairs for severely disabled people.* London: Department of Health, para 9.

209 NHS MEL(1992)67. *National Health in Service in Scotland Management Executive. Indoor/outdoor powered wheelchairs.* Edinburgh: Scottish Office. See also followup letter issued 25 May 1994 about revision of the criteria and insurance. Also: *Hansard,* House of Commons, 18 January 1996, Written Answers, col 757, Lord James Douglas-Hamilton.

210 National Guidelines for Wheelchair Services (1994). *Current views for purchasers and providers.* Birmingham: Regional Rehabilitation Centre, Southern Birmingham Community Health NHS Trust, p.31.

211 Smith, S.; Goddard, T. (1994). *Wheel power? Case studies from users and providers of the NHS wheelchair services.* London: Spastics Society, p.16.

212 Aldersea, P. (1996). *National prosthetic and wheelchair services report 1993–1996.* London: College of Occupational Therapists, Part 2, p.15.

213 EL(93)54. *NHS Management Executive. Priorities and planning guidance 1994–95.* Leeds: Department of Health, 1993, Section B.

214 National Audit Office (1992). *Health services for physically disabled people aged 16 to 64.* London: NAO, p.20.

215 Smith, S.; Goddard, T. (1994). *Wheel power? Case studies from users and providers of the NHS wheelchair services.* London: Spastics Society, p.16.

216 *Hansard,* House of Commons, 27 November 1995, Written Answers, col 516, Mr. Bowis.

217 NHS MEL(1992)67. *National Health in Service in Scotland Management Executive. Indoor/outdoor powered wheelchairs.* Edinburgh: Scottish Office.

218 Aldersea, P. (1996). *National prosthetic and wheelchair services report 1993–1996.* London: College of Occupational Therapists, Part 2, pp.6–7.

219 Cooper, J. (1991). Chair policy. (Letter). *Therapy Weekly:* 1 August 1991. Also: Cornwell, M. (1991). Wheelchair loan scheme. (Letter). *Therapy Weekly:* 5 September 1991, p.5.

220 Aldersea, P. (1996). *National prosthetic and wheelchair services report 1993–1996.* London: College of Occupational Therapists, Part 2, p.22.

221 On the variation in transport provided by education authorities for disabled children: McMillen, P.H. (1992). A survey of transport for children in wheelchairs. *British Journal of Occupational Therapy:* May 1992; 55(5), pp.179–182.

222 Aldersea, P. (1996). *National prosthetic and wheelchair services report 1993–1996.* London: College of Occupational Therapists, Part 2, pp.11–12.

223 Swaffield, L. (1995). It could be you...your chances of getting the wheelchair that gives you maximum independence are as unpredictable – and sometimes as hopeless – as your chances of winning the National Lottery. *Therapy Weekly:* 23 February 1995, p.10.

224 Automobile Association (1995). *Shopmobility: good for people and towns.* Basingstoke, AA.

225 Disabled Living Foundation. *DLF Hamilton Index.* London: DLF (looseleaf), Part 2, Section 7.

226 SI 1989/419. *National Health Service (Charges for Drugs and Appliances) Regulations 1989.* Also: SI 1988/551. *National Health Service (Travelling Expenses and Remission of Charges) Regulations 1988.*

227 North West Thames Regional Health Authority. *MHM 50: provision of medical and surgical appliances.* (Looseleaf: now obsolete).

228 Cheesbrough, M. (1989). Wigs. *British Medical Journal:* 9 December 1989; 299, pp.1455–1456.

229 Bowker, P.; Rocca, L.; Arnell, P.; Powell, E. (1992). *A study of the organisation of the orthotic services in England and Wales: report to the Department of Health.* Salford: Salford Health Authority Physiotherapy Service; University of Salford, Department of Orthopaedic Mechanics; North Western Orthotic Unit, p.91.

Index

In addition to this index, an A–Z list of equipment types, with details of how they are provided, forms part IV of this book. This list should be used in tandem with the index, since only a few of the major entries on the list are included below. The index also contains references to a few of the legal cases cited in the text which are central to the themes of the book.

Community Care Practice and the Law

Michael Mandelstam with Belinda Schwehr

ISBN 1 85302 273 X pb

'...a comprehensive and up-to-date guide to community care law which discusses in detail, and with knowledge and insight about policy and practice, how the law provides both the framework for the delivery of services and the means by which decisions and services can be challenged... valuable for students and for others trying to make sense of how law and practice should and do interact. Planners and managers will also find the book invaluable... this should serve as a valuable reference book for many years.'

– *Issues in Social Work Education*

'this book has to be a must on any occupational therapist's bookshelf for reference by both the independent practitioner and those employed in the statutory services. It is also an important work of reference for occupational therapy education establishments and their students as they prepare new practitioners for the increasingly complex and litigious world in which they will be providing services.'

– *British Journal of Occupational Therapy*

'This book fills a gap in describing the legal framework of the new legislation and relating that to day-to-day questions that arise amongst those administering services or receiving them...will be of great benefit in dealing with the knotty questions around health or social care, the definition of the need and the role of the NHS in long-term care...exceptionally clear and impressively up-to-date. All those who read it will be significantly better informed.' – *Care Weekly*

'Anyone looking for a practical guide to the legal implications of community care practice will find this book by Michael Mandelstam and Belinda Schwehr of immense help. Their practical approach makes *Community Care Practice and the Law* equally suited for service managers and practitioners, voluntary organisations, service users and carers, as well as lawyers, lecturers and students.'

– *Disability News*

'This book appears to be the first real attempt to provide a complete and comprehensive guide to application of community care policy and practice... The back cover of this book declares that it is 'an essential work of reference for managers in the social and health services in both the statutory and voluntary sectors, and for the legal profession, it will also be a useful text for students of social work and social policy'. It is difficult to fault this claim save that the work essential ought to be underlined.'

– *Therapeutic Communities*

'...indispensable...the material is well presented in an accessible way and the authors analyse some of the more contentious aspects of community care' – *Baseline*

'Using non-legal language this book provides practical assistance... It deals objectively with controversial issues and will be of considerable help to workers in this field.'

– *Aslib Book Guide*

'Excellent and much needed text for students and practitioners'

– *Peter Storey, Senior Lecturer, Stockport College of Further and Higher Education*

Jessica Kingsley *Publishers*

116 Pentonville Road, London N1 9JB

Disability and the Law

Jeremy Cooper and Stuart Vernon

ISBN 1 85302 318 3 pb

'This new work will be used by all practitioners, students and teachers involved in providing information and advice on all aspects of disability. As experienced law teachers, the authors are well placed to examine issues from the perspective of the legal and regulatory system... The style of the book is clear and crisp and succeeds in avoiding political criticism for its own sake...a very useful volume, not least for its assembly of many related topics in one place.'

– *Disability Awareness in Action*

'This authoritative and comprehensive book provides a useful and detailed insight into current and future disability legislation in the UK, the European Union and 15 other countries with its implications for people with disabilities...a very useful text for students working with people with disabilities.'

– *Nursing Times*

Jessica Kingsley *Publishers*
116 Pentonville Road, London N1 9JB